The Economy of Medieval Hungary

East Central and Eastern Europe in the Middle Ages, 450–1450

General Editors

Florin Curta and Dušan Zupka

VOLUME 49

The titles published in this series are listed at *brill.com/ecee*

The Economy of Medieval Hungary

Edited by

József Laszlovszky
Balázs Nagy
Péter Szabó
András Vadas

BRILL

LEIDEN | BOSTON

Cover illustration: (Front) Saint Anne Trinity, St Anne with the Virgin and Child (known as Metercia), 1513, Cathedral of the Assumption of Virgin Mary, Rožňava (Katedrála Nanebovzatia panny Márie v Rožňave). (Back) Golden florin from the period of King Charles I with the inscription Karolu[s] rex, Coin collection of the Hungarian National Museum, Budapest (Magyar Nemzeti Múzeum. Éremtár).

The Library of Congress Cataloging-in-Publication Data is available online at http://catalog.loc.gov
LC record available at http://lccn.loc.gov/2018001835

Typeface for the Latin, Greek, and Cyrillic scripts: "Brill". See and download: brill.com/brill-typeface.

ISSN 1872-8103
ISBN 978-90-04-31015-5 (hardback)
ISBN 978-90-04-36390-8 (e-book)

Copyright 2018 by Koninklijke Brill NV, Leiden, The Netherlands.
Koninklijke Brill NV incorporates the imprints Brill, Brill Hes & De Graaf, Brill Nijhoff, Brill Rodopi, Brill Sense and Hotei Publishing
All rights reserved. No part of this publication may be reproduced, translated, stored in a retrieval system, or transmitted in any form or by any means, electronic, mechanical, photocopying, recording or otherwise, without prior written permission from the publisher.
Authorization to photocopy items for internal or personal use is granted by Koninklijke Brill NV provided that the appropriate fees are paid directly to The Copyright Clearance Center, 222 Rosewood Drive, Suite 910, Danvers, MA 01923, USA. Fees are subject to change.

This book is printed on acid-free paper and produced in a sustainable manner.

Contents

Note on Names IX
Acknowledgements X
List of Figures and Tables XII
Abbreviations XVI
Notes on Contributors XVII

Introduction: Hungarian Medieval Economic History: Sources, Research and Methodology 1
   József Laszlovszky, Balázs Nagy, Péter Szabó and András Vadas

PART 1
Structures

1 Long-Term Environmental Changes in Medieval Hungary: Changes in Settlement Areas and Their Potential Drivers 39
   László Ferenczi, József Laszlovszky, Zsolt Pinke, Péter Szabó and András Vadas

2 Demographic Issues in Late Medieval Hungary: Population, Ethnic Groups, Economic Activity 48
   András Kubinyi and József Laszlovszky

3 Mobility, Roads and Bridges in Medieval Hungary 64
   Magdolna Szilágyi

PART 2
Human-Nature Interaction in Production

4 Agriculture in Medieval Hungary 81
   József Laszlovszky

5 Animal Exploitation in Medieval Hungary 113
   László Bartosiewicz, Anna Zsófia Biller, Péter Csippán, László Daróczi-Szabó, Márta Daróczi-Szabó, Erika Gál, István Kováts, Kyra Lyublyanovics and Éva Ágnes Nyerges

6   Mining in Medieval Hungary   166
     Zoltán Batizi

7   Salt Mining and Trade in Hungary before the Mongol Invasion   182
     Beatrix F. Romhányi

8   Salt Mining and Trade in Hungary from the mid-Thirteenth Century until the End of the Middle Ages   205
     István Draskóczy

9   The Extent and Management of Woodland in Medieval Hungary   219
     Péter Szabó

10   Water Management in Medieval Hungary   238
     László Ferenczi

PART 3
Money, Incomes and Management

11   Royal Revenues in the Árpádian Age   255
     Boglárka Weisz

12   Seigneurial Dues and Taxation Principles in Late Medieval Hungary   265
     Árpád Nógrády

13   Minting, Financial Administration and Coin Circulation in Hungary in the Árpádian and Angevin Periods (1000–1387)   279
     Csaba Tóth

14   Coinage and Financial Administration in Late Medieval Hungary (1387–1526)   295
     Márton Gyöngyössy

PART 4
Spheres of Production

15   The Ecclesiastic Economy in Medieval Hungary   309
     Beatrix F. Romhányi

CONTENTS   VII

16   The Urban Economy in Medieval Hungary   335
     Katalin Szende

17   The Medieval Market Town and Its Economy   359
     István Petrovics

18   Crafts in Medieval Hungary   369
     László Szende

19   The Economy of Castle Estates in the Late Medieval Kingdom
     of Hungary   394
     István Kenyeres

     PART 5
     Trade Relations

20   Domestic Trade in the Árpádian Age   419
     Boglárka Weisz

21   Professional Merchants and the Institutions of Trade: Domestic
     Trade in Late Medieval Hungary   432
     András Kubinyi

22   Import Objects as Sources of the Economic History of Medieval
     Hungary   455
     István Feld

23   Foreign Trade of Medieval Hungary   473
     Balázs Nagy

24   Foreign Business Interests in Hungary in the Middle Ages   491
     Krisztina Arany

     Appendix   509
     List of References   511
     Index of Geographic Names   625
     Index of Personal Names   636

Note on Names

If a settlement lies outside the territory of present-day Hungary we always use its official current place name. In order to make identification easier in the index we will also refer to the Hungarian or other relevant forms of the settlement name. If a settlement is lost or integrated into a modern settlement with a different name we will use its medieval or early modern name. With rivers having sections in present-day Hungary we will use the Hungarian names unless they have an English version. With rivers outside of present-day Hungary we use the form of the name used in the relevant countries. We will use Hungarian forms for the historical county names. Kings and queens will be referred to in their English name forms but will always indicate their title as kings and queens of Hungary.

Acknowledgements

The concept of this volume originated in the scholarly *oeuvre* of the late professor András Kubinyi (1929–2007), a leading scholar of medieval Hungarian economic and social history. Most of the authors of the individual chapters were his students or colleagues. The editors are indebted to Professor Kubinyi for inspiration and the motivation he provided.

The present volume is a late but closely connected outcome of the project *Medieval Hungarian Economic History in the Light of Archaeology and Material Culture*, supported by OTKA (the National Scholarly Research Fund, OTKA TS 49866) between 2005 and 2008. The project was directed by András Kubinyi, and after his death by József Laszlovszky.

The results of this research project have been summarized in a Hungarian-language collective volume that was published in 2008 (*Gazdaság és gazdálkodás a középkori Magyarországon. Gazdaságtörténet, anyagi kultúra, régészet* [Economy and farming in medieval Hungary. Economic history, material culture and archaeology], eds. Kubinyi, A., Laszlovszky, J. and Szabó, P. Budapest: Martin Opitz). A later grant from OTKA also financed the English translation of the volume (OTKA PUB-K 80703). Many of the chapters were translated by Alan Campbell, and the editors hereby wish to express their gratitude to him for his precise and dedicated work as well as for Simon Milton for proofreading the entire manuscript.

This volume, however, is not a simple translation of its forerunner in Hungarian, but is basically a new volume which includes a number of new chapters, covering – among other topics – royal revenues, environmental changes, and roads and communication networks. All the chapters have been re-written and adapted according to the needs and interests of non-Hungarian readers. The authors have also endeavored to define and clarify all the concepts and terminology that are less well known among non-Hungarian readers.

The editors express their gratitude to the series editor Florin Curta for accepting this volume to the series *East Central and Eastern Europe in the Middle Ages, 450–1450* and for his numerous advices to improve the quality of the text. Marcella Mulder from Brill helped the editorial work from the beginning until the last moment with special patience and care. The editors thank Jozef Markotan, great provost of the Rožňava Cathedral Chapter for giving permission to reproduce the painting of Saint Anne Trinity on the cover of this book and also Stanislava Kuzmová for easing communication with him.

János Bak maintained a supporting role throughout the process of publishing this volume. His close and critical reading of the manuscript, questions, and advice have been of great help.

The editors

List of Figures and Tables

Figures

0.1　The surface of the Carpathian Basin and its main regions　36
1.1　Geomorphological map of the studied part of the Transtisza region　43
2.1　Route of the Mongol troops in 1241 and 1242　53
2.2　Coin hoards uncovered from the period of the Mongol invasions　55
2.3　Map of different ethnic groups living in medieval Hungary　61
3.1　Medieval road leading from Râșnov to the market town of Bârsa Chute preserved as a holloway　69
3.2　Gothic stone bridge at Dravce in Slovakia　72
3.3　Gothic stone bridge near Leles in Slovakia　72
4.1　Social groups of rural population in the thirteenth century after Szűcs　96
4.2　Sickels from Nyáregyháza-Pusztapótharaszt and Iron depot from Cegléd-Madarászhalom　98
4.3　Remains of the medieval field system near Tamási　106
5.1　The number of medieval animal bone assemblages studied by settlement type and chronological groups　116
5.2　The size distribution of assemblages (NISP) by settlement types　118
5.3　Proportions between the remains of the most important meat producing animals at rural settlements　119
5.4　Excavation of a pot buried upside-down at the site of Budapest–Kána and remains of an articulated puppy skeleton found underneath the pot　122
5.5　Proportions between the remains of the most important meat producing animals at high status settlements　125
5.6　Proportions between the remains of the most important meat producing animals at urban settlements　128
5.7　Depiction of straight-horned Racka sheep by Luigi Fernando Marsigli from 1726　131
5.8　The diversity of bird species by settlement type　134
5.9　Hungarian nobility in decorative plumage at the turn of the sixteenth and seventeenth centuries　136
5.10　Articulated leg bones of an imported Lanner falcon from fourteenth-century Buda Castle　137
5.11　The taxonomic distribution of 1029 fish bones from 23 medieval sites in Hungary　139

LIST OF FIGURES AND TABLES   XIII

5.12 Landing and processing great sturgeon on location in the Iron Gates Gorge of the Danube   141
5.13 Debitage from the bone bead manufacturing workshop in fourteenth–fifteenth-century Visegrád   145
5.14 Late medieval elephant ivory comb from the Lower Castle of Visegrád   147
5.15 Oral section of a late medieval leopard skull from Segesd–Pékóföld (right) and the anatomical location of the worked bone (shaded, left)   148
6.1   Mining areas and minting chambers in medieval Hungary   181
7.1   Organization of salt transportation before the Mongol invasion   201
8.1   Organization of salt mining in fifteenth-century Hungary   218
9.1   The percentage of woodland cover in each county in the fifteenth century as reflected in estimations. No data from counties left blank   226
9.2   The proportion of the area covered by different types of woodland (or combinations of different types) as recorded in estimations   229
10.1 Medieval fishponds of Pauline monastery of the Holy Cross in the Pilis   246
12.1 Weekly wages and the price of oats in Prešov   266
15.1 Estimated incomes of the Hungarian dioceses between the end of the twelfth and the beginning of the sixteenth century   314
16.1 The market zone of lime produced in the kilns run by the municipality of Sopron   345
16.2 Layout of the new town wall of Pest in the late fifteenth century   346
16.3 The marketplace of medieval Óbuda as reconstructed by archaeological research   349
16.4 The marketplaces of medieval Veszprém   350
16.5 Layout of medieval Košice with the marketplace at the center   351
16.6 The topography of medieval Trnava with the marketplaces   353
16.7 The marketplaces of medieval Sopron   354
16.8 Medieval marketplaces of Buda   356
17.1 Towns and market zones in the Great Hungarian Plain in the Late Middle Ages   363
18.1 Sabretache plate fom Hlohovec   373
18.2 The seal of the Latins of Esztergom   376
18.3 Bell from Drăușeni   381
18.4 Mounts of caskets from Limoges   384
18.5 Drinking cup with representation of the *Agnus Dei*   385
18.6 The Benedek Suki chalice   386

18.7	Chausble of Košice 388
18.8	The Matthias stalls at Bardejov 390
18.9	Majolica ware from the Buda workshop 393
19.1	Cash income from the Hunedoara, Gyula and Magyaróvár estates (1511–1541) 402
20.1	Customs places, fords, markets and thirtieth customs places until the mid-fourteenth century 430
22.1	Fragments of the chandelier of Ozora 459
22.2a	Knives imported from Austria. Apart from their type the masters' signs also testify their origin 462
22.2b	Knives imported from Austria. Apart from their type the masters' signs also testify their origin 463
22.3	Glassware fragments originating from Venice 466
23.1	Main trade routes in the late medieval Kingdom of Hungary 487

Tables

5.1	Summary of mammalian assemblages by settlement type 150
5.2	Animal remains from rural settlements 154
5.3	Animal remains from settlements in central positions 156
5.4	Animal remains from urban settlements 158
5.5	Bird remains from rural settlements 160
5.6	Bird remains from settlements in central positions 162
5.7	Bird remains from urban settlements 164
7.1	Salt donations to churches before 1233 198
7.2	Salt donations to churches in the 1233 Bereg charter 198
7.3	Total amounts per types of institutions in 1233 Bereg treaty 200
7.4	Total amounts per types of institutions (with institutions not mentioned by name in the Bereg charter) 200
9.1	The extent of the four basic land-cover types in the Carpathian Basin in the fifteenth century as reflected in estimations 225
12.1	Towns/villages, numbers of taxpayers, total dues collected and average dues (in florins) 271
14.1	Ordinary revenues of the king of Hungary in the fifteenth century (in florins) 303
14.2	The profit from mint chambers in the first half of the fifteenth century (florins) 304
15.1	Incomes of and taxes paid by the Hungarian bishops between 1184 and 1525 312

LIST OF FIGURES AND TABLES

15.2 The incomes of two bishops of Eger, Tamás Bakóc and Ippolito d'Este (sums in golden florins)   315
15.3 The incomes of Ippolito d'Este, archbishop of Esztergom (sums in golden florins)   315
19.1 Income of the Hunedoara estate (1518, 1521–1522)   403
19.2 War dues and extraordinary dues in Hunedoara (1512–1522)   405
19.3 Income of the Gyula estate (1524–1526)   406
19.4 Income of the Magyaróvár estate (1531–1536)   407
19.5 Expenditure of Hunedoara estate (1521–1522)   409
19.6 Gyula estate expenditure (1524–1527)   410
19.7 Magyaróvár estate expenditure (1531–1536)   411
19.8 Average income in cash and kind of the three estates (florins)   412

Abbreviations

DF	Collection of Diplomatic Photographs (preserved in MNL OL)
DL	Collection of Diplomatics (preserved in MNL OL)
MNL OL	Magyar Nemzeti Levéltár Országos Levéltára / Hungarian National Archives, State Archive (Budapest)
MTA	Magyar Tudományos Akadémia / Hungarian Academy of Sciences (Budapest)
OSZK	Országos Széchényi Könyvtár / Széchényi National Library (Budapest)

Notes on Contributors

Krisztina Arany
is Senior Archivist at the National Archives of Hungary and co-ordinates research of archival records on Hungary in foreign archives. She is also curator of Collection of Diplomatic Photographs. Her main interests are medieval economic and social history. She wrote her PhD dissertation on Florentine-Hungarian trade and family contacts at Central European University (*Florentine Families in Hungary in the First Half of the Fifteenth Century*, 2014). She is currently involved in a source-edition project entitled the "Codex of the Talovci family" led by the Division of Historical Sciences of the Institute of Historical and Social Sciences of Croatian Academy of Sciences and Arts.

László Bartosiewicz
is Professor at Stockholm University and head of its Osteoarchaeological Research Laboratory. He received a degree in animal science at the University of Gödöllő (Hungary) in 1977. Following fifteen years of full-time archaeozoological research at the Hungarian Academy of Sciences he began teaching the same subject at universities in Budapest (Hungary), Edinburgh (UK) and Stockholm (Sweden) where he is currently employed. His main areas of interest include the history of cattle exploitation, the reconstruction of fishing and the development of cultural differences in meat consumption in Europe and Southwest Asia. He is author of the monograph *Animals in the urban landscape in the wake of the Middle Ages: a case study from Vác, Hungary* (Oxford, 1995).

Zoltán Batizi
is a freelance archaeologist who has worked at great number of excavations in Pest County as leading archaeologist. He has been working at the Tragor Ignác Museum at Vác for more than a decade. His main research interests span medieval history and the archaeology of Pest County, especially of the Danube Bend, historical navigation on the Danube, medieval mining and minorities to early modern peasant living conditions and the history of the formation of family names.

Anna Zsófia Biller
is archaeozoologist at the Aquincum Museum in Budapest. As a freelance archaeologist she has also processed animal bone materials for several other institutions in Hungary (such as the Institute of Archaeology of the Hungarian Academy of Sciences, the Institute of Archaeological Sciences of Eötvös

Loránd University, the Hungarian National Museum, etc.). She has been involved in research projects as an archaeozoologist in Metaponto in southern Italy (University of Texas, Austin) and Butrint in southern Albania (University of Notre Dame).

Péter Csippán
is Research Fellow at the Department of Archaeometry and Archaeological Methodology, Eötvös Loránd University. His main research interest is the archaeozoology of Prehistory. He defended his PhD dissertation in 2012 related to the same issue: *Őskori települések kulturális ökológiai és zooarchaeoloógiai vizsgálata A késő rézkori háztartások és a konyhahulladék kapcsolata* [Cultural ecological and zooarchaeological research of prehistoric settlements The connections between the late Copper Age households and the household rubbish]. His recent research focuses on new methodological and computer applications in archaeozoology.

László Daróczi-Szabó
is working as a freelance archaeozoologist for numerous institutes in Hungary, analyzing assemblages dating from the Neolithic period up to Modern Times. He is currently working on his PhD dissertation about archaeozoological finds in the medieval Buda Castle.

Márta Daróczi-Szabó
is working as a freelance archaeozoologist for numerous institutes in Hungary, analyzing assemblages dating from the Neolithic period until the Modern Times. She defended her PhD thesis in 2014 on the animal remains at Kána village in the twelfth–thirteenth centuries (*Az Árpád-kori Kána falu állatcsontjainak vizsgálata* [Animal bone remains of the Árpádian-age village of Kána]).

István Draskóczy
is Professor of Medieval History at Eötvös Loránd University, Budapest. His main research interest is the economic and social history of late medieval Hungary. He has published a number of studies on personnel involved in the financial administration of the kingdom and on royal income. In the last two decades he has extensively published on the history of mining and trade in medieval Hungary, with special regard to salt. Currently he is working on the topic of the university peregrination of Hungarian students. He is the head of the joint research group of the Hungarian Academy of Sciences and Eötvös Loránd University on this topic.

István Feld
is Associate Professor at the Department of Hungarian Medieval and Early Modern Archaeology, Institute of Archaeology at Eötvös Loránd University. He has also worked at the Budapest History Museum, as well as at the Rákóczi Museum of Sárospatak, a branch of the Hungarian National Museum. His main research interests include building archaeology, castle research and material culture. He co-authored monographs on the castles of Heves and Borsod-Abaúj-Zemplén counties in the series entitled: *Magyarország várainak topográfiája* [Topography of Hungarian castles].

László Ferenczi
is a historian and archaeologist. His main research interest is the economy of the monastic orders, most importantly the Cistercians. He is about to finish his dissertation at the Central European University on the Cistercian economy in medieval Hungary with special regard to the management of granges (*Management of Monastic Landscapes. Spatial Analysis of the Economy of Cistercian Monasteries in Medieval Hungary*). His publications include landscape history, environmental history and water management.

Erika Gál
is a Senior Research Fellow at the Institute of Archaeology, Research Centre for the Humanities, Hungarian Academy of Sciences. She is the author of the book *Fowling in Lowlands: Neolithic and Chalcolithic bird exploitation in South-East Romania and the Great Hungarian Plain* (2007). Her main research interests include the archaeozoology of birds and mammals in the Carpathian Basin and other parts of Europe.

Márton Gyöngyössy
is Associate Professor at the Department of Auxiliary Sciences of History, Institute of History, Eötvös Loránd University, Budapest. His main research interest is the monetary history of medieval Hungary. He defended his PhD dissertation in 2002 on the monetary reform of King Matthias Corvinus and its continuation until 1521. He is the author of various studies and articles on topics such as numismatics, monetary history, late medieval coinage, Ottoman coinage, religious medals and the legal regulations of archaeological excavations.

István Kenyeres
is General Director of the Budapest City Archives. His main research interests are late medieval and early modern economy, administration, finance

and urban history. His publications include the edition *XVI. századi uradalmi utasítások. Utasítások a kamarai uradalmak prefektusai, udvarbírái és ellenőrei részére* [16th-century instructions to the prefects, stewards, and controllers of estates of the royal chamber] (2002) and the German Butchers' Guild book (*Zunftbuch und Privilegien der Fleischer zu Ofen aus dem Mittelalter*, 2008). He authored the monograph *Uradalmak és végvárak. A kamarai birtokok és a törökellenes határvédelem a 16. századi Magyar Királyságban* [Lordships and border castles. Estates of the Hungarian Chamber and the anti-Ottoman border protection in the sixteenth-century kingdom of Hungary] (2008).

István Kováts
is a field archaeologist and archaeozoologist at the King Matthias Museum in Visegrád, a branch of the Hungarian National Museum. He has directed excavations in several areas of the late medieval town and citadel of Visegrád and has organized regular meetings for archaeozoologists at the museum. He specializes in the Middle Ages and the Early Modern Period and works with osseous materials in particular.

András Kubinyi
(1929–2007) late Professor of Medieval Archaeology at Eötvös Loránd University in Budapest and member of the Hungarian Academy of Sciences. His main research interests were late medieval urban, social, ecclesiastical and economic history, the history of everyday life and material culture. He has dedicated a number of works to the history of medieval Buda, Pest and Óbuda, as well as of their suburbs. His works include: *Die Anfänge Ofens* (1972); and *König und Volk im spätmittelalterlichen Ungarn. Städteentwicklung, Alltagsleben und Regierung im mittelalterlichen Ungarn* (1998). His collected studies on the history of Budapest were published posthumously in two volumes: *Tanulmányok Budapest középkori történetéről* [Studies on the medieval history of Budapest] (2009).

József Laszlovszky
is Professor of Medieval Studies at the Central European University, Budapest and director of its Cultural Heritage Program. He is also a regular guest lecturer at Eötvös Loránd University, Budapest. His research interests span the archaeology of the countryside and monastic landscapes through the preservation of cultural heritage to the history of English–Hungarian relations in the Middle Ages. He has conducted a number of excavations in medieval sites such as the Cistercian grange at Pomáz-Nagykovácsi and the Franciscan friary at

Visegrád. He recently co-authored and co-edited the two-volume English survey of the history and archaeological heritage of Visegrád (*The Medieval Royal Palace at Visegrád*, ed. with Gergely Buzás, 2013 and *The Medieval Royal Town at Visegrád: Royal Centre, Urban Settlement, Churches*, ed. with Orsolya Mészáros and Gergely Buzás, 2014).

Kyra Lyublyanovics
works as a freelance archaeozoologist at various museums in Hungary, as well as at the Hungarian Academy of Sciences, Research Centre for the Humanities. She earned her PhD in 2015 at the Central European University with a dissertation dealing with the animal husbandry of the medieval Cumans (*The Socio-Economic Integration of Cumans in Medieval Hungary. An Archaeozoological Approach*). Her research interest focuses on human-animal relationships in nomadic societies, animals in burial practices, and the history of veterinary treatment and care.

Balázs Nagy
is Associate Professor of Medieval History at the Eötvös Loránd University and visiting faculty at the Department of Medieval Studies at the Central European University, Budapest. His main research interest is the medieval economic and urban history of Central Europe. He is co-editor of the Latin-English bilingual edition of the autobiography of Emperor Charles IV (ed. with Frank Schaer, 2001), has edited with Derek Keene and Katalin Szende *Segregation – Integration – Assimilation: Religious and Ethnic Groups in the Medieval Towns of Central and Eastern Europe* (Ashgate, 2009) and with Martyn Rady, Katalin Szende and András Vadas *Medieval Buda in Context* (Brill, 2016).

Árpád Nógrády
is Senior Research Fellow at the Medieval History Research Team, Research Centre for the Humanities, Institute of History of the Hungarian Academy of Sciences. His main research interests are historical geography, the history of everyday life and the history of social relations in medieval Hungary. His main ongoing project is the continuation of the *Árpád-kori Magyarország történeti földrajza* [Historical Geography of Árpádian Age Hungary]. He is about to finish a volume that discusses the history of Sáros County from the tenth to the fourteenth centuries. He recently published the account book of the incomes of a Hungarian aristocrat in late medieval Hungary (*Kanizsai László számadáskönyve* [The account book of László Kanizsai], 2011).

Éva Ágnes Nyerges
is Assistant Research Fellow at the Institute of Archaeology at the Hungarian Academy of Sciences, Research Centre for the Humanities. She graduated as an archaeology major from Eötvös Loránd University where currently she pursues her PhD studies. Her dissertation deals with the process of domestication in the Neolithic in the light of hunting and animal husbandry at the archaeological site of Alsónyék-Bátaszék in Hungary. Her research interests are animal-keeping, husbandry and farming in Prehistory.

István Petrovics
is Associate Professor at the Department of Medieval and Early Modern Hungarian History at the University of Szeged from where he graduated in 1977. His special field of research is medieval Hungarian and European social and urban history, but his research interests also include medieval church, legal and military history. He has participated in several national research programs, the most important of which led to the publication of the *Early Hungarian Historical Lexicon* in 1994. He also acted as associate-editor and author of the *Medieval Warfare and Military Technology. An Encyclopedia* (Oxford, 2010). He has published four books and more than one hundred and fifty studies, a significant part of which are in English.

Zsolt Pinke
is a historian and a PhD candidate in environmental science at Szent István University in Hungary. He recently defended his dissertation that addressed the possible impacts of the Little Ice Age on the land-use patterns and habitat areas in the Great Hungarian Plain (*Alkalmazkodás és felemelkedés – modernizáció és leszakadás: Kis jégkorszaki kihívások és társadalmi válaszok a Tiszántúlon* [Adaptation and Rise – Modernization and Decline: Little Ice Age Challenges and Social Responses on the Trans-Tisza Region], 2015). His works include studies on river regulations, habitat restoration, agricultural and landscape history.

Beatrix F. Romhányi
is Associate Professor at the Department of Medieval History at Károli Gáspár Calvinist University, Budapest. Her fields of interest and range of publications include medieval ecclesiastical history, especially the history of monasticism, economic history and historical demography. Her recent research focuses on the economic activity of the Paulines and the mendicant orders in Hungary and in Central Europe. Her most recent monograph *'A lelkiek a földiek nélkül*

nem tarthatók fenn'… Pálos gazdálkodás a középkorban [The spiritual cannot be kept up without the earthly. Pauline farming in medieval Hungary] was published in 2010.

Péter Szabó

is Deputy Head at the Department of Vegetation Ecology, Institute of Botany of the Czech Academy of Sciences in Brno. His main research interest is historical ecology and environmental history, especially the history of Central European woodlands and landscapes from the beginning of the Holocene until the present. He works towards the integration of natural sciences and humanities using an interdisciplinary framework. His works include *Woodland and Forests in Medieval Hungary* (2005), several edited volumes on environmental history, and ca. 50 papers in edited volumes and journals including e.g. the Journal of Historical Geography, Landscape Research, Quaternary Science Reviews, Conservation Biology and Biological Reviews.

Katalin Szende

is Associate Professor of Medieval Studies at the Central European University, Budapest. Her research concentrates on medieval towns in the Carpathian Basin and Central Europe, with particular regard to society, demography, literacy, everyday life, and topography. Her previous publications include *Otthon a városban. Társadalom és anyagi kultúra a középkori Sopronban, Pozsonyban és Eperjesen* [At home in the town: Society and material culture in medieval Sopron, Bratislava and Prešov] (2004); ed. with Finn-Einar Eliassen, *Generations in Towns: Succession and Success in Pre-industrial Urban Societies* (2009); ed. with Derek Keene and Balázs Nagy *Segregation – Integration – Assimilation. Religious and Ethnic Groups in the Medieval Towns of Central and Eastern Europe* (2009) and ed. with Balázs Nagy, Martyn Rady and András Vadas *Medieval Buda in Context* (Brill, 2016).

László Szende

is Head of the Central Data Warehouse and Informatics Department of the Hungarian National Museum. His main research interests are the history of crafts and history of courts with special regard to the courts of queens. He defended his PhD dissertation at Eötvös Loránd University on the organization of the court of the queen consort to King Charles I (*Piast Erzsébet és udvara, 1320–1380* [Elizabeth Piast and her court, 1320–1380], 2007). He has published a number of studies on crafts, the history of archaeology and museology, as well as on diets and queenship in medieval Hungary.

Magdolna Szilágyi
is Associate Research Fellow of the Medieval History Research Team at the Research Centre for the Humanities, Hungarian Academy of Sciences. She obtained her PhD degree in Medieval Studies from the Central European University (*Árpád Period Communication Networks: Road Systems in Western Transdanubia*, 2013). Parts of her doctoral dissertation were published as a monograph titled On the Road: The History and Archaeology of Medieval Communication Networks in East-Central Europe in 2014. Her research interests involve medieval history and archaeology, landscape archaeology, and historical geography with special regard to the road system of medieval Hungary.

Csaba Tóth
is numismatist at the Hungarian National Museum, Budapest. His main research interest is the monetary history of medieval Hungary with special regard to the Angevin period. He defended his PhD dissertation in 2002 on the minting and money circulation of the Angevin period (*Pénzverés és pénzforgalom az Anjou-kori Magyarországon*). He is the author of dozens of studies and articles on topics such as numismatics, money circulation, coin-hoards and monetary history. He has also been involved in numerous exhibitions held at the Hungarian National Museum.

András Vadas
is Assistant Professor of Medieval History at the Eötvös Loránd University, Budapest. His research interest is the environmental and economic history of the Middle Ages and the Early Modern Period. His works discuss the problem of the environmental change brought by military activities in the Carpathian Basin, as well as on mills and milling in medieval Hungary. His monograph *Körmend és a vizek. Egy település és környezete a korai újkorban* [Körmend and the waters. A settlement and its environment in the Early Modern period] was published in 2013, and he also and co-edited with Balázs Nagy, Martyn Rady and Katalin Szende *Medieval Buda in Context* (Brill, 2016).

Boglárka Weisz
is Senior Research Fellow at the Institute of History of Research Centre for the Humanities, Hungarian Academy of Sciences, Budapest and leader of the Research Centre for the Humanities, Hungarian Academy of Sciences "Lendület" Medieval Hungarian Economic History Research Group. Her research concentrates on the medieval economic history of Hungary. She has published a complete register of tolls in the Árpádian age (*A királyketteje és az ispán harmada. Vámok és vámszedés Magyarországon a középkor első felében*

[Customs and Customs Duties in Hungary in the First Half of Middle Ages]) (2013) and written a monograph on the institutions of medieval Hungarian trade, fairs, markets and staples (*Vásárok és lerakatok a középkori Magyar Királyságban* [Markets and staples in the Medieval Kingdom of Hungary]) (2012). She has also published a number of studies about the problem of royal taxation and revenues, as well as financial administration, chambers and chamber counts.

INTRODUCTION

Hungarian Medieval Economic History: Sources, Research and Methodology

József Laszlovszky, Balázs Nagy, Péter Szabó and András Vadas*

This book attempts to survey the economic history and production of medieval Hungary using an up-to-date approach, and draws on a wide range of sources. Correspondingly, the characteristics of the sources that are available, problems with methodology, and historiographical legacy are considered in this chapter.

Traditional methods of understanding economic history involve the analysis of quantifiable data of the kind used to characterize the modern economy. These data are used to produce economic indicators, and the way these change over time is used to describe the processes of economic history. This procedure is then applied systematically to specific areas of economic activity. The indicators characterize the basic structural elements of the economy, the relative size of economic sectors and their output, as well as characteristics relating to quality. This approach is clearly not applicable to the economic affairs of medieval Hungary: as a starting point, we would need to know the size and regional distribution of the country's medieval population and the conditions of the settlements people lived in. To be able to assess specific economic sectors and develop a full picture, we would need somewhat more detailed data. In the case of agriculture (the most prominent sector of the medieval economy) such an account would have to include demographic data about the peasant population which was mainly responsible for this sector, the area and spatial distribution of land under cultivation, and related structural indicators. First, we would have to know which crops were grown during different seasons and how much land they were grown on, the kinds of animals that were kept, and their various proportions on different kinds of farms. This would provide the basis for determining which products were being grown – and in which quantities – for the purposes of self-sufficiency or local consumption, which were handed over as local or crown taxes and duties, and which kinds of goods – and in what quantities – had become commercial commodities

---

* The research done by András Vadas was supported by the ÚNKP-17- 4 New National Excellence Program of the Ministry of Human Capacities.

through local or long-distance trade. Establishing the general economic position of the country would require even more far-reaching quantitative indicators. Traditional indicators such as those concerning the balance of foreign trade would have to be analyzed over a period of several centuries. After this study of the country as a whole, we could then examine the regional specifics of economic activity, the magnitude and distribution of the sectors of the economy in different smaller spatial units such as estates and village fields, and the areas and centers of production and their spatial arrangement. After this, we should undertake a historical review of the basic information concerning each sector of the economy, covering the extent of its application and level of development of various production techniques. For agrarian production, this would mean analyzing how village fields were used, characterizing agricultural implements, and producing a detailed treatment of taxes and dues connected with production. In addition, for the most important sector, arable farming, we would need biological information about crops. In conclusion, it is quite clear that the number, character and content of contemporary sources rule out the application of such an approach to economic history. We simply lack the economic indicators, quantifiable data and information about qualitative characteristics that would be required. These omissions are not merely a matter of gaps in time series; we hardly have any data even for discrete moments in time. Even when some extended data series exist (such as those concerning some types of dues and their amounts), they are usually severely restricted in space and time, and only a very small proportion survive from any time before the two final centuries of the Middle Ages. As a result, the major structural changes that took place at the turn of the tenth and eleventh centuries, and then again at the turn of the thirteenth and fourteenth centuries, which affected all of the sectors of the country's economy, can hardly be demonstrated at all in economic historical terms. Furthermore, data from later times cannot be applied to the conditions of earlier centuries, even in areas (such as agricultural cultivation) where changes are usually expected to be relatively slow. This scarcity of sources obstructs the creation of an overall picture of certain geographical areas and economic sectors during certain periods. Thus, all we can do is make very specific analyses of a kind that cannot be generalized to the national scale, or over the longer term. We therefore start with a review of the main groups of sources available for the purposes of research. We then discuss the most typical methodological problems and examine the research that has been carried out to date. This historiographical review does not cover the development of every area of research, but only some characteristics of the main historiographic periods. This review locates economic history studies within the broader Hungarian, and to some extent international, historiography.

The period the book touches upon is what traditionally is considered as Hungarian Middle Ages. This is somewhat different from that of the traditional periodization of Western European history. The beginning of the period is the tenth century when the Hungarians settled in the Carpathian Basin and began to exploit the resources of this area. The end date of the present investigation is the fall of the medieval Kingdom of Hungary to the Ottoman Empire is 1526 which was followed by a gradual expansion of the Turks to the central part of the country.

Characteristics and Availability of Sources

Written Sources

The medieval documents that are least informative about economic matters are narrative sources (chronicles, *gestae*, and saints' lives). They make very infrequent references to agricultural activities and produce, and have little to say about crafts. Any connections they might have with the subject of study are at best indirect, such as the often-quoted story of the servant girl grinding grain with a hand mill by night in the Legend of St Gerhard. This source, for example, permits only vague inferences to be made about grain production and processing.[1] The best information in foreign chronicles is found in the accounts of authors who spent some time in Hungarian lands. These can tell us something about the economy of a specific period.[2] There are numerous reports from the time of the Crusades; for example, when individuals – mainly clergy who traveled with armies as they crossed the country – recorded details about what they considered interesting or strange phenomena. These reports contain solid information about the storage of harvested produce, and more generally about a country, which was always considered by foreigners to be very fertile and to have other good qualities, and also about what these travelers considered to be adverse money exchange rates. In the case of Bishop Otto of Freising, for example, we may ask how much the relative backwardness of towns was responsible for his judgment that the country lagged behind his own land in terms of development. Bishop Otto made similar comments about the kinds of buildings he found in villages. Similarly, descriptions by foreign travelers and merchants from both the East and West have generated dispute about the kinds of towns that existed in Hungary in the Árpádian age,

---

1 On the interpretation of this episode, see: Vajda 2016 and Vadas 2018.
2 Nagy 2009.

and what they tell us about the wealth of urban settlements in that period.[3] Normative sources are of greater value. Since written laws were intended to regulate general trends and countrywide problems, anything they contain pertaining to economic history merits particular emphasis.[4] They are what we rely on, above all, in the areas of state taxation and royal minting, financial administration, and monetary management.[5] Laws such as the ban on horse exports provide important information about animal breeding and foreign trade, and can also be indirectly linked to cultivation practices. An even more important category of legal documents, even though the economic information they provide is indirect, concerns the regulation of the collection of various taxes and dues (e.g. tithes and ninths), many of which were built on income from the most basic categories of agricultural production.[6] Laws governing the tithes imposed on viticulture and wine making, and documents about related litigation, are of similar indirect application in determining the extent and significance of this very remunerative and thus prominent branch of the economy.[7]

Much more information about economic issues, if also mostly of an indirect nature, may be found in the most numerous surviving medieval documents: the charters.[8] Documents recording legal transactions and procedures go into great detail about matters of ownership and the use of estates. Among the most abundant types of charters that are of use to economic historians, and which existed even in the earliest periods of written records in Hungary, are the royal grants of land and their confirmations. The early grants are mainly of royal estates to church institutions (mainly monasteries), but some early private grants were made from which we can make indirect inferences about the character of the estates being transferred. These help generate fairly precise knowledge about an estate's structure and the physical location of certain branches of agriculture, especially if the texts include a description of boundaries.[9] Hardly any of the hundreds of thousands of surviving Hungarian medieval charters, however, tell us with any great precision about the extent and magnitude of specific branches of agriculture. Estate divisions, land conscriptions and estimations are much closer to the kind of sources we need to

---

3 Györffy 1975, 235–247.
4 For the – until the time of publication of this book – most comprehensive collection of the medieval laws of Hungary in a Latin–English bilingual edition, see: Bak et al. (eds.) 1992–2012, I–V.
5 See the contribution of Márton Gyöngyössy in the present volume.
6 See the contribution of Boglárka Weisz in the present volume.
7 Solymosi 1990, Solymosi 1996a, Solymosi 1998 and Solymosi 2009.
8 For an overview of legal evidence: Hunyadi 1999.
9 On the potential of perambulations as source types, see: Szabó 2003, 268–271. On the localization of settlements in rural countryside: Laszlovszky 2003. See also: Zatykó 2015.

determine the significance of specific branches of agriculture and their relationships and extent in specific areas.[10] In fortunate cases, however, there are other ways in which charters can provide data about land use and the fields around villages. Some of the Latin words in these texts (e.g. *mixtim*) may refer to the locations and use of tracts of land, and some Hungarian expressions used in Latin texts, such as *nyomás* (fields in a rotation system), *tanór* (enclosed fields), *telek* (plot or toft), *árok* (ditch) and *füvönosztás* (arable fields divided by strips of grassland), help us to infer the existence of special forms of land use or types of cultivation. For this, we usually need to identify a Latin explanation of the Hungarian term, such as *telek* = *terra fimata, terra culta* (manured field, cultivated field), or ethnographic findings that link a form of land use with a term, such as *nyilas osztás* (annual relocation of fields by drawing lots). For other terms, such as *nyomás*, historical etymological investigation can explain the historical development and agricultural techniques that lie behind their use in charters.[11] Similar inferences, particularly for land use, may be made from toponyms and field names that occur in the charters. Similarly, the changing meanings and uses of various Latin words that occur in charters to classify agrarian settlements (*villa, possessio, terra*, etc.) indicate changes in settlement structure and the structure of agricultural labor, as has been identified in connection with the *praedium* (village or estate).[12] Similarly, toponyms recorded in charters help identify the settlements of serving people and may indicate particular branches of cultivation (e.g. names that include *Szántó* [arable] or *Szőlős* [vineyard]), crafts (*Kovácsi* [blacksmith]) or beekeeping (*Födémes*).[13] Censuses, including those of Árpádian-age portions of monastic estates and the people that lived on them and the services they rendered, can yield fairly precise information about the monastic economy of an era, particularly the significance of agriculture.[14]

A number of other groups of medieval place names, preserved mostly in charters, can be used as sources of economic history, especially when their dating and etymology is clear.[15] In the nineteenth century, Hungarian historical linguistic research naturally focused on the origin of Hungarian and related languages, as by that time it was already obvious that the Hungarian language is different to the languages of neighboring language groups such as Slavic, Romance, and Germanic. This consideration was also important in onomastic

---

10   For an overview, see Szabó 2003.
11   See the contribution of József Laszlovszky in the present volume.
12   Szabó 1963.
13   E.g. Györffy 1972.
14   See the contribution of Beatrix F. Romhányi in the present volume.
15   For an overview of the etymology and dating of place names, see: Kiss 1998.

studies. The study of place (mostly settlement) names in charter evidence that survives from the eleventh century onwards was used to identify which ethnic groups inhabited the Kingdom of Hungary in the age of St Stephen, and in general, in the Árpádian age. The works of István Kniezsa are of primary importance in this respect, as medieval settlement history research for a long time used his chronology of the temporal and geographical range of different settlements.[16] Although his dating of the early settlement names has been challenged at different points in recent studies, the dating of the later layer of settlements, and their importance in settlement- and economic history has remained intact.[17] For instance, the fact that settlement names formed through parasynthesis appear in growing numbers from the thirteenth century onwards is still considered proof of demographic expansion and the extension of the settlement network. Settlement names with *-ülése* (plot of), *-telke* (toft of), *-háza* (house of), *-falva* (village of) are evidence of settling within settlement borders and the colonization of previously less inhabited areas.[18] Placename analysis can also be used in the research of medieval parish networks to provide indirect data about the formation of the settlement networks of certain areas.[19] Recent detailed linguistic history research of settlement names in charter evidence has highlighted the interpolations in important written sources, such as those that describe the lands and the borders of Árpádian-age monasteries, thereby contributing to the more precise dating of the relevant passages and the social and economic features described in them.[20]

The number of surviving charters increases in the late medieval period, allowing us to identify the structure, character and use of the inner and outer fields of tenant peasant villages and other areas in collective use, and the systems of cultivation used therein (such as rotation).[21] Some settlements and systems of land use described in medieval charters retained their basic character until the early modern period, enabling us to include even eighteenth-century documents and maps in reconstructions of some farming units. The relatively coherent system of tenant peasant villages, however, allows us with certain constraints to apply data from such detailed sources to the fields around other settlements. Other useful medieval charters are those that record 'acts of might' (*factum potentiae*) and the damage they caused. These contain

16   Kniezsa 1938.
17   Kristó, Makk and Szegfű 1973–1974 and Kiss 1997b.
18   Kázmér 1970.
19   Mező 1996.
20   Szőke 2015.
21   Laszlovszky 1999.

important details about material culture and everyday life, including the peasant economy, farming, and the techniques these employed. Documents generated by the ensuing litigation recorded the value of damage that was caused and mentioned the object, building or produce that was affected[22] (care must be taken when using such sources, however, because it was in the interest of the victims of such incidents to inflate the value of the damage to an unrealistic extent). These data also tell us about the price of farm produce, and where they are available in sufficient quantities, they permit us to draw conclusions about the economy in general. Sources relating to the economic management of specific estates become increasingly significant from the fifteenth century onwards. They provide data, above all, about agricultural income and costs that the older sources do not. Data series about price and wage conditions can provide important indirect information about the development of the agrarian economy, and possibly on the crises it faced. Studies of German economic history in particular have shown the utility of this approach, but the relative scarcity of such data in Hungary and the lack of monographic treatment and analysis prevent us from drawing any general conclusions from them at present. Sources involving tithes, state taxes and landowners' income have already been used with somewhat greater confidence. Although there are also large gaps in these records,[23] they can tell us indirectly about economic affairs in specific areas. Interestingly, this is also true of sources dating from the early post-medieval period, as analyses of Ottoman censuses have shown.

Sources relating to the life and internal workings of medieval villages also have much to say about certain segments of medieval economic history, as have sources related to royal administration. These include charters of grant and privilege. Specifically, grants of privilege to hold markets and impose customs duties are among our most important sources relating to the history of trade in the Árpádian age, and later.[24]

Written sources relating to towns survive in large quantities, although they are highly fragmentary. There are documents concerning towns of different size and legal status. Their value as sources of economic history varies greatly depending upon the local government that produced them. The type of source that emerged as a documentary record for towns in the second half of

---

22   Kubinyi 1984c. See the recent works of István Tringli. For an overview of the literature in German: Tringli 2014.
23   E.g. Solymosi 1984, Kredics, Madarász and Solymosi (eds.) 1997. See more recently Nógrády (ed.) 2011 and his contribution in the present volume.
24   See the contribution of Boglárka Weisz in the present volume, and further on the sources of the history of trade in Hungary: Solymosi 2016a and Draskóczy 2016a.

the medieval period is not available for villages.[25] Municipal accounts, which are of different types, are very rich sources for many segments of the urban economy.[26] Some sources that concern towns, despite containing little quantitative data, form the basis for determining medieval forms of working organization and the structure of production. Among the most important of these are sources relating to the organization of guilds and their legal affairs, and the same texts often make – usually indirect – references to products made by guild members, and their means of manufacture and sale.[27] Wills are of similar importance in the study of the urban economy and have been the subject of systematic treatment in recent decades.[28] Certain account books and tax lists contain more quantitative information. Tax lists have survived for several major towns such as Sopron and some towns now in Slovakia, such as Košice, Bratislava, Prešov and Bardejov. Except for Bratislava, however, continuous municipal accounts are only available from the sixteenth century, and mostly from the middle of the century.[29]

Written sources thus mostly provide information about specific branches of the economy, and most are of only local or regional relevance. There is an almost complete lack of 'national' economic data – documents that provide information about specific forms of economic activity, craft industries, or any other sphere of the economy that has relevance to the whole kingdom. The exceptions – some very rare sources on national tax income – are of crucial importance for assessing Hungary's economic role in the Middle Ages.[30] As several chapters in this book show, although such census-like documents characterize a branch of the economy or one of its important elements in sufficient detail, as well as possibly offering a broader picture, they provide no more than snapshots, and do not tell us how phenomena changed with time. In other cases there may be several series of data that apply to an area or branch of the economy, but the sources are limited in space or subject matter, and

---

25 Szende 2013b.
26 On town books in the Hungarian Kingdom, see Majorossy and Szende 2012, and on sources of medieval towns, see the contribution of Katalin Szende in the present volume.
27 On guilds in general: Skorka 2012b. For a publication about the most intact medieval source on a guild in Hungary, see: Kenyeres (ed.) 2008. On the administration of guilds: Majorossy and Szende 2012, 345.
28 For an edition about the preeminent last will series from medieval Hungary, see: Majorossy and Szende (eds.) 2010–2014, and for its analysis from the point of view of material culture: Szende 2004b, and several further studies of Katalin Szende and Judit Majorossy.
29 For tax lists and the opportunities for their interpretation, e.g. Fügedi 1957–1958 and Granasztói 2012. On account books: Kováts 1902b. For the town books of Bratislava, see: Goda and Majorossy 2008, 87–99, for the account books of the town, see: 96–97.
30 See recently e.g. Kenyeres 2012 and C. Tóth 2016.

generalizing them over a larger area can only be done with reservation, if at all. Finally, a problem typical of such census-like sources is that they leave out vital information. We know that there were groups and sectors of society, which, for some reason (such as tax exemption), did not feature in tax censuses of different kinds. In addition, we must allow for the errors of those who drew up the censuses and the plethora of techniques by which people got away without paying their dues. Hungarian research into late medieval state taxes, and the pitfalls of the demographic studies built on them (for example) clearly show the serious contradictions to which the analysis of such sources leads.

Some isolated examples of written sources, however, give an impression of the range and complexity of economic affairs in the medieval period. They do not provide a basis, however, for determining the full structure of export or import commodities. The former gives a glimpse of the framework of trade in luxury items and the prices of jewelry and expensive textiles, while the latter provide data about trade and the relative values of ordinary goods. Specific commodities can act as indicators, because the occurrence of certain types of objects in a household may tell us something about the purchasing power of the person or community involved. In the absence of detailed sources that can be analyzed to reveal the wealth of different sectors of society, such indicator sources have great significance.

One widely used source for assessing economic processes and general levels of wealth is data about building projects. A written agreement concerning the construction of the cathedral in Alba Iulia, for example, in addition to providing valuable data about the work organization and costs of a large-scale church building project, indirectly tells us about the scale of the investment it represented.[31] Such building data is of particular importance in the absence of reliable figures concerning the income of bishoprics. Similarly, the alterations to Bratislava Castle during the reign of King Sigismund are also a crucial source of information about royal building activity in Hungary, but these data cannot be generalized to every form of construction.[32]

Pictorial Representations

Pictorial representations have always constituted an important set of sources in the study of medieval history. For the economic history of medieval Hungary, however, there are far fewer pictorial than written sources. Of the very few codex pictures and illuminations that concern Hungarian economic affairs, agriculture or crafts, many were definitely not made in Hungarian workshops. Thus the very few landscapes and representations of agricultural

---

31 Entz 1958.
32 Szűcs 1958.

work that we have do not necessarily depict things as they were in Hungary. The more numerous mural paintings and panel paintings that survive in, or originally came from medieval churches are somewhat more informative. This representational group has proved to be very useful in research into the history of costume and certain ethnic groups in Hungary.[33] Some details of interest for agricultural history have emerged from interpretations of biblical scenes, such as those of Cain and Abel, and scenes from the lives of saints. Similar and particularly useful in this respect are illustrations of the months, which typically show relevant agricultural activities such as plowing, sowing, harvesting and wood-cutting, with regional variations in details and chronological order. Early modern almanacs that feature the same series of month-illustrations are also informative about late medieval forms of cultivation. Pictures with religious themes can also provide information about specific craft products and even craft operations. Pictures in medieval churches (which make up the bulk of pictorial representations) depict biblical scenes or stories from the lives of saints. These were not attempts to reconstruct how things looked in biblical times, and usually recorded the conditions, material culture and costume of the time of their making, even when representing the Last Supper or Christ on the Cross. These pictures are thus crucial sources for the study of medieval material culture. Medieval archaeologists in Hungary have long used this group of sources, particularly in the study of the appearance and distribution of objects of different types. There are also fortuitous forms and subjects of pictorial representation that are highly informative about specific economic activities and branches of craft and trade. A representation of St Joseph, for example, may depict a carpenter's workshop and tools, and pictures of the birth of Jesus can be used to study contemporary stables and shepherds. In other cases, the important information lies in the background of a biblical scene or an illustration of the life of a saint. This may take the form of a cultivated landscape or a tiny detail related to contemporary mining, such as that depicted on St Anne's altar in Rožňava (the cover of the present volume). Such pictures survive in much smaller numbers, however, than panel paintings in other areas of Central Europe and miniature representations in Western Europe.[34]

Archaeology

Archaeological findings constitute one of the fastest-growing groups of sources for medieval economic history. In the past, random finds of agricultural

---

33   E.g. Pálóczi Horváth 1980 and Baráth 2015.
34   On the role of visual sources in the study of medieval material culture, see: Kubinyi and Laszlovszky (eds.) 1991. On visual sources in general: Szakács (ed.) 2001.

implements provided the starting point for the study of the history of objects. In the Middle Ages (principally in the Árpádian age, and later during the Ottoman occupation), iron agricultural implements and iron parts (plowshares, moldboards, coulters, etc.) were regularly buried in times of danger, in the same way as money and jewelry. Such finds of tools and treasure are important for chronological reasons, providing clear evidence that such agricultural implements were used during the period.[35] Recent village excavations – particularly some fortunate discoveries of full sets of household equipment preserved in place by sudden acts of destruction – provide more than mere evidence for the use of specific agricultural implements in the period; they help us reconstruct the operation of a small economic unit – the household. Recent urban excavations have turned up even larger numbers of agricultural items than have been found in hoards of agricultural implements. For example, in the case of the sickle, the most important harvesting implement, we now have a very clear picture of the types that were in use, their places of manufacture, and how they changed over time. Because items such as plows were of very high value, they are very rarely found in excavations of settlements, and many of the implements used on peasant farms (forks, harrows, rakes, etc.) – even in the period of ethnographic research – were made of wood and have not survived in the ground except in very special environments.[36]

Major discoveries during settlement excavations in recent decades have not been confined to agricultural implements, and have contributed to our knowledge of farming in general. Most notably, these have included remains of buildings for keeping livestock (livestock pens, pigsties and byres), as well as milling, and processing and storing produce. Systems of ditches found in villages of the Árpádian age indicate their division into areas for cultivation and livestock grazing or enclosure. This represents nothing less than the imprint of agricultural techniques on the layout of a settlement. Recent discoveries of similar but much more extensive ditch systems that covered even wider areas have been the subject of comprehensive archaeological and historical research, proving the existence of large systems of channels that exploited river floodwaters. These new sources have greatly expanded our knowledge of complex forms of agriculture – fishing, animal husbandry and cultivation.[37] Archaeological remains of farmstead-like settlements scattered in the areas between villages of the Árpádian age and a small number of related documentary sources have thrown light on the use of fields around villages and the way they were brought

---

35 E.g. Balassa 1973 and Müller 1975. Cf. Vargha 2015.
36 For ethnographic research on tools of the peasantry: Fél and Hofer 1997.
37 Takács 2003.

under cultivation.[38] Archaeology has added to our knowledge of late medieval agriculture in two major areas other than agricultural implements. First, the study of the internal structure of medieval villages, house sites and buildings on inner plots tells us about the proportions of settlements assigned to the various branches of agriculture (cultivation and animal husbandry, respectively). Second, using landscape archaeology and land surveying methods it is possible to trace medieval terrace-system, arable lands in hill and forested areas.[39] Their size, structure and location constitute an important source for addressing questions related to land use, and may be studied as indirect sources in relation to forest clearance and individual or collective attempts at colonization. This situation is mainly applicable to the identification and surveying of traces of arable land on areas where medieval arable fields later served as pasture or forest and thus retained their artificial terraces and other traces of plowland. Large numbers of these have been identified in elevated areas of the Carpathian Basin (in medieval Transylvania, Upper Hungary, the western borderlands, etc.), although they have not yet been the subject of detailed treatment or systematic landscape archaeology investigation. Their situation sharply contrasts with conditions in the plains of modern Hungary, where continuous arable cultivation, particularly the deep plowing of the last century, must have destroyed all such traces. For some lowland areas of Transdanubia, however, there are early modern maps, which show the traces of a centuriation system (a form of land use involving regular square parcels arranged along oriented axes) dating from the Roman period. Although these areas were used in completely different ways in the Middle Ages, the system of fields established several centuries earlier could still have provided the framework for cultivation and land use.[40] It may be possible to derive much more information about this by using historical sources combined with landscape archaeology.

Further archaeological finds of great value for economic history are medieval craft products. Ceramics, the one category of artifacts that is found in the greatest quantities, are important to archaeologists primarily as a means of dating, but changes in motifs, manufacturing techniques and morphology pointing to domestic and foreign manufacturing centers provide data useful in the study of economic history with which we can analyze the development of craft techniques and the wealth and living standards of the users. This is

---

38 Laszlovszky 1986.
39 See the volumes of the Archaeological Topography of Hungary. For the published volumes: http://ri.btk.mta.hu/hu/kiadvanyok/sorozatok/mrt-1966-2012 (last accessed: 24 August 2016).
40 See the overview of Zatykó 2015 on research history in the field in Hungary.

particularly true of stove tiles and stove tile decorations, which have an elevated place among ceramic finds. Some types of tile carry figural or heraldic designs, and in fortuitous site conditions, it is possible to identify the building work associated with a particular social group, family, or even individual.

Similarly, some building ceramics, such as ornamental floor bricks, also enable us to determine medieval market regions, as was done for the Cistercian abbey of Pilis. Characteristics of the molds used to make the patterns and slight differences between them enable us to identify the Pilis monastic workshop as the place of manufacture of floor bricks used for other monasteries, as well as the royal chapel in Visegrád.[41] To be able to trace medieval glass objects to the workshops in which they were made, however, knowledge of typology and ornamentation is not enough. Chemical and physical material tests are required, and individual glass objects and window glass finds thus require the use of archaeometric methods involving chemical and physical material tests to identify their origins. The glassworks uncovered in Visegrád and Pilis, however, are of a scale that indicates that there were enough sufficiently wealthy customers – possibly the royal court – to constitute a market for the large quantities of window and other glass artifacts produced in monastic or urban glassworks.[42] This is an example of how some archaeological finds can act as indicators in economic history research. Similarly, the standard of home furnishings provides indirect data about the living standards of a group, and building projects tell us about the economic conditions that made them possible. Indirectly, medieval grave goods[43] and the household culture[44] of different sectors of late medieval society may also be used as economic information, because social stratification and the material culture of different groups are in themselves indicative of economic processes. For example, one analysis of source groups (written, archaeological, etc.) that involved an examination of social stratification showed clearly that each group of sources illuminates different aspects of a different social group (e.g. legal status, wealth and material culture) which can be brought together to show the economic role and social position of a particular sector of society.[45] Building projects that consumed resources on a large scale are in every case potential indicators of the wealth of those who financed them. Presently, information on the size and nature of

---

41 Holl 2000.
42 Mészáros 2008, Buzás, Laszlovszky and Mészáros 2014, 59–62 (the relevant section is the work of O. Mészáros) and Laszlovszky et al. 2014.
43 Vargha 2015.
44 K. Csilléry 1982.
45 Laszlovszky 1991.

building projects mostly comes from architectural history/art history sources, in addition to expanding amounts of, but still relatively scarce, archaeological data. The adoption of approaches rooted in social for understanding economic history – relying to a great extent on the analysis of material culture and incorporating the concept of living standard – has thus become a means of addressing the scarcity of sources in the study of the medieval period. The complex living standard concept applied by Christopher Dyer, for example, considers as equally important the structural and interior features of dwellings and the material culture of different households and direct written sources about wealth and economic activities.[46] This approach has yielded significant results, even in countries with a much greater abundance and range of written sources than Hungary.

Bioarchaeological Sources and Scientific Research

Archaeological excavations conducted using up-to-date techniques are increasingly producing material that can be analyzed using scientific methods. The discipline of archaeobotany derives very useful information from medieval plant remains. Such remains generally survive – i.e., escape the usual biological degradation – in two forms. The first is through carbonization, which preserves remains for centuries. The other is by preservation in an anoxic environment, usually waterlogged ground or mud. This process is typical of seed and crop remains and branch fragments in filled-in wells, and pollen that has settled into the mud of lake-beds. From an analysis of such samples, it is possible to compile lists of species that lived in the cultivated or natural environment in a specific period. Such research, particularly when linked with settlement archaeology, allows us to build a general picture of medieval land use across an entire region, especially as regards the relative proportions of land-use elements (cultivated land, forest, pasture, marsh, etc.).[47] In other cases, and using similar techniques, we can acquire data about the characteristic features of a specific farm or branch of agriculture. This requires special excavation and sampling techniques (such as flotation). Some fortuitous finds (such as the large quantity of carbonized grains obtained during the excavation of the Cistercian abbey of Pásztó) may be used to understand how cereals were grown – autumn or spring sowing – and the presence of weeds alongside crops. Other special conditions of finds (such as carbonized bread or other food remains) tell us about how agricultural produce was prepared and consumed, as does the infill contents of latrines in settlements. In many cases,

---

46   Dyer 1989 and Dyer 1994.
47   Kovács and Zatykó (eds.) 2016 and the works they refer to.

seed and crop finds date the earliest occurrence of some crops to well before the dates previously established on the basis of Hungarian documents.[48]

Also of great significance among archaeobiological sources are animal bone remains, the research material of historical zoology. Given the soil conditions in Hungary, the most common finds of bones at archaeological sites are of those that were deposited as food waste or as raw material or by-products of craft operations. Biological and statistical analysis of these bones and investigation of craft techniques yield what is now the most important data we have about the animals that were bred in different areas, the characteristics of their features, and their role in trade. Analysis of animal remains has also become a means of characterizing major economic changes, a very important task in the study of different medieval periods. Animal bones from village-like settlements have been used to precisely trace the pattern of settlement following the Hungarian Conquest, and similar finds from the late medieval period have provided significant information about the export of large animals (mainly cattle) that played a key part in foreign trade. Finds in places such as Vác have also told us a lot about livestock transportation routes. The increasing availability of scientific tests makes more sources available for research, and this has an effect on the major issues of economic history.[49]

Another area of study that has made considerable headway in recent decades and which partly makes use of archaeobotanical and archaeozoological material is environmental archaeology. This applies a range of scientific techniques to observations of the soil and other material uncovered in archaeological excavations to acquire information about environmental change in historical eras, and the environmental factors that influenced, for example, the agriculture of a single period.[50]

Yet another major contribution to understanding late medieval economic affairs is the increasingly well-known area of landscape archaeology. This often overlaps with the territory of environmental archaeology, but the areas of study are nonetheless separate in terms of methods and approaches. Landscape archaeology examines and interprets archaeological phenomena from two perspectives. It starts out by employing the fact that all kinds of human activity (cultivation, animal husbandry, the extraction of raw materials, water regulation, etc.) result in far-reaching changes in the landscape that survive in

---

48 Gyulai 2010 and the further works of the author. See also the chapter by József Laszlovszky in the present volume.
49 See the chapter written by László Bartosiewicz and his colleagues in the present volume. See also: Lyublyanovics 2017.
50 Juhász, Sümegi and Zatykó (eds.) 2007 and Kovács and Zatykó (eds.) 2016.

some form today, so that elements of the present landscape have potential as sources for understanding historical epochs. It applies appropriate archaeological methods to render these landscape elements 'readable' to historians. In Hungary, the most abundant landscape elements that survive from the medieval period are traces of arable fields, remnants of former fishponds, and elements related to water regulation.[51] An analysis of these yields information of direct use in the study of economic activities. The other essential feature of landscape archaeology is that its investigations go beyond interpretation of archaeological find spots and individual landscape phenomena by integrating all of this information to the landscape scale. The approach involves examining the interaction of natural features and human intervention in terms of landscape units that bear the effects of this interaction in both their extent and their structure, even if the factors that influence them have changed. Using this approach, we can speak of the medieval monastic landscape (for example), a subject excellently suited to landscape archaeology.[52] This indicates, first of all, a conscious choice of location: a group of monks following a specific monastic culture (an order) chose a location for the monastery that met the spiritual and religious aims of the community and possessed the natural and economic features that would ensure the community's survival. Reference to a monastic landscape also implies the possibility of observing the features of a conscious transformation of the natural environment that is related to the architectural, economic and even religious activities of a monastic community.

Archaeometric (material-testing) methods have been applied to metal finds, cinder remains, glass finds, glassmaking products and by-products acquired from archaeological excavations. These have helped to establish the origins of raw materials, identify manufacturing techniques, and assess the levels of technical development and sophistication in the centers of production. This provides the kind of technical information that is almost absent from written sources, and the resulting reconstructions also shed light on economic history. Material testing is of similar use in researching medieval objects held in collections. Recently, it has been applied to a very numerous set of sources – medieval coins. Numismatic observations are very usefully supplemented by scientific determination of the metallic composition of coins. This allows the standard of coinage and minting proportions given in contemporary sources to be checked against established data about coin series, informing us about the extent to which medieval monarchs employed debasement, a known long-term cause of inflation, with all of its concomitant economic effects. Material

---

51 Zatykó 2015.
52 Laszlovszky 2004 and Pető 2015.

testing can also help us analyze the products of medieval money-counterfeiting workshops that have been revealed at many find spots. Complex means of investigation, employing all available types of sources, are now in general use for workshop finds (bronze and cannon foundries, glassmaking workshops, etc.). Investigation of the furnaces of medieval ironworks, involving archaeometric tests among other methods, tells us about more than just the raw materials and the technologies used there. We can also draw quantitative conclusions about the ironwork's average output and its consumption of raw materials and fuel. The same is true of brick kilns, pottery and lime kilns, and glass melting kilns. Increasingly important in the interpretation of such workshop finds, besides material testing methods, are observations from experimental archaeology.

Research Issues and Historiography

The first treatments of the medieval economic history of Hungary appeared in the late nineteenth century, although some historians had earlier researched sources with relevance to economic history and written about certain branches of the economy during the Middle Ages. Some of these older studies, although not dealing expressly with economic history in the classic sense, are still useful in reconstructing the medieval economy and medieval agriculture, particularly when a wide-ranging methodological approach and broad source base is employed, as was the case for the research described in this book. This historiographical review regards this early work as part of the background, but for reasons of space we cannot fully survey the literature and subject it to historiographical analysis. There exist detailed historiographical reviews concerning specific branches of the economy and issues of economic history, some with detailed bibliographies, in chapters of the Hungarian-language book that forms the basis for the present volume,[53] certain chapters of which also mention historiography and characteristic periods of research when discussing specific issues. Thematic bibliographies and historiographical reviews are available in some areas (such as numismatics and agrarian history) but are completely absent in others. Consequently, here we can only present the main results of research about these issues, pointing out the characteristic historiographical periods and the main trends. For each period, we have focused on the viewpoint and approach from which these authors, largely writing only in Hungarian, have discussed the features of medieval economic history and the development of branches of agriculture we consider to be important and

---

53   Kubinyi, Laszlovszky and Szabó (eds.) 2008.

susceptible to analysis today. This introductory chapter is specifically designed to indicate which issues and research areas have received Hungarian input in international historical debates, and to mention areas, which have benefited significantly from contributions by non-Hungarian researchers. The special importance of this task derives from the failure of much work on the medieval economy and agriculture of Hungary to elicit an international response, primarily because most of it was published solely in Hungarian. As a result, many findings which would clearly have been of interest to historians engaged in undertaking comparative studies have failed to enter international circulation. We therefore place particular emphasis on these aspects of historiography.

The Beginnings of Economic Historiography and the Period of Positivism

Work on the economic history of the Middle Ages started with the collection of sources and attempts to systematize and publish them. Such are the numismatic catalogues that started to appear in the late eighteenth century.[54] The systematic publication of descriptions and depictions of coins, usually connected to collections, were usually spurred by interest arising from the collection and trade of antiquities, but became the starting points for academic studies in numismatics and the history of money. This process commenced at about the same time as the publication of written sources, mostly by ecclesiastical historians of the Middle Ages, focusing principally on (narrative) sources for political history and written evidence for (ecclesiastical) institutional history. The next important stage was the positivist collection of medieval written sources and their publication. In the late nineteenth and early twentieth centuries, as source editions appeared in large numbers and the concepts they contained were identified, historians started to address the history of medieval society and to deal with the economic data contained in these sources. For example, Ignác Acsády's[55] book on tenant peasants put the emphasis on investigating the stratum of society they constituted. Similarly, identifying the various groups among the rural population was the focus of work by László Erdélyi[56] and Károly Tagányi.[57] These authors added many new sources

---

54 See e.g. Weszerle 1911.
55 Acsády 1906.
56 László Erdélyi and Károly Tagányi engaged in a long debate about the social history of the Árpádian age, which at a number of points touched upon the question of the population involved in agricultural activities. Erdélyi 1914, 517–561, Erdélyi 1915, 32–50, 202–226, 334–352 and 481–514, Erdélyi 1916, 39–63 and Tagányi 1916, 296–320, 409–448 and 543–608.
57 Erdélyi and Sörös (eds.) 1902–1916 and Tagányi (ed.) 1896.

to the charters that had been published in growing numbers since the eighteenth century, and Tagányi was the author of one of the earliest treatments of agricultural history (regarding the history of common land) that are still of relevance today.[58] He also collected sources on forests,[59] creating a source base that is still useful for research in this area.[60] The great source editions of that period, including those on the history of Pannonhalma Abbey and the Benedictine Order in Hungary, are similarly still important for research about medieval farming, agriculture and the estate system.[61] The increasing number of source publications also prompted thematic treatments at this time. One was the *Oklevél-szótár* ('Charter Dictionary'),[62] which systematized Hungarian expressions that occur in Latin medieval charters. Besides constituting the basic starting point for studies in linguistics and historical etymology, these are important reference documents regarding the use, changes in meaning and dating of expressions, concepts and words related to nearly every branch of the medieval economy. A similar collection of names, toponyms and words related to medieval water bodies and fishing ponds[63] is still important for the study of the medieval history of water management and fishing. Even more important was a systematization and monographic publication about medieval coins, which remained the reference book on the subject for nearly a century.[64]

The publication of sources and the related upsurge in research activity gave rise to new independent areas of study, which in turn published sources for their own use. Economic history is one of the best examples. Although the journal *Magyar Gazdaságtörténelmi Szemle* ('Hungarian Economic History Review') existed for only thirteen years, it published dozens of basic sources and treatments that are still cited by historians. During the long wait for the establishment of an independent department of economic history at a Hungarian university, the journal and its editorial staff were the most important intellectual reference point for medieval and early modern economic history. The outstanding figures behind the journal's work – and moreover, the editors – were Károly Tagányi and his successor Ferenc Kováts. The journal started out in 1893 with the objective of publishing the most important sources of Hungarian agricultural history. In a lecture connected with the foundation of the journal,

---

58 Tagányi 1894.
59 Tagányi (ed.) 1896.
60 E.g. Csőre 1994 and Szabó 2005.
61 Erdélyi and Sörös (eds.) 1902–1916.
62 Szamota and Zolnai (eds.) 1902–1906.
63 Ortvay 1882.
64 Réthy 1899–1907.

Tagányi presented a long list of research issues for which unexplored sources were available for the period between the eleventh and eighteenth centuries.[65] A separate series of charter publications was also planned, but eventually the journal itself carried source publications of various lengths. Each issue was divided into three sections: essays, data, and miscellaneous, to which a fourth – reviews – was added in 1896. The essays were historical treatments, while the data and miscellaneous sections mainly published sources, sometimes with introductions and explanations, but often simply as freestanding information. Although the founding documents declared that the journal's primary aim was to publish agricultural history sources, it represented a wider spectrum of interest right from the start. The craft industry, trade and transport were as well represented as agriculture.[66] Perhaps the most important essay carried by the journal, however, was concerned with the history of agriculture. Tagányi's article on common lands, written more than hundred years ago, is still routinely cited in Hungarian work on economic and social history.[67] Although his conclusions are by now largely obsolete, his work still stands as an example of how to research sources for the purpose of explaining agricultural history. In 1893, Tagányi produced another striking example of his highly ambitious plans for economic history: an outline for the Hungarian Academy of Sciences of a multi-author history of Hungarian agriculture (in fact, general economic history) which would have run to six to seven million characters in length![68]

The *Magyar Gazdaságtörténelmi Szemle* is still much cited, and a sign of its enduring legacy was the decision by Hungarian economic historians to relaunch the journal in 2015. Besides the undisputed influence of the original *Szemle*, the rising interest in economic history at that time was clearly indicated by the launch of a series of books expressly intended as economic history monographs. The first volume published a key source for Hungarian research, the register of the Bratislava thirtieth customs duty for 1457/1458.[69] Ever since, the thirtieth register has been regarded as possibly the most important source for the history of Hungarian medieval foreign trade.[70] Another book in the series that was written by its editor, Gyula Mandelló analyzed wage data from the medieval municipal accounts of Bratislava, but did not make the best use of sources and has not often been cited.[71]

---

65 Tagányi 1893.
66 On the journal, see: Vardy 1975, Kövér 2016 and Bognár 2010, 80–100.
67 Tagányi 1894.
68 The plan was published in: Bognár 2010, 304–310.
69 Kováts 1902a.
70 On this, with further literature on the topic: Nagy 2016. See also Nagy 2012.
71 Mandelló 1903. Cf. Kövér 2013, 221–222.

In many respects, it was this period that gave rise to one of the most comprehensive and definitive works of medieval economic history, although it was actually published during World War I. Bálint Hóman's *Magyar pénztörténet 1000–1325* ('Hungarian Monetary History 1000–1325')[72] was ahead of its time, and remains influential today. One of the foremost historians between the two world wars, as well as a government minister in charge of cultural affairs, Hóman also made use of written sources to analyze monetary administration and pricing systems. The book's content thus included both numismatic and monetary history and drew on a wide range of international data and research – an approach that was not to be repeated in this area for several decades.

Research between the Two World Wars

The consequences for historical research of the political changes following World War I affected every area and persist to the present-day. Under the Treaty of Trianon, much of the territory that had belonged to the medieval Kingdom of Hungary became part of neighboring countries (Austria, Czechoslovakia, Romania and Yugoslavia), leaving only the central part for the new state of Hungary. As a result, much regional research, including studies of economic centers such as towns, mining areas and craft centers and local history research, took place in frameworks defined by new states, and still does. As a result, publications concerning many aspects of medieval Hungary, including questions of economic history, having previously been written in Hungarian or the language of the sources (mostly Latin, but also Hungarian and German), began to appear in many different languages. The most important topics in this respect are the urban centers, mining areas and minting centers that are now located in Slovakia and Romania. To carry out a proper review of the work that has been produced about these areas since World War I would involve reviewing the economic historiography of all of these countries. This task is beyond the scope of this book, and we confine ourselves to mentioning key works in specific areas.

Medieval history enjoyed a revival of interest after World War I, but economic history attracted relatively little attention. Although important work was done in several areas, none could be compared with the source publications and early treatments of the late nineteenth and early twentieth centuries. Nonetheless, some lines of enquiry and areas of research did deliver important results. One of the dominant figures of the time was Sándor Domanovszky, who produced several studies of economic history in the classical sense,[73]

---

72   Hóman 1916.
73   Domanovszky 1916. Some of his works on economic history were later published in a volume: Domanovszky 1979. His most important work on agricultural history: Domanovszky 1938, II, 311–333, repr. Domanovszky 1979, 17–48.

including a history of agriculture. Equally important was his work in founding the Hungarian school of cultural history. The major achievement of this school was the series *Magyar Művelődéstörténet* ('Hungarian Cultural History'),[74] and, although it was not conceived of as economic history, in this work Domanovszky and his associates interpreted cultural history to include a historical approach to horticulture, crafts and medieval costume. The volumes in this series also stand out due to their use of a very broad range of sources that include written material, pictorial representations, items of what we would now call material culture, and archaeological finds.

Some areas outside the main scope of historical research and thus not covered in these major works were the subject of some minor studies which proved to be of considerable value in later, more systematic research. Studies of agricultural history based mainly on documentary data, for example, made progress in several areas in the first half of the twentieth century, although peasant farming, the central element of medieval agriculture, cannot be said to have preoccupied historians at that time. Important work was done, however, on the largest estates[75] and the farming by monks of the Cistercian Order, regarded as great innovators in agricultural technique.[76] Most studies of estate history appeared in a series entitled *Tanulmányok a magyar mezőgazdaság történetéhez* ('Essays on the History of Hungarian Agriculture'), published between 1930 and 1943, and in the cultural history series edited by Domanovszky. Nothing in the field of economic history at that time, however, can be compared to the achievements of ethnographic research and the resulting monographs. Ethnographic studies have occupied a prominent place in Hungarian academia since the late nineteenth century.[77] From the beginning, they paid particular attention to traditional peasant farming, many facets of which had strong parallels with medieval land cultivation methods and other production techniques. The same is true of ethnographic work on animal husbandry, fishing and peasant dwellings. The foundations of the broad ethnographic approach to farming, material culture and customs in such areas as outdoor animal husbandry and fishing were laid by Ottó Herman in the late nineteenth century.[78] These parallels all stemmed from the realization that, in Hungary, as in the other countries

---

74   Domanovszky (ed.) 1939–1941 and Sinkovics 1933.
75   Holub 1943 and Sinkovics 1933.
76   Kalász 1932.
77   On the evaluation of this research: Kósa 2001.
78   Herman 1887, Herman 1914. On the scientific works of Ottó Herman: Kósa, Keve and Farkas 1971; on his political role: Erdődy 1984.

of Central and Eastern Europe, the delayed industrial revolution had caused traditional forms of farming, production and other practices to survive much longer than in Western Europe, permitting ethnographers, whose objects of study were recent phenomena, to extend their research to archaic forms of agriculture and social frameworks. The new research questions and debates that this gave rise to, such as the origins of *tanya* (isolated farmstead) settlements, had a definitive influence on the ethnographic approaches employed between the world wars. Ethnographers consistently maintained an interest in traditional forms of peasant farming on equal terms with their study of folk material culture and folk art. The great survey of Hungarian ethnography produced at that time, *A magyarság néprajza* ('Ethnography of Hungarians')[79] which is thus an important source of much writing on economic history (the folk occupations involved in archaic forms of agriculture in the modern age, along with still-maintained ancient techniques such as tillage and animal husbandry, and especially ancient occupations such as fishing, hunting and gathering, often provide starting points for understanding or reconstructing medieval conditions). This highly influential area of ethnography, whose three chief figures at the time were Zsigmond Bátky, István Györffy and Károly Visky, also put its stamp on studies that are connected to the medieval history of farming in other ways. It also played a part in the first excavations of abandoned medieval villages.[80] Discoveries about village material culture deriving from the excavation of villages around Kecskemét had a considerable influence on subsequent research. The findings of these early archaeological excavations had considerable international relevance and were also published in German, thereby becoming accessible to authors in other countries. At the same time, and also on the basis of ethnographic research, Márta Belényesy started investigating the *tanya* system, a central issue for the ethnographic approaches of the time.[81] Belényesy extended her investigation to the medieval roots of the *tanya* and was to become one of the dominant figures of the next historiographical period, and in many respects of Hungarian agricultural history in general. It was also under the influence of the broad-based ethnographic approach that Gyula László pursued his highly influential archaeological work.[82] He first attempted

---

79   Bátky, Györffy and Viski 1934 ([2]1941).
80   Papp 1931, 137–152. Szabó 1938, Csalogovits 1935, 1–10, Csalogovits 1937, 321–333 and Bálint 1939, 146–160. On the significance of the first major piece of research by László Papp from a research history perspective: Filep 2006, 403–404.
81   Belényesy 1948.
82   László 1944.

to bring together data about the Hungarians who had arrived at the time of the Conquest, devoting particular attention to addressing questions about their agricultural techniques and lifestyle.

Another important area of pre-World War II research was the historical etymological study of the Hungarian language, and particularly of its vocabulary. This greatly contributed to determining the pre-Conquest Hungarians' knowledge of agriculture, as addressed in another major work of history from this period: the *Szent István Emlékkönyv* ('St Stephen's Memorial Book').[83]

Another important approach of interwar historiography was geographical and historical-geographical. The institution headed by Pál Teleki (an outstanding scholar of human geography and leading politician of the period) and the work it engendered[84] developed an interpretation of landscape history and human geography which placed great emphasis on economic issues. This laid the foundation, together with international research, for the first modern studies in urban geography.[85] These were the basic starting points for the study of medieval settlement types and their economic characteristics. Of outstanding importance for understanding the settlement system were studies by the school associated with Elemér Mályusz. This included research based on documentary sources about towns and villages in the peripheral areas of the Carpathian Basin – medieval Hungarian counties that were by that time located in other countries (Czechoslovakia and Romania).[86] These urban geographers and historical geographers thus did not expressly address economic questions, but the changes in towns and villages they documented through their exploration of the sources threw considerable light on economic processes.

The Boom in Economic History after World War II: Marxism and Its Contradictions

There was an upsurge in interest in nearly every aspect of economic history after World War II, and many of the studies published at that time remained points of reference for the authors of this book. This development stemmed partly from progress in historiography, but there were also some ideological

---

83 Domanovszky 1938 and Domanovszky 1979.
84 Princz et al. (eds.) 1936–1938.
85 Mendöl 1963.
86 For the volumes of the co-called Mályusz School, see the book series: *Település- és népiségtörténeti értekezések* [Studies in the history of settlement and ethnological history].

reasons behind it. Hungary and other countries of the region came under communist control through the influence of the Soviet Union. Communist ideology and historical research in the 1950s and 1960s put particular emphasis on 'working people' and thus promoted studies of peasant history and culture. Secondly, according to the predominant Marxist – or rather, vulgar Marxist – ideology, research into the 'foundations' that determined the 'superstructure' (meaning the understanding of economic processes and systems), was the favored topic. This led to a distorted and oversimplified conception of medieval feudalism, but in historiographical terms it opened up some special features of interest for Hungary. Despite being politically driven and ideologically restricted, this historical approach brought some fortunate results for research into the Middle Ages, especially medieval economic history, even in the 1950s. Research teams (that included some fine historians) produced studies that met the highest academic standards while attempting to satisfy the political-ideological demands of the time. Their subjects included the fourteenth-century history of the peasantry,[87] the traditional material culture of the Hungarian people,[88] the archaeological excavation of medieval towns and villages[89] and the relationships between towns and crafts.[90] Research groups set up at that time were to produce work that would define the direction of research for decades to come. The material culture research group and historians at the Hungarian Agricultural Museum engaged in lively research into agrarian history, leading to several publications. The main channel of publication was the newly-launched journal *Agrártörténeti Szemle* ('Agrarian History Review'), which was an international venture that presented Hungarian findings to the world in the form of an international agricultural history bibliography.[91] Several of its supplements were produced in foreign languages, making much influential work accessible outside Hungary.[92] The work on agricultural history from this period well illustrates the importance

---

87 Székely (ed.) 1953.
88 An example of this is the research group lead by Márta Belényesy. On its activity: Belényesy 1954, 612–615. On this phase of ethnographic material culture and agricultural history research: Tálasi 1965a, 5–56 and Tálasi 1965b, 27–57.
89 For a program that offers an overview of these archaeological investigations: Méri 1948.
90 Szűcs 1955. The work not only discusses the issues indicated in the title, but also the participation of burghers in agriculture, thereby significantly clarifying the problem of agriculture.
91 *Bibliographia Historiae Rerum Rusticarum Internationalis*. The series started with the volume of 1960–1961.
92 Makkai 1974 and Maksay 1978.

of economic history research and the lasting value of much of its output. The most outstanding work on agricultural history was by Márta Belényesy, who produced a series of studies[93] that brought together diverse information on agriculture and animal husbandry, particularly land use. Working with the outcome of the above mentioned earlier large-scale collaborative effort between ethnographers and historians on agricultural sources, she studied the history of the material culture of the Hungarian people. This research program still stands as an example of how collaboration among different branches of study and the incorporation of the widest possible range of sources can create a completely new perspective about issues such as types of animal husbandry and viticulture. Her findings were also published in foreign languages, so that they could, in principle, find their place in the international literature.

One product of research of lasting importance from that time was Jenő Szűcs's work on the special features of Hungarian urban development.[94] Although historians today generally do not accept some of his judgments, it was outstanding work in terms of the approach and the range of sources he deployed. Particularly important were his findings on the role of the urban bourgeoisie in viticulture and late medieval agriculture. Even historians most strongly influenced by Marxist ideology[95] at that time recognized significant regularities in social structure and economic relations. For others, the 'ideological shackles' meant no more than having to use the term 'tithe exploitation' for the form of taxation that most burdened the medieval peasantry; this did not undermine their work or diminish its value in terms of methodology or source criticism.[96] Documentary sources about peasant land use[97] were placed in a Marxist framework, as in a study of the history of the peasantry in the fourteenth century. The same treatments also covered important aspects of Hungarian economic development such as the problem of market towns (*mezőváros*),[98] in some respects laying the foundations for later research in this area.

---

93   Belényesy 1953, Belényesy 1954, Belényesy 1955a, Belényesy 1955b, Belényesy 1955–1956, Belényesy 1956a, Belényesy 1956b, Belényesy 1956c, Belényesy 1958a, Belényesy 1958b, Belényesy 1958c, Belényesy 1960a, Belényesy 1960b, Belényesy 1964, Belényesy 1967 and Belényesy 1969. Recently her works written in Hungarian were published in two volumes: Belényesy 2011 and Belényesy 2012.
94   Szűcs 1955.
95   Lederer 1959 and Elekes 1964.
96   Mályusz 1953a, 320–333.
97   Székely 1953, 80–103.
98   Mályusz 1953b, 128–191.

In the somewhat freer political atmosphere of the 1960s and 1970s, historians were subject to somewhat less direct ideological pressure. They did not reject the features of economic history that received such strong emphasis in Marxist historiography, but put them to positive use.[99] This gave rise to monographs and treatments of epochal significance. The historian István Szabó produced monographs and studies covering the main points of agricultural work organization[100] and addressed questions about the medieval settlements most involved in agricultural production:[101] the villages.[102] Another major achievement was his use of a broad range of international literature to place the changes in Hungarian villages within the European context. Of similar importance was Ferenc Maksay's work on settlement structure, an excellent example of the juxtaposition of medieval written sources and early modern cartographic representations. Research into forest use and clearance agriculture in the medieval period made interpretative use of early modern data that had been created by ethnographic research, particularly on forms of economic activity.[103] István Méri[104] first engaged in modern medieval village archaeology and uncovered many details about settlements that were of indirect importance in efforts to characterize methods of cultivation. Archaeological excavations of the major medieval royal centers (such as Buda)[105] at the same time resulted in an enormous quantity and great diversity of finds. These helped illuminate in a fundamentally new way the objects imported into Hungary through medieval trade. Archaeological research on historic buildings in towns produced a clear picture of the bourgeois houses of the main towns, and the economic activities (trade, crafts, viticulture and winemaking) that went on in certain parts of the buildings. Medieval archaeology went through similar expansion, generating a huge increase in the number of sources in neighboring countries (mostly Czechoslovakia, but also Romania) in this period.

In the 1960s, many historians applied these foundations to areas that were clearly, if indirectly, related to economic history, most notably in the field of medieval social history. These included the history of the Árpádian-age peasant society,[106] the significance of market towns in late medieval economic

---

99   Pach 1963.
100   Szabó 1963, 1–49 and 301–337.
101   Szabó 1975.
102   Szabó 1969 and Szabó 1971.
103   Hegyi 1978, Takács 1978 and Takács 1980.
104   Kovaloszki (ed.) 1986.
105   Gerevich 1966.
106   Bolla 1961, 97–120, Bolla 1983 and Szűcs 1981, 3–65 and 263–314.

development (Vera Bácskai), the influence of trade in goods, and the economic role of the late medieval capital of the country, Buda (András Kubinyi).[107] There were also studies of the economic and social effects of foreign settler populations,[108] the structure of village-like settlements,[109] late medieval grain production[110] and the change in structure of monastic cultivation.[111] László Makkai investigated how market towns and their patterns of land use[112] influenced agriculture and internal trade, and surveyed the development of the agricultural structure of early Hungary within the European context.[113] There were lively historical debates about foreign trade and Hungary's economic weight, some of which were connected to the history of cultivation and animal husbandry. For example, Elemér Mályusz addressed the question of livestock exports, an activity of major economic significance at the end of the medieval period,[114] using written sources on livestock transport to Bavaria. Several studies launched in the 1960s and 1970s such as surveys of historical geography had important outcomes, and nowadays constitute the starting point for all kinds of work on economic history. Standing out among these is György Györffy's series on the historical geography of the Árpádian age, built on almost all of the documents that survived from the time.[115] This was the first attempt at a full reconstruction of the settlement system. Some debates that started or re-emerged at this time were to remain subjects of publications for decades to come. One was the issue of Hungary's foreign trade balance, and another the study of economic aspects of regional changes at the end of the medieval period that 'diverged' from Western developments.

The elevated position of economic history in the 1950s and 1960s is inextricably bound up with the work carried out in the Department of Economic History of what was then the Marx Károly University of Economics, whose best-known professors included Zsigmond Pál Pach and Iván Berend T. Pach extended his work on economics to the Late Middle Ages and the early modern age. He expounded his 'theory of divergence', which states that developments

107 Bácskai 1965, Kubinyi 1971a, 58–78, Kubinyi 1964a, 371–404, Kubinyi 1964b, 1–21 and Székely 1961, 309–322.
108 Ladányi 1977, Fügedi 1953, 225–239 and Fügedi 1975, 471–507.
109 Maksay 1971.
110 Maksay 1962, 14–24 and Maksay 1978, 83–108.
111 Maksay 1972, 1–47.
112 Makkai 1957, 463–478.
113 Makkai 1974. On the same question as earlier, partly based on comparative ethnographic material: Hoffmann 1968.
114 Mályusz 1986, 1–33.
115 Györffy 1963–1998, I–IV.

in Hungary followed the same direction as those in the rest of Europe until the great geographical discoveries, but in the sixteenth century, together with other areas to the east of the Elbe, it followed a divergent route.[116] This concept set off intensive debate in the international literature, and Pach's line of research drew attention to important questions for economic and social history that have recurred in recent work.

One of the furthest-reaching debates of the 1970s emerged from a study by Oszkár Paulinyi in the area of medieval Hungarian economic history. Since there are only sporadic surviving sources on the country's late medieval foreign trade, interpreting them properly was recognized as being of crucial importance. One source that is suitable for quantitative analysis is the above referred 1457/1458 register of the thirtieth customs duty of Bratislava. Ferenc Kováts had already used this source to infer the existence of a significant deficit in Hungarian balance of foreign trade. Oszkár Paulinyi provided his own conclusion in the title of the study: 'Rich Land, Poor Country'. He claimed that, despite the wealth of late medieval Hungary in terms of mineral deposits, particularly precious metals, this wealth flowed out of the country mainly to pay for industrial goods brought in from abroad, primarily broadcloth and other textile goods.[117] Several historians contributed to the ensuing debate. András Kubinyi and Elemér Mályusz variously disputed and refined Paulinyi's claim, arguing that one customs register is not a suitable basis for reconstructing the foreign trade of an extended period, and that the cattle that constituted a large proportion of exported goods were registered for customs in a different way and at a different time from other items of foreign trade.[118]

Although it is almost a cliché that the output of Hungary's mines was more responsible than anything else for the country's wealth in the late medieval period, this is an area that economic historians have almost completely neglected. The reference book on mining history, still in use today, was published by Gusztáv Wenzel in 1880, and naturally reflects the preoccupations of that time.[119] It reviews mining activities in Hungary region by region. Mining history has been treated by historians of technology and local historians, and Oszkár Paulinyi and Gusztáv Heckenast also deserve mention in this respect. Paulinyi concentrated on examining the extraction of copper and precious metals and

---

116   Pach 1963 and Pach 1991.
117   Paulinyi 1972a and Paulinyi 1972b.
118   Mályusz 1986, Kubinyi 1992 and Kubinyi 1998a.
119   Wenzel 1880.

the social history of mining,[120] while Heckenast[121] dealt with iron mining and metallurgy. In the last two decades, István Draskóczy has published several studies of salt mining, and the Slovak historian Martin Štefánik has researched the history of mining in medieval Upper Hungary (present-day Slovakia).[122]

The most drastic change in the methodology of acquiring sources relates to the increasing influence of archaeology, particularly the contributions of zooarchaeological and paleobotanical studies. Determination of animal and plant remains[123] has provided historians with completely new and highly valuable sources. Excavations of medieval villages[124] have uncovered, besides agricultural implements, many phenomena of importance to the agrarian economy. Syntheses based on the expanding base of archaeological finds, embracing much more than agricultural implements, and on archaeological research have been essential in many areas of economic investigation.[125]

In the 1970s, Hungarian and, to some extent, foreign economic historians increasingly turned their attention to the medieval Carpathian Basin's interregional trading links. For example, Wolfgang von Stromer studied the appearance of German merchants and capital in Hungary, and Zsuzsa Teke did the same for Italian traders.[126] This research contributed to the increase in the number of publications on foreign trading relations with specific areas of the Carpathian Basin. One such area was medieval Upper Hungary. Slovak and Polish historians have drawn attention to some previously little-studied sources in recent decades.[127] A survey of the economic history of medieval Transylvania has also appeared. Interestingly, it was a young Italian historian,

120 Paulinyi 2005.
121 Heckenast 1991.
122 Draskóczy 2008, Štefánik 2004b and Štefánik 2012. See the studies by Zoltán Batizi and István Draskóczy in the present volume.
123 P. Hartyányi and Nováki 1967–1968, 5–58, P. Hartyányi, Nováki and Patay 1973–1974, 23–73, Füzes 1972, 285–290, Skoflek and Hortobágyi 1973, 135–156, Facsar 1973, 157–174, Hartyányi 1981–1983, 95–113, Zólyomi 1980, 121–126 and, Skoflek 1985, 33–44. For an overview of medieval agriculture of the Carpathian Basin based on archaeobotany: Gyulai 2010. On the research potential of archaeozoology in Hungary, see e.g. Bartosiewicz 1995a, Lyublyanovics 2017, and their study in the present volume.
124 Takács 2003, 7–54, Pálóczi Horváth 2003, 221–260, Méri 1952, 49–65, Méri 1954–1956, 138–152, Méri 1962, 211–218, Méri 1964, Méri 1969–1970, 69–84, Holl and Parádi 1982 and Pálóczi Horváth (ed.) 1996. Most recently: Takács 2010.
125 Müller 1975, 59–102 and Müller 1982.
126 Von Stromer 1970 and von Stromer 1971. See also: Teke 1984, Teke 1995a, Teke 1995b and Teke 1995c. More recently, see the works of Krisztina Arany and Katalin Prajda.
127 Halaga 1967 and Halaga 1975, Sroka. See also: Draskóczy 2016b.

Andrea Fara, rather than anyone from Romania or Hungary, who recently produced a monograph that placed Transylvania on the economic map of medieval Central Europe.[128] Fara examined how Transylvania, wedged between Byzantium and Western Christendom, was connected with the European economic current. Eastward economic links had previously also attracted the interest of several other historians. Zsigmond Pál Pach had first considered the problem in the 1970s. In several essays, he examined whether the Levantine trading route had passed through medieval Hungary.[129] Pach's work was followed by research into the customs registers of the late fifteenth and particularly the early sixteenth centuries. Mária Pakucs studied trade in goods to and from Sibiu and Braşov,[130] and Zsolt Simon used data from three thirtieth customs posts to analyze the volume and composition of Ottoman-Hungarian trade in the early sixteenth century.[131]

The Eclipse and Re-Emergence of Medieval Economic History in the Last Three Decades

The post-World War II period brought a major revival in all forms of medieval economic history. This remains true despite the undeniable distortions forced upon it by the ideological demands of the period, particularly in the 1950s and 1960s. There was a gradual opening up of Hungarian historical research in the 1970s, and the trend strengthened in the 1980s. Historians started to make greater use of foreign contacts and sought out new areas of study. At the same time, economic history sank into the background, although several outstanding medievalists of the time completed works of fundamental importance on economic matters. György Györffy, Gyula Kristó, Erik Fügedi, Pál Engel and András Kubinyi produced several studies of important subjects, ranging from Árpádian-age agriculture to the fundamental changes of the late medieval period.[132] This work is almost completely free of Marxist conceptions, particularly the simplified versions, while much more apparent are the methodological and theoretical approaches taken by foreign historians. Thus we encounter, for example, the viewpoints of the Annales School and of Central Place Theory. These provided much more textured accounts of economic phenomena and,

---

128   Fara 2010.
129   Pach 1972, Pach 1975a and Pach 1975c.
130   Pakucs-Willcocks 2007.
131   Simon 2014. On the trade of Moldavia and Wallachia in the earlier period: Simon 2009.
132   Kubinyi (ed.) 1998.

particularly in conjunction with social history, were much more open to completely new lines of inquiry as regards such matters as medieval castles[133] and many aspects of urban research. At the same time, some areas of medieval history that had been out of favor for several decades re-emerged. These included church history, religious history, and work on the cults of saints and religious orders. Understandably, these revived lines of research, in attempting to fill gaps in research that had built up over several decades, were little concerned with economic issues.

International contacts – a vital factor in academic work – re-asserted their influence in the 1970s and 1980s. There was a reappearance of foreign historians interested in subjects of Hungarian relevance, and not only from neighboring countries. Many fruitful studies about specific mining and manufacturing products and their appearance in international trade were completed at this time. The highly significant cattle trade of the late medieval and subsequent periods was also highlighted in research. Following the Hungarian works mentioned above, Ian Blanchard reviewed the main routes of late medieval and early modern cattle exports from the region, this time in a regional context.[134] Further contributions to this were made by Andrea Fara in a study of trade to and from Italy. The author devoted particular attention to the issue of cattle exports, which had previously only been studied in the context of the early modern period.[135] Animal products joined precious metal mining, salt mining and trade as subjects of fruitful research by medievalists. Connected with all of these was the upsurge in work on medieval monetary history and numismatics, in which the previously compartmentalized topics of coin types, coin finds, and the organization of monetary administration were dealt with as a whole.[136]

Among the new developments of the 1990s we can trace some of the processes that have come to dominate Hungarian work on medieval economic history. Some of these involve indirect contributions from interdisciplinary studies in areas such as environmental change and specific craft occupations, bringing in new sets of sources and methodological approaches. Climatic and environmental phenomena have received increasing attention in historical research and have been identified as major drivers of the transformations of the medieval period. Landscape archaeology, together with environmental history studies based on data from scientific testing and environmental archaeology, has deepened our understanding of how human activity interacts with nature. A

---

133   Fügedi 1986.
134   Blanchard 1986.
135   Fara 2015a and Fara 2015b. For the early modern period, see: Zimányi 1972.
136   See the studies by Csaba Tóth and Márton Gyöngyössy in the present volume.

similarly complex approach has recently been applied to understanding forest use and water management systems.[137] This research proceeds by comparing written sources with topographical archaeological data, and also incorporates the results of botanical and soil research. A similar combination of scientific enquiry – in this case, material examination – using traditional methods of investigating the history of objects formed the basis for Elek Benkő's monograph on an entire craft industry: medieval bells and bronze objects.[138] The findings of several academic areas have also been brought to bear on craft history and industrial archaeology,[139] in a sense following on from initiatives of the 1980s. In this, analysis of archaeological findings and archaeometric research has been supplemented with work in experimental archaeology, particularly in the field of ferrous metallurgy.[140] Good examples of collaboration among disciplines are the thematic books on the processing of wood, bone, leather and other organic materials that also touch on specific economic activities and often extend beyond the chronological boundaries of the Middle Ages.[141] Work on glassmaking, which was previously strongly object centered, has been extended in the last decade to incorporate workshop research and technological observations.[142]

Another area of research which has combined increasingly detailed analysis of written sources with work on other sources involving different methods is trade and the exchange of goods. István Draskóczy has drawn attention to the level of salt imports in the west of the country and from Polish lands when the royal salt monopoly was in place. The author also identified the export of some salt exports to the Balkans, revealing that foreign trade in salt was not confined to imports.[143] The textile trade concerns one type of finished products that has been a prime subject of research in recent years. The research potential of a previously neglected set of sources, textile lead seals, has been demonstrated above all by Maxim Mordovin.[144]

In addition to the merchandise itself, the physical setting of trade – trade routes – have again become a subject of research after a break of half a century.

---

137   See the studies by László Ferenczi and Péter Szabó in the present volume.
138   Benkő 2002.
139   E.g. Gömöri (ed.) 1981, Gömöri (ed.) 1984.
140   Gömöri (ed.) 1999.
141   Gömöri (ed.) 2007, Nagy and Szulovszky (ed.) 2009, Gömöri and Körösi (ed.) 2010, Szulovszky (ed.) 2012.
142   H. Gyürky 1991, Mester 1996, Mészáros 2008 and Laszlovszky et al. 2014.
143   Draskóczy 2008, 205–238.
144   Mordovin 2013 and Mordovin 2014.

The most fruitful research has used the methods of landscape archaeology, and there has also been a systematic study of the typology of roads and their toponyms.[145] This research covered the changes and rearrangements of national trading routes and regional (county) connections.[146]

Economic history took on perceptibly greater significance after 2000, and new lines of research incorporated findings of studies from outside the subject itself. For example, work by Beatrix F. Romhányi has extended the study of medieval religious orders beyond church and religious history with analyses of the monastic economy.[147] Similarly, just as certain buildings can act as indicators of economic activity or the wealth of an area, the founding of monasteries demonstrates the economic capacity of an area, the economic strength of market towns, or certain sections of the nobility.

These developments led to the creation of a major medieval economic history research project that ran between 2005 and 2008. Entitled *Középkori magyar gazdaságtörténet a régészet és az anyagi kultúra tükrében* ('Medieval Hungarian Economic History in the Light of Archaeology and Material Culture'), it was financed by the Hungarian National Scientific Research Fund and represented the culmination of András Kubinyi's work in establishing a new school of research. Kubinyi was an outstanding figure in Hungarian medieval studies, a renowned researcher and professor of medieval history and archaeology, and the author of many publications on economic history. He and his students and colleagues, who included art historians, numismatists and zooarchaeologists as well as historians and archaeologists, drew up a research program for investigating medieval economic history of a kind that was unprecedented in Hungary, making use of a broad base of sources and methodological approaches. The project was designed to sum up Kubinyi's life's work in a way that his students and colleagues – under his guidance and instruction – each worked on one of his major areas of interest, particularly the topics of the university lectures and seminars he had delivered over a period of several decades. The outcome of the program thus tallied with Kubinyi's conception, but it was not his intention to bring it together in a monograph of his own. In fact, he did not see the publication of the book that resulted from this endeavor due to his death in 2007. In the last days of his life he continued to work with the research team, and looked at the manuscripts. After his death, his student

---

145 On water transport, see: Tóth 2010, Toda 2014; on land routes: Szilágyi 2014.
146 Szende 2011b and Skorka 2013. For a typology of roads, see Szilágyi 2014 and her contribution in the present volume. For different counties: Szilágyi 2013 (Vas County) and K. Németh 2014 (Tolna County).
147 See the contribution of Beatrix F. Romhányi in the present volume.

József Laszlovszky took over as director of the program and the editor of the Hungarian-language book that resulted from it.[148] The project team consisted of László Bartosiewicz, Gergely Buzás, István Feld, László Ferenczi, Márton Gyöngyössy, József Laszlovszky, Balázs Nagy, Beatrix F. Romhányi, Péter Szabó, Katalin Szende and Csaba Tóth, together representing many different institutions. Several other – mostly young – scholars were also involved in the work that led up to the final Hungarian-language book that is the basis of this present volume.

The program of 2005–2008 and the latest work by a young generation of historians give every sign that we will look back on the first decades of the new millennium as a period of renewed vigor in medieval economic history in Hungary. Hungarian work on markets and the customs system, for example, has produced new results in recent years. Boglárka Weisz has investigated the characteristics of weekly and annual markets and produced a comprehensive survey of Árpádian-age custom posts.[149] Also important for economic and monetary affairs during the Árpádian age is the comparative study of archaeological finds, particularly graves and hoards of treasure, which has provided information about the framework of the money economy.[150] A research group led by Boglárka Weisz embarked on a major piece of economic history research in 2015. Rather than aiming to conduct a general survey, this project set out to examine specific issues particularly susceptible to research, and to systematically analyze several of the above-mentioned problems that have not been examined for several decades. These include some specific features of mining in Hungary: precious metal and salt mining, as already mentioned, and incomes related to copper mining. The project members intend to devote even more energy to investigating – more systematically than has been done before – the main players in economic life and the organization of the economy, and the role of towns (above all, mining towns) in the Hungarian economy. One of the related aims is to determine the role of specific town privileges.[151] The project is employing a complex, interdisciplinary approach to analyzing economic processes and agents and the role of certain phenomena as economic indicators. This strongly indicates that Hungarian medieval economic historiography, more than a century after it started, has received new impetus and is benefiting from the methodological principles formulated by the research programs of the previous decade.

---

148 Kubinyi, Laszlovszy and Szabó (eds.) 2008.
149 Weisz 2012b and Weisz 2013b. See also Tringli 2010.
150 Vargha 2015.
151 On the research programme: Weisz 2015a. The first results: Weisz (ed.) 2016.

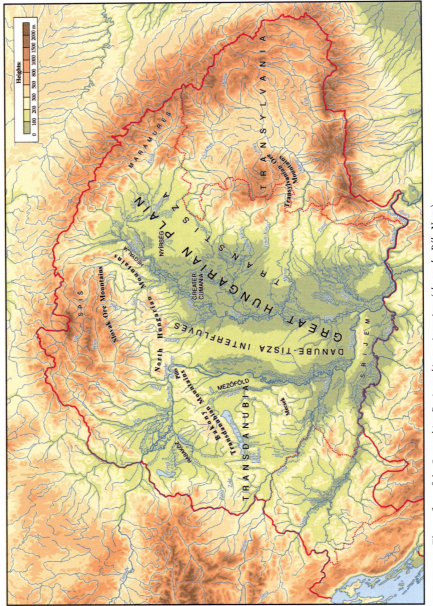

FIGURE 0.1 *The surface of the Carpathian Basin and its main regions (drawn by Béla Nagy).*

PART 1

Structures

∴

CHAPTER 1

Long-Term Environmental Changes in Medieval Hungary: Changes in Settlement Areas and Their Potential Drivers

*László Ferenczi, József Laszlovszky, Zsolt Pinke, Péter Szabó, András Vadas**

Introduction

The natural relief of the Carpathian Basin is favorable for all kinds of economic activities. The central, wide plain area is in general suitable for growing crops, raising herd animals, or undertaking any other agricultural activity, while the ring of mountains that surrounds the plain, the Carpathian Mountains, are rich in wood as well as a number of minerals that have been mined in some cases since prehistory. However, the actual landscape is much more complicated than this general picture. The Carpathian Mountains are scattered in themselves with dozens of minor basins, and the Great and the Little Hungarian Plains in the center of the basin were certainly not everywhere suitable for agricultural production a millennium ago (*see* Fig. 0.1).

The elements of the environment of economic life underwent different kinds of transformation. Apart from the natural relief, which except for some minor transformations may not have changed in the last millennium, forest coverage and the extent of plowlands and water-covered areas certainly did. The extent of forest cover and plowlands is closely connected, as growth in plowland usually goes hand in hand with the rolling back of forests. Waterlogged areas may be less significant in regions where rivers run in deeper beds, but are significant components of the flat and low-lying parts of the Carpathian Basin, where before extensive drainage works in the eighteenth and nineteenth centuries water had covered large areas for a considerable part of the year. The extent of plowlands and the issue of forest cover and silviculture are discussed in separate subchapters as they were responsible for a substantial proportion of the economic output of the medieval Hungarian Kingdom.[1] The economic role of

---

* The research done by András Vadas was supported by the ÚNKP-17-4 New National Excellence Program of the Ministry of Human Capacities.
1 See the chapters by József Laszlovszky and Péter Szabó in the present volume.

waters is also discussed in detail below, although it is worth obtaining a more general overview of the role that hydrography plays in the settlement network and local economies.[2]

In recent years, historians, archaeologists and natural scientists have paid more attention to demonstrating the changes in the environment of the Carpathian Basin in historical times. Archaeologists, palaeoecologists and scholars of various Earth sciences have shown that numerous transformations in environmental conditions can be identified using more sensitive sampling methods and excavation techniques, while historians have argued that despite the general scarcity of narrative and partly archival sources, environmental conditions can be associated with numerous shorter or longer periods of crisis. This chapter cannot provide a critical overview of all the recent work that has been carried out with regard to the environmental changes in the Carpathian Basin, but rather summarizes major transformations in environmental conditions from the perspective of their relevance to long-term land-use patterns. We also discuss the potential driving forces of these changes.

The Extent of Waterlogged Areas and Changes in the Water Levels of Rivers and Lakes

In choosing a site for permanent settlement, people had to consider several factors. Among the most typical areas with a higher population are transition zones between different types of landscapes. For example, transition zones between water-covered and waterlogged areas seem to have always been attractive because of their multiple economic benefits. However, even minor environmental changes in such regions could lead to changes in hydroclimatic conditions that forced local populations to abandon these areas.[3] Historians who focused on studying the settlement network of the Great Hungarian Plain[4] addressed the problem of access to water resources as early as the first half of the twentieth century. In recent decades, archaeologists and Earth scientists have drawn attention to the research opportunities connected with understanding hydroclimatic conditions and settlement patterns.[5] Water-level changes have been demonstrated to have played a major role in forming

---

2 See the chapter by László Ferenczi in the present volume.
3 Turner et al. 2003, or more recently in the context of seasides: Gillis 2012.
4 Glaser 1939.
5 See e.g. Bálint 1980.

settlement strategies, not only in a medieval context, but also in Roman times.[6] The geographical scope of these studies was not limited to lake basins but also included some river valleys. Two features captured the attention of scholars. One was the relatively low water level in most parts of the Basin during Roman times,[7] while the other was the significant rise in the water levels of different water bodies from the late medieval period to the early modern period. In what follows we provide a brief survey of studies that have demonstrated the late medieval changes in the water level in the Carpathian Basin. Such changes had a considerable impact on economic opportunities in many lowland areas.

Because the landscapes around the two largest lakes in the Carpathian Basin (Lake Fertő [Neusiedler See] and Lake Balaton) are flat, even small water-level changes could have had extensive effects. Through the study of written sources, especially charters that discussed the characteristics of these lakes and the hydrography in their surroundings, dry or wet periods were determined.[8] Such studies, however, ran the methodological risk of missing out on the significance of the direct influence of humans on hydrography (sluices, dams, etc.). In the case of the Balaton, for example, there have been regular debates concerning the issue of control of the water level in Roman times.[9] In recent years, rescue excavations shed light on the supposedly permanent low level of water throughout this period, and showed that even in Roman times (the third century) some previously inhabited areas were abandoned because of rising water levels. However, these changes seem to have been temporary, as in the fourth century parts of the areas were again settled permanently.[10]

Medieval water-level changes have been discussed in the Hungarian scholarly literature since the 1960s, when (in addition to written evidence and cartographic data) relevant archaeological data became available for the first time. As for the early medieval period (i.e. before the Hungarian Conquest in the late ninth century) archaeological data is less abundant. Apart from cemeteries, the settlement complex at Zalavár (Mosaburg) – situated along the shore of the Little Balaton, a huge wetland area southwest of Lake Balaton – received considerable attention.[11] Besides various archaeological and environmental

---

6 E.g. recently the case studies by Viczián et al. 2014 and Viczián et al. 2015.
7 Sági 1968a, Horváth and Viczián 2004, Nagy B. et al. 2013, Horváth 2000, Zsidi 2007 and Nagy [no date].
8 Kiss 1997–1998 and Kiss and Piti 2005.
9 Virág 1998. For the medieval period, see: Virág 2005 and moreover Kiss 2009b.
10 Marton and Serlegi 2007, Serlegi 2007 or Serlegi 2009.
11 Sági 1968b and Pálóczi Horváth 1993. See more recently, with a slightly different result: Mordovin 2006, 12.

investigations, it is a charter from here (dated 1335) that allowed the reconstruction of the water level with relative accuracy.[12] For this period, scientific data suggest rising water levels around the Balaton. However, reconstructions by different authors showed considerable differences in the extent of the area affected by this process. Excavations of the last twenty years at the southern shoreline of the Balaton have brought to light settlement archaeological evidence that proved that many of the Árpádian age sites had disappeared by the late medieval period, as they were situated at lower altitudes, and it is likely that they were endangered by rising water levels around the lake.[13] As was also demonstrated at the western (and partly at the northern) shore of the Balaton,[14] the underground water table also changed, which could have affected large areas previously inhabited and suitable for cultivation. Some authors, however, have pointed out that the water level of the Balaton was regulated in the medieval period. While not claiming that a sluice was constructed primarily for water-level regulation, the huge mill complex not far from the present-day sluice at Siófok may have functioned partly as such.[15] Despite doubts concerning the correlation between the fluctuations in the water level of the Balaton and precipitation in its catchment area, rising water levels have also been demonstrated along the shores of other lakes such as Lake Fertő and a number of smaller lakes in the Great Hungarian Plain.[16]

The Great Hungarian Plain is particularly interesting from this point of view, as in certain places settlements were almost completely abandoned in the fourteenth–sixteenth centuries. Possible causes of this settlement desertion have been widely discussed in Hungarian historiography. Since written sources did not provide explanations, some historians have concluded that only scientific investigation can provide a comprehensive answer.[17]

In the case of the Great Hungarian Plain, changes in the water level can be also statistically evaluated.[18] In a recent study, the means of the elevation of the Árpádian-age and late medieval archaeological sites were compared – including settlements, churches and cemeteries situated in the heartland of the wetlands that covered a huge part of the Great Hungarian Plain over

---

12   MNL OL DF 253 832, published in: Nagy, Véghely and Nagy (eds.) 1886–1890, I, 294–307 (no. 206).
13   Mészáros and Serlegi 2011.
14   Pusztai 2013, 161.
15   For the mills there, see: Kiss 2009b.
16   Kiss 1998 and Vadas 2011a.
17   Fügedi 1992, Pinke 2011.
18   Pinke 2015.

an area of 4128 square kilometers (*see* Fig. 1.1). The results suggest that late medieval sites were situated significantly higher than those of the Árpádian age. Research has also indicated that it could partly have been vulnerability to direct flooding, and in some cases also the risk of inundation of roads and

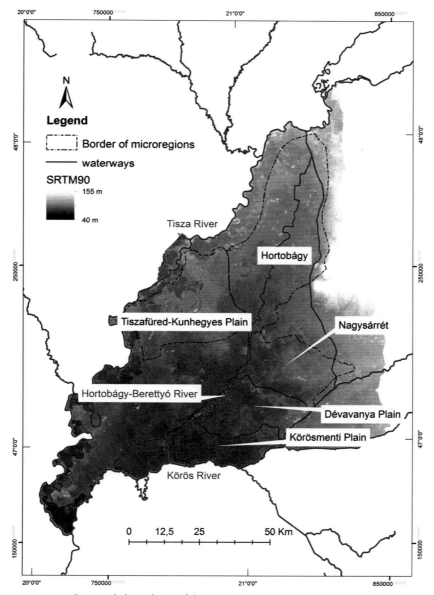

FIGURE 1.1   *Geomorphological map of the Transtisza region under analysis.*

restricted access (i.e. of being cut-off) that resulted in the desertion of specific areas and settlements.[19]

This knowledge concerning roads and access highlights the importance of other factors (in addition to the increasing flood proneness of settlements with waterfront locations) that could have influenced water-related features in settlement patterns. How, for example, did lifestyles, cultural traditions, land-use or logistics affect settlement desertion? With important implications, GIS-based zonal analysis was carried out in this lowland landscape and suggested a strong spatial connection between certain geomorphological features and agro-ecological suitability, both of which appeared as decisive factors in the stability (instability) of settlement patterns with respect to the changes that occurred in the Late Middle Ages.[20] The investigation showed not only that populated zones had shrunk significantly by the end of the Árpádian age and that the mean elevation of archaeological sites in deserted zones was significantly lower than that of those situated in zones with stable settlement patterns, but it also demonstrated that there was significant correlation between agro-ecological potential and settlement abandonment. The proportion of areas with good agro-ecological potential was considerably higher in stable settlement zones than in deserted or uninhabited zones.

In summary, hydrological challenges in areas with different geomorphological features forced the local population to respond in an adaptive manner, and there were basically only two options. First, the border zones of deep floodplains were affected by massive depopulation and the number of settlements located at such sites decreased greatly from the Árpádian age to the Late Middle Ages. Second, areas with the high and wide levees saw relatively little vertical displacement of surviving settlements. Historical data show that at least part of the population of deserted villages migrated towards these flood-free areas with excellent soil conditions, where rapidly growing towns – usually built on small plateaus – emerged from the second half of the Angevin Period onwards.[21] The croplands of abandoned villages were converted into pasture for the extensive cattle husbandry that was managed by these towns, and this became the typical farming method in the Hungarian lowlands that allowed for economic expansion from the sixteenth century onwards.

---

19   Szűcs, 1965 and Pfister 2010.
20   Pinke et al. 2016.
21   E.g. see the studies in the volume: Bárány, Papp and Szálkai (eds.) 2011. On migration towards towns in the Great Hungarian Plain, see most importantly: Gulyás 2015. See also: Pinke et al. 2017.

Climate as a Driver of Environmental Change and Farming Opportunities

In addition to noting the changes in water-covered areas in the Carpathian Basin, it is worth examining the potential drivers of these. Rising water levels and increasing flood vulnerability from the fourteenth century onwards has been observed in several regions of Western Europe: along the Atlantic Coast,[22] in the valleys of the Thames,[23] as well as by the Danube[24] and the Volga.[25] Thus one of the possible explanations for the changes in land-use opportunities and settlement networks is certainly climatic change. The late medieval period is usually referred to as the age of transitions, from the Medieval Climatic Anomaly to the Little Ice Age.[26] The fourteenth century witnessed a significant number of extreme weather events in various parts of Western and Central Europe that partly coincided with major epidemics. This period exactly corresponds with the most important period of transformation of land-use in the lowlands of the Carpathian Basin.[27] However, not enough is known about medieval climate in the Hungarian Kingdom to safely argue that climate was the driving factor behind the changes.

Studies that deal with the (medieval) climate history of Hungary usually represent one of two strands of thought. Some studies demonstrate that the climatic fluctuations in Western Europe which took place from the tenth to the sixteenth century also happened to some extent in the Carpathian Basin. However, none of these pieces of research is based on historical or scientific evidence from the region.[28] Because of the limited opportunity to study the former issue, in recent years the focus has shifted and most historians who are interested in the topic deal with weather events, or study the impact of changes in climate. Based on the historical evidence, it is impossible to reconstruct climatic changes at high resolution as regards the period under study.[29] The scarcity of relevant historical data with which to reconstruct climatic conditions does not mean that no effort has been made to discover the main trends in the fluctuation of the climate. In the past decade a number of studies

---

22 Lamb 1965, Nicholas 1992 and Grove 2004.
23 Galloway and Potts 2007.
24 Kiss 2011, Vadas 2011b, Vadas 2013a and Kiss and Laszlovszky 2013.
25 Panin and Nefedov 2010.
26 See Brázdil et al. 2005 for a systematic overview of the data.
27 See the chapter by József Laszlovszky.
28 E.g. Rabb 2006 and Rácz 2008.
29 For a detailed and critical overview of the research in the field until 2009, see: Kiss 2009a.

have demonstrated the potential of dendroclimatology, pollen-analysis and geochemistry for the study of the medieval climate in the Carpathian Basin.[30] However, it remains to be seen whether these results can be extrapolated to create general conclusions concerning a broader area.

Due to the independent water-level fluctuations of almost a dozen rivers and lakes, there are reasons for assuming that the climate played at least some role in the process. It is important to underline, however, that climate change may only have been one of the factors that affected the hydrological system of the Great Hungarian Plain, and other lowlands. Permanent surface subsidence of certain lowland areas – a more quantifiable phenomenon than climatic processes – could also have triggered a transformation of flow conditions in the Great Hungarian Plain during the study period of five and a half centuries, for example.[31] This process speeded up runoff towards depressions, but slowed down efflux from these. Due to the medieval intensification of runoff, soil erosion and the increased sedimentation of basins that happened as a result of the rapid development of settlement patterns and mining activities in hilly regions, it is also reasonable to assume that the elevation of levees decreased and sedimentation in stream networks increased, thus variability in elevation declined. Such 'longue durée' processes likely aggravated the flood vulnerability of lowland communities in the Great Hungarian Plain and increased hydrological pressure. Such long-term structural changes and short-term hydrological extremities may have transformed not only the living conditions of human communities, but also natural habitats (e.g. steppe-forests), and were key factors in landscape evolution.

Outlook

Foreigners who passed through Hungary throughout the Middle Ages always mentioned the fertility and wealth of the land, although the people and more urban settlements seemed to them to be poorer than the people and towns of contemporary Western Europe. In terms of the agricultural techniques in use and environmental conditions, however, Hungary was no worse off than the western part of the continent at that time. In general, the environmental conditions of the Carpathian Basin were favorable to agricultural production in the Middle Ages. The most productive areas for these activities were lowland

---

30   For an overview, see: Vadas and Rácz 2013.
31   Timár 2003.

areas, as well as the foothills around the margins of the Great Hungarian Plain. The dense network of rivers and substantial arable land supported a relatively stable supply of food and had good agricultural potential. Despite these generally stable and favorable conditions, major shifts in production occurred in medieval Hungary, triggered by a number of factors. Hydrological changes were certainly amongst these, as well as the changing needs and markets of the region.

CHAPTER 2

Demographic Issues in Late Medieval Hungary: Population, Ethnic Groups, Economic Activity

András Kubinyi and József Laszlovszky

Introduction

By examining the natural features of medieval states and the interaction of their people, we can assess their economic potential and the range of economic activities open to them. Having been constrained primarily by the extent and location of land suitable, or made suitable, for agricultural cultivation in the earlier centuries of the Middle Ages, these factors later became much more complex. Economic development in Hungary during the Árpádian age, for example, was unambiguously connected to the expansion of agriculture to previously uncultivated areas. In a period when the economy was dominated by cultivation and animal breeding at a subsistence level, and there was – as in medieval Hungary – an abundance of fertile land, the only restraint to development was insufficient population. During these centuries, the value of land was determined by its fertility and the presence of inhabitants in sufficient numbers and with the appropriate agricultural skills and tools to work the land or bring it under cultivation. Land had little value without these, so the presence of the right people was what made it viable. Colonization (bringing previously unused land into cultivation) and the presence of *hospes* (meaning 'guests'; i.e., settled incoming population) were thus crucial to the process of raising the country's economic potential.[1]

From the thirteenth century onwards – the period under scrutiny here – several aspects of this situation changed. The vast majority of the population continued to obtain the essentials of life from agriculture, principally arable cultivation, but no longer on a subsistence basis. More complex division of labor appeared, even within agriculture.[2] Products increasingly changed hands

---

1 On the issue of *hospites*, see: Fügedi 1975. See also Körmendy 1995.
2 See the diversification of agriculture in the numerous publications of Márta Belényesy and the contribution of József Laszlovszky on agriculture in the present volume.

at markets and fairs, in large part via monetary transactions.[3] Some branches of agriculture, such as viticulture, could produce several times more value per unit of land area than arable cultivation. The value of such produce was by then definitely realized through the mechanisms of internal trade at markets and fairs within the kingdom, and even (in the form of wine) in foreign trade. Producers received value in money, not goods.

At the same time, another set of natural attributes was appreciating in value. In the thirteenth century, and even more so in the fourteenth, some countries drew an increasing part of their economic strength from mineral resources.[4] Geological resources from which to extract precious metals – ores suitable for mining with the technology of the time – increased in value, and greatly contributed to the country's general wealth. The ability to reap the benefit of these natural features was of course highly dependent on the presence of a population with specialized knowledge and skills. This explains the effort made in the Late Middle Ages to bring to the area, sometimes from a great distance and by granting special privileges, groups of people capable of exploiting these natural features and thus enabling a much larger source of wealth to be tapped. There were also other areas where the division of labor in society intensified in this way and the value of groups specialized in such activities appreciated. Such functions were fulfilled by a diversity of ethnic groups, often of foreign origin, their activities embracing certain branches of agriculture, mining, crafts and long-distance trade.

Thus in the final centuries of the Middle Ages, the factors which increasingly determined the potential for national economic growth – besides natural features and the size of the local population – were the specialized activities pursued by certain ethnic groups and the economic efficiency of these activities. In understanding the economic history of medieval Hungary it is an absolutely crucial question how big the population was, and of what origin. In this case, even the most basic sources with which to quantify these pieces of information are lacking, as stated in the introductory chapter about the sources of economic history. For this reason it is essential that some basic issues relating to hints about sources and conclusions that can be drawn from them are clarified when trying to reconstruct the population of Hungary in the Middle Ages.

Of the basic questions, two should be emphasized: the sources for the population estimates, and the proportion of the different ethnic groups, especially in the context of their economic activities. We lay stress on discussing

---

3 Weisz 2012b and Weisz 2013b on the markets in the medieval Kingdom of Hungary until the mid-fourteenth century. On the organization of fairs, see also: Tringli 2010.
4 See the contribution of Zoltán Batizi in the present volume.

the arrival of ethnic groups which brought new production techniques and lifestyles to the region. This helps in the acquisition of information about the sources of internal growth in production that may not be connected with internal development.

Ways of Determining Hungary's Medieval Population and Their Limitations

Determination of Hungary's medieval population is a major problem for historical demographic research, and has been the subject of academic dispute for several decades. As with general quantitative economic-history indices, there is a problem with the number and nature of usable sources. At first sight, calculation of the late medieval population appears to be based on two sets of sources: the papal tithe registers of the 1330s, and the sum of the royal tax censuses of the 1490s. A closer look at the data and the 'methods of calculation' used to determine the population, however, prompts the conclusion that the population of late medieval Hungary cannot be determined with certainty, and any estimate has a large margin of error. No related sources are available at all for earlier periods, thus even estimations which do exist from the period of the Conquest to the turn of the thirteenth century are unfeasible. The numbers that have been published regarding the local population for this period lack scientific validity, and attempts to estimate, based on different demographic models and fertility rates, the population of the Conquest period or the eleventh century based on data from the early fourteenth century – which, as will be discussed here, are also highly problematic – are also entirely speculative.

These attempts do not take into an account the lack of precise data concerning the number of people who settled in the country, mostly between the mid-twelfth to the early fourteenth century, and thus the application any demographic model is therefore spurious. There is no question that between the tenth and the middle of the thirteenth century there was considerable population growth, as is well reflected in the growth in the number and the sizes of settlements, as well as settling at the margins of the Carpathian Basin which before the mid-twelfth century were sparsely inhabited.

Consequently, regarding the usual demographic criteria and with due heed to arguments about sources, the population of medieval Hungary is indeterminate. All attempts at calculations and estimates of population and therefore of demographic indices from the time of the Conquest up to the early sixteenth century are thus doomed to failure. Similarly, calculations of the same indices based on extrapolating the population in the Modern period do not comply with the rules defined by demographers. The two sources discussed below do, however, permit estimates of the country's population in the fourteenth and fifteenth centuries. Even these two sources are problematic, thus calculations based on them cannot be regarded as estimations from a statistical or demographic perspective.

The papal tithe registers drawn up in the 1330s were based on surveys carried out to determine the tithe revenue of the country's parishes. The sources from the last decade of the fifteenth century are made up of surveys of certain components of state tax revenue. Basically, therefore, the two sets of sources cannot be compared, although the lack of other sources obliges us to do this. Each set of sources also has its own individual problems. First, the units they are based on do not cover the entire territory of the kingdom, so that supplementary estimates are required to obtain figures for the country as a whole. Second, the censuses suffered from omissions, some systematic, others random, of data which ostensibly fell within their scope, and so the sources are incomplete. Finally, it is very important to bear in mind that the fourteenth century dataset permits only a highly indirect estimate of population, because what was being surveyed was not the number of people but the church revenue of certain geographical areas. Although the figures are clearly related to the local population, their geographical variation, owing to differences in economic potential (e.g. of grain- or vine-growing areas), may not match actual differences in population.[5]

The accounting books of 1494 and 1495 contain figures entered by Zsigmond Ernuszt, the royal treasurer. They are actually summas of county tax censuses which were carried out to determine the tax base of the country. The census covered Transylvania and Slavonia, but fourteen counties are missing. The figures for these fourteen counties are estimated partly from other censuses and partly by other methods.[6]

One serious drawback of both estimates is the lack of basic demographic data, which can only be obtained very indirectly. Prominent among this is the size of the family or household. The royal census did not set out to measure population like modern censuses do, but to survey the basic units of taxation, which were households. This means that even a full set of data only tells us the number of heads of families among the peasantry (which researchers claim represented 90 % of the country's population). Since there are no general data on how many people lived in one household or how big the average family was, we have to look at censuses where for some reason all members of the family (including children) were included. Since there are very few such

---

5   Györffy 1984b. For the source: Fejérpataky (ed.) 1887 and Ortvay 1891–1892.
6   Solymosi 1984 and Sclymosi 1985. A critical edition of the account book of Ernuszt is under publication by Tibor Neumann.

censuses available, and these were not intended to measure the number of people, the population has to be determined by multiplying. There are similar problems, if of a lesser degree, with determining the number of nobles or clergy. Consequently, the final figures for population stated in the research cannot be applied in the same way as data from modern population censuses. Reconstruction of population densities using known regional differences and areas, however, does permit the making of some general conclusions which provide information useful in describing the history of the medieval Hungarian economy and economic activity.

Population and Population Density Trends in Late Medieval Hungary

Most research into these sources has accepted as a usable estimate that the population of the country in the late fifteenth century was nearly three million (2,900,000).[7] We thus have a figure to go on for the end of the period. However, this number cannot be placed alongside figures of similar accuracy (or inaccuracy) for the thirteenth or fourteenth centuries.

Other types of transitions, such as those between eras of political history, are also important considerations in historical demographic analysis. An appropriate starting point for the analysis of demographic trends, as with economic trends, is one major event early in the period. The devastating 1241–1242 Mongol invasion may be regarded as the dominant factor to affect the late medieval population, since it resulted in a dramatic fall in the number of people living in the country (*see* Fig. 2.1).

The actual magnitude of this population decline, however, is the subject of long-standing academic debate. Published figures about the percentage of the population that died during the Mongol invasion and in the subsequent famine and other disasters are highly contradictory. In the absence of exact data, researchers have tried to assess the level of devastation from indirect evidence. The analysis starts with written records of towns and villages, from which changes in numbers may be determined. The large-scale destruction of settlements in the thirteenth century was previously explained by the Mongol invasion and the famine and epidemic which followed. It is now known, however, that there were also other factors behind the loss of settlements. Archaeological excavations and – even more usefully – topographical

---

[7] For the different opinions until ca. 1990, see: Fügedi 1992. For the different numbers and an overview of the topic since then: Romhányi 2015.

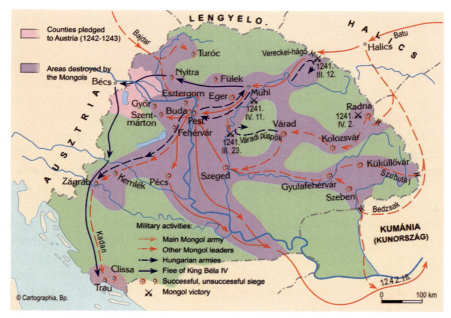

FIGURE 2.1 *Route of the Mongol troops in 1241 and 1242 (after http://tudasbazis.sulinet.hu).*

studies have found that only a few of the very large number of abandoned Árpádian-age settlements (which the written sources do not even mention) could have directly fallen victim to the ravages of the Mongols.[8] This is particularly true of the very small, scattered farmstead-like settlements which have recently been found in increasing numbers. Only a small number of finds or circumstances display direct evidence of destruction. Until very recently, burned-down, destroyed settlements with traces of unburied residents have been found on the relatively sparsely-populated areas of the Great Hungarian Plain.[9] Despite the growing number of destroyed settlements that have been identified by archaeological research, this process took place only in certain areas and probably less often than previously thought. However, the coins and jewelry found across the country, and the traces of the destruction of quickly-erected defensive structures, do suggest that the destruction of large sections

---

8 See the fundamentally important work of Szabó 1963, as well as the case studies carried out recently, for instance: Bálint et al. 2003, Vadas 2011a, Belényesyné Sárosi 2013, Rosta 2014 and Pinke et al. 2016.

9 For a highly comprehensive study volume on the archaeological heritage of the Mongol invasion, see: Rosta and V. Székely (eds.) 2014.

of the population, as dramatically recorded in the written sources, does have some historical basis (*see* Fig. 2.2).[10]

Other data, however, indicate that the complete abandonment of settlements was actually due to a process of integration which occurred after, and partly as a consequence of, the Mongol invasion. Rather than a sudden transformation, this process spanned several decades, or even a century. The important conclusion is that the abandonment of a large number of villages was not necessarily linked to large-scale population decline. This claim applies particularly to periods such as the second half of the thirteenth and the early part of the fourteenth centuries when – as known from other data – some villages were being abandoned, while others – notably some towns, which were starting to grow at the time – were experiencing a significant rise in population.

A comparison of historical, urban-historical and archaeological data suggests that the Mongol invasion caused the death of no more than 15–20 % of the population, much less than many previous estimates, which estimate up to 40 or 50 %.[11] Even if the decline was as severe as the higher estimates, and the country experienced severe trauma, there is very clear evidence that it was followed by a substantial increase in population within a short historical time. An increase in reproduction after the collapse of the kind which has occurred in other eras could only partly have been responsible for this, suggesting that a major factor in making up for the decline was large-scale immigration. The process started in the twelfth century, before the Mongols came, but the second half of the thirteenth century saw a distinctive change in the form of mass immigration, which continued to some extent in the early fourteenth century. Most incomers were from more developed areas of Europe (German lands and western and southern parts of Europe) and the eastern steppe. The first group were mostly accommodated in the *hospes* settlements. Those coming from the east during that period were mostly Cumans, and had a different pattern of settlement.[12] The appearance and settlement of these groups greatly contributed to the flourishing of life in Hungary from the fourteenth century onwards. The overall effect was that, by the mid-fourteenth century, even in demographic terms, the country had recovered from the destruction of the mid-thirteenth century and was experiencing a continuous and substantial rise in population. This may partly have been due to the clear improvement in living

---

10   For the jewelry and hoards that can be connected to the Mongol invasion, see: Vargha 2015.
11   Cf. the related studies in Nagy (ed.) 2003.
12   Pálóczi Horváth 1989, Pálóczi Horváth 2014, Berend 2001 and Zimonyi and Kovács (eds.) 2016.

DEMOGRAPHIC ISSUES IN LATE MEDIEVAL HUNGARY 55

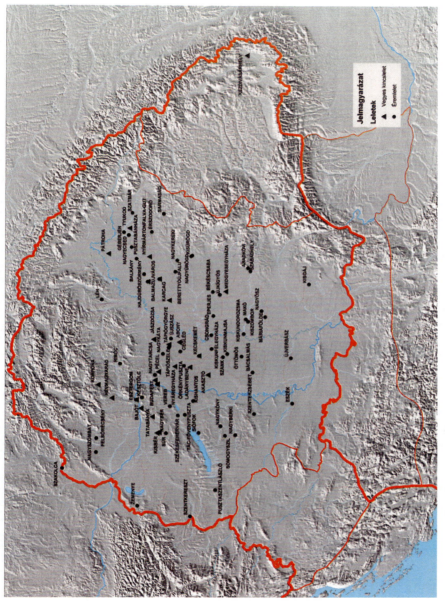

FIGURE 2.2 *Coin hoards uncovered from the period of the Mongol invasions (after Tóth 2007).*

standards among the largest segment of society, the peasants. Archaeological excavations quite definitely show that the increase in the size of peasant houses, the modernization of heating equipment, and the spread of village houses with several rooms are good indicators of a rise in living standards. Underlying this process were the major social changes during which many more peasants gained more freedom than in the thirteenth century. By the early fifteenth century, this combination of factors had led to a steady and relatively large population increase.

It seems that Hungary was not seriously affected by the so-called 'fourteenth-century crisis', as there are hardly any traces of major demographic or alimentary crises in the period.[13] In Western Europe and parts of Central Europe, a clear change in climatic conditions and agricultural opportunities, along with other political, economic and demographic factors, gave rise to a period in which economic growth significantly slowed down, if not declined. However, for the Hungarian Kingdom, as the studies in the present volume attest, this period cannot be considered a time of crisis.[14]

In recent decades, historians working on the Carpathian Basin have attempted to test the validity of the claim of a series of periods of crisis, which in a Western European context have already been analyzed. Since the pioneering monograph of William Chester Jordan (*The Great Famine*) historians have addressed the regional validity of the processes the author described. Numerous studies have investigated the appearance of famines and floods in the 1310s in the Carpathian Basin which are well documented in Western Europe. Earlier research into contemporary Hungarian sources did not find any record of such an environmental crisis in the Carpathian Basin, but recently published results permit the conclusion that extreme weather may have affected this area as well. However, only a few sources mention food shortages or famine in the whole country, unlike in Western Europe.[15] Similarly well studied are the 1340s, which are better documented as a crisis period than the 1310s, in Hungary at least. Many weather extremes (mainly floods) undoubtedly occurred in these years, as was the case in other Central European countries and parts of Western Europe.[16] Charters mention the flooding of several rivers in the spring and summer of 1342, followed in September by snow and more floods. Although there are fewer sources on the weather of subsequent years, Andrea

---

13   Laszlovszky 1994.
14   See also the study by László Ferenczi and his colleagues in the present volume.
15   Kiss 1996, Szántó 2005a, Szántó 2005b, Szántó 2007, 159–164, Vadas 2009 and Vadas 2010. See most recently the comprehensive study on famines in fourteenth-century Hungary: Kiss, Piti and Sebők 2016.
16   Kiss 1996, 65–66.

Kiss found data about floods in the country in 1343, and then nearly every year in the second half of the decade.[17] Although in some cases the weather and connected events that caused serious environmental crises in Western Europe did occur in Hungary, there is no mention of major alimentary crises in the periods in question in the narrative sources or other textual data for the period. As noted, there are only some elements of the 'fourteenth-century crisis' that sources from the Hungarian Kingdom tell us about. One of them is certainly the great epidemic of the mid-fourteenth century, the so-called Great Plague, and in connection with this, the demographic crisis.[18] The (probable) increase in precipitation during the later medieval period may have expanded the areas under permanent or temporary inundation,[19] but may also have reduced the problem of drought typical to continental areas, partly contributing to better opportunities for agriculture and animal husbandry. This, along with growth in the use of mining goods, may have contributed to the hypothesized population growth of the fourteenth century.

The rise in population in the fourteenth and fifteenth centuries also caused population density in certain parts of the country to rise substantially, and previously sparsely-populated areas to be settled. The most densely-populated counties were in the western and south-western parts of the country, as evidenced by the density of settlements, the large number of markets and central points in these regions, and the large number of churches identified from research into ecclesiastical topography. That these areas had considerable economic potential is a conclusion which follows indirectly from this data and is further reinforced by factors such as the scale of construction of private castles – those built after the Mongol invasion were larger.[20] These are most densely grouped in the western and to some extent the northern parts of the country, and not in the direction from which a Mongol attack would be expected (i.e., the east). Other factors, however, were behind the major population expansion in the west and north and the resulting increase in population density. The main engine of regional population growth in northern Hungary and some parts of Transylvania was the exploitation of mineral reserves, which took on new momentum in the fourteenth century and gave rise to new mining towns and other urban settlements.[21] New kinds of economic activity in Hungary in

---

17   Kiss 2009c, 37–47 and Kiss 2012, 483–509.
18   Laszlovszky 1994.
19   See the study of László Ferenczi and his colleagues in the present volume, and Pinke et al. 2016 (both with extensive further literature on the topic).
20   Fügedi 1986.
21   Weisz 2013a, which includes a summary of earlier research.

the late medieval period, however, were not confined to those relatively densely-populated areas. Indeed, there were some regions where the relatively low population and settlement density themselves presented opportunities for new branches of the economy, including activities with significance for foreign trade. The most obvious example is extensive animal husbandry, which took on an increasing role in various parts of the Great Hungarian Plain in the late medieval period, and in production for foreign trade. Densely-populated Italian and German towns whose demand for high-quality meat could not be satisfied by the animal-breeding capacity of the surrounding countryside proved a ready market for livestock from Hungary.[22] By contrast, having been substantially depopulated after the Mongol invasion and then partly settled by Cumans, the Great Hungarian Plain was capable of producing several times as much meat as could be consumed by the local population. The relatively high variation in population density in late medieval Hungary therefore does not imply that only the high-density regions contributed to the country's economic production.

It is difficult to judge the extent to which this relatively large population growth, together with substantial differences in population density, were typical of the country. Several researchers have detected the signs of decline in the second half of the fifteenth century, and particularly the beginning of the sixteenth. In this interpretation, the population estimated for the late fifteenth century may therefore be less than that of the first half of the century. These conclusions, however, face the same kind of problems as the data and censuses used for the estimates. The most intense debate surrounds the proportion of *inquilini* (peasants who owned less than one-eighth of a plot, or no land at all) and particularly the house-owning *inquilini*. The increase in the number of abandoned plots (uninhabited plots within villages) recorded in tax and service censuses may imply a decline in population, but could also be explained by attempts to avoid royal taxes.[23] In the latter explanation the population did not decline as the tax base shrank because tax was paid on plots, and if more than one family moved into one plot the tax burden per family was reduced. The details of this argument will not be presented here, but there is compelling evidence that there was no major decrease in population during this period. In the southern areas of the country, occasional incursions by the Ottomans must have caused some destruction,[24] but this was probably compensated by the immigration of refugees from the Balkans and the south of the country –

---

22 See Blanchard 1986.
23 See the recent results for a different region: Neumann 2003 and Nógrády 2015.
24 For the population loss caused by the Ottomans on the example of Valkó County, see: Engel 2000.

people displaced by the same Ottoman advances. Our knowledge of taxation during the second half of the fifteenth century, especially the almost annual collection of extraordinary tax, shows that there was no major change in the tax base or the number of taxpayers. Otherwise, it is almost inconceivable that this tax could have been collected so often and at such a level. The mining and metalworking ventures in the north of the country also showed signs of development, although this was not necessarily associated with population increase.

Suggestions of economic decline and population decrease in the late fifteenth century must thus be treated with caution in the light of the increasingly clear picture of demographic trends in the sixteenth century. Contrary to previous claims, the first half of the sixteenth century saw no collapse of settlements or dramatic population decline in the Great Hungarian Plain or in other regions affected by the early phases of the Ottoman conquest. Such phenomena occurred only at the end of the century, during the Fifteen Years' War (1591–1606), not solely as the result of military events, but through a combination of civil-war conditions, denominational squabbles, ongoing Ottoman–Hungarian battles, double or even triple taxation, changing climate, and epidemics and animal diseases. Similarly, the development of areas that produced livestock for foreign markets, and the local and transit marketplaces built on this trade, only faltered in the second half of the sixteenth century. This claim is borne out by the censuses and archaeological data from excavations of relevant settlements (e.g. Muhi) and analyses of animal bones (e.g. Vác).[25] The signs of economic crisis in the period prior to the decisive loss against the Ottomans during the battle of Mohács in 1526 are therefore linked not to a demographic crisis but to the struggles against the Ottomans, which absorbed increasing amounts of the country's economic strength.

In sum, then, the period between the Mongol invasion (1241–1242) and the defeat at Mohács (1526) was clearly one of demographic advance for Hungary. This does not mean that growth was steady and without downturns, but the general trend is clear. Whether this population increase is estimated at more or less than one million, the fact of its occurrence is substantiated by written sources, archaeology and urban history research. The increase in population in itself represented major potential for economic growth in a country where the exploitation of diverse natural resources (cultivable land, mining, etc.) was growing at the same time. This, combined with the trends of other demographic changes, made the country, if for a short time, one of the most prominent powers in the region, capable of financing the major military ventures, domestic construction and spectacular art patronage embarked on during the

---

25   Bartosiewicz 1995a.

reign of King Matthias. The growth in the number of market towns and in their economic role, as well as in the number of Mendicant friaries frequently connected to these settlements, show that the general trend was rather to population growth or stagnation rather than decrease in the period.[26] The break in the process, the over-exploitation of human and economic reserves, was the consequence not so much of a deterioration in demographic conditions or of economic production, but of the large-scale power shifts in the neighborhood of the country.

Ethnic Groups and Economic Processes

Late medieval Hungary was in every respect a recipient country in demographic terms. It was host to a large number of ethnic groups of foreign origin and diverse customs. This ethnic and cultural diversity also played a major role in the country's economic life.[27] In the Árpádian age, oriental ethnic groups were of importance mainly in terms of the border defense system, long-distance trade and finance; and Muslim and Jewish groups mainly as regards trade and finance.[28] While the first non-Christian population was present in urban, proto-urban and rural settlements, the second was mainly connected to early towns and cities.[29] In the Late Middle Ages, the situation became even more colorful and complex via a process which started even before the Mongol invasion and persisted throughout the thirteenth century, giving rise to a state of affairs which proved durable thereafter. A major difference to the first half of the Árpádian age was the mass settlement of certain ethnic groups in concentrated areas. Three of the regions which took shape in this way stand out in terms of population and economic effect. These are the areas inhabited by the Saxons in the Spiš region[30] and Transylvania,[31] and the Cuman settlements.[32] Each of these had a complex structure, but relatively contiguous areas took shape through the charters which granted privileges to ethnic groups of

26 Romhányi 2015.
27 Függedi 1975.
28 Berend 2001. See also Mátyás 2014. On the Jewish population, see also: Kubinyi 1995b. More recently, on Jewish-Christian connections, see: Szende 2014.
29 On the Muslim settlements in the rural countryside, see: Rózsa et al. 2014.
30 Homza and Sroka 2009.
31 Kristó 2003 and Kristó 2008.
32 See the pioneering work of Lyublyanovics 2017. Also see: Pálóczi Horváth 2014 and Zimonyi and Kovács (eds.) 2016.

various origins. The people who appear in the sources as "Saxons" were not only from Saxony, but the word was used for all German-speaking settlers. It was largely economic considerations which prompted their invitation to settle. The agricultural techniques and systems of cultivation they brought with them were excellently suited to the colonization of specific areas and the construction first of villages, and later systems of towns. German-speaking people with a different set of special skills were brought in to populate the mining towns, a process that fitted well with the history of the German component of the evolving urban population in Hungary. All of the towns which ranked highest in the Hungarian urban hierarchy included a German population, and in many cases the granting of their privileges may be regarded as the defining point in the development of these towns. For example, one major economic resource for Buda in the thirteenth century, and indeed at later points in the city's development, was the system of contacts maintained by German trading and craft families, who were in many cases related to prominent burghers in other regions (*see* Fig. 2.3).

Another group who exerted a major economic effect and contributed to Hungarian urban development were the people referred to in the sources as "Latins". They also came to the country in the hope of *hospes* privileges, and were classified according to their various neo-Latin languages. In Hungarian,

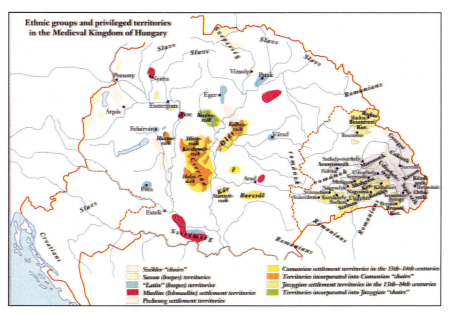

FIGURE 2.3 *Map of different ethnic groups living in medieval Hungary.*

they were usually called *olaszok* (Italians), but in fact they came from western parts of Europe as well as Italy. There was hardly a major town of the time, especially in the central parts of the Hungarian Kingdom, where the Latins did not have a quarter of their own, with separate rights. There were also some areas (such as the Bodrog Valley) where they lived in villages and exerted their economic influence by applying new viticulture techniques. It is no coincidence that the best wines of the Middle Ages were often linked to areas they inhabited. As trade and the economy developed in Italy, relationships led to more such groups arriving in the second half of the late medieval period, particularly to trade in special products or deal in financial affairs. Despite their relatively small number, they were of substantial economic significance.[33] The *hospes* groups of the twelfth and thirteenth centuries also played a crucial role in the social development of the rural countryside. Not only were urban privileges connected to the legal systems of the *hospes* settlements of different origins, but also the emerging new peasantry derived many of its basic legal status and conditions of service from the new settlers.

Also small in terms of population were the Jewish communities, of which there are records in several dozen Hungarian towns in the Late Middle Ages.[34] In Buda and Sopron, besides the written records, relics of Jewish material culture and excavated remains of synagogues convey their significance in urban life, and particularly their effects on the economy. They lived in separate streets or quarters, an indication of their importance, and were not at that time subjected to ghetto-like segregation. Their development was at several times interrupted by their banishment, although in Buda, for example, several Jewish residential areas and religious buildings can clearly be traced.[35] The Jewish communities were not comparable in size and significance to their counterparts in some large medieval German towns, but they nonetheless played a very prominent role in Hungary. A good indication of their special situation is the separate set of privileges and legal system they enjoyed during the reign of King Matthias (the second half of the fifteenth century).[36]

The Cumans formed another group of major economic significance. They were one of the largest settler groups and inhabited a large area. They were initially brought to the country not for economic purposes, but to satisfy King Béla IV's need to defend the country against the approaching Mongols in 1241.

---

33   Petrovics 2009, Draskóczy 2016c or Arany 2007 and her contribution in the present volume.
34   Berend 2001 and Szende 2015b.
35   For Buda, see: Végh 2006. For the Jewish districts of other towns, see: Szende 2015b, 51–63.
36   See e.g. Draskóczy 2016c (with a summary of the aforementioned literature).

The Cumans' assistance was not successful in this respect, but the king subsequently settled them in the largely deserted areas of the Great Hungarian Plain and to a lesser extent in the west of the country (Transdanubia). They had earlier and for a long time inhabited an area directly adjacent to the country, east of the Carpathians, and Béla's intention was to win over an ethnic group that represented considerable military strength. The Cuman forces and nobles retained their important military role beyond the late Árpádian age, into the Angevin period. Their settlement was also a relatively rapid way of repopulating parts of the country which had been left without inhabitants. It was a process not free of conflict, as is reported in written sources from the time. Having a different way of life, with large animal herds, the "pagan Cumans" constantly clashed with the agricultural villages in adjoining areas.[37] The mission to the Christianization of the Cuman settlers and the formation of settlements on their lands similar to Hungarian villages contributed to their gradual integration into their surroundings, although they retained their separate legal status in the areas they farmed and inhabited. Animal husbandry, particularly involving large animals, remained one of their distinctive pursuits throughout the Late Middle Ages, and was undoubtedly a factor in their becoming, in the fifteenth century, the starting point for long-distance cattle trading. In the process, they gradually lost their prominent military role, but gained increasing economic influence.[38]

There were many other ethnic groups of diverse origin living on the territory of late medieval Hungary. Although their economic significance was in no way comparable to those already mentioned, they did contribute to the economic system of the Kingdom of Hungary by developing a wide range of activities that effectively exploited the assorted natural features of the country in the fourteenth and fifteenth centuries. It was this diversity, and the culture and adaptive capabilities of the various ethnic groups, which underlay the vigorous development of the most disparate branches of the economy. The southern Transylvanian Saxon towns' trading links with the Romanian principalities, the Spiš Saxons' contacts with Polish urban centers, and the business and family connections of the German burghers of Sopron with Wiener Neustadt, Vienna and other Austrian towns played an important role in the country's economy, as did the cattle driven from the Great Hungarian Plain to German and Italian towns, and the Hungarian wine sold on foreign markets. This diversity, along with generally positive late medieval demographic trends, is thus one of the keys to understanding the successful economic development of the period.

---

37   On the animal husbandry of the Cumans, see: Lyublyanovics 2017.
38   Pálóczi Horváth 1989 and Pálóczi Horváth 2014.

CHAPTER 3

Mobility, Roads and Bridges in Medieval Hungary

*Magdolna Szilágyi**

The communication system of the Hungarian Kingdom was a complex, multi-layered, and ever-changing network of roads, paths and different river-crossing places that combined the elements of human and natural landscape into one living, cohesive unit. The road network was at the same time the backbone of the settlement system, and the two developed in a closely related way, any changes in one affecting the other. The purpose of the present chapter is to provide an overview of the overland communication network in medieval Hungary with special regard to the following issues: (1) forms of mobility in medieval times, (2) the hierarchy of types of roads, (3) types of river-crossing places, and (4) royal policy towards roads, bridges and ferries. Communication and transportation routes were the arteries of administration, economic and social life. As the economic components of these (namely, domestic and foreign trade) are discussed in detail by other authors in the present volume, they are addressed here only briefly, with a special focus on the trade routes themselves.

Mobility in the Middle Ages

The Middle Ages is often considered to be an era when, due to the poor quality of roads, the fatigue involved with traveling on them, the slow speed and high cost of traveling, and the numerous perils lurking en route, few people ventured onto the roads. Regular travel is regarded to have been the privilege of sovereigns and feudal lords, who were required to travel around their dominions escorted by their entourage of dignitaries to confirm their authority, and for reasons of emphasizing their political and social status. Besides these individuals, it was mainly 'professional' travelers, namely missionaries, merchants, messengers, envoys, soldiers, and artists who were regularly on the move.[1] The majority of society, however, generally lived isolated lives in inward-looking communities and left their places of residence only infrequently.

* The research was supported by the Hungarian Town Atlas research project (OTKA K 116594) funded by the Hungarian Scientific Research Fund.
1 On the role of religion, trade and communications in traveling, see Ohler 1989, 56–73.

The popular notions listed above, however, should now be reconsidered in accordance with the research findings of the past few decades about travel and mobility.[2] The medieval population, especially when compared to modern people, had very limited opportunity to travel, but this does not mean that they were not sometimes able to visit even distant areas. Even peasants were able to leave their settlements if they fulfilled certain requirements.[3]

The requirement to learn and acquire professional skills also caused many people to migrate. Guild masters sent apprentices who had learnt craftsmanship from them to other cities or market towns to broaden their professional skills. Subsequently, these individuals either returned to their former places of residence (i.e., temporary change of location), or settled in a new place where they acquired full membership of a guild (i.e., permanent change of location).[4] Intellectuals generally had to travel farther than craftsmen to study theology, law, and medicine. Before the foundation of the first Hungarian university in Pécs (1367), Hungarians could only go abroad to university. Hungarian students are known from the universities of Paris and Oxford from the twelfth century onwards, and at the universities of Bologna and Padua from the thirteenth.[5]

In addition to the economic and social factors listed above, religion was an equally important motive for travel. Medieval men and women would visit remote places of worship for a number of reasons. Most often they undertook long journeys – and managed the inconvenience and costs associated with them – for reasons of piety (pious pilgrimage), in the hope of forgiveness (ascetic pilgrimage) or due to their assignment (deputy pilgrimage). There is evidence of Hungarian pilgrims visiting Jerusalem (seven persons), Rome (six persons), Santiago de Compostela (one person) and Aachen (one person) as early as the Árpádian age. In the fourteenth century, and especially in the fifteenth, the number of pilgrims traveling abroad and the number of places of worship increased dramatically.[6] Frequenting of divine services involved shorter journeys (walking) and thus involved greater proportions of society. In the early eleventh century, there was a church within 15–24 kilometers

---

2   For a bibliography of international scholarly literature published before 1990 (especially in German) on traveling between 1350 and 1600, see: Matschinegg and Müller 1990.

3   In the second half of the thirteenth century, these conditions were the permission of the *seigneur* and payment of rent (*terragium*), which were later complemented with the payment of debts. See: Kubinyi 1991c, 230.

4   Kubinyi 1991c, 234.

5   Before the foundation of the University of Pécs, 40 universities had been founded in Europe: 18 in Italy, ten on the territory of what later became France, seven in the Iberian Peninsula, two in England and three in Central Europe. Szögi 1995, 6. On Hungarian university peregrination to Paris and Bologna, see also: Mezey 1979, 144–150.

6   Csukovits 2003, 25–26, Table 1.

(that is, three–four hours' walk) from most villages, which made possible regular attendance at Holy Mass, albeit sometimes with difficulty.[7] Moreover, due to the building of more churches, this distance gradually decreased in subsequent centuries. As a result, by the fifteenth century every second village had its own church,[8] which means that the distance from villages without a church to the nearest parish church had decreased to approximately 5 kilometers; that is, about one hour's walk.[9]

Types of Road

Similarly to the motivation of travelers, the functions and use of roads were also extremely diverse in the Middle Ages. The various types of travel (military movements, university peregrination, pilgrimage, trade, etc.) brought into being different types of roads which can be categorized into four main hierarchical groups: (1) long-distance roads linking the major cities of the country and leading abroad; (2) provincial (or inter-regional) roads connecting distant parts of the country; (3) regional roads linking various centers (cities, market towns, castles, monasteries, etc.) with their surroundings; and, (4) local roads that typically connected villages with each other (inter-village roads) and with the fields belonging to them (intra-village roads).

The earliest long-distance roads were certainly for military purposes (*via exercituum*,[10] *via exercitus*,[11] *hadút*,[12] *hadinagyút*[13]); namely, marching routes controlled by castles. They often took the form of straight paths across the countryside which avoided settlements and thus allowed armed forces to

---

[7] Györffy 1983a, 186.
[8] Szabó 1969, 184–186.
[9] On the territory of late-medieval Tolna County, András K. Németh defined the average distance of settlements to the nearest church as 4–5 kilometres, while Máté Stibrányi arrived at the same conclusion after studying the Sárvíz valley area. K. Németh 2015, 238 and Stibrányi 2008, 195. On the archaeology of medieval roads leading to churches, see K. Németh 2014, 180–182.
[10] For example, 1086: *ad viam exercituum* (Koppány, Veszprém County), Erdélyi and Sörös (eds.) 1902–1916, VIII, 267.
[11] For example, 1209: *a publica strata, que vulgo via exercitus dicitur* (Trstenik, Zágráb County), Wenzel (ed.) 1860–1874, XI, 98.
[12] For example, 1055: *ad viam, quae dicitur Haduth* (Gamás, Somogy County), Fejér (ed.) 1829–1844, VII/5, 62.
[13] For example, 1335: *ad quandam viam Hadinogoth vocatam* (Zalavár, Zala County), Nagy, Véghely and Nagy (eds.) 1886–1890, I, 301.

move quickly. The earliest references to medieval military roads date to the early Árpádian age. In Transdanubia, some of these roads followed the remains of ancient highways constructed by the Romans. The Roman military road leading along the fortified Danubian frontier of Pannonia (and at the same time, that of the Roman Empire) called *limes*, for example, was again of outstanding military importance in the eleventh century. This road was used by the armed forces of King Stephen when Hungary joined the last military campaign of Emperor Basil II against Bulgaria led in 1014–1018,[14] and the road was also partly used by Western European Crusaders marching to the Holy Land in 1096.[15] Pilgrimage roads crossing the borders of several countries are also representative examples of European long-distance roads. The earliest pilgrimage road in Hungary was the overland route to Jerusalem following the course of the Roman military road along the right bank of the Danube, as mentioned above. This route was made accessible for Western European pilgrims by King Stephen after his military campaign to the Balkans in 1018.[16] The third main type of long-distance road involved foreign trade routes,[17] the directions and lines of which were defined by the exchange of goods with neighboring countries, natural landscape (especially rivers and hills), and the urban network[18] of Hungary. Long-distance trade routes to the West and to the Balkans, for example, followed the course of the Danube. Further important early Árpádian-age trade routes led from Buda across the Verecke Pass (*Veretskyy pereval*, transcribed from Ukrainian) to Kiev, as well as along the eastern foothills of the Styrian Prealps, linking Venice with Vienna. After the occupation of Kiev by the Mongols in 1240, trade with Buda died away, and the trade route across the Verecke Pass ceased being used. The north-south road across western Transdanubia also lost its role in transit trade in the late twelfth century when a new trade route was opened between Venice and Vienna via the Semmering Pass.[19]

Secondary roads are represented by provincial (inter-regional) roads that often served to facilitate the exchange of goods between different regions of the country. Beginning in the mid-twelfth century there were two types of goods whose trade in Hungary created provincial roads between distant parts

---

14 Györffy 1983a, 288–289.
15 Borosy and Laszlovszky 2006, 80–82.
16 Györffy 1983a, 293–308.
17 For an overview of long-distance trade in the Árpádian age, see: Szűcs 1993, 230–241.
18 On the connection between long-distance communication routes and urban development in medieval Hungary, see: Szende 2011b.
19 Szűcs 1993, 230–235.

of the country: wine, and salt.[20] Roads along which wine was transported (*borhordó út*[21]) from the wine regions of Srijem and Lake Balaton (Somogy and Zala Counties) to Esztergom, and from there to Upper Hungary became the most important north–south directed trade route[22] in the country. Salt roads (*via salifera*,[23] *sóhordó út*,[24] *sóút*,[25] *sajtút*,[26] *sajtosút*[27]) leading from the salt mines of Transylvania, and (beginning in the early fourteenth century) from the Maramureș region to Buda and Transdanubia, on the other hand, formed the main east–west oriented communication axis of the kingdom.[28]

Tertiary roads provided access to the regional centers (towns, markets, fairs, castles, monasteries, seigneurial centers, etc.) of the county.[29] From a functional perspective, these roads were often of economic or administrative use. The regional exchange of goods, for example, created a star-shaped pattern of market roads (*via forensis*,[30] *via ad forum*,[31] *vásárút*,[32] *vásárosút*[33]) around marketplaces (*see* Fig. 3.1). The driving of livestock, such as cattle and horses,

---

20   Szűcs 1993, 256–266.
21   For example, 1382: *ad quondam magnam viam Borhordouth nominatam* (Kemecse and Tótmező, both Veszprém County), Érszegi and Solymosi (eds.) 2010, 323.
22   Wine from the southern slopes of the Fruška Gora in Srijem was either carried by wagons along the so-called *Baranyai nagyút* (the Great Road of Baranya) or shipped on the Danube. Szilágyi 2014, 134–135.
23   For example 1235: *usque viam que vocatur salifera* (Pityord, Győr County), Wenzel (ed.) 1860–1874, II, 35.
24   For example, 1368: *magnam viam wlgo Sohorowth vocatam* (Ikus, Arad County), MNL OL DL 25 769.
25   For example, 1411: *penes quandam viam de possessione Zalard ad possessionem Marya ducentem, Soowth dicatam* (Szalárd and Marja, both Bihar County), Mályusz et al. (eds.) 1951–2017, III, no. 3191. See the studies of Beatrix F. Romhányi and István Draskóczy on the salt trade in the present volume.
26   For example, 1271: *iuxta magnam viam Sahtuth a vulgo vocatam* (Veszprém, Veszprém County), Wenzel (ed.) 1860–1874, III, 269.
27   For example, 1431: *viam Saythwsuth* (Cluj-Mănăştur, Kolozs County), MNL OL DL 31 132.
28   Szűcs 1993, 256–266.
29   Cf. Aston 2002, 144–145.
30   For example, 1240: *ad unam viam forensem* (Gortva, Gömör County), Marsina (ed.) 1971–1987, II, 49.
31   For example, 1247: *iuxta viam, que ducit ad forum* (Sálfölde, Baranya County), Wenzel (ed.) 1860–1874, VII, 248.
32   For example, 1406: *usque viam Vasaruth* (Apsa, Zala County), Nagy, Véghely and Nagy (eds.) 1886–1890, II, 327.
33   For example, 1344: *ad magnam viam Vasarusvth dictam* (Badacsonytomaj, Zala County), Nagy, Véghely and Nagy (eds.) 1886–1890, I, 417.

FIGURE 3.1 *Medieval road leading from Râșnov to the market town of Bârsa Chute preserved as a holloway.*
PHOTOGRAPH BY OANA TODA, 2011.

on foot to market or to seasonal pastures produced drove roads (*via gregum*,[34] *csordaút*;[35] *ménesút*[36]) which are again typical examples of regional roads. Similarly, mention must be made of transportation routes along which natural resources were carried from their provenances to their places of use. For example, the transportation of blocks of stone by wagons from a quarry to the construction site of a church or castle created a special type of road for this specific purpose (*kőhordó út*[37]).

---

34 For example, 1277: *per viam gregum* (Zahara, Nógrád County), Wenzel (ed.) 1860–1874, IV, 93.

35 For example, 1293: *via vulgariter Churdauta dicta* (Veszprém, Veszprém County), Fejér (ed.) 1829–1844, IX/7, 711–712.

36 For example, 1381: *viam Menesuth* (Kesztölc, Tolna County), Fejér (ed.) 1829–1844, IX/6, 264.

37 For example, 1323: *ad viam Keuhorovth* (Veszprém County), Nagy, Véghely and Nagy (eds.) 1886–1890, I, 169.

At the fourth hierarchical level, one finds roads, paths, and tracks that served the purpose of local communication. Based on ethnographic analogues, local roads showed much greater variability and adaptivity than larger roads, which means that due to external (natural, social, economic and other) impacts they came into being or ceased to exist more frequently. In some cases, even whole networks could be reorganized. Their orientation and density were considerably influenced by local economic and social conditions.[38] Medieval sources often refer to local roads or tracks leading to areas around a village (plowlands, meadows, forests, vineyards, etc.).[39] These were, for instance, roads used for carrying hay (*szénahordó út*[40]) and wood (*via lignaria*,[41] *erdőlőút*[42]), and those leading to mills (*via molendinaria*,[43] *via ad molendinum*,[44] *malomuta*,[45] *malomút*,[46] *malomló út*[47]). Roads and footpaths linking a farmstead or a settlement without a church to a neighboring parish church (*via ad ecclesiam*,[48] *semita ad ecclesiam*[49]) were also of local significance. These church paths were primarily used by parishioners for going to Mass. However, the dead also needed to be carried to the churchyard for burial, which created a special type of road: the corpse road (*holtasút*,[50] *halotthordó út*[51]).[52]

---

38 Máté 2014, 572–574.

39 Aston 2002, 145–146.

40 For example, 1326: *usque viam scenahurdout vocatam* (Smolenice, Nyitra County), Nagy and Tasnádi Nagy (eds.) 1878–1920, II, 248.

41 For example, 1420: *per quandam viam lignariam* (Nyárád, Borsod County), Mályusz et al. (eds.) 1951–2017, VII, no. 2276.

42 For example, 1413: *inter viam Erdelewth et Zelewsuth vocatam* (Zombor, Zemplén County), Mályusz et al. (eds.) 1951–2017, IV, no. 853.

43 For example, 1342: *infra viam molendinariam* (Asszonyfa, Vas County), Nagy, Véghely and Nagy (eds.) 1886–1890, I, 403.

44 For example, 1342: *viam magnam ... que vadit ad molendinum* (Rum, Vas County), Nagy, Véghely and Nagy (eds.) 1886–1890, I, 401.

45 For example, 1277: *ad viam, que Molumuta vulgariter vocatur* (Mikófölde and Soponya, both Fejér County), Fejér (ed.) 1829–1844, VII/2, 56.

46 For example, 1400: *iuxta viam Malumvth* (Szécsény, Vas County), Házi 1970, 135.

47 For example, 1400: *iuxta viam Malonlowth* (Szécsény, Vas County), Házi 1970, 135.

48 For example, 1358: *ad viam magnam, qua itur ad ecclesiam sancti Nicolai* (Nick, Vas County), Nagy, Deák and Nagy (eds.) 1865–1891, IV, 143.

49 For example, 1314: *semitam qua itur ad ecclesiam omnium sanctorum* (Mindszent, Vas County), Nagy and Tasnádi Nagy (eds.) 1878–1920, I, 372.

50 For example, 1398: *ad quandam viam holthaswth vocatam* (Füle, Veszprém County), Szamota and Zolnai (eds.) 1902–1906, 343.

51 For example, 1489: *penes quondam viam herbosam que halothorowth diceretur* (Leányfalu, Veszprém County), Szamota and Zolnai (eds.) 1902–1906, 343.

52 Cf. Hindle 1993, 57–61.

Types of River-crossing Places

River-crossing places represent the prolongation of roads over water. As passing over watercourses was limited to bridges, ferry ports, and fords, these places topographically directed traffic to one point and thus turned into larger or smaller nodes of the road network. This also meant that the construction of a new bridge or ferry port (or the demolition of an old one) reshaped the road network of an area, with effects on further areas as well.

In medieval Hungary, bridges were constructed over rivers, streams, ditches and other places.[53] These were predominantly made of timber as this material was more easily accessible and worked than stone.[54] Wooden bridges could be constructed at low cost in a few days, a damaged bridge could be replaced by a new one at any time, and at times of war they could be easily destroyed, thereby holding up the enemy. In addition to references to wooden bridges (*pons ligneus*,[55] *fahíd*[56]) in written documents, the names of settlements such as Fahíd[57] and Nyárhíd[58] preserve the memory of bridges made of timber (Hungarian: *fa*) and poplar wood (Hungarian: *nyár*), respectively. Similarly, there is both written and place-name evidence for the existence of stone bridges (*lapideus pons*,[59] *kőhíd*[60]). The latter involve, for example, the Árpádian-age settlement Kőhídpordány[61] (present-day Wulkaprodersdorf, in Austria), and the name of the post-medieval settlement Sopronkőhida[62] must also testify to the existence of a nearby medieval stone bridge (*see* Figs 3.2–3.3).

In the early Árpádian age all bridges belonged to the king, who collected tolls for their upkeep from those who used them. Beginning with the twelfth century, there is evidence that some monasteries, towns, and nobles were

---

53 1417: *pontes ligneos seu lapideos super quibusvis fluminibus, fossatis et locis construere et edificare*, Mályusz et al. (eds.) 1951–2017, IV, no. 178.
54 For an overview of bridges in medieval Hungary, see: Bolla 1980.
55 For example, 1413: *duobus pontibus ligneis* (Zalavár, Zala County), Nagy, Véghely and Nagy (eds.) et al. 1886–1890, II, 391.
56 Szamota and Zolnai (eds.) 1902–1906, 209.
57 1330: *datum in Fahyd* (Fehér County), Nagy and Tasnádi Nagy (eds.) 1878–1920, II, 484. See also: Györffy 1963–1998, II, 142.
58 1183: *Narhyd* (Nyitra County), Marsina (ed.) 1971–1987, I, 90. See also: Györffy 1963–1998, IV, 428.
59 1254: *descenderet per lapideum pontem Sasaag et iret usque ad metas Peresnye* (Rákos, Sopron County), Wagner et al. (eds.) 1955–1999, I, 234.
60 Szamota and Zolnai (eds.) 1902–1906, 530.
61 1307: *Kuhidparadan* (Sopron County), Wagner et al. (eds.) 1955–1999, III, 30.
62 Kiss 1997a, II, 490.

FIGURE 3.2 *Gothic stone bridge at Dravce in Slovakia (fifteenth century)*.
PHOTOGRAPH BY AUTHOR, 2014.

FIGURE 3.3 *Gothic stone bridge near Leles in Slovakia (fourteenth century)*.
PHOTOGRAPH BY AUTHOR, 2014.

exempted from paying these tolls.[63] Sometimes the king assigned the right to collect bridge tolls to his subjects, irrespective of the proprietorship of the estate in which the bridge was located. After the mid-thirteenth century, however, the monarch normally gifted bridge tolls together with landed properties. While in 1183, for example, King Béla III transferred only one third of the bridge toll collected at Nyárhíd to the bishop of Nitra,[64] in 1264 King Béla IV donated the same settlement along with all its belongings (including its bridge toll) to the Premonstratensian monastery of Csőt.[65]

Beginning in the thirteenth century, the number of privately owned bridges increased. This fact is suggested, among other ways, by settlement names that are compounds formed of the term *-hida* ("the bridge of") and the name of the person that owned the landed property with a bridge on it (who may have been the same individual who erected the bridge), such as Barlabáshida, Péterhida, Mórichida, Bonchida, Pelbárthida, and Jánoshida.[66] Sometimes the owner or builder of the bridge was indicated by their title in a toponym, like in the cases of Apáthida ("abbot's bridge")[67] and Úrhida ("lord's bridge").[68]

Since rivers were incorporated as natural impediments into the Árpádian-age military defensive lines constructed along the frontiers (*gyepű*), bridges built over these rivers were of great strategic importance, and therefore needed to be strongly fortified and defended. The guards (*custodes*) of the bridge over the River Rába who settled at Hídvég in Vas County,[69] for example, are known

---

63 In 1208, for example, King Andrew II exempted the monastery of Lébény from the toll collected at Kenézhida on the Rába River (*in ponte Kenéz super Rabca*), Wagner et al. (eds.) 1955–1999, I, 55.

64 1183: *tertia parte pontis Narhyd* (Nyitra County), Marsina (ed.) 1971–1987, I, 90.

65 Knauz et al. (eds.) 1874–1999, I, 514.

66 1230: *terra Barlabashyda vocata sita iuxta Zala* (Barlabáshida, Zala County), Nagy, Véghely and Nagy (eds.) 1886–1890, I, 5; 1231: *Peterhyda* (Somogy County), Nagy, Deák and Nagy (eds.) 1865–1891, VIII, 27; 1251: *Mauruchhida* (Győr County), Wagner et al. (eds.) 1955–1999, I, 230; 1263: *Bonchhyda* (Bonțida, Doboka County), Nagy, Deák and Nagy (eds.) 1865–1891, V, 40; 1271: *Priuarthyda* (Bihar County), MNL OL DL 990; 1283: *Iwanushyda* (Heves County), Wenzel (ed.) 1860–1874, IV, 254.

67 1263: *Apathida/Apathyda* (Apahida, Kolozs County), MNL OL DL 37 213. The bridge belonged to the Cluj-Mănăștur Abbey together with the toll collected at it. See: Györffy 1963–1998, III, 342.

68 1009: *Hurhida* (Úrhida, Fejér County), Györffy (ed.) 1992, 52–53. The name Úrhida must refer to a bridge that belonged to a prince around the turn of the millennium. Györffy 1963–1998, II, 412.

69 1280: *custodes pontis Raba de comitatu Castri Ferrei* (Hídvég, Vas County), Wagner et al. (eds.) 1955–1999, II, 145.

among the guards of the western frontier of Hungary.[70] Since bridges along the frontiers were fortified places that defended the territories behind them, their defense (or loss) played a decisive role in the outcome of wars, making them likely to become the sites of battles.[71]

Ferries (*portus, rév*[72]) were traditionally used to cross deep and extended bodies of water that could not be bridged. Similarly to bridges, ferry ports are known by medieval toponyms. The name of the locality Lórév[73] ("horse port") at the southern end of Csepel Island, for example, evokes the memory of a ferry port on the Danube from which royal stud reared on the island were shipped.[74] Other toponyms inform us about the natural environment of the ferry port. The name of the site Kőrév[75] ("stone port") established where the Bodrog and the Tisza Rivers meet (near Tokaj) refers to its rocky, stony environment. The name Homokrév[76] ("sand port") suggests that the port was sandy, whereas Laposrév[77] ("marshy port") was named after the swamps and marshes (Hungarian: *láp*) which surrounded the port.[78]

Ferries were not only operated on watercourses, but also on major lakes. Lake Fertő (*lacus Ferthew*), for example, had ferry ports at Rákos[79] and Illmitz[80] with ferries passing between them. There is also written evidence of a ferry port on Lake Balaton (*aqua Balatini*) established at Burul, near Zalavár.[81] Based

---

70 For an overview of the *gyepű* in Western Hungary, see: Göckenjan 1972 and Kiss and Tóth 1996.
71 A battle between King Stephen V and the king of Bohemia was, for example, fought at the bridge of Abda (*apud pontem Abada*) over the River Rábca. Wagner et al. (eds.) 1955–1999, II, 143.
72 Szamota and Zolnai (eds.) 1902–1906, 810–811 (*rév*).
73 1259: *datum in Portu Equorum* (Pest County), Wenzel (ed.) 1860–1874, VII, 506; [1267]: *Datum in Lureu*, Wenzel (ed.) 1860–1874, VIII, 265.
74 Györffy 1963–1998, IV, 203.
75 1067: *versus Kuurew, vsque dum Tyza et Budrug in unum coniunguntur* (Zemplén County), Wenzel (ed.) 1860–1874, I, 26.
76 1274: *Homukrew* (Csanád County), MNL OL DF 254 787 and Györffy 1963–1998, I, 859.
77 1283: *Lopusreu* (Nógrád County), MNL OL DL 65 717 and Györffy 1963–1998, IV, 265.
78 Cf. Szamota and Zolnai (eds.) 1902–1906, 575.
79 1254: *super portu seu tributo portus, videlicet stagni et lacus Ferthew* (Rákos, Sopron County), Wagner et al. (eds.) 1955–1999, I, 233–234.
80 1299: *ad portum arundineti per aquas Ferteu* (Illmitz, Sopron County), Wagner et al. (eds.) 1955–1999, II, 326.
81 1024: *insula aque Balatini una cum silvis adiacentibus villis ipsius ecclesie Zalauar et Burull nuncupatis, cum duodecim piscatoribus in portu eiusdem aque commorantibus* (Zalavár and Burul, both Zala County), Györffy (ed.) 1992, 101–102.

on the 1208 perambulation of Lébény, Lake Sóstó (*Zoustou*) also had a ferry port called *Boldazorma*.[82]

Small rivulets and the shallow parts of streams and rivers were generally crossed at fords (*vadum*[83]) by wading, horseback, or by using a vehicle. In written documents these fords are alternatively called crossing places (*vadum seu transitus*[84]) and ports (*vadum seu portus*[85]), which suggests that during floods persons and goods were transported across the river by ferries. At times of low water, however, one could easily cross over these watercourses on foot at a dry and stony place (*per portum siccum et saxosum*).[86] Stony fords (*vadus lapideus*,[87] *kövecses rév*[88]) developed either naturally due to the accumulation of river drift, or were created by the placement of heaps of stone or large rocks at river shallows.

Royal Policy towards Roads and River-Crossing Places

In the Árpádian age, all those who traveled, including merchants with loaded and empty wagons, riders, wayfarers, and even people simply moving from one place to another, had to pay toll to the king. These tolls were collected along roads (*tributum de via*,[89] *tributum in via*,[90] *tributum viaticum*,[91] *tributum*

---

82   1208: *portus qui dicitur Boldazorma* (Lébény, Moson County), Wagner et al. (eds.) 1955–1999, I, 53.

83   For example, 1249: *in vado magno* (Hermán, Vas County), Wagner et al. (eds.) 1955–1999, III, 262.

84   For example, 1389: *in vado seu transitu fluvii Mura* (Szemenye, Zala County) and Mályusz et al. (eds.) 1951–2017, I, no. 944.

85   For example, 1301: *in quodam vado seu portu super fluuium Sygriche vocatum* (Žehra, Szepes County), Nagy, Deák and Nagy (eds.) 1865–1891, V, 88.

86   1263: *ad fluuium Olchua vocatum, quem transeundo per portum siccum et saxosum* (Zvolen, Zólyom County), Fejér (ed.) 1829–1844, IV/3, 143.

87   For example, 1341: *ad vadum lapideum Kwrew nuncupatum* (Irshava, Bereg County), Fekete Nagy and Makkai 1941, 92.

88   For example, 1390: *penes vadum Keueches reu vocatum* (Vinohradiv, Chornotysiv and Rokoszovo, first two in Ugocsa, the last in Ung County), Mályusz et al. (eds.) 1951–2017, I, no. 1554.

89   For example, 1238: *in Comitatu Soproniensi concessimus illas duas partes tributi, de foris et viis omnibus, quae vulgariter apellantur Kyralkettei* (Sopron County), Fejér (ed.) 1829–1844, IV/1, 106.

90   For example, 1346: *Ruhtukewr cum tributo in via* (Röjtökőr, Sopron County), Wagner et al. (eds.) 1955–1999, V, 140.

91   For example, 1346: *Kwesd … cum tributo viatico* (Kövesd, Sopron County), Wagner et al. (eds.) 1955–1999, V, 140.

terrestres,[92] *pedagium*[93]), at bridges (*tributum pontis*,[94] *telonium pontis*[95]), and at ferry ports (*tributum portus*,[96] *tributum de portu*,[97] *tributum transitus*,[98] *redditus portus*[99]).[100] The fact that not only merchants but everyone, even wayfarers, were required to pay tolls suggests that the money was not collected for the maintenance of roads, bridges and ferries, but for the royal protection of people using public roads (*via publica*,[101] *strata publica*[102]) in the kingdom.[103] The protection of travelers was, however, not unique to Árpádian-age Hungary. Several law codes from contemporary Europe contain references to the protection of pilgrims, travelers and merchants on public roads, the origins of which appear to lay in the desire to protect travelers who were otherwise defenseless, such as strangers and women.[104] As the *Legenda minor Sancti Stephani Regis* demonstrates, strangers arriving in Hungary were also under royal protection, starting with the reign of King Stephen. According to the legend, when King Stephen was informed that the Pechenegs who had come to Hungary with their wagons had been attacked, beaten and robbed on their way to court, he sent for the offenders and had them hanged in pairs along roads in every part of the country.[105]

92　For example, 1263: *tributo … terrestres* (Füzitő, Komárom County), Kubinyi (ed.) 1997, 56.

93　For example, 1239: *tributum seu theolonium aut pedagium* (Esztergom, Esztergom County), Kubinyi (ed.) 1997, 33.

94　For example, 1266: *tributum pontis … prope Monasterium de Saagh, in fluuio Ipul* (Ság, Hont County), Fejér (ed.) 1829–1844, IV/3, 313.

95　For example, 1247: *cum … telonio pontis in fluvio Zala* (Barlabáshida, Zala County), Nagy, Véghely and Nagy (eds.) 1886–1890, I, 18.

96　For example, 1148: *tributum portus Pest* (Pest, Pest County), Kubinyi (ed.) 1997, 11.

97　For example, 1037: *tributa … de foro Zyl et de portu Arpas in Raba* (Árpás, Győr County), Györffy (ed.) 1992, 118.

98　For example, 1075: *tributum transitus super Tizam, qui nuncupatur Benildi* (Bőd, Csongrád County), Györffy (ed.) 1992, 218.

99　For example, 1238: *reditus dicti portus* (Bečej, Bács County), Fejér (ed.) 1829–1844, IV/1, 109.

100　For an overview of customs levied on travelers in the Árpádian age, see: Weisz 2013b, 13–14.

101　For example, 1093: *in via publica* (Apáti, Zala County), Wenzel (ed.) 1860–1874, I, 69.

102　For example, 1263: *in stratam publicam Supruniensem* (Sopron, Sopron County), Wagner et al. (eds.) 1955–1999, I, 293.

103　Weisz 2012b, 112.

104　Cooper 2002, 42–45.

105　Legenda Sancti Stephani Regis, cap. 6: *per omnem regionem in ingressu viarum duo et duo suspendio perierunt*, Szentpétery (ed.) 1937–1938, II, 398–399. This part of the legend was also taken over verbatim by Bishop Hartvik, see: Szentpétery (ed.) 1937–1938, II, 426–427.

Among public roads, the king's highways (*via regis*,[106] *regia via*,[107] *via regalis*,[108] *királyút*,[109] and *királyuta*[110]) were specifically associated with the king in legal terms. The king guaranteed the safety of everyone who used these highways, and crimes committed along them came under royal jurisdiction. With the royal donation of landed properties to private landowners, roads found on these estates were also transferred to landowners. Highways, however, still remained in royal hands. Beginning with the fourteenth century, written sources start using a new term, the so-called *via libera*, referring to public roads that anyone could use freely, while the safety of their person and the goods transported by them was guaranteed by the king. However, contemporary testimonies in which plaintiffs relate that they themselves, their servants or relatives had been halted, beaten, and deprived of their draft animals or goods while traveling on a *via libera* attest to the fact that, despite their special legal status, acts of might (*potentia, factum potentiae*) also occurred on these roads.[111]

From the thirteenth century on, tolls were collected for the maintenance of roads, bridges, and ferries rather than for royal protection, but the king continued to guarantee the safety of travelers on highways. Furthermore, merchants on their way to and back from "free fairs" (*forum liberum*) were under the protection and special defense of the king, together with their goods.[112]

By the late Árpádian age, toll-collecting places had become so numerous throughout the country that the king himself had to put an end to their abuse. In 1284 King Ladislas IV ordered the abolition of tolls that were set up after the

---

106 For example, 1214: *ad quandam publicam stratam, que ...via regis vocatur* (Szepnice, Zágráb County), Wenzel (ed.) 1860–1874, XI, 128.

107 For example, 1217: *ad regiam viam, per quam ad Hegeshalm usque pervenitur* (Hegyeshalom, Moson County), Wagner et al. (eds.) 1955–1999, I, 69.

108 For example, 1247: *ad viam regalem* (Szekcső, Baranya County), Marsina (ed.) 1971–1987, II, 194.

109 For example, 1274: *ad quandam viam kyralwt vocatam* (Halogy and Tófalu, both Vas County), Wagner et al. (eds.) 1955–1999, II, 73.

110 For example, 1256: *iuxta stratam Kyraluta* (Novaj, Abaúj County), Fejér (ed.) 1829–1844, VII/5, 321.

111 For example, 1319: *filii Benedicti, et Petrus, filius Nicolai, Beken filium Iohannis, in libera via sua occidissent sine culpa et res triginta marcas valentes ab eodem recepissent*, Fejér (ed.) 1829–1844, VIII/1, 479. For cases of violent trespass committed against peasants traveling to weekly market, see the study of András Kubinyi in the present volume.

112 For example, 1360: *saluis rebus vestris et personis sub nostra protectione et tutela speciali* (Săsarm, Szolnok County), Fejér (ed.) 1829–1844, IX/6, 109. On the meaning of *forum liberum*, see Fügedi 1981b, 241–246, Weisz 2007c, 895–897, Weisz 2010b, 1414–1417 and the study of András Kubinyi in the present volume.

death of King Béla IV.[113] In 1289 he also abolished tolls established after the death of his father, King Stephen V.[114] These measures, however, seem to have had little impact, as King Andrew III needed to reconfirm them in 1290[115] and again in 1298.[116] King Louis I went further by declaring the collection of all tolls on dry land and on rivers to be unlawful, also decreeing that only those who crossed by bridge or in ferries had to pay.[117] According to the testimony of the 1435 decree of King Sigismund, landowners collecting tolls for bridges and ferries were legally bound to "keep the bridges and ferries in good repair so that the travelers and toll-payers can cross these bridges and ferries freely and unimpeded without any hindrance." Those who neglected to do so were "forced by suitable penalties and fines issued by the county's *ispán* ... to make the necessary repairs and maintenance on their bridges and ferries."[118]

113 Wenzel (ed.) 1860–1874, IX, 400.
114 Anon. 1866, I.
115 Bak et al. (eds.) 1992–2012, I, 44.
116 Bak et al. (eds.) 1992–2012, I, 49.
117 Cap. 8: *Tributa etiam iniusta super terris siccis et fluviis ab infra descendentibus et supra euntibus non exigantur, nisi in pontibus et navigiis ab ultra transeuntibus persolvantur, cum in eisdem nobiles et ignobiles regni nostri multo et nimium percepimus agravari.* Bak et al. (eds.) 1992–2012, II, 10–11.
118 Cap. 21: *Habentes insuper et exigentes tributa ratione pontis vel navium pontes huiusmodi aut naves sub debita reformatione semper studeant conservare taliter, quod viatores et tributa solventes absque impedimento per pontes et naves eorum transitum liberum et non impeditum facere possint; id vero facere negligentes penis et gravaminibus opportunis ad debitam reformationem et conservationem suorum pontium et navium in dictis congregationibus promulgandis per comites eorum parochiales astringantur toties, quoties eorum negligentia exigente fuerit opportunum.* Bak et al. (eds.) 1992–2012, II, 75.

PART 2

Human-Nature Interaction in Production

∴

CHAPTER 4

Agriculture in Medieval Hungary

József Laszlovszky

Introduction

Farming and animal husbandry in medieval Hungary has yet to be treated by an integrated monograph based on modern interdisciplinary research and the full range of possible sources, although much intensive research into certain aspects has been pursued over several decades.[1] Although the topic was at the center of economic history studies in the 1950s and 1960s, yielding many treatments whose details have retained their influence to the present-day, we still do not have a book that covers the whole era.[2] However, Hungarian ethnography has produced very significant monographic studies related to different aspects of agricultural production.[3] These represent very valuable sources for medieval agrarian techniques, land use and animal husbandry. Comparative approaches related to ethnographic studies can be interpreted as one of the key elements of research history, particularly before the recent developments of research methodology and source analysis. One reason for this is the multiplicity of new sources available to research nowadays, with archaeological findings particularly gaining ground alongside the standard and long-studied written sources. The greatest changes have occurred in the history of agricultural implements,[4] although archaeozoology,[5] archaeobotany[6] and environmental history[7] have also contributed important new science-based methods. Landscape history and landscape archaeology have made considerable progress

---

1   Bak 1964, Hoffmann 1968, Balassa 1973, Makkai 1974, Maksay 1975, Maksay 1978, Györffy 1983b, Pálóczi-Horváth 2000a and Bende and Lőrinczy (eds.) 2000.
2   Belényesy 1955, Belényesy 1958c, Belényesy 1960b and Szabó 1975.
3   Balassa 1973, Andrásfalvy 1973, Fél and Hofer 1997, Fél and Hofer 1974, Takács 1978, Takács 1980, Paládi-Kovács 1979, Füzes 1984 and Bellon 1996b.
4   Müller 1975, Müller 1982 and Takács 2016.
5   See the relevant chapters on animal husbandry in this volume.
6   Hartyáni and Nováki 1967–1968, Hartyáni and Nováki 1973–1974, Skoflek and Hortobágyi 1973, Facsar 1973, Zólyomi 1980, Torma 2003, Gyulai 2010, Juhász, Sümegi and Zatykó (eds.) 2007 and Kovács and Zatykó (eds.) 2016.
7   See the relevant chapter by László Ferenczi and his colleagues in this volume.

in studying traces of cultivation and systems of land use around villages.[8] This chapter, then, cannot substitute for a full monograph on the subject, but provides the opportunity to survey the main conclusions of Hungarian agricultural history in the medieval period, and outline current areas of research and problems requiring treatment.[9] The subject is closely bound up with the medieval history of animal husbandry, dealt with in another chapter of this book. Here, animal husbandry will only be touched on where it is inseparable from arable cultivation.

The Environmental and Climatic Conditions of Agriculture in Medieval Hungary

Plowland and Agrarian Production

The vast majority of the lands of the Carpathian Basin have soil and climatic conditions which suit them to any of the techniques of farming known in the Middle Ages. Much land – at least in the Late Middle Ages – was used for cereal production, and furnished satisfactory yields from both autumn and spring sowing. Cereals sown at these different times provided protection against extremes of winter and summer weather; i.e., in years when the temperature or rainfall severely departed from the average. Low-lying areas and the lower hilly areas in the center of the country had rainfall and average temperatures which suited them to the strains of wheat which gave the highest-quality flour, whereas areas on the periphery of the Carpathian Basin, particularly eastern Transylvania and the north of the kingdom (now the highlands of Slovakia), where the climate was more definitely continental, were restricted to hardier cereals tolerant of wider extremes of temperature – rye, barley, oats and millet. These areas, however, were also suited to animal husbandry in some parts of the year, through the use of fallow land or stubble pasture after harvest. Even in the late medieval period, however, natural conditions prevented the general emergence of a strict rotation system for this form of grazing. Instead, the diverse natural vegetation and hydrological conditions favored mosaic land use in which gallery forests, open forests in hilly regions and mountain pastures in many cases supplemented the areas of grassland and fallow fields.

The extent of arable land was constrained by three basic factors. The upper reaches of highland areas – mostly the eastern and northern parts of the medieval kingdom and the high-up steep hillsides or enclosed but cold plateaus

---

8 Laszlovszky 1999, Zatykó 2003 and Zatykó 2015.
9 Short summary of research results: Bende and Lőrinczy (eds.) 2000.

of the North Hungarian Mountains and Transdanubian Mountains – were not suited to growing crops, but did support animal rearing. Another factor, dense forests, applied mostly in the highlands. Forests covered a much greater proportion of the Carpathian Basin in the Middle Ages than they do today. The extent of forested area in the Carpathians was certainly not less than the present, and there were considerable changes to forested areas in the center of the country – the Great Hungarian Plain, the lower-lying hills and the central ranges – over the centuries of the Middle Ages. However, there were also regions, mostly in the hilly areas which are nowadays covered in forest, that were used in the late medieval period as plowlands. This phenomenon was connected to the steady shrinking of forests on the Great Hungarian Plain and Transdanubia between the thirteenth and sixteenth centuries, by which time there was substantially less forest than in the Árpádian age.[10]

The principal cause of this contraction was undoubtedly the spread of agricultural activity. Nonetheless, forests still no doubt covered a greater proportion of the plains than in the early modern period, from when more reliable data is available. This is probably the case even if we allow for some return of forests to such areas during the Ottoman occupation. The fastest change in forested areas took place in hills of medium height and central hill ranges (the North Hungarian Mountains and the Transdanubian Mountains). There are reports of forest areas cleared for cultivation dating to the Árpádian period, and the process clearly accelerated in some areas in the thirteenth and fourteenth centuries as internal colonization extended the area of cultivation and plantation. Clearance for agriculture caused arable cultivation in these geographical regions to spread to higher altitudes, and areas covered by forest in the modern age (i.e. not under cultivation) extended further in the modern period than in the Middle Ages. This phenomenon has made it possible to observe medieval cultivation in higher hilly areas where land was tilled and agricultural villages founded in the Late Middle Ages which no longer exist in the modern age, their lands having been reclaimed by the forest. Landscape archaeological features of medieval fields or field systems have recently been found in these areas,[11] while remains of large-scale transformation of former woodland areas by creating terraced long strip fields on the terraces of hill slopes (lynchets) can be detected in the northern and eastern hilly parts of the medieval Kingdom of Hungary (in present-day Slovakia and Transylvania).

---

10   On the history of forests, see the chapter by Péter Szabó in the present volume.
11   Laszlovszky 1999.

Another factor constraining the expansion of areas under cultivation in the medieval period was the extent of flood-prone land.[12] This was located mainly in flat countryside near the large rivers, where enormous areas could be inundated or were permanently under water. In some parts of the Great Hungarian Plain, these areas were larger than those which were free of flooding. There were often 4–5-kilometer wide flood plains beside the large rivers, and continuous expanses of water up to 10–15-kilometers wide could form at confluences (Tisza–Körös, Tisza–Maros, Danube–Tisza, etc.) when the floods came. Large-scale reclamation projects for regulating these only started in the nineteenth century, which greatly increased the land available for cultivation at the expense of the flood plains. These areas, despite having suitable soil, could not support cereals in the Middle Ages. The second flood wave of late spring or early summer often reached these lands so late that grain sown there afterwards would not have ripened. This does not, however, mean that the flood plains had no agricultural utility. Medieval farmers on the flood plain combined fishing, pasture and fodder-gathering, often with artificial water regulation and level-balancing systems. The latter were not usually built to keep out the floods, but kept some of the flood water in the flood plain so that it could be used later. It is possible that this large expanse of surface water affected the micro-climate and ground-water level in such a way as to reduce the danger of drought on neighboring flood-free land. Similar farming went on in marshlands of similar extent (Sárvíz, Little Balaton, etc.) where the land supported a substantial population despite the near absence of arable farming.[13]

The extent of medieval arable land surpassed that of the Modern period in more than just the hilly forest clearings. The *puszta* or dry steppe lands (Hortobágy and the Kecskemét area) and sand dunes (Nyírség and the Danube–Tisza Interfluve) have been found by settlement history research to have supported a dense network of agricultural villages in the Árpádian age and to some extent even in the late medieval period. The modern, sparsely-inhabited *puszta* environment only formed during the Ottoman and early modern periods, although some of the phenomena involved in the change may have started in the late medieval period.[14] In the latter case, the plowlands may have receded because of the growth of extensive (mostly cattle) herding initiated by the long-distance livestock trade. This increase in extensive animal rearing, possibly combined with climatic–environmental changes and other processes that are not yet fully understood, caused villages engaged in arable cultiva-

---

12   Pinke et al. 2017.
13   Ritoók 2007.
14   Sárosi 2016.

tion to wither and perish as their land became unsuitable for growing crops. The reversion of some areas to wilderness (e.g. Danube–Tisza Interfluve) may to some extent have been caused by tillage and intensive animal rearing. For example, movement of sand dunes may have been exacerbated by intensive agricultural production over a long period. In some areas, there is evidence that overgrazing caused by too much livestock caused previously fixed sand to resume its movement. This process recurred periodically, but we can identify changes in the interaction of natural processes and human impact as it took place that could have affected the abandonment of agrarian villages and the diminution of plowlands.[15] Of greater significance, however, were the wars and drastic environmental changes (particularly severe periods of the Little Ice Age) of the later period (sixteenth and seventeenth centuries) and the general decline in the population caused by the hostilities of the Ottoman period. In other areas, however, such as the flood plains and alluvial areas along the River Dráva, forest clearance was not accompanied by the spread of plowlands. The forest clearance phases recurring in 100–120-year cycles show that trees were cut down at their most valuable age and the land was left to let the forest regenerate. Other forms of animal husbandry (e.g. pigs kept on mast in forests) probably hindered the spreading of plowlands in this region.[16]

Viticulture and Fruits

The geographical features of the Carpathian Basin and its medieval climatic conditions were favorable for viticulture and fruit growing, as well as arable farming. Apart from the highlands and northern parts of the country, nearly every village had 'vine slopes' nearby that at least satisfied the local demand for wine. The grapes of some areas were not of particularly high quality, and the wine typically remained fit for consumption only until the next year's new wine was ready. The grapes from some areas, however, like the Buda Hills, Hegyalja and several larger towns (Sopron, Bratislava) went into wine that was traded over longer distances, and wine for local sale generated substantial revenue for the villages around the town.[17] The highest-rated wine, however, came from Srijem. This was the region that provided the especially fine wines served on the tables of the royal court. Some historical wine regions (like Tokaj) were already producing in the Middle Ages, but did not enjoy the fame

---

15 Bálint 2003, 157–174 and Bálint et al. 2003, 383–385.
16 Viczián and Zatykó 2011.
17 Kubinyi 1996d.

they achieved in the modern age. Fruit growing was also very widespread, and even climatically unfavorable regions had some fruit trees, although they produced considerably smaller fruits than we are used to today. Fruit trees constituted part of the horticulture of nearly every village, although they were not necessarily grown in the form of orchards. Planted fruit trees first occurred in the gardens of ecclesiastic domains and in those of royal and aristocratic residences. According to the testimony of medieval perambulation charters, there were fruit trees at the edges of wooded areas and parklands, which in many cases were used as boundary markers.[18] Some forms of animal husbandry are also connected to orchards, either taking into consideration flood plains or other pastures.

These forms of mixed land use became most common in hilly areas and areas criss-crossed by rivers and streams. Ethnographical research has found that fruit played an important part in the traditional peasant diet, mainly in summer, although a lot of fruit was also dried or conserved in other ways for the rest of the year. This also tells us of its role in land use. Mosaic land use permitted the gathering of forest fruit and the tending of fruit trees in all areas of the country, despite widely varying geographical and climatic conditions. Vegetables were also of nutritional importance, although there are very few sources on this, and expenditure items in account books sometimes provide the only evidence that they were grown at all.

The natural geographic features of the Carpathian Basin were also suited to rearing livestock on a large scale. The varied relief and hydrological features and the diversity of flora were capable of supporting many different forms of animal husbandry, and some of these were pursued simultaneously.[19] Flood plain animal rearing, the keeping of livestock as an adjunct to intensive arable cultivation (sometimes involving a two- or three-field system), and extensive pastoral husbandry on land of low fertility were all characteristic of different areas. These environmental characteristics and the forms of agriculture they supported ensured a stable supply of food crops in the medieval period. Only very rarely were harvests so poor or crops so severely devastated as to threaten famine. Even in these cases, it was possible to offset losses in harvests with the abundance of food from animal sources. The whole territory of medieval Hungary was always rich in wild animals, as frequently reported by foreign travelers, and there are also records of large-scale royal hunts. Nonetheless, game was not a basic source of food in any century of the Middle Ages. The

---

18   Szabó 2005, 99–102.
19   For different forms of animal husbandry, see the chapter by László Bartosiewicz and his colleagues in this volume.

animal protein which was definitely predominant in medieval nutrition therefore fundamentally came from farmed animals, some of which also served as pack or draft animals. In nearly every area, cultivation of the land was closely interlinked with animal husbandry. This mutual support, combined with favorable geographical features, resulted in an abundance of livestock. This permanent rearing of large animals is confirmed by descriptions of the wealth and abundance on display at livestock fairs, and was the economic function that underlay the significance of medieval Pest.[20] The animal bone record shows greater and smaller fluctuations in the quantities of smaller animals (pigs, goats, sheep), but there were fairly large areas of forest for masting and more meagre pastures that could not support large animals, so the rearing of these animals can also be traced continuously throughout the Middle Ages. Another source of nutrition of comparable significance to that of meat was fish. The sources tell us much about fishing, but archeozoology has fewer finds to work on because fish remains are less likely to survive and are more difficult to gather in excavations.

In summary, medieval Hungary had excellent resources for cultivation and animal rearing, supplemented by fishing on a substantial scale. This implies that all levels of society were generally well supplied with a good and varied diet. Contemporary sources hardly mention shortages of food, and there are records of major famines only in extreme conditions (e.g. the Mongol invasion). Human bone records from archaeological excavations confirm this picture, showing only few signs of deficiencies indicative of nutritional problems (tooth wear, articular problems, etc.). It can therefore be confidently stated that farming of crops and livestock provided food of satisfactory quantity and quality throughout the Middle Ages, for a population which grew steadily for long periods.[21]

There were also climatic changes in Europe during the Middle Ages. These do not, however, seem to have had such a severe effect in East Central Europe, and neither the Black Death nor the generally adverse economic effects of the agrarian crisis can be detected in Hungary in the fourteenth or fifteenth centuries.[22] It is clear that in the early fourteenth century, previously dry areas were flooded and fields around villages were often inaccessible, especially on

---

20 Bak and Vadas 2016 and Benda 2016b.
21 See also the contribution of András Kubinyi and József Laszlovszky on the demographic issues in the present volume.
22 Laszlovszky 1994.

the plain areas.[23] Although lost to arable production, however, the land was unlikely to have become much less productive because the periodic flooding did not prevent its use for grazing. Furthermore, the effects of the wetter weather must easily been offset in hilly areas such as the Transdanubian and North Hungarian Mountains where forest clearance was widespread. In these areas, the wetter periods did not create problems with flooded fields, and even elsewhere, in relatively dry flat areas of the Great Hungarian Plain, the effects were not always adverse or even led to improved harvests.[24] The area of land under arable cultivation, the agricultural techniques used on it and the yields that were achieved proved sufficient for the agricultural population to provide for both itself and the large urban or urban-like population that evolved in the late medieval period. Foreigners who passed through Hungary at any time during the Middle Ages always mentioned the fertility and wealth of the land, even if the people or the more urban settlements seemed to them poorer than the people and towns of contemporary Western Europe. In terms of the agricultural techniques that were applied and the environmental conditions, Hungary was at that time no worse off than the western part of the continent.

The Place of Farming and Animal Husbandry in Hungary's Medieval Economy

Throughout the Middle Ages, village inhabitants who cultivated the land or kept livestock made up the largest portion of the Hungarian population. In the Árpádian age, apart from a relatively small number of aristocrats, ethnic groups who served military functions, those who made their living purely from crafts or trade, and the clergy, nearly everybody was involved in agricultural activity. Consequently, every segment of society lived according to the annual cycle of agricultural work, the seasonal calendar of sowing and harvesting, and the slaughter of animals in winter.[25] This even affected the movements and life of the royal court, because monarchs at that time regularly traveled around the royal estates and the castles in royal county centers, where the produce and products of surrounding areas and estates were accumulated, to be consumed, in part, by the king and his retinue.

---

23   Kiss 2018. See also the contribution of László Ferenczi and his colleagues in the present volume.
24   Kiss and Nikolic 2015.
25   Györffy 1983b, 33 Fig. 2.

By the end of Árpádian age, the area of land under cultivation in Hungary had grown considerably, although very large animal herds were still a distinctive feature of the country. The resulting increase in output formed the basis of two major changes. One was the general and substantial increase in population. Indeed, growth may have been even faster, especially if incoming ethnic groups are included. The other was the formation of urban centers with significant concentrations of population, where most of the inhabitants made their living from crafts and trade, but naturally could only be maintained by higher levels of agricultural production. Such towns had a significant demand for food. A town the size of Esztergom, for example, required a 20- or 30-kilometer deep hinterland to provide its daily supply of grain and meat and cover the food requirements of an even larger area. In addition to these expanding urban settlements, the burgeoning amount of agricultural produce was capable of supplying a larger number of clergy, such as monks of the mendicant orders (Franciscans, Dominicans, etc.) who took limited part in agricultural work. This trend was halted by the Mongol invasion, which caused a severe fall in the population as a whole and must have disproportionately afflicted those who were less mobile; i.e., the land-bound peasantry.

Following the Mongol invasion, agriculture underwent substantial growth during the remainder of the thirteenth century. Subsequently, from the early fourteenth century until the first decades of the sixteenth, the area of agricultural land and the produce it yielded steadily increased. This permitted a considerable rise in the country's population and the formation of several large social classes and groups whose economic base was no longer agriculture: people who were maintained by the agricultural produce of the peasant population. As in the two centuries preceding the Mongol invasion, the population growth during this period brought rapid and substantial changes, although a lack of satisfactory sources means that little is known of the details. The first national census which permits even an indirect derivation of the number of basic taxpayers – tenant peasants – was taken in the late fifteenth century, and the sizes of other segments of society can only be estimated. These issues are also relevant for the interpretation of agricultural production. There is a problem, for example, in deciding how to determine the number of landless peasants or *inquilini*, who were treated differently for taxation purposes.[26] It is also difficult to say whether the abandonment of peasant plots recorded in the sources resulted from an actual drop in the village population or was due to families moving together or making other attempts to avoid paying royal taxes. Not every census mentions *inquilini*, and only a few refer to "*inquilini* without

---

26   Nógrády 2015.

houses". The latter were often left out by the census-takers, unlike *inquilini* who had their own houses. The problem this causes for studies of medieval agriculture is that *inquilini* without houses may have had land, tenancies, vineyards and forest clearings, and they certainly accounted for some inhabitants of market towns. The taxable unit in agricultural villages is also a source of difficulty: how many people, and what family structures, did it embrace? The possible variations have caused some researchers to calculate the population at as high as 3.5 million. What is certain is that village peasants constituted the most numerous segment of the population, although their agricultural output supported a nobility which was outstandingly large even by European standards (although its lowest stratum, the 'one-plot nobles', themselves took part in farming), and satisfied the demands of the by-then well-advanced towns and market towns for food and other agricultural products. The same is true of the maintenance of military people (the royal professional army and garrisons of the line of forts built to stem the advance of the Ottoman Empire), who became considerably more numerous towards the end of the period. In addition, the breeding of cattle grew to such an extent as to make Hungary one of the major suppliers of livestock to Central and Southern Europe, resulting in substantial foreign trade with these areas. Research into this subject has shown that in some flat areas of the country, notably the Great Hungarian Plain, the relatively dense distribution of villages gave way to large market towns which used the *puszta* around the abandoned or destroyed villages to practice extensive animal husbandry. This means that the abandonment of villages was offset by the use of former arable land for more profitable livestock rearing, concentrated on foreign exports, and the resulting expansion of market towns prevented a decline in population. Other regions were able to make up for the loss of arable land, and the market towns provided suitable infrastructure for the exchange and trade of agricultural products. The sources also tell of horse breeding on a large scale, although exports of horses were restricted.

Consequently, agriculture, the most significant branch of the economy in medieval Hungary, was capable of satisfying the country's demand for food and left a considerable surplus for export.

Transformation Processes of Agriculture in Medieval Hungary

The first and most far-reaching phenomenon in the development of Hungary's medieval agriculture occurred immediately after the Conquest in the last decade of the ninth century, as the Hungarians, having moved into the Carpathian Basin, completed their settlement and in a relatively short period (tenth–

thirteenth centuries) set up a dense network of agricultural villages.[27] The agrarian conditions of late medieval times, the fourteenth and fifteenth centuries, clearly preserved many of the features that took shape in that initial period. Earlier research frequently concluded that nomadic Hungarians coming from the East took a long time to settle, and that tilling the land was of little significance for the population of the tenth and eleventh centuries. The persistence of nomadism was the subject of a long dispute among historians, but combined studies of archaeological, botanical and animal-bone finds increasingly support the view that few people could have been nomadic at that time.[28] Instead, recent research sees the conquering Hungarians as a semi-nomadic people, a substantial part of whose lives, besides tending herds, was taken up by the planting of crops. Settlement archaeologists have developed a similar picture.[29] The view that medieval villages evolved from the winter residences of gradually-settling nomads cannot be convincingly maintained. Although the settlements of ordinary people at that time undoubtedly did not stay fixed for long periods, this is not a sign of nomadism, but follows from how people used the land and kept their animals at that time. Further evidence for this comes from studies of loan words in the Hungarian language and findings of archaeozoology and archaeobotany. Most crop names and cultivation-related words in Hungarian are Bulgarian-Turkish loan words, which means that they were acquired when the Hungarians – some time before the conquest of the Carpathian Basin – were in contact with ethnic groups that spoke Bulgarian-Turkish languages. Many expressions concerning forms of animal husbandry originate from the same source, showing that the Hungarians were already combining tillage of the land with the herding of large animals when their homeland was the East European Plain. Descriptions of the Hungarians' pre-Conquest homeland also allude to plowland, so that there is even confirmation from written sources of the combined role of cultivation and animal husbandry. Crop remains from the early Árpádian age found at the sites of settlements of that time also prove the growing of cereals of various kinds. In addition, animal-bone finds from the period show no signs of nomadic animal husbandry affecting large areas. Cattle and horse bones account for a high percentage of these, but pig and poultry bones are also well represented. Casting further doubt on the nomadic character of herding is the probable difficulty of moving large herds parallel or perpendicular to the rivers and flood plains that criss-cross all of the large plains of the Carpathian Basin. Such movement,

---

27 Hoffman 1968.
28 For the history of research concerning the Conquest Period, see: Langó 2005.
29 Takács 2014.

typical of life on the dry eastern steppe, was unnecessary in any case because the annual rainfall in the region and the pastureland vegetation permitted the upkeep of large herds without exhausting the pasture. Thus the Carpathian Basin offered the Hungarians perfect conditions for the semi-nomadic but increasingly settled way of life which had been under development in their old eastern homelands.

A large proportion of the villages which formed during the Árpádian age, even the first half, existed throughout the Middle Ages and were sites of agricultural production. Although agriculture went through a great process of transformation at the end of the Árpádian period, resulting in a completely different system overall, its practices were largely rooted in those of the earlier period. Excavations of Árpádian-age villages show many of them to have comprised houses separated by considerable distances and by empty areas enclosed by ditches. These systems of ditches themselves made them suitable for the alternate cultivation of crops, keeping animals kept near the villages away from grain – or possibly from garden-like crops –, and at other times acting as fences for keeping a large number of livestock in one place. Thus the relatively high stubble left after harvesting grain could be used for pasture, and animals provided manure that maintained the fertility of the land. This does not indicate any kind of regulated system of use of fields, or of leaving them fallow. Rather it suggests a permanent one-field tillage system, maintained until the land was exhausted – a process which the natural fertilization of the animals that were kept could at most slow down. It is therefore not appropriate to think in terms of the later plot system of agricultural villages. There were at most household plots beside houses, and they frequently changed their positions within the boundary of the village because the buildings did not remain habitable for a long time. These boundaries of villages have already been detected in charters of the eleventh century. The boundaries of royal estates granted to monasteries, for example, must therefore have been well established, and there may have been one or more settlements on the land. Another unavoidable conclusion is the absence of nomadic herding across large areas. The expressions used in written sources of the time and the changes in their meaning also clearly mark out the course of settlements and changing land use. The Hungarian word for "plot of land", *telek*, which may be found in written sources dating even from the first half of the Árpádian age, at that time referred to land whose natural characteristics made it fertile (from *televényes* – humic; having satisfactory soil moisture), and its meaning gradually changed to that of *terra culta*; i.e., cultivated land. This shows that land with such good properties was increasingly brought under cultivation, so that after a time *telek* arose as a general synonym for cultivated land. It was not only natural features, however, that made this land fertile and easily cultivable. The process could be influenced by human action. Keeping animals on land fundamentally improved its fertility if the soil had suitable characteristics – manure rich in organic matter created greatly improved conditions for crop growing. Consequently, keeping livestock (primarily cattle and horses) periodically in one place generated *terra fimata*; i.e., fertilized land, and after a while this meaning also became attached to the word *telek* in the charters.[30] This well illustrates the change in the significance of cultivation and the nature of the land being tilled. As constantly-used arable land became exhausted, fields within the settlement had occasionally to be abandoned or changed over, and after a long time whole settlements had to be relocated. The movement of villages, which laws of the late eleventh century tried to inhibit, was the consequence of this distinctive form of land use. The problem was not lack of land, but the fact that the villages wanted to move away from the village churches which were appearing in ever greater numbers after the adoption of Christianity, and thus endangered the economic base of the churches set up through the early local parish system. The law banning removal should not, therefore, be seen as evidence of late nomadism, but rather as the outcome of conflict between the land-use system of a gradually-settling people, increasingly turning to growing crops, and the newly-formed church organization. Around these stabilizing – although perhaps still moving – villages, were borders clearly marked by natural features or artificial signs recognized by the village communities and their neighbors, and increasingly defined in charters. Much of the land within village boundaries, however, was still not under permanent cultivation, and boundaries often enclosed more than one settlement or embryonic village. The extent of land available and the large areas of unoccupied land meant that its value was not determined by its size, but by the people who belonged to it, cultivated it, and were bound to its service. Charters issued at the time and measures taken to encourage settlement show that an estate or tract of land would only be profitable for a landowner if, in addition to favorable natural features, it contained a village with a sufficiency of inhabitants bound to provide appropriate service.[31]

The general predominance of animal husbandry in the first half of the Árpádian age is indisputable. The Legend of St Gerhard contains a reference which may be taken as illustrative of the general situation: Ajtony, a powerful chieftain in the period of St Stephen who in the eastern part of the country established almost independent rule, had innumerable livestock, "cattle", kept on the fields outside the village and watched over by herders, but there were also

---

30   Laszlovszky 1986, 248–254 and Zatykó 2007, 262–264.
31   Takács 2013.

other animals kept in villages in purpose-built byres. The latter have been identified in village excavations, and are not evidence of indoor animal husbandry, having only held a small proportion of the villagers' livestock – animals which for some reason were more important and valuable. They were built for some saddle-horses and those dairy animals which needed better protection, but there were also open pens surrounded by ditches which also served the purpose of keeping the animals together. Archaeologists have found remains of these in the inner parts of villages and a similar purpose was served by trench-based structures similar to the lean-to buildings recorded by ethnographers as being used by pastoralists. All of this implies that animal rearing involved a highly developed and complex structure involving very large herds. Indeed, livestock also served as a measure of value and wealth at the time, the "cow equivalent" being a generally-accepted unit of exchange in barter.

The constant transformation of agriculture in the Árpádian age was also driven by external influences which brought new techniques and caused it to become more intensive. In particular, it was external effects which speeded up the spread of arable farming and the growing of fruit and vegetables. Although several factors – internal and external – were involved in the development of the agricultural system in late-medieval peasant villages, the specific extent of each is still not clear. One of the earliest external influences was the appearance of Benedictine farming.[32] Large and important Benedictine monasteries, in line with the international models of the faith, set up complex estates on the land it was endowed with and introduced the most advanced farming techniques of the time. Intensive horticultural techniques appeared in the gardens and vineyards which were in the direct vicinity of the monastery, tended by the monks themselves. Crops and herbs previously unknown to the area, certainly to peasants, also came in with the monks. The servants of the monasteries, especially the largest Benedictine abbeys, frequently became specialized in particular areas of farming, although in addition to the product of their bonded labor they had to provide for their own subsistence. In the twelfth and thirteenth centuries, the Cistercian order brought an even more advanced form of monastic farming to Hungary, with manor-like estate centers which created special sources of income to support the monasteries, even though the Cistercians in Hungary did not engage in large-scale land improvement and colonization.[33]

---

[32] For the monastic economy, see the relevant chapter of Beatrix F. Romhányi in the present volume.

[33] Romhányi 1993–1994, 180–204 and Ferenczi 2006, 83–100.

The monastic estates certainly made a major contribution to the spread of fruit-growing and viticulture. Archaeobotanical studies have shown that, despite the great movements and transformations stemming from migration of peoples, some elements remained from the culture of vine and fruit growing set up by the Romans. The adoption of Christianity and the spread of ecclesiastical estates also contributed to the spread of viticulture. The extent of villages whose inhabitants worked in the vineyards, and a comparison of contemporary data with historical ethnographic observations, suggest that vines were mostly grown fruit trees in a kind of trellis arrangement in the early period, the new system of vineyard plantation only becoming common later. Fruit growing should not be imagined as regularly laid-out monocultural orchards; it mainly involved single trees surrounded by other crops. Archaeological excavations of church estates even from that period, however, have found remains of artificially laid-out orchards where the trees were planted in holes dug at regular intervals.

In addition to clerical-monastic estates, a major external influence in the transformation of agriculture was the arrival of settler (*hospes*) peoples. They usually came from areas with more advanced agricultural techniques where partial overpopulation occurred in the twelfth and thirteenth centuries, and entire village communities took up the offer, on good terms, of settlement in other areas. Largely from German lands (called "Saxons", but also originating from other regions) or Romance areas (*Latini*), the settlers were guided by *sculteti* or *locatori* to particular regions and set up new kinds of villages, employing new systems of land use in the vicinity. Their arrival fitted with another significant development, the expansion of cultivated land. A substantial increase in the area of cultivated land is detectable in the second half of the twelfth and particularly in the thirteenth century.[34] One consequence of this was more intensive settlement of the country's peripheral lands, and another the increase in cultivated area in the interior, partly by clearing forests in the highlands and partly by the increasingly intensive use of land around the villages on the plain. The German (Saxon) people who came to the north of the country (Spiš) and to Transylvania brought both advanced agricultural techniques – in many cases involving a special, more highly regulated village structure – and craft skills that led towards the development of urban settlements, giving rise to a legal framework based on the *hospes* privileges (*see* Fig. 4.1).

The appearance of new kinds of plow can also in some respects be linked to the settlers, because it was from this time that the slightly asymmetric plow,

---

34   Körmendy 1995.

capable only of breaking the soil, gradually gave way to the larger, highly asymmetric plow which had iron components and turned the soil over. The new plow had a large coulter capable of breaking the surface of soil which had never, or only long before, been cultivated, and the oblique plowshare, which cut deeper, turned over the top layer of soil to produce a real furrow. This resulted in much more intensive tillage and preparation of the soil, helping to raise the fertility of the land and better enabling new land to be broken and wasteland and fallow land to be reclaimed (*see* Fig. 4.2).

These types of plow required substantial draft power, but the main change was not from light to heavy plow, but in the plow type and its fabrication. The larger plowshare and the plow's other iron components demanded a more complex wooden construction, of which a later development, eventually to become widespread, was the wheeled plow. Another major change was in the shape of the land being tilled. Long narrow selions, more suited to the new

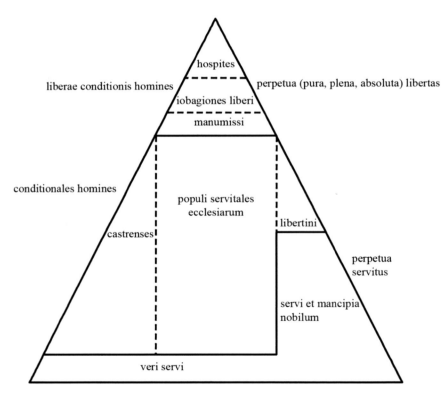

FIGURE 4.1A   *Social groups of rural population in the thirteenth century, after Jenő Szűcs.*
PUBLISHED IN LASZLOVSZKY 1991.

AGRICULTURE IN MEDIEVAL HUNGARY

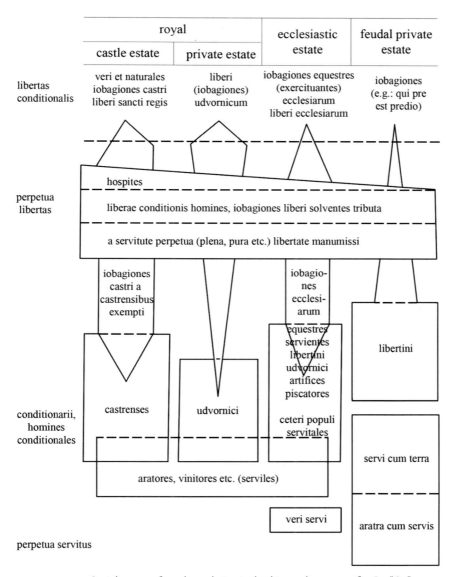

FIGURE 4.1B *Social groups of rural population in the thirteenth century, after Jenő Szűcs.*
PUBLISHED IN LASZLOVSZKY 1991.

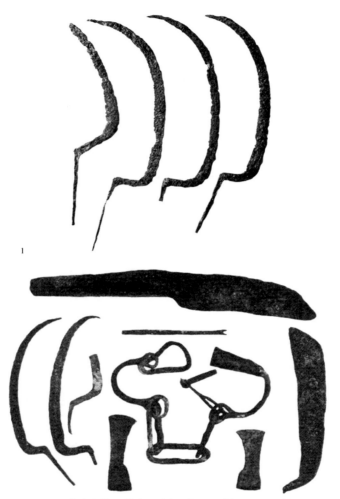

FIGURE 4.2 *Sickels from Nyáregyháza-Pusztapótharaszt and Iron depot from Cegléd-Madarászhalom (thirteenth century; after Vargha 2015).*

kind of plow, replaced what had mainly been small square fields. In contrast to the relatively short rectangular plots bounded by the systems of ditches in Árpádian-age settlements, the land cultivated in the Late Middle Ages was divided into long stripfields. Symmetric or slightly asymmetric plows were used in short runs, sometimes in both longitudinal and transverse plowing. The advantage of a field that was square or almost square was that the ditch and embankment enclosing it were relatively short. The highly asymmetric plow was better suited to fields with long runs, and such fields were no longer enclosed. The plow and its draft animals could continue in one direction for a greater distance, leaving an uninterrupted and completely turned-over furrow, the plow having to be lifted and turned round only once, at the end of the tract. Another aspect of enclosed fields was that the farmer had individual control of when he kept animals there, so as to provide manure during periods when the field was out of cultivation. Unfenced long stripfields, however, demanded communal decisions about the phases of rotation. This plow also allowed terrace-like tracts to be laid out on slightly-sloping hillsides, perpendicular to the slope, a technique widely used in forest clearances. Such cultivated terraces (lynchets) may be observed in many hilly areas of what was medieval Hungary. Although these terraces cannot yet be dated with precision, they are associated with settlements that were founded in the thirteenth century, and their close proximity to these settlements implies that they started at an early stage. They gradually extended over wider areas, making up much of the cultivated land around the villages. The extent of these areas proves that the process of clearing the forests and forming lynchets could have taken several centuries. Archaeological research of late medieval arable land, however, has found that it may be classified into different categories, implying major local variations in the process. None of the surface traces of ridge-and-furrow plowland that landscape archaeological methods have detected on plain areas, however, date from this era. The form of cultivation they represent was confined to relatively small areas of the Carpathian Basin, even in the modern age.

Having come into use in the thirteenth century, the new type of plow, combined with a more systematic way of regulating the land around the villages which the settlers brought in, led to a new layout of village land. One aspect of this process, however, was an internal development not linked solely to the arrival of the *hospes* peoples. It was a logical consequence of animal rearing that large herds kept by villagers on the plain, where the surrounding land was not covered in forest, were moved from place to place around the village to make best use of pasture. This rendered some land more suitable for cultivation, the animals trampling and grazing down larger vegetation, thereby suppressing weeds and increasing fertility with their manure. Land "converted into fields" in this way then became capable of supporting tillage. There is much evidence in the written sources about land around villages becoming agricultural plots which were given individual names like Kökényestelek or Páltelke, comprising the name of one characteristic feature of the land (with some type of bushes, *Kökényes*) or of the owner (*Pál*) and *telek*, the above mentioned word for plot. These plots constituted scattered farmstead-like settlements in the vicinity of villages. These little, scattered settlements – seeds of villages – left remains in several areas which have been discovered by archaeologists. Archaeological field surveys of modern arable land in locations scattered throughout the country have discovered surface concentrations of Árpádian-age pottery spread across circles of 30–50 meters in diameter. Excavations of some such isolated farmsteads show that they consisted of the same kinds of buildings and structures as are found in contemporary villages: pit-houses, outdoor ovens and ditches. Some of the latter clearly served as paddocks or pens for holding livestock.[35] Farms consisting of a single house and its outbuildings have been found spaced 80–100 meters or even further apart. This corresponds to information from some written sources from the second half of the thirteenth century, stipulating the distance of an arrow's flight between such an outlying dwelling place and a small settlement, and an axe-throw as the shortest distance that a person altering a plot in the land around the village could locate his house from another dwelling place.[36] Thus, the division of the land around the village could reach a level where the placing of the outfield plots and their associated house plots (*sessiones*) had to be regulated, because if they were too close together, one farmer's animals could cause damage to the tilled land of his neighbor. These regulatory measures, and the more systematic use of the land around the village by the settlers, supplemented by the sophisticated manor-like organization of labor in certain monasteries, combined to produce the layout, land-use and labor system of the peasant village that was distinctive of the following era. This process has left clear archaeological traces. Traces of furrows in previously unbroken land, clearly made by an asymmetric plow, have been found in the sandy soil in the Danube–Tisza Interfluve area. Surface finds date this to the thirteenth century. It represents the use of the plow to break the grassland of the relatively abundant area still available around the village. Unlike the trend in most plains in the country, however, the land brought under cultivation in this way did not remain arable throughout the medieval period.[37] The example mentioned here involved only a single plowing which was later covered by shifting surface sand. Subsequently, the land was probably used for extensive animal husbandry, while the plowland, covered with sand, retained its form so that archaeologists could determine its story.

The increasingly regular form of enclosed plots beside houses (precursors of tofts) also left archaeological traces. In an Árpádian-age find near Budapest, the houses and their plots lie in a single row and are approximately the same

---

35   Laszlovszky 1986.
36   Laszlovszky 2011, 103–118.
37   Nyári et al. 2006 and Nyári, Kiss and Sipos 2007.

size, similar to the arrangements of late medieval settlements. Excavations in the late medieval market town of Muhi, previously a village, have shown the fixing of house sites starting in the thirteenth century. Although these went through major changes in shape and size, the center of the settlement grew up continuously in the same place from that time, and this also determined the sizes of inner plots. Another result of this process and complex of influences was the regular system of ley farming and fallowing, eventually in its classic forms: the two- and three-field systems. These are recorded in sources from as early as the thirteenth century, but only became widespread in the fourteenth. The various environmental conditions and the size and nature of herds, however, also greatly influenced the local application of such systems in the closing years of the Middle Ages. Certainly, systematic fallowing and the new type of plow combined to promote the sowing of wheat in favor of lower-grade millet and more generally to enable higher yields from cultivated land. A clue to how these developments took place comes from the Hungarian word *nyomás*, meaning a field with several selions or furlongs used in a system of two- or three-field rotation. The same word is used for "pressing" or "trampling", indicating that this was land which the animals had previously "trampled"; i.e., fertilized and made fit for plowing. Another Hungarian peculiarity is that the single word *telek* was used for both parts of the croft – i.e., both the toft and the plot on the outskirts of the village, so that the piece of land made fertile around the house and the land with similar properties around the village evolved as part of the same process. Only when the land around the village was regulated into an open-field system were the two connected, based on possession and cultivation by the same family. All of these developments led up to the legally coherent system of tenant peasant villages that characterized the late medieval period. Peasant farming was based on the system of tofts and outer plots; i.e., the individual peasant possession of land and village owned by the landowner. While cultivation of the plots was the responsibility of individual peasant farmers (on land that was redistributed annually by drawing lots or was acquired by inheritance), the system of farming (rotation or the two- or three-field system) and the utilization of areas in common use (forests and meadows) were decided by the village community.

The expansion of area brought under tillage was accompanied by increasing intensity of cultivation, but there was also an opposing trend that started in the thirteenth century. The decline in population and destruction of villages caused by the Mongol invasion were most severe in the center of the country, on the Great Hungarian Plain. Whole areas were left empty as a result, and it was here that Béla IV settled the Cumans (a smaller group of whom were located on the plains of Transdanubia).[38] These settlers had large herds and their way of life was closer to the semi-nomadic type than to life in Hungarian villages, based primarily on arable cultivation. This was a constant source of friction in the areas where Hungarian villages lay close to Cuman lands, because the free-ranging herds of large animals destroyed villagers' crops, and these differences in way of life were easily linked to the differing customs and pagan beliefs of the incomers.[39] The formation of agricultural villages in Cuman lands was a very long process. Archaeological excavations (e.g. in Szentkirály) show that it took at least a century and a half.[40]

The changes of the thirteenth century also affected other areas of food production. Some groups of the *hospes* population brought with them new vinicultural skills. Vineyards, which required more labor but yielded greater income, took up steadily greater areas through new forest clearance or other means of rendering land fit for cultivation. This phenomenon was particularly marked among settlers from Romance (neo-Latin) language-speaking areas of Southern or Western Europe.[41] A major economic drive for this activity came from another development which was strongly linked to the appearance of *hospes* groups and the growth of early towns.[42] The inhabitants of the new urban settlements presented a great demand for wine which had to be satisfied by local markets whose economic significance was steadily increasing. They in turn were supplied by the steadily-expanding vineyards near Buda, Sopron or other urban centers, and the civil architecture of these towns also bore the traces of this trade. Building archaeology and historic buildings research have found that distinctive house types in both towns evolved through the influence of pressing and processing grapes, storing large quantities of wine in cellars (Buda) and storing wine on the ground floors of buildings (Sopron).[43] These urban settlements and their markets also drew in locally-grown fruit and vegetables, of which an ever-wider range has been revealed by the contents of filled-in wells in these towns, the remains of produce and seeds giving a good picture of the fruit which was consumed.[44]

---

38   Pálóczi-Horváth 1989 and Berend 2001, 68–73 and 87–93.
39   Berend 2001, 134–140.
40   Pálóczi-Horváth 2002c and Pálóczi-Horváth 2005.
41   Székely 1964.
42   Kubinyi 1996b.
43   Feld 2004, 9–38.
44   Facsar 1973, Skoflek and Hortobágyi 1973 and Torma 2003.

There were fewer changes in the structure of animal rearing during this time, although it was affected by the changing nature of tillage.[45] Complex forms of farming evolved, affecting the land used for growing crops and keeping livestock (ley farming) and special land use in some regions. On the flood plains of the large rivers, in addition to ordinary flood-plain farming, some areas were regulated by ditches to control the flow of water onto the land and hold it there, thus stabilizing the soil moisture content and permitting fishing, grazing and crop-growing at different times of year.[46] This combined to raise the overall quantity of grain produced, as indicated by the rising population and the spread of water mills, which took on an increasingly central role in cereal processing.[47]

Throughout the Árpádian-age, in addition to continuously supplying the peasantry with sufficient food, the agricultural sector of the economy provided the basis for a rising number of urban settlements, especially in the second part of the period. The village population also managed to pay their tithes, the monastic estates provided for the ecclesiastical establishment, and – especially from the twelfth and thirteenth centuries – more and more produce came into direct trade. The change in farming structure on monastic estates shows up clearly in the tendency for dues payable in produce to be replaced by payment in money.[48] This also meant that a large proportion of agriculture products were sold on the market. The formation of tenant peasant villages also provided a strong agricultural base for the economy, enabling the growth of towns and the initial impetus for the formation of market towns based on the local exchange of goods. Treasure-hoards dating from the Mongol invasion also prove that in the mid-thirteenth century a large part of this trade in goods, which still largely comprise agricultural produce, involved monetary transactions.[49] This meant that freemen could pay their denars and monasteries, and as their economic structure changed, could increasingly demand the services due to them in money. All of these economic changes were inevitably linked to equally far-reaching changes in society.

---

45 Belényesy 1969.
46 Takács 2003.
47 For water mills see the study of László Ferenczi in the present volume and Vadas 2018.
48 Maksay 1972.
49 Laszlovszky 1991 and Vargha 2015, 65–81.

The Late Medieval Agricultural Economy

The major technical advances in agriculture in the thirteenth century were associated by an even deeper socio-economic transformation. In the century or so following the Mongol invasion, the complex layers of status and obligation among the peasant population which had developed by the late Árpádian-age changed into the single and more modern legal status of *jobbágy* (*iobagio* in Latin texts, meaning tenant peasant). The final stage in the process was the law regulating the seigneurial due (*kilenced*, Latin *nona*) of 1351, which shows that one of the fundamental obligations of the new social class was service to the landlord, which from that time on constituted a more or less constant burden together with church tithes that had been in place since the Christian state was founded, and the frequently-changing state taxes.

This was accompanied by a major rearrangement in the structure of towns and villages.[50] The complex diversity of small villages gave way to a system of villages which had many things in common. Instead of tilling fields in the direct vicinity of the house, peasants were concentrated into villages with a distinctive inner layout and there arose an open-field system of tofts and outfield plots. Peasant houses were regularly arranged around the church and the neighboring lord's mansion. They were often laid out in rows, with a long plot stretching out behind each house perpendicular to the street.[51] In the direct vicinity of the building were outbuildings and barns for animal fodder, very similar to what ethnographic researchers observed in Modern-period village houses. The buildings were no longer single-room pit-houses but mainly two- and three-room peasant houses built at ground level with walls of varied construction. The basic types evolved in the first half of the fourteenth century, and developments of these persisted in village architecture right up to the early twentieth century.[52] Their evolution, as well as reflecting the technical developments in house-building, provides evidence of the economic base that permitted peasants to build houses with a larger and more refined living space than had previously been possible.[53] After doing their agricultural work and rendering their dues and services to the lord, they still had time, financial resources and building materials to erect such houses. The substantial outbuildings beside the houses prove that there were surpluses that needed storing,

---

50   Maksay 1971.
51   Pálóczi-Horváth 1998, 192–204.
52   Tálasi 1965b.
53   Pálóczi-Horváth 1997, 507–513, Pálóczi-Horváth 2002a, 308–319 and Pálóczi-Horváth 2002b, 196–202.

from which we may conclude that agriculture was making advances. There was also more livestock, held in sunken pens or ground-level structures. In the Árpádian age, more and more pigs were raised on what were basically cattle and horse farms, although their significance later dwindled. The proportion of small grazing animals also fluctuated somewhat over the same period. The area that constituted the kitchen garden, used for growing fruit and vegetables, also usually lay behind the house on the internal plot. Most of the open-field area was under cultivation by that time, divided into furlongs which were in turn subdivided into strips. The geographical preconditions of agriculture significantly differed in the different areas of the country, but long strip field as a general form became dominant everywhere. The reason for this was the plowing technique and the usage of the asymmetric plow. At the same time, some scattered late medieval data on draft animals and many ethnographic examples tell of a great variety in the equipment and means of plowing within this basic type. Peasants were allocated strips here and there in different parts of the field, either permanently or by drawing lots every year. Work on this land followed the regulated fallowing or two/three-field system, mostly involving cereals. Archaeological investigations of traces of cultivation have given us a way of envisioning this land by a means other than parallels with modern ethnographic findings. Traces of hillside terraces, for example, can show us where the selions were. One fortunate find is a unit of three roughly equal-sized terraces, which could have been used in a three-field system of rotation (see Fig. 4.3).[54] The most recent finds of cultivation traces have even provided archaeologists with a relatively accurate picture of the type of plow that made them, and this is confirmed by iron finds in hoards and on the sites of agricultural settlements.

Besides the relatively regular system of outer plots, the land around the village included the lord's demesne with its cultivated fields and areas of meadow, pasture and forest which were fundamental to the life and needs of the village and most often used in common. Although most arable land in the country was cultivated using the two- or three-field system in the late medieval period, the mosaic of soils in some areas favored cultivation of the whole field with the same crop in one year or many individual forms of peasant farming. This involved the use of forest clearings, a continuing process that transformed previously forested areas, and the cultivation of parcels laid out on unbroken parts of the outfield. In villages inhabited by lower or "one-plot" nobles, the diversity of land ownership and cultivation was inherent, and plots were constantly being divided and united. This resulted in villages with many patterns of land

---

54 Torma 1986.

FIGURE 4.3 *Remains of the medieval field system near Tamási (after Torma 1986).*

use other than the two- and three-field systems.⁵⁵ There were also changes in time as the result of changing markets, and incidental elements sometimes became dominant in certain areas. Such were regions or areas specializing in viticulture near large towns. A similar process engendered new ways of using the outfields of abandoned villages on the Great Hungarian Plain, where extensive animal herding became profitable.⁵⁶ Hayfields, important for provision of animal feed, may have been in individual possession in this period, and they took on steadily-growing importance in line with developments in livestock rearing. This claim is borne out by the evolution of agricultural implements. The main harvest implement remained the sickle, of which several types were in widespread use, but the straight-edged scythe also appeared, at that time a tool for making hay rather than harvesting.⁵⁷ The gallery forests and pastures along the rivers were a further addition to the area for keeping livestock, enabling large numbers of animals to be kept at some parts of the year without causing problems for the extensive cultivated land where grain was grown. This was particularly important in the dry summer months, when areas beside water provided ample grazing.

There were also areas around the villages which lay outside the plot system and the lord's demesne. Important among these was the area used for systematic forest clearing. This in many cases was formed in a single large-scale clearing operation through communal action by the village, although the piece-by-piece expansion of villages' cultivated land still continued. The clearings were of small area and did not have the comparative uniformity of furlongs and strip plots. Excavations and field surveys of the medieval village of Sarvaly in Veszprém County have found an array of terrace-like fields in the vicinity of assorted sizes, suggesting forest clearance.⁵⁸ The implements used for clearing and exploiting forests are a well-known part of medieval material culture and have close ethnographic parallels.⁵⁹ A reconstruction of the clearing process, based primarily on ethnographical observations, has shown that single peasant farmers tried to extend the land under cultivation in some areas through a form of forest use that initially enabled a system of forest pasturage and gradually eliminated the original forest-scrub vegetation.⁶⁰

---

55   Zatykó 2003.
56   Sárosi 2016.
57   Takács 1972, Müller 1975 and Müller 2014.
58   Laszlovszky 1999, 439–440.
59   Belényesy 1958a.
60   Takács 1978 and Takács 1980.

Cutting down the large trees enabled plowing to begin, but the stumps could take several decades to rot. Only after they completely disappeared did the newly-cultivated land become truly suitable for plowing. These areas were mostly in hilly regions, and the stones that constantly came to the surface during plowing were taken to the edge of the field so that they did not hamper cultivation. Rows of stones at the edge of the plowed field also prevented erosion of the land and helped the formation of arable terraces. Clearing the forest was not always a matter of individual effort. It could also take communal forms. We primarily know of these from written sources. Village names have also incorporated some aspects of the expansion of farmland and the formation of new settlements based primarily on forest clearance. Some endings of late medieval settlement names show that they were originally isolated farmsteads. Names ending in *laka* or *háza* (house of) and *telke, ülése* or *földje* (plot of, land of) may allude to initial habitation by individual settlers, where a small clearing could have been the starting point for a new settlement. The latter form is also implied by place names ending in *vágása* (clearing of). Other kinds of internal colonization are apparent in place names ending in *falva, fala* or *fa* (village of) and their spatial distribution. The great majority were in the Transdanubian Mountains and the North Hungarian Mountains, but not the highest regions. This shows a process of community (clearing village) rather than individual colonization. In the perimeter regions of the country, particularly where there were large expanses of forest, even larger units of land were taken under cultivation. These required the support of royal settlement policy, as we can see in the Spiš region and the south of Transylvania. Although the classical period of this settlement policy fell in the thirteenth century, the process continued into the fourteenth and fifteenth centuries as land under cultivation spread out from these areas or gradually expanded within the outfields of older-established villages. The growing number of agricultural villages in these regions and the expanding area of land under cultivation also contributed to the country's ability to support its greatly increased population.[61] Much produce was also available for export. The steep rise in population certainly continued up to the end of the fifteenth century or even the middle of the sixteenth, except for the areas – mainly in the south – that were devastated by the Ottoman advance. In addition to the overall expansion of the population, the proportion of people who were not involved in either cultivation or animal husbandry is itself an indicator of how much agricultural production increased. Most of these people lived in towns with charters of privilege, although the substantial populations of mining towns and settlements, with their major economic

---

61   Pálóczi-Horváth 2000b, 60–68.

importance, were dependent on the agricultural production of other areas. The nobility, accounting for a large proportion of the population, also became increasingly involved in the production of goods through the use of land controlled by landowners. An indirect indicator of Hungary's population carrying capacity is that it was the country where the mendicant orders experienced their most spectacular development in Europe in the fifteenth and sixteenth centuries. It is true, however, that these friaries themselves became involved in agricultural production, and some owned tracts of land in the late fifteenth and early sixteenth century.

Another form of land use on areas newly brought under cultivation in the late medieval period was viticulture.[62] Vineyards lay outside the plot system because they required much labor to establish and provided a return only in the long-term, after the vines started to fruit. Nonetheless, there were vine slopes nearly everywhere, either on hills separate from the village or merely separated from other land. The main exceptions were in upland areas where vines would not grow. Possession of vineyards was not confined to peasants; in the late medieval period several wealthier burghers owned vineyards which provided them with revenue and they employed hired workers to tend them. This is a relatively well documented area. In Buda, for example, the phases of viticulture may be traced from the start of work in spring through the summer hoeing to the autumn grape-picking.[63] We also have knowledge of pruning through archaeological finds of vine pruning knives. These vineyards created one of the most remunerative branches of agriculture at that time. There was substantial local consumption, but wine from several areas was also sold further afield. In the emerging vine-growing regions, the returns from this form of cultivation caused its adoption on nearly every available stretch of land, whether owned by land-owning nobles, churches, peasants or even burghers. Wines from the above-mentioned Srijem were held to be of particularly high quality, and good wine was also made from the vines on the southern slopes beside Buda, mostly for the cellars of town citizens.[64] In the regions to the north of the Great Hungarian Plain, mainly in the hills, wine was made for foreign export, mainly to Poland. Wine export was a major source of income for the agricultural populations of whole regions.

Livestock was the other agricultural commodity with a major role in foreign trade. The rapidly-growing urban populations of southern Germany and Italy represented good markets for meat, and the relatively hardy cattle raised on

---

62   Gyulai et al. 2009 and Mravcsik et al. 2015.
63   Kubinyi 1964b.
64   Kubinyi 1996d.

the Great Hungarian Plain, which could withstand being driven long distances, were well placed to satisfy this demand. Exports on a large scale started in the fourteenth century and reached a peak in the fifteenth. This phenomenon left its mark in the town of Vác, for example, which lay on one of the main driving routes. Extensive herding and driving for long distances did not degrade the condition of the cattle, and its meat was always highly rated and sought-after in the region to which it was exported. The size, and particularly the sturdiness of these cattle surpassed those of the livestock strains bred there, but the long-horned grey cattle cannot be said to have been the main breed among them. The process remained uninterrupted at the start of the sixteenth century and during the Ottoman occupation. Livestock was driven from the Plains every year to gathering points from where they were taken on to their destinations abroad.

Some pig-rearing also involved a lot of movement. Semi-wild pigs were sent out for masting in the forest during the autumn, thus gaining weight and becoming an important source of food during the winter slaughter season. These omnivorous pigs, however, may have thrived in areas other than those identified by ethnographic research. Flood plain areas could also have supplied them with sustenance, and in the marshy shallows they may even have eaten fish.

Animal protein from the plentiful and varied livestock was still supplemented to a significant degree by fish. Ways of catching them, and fisheries regulated by technical means, were widespread in this period. The Late Middle Ages, then, was a time when every section of society had increasing access to varied sources of nutrition.

Revenue from agriculture and agricultural products were also basic factors in the development of a special kind of settlement, the market town. Market towns grew up most densely on areas where the regional centers of trade in agricultural products – markets and fairs – were established.[65] These functions were increasingly linked to crafts, and in a few cases the largest market towns took on the functions of fully-fledged towns in areas which lacked them. The economic base of such market towns probably also shifted strongly from agricultural activities towards crafts and long-distance trade. In the legal sense, market-town inhabitants were tenant peasants obliged to serve the lord, but population concentration and complex economic functions led to the development of an entrepreneurial class in market towns which, towards the end of the medieval period, gathered increasing strength and earned substantial income, primarily through trade in agricultural produce. Foremost among them were towns involved in the long-distance livestock trade. Enterprise activity

---

65 For market-towns, see the study of István Petrovics in the present volume.

may also be detected among the village population, and some lords also moved towards the production of agricultural commodities. The same period also saw the intensification of the economic stratification of the peasant population, resulting in increasing numbers of *inquilini*. Thus a section of society working increasingly as hired laborers was formed, although the extent of this is strongly disputed among modern historians. All of these processes accelerated in the late fifteenth century and caused major structural rearrangements in both the work of the peasant population and the system of rents and income of the lords. Many forms of production that started at this time were similar to the structure of agriculture characteristics of the early modern period. This is the area where research into historical sources over the last decade has borne the most substantial results. The views about the rising numbers of *inquilini* previously widespread among historians have been proved to be unsustainable. At the same time, the peasantry involved in the market economy must have generated significant revenue. We see with increasing clarity that a broad section of the peasantry had agricultural output that permitted a substantial rise in central taxes, but also that various techniques were employed to avoid paying them. The same process took effect on demesne farming and seigneurial rents, frequently causing severe conflicts between parties with differing roles in the economic system. It is not clear, however, how much these processes of structural transformation contributed to changes in farming techniques, open field use or the proportions of crops and livestock. These issues also suggest that we might rethink the causes of the 1514 peasant uprising, the most serious of its kind in medieval Hungary.[66] Hungarian historians have long since moved on from class-war oversimplifications and put forward somewhat more complex explanations. It is now possible, drawing on the results of recent findings in economic and social history, to detect in the background of these events structural problems which may well have included historic changes in agriculture. Another contribution to the elucidation of these issues could come from archaeological research into market towns, which has undergone resurgence in recent decades. A reconstruction which incorporates the houses and agricultural implements found in the settlements and the nearby buildings and places for keeping livestock could have a considerable influence on the determination of the role of these settlements in commodity production and the market economy. This could in many respects alter our views about the economic role of Hungarian peasants in the late medieval period, especially concerning the economically-significant changes to the ways they tilled their fields and raised their animals. In general, the substantial growth experienced

---

66   C. Tóth and Neumann (eds.) 2015.

in the period up to the late fifteenth or early sixteenth century was derived less from improvements in agricultural techniques than from regional specialization. The prevailing agricultural technologies had been in use since the early fourteenth century, and it was estate management, the market economy and the changing proportions of branches of agriculture that provided landowners with sources of additional income. Specialization in grain growing, viticulture and extensive livestock rearing, combined with the role of market towns as centers of distribution enabled agriculture to steadily increase its output until the turn of the fifteenth and sixteenth centuries.

These forms of agriculture were largely responsible for preventing major decreases in population and the abandonment of villages in the war-torn periods of the sixteenth century and the early decades of Ottoman occupation. When the situation changed in the second half of the century, and particularly in its closing decades, a major factor was the loss of land under cultivation and the consequent fall in agricultural output. Exacerbating the process was a combination of climate change and several kinds of epidemic, leading to outbreaks of famine and the almost complete depopulation of some areas. Large expanses of some regions (such as the Great Hungarian Plain) lost their cultivated character for more than a century, and the system of tenant peasant villages gave way to very large peasant towns. In other parts of the country, however, agriculture continued under unchanging conditions and preserved its form. There were large areas, not surprisingly in the parts of the country spared the afflictions of Ottoman occupation and war, where the peasant villages retained their internal structure and even their pattern of outfield use until the start of the early modern period or beyond.

CHAPTER 5

Animal Exploitation in Medieval Hungary

*László Bartosiewicz, Anna Zsófia Biller, Péter Csippán,
László Daróczi-Szabó, Márta Daróczi-Szabó, Erika Gál,
István Kováts, Kyra Lyublyanovics and Éva Ágnes Nyerges*

Introduction

During the last few years there has been an upswing in interest in animal studies among medievalists. Historical research into medieval animal husbandry and the use of related products has intensified in terms of the analysis of documentary (and to some extent, iconographic) sources, but the help of archaeologists has also been enlisted. Eventually, the study of animal bone finds also began, although this type of inquiry is far better developed in the field of prehistoric archaeology: in the absence of written sources, prehistorians had to turn to less spectacular evidence, including animal remains. Archaeozoology is devoted to the identification, analysis and interpretation of animal remains from archaeological sites. Although the detailed analysis of written sources and animal iconography fall outside the scope of archaeozoology, familiarity with this process is indispensable for properly interpreting the archaeological traces of medieval animal exploitation.[1]

In contrast to contemporaneous documents, archaeological finds directly represent material culture and, in the case of animal remains, consumption rather than production. The study of animal bone assemblages therefore represents an entirely new dimension in the reconstruction of the medieval economy – one which is complementary to the historical record. Recent advances in medieval archaeozoology in Hungary have resulted in the rapid growth of information, resulting in its syntheses within a broader European context at regular intervals.[2]

Analysis of animal exploitation in the Árpádian age (tenth–thirteenth centuries) is dominated by the interest in understanding how mobile pastoralists adapted to sedentism. Late medieval research tends to be interested in the formation and import of new animal breeds, and even exotic species.

---

1 Choyke, Lyublyanovics and Bartosiewicz 2005.
2 Bökönyi 1995, Bartosiewicz 1999a, Vörös 2000, Bartosiewicz and Gál 2010.

In Hungary, much debate has been focused on the animal husbandry of the tenth century (the period of the Conquest), both in professional and lay circles. The first archaeozoological monograph in Hungary was written by Ferenc Kubinyi in 1859 with the title "On Camels and Horses from a Zoological and Paleontological Point of View, with a Discussion of their Historical Role in the Migration of Hungarians from the East". Although the piece of camel bone Kubinyi identified later turned out to have been a Pleistocene specimen, Kubinyi's train of thought was the most up-to-date of his time. The first burials of mounted Hungarian warriors were discovered as early as 1834 at Benepuszta, near Kecskemét.[3] At that time, however, animal remains were not given much attention. Nonetheless, by the turn of the nineteenth and twentieth centuries, József Besskó had published a craniological study of the horses of the conquering Hungarians. Another significant contribution was Gyula Brummel's set of articles about domesticates from the period of the Hungarian Conquest.

The biologist Béla Hankó (1886–1959), founder of systematic archaeozoological research in Hungary, represented a historicizing perspective inspired by a respect for tradition. His "archaeozoological" research, however, rather involved the study of cranial measurements taken from modern domesticates assumed to have ancient Hungarian origins. Sándor Bökönyi (1926–1994) started systematically analyzing archaeological bone assemblages stored in the Natural History Museum in 1951, and conducted a thorough identification of faunal remains, assisted by quantitative and morphological evaluation. His works paved the way to the modern research of animal remains due to his success in supplementing previously obscure theories about the origins of medieval domesticates with meticulously collected, objective osteometric data.[4]

During the nineteenth century, construction of national identities and equestrian tradition as represented by the Scythians was often confused with Hungarian ethnogenesis. Another important issue was whether the conquering Hungarians (who led a mobile, pastoralist way of life) could have brought swine with them from the Eurasian steppes to the Carpathian Basin. The debate was partly ideological in nature, as the prevalent historical viewpoint in the newly (1867) founded Austro-Hungarian Monarchy was of an ingress of valiant mounted warriors, rather than swine-herders. However, it seemed hard to believe that a people with highly developed animal husbandry skills were not familiar with swine-keeping. At the settlements of mobile pastoralists (Sarmatians, Avars, Hungarians, Cumans) at least sporadic remains of swine are regularly found. This is generally considered to reflect the process of

---

3   Fodor 1996.
4   Bartosiewicz and Choyke 2002.

increasing sedentism; however, it is hard to avoid the pitfall of circular reasoning if the issue of nomadism and sedentarization is viewed only through the presence or absence of swine.[5]

One of the most important late medieval export goods of Hungary was livestock, predominantly cattle, driven on foot to urban markets in the west. This practice of extensive animal husbandry that ensured a supply of meat for cities and towns is well-known from later written sources.[6] It is easy to mistakenly conflate nomadic and extensive early modern pastoralism; any similarities, however, are due to the general practicalities of animal herding, irrespective of ownership. Nomadic families usually moved along with their herds; in a newly emerging economic system, however, drovers in the early modern period were hired as wage-workers for driving cattle to market or slaughterhouse.

Animal Exploitation at Medieval Settlements

As with other archaeological finds, a considerable amount of information is lacking in historical sources, making their interpretation increasingly difficult as we proceed back in time. It is nevertheless clear that this loss of information is not simply time-related but also depends on the variability in intensity of a complex taphonomic process. Animal representations in codices, panel paintings or stone reliefs have different chances of surviving, while it is also questionable whether various animals were depicted at the same frequency by medieval artists in various media.[7] The three main types of sources – that is, the written, the iconographic, and the biological (i.e., archaeozoological) – are affected differently by taphonomic processes:

- their original content was selected for different purposes,
- their chance of survival and the pace of their destruction differ,
- their frequency varies in time and space, in relation to their original purpose.

Thus, the methodologies suitable for their integrated scholarly analysis are difficult to harmonize. Consequently, only complementary studies of various types of sources can provide a proper academic understanding of many of the aspects (animal breeding and exploitation, consumption customs, trade,

---

5 Bartosiewicz 2003a.
6 Bartosiewicz 1995a and Bartosiewicz 1999b. See the chapter by Balázs Nagy in the present volume.
7 Bartosiewicz 2011.

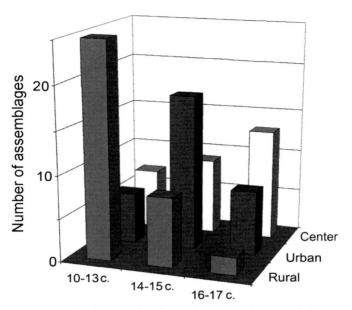

FIGURE 5.1 *Number of medieval animal bone assemblages studied by settlement type and chronological group.*

craftsmanship and beliefs) of medieval culture. Similar difficulty is faced when trying to compare the animal bone assemblages brought to light at different archaeological sites. There are notable discrepancies in the number of excavated, analyzed and published sites according to settlement type and dating – as analyzed in this chapter (*see* Fig. 5.1; Appendix, Table 5.1).

Columns in *Fig*. 5.1. suggest a diachronic decrease in the number of known rural assemblages, while bone materials from towns and various centers show somewhat different patterns. Members of this latter, very heterogeneous group of settlements[8] are primarily characterized by their relatively small population and dependence on a rural network for meat supplies. For the purpose of this study, this group was further sub-divided into elite (royal palaces, administrative centers), residential (castles of nobility,[9] manorial houses[10]) and military (garrisons, Ottoman-period forts[11]) sites. The position of individual settlements within this hierarchy often changed during medieval history. Some

---

8   Bartosiewicz 1999a.
9   E.g. Bartosiewicz 2016.
10 Bartosiewicz 2009.
11 E.g. Gál and Bartosiewicz 2016.

sites (e.g. Segesd[12] and Visegrád[13]) suffered a decline from royal status to neglected rural settlement in later times, and thus appear in all three categories depending on their status in the given time period. These discrepancies may undermine the credibility of the comparative analysis of settlement types and broad time periods. However, according to a Chi-squared test, medieval archaeozoological assemblages were not statistically significantly different in terms of typo-chronological site distribution. The overall picture is influenced by historical realities. These include the disintegration of the Árpádian-age village network from the late Árpádian-age, and centuries later, the increasing pace of urbanization.

An important geographical limitation must also be noted here: following World War I the territory of modern-day Hungary became limited to the central, lowland section of the Carpathian Basin. Important, highly developed regions of medieval Hungary, undisturbed by Ottoman occupation (including sites such as mining towns and forts in the Carpathians), were left outside the newly drafted political borders, largely in Romania and Slovakia.[14] While the archaeological study of the Middle Ages seems to be similarly developed in all neighboring countries, the analysis of animal bones appears to have been carried out most consistently in Hungary.

Coincidentally, the central third of the medieval kingdom of Hungary was also the open, strategically vulnerable area affected by the sixteenth–seventeenth-century Ottoman occupation. The Ottoman Empire covered the southern half of present-day Hungary, offering researchers a special opportunity to study the culturally diverse end of the Middle Ages in this area.

Medieval sites in Hungary do not simply vary in terms of location, chronology and known function. Largely depending on the widely differing opportunities for sampling and excavation, assemblage sizes (referred to here in terms of the number of identifiable bone specimens, henceforth 'NISP') vary between handfuls of animal bones and thousands of remains at better-known sites. These data, whose distribution is skewed by the significant dominance of assemblages containing fewer than 1500 identifiable bones, are summarized in *Fig.* 5.2. The smaller the number of finds, the greater the risk of random bias in calculating their relative frequencies (e.g. percentages), thus the discussions in this paper are focused on assemblages where the number of identifiable animal bones exceeded 400.

---

12   Bartosiewicz 1996a.
13   Twigg 2012.
14   Bartosiewicz, Mérai and Csippán 2011.

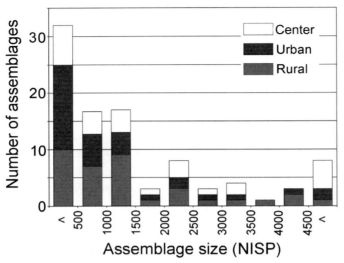

FIGURE 5.2 *Size distribution of assemblages* (NISP) *by settlement type.*

The availability of assemblages has also been determined by archaeological strategies in the second half of the twentieth century (rescue archaeology vs. research excavations), the varying degrees of attention individual archaeologists have paid to collecting faunal materials from given sites, and whether excavators had personal working contact with archaeozoologists.

Archaeozoological studies of early medieval settlements were conducted by Sándor Bökönyi and János Matolcsi in the 1960s and 1970s, and later their pupils László Bartosiewicz, István Vörös and István Takács continued this research. Today, a number of new-generation archaeozoologists (who have contributed to this chapter) are involved in the analysis of animal remains at medieval sites, in addition to their broader interests in all archaeological periods.

Rural Settlements

The first group of medieval settlements discussed here is best known from the relatively early period of the Árpádian dynasty. Research at medieval rural settlements in Hungary began in the 1920s–1930s and became fully established after World War II.[15] There are fundamental chronological as well as geographical differences between these sites and assemblage sizes also vary extensively (Appendix, Table 5.2).

---

15   Bartosiewicz 2017.

ANIMAL EXPLOITATION IN MEDIEVAL HUNGARY 119

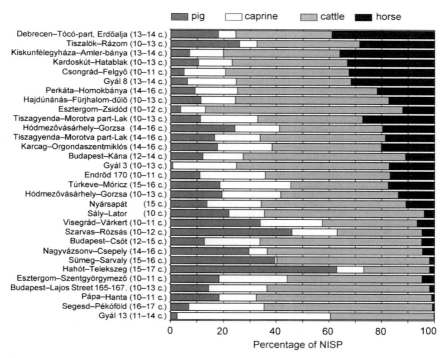

FIGURE 5.3 *Proportions of most important meat-producing animals in remains at rural settlements (for details, see Table 5.1).*

Most rural assemblages are dated to the Árpádian age. Proportions of the most important meat-producing animals, cattle, sheep/goat (caprine), pig and horse, are summarized in *Fig.* 5.3.

In general, from rural deposits the remains of cattle appear in the greatest proportions, while the ratio of domestic fowl and wild animals is quite low. In the case of other domestic mammals (horse, pig, sheep, goat and dog) proportions are sometimes very variable at different sites. The popularity of cattle is due to its versatile primary and secondary uses. Sheep and goat can also be exploited in many ways.

Sheep and goat are different species in many respects (e.g., habitat preferences, modes of exploitation); their bones, however, are hardly distinguishable from one another with the notable exception of skulls, horn cores, and metapodia. Even though goat is hardier and produces more milk compared to its body size, sheep remains are usually found in much greater numbers in Hungary (there are usually three–four times as many sheep as goat remains in medieval assemblages, although in some cases there may be seven–eight times as many).[16] In contrast to small ruminants, swine is an animal kept exclusively for meat.

The ratio of caprine (sheep and goat) to swine changes by site. It should be kept in mind, however, that the husbandry of these species is highly environment-dependent (relief, hydrogeography), as swine require more water than sheep and goat. Acorns were also an important source of fodder for these animals, making their keeping successful in woodland. Swine-keeping was successful in marshy areas and gallery forests, especially in Transdanubia.[17] In the swampy region of Greater Cumania (in present-day eastern Hungary), even in villages associated with the Cumans (a population that previously inhabited the steppe region and had no tradition of pig herding before their thirteenth-century migration to the Carpathian Basin) pigs were also kept and consumed in relatively large numbers due to favorable environmental factors.[18] On the other hand, pig bones are almost completely absent from some Árpádian-age sites, possibly because of an early, non-Christian avoidance of pork.[19]

Horse was included in *Fig.* 5.3 because in early medieval rural assemblages it often constitutes a considerable part of faunal materials. Even though Pope Gregory III raised objections against the eating of horse meat during the mid-eighth-century conversion of Germanic tribes, Hungarians seem to have kept up this custom well after having officially adopted Christianity in the year 1000. Following the tenth-century Hungarian Conquest of the Carpathian Basin, a number of peoples of eastern origins (such as the Cumans) arrived in the same area and horse consumption formed part of their tradition as well.[20] The custom survived for a longer time in the Great Hungarian Plain (eastern Hungary, e.g. Tiszalök–Rázom,[21] Csongrád–Felgyő,[22] Gyál,[23] Hajdúnánás–Fürjhalom-dűlő[24]) where influx by mobile pastoralists remained more intensive.[25] At these sites, the presence of horse bones appears complementary to those of cattle. Sites in *Fig.* 5.3 may be categorized by reference to the

---

16 Bartosiewicz 1999c.
17 Vörös 2000.
18 Lyublyanovics 2015 and Lyublyanovics 2017.
19 See for example, Rózsa and Tugya 2012.
20 Lyublyanovics 2015, Lyublyanovics 2016 and Lyublyanovics 2017.
21 Bökönyi 1974.
22 Matolcsi 1982a.
23 Biller 2007 and Kőrösi 2009.
24 Gál 2010a.
25 Vörös 2000.

decrease in the ratio of horse/pig bones, considered diagnostic from a dietary point of view. The trend of pork replacing horse flesh in diets is clear from the illustration. Sites located in the hillier western part of the country (such as Hahót–Telekszeg,[26] Csőt or Esztergom–Zsidód[27]) have far smaller proportions of horse bones, while pig tends to be relatively better represented than in the Great Hungarian Plain. Potential connections between the dates assigned to sites and the horse/pig NISP ratio were tested by calculating the Spearman rank order correlation between the two variables. On the basis of the resulting coefficient (R=0.282) and probability value (P=0.138), the association between historical time and the increase in pork consumption at the expense of horse flesh cannot be considered statistically significant. The complementary roles of beef and mutton tend to increase the complexity of the situation.

In addition to signs of butchery for food, fine, transversal cut marks on the bones of the feet often testify to skinning, i.e. the use of hides.[28] Horse metapodia were also frequently manufactured due to their strength and straight shape. In Hungary, horse bone 'skates' (or runners) occur commonly in communities with a steppe tradition and were already typical of Roman-age Sarmatian assemblages in the Great Hungarian Plain. Ethnographic analogies indicate that horse skulls deposited at some rural settlements served apotropaic purposes.[29] A healed fracture was found on a horse pelvis from the fourteenth–sixteenth-century Cuman village of Orgondaszentmiklós, an injury that is troublesome to treat and probably prevented the animal from working for the rest of its life. The care taken of this horse testifies to the special place this species occupied in such rural communities.[30]

Dog meat was not consumed, so remains of this animal have a smaller chance of ending up in archaeological material mainly consisting of kitchen refuse. On the other hand, dog carcasses are more likely to be discovered intact and in anatomical order. In the Late Middle Ages, dog breeding was practiced by the aristocracy and at the royal court, resulting in a number of 'breeds' of different character. This situation is, however, not typical of small rural settlements.[31] Dog skeletons recovered from villages sometimes belong to large, muscular individuals, presumably herding dogs, but most of them

---

26   Bartosiewicz 1997.
27   Vörös 2004 and Vörös 2009.
28   Bartosiewicz 1993.
29   Takács 1996a.
30   Lyublyanovics 2015, Lyublyanovics 2017 and Bartosiewicz 2013a.
31   Daróczi-Szabó 2006.

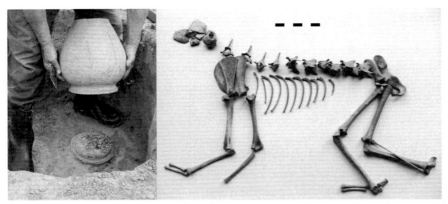

FIGURE 5.4 *Excavation of a pot buried upside down at a site in Budapest – Kána and remains of an articulated puppy skeleton found underneath the pot.*

indicate middle-sized, pariah dog-like animals. Attitudes toward dogs were ambiguous: they were symbols both of loyalty and envy.[32]

Dog remains are mostly brought to light from pits, trenches or wells, but in some cases they were deposited in special, structured contexts. Dog skulls were identified in ceramic pots at the site of Fancsika near Debrecen in northeastern Hungary,[33] and the skeletons of several puppies were found buried under upside down pots (*see* Fig. 5.4) across the Árpádian-age village of Kána.[34]

Dog remains buried in the hearth or the house, as well as dogs cut into pieces and thrown into the Árpádian-age grave of a woman quartered and buried outside a consecrated cemetery (Visegrád–Várkert) are also known.[35] These archaeological phenomena are of special interest, as such customs are not mentioned in the sporadic contemporaneous written record. They illustrate the continuity of archaic beliefs and their coexistence with Christianity.

Bones of cats are only rarely discovered, although the number of rodents must have been high at rural settlements. The hen was the main domestic fowl in all cases. Domestic goose is found only sporadically, while duck remains have been unearthed only at one fifteenth–sixteenth-century rural site. Identifying domestic geese poses a challenge, as their bones do not anatomically differ from those of their wild ancestor, greylag goose, and it is usually only their somewhat larger size that makes them recognizable. Nevertheless, sources

---

32   Bartosiewicz 1998b.
33   Vörös 1990b.
34   Daróczi-Szabó 2010.
35   Vörös 1991.

describing the selection of geese by color in thirteenth-century Hungary speak for the importance of this species.[36] Differentiating between the bones of domestic ducks and mallards is similarly problematic.

The percentage of game animals is low, in most cases not exceeding 2 % of all mammalian NISP. Red deer, roe deer, wild boar and hare are the most common species.[37] Deer are often represented only by antlers, which may have simply been collected in the forest without hunting the animal itself. Recent individuals of some species, especially fox, badger and hamster, may have ended up in the archaeological bone assemblage by dying in their burrows. In such cases, the only evidence that supports medieval dating is a sign of human alteration, such as skinning marks.[38]

Settlements of Central Position

These assemblages originated from high status sites of distinctly non-agrarian character where the opportunities for animal keeping were obviously limited within the habitation area. Meat supply to residences of the aristocracy, ecclesiastic or military complexes (similarly to that of free royal cities and mining towns) depended on food production by villages and market towns (to be discussed later). Beef played a crucial role in the everyday diet of the segment of the population in Hungary who had access to meat. In addition to high status centers, the inhabitants of the free royal towns and mining towns as well as the military generated constant demand, even during late medieval times when the main goal of cattle rearing was the export of live animals. Animal keeping within high-status settlements was hindered by the lack of space: inside the walls there was simply no room for pasturage and water supplies were often limited. Only animals suitable for confinement in small places (swine, hen), and non-meat purpose horses, dogs and cats could be kept in relatively large numbers in such complexes.

Thus the meat supply of these settlements had to be organized in a way that the animals which were slaughtered would often be driven to the complex only at the time when they were to be culled and butchered. Only four of the high-status animal bone assemblages discussed here are dated to the Árpádian age (just the opposite of the chronological distribution of excavated and previously analyzed rural settlements among which this period dominated).

---

36 Matolcsi 1975b.
37 Bartosiewicz, Gyetvai and Küchelmann 2010 and Beast 2010.
38 Bartosiewicz 2003a.

On the other hand, administrative and military centers are more frequently mentioned in charters due to their central social and often geographical position, as well as their later existence when tax rolls and inventories also help in reconstructing the roles of animals in provisioning. Osteological evidence from the 31 sites of the three different types of sources under discussion here is summarized in the Appendix, Table 5.3.

According to the proportions of identifiable bones, cattle were undoubtedly the most important source of meat at many of the later sites, providing not only beef but also dairy products, draft power, as well as the bone and leather used in craft industries. Sheep and goat could be exploited for meat, milk and wool. Pork seems to have dominated at sites where less beef was consumed. The multiparous and omnivorous nature of swine made them an ideal backyard animal at settlements with limited space. Poultry, especially hen keeping, required a minimal investment of labor and fodder, while eggs and feathers could also be utilized.

Although game constituted only a small part of the meat diet it was included in *Fig.* 5.5 instead of horse as hunting seems to have been practiced by the inhabitants of high status sites more often than by common people. Bones of wild boar, red deer, roe deer and hare are usually found at medieval centers. At the Árpádian-age administrative and military center of the *comes* (royal representative) at Szabolcs (in addition to Esztergom) remains of European bison were discovered; hunting of this large beast was probably only a privilege of the aristocracy.

Game gradually lost its dietary significance, although hunting continued as an aristocratic sport, form of military drill, or contingency type of meat provisioning. The fundamental role of game meat in high-status diets[39] is shown by the relatively major contribution of wild animal remains to assemblages from elite settlements (with the exception of the queen's seat at Segesd, and the pasha's palace in Ottoman-period Buda). In addition to the rare findings of bison bones, remains of fur-bearing animals (bear, wolf, beaver), were also found. Sixteenth-century animal remains from the Dominican friary in Buda stand out both in terms of the contribution of swine and game – potential indicators of a very high status diet.

Of the residential sites, the significant contribution of red deer bones in the assemblage from the manorial center at Baj–Öreg-Kovács-hegy is attributable to hide-processing on location.[40] Game played a much lesser role in the provisioning of military garrisons. On the other hand, it was at these settlements

---

39   Bartosiewicz, Gyetvai and Küchelmann 2010.
40   Bartosiewicz 2009.

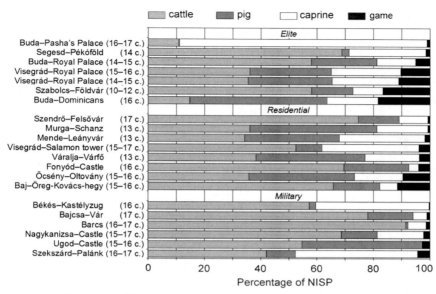

FIGURE 5.5 *Proportions of the most important meat-producing animals in remains at high status settlements. The diachronic sequence begins at the bottom of each graph (for details, see Table 5.2).*

where numerous Ottoman period camel bones were found. These animals, however, are not considered an integral part of the medieval fauna in Hungary, and the eight sites that have so far yielded camel bones have been discussed in a separate study.[41]

As mentioned earlier, in contrast to widely spread *topoi* in the contemporary literature, the consumption of horse meat was not explicitly prohibited by the Catholic Church in medieval Hungary. It is nevertheless unlikely that the few horse bones excavated at high status complexes were deposited as food refuse. Horse consumption seems to have declined only following the aforementioned mid-thirteenth-century appearance of western settlers who introduced a more pork-based meat diet to Hungary. Occasional horse remains showing butchering marks prove that horse meat was sometimes consumed, even in high-status settlements. Donkey remains are extremely rare among food refuse. These animals were already in use for the local transport of water and lightweight products during the Árpádian age.[42] Mules, and especially hinnies,

---

41 Daróczi-Szabó et al. 2014.
42 Bartosiewicz 2004.

must have been used as high-status mounts,[43] but as their bones cannot be clearly distinguished from those of donkey and small horses, it is difficult to appraise their actual significance on the basis of the archaeozoological record.

Dogs and cats lived around the house mostly as self-sufficient, commensal animals often scavenging on refuse. Some of them may have been kept as pets, and were used for protection against vermin, especially rodents. The presence of dogs (used as hunting companions or lap dogs) is associated with high status mostly at central settlements.[44]

The early example of the domestic water buffalo found at the Buda Castle,[45] and the rabbit (not native to the Carpathian Basin) that first occurs in late medieval assemblages in the Royal Palace of Visegrád may be considered exotica among domestic animals.[46] By the early modern period, some of these peculiar animals had become fashionable means of self-representation among the elites. Such curiosities included crested hens, bred from individuals with inherited cerebral hernia.[47]

The general characteristics of animal exploitation in royal centers and castles are clearly recognizable in most of the assemblages; nevertheless, it is hard to reconstruct the precise proportions of various species. The remains of domesticates prevail in all cases, but their share varies. Cattle are usually identified as the dominant species, but as their bones are the largest, they were cut up during butchering and cooking, producing more numerous fragments than the bones of small stock. Moreover, even though there is a general assumption that in the Late Middle Ages the number of sheep and goats gradually decreased as pork became more important in the diet, no such trend can be observed at medieval centers.

Various explanations exist for the great variation in proportions shown in *Fig.* 5.5. The natural environment of any site is of utmost importance: forested, scarcely inhabited areas surrounding some of the castles were ideal for hunting, as well as free-range swine herding; dry slopes were suitable for caprine grazing, while in addition to dense forests marshy areas were favorable for pig-keeping. Customs of meat consumption among the medieval population also varied: sometimes assemblages of entirely different composition come to light from high status sites located close to each other. The share of fish bones remains very low in these assemblages, chiefly due to the lack of fine recovery

---

43 Bartosiewicz and Gyöngyössy 2006.
44 Daróczi-Szabó 2006 and Bartosiewicz 2011.
45 Matolcsi 1977.
46 Bökönyi 1974.
47 Gál et al. 2010.

techniques, especially water-sieving. Although written medieval sources on the topic are few and far between, cookbooks from the early modern period attest to the significance of a great variety of fish in high-status diets.[48]

One assemblage brought to light from the Buda Castle is an interesting example of special dietary customs within a high-status settlement. The castle was built to become the royal center after the mid-thirteenth century. A well (no. 8), excavated at Szent György Square and dated to the period of King Sigismund provides evidence of religious dietary restrictions. Artifacts found in the lower layers are indicative of a Jewish community, and indeed the site was located in the first medieval Jewish district. Historical data have also been supported by the animal bone assemblage. In the upper layers, accumulated by a later, Christian population, pig bones were present, but they suddenly disappeared in the lower layers associated with Jewish inhabitants,[49] whose religious prohibitions strictly forbade the consumption of not only pork but also fish species without scales. Remains of catfish and sturgeon were thus only found in the Christian deposits in the well.[50] Meanwhile, the material left behind by the Jewish community contained an unusually high proportion of bones from poultry.

Since Christianity became strongly dominant during the Middle Ages, animals are rarely interred in the company of humans. One example of special animal remains in a high-status context is a stallion discovered in the thirteenth-century grave of a Cuman nobleman at Csengele. This ritually sacrificed stallion was probably brought from the east; genetic tests revealed its resemblance to Arabian horses.[51]

Urban Settlements

Urbanization was a protracted process in medieval Hungary, but the nature of animal exploitation differed between 'proper' towns – such as free royal cities, mining towns, and manufacturing centers[52] – and rural, so-called market towns (*oppida*). A special taphonomic feature of urban archaeology is that many sites are buried under modern towns, so recovery is often carried out in the form of

---

48   Bartosiewicz 2013b.
49   Daróczi Szabó 2004a.
50   Bartosiewicz 2003b.
51   Vörös 2006 and Priskin 2006.
52   E.g. Ringer et al. 2010.

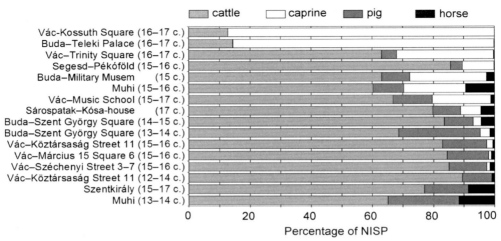

FIGURE 5.6 *Proportions of remains of the most important meat-producing animals at urban settlements (for details, see Table 5.3).*

small rescue excavations.[53] As a result, only about half (seventeen of the thirty-two) of the urban assemblages thus studied exceeded the NISP=400 minimum value considered representative in this study (*see* Fig. 5.6). The towns of Vác and Székesfehérvár[54] are especially well represented by small sets of medieval animal bones that could not be included in the graph. These provide valuable qualitative information (e.g. an Ottoman-period turkey bone is known from Székesfehérvár[55]), but are unfit for statistical evaluation (Appendix, Table 5.4).

In *Fig.* 5.6, two settlements stand out at either end of the scale: Ottoman urban deposits in Buda and Vác are characterized by an overwhelming dominance of caprine remains and a lack of horse bones. At the other extreme, the market towns of Szentkirály, and especially Muhi, stand out due to the relatively large contribution of horse remains, indicative of a meat diet of a more rural character. In the case of Muhi, a diachronic increase in beef consumption in the fifteenth–sixteenth centuries may be a reflection of increasing supply, attributable to the conjuncture in livestock trade.

Even though the Hungarian name *mezőváros* (i.e. non-fortified market town) has little to do with agriculture, animal products maintained a crucial

---

53 This contrasts with situation at the rural site of Budapest–Kána, where an entire late-Árpádian-age village was excavated in the open field: Daróczi-Szabó 2013.
54 Bartosiewicz 1995a and Bartosiewicz 1997.
55 Bartosiewicz 2006.

role in the economic life of these medieval settlements. Animal production in the extensive outskirts of market towns provided the basis for medieval animal husbandry in Hungary after the deterioration of the Árpádian-age network of villages. It is doubtful, however, whether it is possible to speak about animal-keeping within market towns in general terms, since this settlement category was far from homogenous,[56] and although some market towns in the Great Hungarian Plain were mainly involved in extensive animal keeping, others specialized in large-scale grain or wine production.

The prosperity of market towns was often closely connected to animal production and the acquisition of newly accessible land due to the desertion of the Árpádian-age rural settlement network. The natural environment of the Great Hungarian Plain in the east was especially suitable for grazing both large stock and caprines. From the fourteenth century onwards, newly acquired lands were often handled as common property by towns, instead of being divided into individual plots. At the beginning of the fifteenth century, a number of large market towns (e.g. Debrecen, Kecskemét, Nagykőrös, Hódmezővásárhely) already had extensive pastures. At the same time, a higher, affluent social stratum developed in market towns specialized in animal production and trade. This may explain the massive dominance of beef in the diet of several late medieval towns located in the proximity of important cattle trading routes.[57]

Three main routes existed for driving cattle to markets abroad: the most important one led to Austria and southern Germany, but cattle traders drove large numbers of animals to Italy and Moravia as well. In the sixteenth century, tens of thousands of cattle were driven on an annual basis from Hungary to Vienna, southern Germany and Venice. Market towns in the Great Hungarian Plain (e.g. Debrecen, Kecskemét, Jászberény, Cegléd, Heves, Mezőtúr, Szeged, Kiskunhalas, Nagykőrös) were the most important hubs, with a vested interest in cattle trade.[58] Earlier data about cattle exports to Austria exist, even though market towns joined in this activity in large numbers only in the fifteenth century when livestock itself became a more important export good than other, processed products (leather and wool, in the case of sheep). The economic historian Vera Zimányi called this period the "Golden Age of Cattle".[59] Cattle

---

56 Bácskai 1965, Fügedi 1981c, Mályusz 1953b, Mályusz 1986, Bellon 1996a, Makkai 1961, Székely 1974 and Kubinyi 2000b.
57 Bartosiewicz 1999b.
58 Plentiful literature exists about this issue: see e.g. Takáts 1927, Makkai 1971, Makkai 1988, Kocsis 1993, Mészáros 1979, Blanchard 1986 and Pickl 1979.
59 Zimányi 1976.

owners ranged herds extensively outside settlements, grazing all year round. Merchants in market towns bought up the livestock and had the animals driven to the markets where they were sold. This was an expensive enterprise: drivers had to be paid, and the broad driving roads (*viae bovariae*) and their infrastructure (pastures and watering places along them) had to be maintained.

Many market towns became *de facto* centers, if only in an economic rather than a legal or administrative sense. Such towns started becoming involved in the large-scale trade in livestock and animal products in the second half of the fifteenth century, with cattle and sheep being the most important species. In post-medieval times, this trend was maintained or even promoted by the occupying Ottoman authorities; it should be considered a *topos* that the Turkish invasion completely precluded peaceful sedentary agriculture for one hundred and fifty years. Nonetheless, Ottoman occupation brought about the deterioration of urban ways of life. Although some coeval accounts may be influenced by Christian propaganda,[60] archaeological evidence points to a change in the management of waste in towns (e.g. the occurrence of large refuse pits in densely-inhabited areas).[61]

Written sources, including toll and tithe records, travel literature and Turkish *defters* from the time of the Ottoman occupation, provide information about extensive cattle herding and livestock trade, but usually remain silent about the everyday practice of these activities, as well as about the animals kept for local consumption and work. Animal bone assemblages, however, reflect kitchen refuse (i.e., consumption, not production); meat composition is also affected by the ethnic background and religious identity of populations. A more precise picture can be obtained by juxtaposing different types of sources; most of the archaeological evidence, however, is yet to be analyzed. Animal production for wholesale trade and local animal exploitation constitute different categories, and it is a relevant question how much the husbandry of animals for immediate consumption and agricultural work differed from animal-keeping practices at rural settlements.

The proportion of cattle bones in eleventh–seventeenth-century animal bone assemblages varies between 50 and 82 %, with a mean value of 70 %. This high share is partly due to intensive cattle trade in the Late Middle Ages, and perhaps the fact that beef is more suitable for large-scale market redistribution in major population centers than for use at the household-level on a subsistence basis.

---

60   Tóth et al. 2010.
61   Daróczi-Szabó 2014.

The proportion of caprines is 18–19 % of the faunal material found in towns. In areas where there are contemporaneous records about wool production, the share of sheep is usually higher in kitchen refuse. Farms specialized in sheep husbandry started emerging in the sixteenth century. Groups of Wallachian shepherds appeared with their flocks in deserted areas of the Great Hungarian Plain by the fifteenth century. Tithe records from the sixteenth century show a concentration of this type of livestock, which seems indicative of specialization in sheep. The presence of the expanding Ottoman Empire must have been a factor, as Turks consumed the most mutton in southeastern Europe and regularly bought sheep to Hungarian soil for the purposes of military supply. Sheep-trading, however, was not comparable to the export of cattle. In many settlements, sheep herds tended to be concentrated in the hands of a few farmers, but tax rolls show that the size of sheep flocks fluctuated.[62]

The forms of both sheep and cattle became varied, with at least half-a-dozen types developing by the early modern period, many of them recognizable by horn conformation in archaeological deposits (see Fig. 5.7).

FIGURE 5.7 *Depiction of straight-horned Racka sheep by Luigi Fernando Marsigli from 1726. The first horn core finds of this curious form began appearing during the Late Middle Ages in Hungary.*

---

62 Káldy-Nagy (ed.) 1985.

Swine were typically kept for local, household consumption. There are legal references to swine-keeping being regulated in medieval urban centers in German areas due to this practice being considered unworthy of great cities.[63] Animal remains from Hungary suggest that in towns that mostly relied on craftsmanship, the number of swine was probably low. Pig herding in market towns, on the other hand, was a non-commercial subsistence activity, serving local demand for pork. This practice did not differ much from rural pig herding. During the summer, pigs could be grazed, while acorn provided fodder in the wintertime. Accordingly, swine husbandry was most successful near oak and beech forests. Extensively kept domestic pigs probably interbred with wild boars. In the archaeological assemblage of towns, swine bone constitutes a small fraction (only around 10–20 %), while in the faunal material of villages this proportion sometimes reached 50 %, indicative of direct, domestic meat supplies. Although horse trade flourished, regular horse meat consumption must have been rather sporadic in late medieval towns, possibly limited to contingency.

Market towns that played a key role in cattle trade contributed to the emergence of conscious attempts at animal breeding. The goal was to produce high-quality beef, leading to strong pressure for artificial selection. Slaughterhouse documents and archaeological data from the sixteenth–seventeenth centuries reflect an increase in the height of withers, as well as the weight of the animals.[64] The stock was, however, heterogeneous. Although the picture that emerges from Bavarian or Austrian cattle markets is quite consistent, the original livestock, geographically distant from the demand markets, probably lacked this kind of homogeneity. At smaller markets along the driving route, the drivers may have tried to sell underweight, lame, injured or less visually appealing individuals, so that only the best part of the herd reached the foreign target market. Variability is testified to by records in which animals were conscribed according to colour or shape of horns. The late medieval cattle stock that continuously increased in number due to the trading boom provided a selection basis for the emergence of the Hungarian grey cattle in the eighteenth century. The cattle horn cores found in a pit in Buda, dated to the eighteenth century, possibly refuse from comb manufacturing, represent impressive evidence of this process. Sizes and shapes of horn cores show clear evidence of

---

63   Pounds 1994.
64   Matolcsi 1970.

the breeding of a robust, long-horned cattle type,[65] but the variability in cattle body shape remained significant throughout the medieval centuries.[66]

The price of beef began falling after 1620, bottoming out in the 1650s.[67] The main cause of this was a decrease in market demand, a consequence of the impoverishment of the Austrian and German bourgeoisie; there were, however, several more subtle causes for the crisis as well. Contemporary documents not only testify to a decrease in demand, but also to an increase in conflict with Austrian and Italian cattle traders, competition posed by Polish cattle suppliers, corruption in administrative matters, and a decline in public safety. The decreasing demand for Hungarian cattle in the seventeenth century may also be explained by the appearance of large-size dairy cattle bred near the North Sea, a dual-purpose cattle type whose meat could have possibly substituted for imports from Eastern Europe.

Fowling in Medieval Hungary

The exploitation of wild avifauna is a special feature of medieval culture. However, the recovery of usually small bird bone fragments is size-selective, thus much depends on the precision of excavation and the application of screening or water-sieving techniques. So far, remains of wild birds have been brought to light from 37 medieval sites in Hungary. Twelve of these sites are dated to the Árpádian age, 14 to the Late Middle Ages, and 11 to the Early Modern Period. The number of identified species is 55. Eleven rural sites have provided remains of wild birds of 21 different species. Most data come from royal, ecclesiastic, residential and military centers: 14 sites provided 39 different taxa. Twenty species were identified in 12 urban assemblages (*see* Fig. 5.8; Appendix, Tables 5–7).[68]

Most of the identified species nest in the Carpathian Basin. Some of them are present in the area all year round, others only from spring to autumn. The common teal and the bean goose migrate and are seasonal in the spring and the autumn, even though the latter often spend the entire winter (from November to April) in this area. Therefore, bird remains known from fourteenth–sixteenth-century Segesd reflect seasonal hunting. From the fourteenth–fifteenth-century Visegrád royal palace, the remains of mistle thrush and fieldfare have

---

65 Csippán 2009.
66 Csippán 2013.
67 Blanchard 1986.
68 Gál 2015, Bökönyi and Jánossy 1965 and Jánossy 1985.

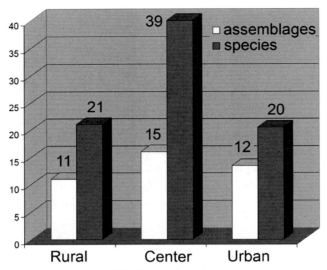
FIGURE 5.8 *Diversity of bird species by settlement type.*

been found. These species appear in the Carpathian Basin only during the winter; consequently, they must have been killed in the wintertime. The tawny eagle, the Lanner falcon and the peacock are not native to Hungary and must have been brought here by trade or as gifts. Although peacocks are counted among the domestic fowl due to their deliberate taming and husbandry, their use as exotic rarities and indicators of high status suggests the existence of attitudes different from those involving ordinary hen keeping.

The basic acquisition of bird meat and eggs was based on poultry keeping from the Early Middle Ages onwards; hunting contributed to nutrition only as an occasional source of meat, a claim supported by archaeological finds. The most commonly hunted wild bird was partridge, discovered at 13 sites. The meat of the great crested grebe, swan, geese and diverse duck taxa, black grouse, hazel hen, quail, pheasant, coot, crane, great bustard, black-tailed godwit, woodcock, wood pigeon, hoopo, starling, mistle thrush and fieldfare was also consumed. Coot and the great crested grebe were approved meats for Lent, as they live in water, like fish. According to contemporaneous data about food traditions, recipes and ethnographic observations, jackdaws, rooks and crows were also consumed.[69] The latter is testified to by the cut ulna of a rook from the Early Modern Period, brought to light at Szendrő–Felsővár. Last but

---

69   Bartosiewicz 2004.

not least, an often diverse choice of wild birds was offered at aristocratic feasts as a means of high-status self-representation.[70]

In Northern Europe, the large-sized waterfowl and wading birds were served – usually stuffed with food – as decoration at the feasts of the aristocracy. We do not know, however, whether the grey heron, purple heron, great white egret, glossy ibis and swan identified from high status centers in Hungary ever played a similar role.

The presence of a varied avifauna in medieval assemblages indicates a role exceeding that of animals hunted merely for consumption. Swans, peacocks and cranes were popular pet birds in noble courts and castle parks. Written as well as iconographic sources speak for the value attached to the plumage of grebes, peacocks, cranes and bustards; it was fashionable to use this material for ornament on clothing and, from the Ottoman period onwards, on horse harness. This custom was probably rooted in the signals used by hunters. Men of lower social status decorated their hats with the plumage of domestic birds (goose, duck or rooster), while members of the elite, including women, used the feathers of exotic ostrich, egret or crane (see Fig. 5.9).

Plume holders made of precious metals ornamented with gems were so expensive that they were used as pawn in times of financial difficulties. Peacock and crane bones recovered from the Árpádian-age site at Balatonkeresztúr–Réti-dűlő are of special interest: according to written records, as well as archaeological data, the area was under the ownership of a wealthy family who could afford to keep these luxurious birds.[71]

Not only did the feathers of birds have a symbolic role, but birds were sometimes used as sacrificial animals. Most of the birds killed as building offerings in the Árpádian age were domestic fowl; their carcasses were often covered with pots.[72] At Csengele–Fecskés, one of the upside-down pots contained the remains of a house sparrow. Two flutes found at fifteenth–seventeenth-century Visegrád–Alsóvár were made of the ulnae of a golden eagle; the choice of raw materials may have had a symbolic meaning.[73] Falconry, an aristocratic pastime of Asian origin, was widely documented, even though more common species (goshawk, sparrow hawk) might have been used in hunting by people of lower status as well.[74] In the elite quarters of medieval Buda Castle, remains of a Lanner falcon were found, suggesting the presence of this expensive,

---

70   Gál 2010b.
71   Gál 2007.
72   Daróczi-Szabó 2010.
73   Gál 2005.
74   Bartosiewicz 2012 and Gál 2012.

FIGURE 5.9 *Hungarian nobility in decorative plumage at the turn of the sixteenth and seventeenth centuries (after Szilágyi 1897).*

imported bird of prey (*see* Fig. 5.10); the bone of a tawny eagle found at the Ottoman-period fort of Bajcsavár (inhabited by Christian forces, today bordering Nagykanizsa) may be seen in a similar context.[75]

---

75   Gál 2002.

ANIMAL EXPLOITATION IN MEDIEVAL HUNGARY 137

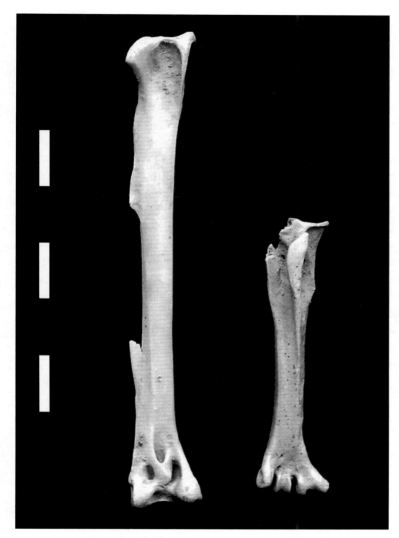

FIGURE 5.10   *Articulated leg bones of an imported Lanner falcon from fourteenth-century Buda Castle.*

Conscious as well as inadvertent impacts on the medieval landscape (forest clearing, plowland cultivation, water regulation) and hunting began adversely affecting not only large game but also the avifauna. Over time, populations of habitat-bound (e.g. black grouse, little bustard) and widely hunted (crane) species became increasingly threatened, and almost completely disappeared from the avifauna of Hungary. Cranes are migratory; their seasonal incubation in

Hungary became rare: the last recorded case was in 1892.[76] The white pelican and the mute swan incubated in the Carpathian Basin until the nineteenth century, while now they rarely appear in this area. The number of golden eagles decreased to five-six breeding pairs.

The living conditions of other species, however, were improved by the expanding towns and the ever-denser network of settlements that provided food resources and shelter from natural enemies. Ethnographic evidence (folksongs, proverbs, counting-out rhymes, etc.) indicates that the white stork, the common house martin and the barn swallow were first associated with human habitats. Their monogamous nature and strong attachment to mates made them the symbols of fidelity in folklore. They were also widely considered beneficial for their role in controlling vermin and insects.

Several birds of the crow family (rooks, hooded crows, jackdaws and magpies) and predatory birds lived close to humans as well; nevertheless, these were not held in esteem. Although flocks of crows can rid a plowland of pests, the damage they cause to crops, the noise they make and their tendency to 'steal' objects made them vermin in the eyes of humans. Perceptions of these birds seems to be of a dual nature: they were usually persecuted, despite their friendly and easily tamable nature. The most bird remains unearthed at one site (82 bones of 14 individuals, from the site of Csepel–Vízművek, a sixteenth-century grain storage pit) belong to the jackdaw. In addition, magpie, jay and kestrel bone fragments testify to the presence of avian species in the towns of medieval Hungary. Written records confirm that magpies and jays were sometimes tamed and kept as pets,[77] which may have been the case leading to the jay bones from the thirteenth–fourteenth centuries brought to light at Szent György Square and from the Teleki Palace in the Buda Royal Palace.

Medieval Fishing and the Great Sturgeon

Screening is a precondition for the reliable recovery of fish remains from archaeological sites. This technique, however, is almost unknown among medieval archaeologists in Hungary. As a result, written information about medieval fishing, especially in legal documents (discussed separately), still dominates over the scantily found archaeozoological evidence.

Due to this recovery bias, the list of species that can be discussed on the basis of bone finds is limited to commonly occurring, large-bodied catfish

---

76 Bartosiewicz 2005.
77 Bartosiewicz 2003c.

(sheathfish), pike, carp and large, anadromous species of the sturgeon family (Acipenseridae). In addition, small cyprinids and pikeperch are sometimes identified in the assemblages. In this subchapter, fish that played a crucial role due to their size and economic importance – that is, sturgeon, and especially the great sturgeon – are discussed. These nearly extinct, large-sized species of the Danube are anadromous; i.e., they regularly left the Black Sea and migrated upstream to spawn in the river and its tributaries. Their migration usually took place between January and June, as well as between October and December, on the way back to the sea.

Fish remains identified to species level are known from 23 medieval sites in the territory of modern-day Hungary. Six of them are villages (of which four are dated to the Árpádian age, and two to the Late Middle Ages). All these villages are located close to the Danube or the Tisza River. The general proportions of pooled fish bones identified to species level are shown in *Fig.* 5.11.

Even though this summary might obscure small differences between sites, it shows the dominance of carp (Cyprinidae) and the low proportion of sturgeon in the medieval diet, as also reflected in written sources. In 1495, when the king was welcomed as a guest at the bishop's palace in Eger, 6,000 carp, sterlet, burbot, catfish and trout were supposedly served, all from the bishop's fishponds. The only species missing from this list but often found in archaeological

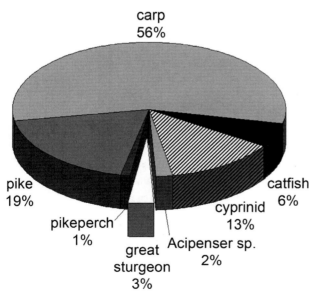

FIGURE 5.11   *Taxonomic distribution of 1029 fish bones from 23 medieval sites in Hungary.*

assemblages is pike, a species that preys on small fish, thus causing damage to stocks raised in fishponds.[78]

Remains of sturgeon have only been found in a single rural context at the site of Győr–Ece. The high-status nature of this fish is evident from legal documents. In 1432, when serfs of the Eger chapter caught two great sturgeon at the chapter's estate in Palkonya and tried to transport them to Eger, a local official confiscated the fish by force. Only one of the two fish assemblages known from towns, the Turkish period Vác–Zeneiskola, contained bones of a great sturgeon. The remaining ten sites were all administrative and/or military centers; bones of fish from the sturgeon family, usually great sturgeon, were found at nine (!) of them. Excavations at the Dominican friary in Buda Castle, the nunnery of the Poor Clares in Óbuda, as well as the Cistercian Abbey in Pilisszentkereszt also brought to light bones of great sturgeon.

Sturgeon are 1–6 meters long and have a lifespan of up to 25 years. The bones of their species are not always distinguishable, a fact exacerbated by spontaneous hybridization between several species within this family of fish. There are two notable exceptions: great sturgeon belongs to a distinct genus, while starlet is adapted to freshwater, and does not migrate to spawn. Sturgeon fish were obviously valued for their size as well as the quality of their meat, as reflected in a 1329 toll record of Zsolca by the Sajó River. The fee for a great sturgeon was two denarii, while a toll of only 1 denar was prescribed for other fish of the Acipenserid family, similarly to horses, oxen or cows.[79]

Great sturgeon, sometimes weighing several hundred kilograms, were often cut up into portable pieces after they were caught; their meat was salted and transported to market, while the largest bones were probably left behind (*see* Fig. 5.12). This technical solution further decreases the number of bones for recovery at sites of consumption. The other option was to keep the large fish alive as long as possible.

Matthias Bél (eighteenth century) noted that great sturgeon were tied to a pole after they had been caught and fatigued in the river before being dragged along the Danube by boat to nearby large markets such as Buda or Vienna.[80]

King Sigismund's 1405 order protecting fishermen and fish traders, according to which only butchers had the right to sell fish of a large size on their chopping blocks and banks, must have applied mainly to great sturgeon. According to the guild documents and letters patent of the medieval butchers of Buda, in 1519 great sturgeons and other fish of the sturgeon family were transported

---

78   See the chapter by László Ferenczi in the present volume.
79   Bartosiewicz, Bonsall and Şişu 2008.
80   Bél 1764.

FIGURE 5.12   *Landing and processing great sturgeon on location at the Iron Gates Gorge on the Danube (after Marsigli 1726).*

to Buda from Paks and Földvár located downstream in the south, and from Esztergom, Nagymaros, Megyer, Óbuda and Szentlászló (across from Óbuda) upstream in the northwest.[81]

Great sturgeon remains are conspicuously frequent at sites near the Danube between Esztergom and Buda. This, however, does not reflect the special abundance of this fish in the Danube Bend Gorge, but rather the geographical location of high-status sites in the focus of archaeological research.[82] Only Sárszentlőrinc and Zirc in Transdanubia and the castle of Szendrő in the North Hungarian Mountains[83] are located far away from these well-researched riparian environments to indicate trade over land.

Fish trapping was practiced using weirs (substantial timber structures usually equipped with additional nets). Side branches of rivers and small tributaries also served as natural traps or could be relatively easily fenced as weirs. The town of Komárno, at the confluence of the Váh and Danube rivers, was a popular sturgeon trapping area where from 1518 onwards great sturgeon

---

81   Kenyeres (ed.) 2008, 185.
82   Bartosiewicz and Bonsall 2008.
83   Daróczi-Szabó 2009.

were allowed to be caught by royal authorities only.[84] Miklós Oláh mentioned that the whole breadth of the Danube could be fenced and turned into a weir, which was, however – as a 1528 lawsuit between the towns of Vác and Buda testifies – a rather undesirable method. Therefore, weirs were rather placed at the confluence of tributaries, or between the river bank and smaller islands. In a 1726 book by Luigi Ferdinando Marsigli, published in Amsterdam, weirs are clearly seen where the Iron Gates Gorge meets the Lower Danube (*see* Fig. 5.12). Building weirs must have been a large-scale enterprise; in the Tisza region in the sixteenth century peasants of several villages were ordered to make weirs under the leadership of a *magister clausurae*, and the oak timbers had to be transported to that location from forested areas, often over very long distances. Peasants who participated in the construction were then given some of the fish caught using the weir, except for the valuable great sturgeons.

The caviar of this species must have been an important delicacy. Although there is little chance of finding archaeological evidence for fish eggs, the consumption of caviar by the aristocracy is mentioned in contemporaneous documents. Interestingly, this coincides with the appearance of water fowl in archaeological assemblages – species that also contributed variety to the 'humble' diet during Lenten fasting. Two water-bound mammals, the otter and the beaver – the latter having scales on its flat tail – were also considered fit for consumption during Lent. Beaver bones were brought to light in large quantities from the Ottoman-period castle of Bajcsa used by Christian mercenaries. Such delicacies at medieval centers signify that it was rather the letter than the spirit of Lent that was observed by the *élites* who strived for both varied food intake and impressive self-representation through their diets.

For observant Jews who followed the Torah, only scaled fish were considered *kosher*. The bony plates of sturgeons were not seen as scales from a religious point of view as they cannot be removed from the body without injuring the skin. Therefore, Jews in Eastern Europe were allowed to consume neither Acipenserid fish nor their roe. While the bones of the great sturgeon and the similarly scaleless catfish are well represented in the assemblage recovered from the medieval castle of Buda, the remains of these species are missing from the kitchen refuse found in the aforementioned well no. 8 of the Old Jewish Quarters at the Teleki Palace in Buda.[85]

---

84   Khin 1957.
85   Bartosiewicz 2003b.

Medieval Bone Manufacturing

Raw materials of animal origin had been regularly used for thousands of years before the Middle Ages in the manufacture of tools and ornaments. Worked bone, antler and tusk objects differ from other archaeozoological finds, as they reflect the manufacturing process, the methods and technical level of craftsmanship, as well as the symbolic meanings of the animals incorporated in certain tools. On the other hand, it is difficult to use these finds in reconstructing the environment, as they were made according to highly traditional individual decisions (e.g. involving the choice of raw material, ever-developing working process, as well as changes in use).

Although in principle any bone of any species can be used for tool-making purposes, the selection of raw material was a conscious process. Radii and metapodia of large ungulates were of special importance. Fragments of these bones of cattle, a species that dominated the medieval diet, could even be picked out from kitchen refuse and reused. Metapodia are body parts associated with meat of secondary quality often left behind at the slaughter house, or taken to tanneries together with animal hides.[86] In addition, their ossification is complete at a relatively early age, creating thick and compact bone material. Therefore, these bones (procured from butchers) constituted the main basis of the raw material supply of the bone workshops that operated in medieval towns.

Large and dense radii and metapodia from cattle and horse were also the skeletal parts most frequently employed as bone anvils. These – sometimes carefully shaped, other times barely modified – bones were used for support during the reparation of serrated iron sickles, thus they bear the characteristic marks of serial use. As a consequence, they incorporate information about agriculture, metallurgy and bone manufacturing alike. The majority of such finds from Hungary were recovered from Árpádian-age deposits. So far they have been identified from 10 sites across the country.[87]

Bone working in the twelfth–thirteenth century was minimally specialized. Finds unearthed from layers representing this period (simple *ad hoc* tools presumably manufactured within the household, pins, 'skates' or sledge runners made of horse metapodia, and rarely, knife handles) testify to manufacturing not exceeding the framework of household production. This is not contradicted by the discovery of the finds of a bone workshop near Orosháza, from

---

86   Bartosiewicz 2009.
87   Gál et al. 2010, Kvassay and Vörös 2010 and Tugya 2014.

the Árpádian age.[88] It was only in the fourteenth–fifteenth century that large numbers of serially produced tools, made from the same type of raw material and by using similar techniques, occurred.

Medieval bone manufacturing workshops known from archaeological contexts (Buda, Visegrád, Miskolc–Diósgyőr, Bratislava, Banská Bystrica, Košice, Prešov, Constance, etc.) seem to have been specialized in the production of certain tool types.[89] Bone beads were produced in several sizes; these were mostly used for rosaries. Rosaries were of Eastern origins; this religious object was spread in Europe by Dominican friars in the thirteenth century, and its liturgical uses, as well as connotations with superstition, are known of.[90] Another product typical of bone processing workshops is dice.[91] These regular cubes with six faces and the methods of their production are known not only from archaeological finds but from contemporaneous representations; their presence is also associated with often-mentioned prohibitions of use by both the clergy and secular authorities.[92]

In the bone-processing workshop of Visegrád, dated to the last third of the fourteenth and the beginning of the fifteenth century, both beads and dice were produced.[93] The process of fabrication has been reconstructed on the basis of workshop refuse (drilled bone plates of different sizes, rectangular, prism-shaped, sawed pieces of bone, complete and damaged dice), the presence of an iron drill with three tips that was once part of a lathe used for making beads, as well as contemporaneous pictorial representations. Drills of various bit sizes were used in the Visegrád workshop, as is attested by the diameter of the holes on the leftover blanks (see Fig. 5.13). In an eighteenth-century workshop that produced bone buttons in Budapest–Tabán, three- and five-armed drills were used.[94]

Specialization in medieval bone working was probably related to the differentiation of related crafts. Another typical product of the workshops, the simple or ornamented knife handle, was attached to the knife itself by a cutler, who later also sold these items. In Steyr in Austria, fifteenth-century cutlers hired "carvers" (*Schroter*) to produce bone and wooden plates for a

---

88 Lichtenstein and Tugya 2009.
89 Kovács 2005.
90 Gróf and Gróh 2001.
91 Petényi 1994.
92 Gróf and Gróh 2004.
93 Gróf and Gróh 2001.
94 G. Sándor 1960.

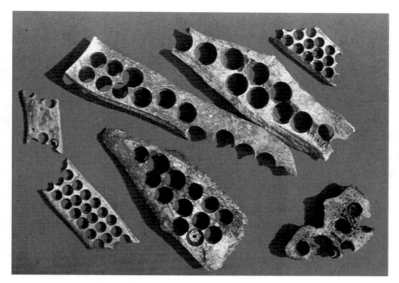

FIGURE 5.13   *Debitage from a bone bead manufacturing workshop in fourteenth–fifteenth-century Visegrád.*

fixed price.[95] Written sources from the beginning of the nineteenth century indicate the mass production of bone items (handles, buttons, gaming pieces, combs, spindles).[96]

In addition to these, belt studs, strap ends or belt stiffeners, most frequently found as grave goods, were also products of bone-processing workshops. Simple bone objects made by individual households ('skates' or runners, sleds, needle-holders, weights for fish nets, flutes made of bird bones, simple toys), however, are present throughout the entire Middle Ages.[97] Most of these objects are known from ethnographic sources to have been in use until the twentieth century.[98]

Horn working is usually evidenced by small, characteristic cutmarks on horn cores of cattle, sheep and goat, made during the removal of the horn sheath from the bone. Buttons, combs and translucent lantern panes were made of horn; these, nevertheless, count among the rare finds, just as do the

95   Holl 1994–1995.
96   Möller 1984.
97   Kováts 2005.
98   Herman 1902.

large drinking horns made of aurochs and bison horns, horn being prone to decay.[99] The presence of horn cores without cutmarks in archaeozoological assemblages may indicate other activities such as tanning.

Antlers of red and roe deer do not constitute a part of kitchen refuse, and their appearance at sites is usually associated with their working.[100] Both shed antler and those of hunted animals were suitable for tool making. Antler was a cheap and easily accessible raw material, especially in forested areas. The systematic collection and processing of shed antlers is also discussed in written sources. Antler is more flexible than bone, it is less likely to crack. This made it an ideal raw material for everyday tools, ornaments or parts of more complex structures, from the Neolithic to the present-day. First and foremost, antler was used to cover the handles of tools (drills, chisels, larger knives). The conscious use of antler as a raw material in fourteenth-century Hungary is shown in the practice of making antler crossbow nuts (cylindrical pawls that retain the string) and covers for crossbow props. Such carved antler pieces are frequently found in castles and towns.[101] Decorated gunpowder flasks were also made of antler, although these are found only rarely. Examples are known from the castles of Ugod, Hollókő and Ozora.[102]

Medieval bone and antler working did not require special tools. Larger pieces of bone and antler were cut up by a type of metal saw used from the Bronze Age onwards. This process included the removal of the epiphyses at either end of long bones, or cutting up the antler beam into smaller pieces, etc. For secondary cuts and shaping of the piece, drawing knives were used. Antlers of older stags were probably softened by boiling, as is attested to by ethnographic observations.[103]

Pole lathes and drills, mechanized tools frequently seen in medieval pictorial representations, were widely used from antiquity onwards; their use is indirectly proven by the aforementioned archaeological finds. Varied ornamental motifs (geometric, floral, figural etc.) were incised using carving knives. The common practice of applying colors is testified to by written sources, in addition to sporadic archaeological evidence: Theophilus in the first half of the twelfth century mentioned red-colored bone objects, while Gionaventura

---

99 MacGregor 1985.
100 Bartosiewicz 2008b.
101 Gömöri 1977.
102 Vörös 1988.
103 G. Sándor 1963.

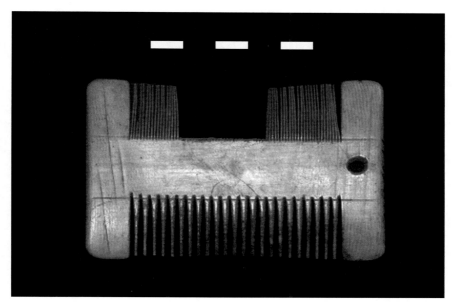

FIGURE 5.14   Late-medieval elephant ivory comb from the Lower Castle of Visegrád.

Rosetti wrote in Venice about solutions and admixtures for coloring bones green in 1548.[104]

Ivory – most commonly, dentine from the upper incisors of elephants – was imported to European markets in the Early Middle Ages mostly from East- and West-Africa, through Byzantium and the Middle East. From the fourteenth century onwards, elephant ivory was transported in huge amounts through French and Flemish harbors to the large processing centers in Western Europe, especially France, Italy, the Rhine region and southwestern Germany.[105] This was the time when ivory objects, such as combs, handles, ornaments and small boxes, appeared in considerable numbers in the area of Hungary as well. Most of these artifacts must have been brought to the centers by trade: elephant ivory objects (mainly combs) have been found in relatively large numbers in Buda and Visegrád[106] (see Fig. 5.14).

One well-known example of ivory working in Hungary is the pommel and crossguard of the sword associated with St Stephen, the first Christian king

---

104   MacGregor 1985.
105   Guerin 2010.
106   Kovács 2005, Choyke and Kováts 2010.

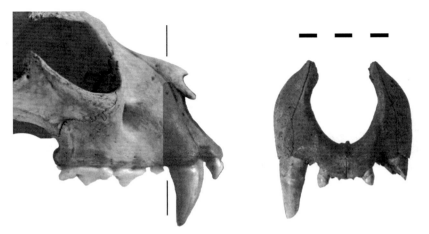

FIGURE 5.15   Oral section of a late-medieval leopard skull from Segesd–Pékóföld (right), and the anatomical location of the worked bone (shaded, left).

of Hungary. It was probably produced in a tenth-century (Viking) workshop, and has been kept in Prague since the fourteenth century.[107] Its raw material, however, is yet to be exactly identified, because the working and trade of walrus tusks in the Middle Ages is associated with Northern Europe (Norway, Denmark, England, and partly northern Germany). During the excavations of the monastery of Veszprémvölgy (part of Veszprém), a richly carved, T-shaped end of a crosier made of walrus tusk was also found,[108] possibly indicative of direct northern or western imports. Luxury objects made of this raw material appear even in the Middle East, probably moved through Russian and Varyag traders. A sixteenth-century walrus ivory belt plaque found at the Turkish fortress of Barcs along the Drava River in Hungary may have been imported through Tartar and Ottoman mediation.[109]

The teeth and claws of bear and exotic carnivores may have been attached to their furs. The sawed-off skull fragment with the canine teeth of a leopard found in the medieval queenly center at Segesd (see Fig. 5.15), was an ornament potentially once attached to a so-called *kacagány*, a traditional type of fur cape for nobility – especially high-ranking officers –, often made from leopard skin. This piece of worked bone is unlikely to originate from a live beast

107   Fancsalszky 2003.
108   Fülöp and Koppány 2004.
109   Gál and Kovács 2011.

imported into Hungary from outside Europe.[110] This example contrasts with the complete skeleton of a lynx recovered from the site of what looks like a late medieval tannery in the town of Vác.[111] The bones of this latter individual showed no modification except for the fine, transversal marks of skinning left on the metapodia.

In summary, there is evidence for the production and use of bone and antler objects in mass quantities in the Middle Ages. It is important to remember that most bone and antler objects could have been carved out of other material as well: handles, spindles, combs and flutes could easily have been made from wood. There are, however, a number of types of object that were consistently made of bone and antler. The primary reason for this practice was that these raw materials were accessible everywhere and relatively easy to work, but were also more durable than ordinary wood. Meanwhile, luxury items in high status areas were often made from imported raw materials or, more likely, brought to Hungary as finished products.

Summary

Animal remains from archaeological excavations are *bona fide* artifacts, legitimately representing material culture. It is not only the way animals were handled and consumed that is revealed in these finds. In addition to helping create a broader picture of meat consumption, some physical properties of the animals can also be recognized. These help with reconstructing the start of the process of conscious breeding.

Attitudes toward animals are reflected in a multitude of physical phenomena, many of which can be read from the bones recovered from medieval settlements. These offer insights into the beliefs and aspirations of people during the Middle Ages.

Even those who doubt the artifactual nature of excavated animal remains will recognize worked bone, antler and ivory as 'proper' archaeological artifacts. The zoological identification of these objects is of utmost importance in reconstructing both local craft industries and patterns of the long-distance circulation of exotica.

The ongoing synthesis of documentary, iconographic and osteological information is creating new research perspectives about medieval economies and society in general.

---

110   Bartosiewicz 2001.
111   Bartosiewicz 1993.

Appendix

TABLE 5.1   *Summary of mammalian assemblages by settlement type*

Rural

No.	Century	Site (NISP)	Source
1	10	Sály–Lator (617)	Vörös 1989
2	10–11	Pápa–Hanta (475)	Vörös 1996
3	10–11	Esztergom–Szentgyörgymező (3546)	Vörös 1989
4	10–11	Endrőd 170 (451)	Bartosiewicz and Choyke 2011
5	10–11	Csongrád–Felgyő (4345)	Matolcsi 1982a
6	10–12	Szarvas–Rózsás (543)	Bökönyi 1974
7	10–12	Esztergom–Zsidód (413)	Vörös 2009
8	10–12	Visegrád–Castle Garden (822)	Bökönyi 1974
9	10–13	Csatár–Cooperative stables (82)	Bökönyi 1974
10	10–13	Sióagárd–Cooperative farmstead (184)	Bartosiewicz 1999a
11	10–13	Csátalja–Vágotthegy (133)	Bökönyi 1974
12	10–13	Hajdúnánás–Fürjhalom–dűlő (1048)	Gál 2010a
13	10–13	Budapest, Lajos Street 165–167 (2043)	Vörös 1989
14	10–13	Tiszagyenda–Morotva-part Lak (1463)	Lyublyanovics 2016
15	10–13	Gyál 3 (2458)	Kőrösi 2009
16	10–13	Kardoskút–Hatablak (886)	Bökönyi 1974
17	10–13	Tiszalök–Rázom (1158)	Bökönyi 1974
18	11–13	Sarud–Pócstöltés (242)	Matolcsi 1975a
19	12	Lajosmizse M5 (102)	Bartosiewicz 1999a
20	11–14	Gyál 13 (1240)	Biller 2007
21	12–14	Budapest–Kána (11 771)	Daróczi-Szabó 2013
22	13–14	Gyál 8 (1826)	Biller 2007
23	13–14	Debrecen, Tócó-part, Erdőalja (580)	Daróczi-Szabó unpublished
24	13–14	Kiskunfélegyháza–Amler-bánya (579)	Tugya 2014
25	12–15	Budapest–Csőt (756)	Vörös 2004
26	14–16	Nagyvázsony–Csepely (412)	Bökönyi 1974
27	14–16	Hódmezővásárhely–Gorzsa (2032)	Lyublyanovics 2016
28	14–16	Tiszagyenda–Morotva-part Lak (4823)	Lyublyanovics 2016
29	14–16	Karcag–Orgondaszentmiklós (1174)	Lyublyanovics 2016

Rural

No.	Century	Site (NISP)	Source
30	14–16	Perkáta–Homokbánya (1406)	Biller unpublished
31	15	Nyársapát (420)	Bökönyi 1974
32	15–16	Sümeg–Sarvaly (1091)	Matolcsi 1982b
33	15–16	Túrkeve–Móricz farmstead (1465)	Bökönyi 1974
34	15–17	Hahót–Telekszeg (1489)	Bartosiewicz 1996b
35	16–17	Visegrád–Lower Castle (2236)	Twigg 2012
36	16–17	Segesd–Pékóföld (1051)	Bartosiewicz 1996a

Center

No.	Century	Site (NISP)	Source
Elite center			
37	11	Vác–Géza Square (334)	Bartosiewicz 1994
38	13	Buda–Palace (198)	Bökönyi 1974
39	14	Segesd–Pékóföld (678)	Bartosiewicz 1996a
40	10–12	Szabolcs–Earthen fortification (611)	Vörös 1990a
41	14–15	Buda–Royal Palace (3544)	Matolcsi 1977
42	14–15	Visegrád–Royal Palace (3980)	Bökönyi 1974
43	15–16	Visegrád–Royal Palace (1195)	Bökönyi 1974
44	16	Buda–Dominican friary (407)	Matolcsi 1981
45	16–17	Buda–Pasha's Palace (1460)	Bökönyi 1974
Residential			
46	13	Váralja–Várfő (1343)	Bartosiewicz 1998
47	13	Murga–Schanz (567)	Gál 2004
48	13	Mende–Leányvár (1255)	Bökönyi 1981
49	13–14	Kőszeg–Castle (239)	Bökönyi 1974
50	15–17	Kőszeg–Castle (120)	Bökönyi 1974
51	16	Fonyód–Castle (545)	Bökönyi 1974
52	17	Szendrő–Upper Castle (7569)	Daróczi-Szabó 2009
53	13–15	Visegrád–Salamon Tower (148)	Bökönyi 1974
54	15–16	Őcsény–Oltovány (2136)	Bartosiewicz 2016
55	15–16	Baj–Öreg-Kovács-hegy (3174)	Bartosiewicz 2009
56	15–17	Visegrád–Salamon Tower (8439)	Bökönyi 1974

TABLE 5.1   Summary of mammalian assemblages by settlement type (cont.)

Center

No.	Century	Site (NISP)	Source
Military			
57	15–16	Ugod–Castle (2277)	Vörös 1988
58	15–17	Szolnok–Castle (147)	Vörös 2003
59	15–17	Gyula–Castle (58)	Bökönyi 1974
60	15–17	Nagykanizsa–Castle (2049)	Bökönyi 1974
61	16	Visegrád–Citadel (367)	Bökönyi 1974
62	16	Békés–Kastélyzug (1814)	Vörös 1980
63	16–17	Érd–Plank fortification (345)	Vörös 2003
64	16–17	Barcs (9568)	Gal and Bartosiewicz 2016
65	16–17	Szekszárd–Plank fortification (6102)	Bartosiewicz 1995b
66	17	Bajcsa–Castle (4375)	Bartosiewicz 2002

Urban

No.	Century	Site (NISP)	Source
67	12–14	Vác–Köztársaság Street 11 (2862)	Bartosiewicz 1995a
68	12–14	Vác–Zeneiskola (243)	Bartosiewicz 1995a
69	13–14	Buda–Szent György Square (1334)	Bartosiewicz 1995a
70	13–14	Vác–Musical School (82)	Bartosiewicz 1995a
71	13–14	Vác–Széchenyi Street 3–7 (169)	Bartosiewicz 1995a
72	13–15	Székesfehérvár–Csók Street (212)	Bartosiewicz 1995a
73	13–15	Vác–Köztársaság Street 11 (80)	Bartosiewicz 1995a
74	13–15	Vác–Tabán Street (20)	Bartosiewicz 1995a
75	14–15	Buda–Palace (58)	Bökönyi 1974
76	14–15	Buda–Szent György Square (1332)	Csippán 2004
77	15	Buda–Military Museum (671)	Vörös 1992
78	15–16	Segesd–Pékóföld (1448)	Bartosiewicz 1996a
79	15–16	Székesfehérvár–Ady Street (60)	Bartosiewicz 1997
80	15–16	Székesfehérvár–Koch Street (69)	Bartosiewicz 1997
81	15–16	Vác–Engineering Highschool (182)	Bartosiewicz 1995a
82	15–16	Vác–Kossuth Square (49)	Bartosiewicz 1995a

Urban

No.	Century	Site (NISP)	Source
83	15–16	Vác–Köztársaság Street 11 (2657)	Bartosiewicz 1995a
84	15–16	Vác–Március 15 Square 6 (432)	Bartosiewicz 1995a
85	15–16	Vác–Március 15 Square 8 (59)	Bartosiewicz 1995a
86	15–16	Vác–Piarist Chruch (102)	Bartosiewicz 1995a
87	15–16	Vác–Széchenyi Street 3–7 (2189)	Bartosiewicz 1995a
88	15–16	Vác–Széchenyi Street 4–6 (307)	Vörös 1986
89	15–17	Vác–Musical School (564)	Bartosiewicz 1995a
90	16–17	Buda–Teleki Palace (2068)	Daróczi-Szabó 2004b
91	16–17	Vác–Engineering Highschool (373)	Bartosiewicz 1995
92	16–17	Vác–Kossuth Square (97)	Bartosiewicz 1995
93	16–17	Vác–Musical School (41)	Bartosiewicz 1995
94	16–17	Vác–Trinity Square (876)	Vörös 2003
95	15–16	Muhi (3983)	Lyublyanovics 2008
96	13–14	Muhi (5665)	Lyublyanovics 2008
97	15–17	Szentkirály (2632)	Nyerges and Bartosiewicz 2006
98	17	Sárospatak–Kósa-house (686)	Ringer et al. 2010

TABLE 5.2 *Animal remains from rural settlements*

	Century	Site (NISP)	Cattle	Sheep
1	10	Sály–Lator (617)	341	
2	10–11	Pápa–Hanta (475)	299	64
3	10–11	Esztergom–Szentgyörgymező (3546)	1742	
4	10–11	Endrőd 170 (451)	213	
5	10–11	Csongrád–Felgyő (4345)	1711	
6	10–12	Szarvas–Rózsás (543)	82	
7	10–12	Esztergom–Zsidód (413)	297	
8	10–12	Visegrád–Várkert (822)	270	
9	10–13	Csatár– Cooperative stables (82)	18	
10	10–13	Sióagárd–Cooperative farmstead (184)	36	
11	10–13	Csátalja–Vágotthegy (133)	53	
12	10–13	Hajdúnánás–Fürjhalom–dűlő (1048)	524	5
13	10–13	Budapest, Lajos Street 165–167 (2043)	1242	
14	10–13	Tiszagyenda–Morotva-part Lak (1463)	517	
15	10–13	Gyál 3 (2458)	1372	569
16	10–13	Kardoskút–Hatablak (886)	277	
17	10–13	Tiszalök–Rázom (1158)	361	
18	12–13	Sarud–Pócstöltés (242)	60	
19	12	Lajosmizse M5 (102)	64	3
20	11–14	Gyál 13 (1240)	475	2
21	12–14	Budapest–Kána (11 771)	5887	
22	13–14	Gyál 8 (1826)	758	5
23	13–14	Debrecen, Tócó-part, Erdőalja (580)	172	
24	13–14	Kiskunfélegyháza–Amler-bánya (579)	245	
25	12–15	Budapest–Csőt (756)	437	
26	14–16	Nagyvázsony–Csepely (412)	217	
27	14–16	Hódmezővásárhely–Gorzsa (2032)	663	
28	14–16	Tiszagyenda–Morotva-part Lak (4823)	2062	
29	14–16	Karcag–Orgondaszentmiklós (1174)	456	
30	14–16	Perkáta–Homokbánya (1406)	710	
31	15	Nyársapát (420)	222	
32	15–16	Sümeg–Sarvaly (1091)	581	
33	15–16	Túrkeve–Móricz farmstead (1465)	441	
34	15–17	Hahót–Telekszeg (1489)	884	6
35	16–17	Visegrád–Lower Castle (2236)	1037	21
36	16–17	Segesd–Pékóföld (1051)	651	93

Note: *4 bison,** 1 aurochs, *** 1 bison.

Goat	Caprine	Pig	Horse	Ass	Dog	Cat	Poultry	Game	Wild fowl	Fish
	76	124	22	2	28			24		
		82	5	9			14	2		
	886	624	161	8	45	1	19	60*		
	112	50	76							
	576	181	1187		517	63	110			
	44	117	12		73	3	25		7	180
	37	15	48					13		3
	177	255	49		3		34	26		8
	15	31	17				1			
	14	43	13		1	13	47			
	27	28	19		4			2		
1	122	102	157		92		12	25	3	5
	446	288	37		4		9	15	2	
	282	147	356		99	3	33	10	12	4
2		18	409	1	35		33	4	2	13
	80	66	209		132		102	18	2	
	60	240	261		60	1	32	48	15	80
		18	156		1			7		
1	35	10	34		6		13			
	702	30	1		25			5		
	1449	1161	1039	6	1355	89	410	144**	28	203
	315	108	548		48		30	12	1	1
	31	85	183				54	51	1	3
1	70	39	199		15		4	1	3	2
	151	91	35	1	21		11	2***	7	
	26	109	17		9			34		
	288	412	335		154	2	74	14	35	55
	741	721	807		337	21	94	16	18	
	228	195	223		31	1	17	9		
	213	123	291		30		10	27	2	
	83	56	44		7	3		3	2	
	9	396	19		4		21	61		
	320	221	209		30	200		1	43	
	136	351	26		4		62	19	1	
6	963	132	14		26	9		54		
18	179	70	8		2		25	5		

ANIMAL EXPLOITATION IN MEDIEVAL HUNGARY

TABLE 5.3 *Animal remains from settlements in central positions*

	Century	Site (NISP)	Cattle	Sheep	Goat
Elite centers					
37	11	Vác–Géza Square (334)	85	25	
38	13	Buda–Palace (198)	107		
39	14	Segesd–Pékóföld (678)	372	84	15
40	10–12	Szabolcs–Earthen fortification (611)	243	45	
41	14–15	Buda–Royal Palace (3544)	1788		
42	14–15	Visegrád–Royal Palace (3980)	942		
43	15–16	Visegrád–Royal Palace (1195)	226		
44	16	Buda–Dominican friary (407)	62		
45	16–17	Buda–Pasha's Palace (1460)	151		
Habitation					
46	13	Váralja–Várfő (1343)	457	29	3
47	13	Murga–Schanz (567)	191	4	1
48	13	Mende–Leányvár (1255)	398		
49	13–14	Kőszeg–Castle (239)	87		
50	15–17	Kőszeg–Castle (120)	25		
51	16	Fonyód–Castle (545)	357		
52	17	Szendrő–Upper Castle (7569)	4659	4	3
53	13–15	Visegrád–Salamon Tower (148)	77		
54	15–16	Őcsény–Oltovány (2136)	785	146	37
55	15–16	Baj–Öreg-Kovács-hegy (3174)	1969	59	12
56	15–17	Visegrád–Salamon Tower (8439)	3053		
Military forts					
57	15–16	Ugod–Castle (2277)	1130	90	1
58	15–17	Szolnok–Castle (147)	16	121	9
59	15–17	Gyula–Castle (58)	11	14	7
60	15–17	Nagykanizsa–Castle (2049)	1267		
61	16	Visegrád–Citadel (367)	75		
62	16	Békés–Kastélyzug (1814)	1024		
63	16–17	Érd–Plank fortification (345)	178		
64	16–17	Barcs (9568)	7474	344	78
65	16–17	Szekszárd–Plank fortification (6102)	1844	427	153
66	17	Bajcsa–Castle (4375)	3252		

Note: * 2 and 3 bison, ** water buffalo, *** camel + 2 turkey, 1 peacock, ++ 1 peacock, 100 rabbit (reported domestic).

ANIMAL EXPLOITATION IN MEDIEVAL HUNGARY 157

Caprine	Pig	Horse	Ass	Dog	Cat	Poultry	Game	Wild fowl	Fish
188	23	2				11			
42	33	3				7	2	1	3
135	14	1		2	1	48	5		1
	69	32		148		4	70*		
423	714	63	3**	13	8	211	157	94	70
617	778	10		7	33	1086+	287	135	103
148	182	1		13	18	451	71	15	70
213	64	13			54		1		
1245	5	2		7		35	15		
226	463	6		24		87	45		3
95	240				2	29	4		1
352	392	12		3		77	21		
33	82					7	17		1
3	11	11		1	2	58	9		
17	119	8		1	3	18	21		1
629	902	6		8	17	1026	49	248	67
25	30	1				12	3		
341	827	3		11		10	210	2	
178	495	77		26		15	343		
2005	534	56	2**	79	84	2102++	224+++	11	89
	884	8		1		110	53		
130		9							
	5	1				1	7	12	
305	234	73	1**	42	9	73	40*	3	2
41	106	1				127	12	2	3
720	40	13	1	6	6		4		
106	17	20							
453	55	36		68	28	929	103	17	4
1753	452	227	14***	117	20	447	191		457
208	667	27	3***	7	3	153	42	16	4375

TABLE 5.4   *Animal remains from urban settlements*

	Century	Site (NISP)	Cattle	Sheep	Goat
67	12–14	Vác–Köztársaság Street 11 (2862)	2233	42	8
68	12–14	Vác–Zeneiskola (243)	165	4	4
69	13–14	Buda–Szent György Square (1334)	643		
70	13–14	Vác–Zeneiskola (82)	42	3	
71	13–14	Vác–Széchenyi Street 3–7 (169)	136	4	1
72	13–15	Székesfehérvár–Csók Street (212)	93	19	3
73	13–15	Vác–Köztársaság Street 11 (80)	59	3	1
74	13–15	Vác–Tabán Street (20)	7	9	4
75	14–15	Buda–Palace (58)	32		
76	13–14	Buda–Szent György Square (1332)	643		
77	15	Buda–Military Museum (671)	458	56	9
78	15–16	Segesd–Pékóföld (1448)	913	103	4
79	15–16	Székesfehérvár–Ady Street (60)	16	14	1
80	15–16	Székesfehérvár–Koch Street (69)	19	6	
81	15–16	Vác–Engineering Highschool (182)	39	4	
82	15–16	Vác–Kossuth Street (49)	25	9	
83	15–16	Vác–Köztársaság Street 11 (2657)	1833	72	4
84	15–16	Vác–Március 15 Square 6 (432)	332	10	1
85	15–16	Vác–Március 15 Square 8 (59)	33		
86	15–16	Vác–Piarist Chruch (102)	83	3	1
87	15–16	Vác–Széchenyi Str. 3–7 (2189)	1514	55	13
88	15–16	Vác–Széchenyi Str. 4–6 (307)	231		
89	15–17	Vác–Zeneiskola (564)	396	13	3
90	16–17	Buda–Teleki Palace (2068)	190	1	1
91	16–17	Vác-Engineering Highschool (373)	209	18	8
92	16–17	Vác-Kossuth Square (97)	86	4	
93	16–17	Vác-Zeneiskola (41)	21		
94	16–17	Vác–Trinity Square (876)	737*		
95	15–16	Muhi (3983)	2661	11	12
96	13–14	Muhi (5665)	2810		
97	15–17	Szentkirály (2632)	1643		
98	17	Sárospatak–Kósa-house (686)	536		

Note: *1 water buffalo, 1 ass, *** 10 turkey.

ANIMAL EXPLOITATION IN MEDIEVAL HUNGARY

Caprine	Pig	Horse	Dog	Cat	Poultry	Game	Wild fowl	Fish
174	238	17	78	1	34	27		10
27	27	5	8		3			
124	250	14	98	13	172	2	5	12
14	16	1	1		3	2		
5	15	7						1
27	46	3		3	15	3		
9	2	1			1	4		
9	12	1			2	2		
124	250	14	98	13	172	4	2	12
	67	19	23	14	8	8	4	5
361	41	2				21	2	1
3	26							
5	6	23	7		2	1		
9	6	1	121		2			
13					2			
231	317	14	25		129	20		12
18	53	4		2	7	2		3
	7				15	4		
3	6	2		1	3			
96	220	27	48	92	80	33	6	5
19	27	1			16		5	1
41	76	7	3		19***	4		2
892	3	2	12	60	863	38		6
106	12	1	13	1	3	2		
5					1			1
11			2		7			
54	57	3**	1		17	1	1	2
357	451	416	29	8	9	20		9
1138	1000	496	61	17	71	37		35
491	222	120	32	13	76	12	1	22
63	53	21	2		8	2	1	

TABLE 5.5 *Bird remains from rural settlements*

Vernacular name	Linnaean name	Balatonkereszttúr–Réti-dűlő 11–15 c.	Csengele–Fecskés 12–13 c.	Csepel–Vízművek 16 c.
White pelican	*Pelecanus onocrotalus*			
Little egret	*Egretta garzetta*			
Grey heron	*Ardea cinerea*	3/1		
White stork	*Ciconia* cf. *ciconia*			
Greylag goose	*Anser anser*			
Mallard	*Anas platyrhynchos*			
White-tailed eagle	*Haliaeetus albicilla*			
Black grouse	*Tetrao tetrix*			
Partridge	*Perdix perdix*	1		
Quail	*Coturnix coturnix*			
Peacock	*Pavo cristatus*	1		
Coot	*Fulica atra*			
Crane	*Grus grus*	1		
Great bustard	*Otis tarda*			
Black-tailed godwit	*Limosa limosa*			
Short-eared owl	*Asio flammeus*			
Fieldfare	*Turdus* cf. *pilaris*			
Jay	*Garrulus glandarius*			
Jackdaw	*Corvus monedula*			82/14
Rook	*Corvus* cf. *frugilegus*	1		
House sparrow	*Passer domesticus*		25/1	
Total (NISP/MNI)		7/5	25/1	82/14

Kardoskút–Hatablak	Ópusztaszer	Ordacsehi–Kistöltés	Szarvas–Rózsás	Tiszalök–Rázom	Túrkeve–Móricz	Üllő 9	Visegrád–Castle Garden
11–13 c.	11–12 c.	10–13 c.	10–12 c.	11–13 c.	15–16 c.	10–13 c.	10–11 c.
						1	
	3/?						
		1					
					1		
							5/1
							1
				1			
17/?							5/1
		1					
1		1					
1					1		
			4/1				
						1	
							2/1
							1
17/?	5/?	3/3	4/1	1	2/2	2/2	14/5

TABLE 5.6 *Bird remains from settlements in central positions*

Vernacular name	Linnaean name	Bajcsa–Castle 17 c. (OP)	Buda–Royal Palace 14–15 c.	Esztergom–Alsósziget 12–14 c.
White pelican	*Pelecanus onocrotalus*	1		
Great crested grebe	*Podiceps cristatus*			
Night heron	*Nycticorax nycticorax*			
Great white egret	*Egretta alba*			1
Purple heron	*Ardea purpurea*	1		
Black stork/White stork	*Ciconia nigra/C. ciconia*			
Glossy ibis	*Plegadis falcinellus*			
Whooper swan/Mute swan	*Cygnus cygnus/C. olor*		5/1	
Mallard	*Anas platyrhynchos*		11/2	
Greylag goose	*Anser anser*		17/3	
Pochard	*Aythya ferina*			
Black kite	*Milvus migrans*			
Goshawk	*Accipiter gentilis*	1		
Sparrow hawk	*Accipiter nisus*	1		
Tawny eagle	*Aquila rapax*	1		
Imperial eagle	*Aquila heliaca*			
White-tailed eagle	*Haliaeetus albicilla*			
Buzzard	*Buteo buteo*			
Kestrel	*Falco tinnunculus*			
Capercaillie	*Tetrao urogallus*			
Black grouse	*Tetrao tetrix*			
Partridge	*Perdix perdix*		7/3	
Peacock	*Pavo cristatus*			
Pheasant	*Phasianus colchicus*		15/6	
Coot	*Fulica atra*	1		
Crane	*Grus grus*			
Great bustard	*Otis tarda*		1	
Woodpigeon	*Columba palumbus*	1		
Tawny owl	*Strix aluco*			
Stock dove	*Columba oenas*		2/1	
Hooded crow	*Corvus* cf. *corone*	1	1	
Raven	*Corvus corax*			
Total (NISP/MNI)		8/8	59/18	1

ANIMAL EXPLOITATION IN MEDIEVAL HUNGARY 163

Érd–Ófalu	Felsőnyék–Castle Hill	Gyula–Castle	Ocland–Kustaly Castle	Târgu Mureș–Castle Church	Pilisszentkereszt
17 c. (OP)	13–16 c.	15–17 c.	10–13 c.	14 c.	16–18 c.
2/?		2/?			
					1
					2/1
					3/1
		3/?			
		1			
					3/1
					3/1
					2/2
		2/1			
		1			
	1				
			4/2		
	1				
	1			2/1	
					2/2
		4/?			1
		1			
				1	
	2/1				7/1
2/1	5/4	14/?	4/2	3/2	24/11

TABLE 5.7 *Bird remains from urban settlements*

Vernacular name	Linnaean name	Budapest–Szt. György Square	Budapest–Teleki Palace	Budapest–Royal Palace	Pásztó–Gothic house
		13–14 c.	14 c.	15/16–17 c.	16 c.
White stork	*Ciconia* cf. *ciconia*				
Bean goose	*Anser* cf. *fabalis*				
Mallard	*Anas platyrhynchos*				
Common teal	*Anas crecca*				
Ferruginous duck	*Aythya nyroca*				
Black kite	*Milvus migrans*				
Buzzard	*Buteo buteo*				
Kestrel	*Falco tinnunculus*				
Lanner	*Falco biarmicus*		2/1		
Hazel hen	*Bonasa bonasia*				
Partridge	*Perdix perdix*	1	1		
Quail	*Coturnix coturnix*				
Pheasant	*Phasianus colchicus*				
Peacock	*Pavo cristatus*			1	1
Crane	*Grus grus*				
Woodcock	*Scolopax rusticola*				
Thrush	*Turdus* sp.				
Magpie	*Pica pica*	6/3	1		
Jay	*Garrulus glandarius*				
Jackdaw	*Corvus monedula*	3/1			
Total (NISP/MNI)		10/5	4/3	1	1

Muhi	Segesd	Cristuru Secuiesc CEC	Cristuru Secuiesc Manor House	Székes- fehérvár– Jókai Street	Vác– Széchenyi Street 3–7.	Vác– Széchenyi Street 4–6.	Visegrád– Calvary
13 c.	14–16 c.	14–16 c.	15–16 c.	16–17 c.	15–16 c.	15 c.	14 c.
				1			
	1						
1							
	1						
1							
							1
1							
			2/1				
			12/6				
1		1	4/2				19/?
			3/2				2/?
				9/1	5/1		
		1					
							1
			2/2		2/1	5/1	
			1				
4/4	2/2	2/2	24/14	9/1	7/2	5/1	23/?

CHAPTER 6

Mining in Medieval Hungary

Zoltán Batizi

A Brief History of Mining in Medieval Hungary

Mined goods were an integral part of medieval economies.[1] Mining was the only source of various precious, ferrous and non-ferrous metals, and a good part of salt production also came from mines. All these materials were essential for medieval artisanship and industrial production, while salt was essential in human nutrition. Besides these factors, medieval mining influences social change and settlement structure in several other ways. In Central Europe, mining was a major factor in attracting foreign settlers, who brought with them their technical expertise, but also their legal customs and various traditions. Mining across the region contributed to the formation of special mining towns, some of which become the focal points of economic prosperity in mining regions.

The Early Middle Ages

There is clear evidence of mining by the Romans in the territory of medieval Hungary. In the province of Dacia, the Romans mined gold around Abrud, Roşia Montană and Zlatna in the Transylvanian Ore Mountains. Tacitus, in his account of the Germanic tribes, mentioned gold mining by the Quades and Marcomans, peoples who at that time (the first and second century AD) lived in the northwestern part of the Carpathian Basin, areas of the modern-day Czech Republic, and southwest Poland. It is possible that these mines were located in the goldfields of northwest medieval Hungary. It is highly probable, however, that peoples of the Carpathian Basin had been extracting gold, perhaps not by mining, but by panning and on the surface, or collecting native gold from outcrops, for a long time before then. Archaeologists have also found evidence of iron being made from surface bog ore as far back as the early Iron Age.[2]

---

1   The most important work as concerns medieval mining: Wenzel 1880. More recent summaries of mining in chapters about the Middle Ages mostly repeat Wenzel's points (e.g. Benke 1996). For a further important overview: Zsámboki 1982a, 13–48.
2   Benke 1996, 30 and Zsámboki 1982a, 14–15 and 24–26.

It is also from archaeology that we know of the high-quality gold and other metal work brought by the conquering Hungarians from the Black Sea region. The Hungarians may have obtained some of the raw material for their jewelry directly from the ground. Since they lived along rivers in Eastern Europe until 895, this would almost certainly have been gathered by paning.

When they arrived in the Carpathian Basin in the late ninth century, the Hungarians found working salt mines in Transylvania. There were also people in the west of Transdanubia who to some extent specialized in making iron. Their number was subsequently augmented by miners taken captive in German areas during the plundering expeditions of the tenth century.[3]

The meager written sources concerning Hungary between the tenth and twelfth centuries contain no direct references to mining, and anything we know comes from archaeological finds, ethnographic analogies and toponyms in charters dating from between the eleventh and thirteenth centuries. The clearest evidence of iron production comes from excavated bloomeries. The large number of metal objects commonly found at excavations – metal parts of tools used for farming and household purposes, weapons and other personal objects – also suggests that the majority of these were made from domestic iron, smelted from local ore, and were not imported. There are settlements called Vasvár ("iron castle") both in western and northern Hungary, and the many early Árpádian-age ironworks reveal the presence of an iron industry, probably under the control of a chieftain, as early as the tenth century. It was common for the inhabitants of a village to specialize in a single trade in the tenth and eleventh centuries, leading to the village becoming known by the name of that trade. Some of the settlements whose names preserve the memory of metalwork trades (and the mixed Slavic–Hungarian population of the time) are grouped around the two Vasvárs; the rest are scattered throughout the kingdom. The old Slavic word *ruda* ("ore") is the origin of the *Ruda* in Rudabánya (*bánya* means mine in Hungarian), where metal ore was mined, and the related toponyms. Rednek, Rendek and Rudnok, as well as Vigne and Kovácsi (the Hungarianized version of another Slavic word meaning smith) refer to iron-ore mining and metal trades. Several other toponyms also appear to belong to this group: the Slavic-origin Rudna, Radna and Kazinc, the Hungarian Vasas ("iron") and Verő ("hammer"), and the Turkish-origin Tömörd and Tárkány. Some of the iron produced from the ore in the bloomeries must have been processed in the villages called Csitár and Csatár (from a Slavic word meaning shield-maker). The paucity of written sources has caused some historians of the tenth and eleventh centuries to ascribe great significance to

---

3   See the contributions of Beatrix F. Romhányi and István Draskóczy in the present volume.

toponyms derived from occupations. From their number, type and distribution within the Carpathian Basin, some of the former have attempted to deduce how the system and location of servant folk specializing in various trades evolved and operated in the early years of the Hungarian state. Other historians have challenged the reliability of this method, citing among their main arguments the fact – backed up by documentary evidence – that many craftsmen lived in villages whose names were unrelated to their trades. Metallurgy was not confined to places with names like Vasas, Rednek, Kovácsi, etc., but also went on in villages named after other characteristics, such as their apple trees (Almás) or their size (Nagyfalu).[4]

King Stephen I probably had his coins minted in Kovácsi (meaning a settlement of smiths) near Esztergom, using silver mined near what is now Banská Štiavnica. This follows from later – thirteenth century – written sources that mention the royal coins of that time as being made by "minters" who were inhabitants of this village. The Arab traveler Abu-Hamid al-Garnati wrote of the Hungarians in the mid-twelfth century that "they produce from the mountains gold and silver."[5] The first written reference to silver mining in the Banská Štiavnica area is in a document of 1228, which mentions an *argenti fodina* (silver mine) in the description of the boundaries of an estate near the town. The place referred to as "Bana" (*baňa* in Slovak means mine similarly to the Hungarian term) whose revenue provided the 300 silver marks a year that the king paid in compensation to his former master of the butlers (*magister pincernarum*) starting in 1217 can almost certainly be identified as Banská Štiavnica. The revenue probably derived from mining, although this fact is not stated. This place retained its name – the word for "mine" without any distinguishing prefix – from the foundation of the kingdom until the late thirteenth century, suggesting that it was the first mine to operate when the minting of silver coins began, and remained the kingdom's most important mining settlement for nearly three hundred years.[6] The high degree of expertise and experience required for extracting precious metals and for mining in general, even in the Middle Ages, was something possessed by only a few inhabitants in Hungary. Consequently, kings and landowners were frequently obliged to bring in foreign settlers, mainly from Austrian and German lands. It was probably the

---

4 On early metallurgy and on the two metal-producing centers: Heckenast et al. 1968. Heckenast and Györffy drew attention to the role of place names in the dispute about servant folk. See: Heckenast 1970 and Györffy 1972, 261–320. On the counter arguments: Kristó 1976. On the origin of the different toponyms: Kiss 1997a.
5 Hrbek 1955, 208.
6 For the charter evidence on Banská Štiavnica see: Györffy 1963–1998, III, 243–247.

boom in silver mining that brought German-speaking miners to what are now called the Slovak Ore Mountains and to the region of the town Rodna in Transylvania.[7]

The author of the *Gesta Hungarorum*, Anonymus, who wrote his gesta in the thirteenth century, knew of salt mines in Transylvania and gold paned from the rivers, and projected these activities on to his account of the Hungarian Conquest.[8] The River Arieş (in Hungarian, Aranyos, "golden") in the Transylvanian Ore Mountains earned its name from the ore it carries in its waters. Paning for gold was also mentioned in two ore-rich areas of northern Hungary in the late thirteenth century and in 1337.[9]

Some early toponyms indicate primitive gold mining that exploited outcrops. The foundation charter of Hronský Beňadik Abbey, dating from 1075, mentions a place called Aranyas beside the River Arieş in Transylvania. A census of the estate of Bakonybél Abbey in 1086 mentions a *mons aureus*, or "golden hill".[10] The name of Zlatna in Transylvania derives from the southern Slavic word *zlato* (meaning gold).[11] This implies that gold was mined here by the Slavs who gave the town its modern name, as well as the Romans, who are known to have been active in mining in the area. Gold mining in the Kingdom of Hungary, particularly the Transylvanian Ore Mountains, became very productive in the second half of the Árpádian age. Written sources from around 1200 tell of substantial precious metal exports to Austria and Venice.[12]

One characteristic of natural ore deposits is that they rarely contain non-ferrous metals in isolation. Rocks bearing mainly silver or copper frequently contain small quantities of gold, and gold mines often produce some copper ore. Because of their much lower value, the early sources rarely mention non-ferrous metals other than gold or silver. A rare exception is the inclusion of copper in a list of goods transported from Hungary to Austria around 1200.[13] We have much more information on Hungarian mining from the second half of the thirteenth century, when operations escalated and related documents

---

7   Wenzel 1880, 23–24 and Zsámboki 1982a, 15–16. On Kovácsi next to Esztergom: Györffy 1963–1998, II, 271–273. The perambulation of 1228 in the surroundings of Banská Štiavnica: Györffy 1963–1998, II, 433.
8   Rady and Veszprémy (eds.) 2010, 60–61 (cap. 25).
9   Györffy 1963–1998, IV, 56–57. The entire text of the 1337 Latin charter (misdated to 1307) Wenzel 1880, 318–319. A summary of the charter with good dating: Kristó et al. (eds.) 1990–2015, II, between nos. 134 and 135.
10 Wenzel 1880, 10–11 and 24.
11 Kiss 1997a, II, 798.
12 Benke 1996, 34–35.
13 Wenzel 1880, 23.

became prolific. The 1255 Buda customs regulations mention copper, silver, iron, and lead among the commodities in trade. Lead was an ingredient of copper alloys, and essential to the contemporary smelting process for precious and non-ferrous metals. The account book of Banská Bystrica from the late fourteenth century mentions mercury produced by residents of the town. This operation was probably based in Ortut, half way between the town and the gold-producing Kremnica, because there is a source from the early sixteenth century that mentions old, out-of-service mercury mines. In addition, *ortut* is the Slovak word for mercury. Mercury was essential for the medieval method of assaying used when gold was bought.[14] The Esztergom customs regulations of 1288, defining the duty payable on lead and copper (which was twice as valuable), probably confirmed the rules from the decades prior to the Mongol invasion of 1241–1242.[15] Iron, lead and tin were mentioned among metals exempt from crown taxation in Jasov in 1290.[16] There is only indirect evidence, however, for the mining of tin in Hungary in the early period. Small amounts may have been produced at some sites that are known to have been worked later, in the modern times, such as Cinobaňa in what was Nógrád County.

The iron industry that grew up in western and northern Hungary around the two Vasvárs up until the thirteenth century must have supplied the raw material for forges in the rest of the kingdom, where iron ore was nowhere to be found. The smiths worked for the crown or large landowners, and transport and distribution were under central control. There is documentary evidence from the second half of the thirteenth century of iron being regularly supplied to the smiths of Pannonhalma Abbey from Vasvár in Vas County. Iron-producing sites at other points of the kingdom met some local needs. For example, sources frequently mention a mining operation around Pécsvárad (in the Mecsek Mountains). Research on this subject is supplemented both by archaeology and written evidence. Excavations of several settlements have found remains of bloomeries and/or iron slag. The iron industry went through radical changes in the thirteenth century. The ore in some areas was worked out, and some iron-producing settlements and their inhabitants fell victim to the Mongol invasion. In the second half of the century, the arrival of settlers from the West with more advanced mining and smelting techniques caused the iron industry to shift to new areas.[17]

---

14   Zsámboki 1982a, 23 and 30 and Benke 1996, 128.
15   Györffy 1963–1998, II, 260–261.
16   Heckenast 1980, 6.
17   Zsámboki 1982a, 25–26.

Several Árpádian-age iron ore pits have been found and excavated in what are now West Hungary and the neighboring territories of Austria. Iron ore was usually extracted from soft ground rather than hard rock, and the pits are in most cases a few meters deep and of similar width. The danger of collapse usually prevented pits or tunnels being dug deeper into the ground. Since iron ore could be found near the surface over a large area, it was simpler and safer to open a new pit than deepen an existing one, which required lining and reinforcing with beams. The bloomeries were set up near where the ore was extracted, usually near a river or stream. Such a smelter could process only a few kilograms of ore each time it was fired.[18]

The Transylvanian salt mines were worked continuously from the Hungarian Conquest onwards. The early seats of the Transylvanian counties (e.g. Dej, Turda, and Cluj) were all located near salt mines. Salt mining may also have started in the first half of the Árpádian age at Solivar (presently part of Prešov) in medieval northern Hungary.[19]

We know from archaeology and the study of historic buildings that stone from Árpádian-age quarries was mostly used to build forts and churches, although some – including marble – was also occasionally used for royal palaces and the residences of prelates and high lords. In the thirteenth century, increasing numbers of town houses started to be built with stone cellars. Limestone, easily-worked but durable, was the favored stone for building. The settlements which grew up beside quarries of good building stone maintained a high level of expertise in quarrying and stone-carving for several centuries, and received orders from far afield.[20]

Limestone was also needed for the lime used in building. Some of the quarries still working today are known to have opened in the Middle Ages, although this very continuity makes their origins difficult to trace, because early workings have been obscured by the activity of later generations.

Most medieval vessels for storing, cooking and serving were made of clay. The same raw material was used for lamps, house walls, floors, ovens and fireplaces. Despite its universality, we know little about where or how the clay was extracted. The problem is similar to that of quarries. The clay pits near some settlements may have been the same as those used in the twentieth century. Those which were abandoned would have swiftly deteriorated, disappeared and become unrecognizable, or at least be impossible to date for lack of finds.

---

18   For an overview of ore mining and working: Heckenast et al. 1968.
19   Draskóczy 2002 and Draskóczy 2005.
20   For a good overview of the problem: Kőfalvi 1980, 241–282.

Later Middle Ages

King Béla IV had plans to bring in settlers when he ascended the throne, although they only started to be realized after the Mongol invasion. With a view to raising sovereign revenues, many mining settlements were founded and some remote forest villages in the Transylvania Ore Mountains and North Hungary were raised to the status of towns in the second half of the thirteenth century. Some decades later, a mining region grew up centered on Baia Mare in the east of Szatmár County.

These events changed the legal status of mining and mines and the social status of mine workers, mostly German speakers, who now formed a considerable part of the population.[21] Mines in the early Árpádian age were appurtenances of the land on which they lay, and so could be worked by ecclesiastical or secular landlords as well as the king. The landowners also took ownership of the precious metals that were mined. In the thirteenth century, the crown adopted from the Holy Roman Empire the institution of mining *regale*. This made mining of precious metals as well as copper a royal privilege, and the king could take possession of land on which they were discovered. Consequently, the king frequently took land away from private landlords who discovered precious metals and intended to open mines. In most cases known from the thirteenth century, the landowner was compensated with land of equal size, but received none of the profits from gold or silver mining. It was only by exceptional royal grace that some nobles or bishops were allowed to keep their mines and enjoy the revenue.

The German freemen miners, like the other *hospites* ("guests") enjoyed many privileges and freedoms (free election of judge and priest, tax benefits, customs duty exemption, freedom of movement, etc.) from the king or landlord who settled them. The wealthiest of their villages grew into free royal towns, and the lesser villages, including those on private and ecclesiastical estates, became *oppida*, market towns.[22] Mining society became more differentiated as the industry developed. The mining entrepreneurs who ran the mines and traded the metal lived in the center of the town, separate from the skilled and unskilled mineworkers in the outskirts, or beyond. This stratification was not rigid in the early centuries, and there are recorded examples of social mobility in both directions. For a long time, a middle stratum of mine workers with some

---

21 For a recent general overview of mining in medieval Germany, with several references to Central European and Hungarian mining: Bartels and Slotta 2012.

22 See the chapters by István Petrovics and Katalin Szende in the present volume. On mining town privileges, see Weisz 2013a.

entrepreneurial status existed between the wealthy mine-owning metal merchants and the hired laborers. New mining technology also came to Hungary from the West, brought by settlers. They also brought expertise in prospecting, and within the hundred years or so following the mid-thirteenth century, all of the ore-bearing areas in the kingdom had been discovered, and their exploitation commenced. This led to a sudden boom in the precious metal production of Hungary in the second half of the thirteenth century. At that time, the emphasis was on silver, the raw material for the coins which were in circulation at the time, denars; documents from that period much more seldom mentioned gold mines (such as Rimavská Baňa, Jasov and Pezinok). Gold sometimes occurred alongside silver as a 'by-product'.

The developments of the second half of the thirteenth century, what is often looked on as the first golden age of Hungarian mining, came to a halt for a few decades during the wars over the throne after the Árpádian dynasty died out in 1301. The weakening of sovereign power and lack of law and order worked to the detriment of the mines.

Around 1320, King Charles I managed to extend his power over the entire territory of the kingdom, including the mining regions in the Carpathians. His economic and financial reforms fundamentally changed the structure of precious metal production in Hungary. What had previously been the kingdom's only coin, the relatively low-value denar, was joined in 1325 by the gold florin, which was of durable value – i.e. was not subject to the annual exchange obligation. The changeover from silver to gold in the cash economy shifted attention to gold in mining and smelting too. Within a few years, new sites based on gold mining had been set up and were flourishing, gaining ascendancy over the previously central silver mining areas. The laws of Charles I resulted in unprecedented development of mining. Inhabitants of royal mining towns and mining settlements could freely prospect for ore anywhere in the kingdom. The king no longer stripped the landowner of title to land where gold or silver was found and a mine was opened, although the mine still worked for the crown. To give ecclesiastical and secular landlords an incentive to prospect for ore deposits, after the Árpádian-age antecedents, Charles I assigned them one third of the *urbura* or rent payable to the king by mine-operators in the whole country. *Urbura* was paid by mine operators, the entrepreneurs contracted to the crown; this was equivalent to one tenth of the gold produced and one eighth of the silver and other metals. Charles I established a monopoly in precious metal, obliging everyone to redeem the gold and silver they mined. It was forbidden to trade in this or take it out of the country. The royal chambers took a 40 % profit on the gold and silver, meaning that the mine operators who redeemed it received in return coins containing that much less gold and silver.

At that time, mining precious metals was a lucrative business even at that rate of redemption, because the gold came from the surface or only just below it.[23]

The measures taken by the first Angevin king gave mining an unprecedented boost. The kingdom's yield of gold and silver was highly variable, often changing from year to year. The discovery of a new goldfield could abruptly increase the annual output, and the working-out of a large mine, or its flooding by groundwater, could reduce it just as suddenly. Even given these fluctuations in production, there is a generally-accepted estimate that Hungary's mines produced at least one third of the known world's gold output, and 80–90 % of Europe's, in the fourteenth century.[24] The crown was concerned with silver as well as gold: several gold-producing settlements were granted charters as towns, and the freedoms of existing towns were confirmed. Hungary's silver production had a distinguished place in Europe, too, second only to Bohemia. Some 2500 kilograms of gold and 10,000 kilograms of silver were produced each year. Signs of falling production proliferated towards the end of the Angevin period, but Hungary remained Europe's leading gold producer in the fifteenth century too. Earlier estimates put the annual amount of gold produced in the kingdom at the end of that century at 1500 kilograms, and silver at 3000 kilograms.[25] However, as recent research based on surviving chamber documents from the late fifteenth century pointed out, the number of gold florins coming out of the country's mints in the late 1480s could have been no more than 327,000.[26] This would have required some 1150 kilograms of gold each year.

Charles I divided the country among ten minting chambers, which collected the *urbura* as well as minting coins. At the chamber seats, raw gold and silver from the mines was assayed and weighed, and minted coins were paid out in exchange for the gold surrendered. The mint further refined the precious metal where necessary and struck new denars, *grossi* and gold florins. There was a count of the chamber at the head of each chamber, usually not a royal official but a wealthy entrepreneur who paid a fixed rent for the lease of the chamber, carried out all of its functions, and took all of its revenue. In order to maximize their revenue, the counts of the chamber had to keep track of everything due to them, which involved strict inspections of the mines under their control

---

23 On the transformations from the mid-thirteenth century to the reforms of Charles I: Zsámboki 1982a, 16–17 and Heckenast 1994, 80–82. Most recently on *urbura*, see: Weisz 2015b.

24 On the significance of gold florins from Hungary in the international market, see: Draskóczy 2004a.

25 Zsámboki 1982a, 17–18.

26 Gyöngyössy 2003, 62.

to determine how much ore was being brought to the surface. In addition to their financial function, the counts of the chamber held the position of judge over their own officials, the mines, the miners and the mine operators. This system fundamentally remained in effect until the end of the medieval period, although changes were made during the rule of Charles I's son King Louis I. The number of entrepreneurial counts of the chamber started to decrease in the second half of the fourteenth century, and more royal officials were placed in charge of the chambers.[27]

Written sources on non-ferrous metals in the late Árpádian age are most numerous in the case of copper. The first mention of copper (among items subject to fair duty in Buda) dates from the same year as the foundation and chartering of Banská Bystrica, 1255.[28] Having initially been a site of silver and gold mining, the town became the center of the copper mining industry of Hungary in the fourteenth century. Other large copper deposits were discovered nearby, at Ľubietová and Brezno. There was also significant copper mining in other parts of what are now the Slovak Ore Mountains. A common characteristic of nearly every copper field is that other metals were also mined there, or that the copper ore contained some gold or silver. A substantial proportion of copper coming out of the mines went for export, to markets as far away as England in the fourteenth century. There were exports to Austria even in the Árpádian age, and Venice was another important destination. Much of the copper was sold in an unrefined state.[29]

Hungarian mining appears from the sources to have suffered from a severe lack of home-grown capital. The mine-owner's job was relatively simple and easy as long as the ore outcrop or lode was wide and formed a rich strip which could easily be followed into the ground or the rock. Even then, mining involved substantial costs arising from processing the ore. Water-driven ore crushers and bellows built with the expertise of millwrights from the West started to appear in Hungary in the first half of the fourteenth century, and water-driven water-raising wheels towards the end of the century. The water to drive these mechanisms often had to be led in from a distance of several kilometers, requiring enormous excavations and/or the construction of wooden

---

27 Benke 1996, 60–61.
28 Štefánik 2004a.
29 Zsámboki 1982a, 23. On the town around the River Hron: Wenzel 1880, 52–68, to the settlements and the mining of the Spiš-Gemer Ore Mountains: Kollmann 2005, 47–122 and Štefánik 2004b.

channels.[30] Once they were built, their operation and maintenance involved considerable further expense. Then there was the enormous amount of wood which had to be cut for digging the tunnels and propping them up, for building other structures, and for firing the smelters; the latter required great quantities of charcoal. The separation of gold and silver also required glassware, which was made in local workshops.

Mines could be profitable even with such expenses for a while, but if the ore-bearing lode narrowed, or the pit ran into harder rock which was more difficult to hew, it soon started to make a loss. Mine operators frequently abandoned rich lodes long before they were exhausted because groundwater had burst into the workings at a rate that was impossible to drain or pump out. In that case, the water could only be drained by cutting an auxiliary tunnel under the first into which the groundwater could be drained. When a working pit was inundated, it could be several decades before an entrepreneur came along who was prepared to meet the costs of the drainage shaft in the hope of profiting from the mine's continued working.

Following its medieval golden age, which lasted from the 1330s to the end of the fourteenth century, Hungarian mining started to show signs of decline in the early years of the fifteenth century. The rich gold- and silver-bearing rocks near the surface had been worked out, and pits had to be dug ever deeper, in pursuit of poorer and thinner lodes. With the technology of the time, draining water from the mines was an enormous challenge. References to inundated, unworkable pits are regularly found even in late fourteenth-century sources. An entry in the so-called Gedenkbuch of the judge of Banská Štiavnica in 1385 gives an idea of how prevalent this problem was in the mining towns along the River Hron. It required any mine operator who ceased operations because of flooding, and had no intention of attempting drainage even in future, to relinquish operation in favor of others. The crown took several measures to support mining in the following decades. These privileges did not bear much fruit, and the production of non-ferrous metals dwindled steadily during the fifteenth century. In 1479, King Matthias exempted the inhabitants of the previously-burgeoning gold-mining town of Kremnica from payment of all taxes and *urbura* for several years, but still failed to stem the town's decline. Most of its mines were standing in water, and remained so for several decades.[31]

---

30   On fourteenth century technical innovations: Heckenast 1980, 3–10. On the long channel systems: Benke 1996, 14–15. See also: Teke 2003.
31   Zsámboki 1982a, 17–18 and Benke 1996, 68 and 78–79.

Hungarian copper mining reached its zenith between the late fifteenth and mid-sixteenth centuries. Its rise was in large part due to János Thurzó's technical and organizational brilliance, combined with capital provided by the German Fugger family. The technical advances were a new means of harnessing water power, the use of manual pumps, and improved means of raising water and purifying copper. The other major factor was the rising demand for copper in western parts of Europe. The introduction of new machinery and techniques also had a favorable effect on other branches of mining, although none flourished to anything like the same extent as copper mining.[32]

Iron production developed in the years following the Mongol invasion through immigration of large numbers of German miners and smelting workers, combined with the harnessing of water power. The center of gravity of the iron industry shifted to the Slovak Ore Mountains region, around Štítnik, Rožňava, Dobšina, Medzev and Gelnica. After the mid-thirteenth century, there was also a major change in technology. Smelters stopped using bog ore – obtainable near the surface – in favor of iron ore, which could be extracted only from deep pits.

Lesser iron mining operations in the thirteenth to fifteenth centuries were those of the Hron region, the valley of the Fekete-Körös River in Bihar County, Rimetea in Transylvania (from the early fourteenth century) and Hunyad County (from the fifteenth century).[33]

Mines and Mine Operators in Contemporary Sources

Until recently, research into mining in medieval Hungary relied almost solely on written sources. Narrative sources, laws and decrees, and – much more numerous but less informative – litigation documents and privileges have at least yielded a reliable list of the places where mining was pursued in the Carpathian Basin at that time. Since only a few dozen documents survive from the eleventh and twelfth centuries, we have extremely little information on this part of the Árpádian age.

To even partially lift the mist surrounding the history of mining, we must call upon the help of scholars of several disciplines. Data on different regions or towns can be mutually complementary, and by comparing them we can gain a much clearer insight into previously unanswered questions. We will now look

---

32   Zsámboki 1982a, 23–24.
33   Zsámboki 1982a, 24.

at some details of the beginnings and development of non-ferrous metal mining and metallurgy between the thirteenth and sixteenth centuries, a story that can be more thoroughly fleshed out than anything in the early Árpádian age.

Mines and lodes generally followed surface outcrops. In 1263, King Béla IV granted settlers in Partizanske Ľupča the privilege of seeking gold, silver and copper freely in the forests and fields if they paid the customary taxes to the king. Several settlements owed their foundation to the discovery of ore on the surface. One such was the former forest estate of Kremnica, granted a royal charter in 1328.[34] Elsewhere, already-existent but minor settlements started to grow when ore was discovered nearby. Despite their privileges, most of the newly-settled miners did not – indeed could not – give up farming, because the exhaustion or flooding of a mine could be followed by several decades when there was no mining activity, and no income. Most of the miners of Rimavská Baňa, in 1268, had land which they regularly tilled and sowed. Old, abandoned gold mines were mentioned there in 1271.[35] The more productive the mines around a village or town, and the more seams were being worked, the less the inhabitants were dependent on agriculture.

Where miners founded a completely new settlement in the uninhabited mountains, they took possession of the entire surrounding area and – usually – had free use of it. Sometimes, however, the miner-settlers found Hungarian- or Slavic-speaking people, tillers of the land with different ways of life, already living in their designated place of habitation. A good example is Nagybörzsöny, where there are both Slavic and Hungarian toponyms in the surrounding area indicative of native populations, who were then joined by German miners in the thirteenth century, and where mining activity was mentioned first in 1312.[36]

Some mining settlements are not recorded in any documents, and the only sources of data are archaeological and art historical. In many cases, church carvings and frescoes indicate a link to mining at some time. There are some undocumented places where only local Germanic place names or family names indicate the coming of an alien ethnic group which has long since assimilated.

We seldom have detailed information on the number of settlers, or the productiveness or means of mining operations. The large mining towns certainly had several pits in operation simultaneously. Elsewhere we hear only of one

---

34 For the Hungarian summary of the charter: Kristó et al. (eds.) 1990–2015, XII, no. 473. On Kremnica: Wenzel 1880, 44–51.
35 Györffy 1963–1998, III, 270.
36 For an overview of the archaeological and archival sources of the medieval settlements: Dinnyés et al. 1993, 205–207.

seam being worked. In such places, when the seam was exhausted, the miners either moved away or turned to farming or crafts for their living.

When a mine was opened – the point where an outcrop of precious metals was found –, only a few workers were required for the first few meters of excavation. The lode of silver-, gold- or other precious metal-bearing ore commonly had a thickness of no more than two spans, and sometimes only a few fingers; it was hewed by one or two miners with chisels, hammers and pickaxes. Since the rock around the ore had no value, as little as possible was broken, so that the tunnels were often very narrow. The miners had to crouch as they worked the lode, and the laborers were similarly bent over as they pulled out the baskets of ore by hand, or on their backs. In broader tunnels, the ore was carried by barrow or handcart. Where the lode descended vertically, pits a few meters across extended downwards to depths of several tens of meters. The ore was brought up either by laborers climbing a ladder with a basket on their back, or on a rope with a wooden hoisting mechanism. In the larger mines there were several such tunnels one under another, so that the ore had to be brought up several 'floors'. In the late medieval period, hoists were driven by workers on horizontal-axis treadmills or by animals, usually horses, walking around a vertical-axis mechanism. These were complex structures comprising several wheels and cogwheels of different sizes, and required special expertise to make and maintain. Similar techniques were used for raising water. The poisonous gases that filled the pits and hampered the work in a similar way to the water had to be led out through ventilation shafts dug for the purpose.

Detailed information about the mining in the Hron region around 1500 has been obtained from surviving regulations, decrees, accounts, descriptions and other related documents. Output was subject to wide fluctuation, as illustrated by the case of Špania Dolina near Banská Bystrica, where 25 miners were employed in 1535. This was just before the discovery of new copper deposits, and only eight years later – in 1543 – the number of miners had risen to 170. At nearby Hodruš in 1535, good ore was extracted for a short time, during which the mines and processing works employed a total of four thousand workers.

As soon as the lumps of ore were brought into the daylight, they were graded so that rocks not bearing copper, gold or silver did not go for further processing. This job was being done by women and children in Banská Štiavnica in 1515. After separation, the ore was taken by wagon from the mouth of the mine to crushers and smelters, which were usually beside rivers. (Before mechanical mills were used, the ore was crushed in opposing hand-driven carved-stone mills.) Having been reduced to pieces a few centimeters across, the ore passed to the smelters where it was heated to a high temperature to separate the nonferrous metals from the rock. The little smelters of the first half of the Árpádian age, taking a charge of only 2–3 kilograms, gave way to much larger versions that used enormous water-driven bellows.[37]

Smelting required large quantities of charcoal, so that each smelter kept a dozen or so woodcutters and charcoal burners busy in forests which could be quite far away. Where gold and silver occurred in the same lode, it was best to separate them. The chemical techniques for this probably came to Hungary with the large number of miners who settled there in the thirteenth century. The *aqua fortis* used for separation could only be withstood by glass vessels, so that it was metal-refining that launched glassmaking in Banská Štiavnica and other mining towns in the late Árpádian age.

In the late medieval period, the mine-owning entrepreneur was obliged to take the raw gold or silver resulting from the smelting and refining processes to the nearest chamber office. There, royal officials assayed the precious metal and redeemed it at the currently applicable rate, which started at 40 % in the reign of Charles I and diminished steadily thereafter. Copper was usually sold in the semi-refined "black copper" state in the late medieval period.

Outlook

Despite the numerous obvious and open questions which remain, it is clear that the metal mining of medieval Hungary was an integral element of European metallurgy from the time of St Stephen. Due to the natural resources and the immigration of foreign, primarily German-speaking miners, Hungary became one of the most important metal-producing countries in Europe from the late thirteenth century onwards, peaking from the 1330s. The market price of silver and especially that of gold could be significantly influenced by the opening or exhausting of mines in northern and eastern Hungary. It is well known that the golden florins given out by King Louis I during his military campaign in Italy in 1347–1348 resulted in a decrease in the exchange rate of gold. After the culmination of mining activity in fourteenth century, there was a clear drop in output, but until the sixteenth century Hungary was among the countries with the highest mining production in Europe (*see* Fig. 6.1).

---

37   For the data about mining in the area of the River Hron, as analyzed in the two last paragraphs, see: Benke 1996, 14–15 and 87–91.

MINING IN MEDIEVAL HUNGARY

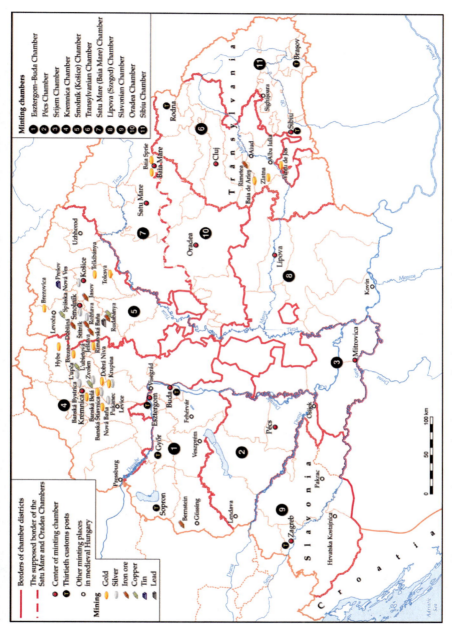

FIGURE 6.1 *Mining areas and minting chambers in medieval Hungary (drawn by Béla Nagy).*

CHAPTER 7

Salt Mining and Trade in Hungary before the Mongol Invasion

Beatrix F. Romhányi

Salt has always been one of the fundamental elements of sustenance. Not only do human beings need it, but animals and even plants, too. Carnivores get the salt they need from the blood of their prey, while herbivores and plants depend on other sources. Domesticated animals may obtain some of the salt they need with fodder, but in historical times their needs were mainly satisfied by grazing. Pasture near the sea contains more salt than continental pasture, which affects ingestion and milking capacity, especially of cattle and sheep. The use of salt deposits and salt-ponds can be proven at least since the Bronze Age, but in certain cases even from the Neolithic. Salt can be extracted from sea water (salt-ponds) or mined out of sedimentary salt deposits. Major areas where salt was made through evaporation include Italy (near Venice), Dalmatia, some of the Mediterranean islands (Sicily, Sardinia, Mallorca), Spain (Catalonia, Biscay), the Camargue, along the Atlantic Coast in Aquitaine and Brittany, southern England (Plymouth) and southern Ireland. Salt-ponds also existed on the northern shore of the Black Sea, as well as in and around the Crimea. Salt deposits can be found in certain regions of Germany, as well as in the Alps (in the region of Salzburg), in Soest, and the region of Halle an der Saale in Lüneburg. Important sites were located in Catalonia near Barcelona, and in English Droitwitch (as mentioned in the Domesday Book), but smaller mines were known in Bosnian Tuzla (the name itself means salt) and in Solivar near Prešov (modern Slovakia) too. These mines produced salt in furnaces; i.e., solubilized rock salt or brine was boiled until pure cooking salt was obtained. Two further European mining regions should be mentioned here: Transylvania and Maramureş, and the salt mines of Wieliczka and Bochnia in Poland. The latter mines were intensively cultivated only from the second third of the thirteenth century. The specialty of these mines was that the salt occurred there in the form of almost pure halite, thus could be used directly. This also meant that pieces of salt (blocks or drums) were cut in the mines[1] and sold in this form to

---

1 Cf. in *partibus Transiluanis sunt maximi montes de sale, et de illis montibus cauatur sal sicut lapides* – Górka (ed.) 1916, 46.

customers. Although many salterns were known from prehistoric times, they were not in use continuously: whether salt was extracted at a given site in a given period depended on demographic conditions, political circumstances and transport opportunities. Since salt did not spoil, it could substitute for money (until very recently, salt was frequently used in lieu of money as salary). However, unlike gold and silver, salt is used in consumption, and cannot be hoarded as treasure.

Early Salt Mining in Transylvania

The most important salt mines of the Carpathian Basin are in Transylvania and in the region adjacent to Maramureş. The major sites are Dej, Sic, Cojocna, Turda, Ocna Mureş, Ocna Sibiului, the 'Sóvidék' ("salt country") around Sărăţeni, and Sărata near Bistriţa in Transylvania, and around Coştiui in Maramureş. The latter salt region extends from Şugatag (Romania) to Solotvino (Ukraine), and is associated with several mines. The first traces of salt exploitation in Transylvania date back as far as the prehistoric times: in the Maramureş region, finds from the Bronze Age testify to early mine working.[2] The sites were known about throughout the last seven or eight thousand years, but this does not mean that they were in constant use. After the Roman occupation of Dacia, not only were metals extracted from the mountains, but also salt. Sărăţeni was called Castrum Salivum and was the center of salt administration in Roman Dacia. Archaeological evidence shows that the mine of Turda (Roman Potaissa) was also exploited. The Roman Empire tried to control trading routes even after it was forced to evacuate the province: recent archaeological research suggests that the gates of the amphitheater of Sarmizegetusa were blocked in the fourth century, indicating the presence of a Roman population even after the Roman military had left. Economic activity at the settlement is proved by the presence of Roman coins dating to the second half of the fourth century.[3] In the Migration Period, the Gepids (fifth–sixth centuries) and the Avars (sixth–eighth centuries) held the mines in Northern and Central Transylvania (cf. the two hoards found at Şimleu Silvaniei, the princely burials of Apahida, and the late Avar burials; e.g. at Câmpia Turzii). In the ninth century, the Bulgarians occupied some strategic points in southern Transylvania in order to control the mines of the region. Cemeteries for this population have

---

2 Bánffy 2015 for further literature on prehistoric salt mining. On the Bronze Age, see also T. Németh 2013.
3 Găzdac and Cociş 2004, 4, 17 and 21.

been discovered, for instance, in Alba Iulia, Blandiana and Zeligrad.[4] Their presence is also attested to in 892 when – according to the *Annales Fuldenses* – the Carolingian emperor Arnulf asked the Bulgarians to hinder salt transports for the Moravians.[5] Similarly, in the late ninth and tenth century the Hungarian elite took hold of the territories around Cluj and Turda, as reflected in the early Hungarian burials with horse and weapons in this area.[6] Medieval exploitation of the mines in the Maramureş region started in the thirteenth century. We do not have sources concerning the organization of salt exploitation and trade before the year 1000, but we assume that the mines became royal estate after the foundation of the Hungarian Kingdom.

Salt Exploitation in the Early Árpádian Age

Since salt was one of the most important minerals and trade goods of the Carpathian Basin, historians dealt with it as early as in the 1880s, although only in the context of the history of mining,[7] or of the economy of the medieval Hungarian Kingdom in general.[8] The first comprehensive piece of research on the Árpádian-age salt exploitation and salt trade was an article by Oszkár Paulinyi, who mainly clarified the evolution of *ius regale* on salt, but also dealt with the relevant parts of the so-called Oath of Bereg.[9] His interpretation was widely accepted until recently.[10] We do not have evidence about the eleventh and early twelfth century organizations through which salt was distributed. The profitability of the salt trade is reflected in the law of King Coloman who ordered the payment of tithes after toll and salt incomes.[11] The first element in the distribution system, Sălacea, is first referred to in 1067, but further hints to the existence of the royal salt depots emerged only from the twelfth century onwards (e.g. at Sâmbăteni, Arad, Szeged, and Vasvár). During the reign of King Andrew II, several depots are mentioned in the sources, some of them on the borders of the Kingdom (Bratislava, Sopron, Vasvár, and an unnamed depot in

---

4   Bóna 1987, 190. On the Bulgarian presence in the Carpathian Basin, see also Katona Kiss 2009. The name Zeligrad is of Bulgarian origin, meaning castle of salt.
5   Pertz (ed.) 1891, 121.
6   Gáll 2013, 656.
7   Wenzel 1880, 20–21 and Iványi 1911.
8   Hóman 1921, 14.
9   Paulinyi 1924, esp. 640–643.
10   Draskóczy 2008, with further literature.
11   Bak et al. (eds.) 1992–2012, I, 27 (Colom. §25).

Zala County[12]), along with others in the core territories (Sălacea, Szeged, and Székesfehérvár).

The existence of an early royal monopoly on salt appears to be supported by an incident which occurred between King St Stephen and the lord of the Maros Region, Ajtony, when the latter – allegedly – broke the law by hindering the transport of royal salt and imposing tolls on it at the riverside.[13] However, the story is known only from the Legend of St Gerhard, and this fact reminds the researcher to be very careful: the final version of this text was compiled in the fourteenth century, the earliest parts being from the twelfth century, but it also contains some elements dating back to the eleventh.[14] The main question is whether the relevant section can be dated to the early period.

Broad consensus also exists about the Oath of Bereg. The charter describes a royal donation of salt to a number of church institutions, mainly located along the Maros River.[15] This privilege is usually interpreted to mean that the different bishops, collegiate chapters and abbeys received the salt so that they could sell of their own volition. But does this interpretation really capture the meaning of the original text? Or was the donation part of a longer-lasting arrangement in Hungary? The number of complementary sources is rather limited; however, it is worth analyzing them using a common framework to better understand the system and help decide – if it is possible – what the intent of the 1233 charter was, and whether the privilege granted by the legate Jacopo Pecorari and sealed by King Andrew II survived throughout the following decades.

In total, we can identify about a dozen privilegial charters to church institutions from before the year of the Oath of Bereg that in some way refer to salt-related donations. Three of them are dated to the eleventh century. According to the foundation charter of the Benedictine Abbey of Pécsvárad (1015), the founder, King St Stephen, awarded significant salt-related privileges to the monastery, including the freedom to mine, transport and trade, without restrictions on quantity.[16] Alas, the charter is interpolated and was compiled

---

12 Karácsonyi and Borovszky (eds.) 1903, §277.
13 Madzsar (ed.) 1938, 489–490. Most probably, Ajtony imposed toll on the royal salt carried on land road from Sălacea or Csongrád to the south at the fords of the Maros River.
14 Madzsar (ed.) 1938, 464–466.
15 Knauz et al. (eds.) 1874–1999, I, 448. About medieval regulations concerning salt, see Kubinyi 1991d.
16 †1015: Györffy (ed.) 1992, 63–80 (with a detailed critical evaluation of the text). The formulation is very odd, and has no parallel in medieval Hungarian charters. It is also suspicious that neither the site of the salt mine, nor the quantity of salt are indicated. Furthermore, there is no reference to transportation.

in the 1220s according to the model of the privileges of the Pannonhalma Abbey. The relevant section is certainly false.

Another charter that mentions a donation of salt income dates from 1075: the foundation charter of the Hronský Beňadik Abbey. According to the text, King Géza II gave the abbey the toll paid after salt near Turda (in relation to its transport [?]).[17] In this case, it is clear that the monks were not directly involved in the salt business, but received some income from it in terms of money or in kind. Furthermore, according to the opinion of Boglárka Weisz based on two thirteenth century charters, the abbey acquired the toll as late as 1209.[18] If the abbey had some connection to the salt trade earlier, this must have been linked to its properties in the Transtisza Region (Tiszántúl) and in Csongrád (the ford of Bőd).[19]

The third eleventh-century donation is connected to the Abbey of Bakonybél (also Benedictine) which – allegedly – in 1086 or in 1092 received a number of salt-transporting boats on the River Maros from King St Ladislas. However, this charter was later complemented (in the first half of the twelfth century), and the paragraph in question belongs to this later addition.[20] The salt-transporting servants and boats were again clearly referred to in the 1130s when the property of the Abbey, after having been occupied by a certain Opus (*comes udvarnicorum* of the king), was restored.[21] Comes Opus did not act as a private person but as a royal official: he was probably required to control the royal incomes and to decide whether some part of them was illegally entering foreign hands. Taking this into consideration, we may suppose that in the first decades of the twelfth century it was not common for abbeys to take part in the salt trade and receive income from this activity.

Thus, we have three charters from the first century of the Hungarian Kingdom that mention different types of salt donations to three different Benedictine abbeys in western Hungary, but unfortunately all of them are either completely forged, or interpolated. Nevertheless, the privilege of Bakonybél Abbey did exist before 1131, as supported by the charter of King Béla II. In this case, the relevant question is: who gave the salt boats to the Abbey? The description of the donation is detailed, similar to the donation given by King Béla II to the collegiate chapter of Dömös, which would support its authenticity. In any case,

---

17 1075: Györffy (ed.) 1992, 206–218.
18 Weisz 2013b, 55–56.
19 Györffy 1963–1998, I, 892 and 899–900.
20 1086: Györffy (ed.) 1992, 247–249, 255.
21 1131: Erdélyi and Sörös (eds.) 1902–1916, VIII, 247.

the privileges of Bakonybél and of Dömös suggest that a new situation arose around 1100.

The first charter we have from the twelfth century is also problematic. According to this text, dated to 1137, but compiled in the first half of the thirteenth century, the abbey of Pannonhalma received two boats and the privilege to carry salt toll free to the abbey.[22] Nonetheless, these details do not contradict those of other, authentic charters.

In fact, the first really reliable charter certainly relates to the donation of King Béla II from 1138.[23] The privileged Dömös Chapter was founded by the king's father, Prince Álmos, thirty years earlier.[24] The description of salt transport is very accurate: the two boats from Dömös were permitted to go and return six times a year on the River Maros, and to transport 24,000 pieces of salt from Transylvania (we later define what weight this quantity refers to) to a place called *forum Sumbuth* (Sâmbăteni). The name of this settlement, situated on the right bank of the river, does not appear again in any of the documents connected to the salt trade, but it is located just opposite the Abbey of Bizere which played an eminent role in the salt trade in the second half of the twelfth, and the first decades of the thirteenth century.

The next charters are different; in 1148, King Géza II gave the Chapter of Óbuda the toll from boats carrying wine and salt on the Danube, among other things.[25] In 1157, the archbishop of Esztergom received the salt tolls of two villages north of the city of Nána and Štúrovo.[26] Similarly, the Abbey of Meseş[27] received a toll-like income in 1165 from King Stephen III: one block of salt went to the abbey from each salt-carrying cart that crossed the Meseş Pass.[28] Despite their differences, there is something similar about these two charters: the churches received only income, without participating in the salt business directly – just as in the case of the Hronský Beňadik Abbey.

An undated charter of King Stephen III contains particularly important information. According to this document, King Ladislas gave the toll of Sălacea to the abbey of Sîniob, but King Coloman cancelled this donation and burnt

---

22 MNL OL DF 206 811.
23 1138: Fejér (ed.) 1829–1844, II, 104.
24 For problems with the early history of the chapter, see Thoroczkay 2012.
25 Weisz 2013b, 307.
26 Weisz 2013b, 212–213 and 275.
27 The Abbey was built on the territory of the antique Porolissum. Its ruins can be found in the confines of the village of Mirşid.
28 1165: MNL OL DL 76 136 – Nagy, Nagy and Véghely (eds.) 1871–1931, I, 2.

the donation charter. However, King Géza II later restored the rights of the monastery.[29] Thus, the first king to award such privileges was St Ladislas before the end of his reign, but Coloman did not support the measures taken by his predecessor.

From the 1180s on, the charters not only multiplied but their content also changed. The first document in the series is the privilege given to the bishopric of Nitra in 1183. According to this text, the bishopric received three boats with the same rights as were granted earlier to the Abbey of Bizere and the collegiate chapter of Arad.[30] Beside the fact that the formulation refers to the earlier privileges of two other ecclesiastical institutions, the charters of which did not survive, it also gives the bishop the permission to have more boats and thus to transport the specified amount of salt in a single shipment instead of in three portions. This infers that – unlike in later periods – there was one type of boat used for this purpose. It is also worth mentioning that the town of Szeged occurs for the first time in this privilege, as an alternative harbor for unloading the boats.

In 1192, less than ten years later, the Abbey of Pannonhalma received the privilege of having three boats on the Maros and transporting salt to the abbey itself.[31] This time it is not documented how many times the boats would go and return. The privilege was repeated by King Andrew II in 1211, with the same formulation as the privilege of Nitra in 1183.[32] A number of further privileges granted by King Béla III and/or King Emeric are referred to by King Andrew II (see below) but the original charters did not survive.

In the thirteenth century, more churches received different salt privileges. Such donations were given before 1204 to the collegiate chapter of Óbuda,[33] before 1196 to the Cistercian Abbey of Heiligenkreuz in Lower Austria,[34] in 1217

---

29   Weisz 2013b, 348.
30   1183: Wenzel (ed.) 1860–1874, XI, 48.
31   1192: Wenzel (ed.) 1860–1874, VI, 183. The privilege was repeated in 1211 (Wenzel [ed.] 1860–1874, VI, 348–349).
32   1211: Wenzel (ed.) 1860–1874, VI, 349.
33   1212: Fejér (ed.) 1829–1844, III/1, 123. By this charter King Andrew II restored the possessions of the Buda Collegiate Chapter awarded by his brother King Emeric before 1204, among them the salary.
34   1208: Weis (ed.) 1856, I, 39. The same privilege was repeated in 1217: Weis (ed.) 1856, I, 54. Confirmed in 1233 through the price regulations in the Bereg treaty in Wenzel (ed.) 1860–1874, I, 184 (1233).

to the Chapter of Zagreb,[35] in 1222 to the Teutonic Order,[36] and in 1225 to the Cistercian Abbey of Klostermarienberg.[37] In the same period (1217) another Benedictine Abbey (Szigetmonostor) received an income – namely 60 marks – from the salt sold in Bratislava, in compensation for half of the Pest toll taken by the King.[38] In 1232 we learn that the Abbey of Bakonybél received, some time after 1217, 30 marks of silver from King Andrew II, and the sum had to be paid from the income derived from salt by the officials of the King at Sălacea at Pentecost.[39] Last but not least, there is the Oath of Bereg itself, issued in August 1233 and including 29 institutions by name, and an unknown number of other churches which are generally addressed. This charter attempted to summarize the whole system of royal salt privileges that had begun to develop from the first half of the twelfth century. In fact, a whole series of charters connected to the Bereg oath were issued on 1st October 1233. Among the privileged institutions we find the abbeys of Pannonhalma, Tihany, Pornó, Szentgotthárd and Heiligenkreuz, and there is even a false charter for the Cistercian Abbey of Klostermarienberg dated to that day.[40]

Thus, we have two types of privileges describing how different ecclesiastical institutions participated in the marketing of salt. The first group – including Hronský Beňadik, Esztergom, Meseş and Szigetmonostor, but also Zagreb and the second privilege of Bakonybél and Pilis – enjoyed incomes through the tolls or received a certain sum of money or (eventually) salt from the chambers of Sălacea or Szeged. If the donation was given in salt, the privileged institutions could sell it, as in the case of the Zagreb Chapter. The other group – including all the institutions mentioned by name in the Oath of Bereg, as well as the Teutonic Order before 1225, Bakonybél, Heiligenkreuz, Óbuda, Klostermarienberg and Tihany – had either boats for salt transport and barns

---

35   1217: Wenzel (ed.) 1860–1874, XI, 148–149. In fact, the salary Heiligenkreuz received from the Hungarian king is dated to before the earliest similar donation given by an Austrian archduke (1219). Cf. Weis (ed.) 1856, I, 55.

36   1222: Zimmermann et al. (eds.) 1892–1991, I, 19. The authenticity of the charter is discussed in: Györffy (ed.) 1992, 248–250.

37   1225: Wenzel (ed.) 1860–1874, I, 428.

38   1217: MNL OL DL 83 – Wenzel (ed.) 1860–1874, XI, 150. The text refers to the earlier donation of King Emeric. According to a later note on the rear of the charter, 40 marks should be given to the nuns of Margaret Island (the monastery was founded in 1252 by King Béla IV).

39   1232: MNL OL DF 292 176 – Wenzel (ed.) 1860–1874, I, 292.

40   According to the false charter of 1233 attributed to King Andrew II, the Abbey of Klostermarienberg would receive 1000 *zuan*s of salt from the Sopron salt depot. See Weis (ed.) 1856, I, 295.

for storage or only barns where they could keep the salt under the seal of royal officials (*salinarii*) and the local prelate until the dates given in the charters (27th August and 6th December). From our perspective, it is this latter group that should be investigated more closely.

To understand what the charters refer to, some details must be ascertained. First of all, the privileges reflect a coherent system as far as the measures are concerned. Even if there were some discrepancies in the outcomes of the measures, theoretically the terms were fixed, and there is no reason to think that any confusion would have been tolerated by the king or the royal officials. As a consequence, we should regard the Oath of Bereg and the charters connected to it as a shared system of contracts that applied to more than thirty ecclesiastical institutions, with fixed measures and fixed, coherent prices. Accordingly, even if there is still some hesitation among historians about whether the amounts of salt that are described can be identified and converted into modern units of measure, I would argue that the source can be unequivocally interpreted, with the restriction that the conversion of the quantities that are described into modern measures has its problems.

First of all, one should understand the character of the charters. Usually, such treaties were regarded as simple charters of donation according to which different churches were given a certain amount of salt that they were allowed to transport toll free across the country to their storage barns, and to sell without restriction. However, looking more closely at the text (see the Appendix) we must reject this simplifying assumption. The respective treaty is much more a freight and store concession, and the right of free sale is restricted to the case that the king did not pay on time. We can imagine that such situations could occur – King Andrew II often had financial problems – but the original conception was certainly that the churches should receive their money on the fixed dates. Thus, the sums listed in the text are not prices for salt, but refer to compensation for shipping and storage costs. This also means that we do not know the actual value of the salt – which was certainly higher than the sums paid to the churches – but we do know its quantity. Although we do not know how much salt was transported on the Maros, nor the percentage of total production it represented, we have at least a figure for the minimum amount of salt that was cut in the mines.[41]

---

41 We should also take into consideration that production was determined by several factors. On the one hand, it was certainly limited by technical conditions (production and transport). On the other, one must not forget the demands of the market. Although it was possible to store salt for years if necessary, the main purpose of production was create income from sales. Thus, there was no reason to increase production if there was no

The charters issued in 1233 after the Bereg treaty, most of them on October 1st, should be analyzed in more detail. At first glance, the privileges of the abbeys of Pannonhalma,[42] Tihany,[43] Pornó,[44] Szentgotthárd,[45] Heiligenkreuz[46] and Pilis[47] appear to have been issued simply because these institutions were not mentioned by name in the charter of Bereg. But then why do we find among them the abbeys of Pilis, Pornó and Szentgotthárd that are also listed in the Bereg oath? In order to supply the answer to this question, we must analyze the measures and the exact meaning of the units provided in the text.

The Measures

When speaking about the measures used in the Middle Ages, we face a number of problems. Since no unified system of measurement existed until the Modern period, the same units may refer to very different quantities. Furthermore, the exact meaning of the related words changed from time to time, and from region to region. However, even if the metric equivalent cannot always be precisely identified, the relationship between the different units can be established. For

---

need for the product on the market. To get an idea of the quantity of salt we are dealing with, we may examine the salt production of the Transylvanian mines in 1530s. In the early modern period, the five salt chambers produced more than 1.6 million pieces of salt (*sales curruales*) per year. This quantity was equivalent to more than 400,000 zuan, just four times the quantity recorded in the Bereg charter. According to written evidence, the production of the mines increased from the fourteenth century onwards. Cf. Draskóczy 2004d and Draskóczy 2014.

42   1233: MNL OL DL 206 929 – Wenzel (ed.) 1860–1874, VI, 520–521. The confirmation of the privilege given by King Béla III (1233): Wenzel (ed.) 1860–1874, XI, 258–259.
43   1233: Pannonhalmi Bencés Főapátság Levéltára (Archive of the Benedictine Archabbey of Pannonhalma), Tihany 1233 – Erdélyi and Sörös (eds.) 1903, X, 519. The text clearly states that the salt comes from the salt chamber in Sălacea.
44   1233: MNL OL DL 99 838 – Wenzel (ed.) 1860–1874, VI, 517–518. *Ecclesie vestre contulerimus mille zuanos, in Woswar a salinariis annuatim circa festum Sancti Joannis Baptiste* (24th June) *in prima via sine omni contradiccione, diminucione et dilacione persoluendos jure perpetuo.*
45   1233: MOL DL 99 839 – Szentpétery and Borsa (eds.) 1923–1987, I/1, 161–162. The Abbey is mentioned in the Oath of Bereg too, but in this charter its rights and incomes are described in more detail. The problem is discussed later in the text.
46   1233: Wenzel (ed.) 1860–1874, I, 184 and 302.
47   1236: Theiner (ed.) 1859, 143. Pope Gregory IX refers to the earlier donation of King Andrew II.

information on the measures used in medieval and early modern Hungary, the work of István Bogdán is commonly referred to.[48] According to this author:

1 *sal navalis* = 5.5 or 10 Viennese pounds = 3.06 or 5.56 kilograms;
1 *lapis* (*kősó*, stone of salt) = 37.80 kilograms;
1 *sal currualis* = 17 Viennese pounds = 9.52 kilograms;
1 *tyminum* (*tömény*) = 10,000 pieces of salt (no weight specified);
1 *tulkó* = a large plate of salt the size of which is not typically quantified; term only used in mines.

In the sources of the Árpádian age we find two further expressions. One of them is *zuan*,[49] which can be identified with the *kősó* in Bogdán's list. The *zuan* as a unit of measure need not have referred to one single piece of salt, although there is a source suggesting that there such large pieces existed.[50] Another measure appears to be a 'boat' (*navis*). It appears that as early as the beginning of the twelfth century, this unit did not simply refer to the vehicle used for transport, but also to a boatload as a measure. Since – unlike in the Modern period – the charters do not speak about different sizes of boats (e.g. the bishop of Nitra was allowed to have 'more boats', not bigger ones) we may assume that a standard-size boat was used on the Maros in the twelfth and the first half of the thirteenth century for salt transport. Fortunately, we have some idea what sort of vehicle this may be, since the imprint of a log boat was recently found during the excavation of Bizere Abbey.[51] This boat was approximately 12 meters long and 1.5 meters wide, and made of oak. Similar types have been found in the River Dráva and near the River Szamos.[52] The maximum loading weight of such a boat would have been approximately 6.3 tons.

Based on this information and the written evidence, the system of measurements can be reconstructed. The starting point is the "salaries" of the Dömös Chapter and the Cistercian Abbey of Szentgotthárd. Dömös received in 1138 24,000 blocks in six shipments of two boats. Thus, a log boat could carry 2000

---

48   Bogdán's works are available online: https://library.hungaricana.hu/hu/view/MolDigiLib_MOLkiadv4_07/?pg=0&layout=s (last accessed: 4 November 2016).
49   The origin of the word is quite obscure, its etymology unclear. Traditionally, linguists suppose that it is a Slavic loanword. However, it occurs in charters only between 1225 and 1233, which arouses suspicion.
50   1208: Weis (ed.) 1856, I, 39. *Preterea eidem cenobio tria milia salium qui regales dicuntur.* In 1217 the formulation of the same privilege is different: *donationem de tribus milibus zuanorum* (Weis [ed.] 1856, I, 54).
51   Rusu and Toda 2014.
52   Tóth 2010 and Tóth 2009.

blocks. This implies that a block weighed around 3.15 kilograms, corresponding to the weight of the late medieval *sal navalis*, specified as *sal aquaticus* in the charter of 1233. The weight of the *zuan* probably did not change – it was around 38 kilograms (37.8 kilograms, according to István Bogdán) at that time. On the basis of this knowledge, 1 *zuan* was equivalent to 12 pieces of *sal aquaticus*.

A larger unit of salt was also carried on boats, called *sal aquaticus maior*. This type appears in connection with the Chapter of Arad, the Cistercian Abbey of Igriş and the Knights Hospitaller. Based on the quantity given to the Chapter of Arad, 1 *zuan* equalled four pieces of *sal aquaticus maior* (i.e., around 9.45 kilograms, or three times the weight of *sal aquaticus*).

The price of *sal aquaticus maior* is given twice in the charter, and is slightly higher for the Cistercian Abbey of Igriş than for the Chapter of Arad (26 and 25 marks, respectively). The salary of the Knights Hospitaller is calculated on a completely different basis. In the first two cases, the reason for the variability may be the different transport distance (Igriş is more than 50 kilometers further from the Transylvanian harbors than Arad), or be connected to a task undertaken by Igriş Abbey,[53] but we do not know why the figure was different in the case of the Knights Hospitaller.

After these three items, the unit of measure changes in the charter. All the following amounts are given in *zuan*, although this unit is not always mentioned explicitly, while the salt was actually shipped in blocks of the normal size (*sal aquaticus*).

In the list of the privileged institutions, we find only these two types, but there is a further expression used in connection with land transport: *sal terrestris*. It is not by chance that this does not appear on the detailed list. The text speaks in general about shipping costs, not the price of salt itself, and this is not different in the case of *sal terrestris* (*Pro salibus vero terrestribus dabimus unam marcam pro centum zuanis, si sales suos debeant habere in confiniis, excepto monasterio S. Gothardi, cui pro octoginta zuanis dabimus unam marcam*). The sum mentioned is marginally higher than in the case of normal

---

53 Although neither this document nor other written evidence hints that the Abbey of Igriş undertook any additional tasks. However, further investigation is required: opposite Igriş is the village of Şeitin, the name of which refers to salt. North of it a canal system has been identified, leading towards the medieval settlement of Pereg (today, Kaszaper) which, based on C14 data, can be dated to the twelfth–thirteenth centuries. Thus, it is possible that these canals played a role in the shipping of salt, and that Igriş – the closest monastery to this transport route – may have controlled or maintained them. Since the archaeological investigation of the territory has only just started, this is a preliminary hypothesis. I am grateful to my colleague Zoltán Rózsa (Szántó Kovács Museum, Orosháza) for sharing his early findings with me.

river transport, and equals exactly the price specified in the Arad Chapter. The charter of King Andrew II issued on 1st October, 1233 tells us how the abbey received the salt. The king refers to a donation by his father, King Béla III, who gave the Cistercians of Szentgotthárd 20,000 pieces of salt (*viginti milia salium magnorum qui in curribus ad confinia Teutonie deferuntur*).[54] It is important that the charter repeats only the price and the method of calculation from the Bereg Oath while the amount of salt is stated in a different way – not in *zuan*, but in pieces of *sal magnus*. This means that the Abbey of Szentgotthárd stored salt from two different sources: 2500 *zuan's* worth of that which was carried on the Maros, and 20,000 pieces of *sal magnus* that arrived from another direction, carried on the land road to Sălacea, and then to other places around the country. Thus, *sal magnus* is determined to be equivalent to *sal aquaticus maior*, the later *sal currualis*. The system of measures was thus as follows:

1 *zuan* (*sal regalis*) = 4 *sal magnus* = 4 *sal terrestris* = 4 *sal aquaticus maior* = 12 *sal aquaticus*

Although Szentgotthárd can be identified as one of the largest salt depots, storing 7500 *zuan* (283,500 kilograms) a year, the same amount was administered by the Abbey of Igriş. The whole quantity generated 86.5 marks of income per year, the major share of which, without doubt, went to cover shipping costs.

This case informs us that the Oath of Bereg mainly concerns salt transport on the Maros River, but also that there was another, probably even older route for exporting salt from Transylvania – through the Meseş Pass to Sălacea – and that other churches participated in this business too. Therefore, the expressions *sal aquaticus* and *sal terrestris* are not equivalent to the later denominations *sal navalis* and *sal currualis*, although the sizes did not change – at least there is no sign of this. *Sal terrestris* specifically referred to the salt carried on land from northern Transylvania, while *sal aquaticus* meant the salt shipped down the Maros River. One question is whether the two routes always remained unconnected.

Although the Legend of St Gerhard speaks about the conflict between King St Stephen and Ajtony over salt transport on the river, there is no direct evidence for the existence of this route before the twelfth century. In fact, it is not only the lack of written evidence, but the lack of institutional background that should be noted. Hardly any central settlements existed in the region before 1100. The town of Cenad, which was the seat of the bishopric, was certainly one

---

54   1233: MNL OL DL 99 839 – Szentpétery 1923, 1/1, 161–162. The false charter of the Klostermarienberg Abbey followed this formulation (cf. fn. 41).

of them, but the early existence of Arad and Szeged is doubtful. In Arad, the collegiate chapter was founded in the first half of the twelfth century, probably by King Béla II, and the earliest church of Szeged was also built in the twelfth century – at least according to the archaeological evidence. The chain of monasteries, whose participation in salt transport is documented from the second half of the twelfth century, also emerged – according to the archaeological data – after 1100. Another hint is that the Oath of Bereg contains detailed regulation about river transport, while land transport appears only in the context of price regulation, suggesting that land transport was older, and the system was well known and established. The relative novelty of river transport is supported by a false charter, too, according to which Pannonhalma Abbey received three boats on the Maros in 1137. In fact, the document was written around 1228, but it is probably not by chance that the falsifier dated it to the 1130s – in this respect, he was more skilled than the scribe of the Pécsvárad Abbey who dated his false charter to the beginning of the eleventh century.

Coming back to the issue concerning the charters issued in 1233 after the Oath of Bereg, it appears that several monasteries were not, or not only, involved in the salt business along the Maros. The Cistercian Abbey of Szentgotthárd had privileges for both directions, while the Abbey of Tihany seems to have been involved only in trade via the land route.

The total quantity distributed in the charter of Bereg was 89,000 zuan (approximately 3364 tons). After adding the quantities known from other charters, the amount totals 105,700 zuan (nearly 4000 tons). Supposing that the quantity carried on the two shipping routes was more or less equal, total production was at least 190,000 zuan (approx. 7200 tons). To put the importance of the Transylvanian salt industry into perspective, the yearly production of Lüneburg, the major center of the Nordic salt industry, was estimated at around 1200 to 5200 tons.[55]

As far as the value of the salt is concerned, it is difficult to calculate. Based on the toll regulation of Buda issued by King Béla IV in 1255, the value of one piece of salt (*sal terrestris/magnus*) was 10 denars, and 10 zuan of salt was worth 1 mark. This information suggests that the value of salt recorded in the Bereg treaty was 8900 marks. The sum promised to churches for shipping and storage was around 10 % of this value (884.6 / 932.6 marks). Furthermore, the cost of production should be clarified. In the second half of the thirteenth century, production costs amounted to 1/30th of the value of the salt,[56] but

---

55 Witthöft 1976, 104–106. Production in Lüneburg increased to 15,000 tons by the end of the thirteenth century.
56 Knauz et al. (eds.) 1874–1999, I, 478.

before the Mongol Invasion, when miners were servants of the king, the cost was probably less. In the 1230s, the estimated value of the total quantity of salt exploited per year was at least 18,900 marks. After deducting an average of 12 % for costs, the remaining income was nearly 16,700 marks (with some part of the salt remaining in Transylvania, it probably exceeded 17,000 marks). This estimation is slightly higher than the 16,000 marks listed on the income register of King Béla III.

It is also worth examining the proportions of different orders, and other church institutions. The bishops and the collegiate chapters received around 40 % of the total quantity, the Benedictines and the Cistercians around 25 % each (the Benedictines had a slightly larger share), and the remaining 10 % was shipped and stored by the Knights Hospitaller. The income register of King Béla III[57] suggests that shipping and storage costs were at least 7 % of the income derived from the salt (the part we know of). Addition of the total amount of other known salaries, and the estimated value of the salt received by Meseş Abbey (at least 500 *zuan*), we find the total value of the silver promised to the churches to be at least 1355 marks – a large sum, but scarcely more than the 0.5 % of royal income in King Béla III's time.

While the treaty of Bereg was very advantageous for the church, it was extremely disadvantageous for the king. On the one hand, the different ecclesiastical institutions obtained the right to carry the salt from mines to depots, and to store it until a predefined date. They also received a fix sum in good silver for this purpose from the king – later paid in foreign currency –, and in addition, they obtained the right to use an unlimited portion of the salt for their own purposes and to sell the salt freely if the king was late in paying. On the other hand, the king had to pay out a considerable sum of cash each year, he never knew how much salt had been used by the churches, and he risked losing all of it if he was unable to provide the privileged institutions with the money they were due. However, it should be emphasized that the ecclesiastical institutions did not receive the mines nor the salt as a property gift. The Bereg Oath described a concession to freight the salt from Transylvania to the official depots where it was stored under the seal of the royal official (*salinarius*) and the local prelate. Money was not paid for the salt itself, but to cover the expenses of the churches.

---

57   Barta and Barta 1993, 443–444.

Conclusions

In summary: what can be said about the Árpádian-age salt trade, and the charter of 1233 in particular? First of all, it must be emphasized that the legal framework of the salt trade appears to be fairly different from what we know from the late fourteenth century. From early times until approximately the end of the eleventh century, the production of Transylvanian salt mines was mainly transported via the northern land route using caravans and carts. In this early phase, the mines were already the property of the king, and the trade in salt belonged to his domanial income (in legal terms, it was not yet *droit de régale* in that period).[58] River transport began to develop by the turn of the eleventh and twelfth centuries. Church institutions, especially monasteries, were involved in salt transport rather early on; the first detailed description of the business model that we know of is the privilege of the Dömös Chapter. The breakthrough happened in the last third of the twelfth century when the number of privileged institutions multiplied: many charters issued by King Andrew II mention that the donation he confirmed was originally awarded by his father and/or brother. There are some traces of an effort to reorganize the salt trade around 1217: it is around this year (and also a few years later) that donations are confirmed, suggesting their earlier existence. The Oath of Bereg was designed to be the final treaty between the king and the church concerning the rights of the ecclesiastical institutions regarding the salt trade, involving most bishops with collegiate chapters, Benedictine and Cistercian abbeys, and the Knights Hospitaller. However, the Oath did not survive the death of King Andrew II. Instead of reconfirming Andrew's regulation (there are no transcriptions of the charter after 1234) his son and successor King Béla IV withdrew the concessions shortly after his accession to the throne, although he continued to support the monasteries from the income from salt.[59]

We have also learned that the units of measure were the same in this period as in the Late Middle Ages, but the denominations were different. They probably changed because of the opening of the Szamos route in the late thirteenth and early fourteenth century. From that time on, there was no reason to differentiate between *sal terrestris* and *sal aquaticus* in reference to two different freight routes.

---

58 About the issue in a broader context, see Paulinyi 1924.

59 Without further enumerating these charters, we refer to his donation to the Cistercian Abbey of Petrovaradin – which he founded – according to which the Abbey was paid the value of 50000 pieces of salt in Szeged. The infirming of the earlier privileges is also reflected in the series of false charters produced by the Cistercian Abbey of Klostermarienberg.

Ultimately, the process is part of the formation of the salt regale which – similarly to in other regions of Europe – probably appeared in the twelfth century, and went through considerable transformation before emerging in its late medieval form. The church played a significant role in this process by building up and managing the younger river route for about a century.

TABLE 7.1 *Salt donations to churches before 1233*

Name	Type of institution	Amount in the charter	in *zuan*
Bakonybél	Abbey (B)	3 boats/4×	2000
Bakonybél	Abbey (B)	30 marks	
Dömös	Collegial	24000 in 2 boats/6×	2000
Heiligenkreuz	Abbey (C)	3000 *zuan*	3000
Klostermarienberg	Abbey (C)	200 *zuan*	200
Nitra	Bishop	3 boats/3×	1500
Óbuda	Collegial	tyminii salium	2000*
Pannonhalma	Abbey (B)	3 boats/2×	1000
Pilis	Abbey (C)	100 marks	
Szentgotthárd	Abbey (C)	20000 sales magni in curru	5000
Szigetmonostor	Abbey (B)	60 marks	
Tihany	Abbey (B)	1000 *zuan*	1000
Zagreb	Chapter	50 marks	
Sum			16700

*Quantity received in 1233

TABLE 7.2 *Salt donations to churches in the 1233 Bereg charter*

Name	Type of institution	Amount in *zuan*
Alba Iulia	Bishop	2000
Arad	Collegial	500
Archbishopric of Esztergom	Bishop	2000
Archbishopric of Kalocsa	Bishop	10000
Bač	Chapter	10000

Name	Type of institution	Amount in *zuan*
Bishopric of Cenad	Bishop	5000
Bishopric of Oradea	Bishop	2000
Bizere	Abbey (B)	4000
Bulci	Abbey (B)	5000
Cârța	Abbey (C)	1000
Ercsi	Abbey (C)	1000
Gyelid	Collegial (?)	500
Hodosmonostor (Bodrogu Vechi)	Abbey (B)	1000
Igriș	Abbey (C)	7500
Izsó	Abbey (B)	1000
Kenéz	Abbey (B)	2000
Knights Hospitallers	Knights	10000
Óbuda[a]	Collegial	2000
Pilis	Abbey (C)	2000
Pornó	Abbey (C)	1000
Prešov	Abbey (B)	3000
Rohonca	Abbey (B)	4000
Székesfehérvár	Collegial	2000
Szekszárd	Abbey (B)	1000
Szentgotthárd	Abbey (C)	2500
Szer	Abbey (B)	1000
Szőreg (Szeged)	Abbey (B)	1000
Titel	Collegial	3000
Zirc	Abbey (C)	2000
Sum		**89000**

a The collegiate chapter received a donation of salt before 1204 from King Emeric. The evidence for this is the charter of King Andrew II (see above) which does not specify the exact quantity, but speaks only about *tyminios salium*. The original charter probably contained a donation similar to that given to Dömös and Szentgotthárd, in which the amount was specified in *sales navales* and *sales curruales*, respectively. The 2000 zuan given in 1233 corresponds to 24000 *sales navales*.

TABLE 7.3   *Total amount per type of institution in the 1233 Bereg treaty*

Type	Zuan	%	Mark	%
Benedictines	23000	25.8	220.8	25.0
Cistercians	17000	19.1	169.2	19.1
Knights Hospitallers	10000	11.2	120.0	13.6
Bishops	31000	34.8	297.6	33.6
Collegiate chapters	8000	9.0	77.0	8.7
Sum	**89000**		**884.6**	

TABLE 7.4   *Total amounts per type of institution (to institutions not mentioned by name in the Bereg charter)*

Type	Zuan	%
Benedictines	27900	25.6
Cistercians	28200	25.8
Knights Hospitallers	10000	9.2
Bishops	32500	29.8
Collegiate chapters	10500	9.6
Sum	**109100**	

Appendix

Detail of the Oath of Bereg
20th August, 1233, in the Bereg Forest
Prímási Levéltár Esztergom (Esztergom Primate Archives) Lad. V nn. 2 & 3 (MNL OL DF 248 771).
Edition: Fejér (ed.) 1829–1844, III/2, 320–323.

Item volumus et concedimus, quod ecclesie libere portent sales suos ad ecclesias ipsas, et ibi sub sigillo salinariorum, et prelati illius eccleie, in qua sales deponuntur, qui pro tempore fuerint, deponantur, depositique serventur usque ad octavas S. Stephani Regis (*27th August*), et tunc ab illo die usque ad nativitatem B. V. Marie (*8th September*) solvatur eis argentum pro salibus, quos tunc ecclesie habuerint penes se, secundum

SALT MINING AND TRADE IN HUNGARY BEFORE THE MONGOL INVASION 201

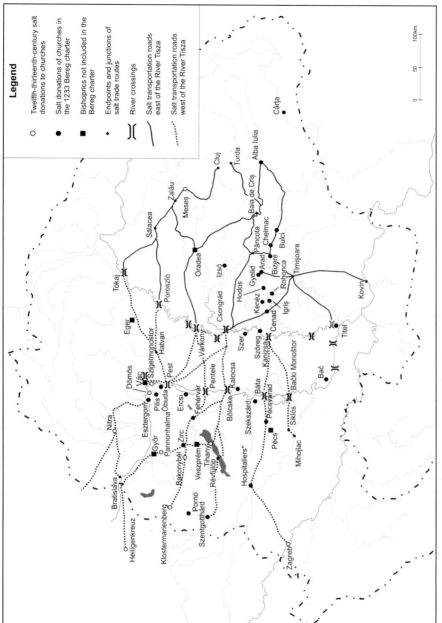

FIGURE 7.1 *The organization of salt transportation before the Mongol invasion.*

estimationem inferius adnotatam. Et si in illo tempore ipsi salinarii ipsos sales non emerent, et ecclesiis argentum, secundum dictam aestimationem, non solverent; ex tunc omni tempore sales illos in proprium usum ecclesiae percipientes, vendant iuxta sue arbitrium voluntatis, et omne lucrum, quod deberemus nos, vel alius rex, qui pro tempore fuerit, vel ipsi salinarii, inde percipere, totaliter cedat in usus ecclesiarum. Nec a salinariis ipsis, vel nobis, vel aliis personis, aliquatenus molestentur, quin possint, quidquid placet eis, facere semper de salibus, ex quo in dicto termino non fuerit eis pecunia persoluta. Item dicimus de secundo termino, ut a festo S. Nicolai (*6th December*) usque ad festum Beati Thome Apostoli (*21th December*) pro salibus, quos apud se habebunt ecclesie sub sigillo salinariorum, solvatur eis argentum secundum aestimationem adnotatam. Quod si factum non fuerit, idem fiat, quod in casu superiore de salibus dictum est.

Argentum vero, quod praedictis ecclesiis persolvetur, erit in bonis Frisaticis, vel in argento, cuius decima pars comburetur. Precia vero salium sunt haec:

> quod pro quolibet timino salium aquaticorum, persoluentur ecclesiis octo marce, excepta domo hospitalis Hierosolymitani, et ecclesiis Colocensi, et Bachiensi, quibus pro quolibet tymino dabimus decem marcas, si dictae ecclesie Colocensis et Baachiensis debeant deferre sales suos in Zegedyn, vel ultra, alioquin octo marcas habebunt. Pro maioribus vero salibus aquaticis, debemus abbacie de Egrus XXVI marcas pro quolibet timino, et ecclesie Orodiensi XXV similiter pro quolibet timino. Pro salibus vero terrestribus dabimus unam marcam pro centum zuanis,[60] si sales suos debeant habere in confiniis, excepto monasterio S. Gothardi, cui pro octoginta zuanis dabimus unam marcam. Nos vero, et quicunque fuerit rex pro tempore, debemus mittere sales ad confinia, secundum tenorem privilegiorum ecclesiarum, et deponi debent in domibus privilegiatorum, ubi stabunt sub sigillis salinariorum usque ad predictos terminos. Et eodem modo omnia serventur a nobis et ab ipsis, sicut dictum est in terminis supra dictis.

---

60 The tradition of giving the price of the salt per 100 pieces was long lasting. In 1397, King Sigismund issued a regulation on the price of salt (MNL OL DL 8861) according to which 100 pieces could be sold for 3 florins in Buda. Cf. Wenzel 1880, 438. In 1511, in a contract between the exchequer Gabriel Perényi and Ambrosius Sárkány de Ákosháza, we learn the actual value of *sal currualis*: Four florins for 100 pieces – higher than the price of the salt fixed by King Sigismund in the early fifteenth century. The amount given by the exchequer is considerable: 25000 pieces of salt weighing altogether 236250 kilograms (more than 110 loads). Cf. Tringli (ed.) 2008, no. 761 (11 November 1511).

Ecclesiae vero retinebunt de salibus suis ad usus suos hoc modo:

> abbacia de Egrus tres timinos;
> praepositus Orodiensis cum capitulo suo duo millia lapidum;
> Hospitale Hierosolymitanum cum omnibus domibus suis de Hungaria IV timinos de talibus salibus, quales habet monasterium de Egrus;
> monasterium S. Gotthardi duo millia et 500 zuanos;
> ecclesia Varadiensis 2000;
> ecclesia de Pernoch 1000 zuanos;
> ecclesia de Zeer 1000 zuanos;
> ecclesia Colocensis unum timinum;
> ecclesia Bachiensis unum timinum;
> ecclesia Albensis Transiluana 2000 zuanorum;
> ecclesia de Bulch 5000;
> ecclesia de Epuryes 3000;
> ecclesia de Bistria 4000;
> ecclesia de Zadust 1000;
> ecclesia de Ysou 1000;
> ecclesia de Roncha 4000;
> ecclesia de Kenaz 2000;
> ecclesia S. Philippi 1000;
> ecclesia de Geleth 500;
> ecclesia de Saxsvar 1000;
> ecclesia Cenadiensis 5000;
> ecclesia Titulensis 3000;
> ecclesia de Chod 1000 zuanos;
> ecclesia Strigoniensis 2000 zuanorum;
> ecclesia Albensis totidem;
> ecclesia Budensis 2000;
> ecclesia de Bokan 2000 zuanorum;
> ecclesia de Pelis totidem;
> ecclesia de Kercz 1000 zuanos.

Aliae vero ecclesiae, quarum nomina non exprimuntur, recipient ad usum suum, secundum quod praelati earum in animas suas dixerint.

Item volumus et consentimus, quod sales in salisfodinis non vendantur carius, quam antiquitus vendi consueverint ecclesiis, quae consueverunt emere sales. Pro reditibus vero ecclesiarum, qui hactenus subtracti sunt in salibus, exceptis decimis, persolvemus 10000 marcarum per quinque annos continuos; qui anni incipiunt computari a proximo Pascha resurrectionis Dominicae; et solutionem faciemus hoc modo:

in primo anno in nativitate B. Virginis solvemus 1000 marcas; in festivitate S. Thome Apostoli 1000 marcas alias; et sic postea quolibet anno continue faciemus, quousque dictam pecuniam decem millia marcarum persolvamus, et totam istam pecuniam persolvemus in dictis terminis; episcopo Cenadiensi, abbati S.Martini de Pannonia, abbati Egriensi (*recte* Egrusiensi), vel eorum procuratoribus, habentibus a dominis suis procuratorias super hoc litteras speciales; vel duobus ex praedictis, vel procuratoribus eorum. Et solvemus eam in domo Fratrum Predicatorum de Pest in presentia Capituli, vel maioris partis, distribuendam et ordinandam secundum voluntatem dicti legati de consilio Strigoniensis, et Colocensis Archiepiscoporum. Et nihilo minus, si praedictam pecuniam decem millia marcarum non solverimus, in singulis terminis, sicut superius est expressum, volumus et consentimus, quod ecclesie, quibus sales sunt subtracti, non obstante ista compositione, libere et integre sint in eodem statu et iure, in quo erant ante compositionem istam.

CHAPTER 8

Salt Mining and Trade in Hungary from the mid-Thirteenth Century until the End of the Middle Ages

István Draskóczy

Nihil enim utilius sale et sole
ISIDORE OF SEVILLE

∴

Introduction

There is salt under the ground in many places in the Carpathian Basin, the territory of the medieval Kingdom of Hungary. The richest deposits are in Transylvania and Maramureș (now in Romania and the Ukraine). Another important location is Solivar in Sáros County, Slovakia, where water from a salt well was evaporated. But the most significant mining areas in terms of output were Ocna Dejului, Sic, Cojocna, Turda, Ocna Sibiului and Albeștii Bistriței in Transylvania. In the Székely Lands, also in Transylvania, salt was mined in the "Salt country" (Sóvidék) or Ținutul Ocnelor. In Maramureș, the mines in Rona de Sus were in the ascendancy towards the end of the medieval period.[1] Salt was certainly mined in Transylvania from the Bronze Age onwards. When the conquering Hungarians invaded Transylvania, they took over mines which had hitherto been controlled by Bulgars. The *comes*' castles and castle estates set up there during the formation of the Hungarian state served to defend the salt mines, as well as the land. In Maramureș, medieval mining started only in the late thirteenth century.[2]

The salt mines became crown property when the kingdom was founded, and although ecclesiastics and, in exceptional cases, landed nobles also gained

---

1 Kubinyi 1988, 213–214 and Sófalvi 2005, 170–183.
2 Bóna 2001, 82–86, Vékony 2004, 655–661, Györffy 1963–1998, IV, 114 and Wollmann 1995, 136–137. For early mining, see the contribution of Beatrix F. Romhányi in the present volume.

possession of salt mines in the Árpádian age, the principal mining areas remained under royal control throughout the Middle Ages. This gave the king power over the mining, carriage and trading of salt, and as a result, salt accounted for 6.6 % of crown revenue in the late twelfth century. Since salt was an essential food and preservative, its place among the main commodities of the time was comparable to that of wine.

Merchants bought salt in the mining areas and transported it into the interior of the kingdom. In addition to the crown, some ecclesiastical institutions had interests in the transport and trading of salt. This was because the crown and the church were the largest landowners in the country, and their lands were home to large numbers of servant folk whose duties included various kinds of carriage. Salt was also a major foreign trade commodity, exported to the West, the Balkan Peninsula and sometimes to Poland. Foreign trade was also under crown control.

Data on salt mining and trade is more plentiful from the thirteenth century. Thus there is a quantity of data on the distribution of this mining good in the country before the Mongol invasion. However, the system sketched out in the preceding chapter by Beatrix F. Romhányi has to be completely reorganized to describe the time following the Mongol invasion in 1241–1242.[3]

Béla IV placed particular emphasis on salt revenues and took great pains to revive mining. Salt offices and salt mines were headed by chambers. Charters dating from the reign of Andrew III refer to the office of chamber count (*comes camarae*).[4] Crown measures to further the development of the towns included the offer of privileges to incomers who settled in mining areas. Transylvanian mining towns were settled by Germans.[5] Production and transport were put on a new footing.

Before this time, workers in the mines were legally servant folk, and transport was the job of other servants specialized in carrying salt for the crown or the church.[6] By the second half of the thirteenth century, charters were referring to freemen in connection with mining. The inhabitants of mining towns were responsible for mining, and in all of these towns they were entitled to spend seven–eight days cutting salt from the royal mines for their own benefit.

---

3 Jakó (ed.) 1997, no. 209.
4 Knauz et al. (eds.) 1874–1999, I, 478, Zimmermann et al. (eds.) 1892–1991, I, 166, 170, 182 and 293 and Weisz 2010a, 81.
5 Szende 2011a, 34–35.
6 On the legal situation of those living off church and royal estates: Bolla 1998 and Györffy 1972, 292.

When Béla IV's conflict with his son Stephen came to an end in 1262, the agreement they made covered salt in some detail, an indication of its importance to the crown as a source of revenue. The charter distinguished two kinds of miners. The group of miners referred to as *salifossores* was shared half-and-half between the King and his son Stephen. The other class of miners, *salium incisores*, were wage laborers hired by both parties at their own expense.[7]

A fragment of a thirteenth-century charter states that earlier a Hungarian abbey (Bakonybél) received 24 *mansiones* with a salt mine and three ships, *ut ipsimet lapides salis efodiant, fossatosque deferant*.[8] In 1248, the bishopric of Eger was granted *unum fossatum sive foveam salifodine liberam* in Ocna Dejului, with entitlement to freely *sales de eadem extractos* and to carry this free of customs duty by land and water to Eger.[9] An early fourteenth-century description of Hungary says of salt mining: *in partibus transiluanis sunt maximi montes de sale, et de illis montibus cauatur sal sicut lapides*.[10] This information suggests that mining originally involved the exploitation of near-surface salt strata, rather than deep underground resources. It was extracted by hole digging, a practice which continued for as long reserves lasted.[11] The "salt diggers" (*salifossores*) mentioned in the agreement of 1262 were probably engaged in this traditional way of extracting salt, and we can presume it was them who opened up the pits. Other workers were the hired *salium incisores* (salt cutters). A 1291 document records that the *incisores* in Ocna Dejului received the equivalent of 4 *pondus* in denars for every 100 salt blocks.[12] We do not know exactly what their work consisted of at that time, but the same term was used in the Late Middle Ages for miners who cut out the salt underground. They probably had similar duties in the thirteenth century.[13] If so, then the start of widespread underground mining can be dated to this period, which can be explained by the growing demand for salt.[14]

Salt in the mines was cut into blocks; these varied in size, probably from the Árpádian age onwards. Those carried over land by wagon were cut to a different size than those taken by boat. The most commonly used cargo

---

7 Knauz et al. (eds.) 1874–1999, I, 478. On the conflict, see: Zsoldos 2007.
8 Györffy (ed.) 1992, 255.
9 Kondorné Látkóczki 1997, 15.
10 Górka 1916, 46.
11 Niedermaier 1997, 124 and Draskóczy 2014.
12 Zimmermann et al. (eds.) 1892–1991, I, 170.
13 Harmatta et al. 1987–, V, 122. In Poland, miners were referred to with the Latin words *sector salis* (salt cutter): Wyrozumski 1968, 133.
14 On the growing population of the country, see: Kristó 2007, 49–56.

boat was supposedly one of the largest vessels of the time,[15] with a constant and well-recognized capacity. This is clear from the fact that in the twelfth and thirteenth centuries, the quantity of salt that church institutions were permitted to carry free of customs was usually specified using a number of boatloads.

The boats carried salt from the mines of Transylvania along the Maros and the Szamos Rivers, and from Maramureş along the Tisza. Szeged, at the confluence of the Maros and Tisza, largely owed its prosperity to salt. In the Árpádian age, salt was carried from Transylvania through the Meseş Pass. The most important point on this land route was Sălacea, chosen as the site of a royal salt chamber.[16] It was at this time when the routes for carrying salt through the kingdom were established.[17]

By the end of the Árpádian age, the crown had strengthened its hold on salt mining and trade, but had not established a monopoly. Some mines were still in private and church ownership. Much is revealed by the fact that trading in salt required a royal permit.[18] It was Charles I who, in the first third of the fourteenth century, finally established a full royal monopoly on mining and trade. With the single exception of Solivar, mines under the control of private owners disappeared. Salt mines could be opened only on the basis of a royal privilege.[19]

The changes in Hungary were paralleled in neighboring Poland, where similar events took place in the second half of the thirteenth century. In Bochnia, and later in Wieliczka, it was not Polish workers but German miners with experience in ore mining who started to bring up rock salt from deep underground. The people of these two towns received major privileges. Boleslav the Shy (Bolesław Wstydliwy), prince of Cracow (1227–1279) and husband of Béla IV's daughter Kinga, abolished all private salt mines in 1278, and withdrew all former salt-related grants. Thus all mining and extraction in Little Poland came under the prince's control, laying the foundations for the state salt business. The salt count (żupnik) of Cracow governed salt affairs starting in the late thirteenth century. Salt imports were banned. It was also during Boleslav's rule that a class of miners known in Latin as *sectores* were granted the privilege of working their own assigned lodes, which were heritable, and replaced on being worked out. They were paid wages for their work. Mining output expanded

---

15   Górka 1916, 47 and Weisz 2007b.
16   Paulinyi 2005, passim, Knauz et al. (eds.) 1874–1999, I, 293–294 and 478 and Niedermaier 1997, 124–125.
17   Benkő 1998, 169–176.
18   Zimmermann et al. (eds.) 1892–1991, I, 104, 133–134, 166, 170 and 182.
19   Paulinyi 2005, passim and Kubinyi 1988, 217.

rapidly after 1278. In contrast to the situation in Hungary, salt commerce in Poland was not organized by the royal administration.[20]

Late Medieval Mining and Trade

In the Angevin period, the salt chambers were built on their Árpádian-age foundations. All salt mines and salt offices (both known as "chambers") were put under the direction of the salt count of Transylvania. The same person frequently held the office of the thirtieth customs count, making for more effective enforcement of the ban on imports of foreign salt into the interior of the country. Hungarian salt was also exported to the Balkans in the fourteenth and fifteenth centuries, but exports to the west and north were eventually stifled by increasing production in Austria and Poland.

Parts of the kingdom which lay far from the mining areas brought in salt from neighboring countries, and in the second half of the fourteenth century, not all of the chamber counts were Hungarian – some Italians are to be found among them.[21]

In a decree of 1397, King Sigismund laid down the rules by which salt chambers worked throughout the remainder of the medieval period.[22] The regulations were the basis of a system which stayed in place until the abolition of the monopoly in 1521. Inside the kingdom, consumers and small traders bought salt from the royal salt chambers. Salt could also be bought at the mines. A royal permit or privilege was required in both cases. King Sigismund also fixed the price of salt. 100 blocks could be purchased for 1 florin in the mining areas, but the official price was 225 denars at Szeged (100 denars=1 florin at that time), 300 denars in Buda, 400 denars at Košice and at Kovin on the Lower Danube, while further away – in places such as Zagreb, Vasvár, Sopron, Győr, Bratislava, Trnava and Trenčín – the official price was set at 5 florins. These prices – as András Kubinyi has verified – did not change until the late fifteenth century. Then there came a differentiation in price between the large blocks carried by wagon and the small blocks carried by boat. In Transylvania, the latter were sold for 1.1 florins and the former for 3 florins. We also know from the 1397 charter that salt from the Maramureş mines was to be sold and used in the land bounded by the Tisza and the Zagyva Rivers in the northeastern region of the country, and the rest of the country had to use salt from Transylvania.

---

20 Wyrozumski 1989, 274 and Piotrowicz 1991, 272–276.
21 Hóman 2003, 155–157 and 237–243 and Draskóczy 2004b, 285–293.
22 MNL OL DL 8861, see Draskóczy 2004b.

The decree banned imports of foreign salt. Sigismund revived some chambers which had lapsed in previous years and set up new ones. The decree defined the River Sava as the boundary within which people were constrained to buy Transylvanian and Maramureş salt. Inhabitants of the lands to the south – Slavonia and Croatia – used salt from the Adriatic Sea.

Although Transylvania and Maramureş supplied different areas, salt was under the administration of a national salt count after 1397. This office was held by the Florentine man of business Pipo of Ozora (Filippo Scolari) from 1400 until his death in 1426, putting the system under unified control. He was responsible for putting the 1397 measures into effect, including the setting up of further chambers. Governance of the chambers changed after his death. Sigismund sometimes assigned different people to each chamber, and other times put them under central control (e.g. the Tallóci brothers between 1438 and 1440). Pipo of Ozora preferred to bring in Italians experienced in administration, and several of them remained in the salt administration after his death, seeing business potential in it. By the 1460s, however, we find only Hungarians working in the chambers. Some of these were local townspeople, and others members of noble families. Italian men of finance were also to be found in the salt offices of neighboring Poland.[23]

King Matthias put through a reform of the treasury, placing all financial administration under a treasurer who was thenceforth in charge of salt mining and the salt trade. Another important post was that of the Transylvanian salt chamber count, whose duties often extended to supervision of Transylvanian taxes, customs and mines. It is remarkable that many treasurers had previously worked in salt administration. When Matthias married Beatrice, daughter of the king of Naples, in 1476, he promised her Maramureş. The queen took possession of the mining area around 1480, together with the North Hungarian salt chambers which sold salt from there. This territory extended to Nitra and brought in substantial revenue for the queen. From then on, Maramureş and its associated salt chambers formed part of the queen's estate.[24]

A large number of chambers were needed to prevent foreign salt from finding its way on to the market, and to enforce restrictions on free trade. The system put in place by the Angevin kings was not equal to this task, which is why more chambers were set up in the fifteenth century. King Matthias' efforts to establish a tight network of chambers ran into opposition from the nobility, who demanded a return to the situation existing under Sigismund's reign. By the end of the Middle Ages, to our present knowledge, there were

---

23   Draskóczy 2002, 281–284.
24   Draskóczy 2004c, passim and Draskóczy 2005, 83–95.

salt chamber offices in seventy places, including mining sites, and all of them were eventually located in towns. The principal locations (such as Košice and Bratislava) controlled larger zones and had branch chambers. Some areas, however, did not have a salt chamber at all. Examples include Somogy County, because its inhabitants lived from selling wine, and it was via this business they obtained their salt.

The writ of the royal chambers did not run to the Székely Lands in Transylvania, where near-surface salt deposits could be mined cheaply. The inhabitants of this area were allowed to buy locally-mined salt through free trade without traveling to a chamber. In the same way, the Saxon Seats near the Székely Lands had the privilege of buying salt mined in the Székely Lands instead of royal salt. Salt from Székely Lands was indeed also smuggled elsewhere in Transylvania, in defiance of royal prohibition.[25]

Chambers which sold and distributed salt controlled a district with a radius of 2–3 miles, and royal officials could inspect everybody within this district. The chamber was responsible for enforcing the salt monopoly. It also ensured that if anybody traded in salt, they did not do so at the chamber price (i.e. not more cheaply). Customers who went to the seat of the chamber for salt were primarily the inhabitants of its district. Two miles were equivalent to one *rast*, while a district (about 16–19 kilometers) coincided with the narrow market zone of a town, the distance that people living there could travel to the center and get home the same day.[26]

Mines and Miners

In the royal mining towns, salt was brought to the surface from deep underground. Two (sometimes three) vertical shafts were dug from the surface. One shaft had at its head a horse-driven mechanism for drawing the rope which raised the salt, stone, soil and water. The second shaft allowed the miners to climb up and down on ladders, and the third, where it existed, provided ventilation. The biggest problem was usually water, which had to be raised or drained. To protect against the destructive effects of water, the shafts were lined with buffalo leather or wood. Where a shaft reached the salt stratum, the interior of the mine developed into a bell shape. The mining itself took place on the floor of the mine.

---

25   Kubinyi 1988, 221–227 and Sófalvi 2005, 177–178.
26   See the chapter of András Kubinyi in the present volume. Also: Draskóczy 2010a, 55–56 and Draskóczy 2016d.

According to an account written by the French knight Bertrandon de la Brocquière in 1433, great rocks of salt were dug out in Hungary and cut into square pieces. The blocks of salt he saw on a wagon measured approximately one foot across. His report tallies with an Italian description dating from 1462/63, stating that salt in Transylvania was cut first into large blocks (one manuscript stating they weighed 3 *cantaros*) and then into smaller blocks of 10–12 pounds.[27]

These descriptions give us an idea of the manual operations involved in salt mining, which were similar to how miners were still working in the first half of the nineteenth century. The miners first cut out large blocks from the ground of the mine, and then cut them into pieces of the prescribed size. This operation inevitably produced some fragmentary and powdered salt. The fragments were loaded into vessels and sold by the chamber. Blocks or fragments that became dirty or covered with soil as they were brought out of the mine were set aside and cast into abandoned mines. The greatest enemy of mining was water, which ultimately caused the pits to be abandoned.[28] There are records from the first half of the sixteenth century telling us how deep the salt mines were. King Ferdinand I mortgaged the Transylvanian salt mines to the Fuggers, whose factor, Hans Dernschwam, produced a report for his employers in 1528. This tells us that salt was brought up from a depth of ca. 140 meters in one Turda mine, and ca. 60 meter in another. One mine in Ocna Dejului in the middle of the sixteenth century went down to ca. 100 meters and another to 70 meters.[29]

In 1453/1454, Ulrich Eizinger made an estimate of crown revenues. This naturally covered salt mining. He noted that the blocks cut in the mines were not of uniform size. He stated that the salt *in gleicher gröss müste hawen und schroten*.[30] We do not, unfortunately, know the size of the salt blocks. Bertrandon de la Brocquière saw them on a wagon and claimed they were one-foot blocks. The equivalent in modern units of the 10–12 pounds mentioned in the Italian description depends on whether the author was using Italian or Hungarian pounds. The weight could have been anything between 3.5 and

---

27   Schefer 1892, 236, Venice, Biblioteca Marciana, Ms IT VI. 276. 106ᵛ: ... *el qual sale se cava de algune montagne, sono in Transilvana che sono quaxi in forma de preda, che par marmoro, e fasene pezi a modo de quareli de peso de 10 in 12 libre el pezo,.. 3 cantaro*. See also for this note in another manuscript: Vatican, Bibliotheca Apostolica Vaticana Urb. Lat. 728. fol. 33ᵛ–34ʳ). It would be between 80–100 kilograms. Cf. von Alberti 1957, 403–404.
28   Strieder 1933, 268–276, Wollmann 1995, 138–142 and Niedermaier 1999–2000, 89.
29   Strieder 1933, 269, Engel 1797–1801, II, 20. The amounts were given in *öls*. On this, see: Bogdán 1978, 101.
30   Bak 1987, 381.

4 kilograms.³¹ The size of the blocks changed in the early sixteenth century, the weight of the blocks carried on wagons being increased. The size of blocks that were produced varied between mining areas. We know that in Turda, "boat salt" weighed 5.5 Hungarian pounds (=2.7 kilograms) and "wagon salt" 17.5 pounds (=8.5938 kilograms). In Ocna Sibiului, the former weighed 10 pounds (=4.9108 kilograms) and the latter 22 pounds (=10.8036 kilograms), so that wagon salt was larger and heavier than boat salt (and so had a higher price), and there were clearly big differences between mining areas. A decree of 1521 standardized the size of blocks throughout the kingdom, and set the chamber price of a hundred blocks at three florins. It seems, however, that the decree failed to take hold, and the old sizes continued to be used.³²

There was a complex division of labor in the mines. At the head of the apparatus was the chamber count. Accounts were kept by the steward. Each mine employed a smith, a bath-keeper, a cook, an equerry, workers specialized in working the hoists, and others who removed salt dust and debris from the mine. The highest-ranking workers were the salt cutters, led by their judge. They were divided into two groups, differentiated by their terms of employment: either hired for one year, or on a casual basis. Those in the former group were supplied with cloth (understandably, because their work wore out their clothes), and received wine on being hired. At the end of the medieval period, they could take home one block of salt a day, and they sometimes received cash subventions. The bulk of their income, however, came from their wages. There were several decrees setting wages, such as in Maramureş in 1435, 1448 and 1498. In the Matthias and Jagiellonian periods, 10 denars were paid in Transylvania for cutting one hundred blocks, despite the change in block size in the early sixteenth century. Later, wages were adjusted to the size of blocks, and more was paid for wagon salt. In the 1527–1528 period, the daily output of a miner in Dej was seventy–eighty smaller blocks, and in Turda, forty–fifty large blocks, so that the average daily rate was 7–8 denars, supplemented by other emoluments. We assume five working days a week, averaged over the year. The hard working conditions and meager wages prompted numerous protests and tensions (e.g. in 1435). Dernschwam was dissatisfied with the miners, whom he saw as doing little and disorderly work, and spending too much time in the tavern. In the summer, casual workers were more likely to work on the harvest.³³

---

31 von Alberti 1957, 403–404. On the Hungarian pound: Hóman 1916, 115–122.
32 Engel 1797–1801, II, 38 and Kubinyi 1991d, 267.
33 Strieder 1933, 273–278, Iványi 1911, 10–30, 98–113 and 187–195, Kubinyi 1991b, 264–267, Vienna, Österreichische Nationalbibliothek, Handschriftensammlung (ÖNB HA), Handschriften nos. 367 and 369.

The chamber was responsible for sending the salt to the interior of the country. Carters were hired for this, mostly inhabitants of mining towns, and some villagers. Land transport was expensive; carters had to contend with bad roads and inclement weather. For peasant carriers, agricultural work always came first. Consequently, most of the salt was transported on carts in May, June and October.

Salt was also transported by boat (and sometimes by raft). The chamber engaged boatmen (*celeristae*) who made their boats at the end of winter and afterwards left them at their destinations because the timber was useful in the Great Hungarian Plain. If one mid-sixteenth-century report is to be believed, they made surprisingly large (probably flat-bottomed) boats. The largest vessel made in Turda could be loaded up with some 60–70 tons of salt. Even bigger boats were made in Dej, which the source claims could carry a cargo of 90–100 tons. The sources imply that transport was timed for when the rivers were in spate in spring (March and April). There were years when the usual spring floods did not appear in Transylvania, and salt did not reach the interior of the country. In the early sixteenth century, the Maramureş Chamber Count, Péter Butkai, claimed that boats could not sail from Maramureş before St George's Day (24 April). The importance of the state of the river prompted considerable efforts in early spring to clear away tree trunks, dismantle mill dams, and prohibit the installing of water mills, which were an obstacle to transport. For the boats to pass along the Maros in safety, they had to be assured of a channel at least 40 meters wide, but smaller boats were also used. The arrangement meant that a large proportion of the mines' annual output reached the main Hungarian salt ports (Satu Mare, Tokaj, Poroszló, Szolnok, Szeged) in early spring, and the salt was taken from there to its destination.[34]

It is difficult to estimate the amount of salt that came out of the mines. The kingdom had a population of about three million in the Late Middle Ages.[35] Assuming annual consumption per head of 8–10 kilograms (including salt used for preserving food and other household purposes), domestic demand must have been about 24,000 tons. Much salt was also used in the rearing of large animals. The overall demand may therefore be conservatively (and very approximately) estimated at 30,000 tons.[36]

Running the salt monopoly was very expensive, but brought in considerable revenue to the crown. During the reign of King Sigismund, this revenue was 100,000 florins. King Matthias' annual salt revenue was 80,000–100,000 florins.

---

34   Draskóczy 2005, 112–116 and Draskóczy 2004c, 42–44.
35   Cf. the chapter of András Kubinyi and József Laszlovszky in the present volume.
36   Hocquet 1988, 39. In contrast, Piasecki (1987, 55–57) counts using 10 kilograms/person.

In the Jagiellonian period, however, the rewards of the monopoly declined radically. From about 50,000 florins at the beginning of the sixteenth century, the annual sum flowing into the treasury dwindled to 25,000 florins in 1516 and 14,000 in 1519.[37] Although the royal monopoly was maintained, increasing amounts of salt were sold outside the chamber organization. The king for various reasons made grants of salt to clerics and commoners, and sometimes made payments in salt. Some had privileges entitling them to a certain quantity of salt. Ecclesiastical institutions were particularly frequent recipients of salt. Salt was important to the economy of the Paulines, and they received salt to the value of 300 florins from Maramureş towards the annual upkeep of the grand chapter of the order. Kings made further grants of salt to the grand chapter, and were also fairly generous to the other Pauline houses.[38]

The list of church institutions to enjoy annual salt allowances was not confined the Paulines, and some received salt in other ways. In 1477–1478, Matthias leased the Buda tithe for 1000 florins. In return for half of this amount, he granted to the Veszprém chapter salt from the Székesfehérvár chamber. In mining areas, priests were due a certain amount of salt. We have information particularly on Khust and the Maramureş towns.[39] In other cases, the king made disbursements to the churches from chamber revenue.

It was common for the king to grant salt to a landed nobleman as a gift or in return for some service. Crown officials received some of their emoluments in salt. In 1504, for example, the castellan of Buda received payment of 1200 florins in cash and 500 florins in salt. Towns were granted salt towards the construction of town walls.[40] Since chambers never had enough money, they paid their staff partly in salt. If the chamber purchased something (such as carriage and shipping), it frequently paid for it in salt.

Defense against the Ottomans demanded more and more money. Pipo of Ozora, the Tallócis and John Hunyadi met some of the military costs from salt revenue. During the Jagiellonian period, there was not enough cash to pay castellans and border fort garrisons, and so they received part of their bounty in salt. At Belgrade, for example, the Vojniks were paid 7 florins a year, of which 2 were paid in salt, 2 in broadcloth, and only 3 in cash. Border fort garrisons received salt of total value 20,558 florins in 1504 and 21,484 florins in 1511

---

37 Kubinyi 1988, 227 and Draskóczy, 2005, 88–89.
38 Romhányi 2010b, 120–124.
39 Kropf 1899, 97 and Iványi 1911, passim. On the tenth of Buda, see the regestas of Elemér Mályusz in the Budapest History Museum (Cartulary of the chapter of Veszprém, Veszprém, Dec. Budenses 20).
40 Kubinyi 1988, 229–230, for the document, see: MNL OL DL 21 279.

(18.2 and 15.2 % respectively of total military expenditure). This was equivalent to more than 400,000 blocks of salt. The soldiers received their salt in the smaller "boat" blocks, but it was still a very large quantity.[41]

The people of Debrecen enjoyed the privilege of traveling to Transylvania or Maramureş to buy salt, which they could then sell at markets. The people of Szeged bought salt at the local chamber and sold it in Somogy County, and bought the well-known wines of Somogy with their income. Anybody who received salt for any reason could sell it freely, unimpeded by the chambers. There were also salt merchants. A condition of operation was that the merchant be able to prove he had bought his wares legally. He could not sell salt at the seat of a salt chamber, and could not sell at the official price (to prevent competition with the chambers). It was only by special royal grace that somebody was allowed to sell salt at chamber prices. Mining chambers in Transylvania and Maramureş also sold salt. Their customers were mainly the people of Dej, Turda, the Maramureş chamber towns and the surrounding villages. Most customers could not pay the full price immediately, and many were indebted to the salt office for years. These debts, in some cases, were never recovered. The mining town authorities were forced to sell salt locally in order to cover their costs.[42]

Production declined during the Jagiellonian period, and revenue from salt fell off drastically. Much of the problem lay in corruption and slovenly chamber administration. A striking illustration of administrative shortcomings is the amount of salt which remained in the Transylvanian chambers instead of being carried into the interior or sold locally. This failure was again due to lack of cash. Sometimes chambers were subsidized from other sources of crown revenue. As more and more salt went on the market in evasion of the chambers, the chamber apparatus found it increasingly difficult to support itself. Not surprisingly, a plan was put forward at the beginning of the sixteenth century to radically reduce the number of chambers. These developments led to the abolition of the salt monopoly in 1521. Trade was freed, and the system of crown salt offices in the interior of the country was dissolved. Some important salt chambers, however (such as Szeged, Satu Mare and Tokaj) remained. They were still needed to organize the river transport which had developed in the Middle Ages. The abolition of the salt monopoly favored the inhabitants of towns already involved in trade (such as the mining towns, Szeged and

---

41 Kubinyi 2004a, in the financial year 1515/16 approx. 2.5 million blocks of salt were produced (ÖNB HA Handschriften no. 373). See also: Kubinyi 1988, 230 and Kubinyi 2007, 126.
42 Kubinyi 1988, 227–232, Draskóczy 2005, 96–112 and Simon 2010, 141–160.

Debrecen) and the villages around the mines. Nonetheless, the disappearance of the system disrupted supply.

Adding to the difficulties of crown salt administration was its inability to prevent imports. The chambers were not always able to maintain sufficient levels of supply to border areas far from the mines, and Austrian and Polish salt was cheaper than the domestic product. Polish salt had regularly been supplied to what is now northern Slovakia since the late thirteenth century.[43] In western Hungary, Austrian evaporated salt presented strong competition to Hungarian mined salt. It first appeared in the fourteenth century, and gained royal approval in the middle of that century. Early attempts at banning imports failed because local inhabitants had little alternative. Account books in Bratislava report sizeable quantities passing through the city in the period between 1444 and 1464. The highest annual figure was 1361.2 tons, recorded in 1448. Imports totaled 1119.8 tons between 22 April and 22 December 1456 and 936.7 tons between 9 May and 13 December 1457. Thereafter, imports went into steep decline. Considerable quantities also came in via Sopron (a calculation based on figures for 1425 puts the amount of salt passing through the customs post there at 400–800 tons). Matthias banned imports in 1464. Towards the end of the fifteenth century, however, salt imports into western Hungary seem to have risen again. There must also have been some smuggling.[44] In the other direction, Transylvanian salt reached the Balkans and the territory of the Ottoman Empire.[45]

The extraction and trade of this essential commodity created mining towns and provided a living for many townspeople and villagers. The salt business thus contributed to the development of Hungarian towns and the Hungarian economy.[46] The monopolies also had economic benefits. Under good management, they provided a substantial source of revenue for the crown. The chamber establishment also took responsibility for mining operations and for transport and distribution, all of which demanded considerable capital and organization, not to mention royal authority (in such things as customs disputes).

---

43 Carter 1994, 125 and Draskóczy 2009, 111–124.
44 Bratislava, Archív Hlavného Mesta Bratislavy, Mesto Bratislava, Kammerrechnungen and Mollay 1990.
45 Hóvári 1989 and Simon 2006a.
46 Kubinyi 1988, passim.

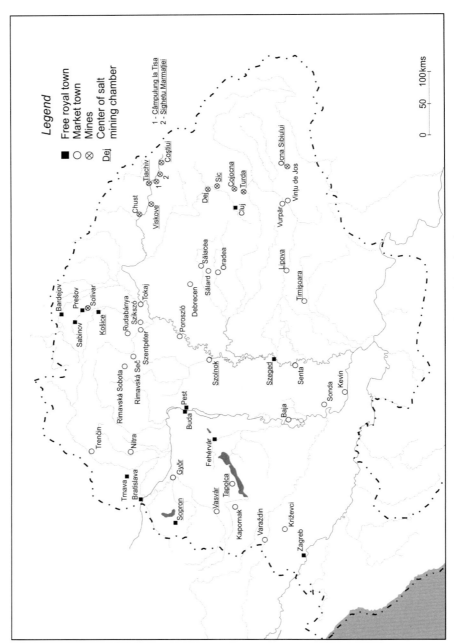

FIGURE 8.1 *Organization of salt mining in fifteenth-century Hungary (after András Kubinyi).*

CHAPTER 9

The Extent and Management of Woodland in Medieval Hungary

Péter Szabó

Introduction

In the past few decades, the study of woodland history has gone through two major changes. On the one hand, it has turned into an interdisciplinary venture. While earlier research could make do with relying on fossilized plant remains or archival sources alone,[1] nowadays many studies combine natural scientific and historical sources and methods in what is increasingly termed 'historical ecology'.[2] On the other hand, the previously unchallenged authority of advocates of twentieth-century plantation forestry regarding the assessment of pre-forestry woodland management has largely vanished. For almost a century, the historiography of woodland management was dominated by a linear development model. The methods of then-modern forestry (rigid planning and artificial forest regeneration through planting) were regarded as the most advanced, and such methods were sought in the past. When not found, early management was labeled 'unmethodical' or even 'primitive.'[3] However, the methods of scientific forestry are well-documented to have developed in the eighteenth and nineteenth centuries,[4] and it is therefore logical that they cannot be evidenced from earlier periods. In fact, looking for them is

---

1 Typical examples for Central Europe and the Carpathian Basin: Firbas 1949–1952 and Zólyomi 1952. For Hungarian woodland history based on written sources, see for example Tagányi 1896, Kolossváry (ed.) 1975 and Magyar 1983.
2 The most comprehensive review of the history of historical ecology so far is Szabó 2015. See also Bürgi and Gimmi 2007 and Russell 1998. In Hungary, the phrase 'historical ecology' (*történeti ökológia*) was and is still sometimes used as a synonym for environmental history, although the two fields are clearly not the same. R. Várkonyi and Kósa (eds.) 1993.
3 Having written an entire book on medieval woodland management, Pál Csőre came to the surprising conclusion that "the Middle Ages in general were characterized by unmethodical management. This holds true for the fifteenth century as well, even though in this century there were several processes in which signs of the idea of rational management can be spotted." [author's translation] Csőre 1980, 227.
4 See for example Hölzl 2010.

anachronistic. Realizing this, in the 1960s and 1970s in England and later also in other countries of Western Europe, researchers tried to comprehend woodland management from prehistory until the nineteenth century as a meaningful system in its own right that served the needs of humans in any period in a rational manner.[5] The Middle Ages played a key role in this paradigm shift, because this is the first period from which written evidence on woodland management is available.[6] More recently, there has been an upsurge in the study of traditional ecological knowledge connected to woodland. Such research uses ethnographic and anthropological methods, including oral history, to understand management decisions and methods unrepresented in archival sources, which are ultimately the products of elite culture.[7]

The present chapter examines two basic questions concerning woodlands in the medieval kingdom of Hungary: how much woodland was there, and how was it managed? To answer these questions in a meaningful manner, I briefly describe the kinds of sources that are available, and also the management methods that are known to have been used in other European countries in the Middle Ages.

Sources

There are two basic kinds of sources for woodland history:[8] natural scientific, and archival (written). The natural sciences in particular comprise a very dynamic field in which new types of information and methods of analyzing them are still being discovered. This chapter is not written to review these sources and methods at length, but is instead intended as a short introduction.[9] The best-known natural scientific methods in woodland history are palynology (the study of fossilized plant pollen), the study of plant macrofossils, dendrochronology (the analysis of tree rings), and anthracology (the study of carbonized micro and macroscopic tree remains, i.e., charcoal). With the exception of dendrochronology, these methods rely on stratigraphy to establish temporal relations and radiocarbon dating to obtain absolute dates. Dendrochronology, as the name implies, was originally developed as a dating technique and serves

---

5   Rackham 1976, Rackham 2003, Tack et al. 1993 and Foster and Aber 2004.
6   Apart from a small number of Roman agricultural documents related to the subject.
7   Parrotta and Trosper (eds.) 2012.
8   Not including oral history interviews. For these, see e.g. Bürgi and Stuber 2013.
9   For comprehensive surveys, see for example Evans and O'Connor (eds.) 1999 and Cappers and Neef 2012.

as the basis for calibrating the results of radiocarbon dating. All four methods can provide information about the entire Holocene (ca. 12,000 years).

Each of these methods has its advantages and limitations. Palynology provides the most comprehensive information about past vegetation, but the results (percentages of various pollen types in pollen assemblage for each time period) are difficult to interpret because not every plant produces the same amount of pollen, and pollen grains themselves differ in their ability to fly and survive. Recently, several mathematical modeling techniques have been developed that provide transparent rather than intuitive pollen-based landscape reconstructions.[10] Plant macrofossils and charcoal allow researchers to gain insights into local rather than regional vegetation patterns. In addition, charcoal can reveal fire history, which is especially useful in fire-prone coniferous forests. Charcoal uncovered in an archaeological context may reflect preferences for certain types of trees for firewood.[11] Dendrochronology is based on the biological phenomenon that each tree in the Earth's temperate zone lays down one tree ring at its circumference each year. The width and the density of each ring mirrors weather and biotic influences (such as caterpillar attacks) but also management history. Dendrochronological investigations can be conducted on macrocharcoal as well, whereby management methods for firewood production can be established.[12]

Archival sources can be of many types. Here, I will only deal with those that occurred in the Middle Ages in Hungary.[13] The most significant shortage of sources is the lack of account books and estate conscriptions.[14] Those few that were compiled contain virtually nothing about woodlands. Other than impressionistic descriptions by travelers,[15] from among the available sources, the most important are perambulations and estimations. The latter I describe in more detail in connection with the amount of woodland in the Middle Ages. The former involve the formal definition of boundaries by walking around them and noting down the most important landscape features.[16] Many trees (identified to the species or genus) were recorded in such perambulations.[17] In addition,

---

10   Sugita 2007 and Felde et al. 2014.
11   Out 2010.
12   Dufraisse 2008.
13   For a more detailed survey, see Szabó 2003.
14   The typical Hungarian estate conscription was the *urbarium*, which, being primarily related to the plots and services of tenants, hardly ever mentioned woodland. Maksay 1957.
15   An attempt to squeeze at least some information out of such sources is Tóber 2012.
16   Takács 1987.
17   Szabó 2002 and Grynaeus and Grynaeus 2001.

many woods were also mentioned, and even entire woods were perambulated, from which process their medieval boundaries can be worked out.

Medieval Woodland Management in Europe

It is a fact that most broadleaved trees (i.e., not conifers) grow back when they are cut down. However, instead of a single-stemmed tree, many smaller stems (shoots) replace the earlier growth. When these shoots themselves are cut down, new shoots arise and the process is repeated. Trees are not like humans; they do not have a predictable life-span. Repeatedly cutting all shoots prolongs the life of a tree through drastically reducing its (trunk-related) energy demand, while leaving its energy intake (the root system) unchanged. A repeatedly cut tree is virtually immortal. By happy coincidence, the young shoots that grow on the trunk (or 'stool') are ideal for human purposes. Before the advent of fossil fuels, most Europeans had to heat and cook using firewood. Especially in colder climates, having access to firewood was a matter of life and death. However, large trunks are very impractical for firewood. Because large pieces simply cannot be burned using household equipment, they have to be chopped up into smaller pieces that can be put onto a fire. People without power tools (such as existed in the Middle Ages), saws (most of prehistory) or even metal tools (Mesolithic and Neolithic) tried to avoid handling large trees if they could. There is copious archaeological and archival evidence from various European regions to prove that in non-coniferous environments people have employed the above-mentioned ability of trees to produce young shoots after cutting to produce firewood since at the least the Neolithic.[18] Most broadleaved forests were cut on short rotations (as little as seven years in the Middle Ages), a system known as coppicing (from the French *couper*, "to cut"). The coppice system was described many times in medieval documents, including the length of the coppice cycle, the size of areas to be cut, and remarks about 'sustainability.'[19] The larger trees (called timber or standard) that were needed to build houses, mills and the like, sometimes grew in timber-only woods (high-forests in modern terminology), but were more often scattered around coppice woods, creating a system called coppice-with-standards.

18   Bishop et al. 2015, Rackham 1979, Rackham 2003, Billamboz 2003 and Haneca et al. 2005.
19   For example, the management plan of Hayley Wood (England) in 1356 mentioned that the wood "contains 80 acres by estimate. Of the underwood of which there can be sold every year, without causing waste or destruction, 11 acres of underwood." Rackham 1975, 26. This implies a 7-year 'sustainability' cycle.

Details about the intensive coppice system usually appeared in written sources in a fully developed form only from ca. the thirteenth century in Western Europe, and research on earlier forms of management, and especially on the transition to coppicing, is rare.[20]

Woodland Cover in Medieval Hungary

The history of the present-day forests of the Carpathian Basin started some 12,000 years ago at the end of the latest Ice Age, when trees that survived in warmer pockets of Hungary and in Southern Europe spread across the region.[21] Palaeoecological data reveal the vegetation of this period. Even though the number of palaeoecological sites is still insufficient to form a coherent picture of Holocene vegetation development for the entire Carpathian Basin, it is clear that even in prehistory the landscape of the region was highly varied, made up of a mosaic of various habitats of large and small scales.[22] Because humans have influenced vegetation significantly for at least 8,000 years, it is beyond doubt that by the beginning of the Middle Ages the forests of the Carpathian Basin were reduced in size and far from pristine.[23] In the Middle Ages, the already existing processes took on new momentum. Direct evidence for the early phases of this process cannot be found in archival material for most of the Carpathian Basin. One of the earliest written sources containing recognizable details about the landscape of the Hungarian Kingdom is the foundation charter of the abbey of Tihany from 1055. This refers to a wood at Gamás (Somogy County) that was surrounded by meadows and valleys, just like most woods nowadays.[24] Practically every medieval document from Hungary referred to these sorts of woods: surrounded by meadows, pastures, arable lands and relatively restricted in size. The immense medieval woodlands imagined by many historians lingered only on the fringes of the kingdom in the Carpathian Mountains.

How much woodland was there in the Carpathian Basin in the medieval period and how did woodland cover change in the course of the six centuries from the Hungarian Conquest to the early sixteenth century? Quantitative

20 But see Keyser 2009.
21 Willis et al. 2000.
22 A short summary is contained in Sümegi and Törőcsik 2007. For sites, see Buczkó et al. 2009.
23 For a comprehensive overview of the same issue in Europe, see Hoffmann 2014, 21–50.
24 For the most recent edition of the charter, see Hoffmann 2010, 21–32.

data directly describing the extent of various land cover types are available for only the fifteenth–sixteenth centuries. Before this period, one has to rely on palaeoecological evidence, which is inevitably limited in spatial coverage, or use settlement history as a proxy for the spread of arable cultivation at the expense of forests. In this chapter, I work backwards from late medieval survey data towards the more speculative accounts of earlier periods.

The only type of medieval source that contains quantitative data about the extent of woodlands is the so-called estimation. Such an estimation (*estimatio* in Latin, *becsü* in Hungarian) was commissioned when, for some reason (estate division, inheritance, distribution of the possessions of someone who was arrested, etc.), authorities wanted to know how much money a certain person's possessions were worth.[25] Possessions included the plots of peasants, land, buildings, livestock or mills. Notably, different land uses were described separately, along with the size of areas. Estimations appeared in the fourteenth century, but were compiled in larger numbers only from the fifteenth century onwards. Despite their appearance, estimations are jurisdictional and not economic sources. Everything had a fixed price, – for example, one royal plow of arable land was always three marks, regardless of quality. Here is an example from 1423, in which the chapter of Eger reported to Miklós Garai, count palatine:

> Item, first in the said Hangon [the surveyors found] the private plot of the same Blasius, one peasant plot and a stone church with a cemetery, one plow of arable land, three plows of acorn-bearing woods, twenty *falcastra* of meadows, all to the royal measure, and a river on which a mill can be built. Item in Susa two plows of arable with *nemora*, eight *falcastra* of meadows, four and a half peasant plots, a wooden chapel without a cemetery, one plow of *permissionalis* woods, of which woods only one quarter belongs to the same Blasius.[26]

Because estimations were connected to specific legal situations, not many were made. A large portion of these were subsequently destroyed during the various misfortunes that befell Hungarian archival sources. One also has to keep in mind that estimations were connected to lands owned by the nobility, because the Church did not have inheritance issues and royalty were not involved in such matters. Furthermore, apart from a few estimation that covered

---

25   The best introduction to estimations remains Kubinyi 1986.
26   Ila and Borsa (eds.) 1993, 140. One plow is about 127 hectares, one *falcastrum*, 8442 m². *Nemus*, here, is a type of woodland. *Permissionalis* woods are coppices.

TABLE 9.1 *The extent of the four basic land-cover types in the Carpathian Basin in the fifteenth century, as reflected in estimations*[a]

	Arable[b] (ha/per cent)	Meadow (ha/per cent)	Woodland (ha/per cent)	Pasture (ha/per cent)	Total (ha/per cent)
Total	122,206 40 %	29,863 10 %	102,519 34 %	48,259 16 %	302,847 100 %

a For the original data, see Szabó 2005, 153–156.
b Including vineyards.

large areas,[27] most documents, like the example above, surveyed only a few villages. Known estimations cover ca. 1 % of the medieval Kingdom of Hungary. From these, the extent of various land-cover types is shown in Table 9.1.

Because most medieval sources were destroyed in the areas of the Carpathian Basin that later became parts of the Ottoman Empire, the geographical distribution of the data is not even. On the other hand, data are widely scattered, which gives us an opportunity to understand the situation in different parts of the country. Out of the seventy-five counties of fifteenth-century Hungary,[28] thirty-three (44 %) are illuminated by the estimation of at least one village. This permits us to draw conclusions about the kingdom with far more confidence than if most data came from just a handful of counties. Nonetheless, Figure 9.1 clearly demonstrates that there is a pattern to the distribution of those counties where some data at least are preserved. While the west (Transdanubia) and the north (especially the north-east) are fairly well-represented, the central parts (the Great Hungarian Plain) and the east (Transylvania) are almost empty of data. Because the Great Hungarian Plain surely had less woodland than most other regions, the overall figure of 34 % woodland cover for the entire Carpathian Basin is arguably too high. Figure 9.1 also depicts the proportion of woodland in each county. Somewhat unexpectedly, there is a clear pattern. Less than 20 % woodland cover was recorded in the inner parts of the kingdom. It is notable that the counties in which the

---

27 Kubinyi 1986. The estimation of the Makovica estate is MNL OL DL 3022. The estimation of the Druget family possessions is MNL OL DF 234 235. The estimation of the Cesargrad estate is Graz, Steiermärkisches Landesarchiv, Urkunden No. 8502, summarized in Kubinyi 2001b.
28 Including the counties accounted for in Engel 2002.

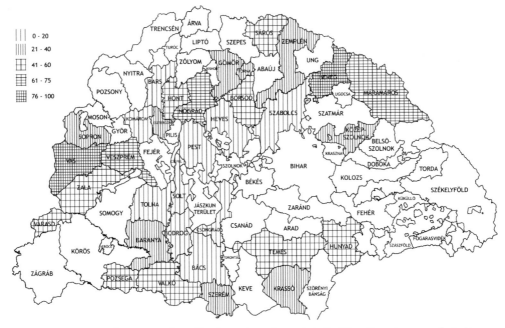

FIGURE 9.1 *Percentage of woodland cover in each county in the fifteenth century, as reflected in estimations (no data are available for counties left blank).*

Great Hungarian Plain adjoins the hills (Komárom, Pest, Heves, and Szabolcs Counties), which have probably the most fertile soils in the Carpathian Basin, form a line of areas with low levels of woodland cover. Up to 40 % woodland is characteristic of the regions in the central parts of northern Hungary and the south. Even more wooded were the border counties, and one cannot fail to notice the stronghold of woodlands in western Transdanubia (Zala, Veszprém, and Vas Counties). How does this situation compare to population density? Comparison with the map compiled by András Kubinyi reveals a relationship that is anything but straightforward.[29] The densest populations of the kingdom (except for the central parts around Buda) were southwest Transdanubia and the northern parts of central Hungary. The northern border counties and certain parts of the Great Hungarian Plain were typically sparsely populated. For the latter, we lack written sources, but in the north much woodland and few people went hand in hand. However, in Transdanubia, a high percentage of woodland combined with high population density. By contrast, the relatively well-populated central northern regions had little woodland.

---

29   Kubinyi 1997a.

THE EXTENT AND MANAGEMENT OF WOODLAND IN MEDIEVAL HUNGARY   227

The late medieval woodland cover of one-quarter to one-third of the Carpathian Basin resulted from a long process that was well developed by the time the Hungarians arrived. Nonetheless, medieval landscape colonization, especially at middle and higher altitudes, was probably responsible for the disappearance of large tracts of woodland in a relatively short time period. A typical example is Ung County (in the northeastern part of the Carpathian Basin), whose settlement history was discussed by Pál Engel. In this county, two medieval conscriptions enumerated settlements, nobles and peasants (1398 and 1427). In addition, a major estimation of the lands of the Druget family survives (1437) that covers about half the county.[30] Ung has three basic geographical components: the lowland region, the hilly parts at the foot of the Carpathians, and the high Carpathian Mountains at the border.[31] In the thirteenth century, only the southern part of the lowland region was populated. Around 1300, 75–80 % of the county must have been covered by woodland. Within two hundred years, the northern lowland region and the hilly parts were moderately populated and, at most, half-wooded. The higher mountains were almost completely without inhabitants until modern times. The 1437 estimation reinforces the impression gained from the settlement pattern. This document describes the northern half of the county, where woodland was extensive even in the fifteenth century. The villages that are recorded were mainly located in the hilly region, with a few tiny settlements up in the mountains. They contained approximately eighty plows of arable, meadow, and managed woodland, plus "woods for 340 pigs". In contrast, the vast woodland "until the border of the Ruthenians" was estimated to be one thousand plows. There was no real surveying, of course, and this number appears to be a synonym for 'very much'. This great wood occupied about half the county, which leaves the other half as mostly cultural landscape with not much woodland.[32] Thus, if the northern part of Ung County (with the Druget lands) was very much wooded, while the southern one was not, we arrive at a figure of somewhere around 60–70 % woodland for the first half of the fifteenth century. We should note, however, that the dividing line between inhabited and uninhabited areas was rather sharp, and probably already established in the eleventh century. A similar process was typical of other border counties as well, and colonization was often carried out in an organized way by foreign settlers.[33] In some areas, cultivation

30   Engel 1985 and Engel 1998. The estimation is MNL OL DF 234 235.
31   This mirrors the conditions of the whole kingdom on a small scale.
32   Unfortunately, this estimation records woodland and arable together, with the exception of timber- and acorn-bearing woods.
33   For Central Europe in general, see Körmendy 1995. For the north, see Teiszler 2007.

extended further in the Middle Ages than in subsequent periods, as evidenced by field remains in what are currently woods.[34]

Medieval Woodland Management in Hungary

Due to the lack of sources that directly describe woodland management techniques, one needs to turn to estimations, because these mentioned several types of woodland based on their styles of management. The meaning of these various terms was explained in guidelines provided for estimations that were compiled to help the work of estimators, and mainly consist of lists of how much money different types of land (and other property) were worth. The best-known such guideline was included in István Werbőczy's *Tripartitum*, a compilation of the customary law of Hungary from 1517.[35] By and large, all guidelines tell the same story: They differentiate between four types of woodland (including wood-pasture): *silva communis*; *silva permissionalis*; *silva glandinosa, sub dolabro et venatione*; and *rubetum / virgultum*. It was indeed these types of woodland that appeared in estimations, perambulations and other sources; the only type one regularly finds in sources but that is missing from the list is *nemus*. In other words, the estimators used a classification that was not imposed from above on an otherwise less-rigid reality, but described the system as it actually worked.

As Figure 9.2 shows, approximately half of the woods in estimations were called simply *silva*. Among those woods that were classified in detail, *silva glandinosa* occupied the largest area, followed by *permissoria* and *rubeta*.

Silva Communis

> a common wood, on which no pig-tithe or other tax is collected, and which has no definite income, is estimated at the same amount as one royal *aratrum* of arable land, that is, at 3 marks.[36]

---

[34] A review of such places with a bibliography may be found in Laszlovszky 1999.

[35] Bak et al. (eds.) 1992–2012, V, 214–223 (I, no. 133). Further estimation guidelines: MNL OL DL 32 012, DL 48 204, DF 283 678, DF 283 386. A comparative analysis of these guidelines is included in Bónis 1972, 162–185. One list unknown to Bónis is MNL OL DF 252 476.

[36] *Item silva communis de qua decima porcorum vel tributum generaliter non exigitur nec habet aliquem certum proventum estimatur sicut terra communis ad unum aratrum videlicet regalis mensurae adiacens ad M. III.* – Bak et al. (eds.) 1992–2012, V, 218–219. (I, no. 133/25).

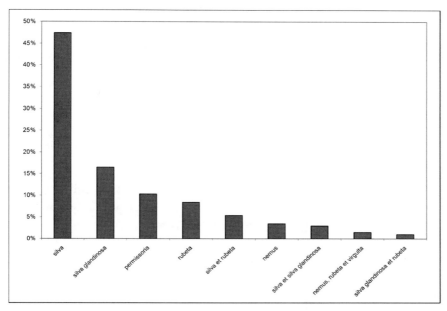

FIGURE 9.2 *The proportion of area covered by different types of woodland (or combinations of different types) as recorded in estimations. Only types and combinations occupying more than 1 % of the overall area are shown.*

The Latin word *communis*, just like the English 'common,' has a dual meaning. It may either mean 'shared by a group', or 'ordinary.' Werbőczy's choice of words in this sentence about common land, for example, suggests that *communis* means 'ordinary.'[37] In medieval times, however, it was often very difficult to differentiate between the two. Arable land was 'ordinary' land, but in the case of many open-fields it was also 'shared by a group.' Nor is distinguishing between the legal and the functional features an easy task with woods. Werbőczy says that a common wood lacks three characteristics that make it non-common: a pig tithe, dues, and fixed income. The first of these defines it as an 'ordinary' wood; that is, one without big oaks. The second and the third, however, more likely refer to a wood 'shared by a group' – namely, a group of villagers. Hence the absence of dues (the lord cannot make anyone pay to use it), and the lack of income (nor can he make money out of selling woodland products). Nonetheless, this type of woodland was by no means the wood "where people

---

37   In the previous sentence, he talks about "common or arable land" (*terra communis vel arabilis*).

casually cut what and how much they needed."[38] Common woods were of the same value as arable land; in other words, they must have been managed. What this management involved, however, it is not possible to say.

Silva Permissionalis

> (alternatively called *permissorium* or *permissoria*[39])
> a large wood, also called *permissoria*, that is suitable for common work and use ... to 10 marks.[40]

All we learn here, except that *permissoria* were more than three times as valuable as common woods, is that a *permissorium* is large, and it is apt for common work. As far as the first claim is concerned, it was certainly not true. Even in the *Tripartitum* there is a long passage about what to do if a *permissorium* happens to be smaller than half a plow (ca. 63 hectares).[41] In charters, we find many *permissoria* much smaller than this. In Kopács (Vas County), for example, the *permissorium* was 20 *iugera* (ca. 17 hectares).[42] The smallest *permissoria* known to the author include the tiny one-*iugerum* (ca. 0.8 hectare) wood recorded in Tilaj (Borsod County) and the half-a-*iugerum* (ca. 0.4 hectare) wood in Kukeč (Vas County).[43] Leaving apart the five giant woods in Bodrog County (450, 3000, 3300, 1500, and 1200 *iugera*), the rest yield an average of 63.2 *iugera* (approximately 53.3 hectares) per *permissoria*. Let us now return to Werbőczy's description. "Apt for common work and labor" is a rather general statement which does not suggest any particular meaning. The question remains: what type of woodland was *silva permissionalis*?

Unlike other types of woodland, *permissoria* had a special medieval Hungarian name: *eresztvény*. This word is not part of the modern language and nowadays only appears in place-names, albeit abundantly. It is a typical Hungarian (that is, agglutinative) construction in the sense that it is made up of a simple root and multiple layers of suffixes. *Eresztvény* shares its root with the Hungarian word for woodland (*erdő*), which originates in the verb *ered* and

---

38   Bartha 2000, 16.
39   The last one is, in theory, the plural of the second, but this distinction was not taken seriously in the Middle Ages. *Permissoria* was often interpreted as a singular noun.
40   *Item silva magna quae alias permissoria dicitur, pro communi opere et labore apta ... ad M. X.* – Bak et al. (eds.) 1992–2012, V, 218–219. (I, no. 133/27).
41   Bak et al. (eds.) 1992–2012, V, 218–219. (I, no. 133/31).
42   1402: Mályusz et al. (eds.) 1951–2017, II/1, no. 1831.
43   Géresi 1882–1897, II, 104–106, MNL OL DL 92 876.

means 'to grow by itself' or 'to spring.' The stem of *eresztvény* is *ereszt*, which, linguists argue, is very similar to *ered*.[44] (They share a common root: *er-*, but have different suffixes.) It is usual for verbs ending in *-ed* to have an *-eszt* ending version, which often has a factitive meaning.[45] Therefore, *ered* means 'to grow,' which implies that something appears on the ground apparently out of nothing, such as flowers or grass. By contrast, *ereszt* implies that someone is making something grow out of something that was already there.

The same tendency can be observed in the second layer of suffixes. *Erdő* contains *-ő*, which is one of the most common suffixes in Hungarian for forming a noun from an active verb. *Eresztvény* includes *-vény*, which presents a number of unresolved problems. Linguists do not agree about its origins and meaning. Some argue that it was a phonetic variant of *-vén*, an adverbial participle.[46] Others claim it to be a compound in itself, made up of *-v* and *-ény*.[47] What is interesting is that in this version *-v* would be an ancient reflexive suffix. A third option is that *-vény* is in fact a compound, but *-v* is not a reflexive but an adverbial suffix.[48] Consequently, what meaning *-vény* implies is also subject to debate. The present author certainly cannot make sense of what does not seem clear even to specialists, although there is one interpretation that offers a handhold. Kálmán Szily discovered that *-vény* was used both more and less actively during distinct periods in its history, and its meaning also changed.[49] To study these changes, he collected words ending with *-vény* from the first active period of the suffix: the thirteenth and fourteenth centuries. All, including *eresztvény*, are strikingly similar. They refer to something that is the result of human activity (*ásvány* = 'a channel that was dug,'[50] *sövény* = 'a wattle-fence that was woven,' *töltevény* = 'a bank that was piled up,' and so on). Applying this logic, *eresztvény* should mean 'something that was made to grow.'

Thus, on linguistic grounds, two separate elements of the name of this type of woodland suggest that people were involved in its creation. It should also be understood that although Latin sources spoke about *silva permissionalis*, in the vernacular *erdő* and *eresztvény* never appeared together. The latter was not a subtype of the former, but an equal variant with a different meaning. A place

---

44 Benkő (ed.) 1967–1984, I, 782–785.
45 Simonyi 1881, 262–263. For example, *reped* ("to crack") and *repeszt* ("to make something crack").
46 Mészöly 1908. *-Vány* and *-vény* are phonetic variants.
47 Bárczi, Benkő and Berrár 1978, 332.
48 Beke 1913, Pais 1933. See also Bárczi 1951, 174–175.
49 Szily 1919.
50 The present meaning of the word ("mineral") is a recent development.

where trees were growing was either an *erdő* or an *eresztvény*. I return to these observations later.

Charters do not reveal much about *permissoria*, but certain peculiarities must not be left without mention. As a direct consequence of their value, they were often differentiated from other types of woodland in estate divisions. While the latter were often left in common use, *permissoria* were, in most cases, divided between parties. In extreme examples, such as on that existed in Opatovská Nová Ves (Hont County) in 1409, only the *eresztvény* was divided by boundary signs, all "the other woods, arable lands, meadows and utilities were rendered to common use."[51]

Some charters use surprising verbs in connection with *permissoria*. In 1411, the villagers of Spišská Nová Ves (Szepes County) complained that although "a certain *permissionalis* wood in a certain colonial place of theirs, within the just boundaries of their settlement, which has newly been created," was exclusively theirs, it was also used by others.[52] The same concept was repeated in Kállósemjén (Szabolcs County) in a lawsuit from 1399, where the defendant allegedly occupied a piece of land, and "created" a *permissoria*.[53] A similar word was used in a case of peaceful agreement in Trencsén County, when common woods, *rubeta*, and *nemora* were given in compensation for other lands, but it was noted that two *permissoria* did not form part of the agreement and remained with their previous owners (again typical of the outstanding position *permissoria* had among different types of woodland). We learn the names of these woods, and also the fact that one of them "was constructed beyond the parish church in the village ... called Wgrogh."[54] These verbs indicate something man-made. This situation is fundamentally different from other types of woodland, and might explain why *permissoria* were so valuable. Without attempting to answer what this 'creation' involved, let us consider some further issues.

There are a number of cases when *permissoria* (or the Hungarian *eresztvény*) were equated with vineyards. These do not, as one might expect, seem to be mistakes or misunderstandings. The reference from Gyulakeszi (Zala County)

---

51 *ceteras autem silvas, terras arabiles, prata ac utilitates ad communem usum deputassent.* – Mályusz et al. (eds.) 1951–2017, II/2, no. 6800.

52 *quedam silva permissionalis in quodam loco ipsorum colonicali intra veros cursus ipsorum metarum metales de novo procreate* – Mályusz et al. (eds.) 1951–2017, III, no. 334.

53 Mályusz et al. (eds.) 1951–2017, I, no. 5986.

54 Lukinich (ed.) 1937–1943, I, 235–238. 1492: *supra ecclesiam parochialem in possessione ... Wgrogh appellata constructa.*

is almost verbose: "Vineyards, which were planted by the said nobles last year and were left to grow, and which are called herezthuen ..."[55] At first this does not make any sense, but if interpreted as one aspect of a broader context, it can be accounted for.

As far as management is concerned, information is again sparse. The present author knows of a charter from 1407 that grants two cartloads of firewood every week for two years from a *permissionalis* wood in Ordzovany (Szepes County).[56] This suggests large-scale coppicing. Some other mentions of the word demonstrate a close relationship between *permissoria* and mining. The most interesting of these is an estate division in Milaj (Szepes County). Here the parties divided, among other things, the *permissoria*. They agreed that if they found a mine on either's land, they would use that mine in common. If the *permissoria* needed for mining were not sufficient for one party, they would buy the wood from the other party. If, however, both had sufficient wood, they would supply it on equal terms.[57] Since there were many other woodlands mentioned in the charters, it is beyond doubt that only *permissoria* were apt for the purposes of mining.

Let me now sum up the pieces of information gathered so far. Linguistic evidence suggests that an *eresztvény* was a place where trees grew from a permanent base that involved human activity. Charters reveal information about the special position of *permissoria* among different types of woodland. The suspicion of human activity is further strengthened by such words as 'create' or 'construct' that were used in connection with *permissoria*. The word *eresztvény* was sometimes equated with vineyards. Finally, there is also written evidence for the connection between mining and *permissoria*. The only way to account for these phenomena is if the meaning of *permissoria* is 'coppice wood'. The word *eresztvény* describes a phenomenon rather similar to coppices. It is man-made in the sense that people cut trees and create permanent bases (stools). Shoots are 'made to grow'. 'Create' and 'construct' also then make sense in connection with *permissoria*. They most probably refer to the construction of ditches, banks, permanent and temporary fences, or any other means of protecting

---

55 Szamota and Zolnai (eds.) 1902–1906, 197. 1255/1415: *vinee vero de anno preterito plantate ab ipsis nobilibus crescendum dimisse que hereztuen dicuntur* ... (the meaning of *crescendum dimisse* is not entirely clear.) Another case of *permissoria* meaning vineyard is found in Nagy (ed.) 1887–1889, II, 438–447. A third case from 1450: MNL OL DL 14 314.

56 Mályusz et al. (eds.) 1951–2017, II/2, no. 5275.

57 1405: Mályusz et al. (eds.) 1951–2017, II/1, no. 4203. Also in 1415: Mályusz et al. (eds.) 1951–2017, V, no. 1146.

new growth.[58] The special position and value of *permissoria* also becomes understandable. If they were protected, capital investment was required. Why vineyards should be called *eresztvény* is also less of a puzzle. Vineyards operate in much the same way as coppice woods. Stock is permanent, just like stools, and young shoots appear every year (although coppice woods are cut less frequently). This fact is reflected in terminology as well: the medieval Hungarian word for a stool was the same as that used for a vine-stock (*tőke*).[59]

These conclusions are supported by early dictionaries. Even in the nineteenth century it was plain that an *eresztvény* is "woodland that is cut and is growing new shoots from the stools."[60] *Eresztvény* woods were a stable part of the countryside, often mentioned at longer time intervals. Their management made them more than three times as valuable as ordinary arable land. The meaning of *eresztvény* has become obscure, partly because writers of forestry history who tried to explain it were unfamiliar with the basic concept of coppicing or were reluctant to accept it as a separate management practice.

One remaining problem is the connection between the Latin and the Hungarian terms. *Permissorium* appears to be the translation of *eresztvény*, but the stem of the former is *permissio*, the equivalent of the English 'permission.' This has nothing to do with trees and this fact has puzzled scholars for over a century. Some have conjectured that a *permissorium* was a wood that everyone had permission to visit, but Tagányi observed that access to *permissionalis* woods was usually prohibited.[61] I propose that *permissorium* is merely a bad translation of *eresztvény*, based on a misunderstanding. *Ereszt* today has another meaning: 'to let someone do something'. This must have been the same in the Middle Ages, when those who had to translate the term *eresztvény*, and were probably ignorant of woodland management practices, understood that it had something to do with permission, and translated it likewise.

Silva Dolabrosa, Glandinosa, et Sub Venatione

> a major wood, that is, a timber- or acorn-bearing wood, which is used for timber and hunting, and is good for any kind of work or craft ... each *aratrum* is estimated at 50 marks.[62]

---

58   Szabó 2010.
59   Szabó 2005, 80–81.
60   Czuczor and Fogarasi (eds.) 1862–1874, II, 386.
61   Tagányi 1896, I, xiii.
62   *Item silva maior puta dolabrosa et glandifera seu sub dolabro et venatione existens ac pro quolibet opere et artificio valens ... quodlibet aratrum aestimatur ad M. L.* – Bak et al. (eds.)

The most important message from this definition is that acorn-bearing (*glandinosa*) woods were very valuable: seventeen times as valuable as arable or common woods, and five times as valuable as coppice woods. This was probably because of the acorns, which represented a source of income, the right to which most often belonged to the overlord and therefore had special economic significance. Domestic pigs were driven into woods in the autumn to feed on acorns (a process called pannage), but it should be noted that mast years (years with abundant acorns) occur only every six to eight years, therefore the significance of pannage for woodland ecology should not be overestimated.[63] However, the medieval history of a wood in neighboring Moravia aptly illustrates that management that promotes oaks can change an entire ecosystem.[64] Acorn-bearing woods may also be classified as *dolabrosa*: in such woods, standard trees dominated over coppice stools and management was extensive as opposed to intensive (i.e., intensively managed coppices). The reason is provided by the fact that oak is the species used almost exclusively as medieval building timber. 'Used for hunting' (*sub venatione*) may have had a legal meaning but obviously no management connotations.[65] In the sources, the generally preferred term was *silva dolabrosa*.

Rubetum or Virgultum

for *rubeta* and *virgulta* the same rule [as for common woods] is applied[66]

This laconic sentence by Werbőczy only reveals that *rubeta* and *virgulta* had the same value as arable land or common woods. The two words appear to have been interchangeable, with *rubetum* being the more often used variant. The meanings of these Latin words make it clear that the reference concerns a piece of land dominated by shrubs. *Virgultum* itself may mean 'shrub' and takes its origin from *virga*, meaning 'twig.' *Rubetum* is linguistically less general; it comes from *rubus* meaning 'bramble' in classical Latin. Rather surprisingly, the

---

1992–2012, v, 218–219. (I, no. 133/29). I have slightly altered the translation in Bak et al. (eds.) 1992–2012.

63 Szabó 2013.
64 Jamrichová et al. 2013.
65 For a short overview of medieval hunting rights, see Csőre 1980, 85–88. See also Zolnay 1971.
66 *De rubetis etiam et virgultis idem est sentiendum* – Bak et al. (eds.) 1992–2012, v, 218–219. (I, no. 133/26). Unlike the translation in Bak et al. (eds.) 1992–2012, I have kept the original Latin terms.

Hungarian equivalent of these terms cannot be traced in the sources. In modern source editions, it is customary to translate them as *cserjés*, which broadly covers the concept of *virgultum*.[67]

Shrubland in theory represent the transition between a treeless state and woodland during a process ecologists call succession. Werbőczy knew about succession. When writing about vineyards, he added the following: "Vineyards, according to the ancient customs of our realm, are usually estimated like *rubeta* and *virgulta*, since when and where the vineyard is not attended, and its cultivation is neglected, it turns into *rubeta* and thorns (*vepres*) easily and quickly."[68] However, *rubeta* were a stable part of the landscape. For example, part of the boundary of Barnag (Veszprém County) in 1284 ran between a *silva* and a *virgultum*.[69] This would have made no sense if the *virgultum* was liable to turn into woodland in twenty years or so. In the context of the Carpathian Basin, the only thing capable of stabilizing *rubeta* was management, and in particular, grazing. *Virgulta* and *rubeta* were therefore probably medieval Latin technical terms for *wood-pasture*. This is sometimes explicitly stated, as it is in connection with the village of Béc (Zala County) in 1373: "rubeta seu silva pascualis."[70]

Nemus

Although missing from the *Tripartitum*, *nemus* was a type of woodland very often mentioned in estimations and charters. The word is usually translated into Hungarian as 'berek.' The linguistic background of this word is unclear. Some argue it is Finno-Ugric, and is based on 'bere,' meaning 'mud, marsh,' which was given the diminutive suffix '-k.' Others claim that it is of Slavic origin and means 'bank of river.' Neither of these explanations, so the *Etymological Dictionary* claims, is very convincing.[71] In any case, 'berek' clearly implies some sort of a wetland environment. In a short sentence, *Glosses of Cluj* (ca. 1550) informs us that a "berek" is "where cattle are grazed and kept warm or pass

---

67   *Cserje* means 'shrub.'
68   *Nam vinee generaliter tanquam rubeta et virgulta de regni nostri antiqua consuetudine estimari solent ex eo quod ubi et postquam cultores vinearum aut defuerint aut earum labores praetermiserint vinee cito defacilique in rubeta et vepres convertentur* – Bak et al. (eds.) 1992–2012, V, 220–221. (I, no. 133/45). Here I have also kept the original Latin terms for woodland types.
69   Nagy, Véghely and Nagy (eds.) 1886–1890, I, 94–95.
70   Nagy, Véghely and Nagy (eds.) 1886–1890, II, 68–69.
71   Benkő (ed.) 1967–1984, s. v. "berek." It should be mentioned that there are cases when the "bank of river" translation occurs in medieval documents: Szamota and Zolnai 1902–1906, 66.

the winter."[72] *Nemus* was therefore most probably a form of extensive wetland wood-pasture once typical of large waterlogged areas of the Great Hungarian Plain.

Conclusions

As in other parts of Europe, woodland management in the Middle Ages in the Carpathian Basin was sophisticated and highly adaptable. The many types of management created varied woodland structures, which served a number of purposes – from firewood through building timber to grazing. Careful management was necessary, because by the Late Middle Ages woodland was already very clearly a limited resource that covered only one quarter to one third of the country.

---

72 *Berek, ubi pasci et aestuare vel hyemare pecudes solent* – Berrár and Károly (eds.) 1984, 195.

CHAPTER 10

Water Management in Medieval Hungary

László Ferenczi

In hydrological literature, water management is generally defined as the reconciliation of *water resources* with *water demand*. This effectively divides into four areas of enquiry: (1) water supply for places of habitation, (2) fishing, where it involves managing natural resources, (3) water regulation (flood defense, agricultural irrigation, military-defensive water management, and (4) water as a source of power. Of these, irrigation, fishing and water power merit the most attention by economic historians. This paper will not deal with water supply or sewage, – even though the construction of urban water supplies, for example, were infrastructural developments that could serve as indicators of towns' economic development –, nor with the military significance or economic-history aspects of later medieval hydraulic regulation, apart from some early examples, these being essentially within the sphere of research into early modern fortification systems. Neither is there space to cover the historical hydrological conditions which fundamentally constrained water management, or the methodological difficulties of reconstructing them, although recent research has attempted more accurate reconstruction and understanding of these through the study of historical sources and maps, as well as scientific observations and landscape archaeology data.[1]

Irrigation and River Regulation

The earliest historical studies of water management[2] were based on scattered data from charters and saw medieval water regulation as a restricted, local affair compared with what came later, the large-scale water regulation projects of the nineteenth and twentieth centuries. These studies assumed that material resources and territorial conflicts constrained the scale of water regulations during the Middle Ages, so that the period up to and including the eighteenth

---

1 See for example Kiss 2001 or Pinke and Szabó 2010 and the chapter by László Ferenczi and his colleagues in the present volume.
2 An overview of the results of late nineteenth–early-twentieth-century case studies about different regions of Hungary is contained in Ihrig et al. 1973.

century is referred to as the "era of scattered irrigation." From a social historical perspective, the role of royal and ecclesiastical (monastic) estates and estate centers has been emphasized, whose importance stemmed from their labor-organization capacity and central functions, and also their connection with foreign settlers (*hospites*) from Western Europe, who could play a part in technology transfer with regard to water management.

These studies also inferred that flood plains were used primarily for fishing, hunting and extensive animal husbandry, and only as the significance of crop cultivation grew was there a demand for the regulation of rivers (monastic estates were probably important here too), especially where accompanied by pressure from natural circumstances (such as flood-prone areas, or frequently changing river courses). Economic historians saw a fundamental change in economic regimes in the late thirteenth and early fourteenth centuries. They assumed that animal breeding was more dominant in the eleventh–thirteenth centuries, and that there was a shift in agricultural activities with more emphasis on crop cultivation in the late medieval period. This was confirmed later by findings from settlement archaeology and archaeozoology (by the shift from the characteristically scattered Árpádian-age settlement forms to more nucleated settlements with open field systems characteristic of the fourteenth and fifteenth centuries).[3] There is insufficient evidence to determine whether these fundamental changes occurred in the case of earlier monastic and royal estates.

A case study concerning the region of Rábaköz placed early documentary sources in a landscape archaeology context.[4] It shed new light on issues that have arisen in earlier literature with regard to the dating and physical extent of water regulation works, and made important observations concerning their complexity and their reconstructed principles of operation. It argued that channels identified in the Rábaköz were part of a complex network system which, in addition to draining and preventing floods, provided fresh water for fisheries and the irrigation of fields. The findings of Károly Takács have been criticized by hydrologists, even though we know of other medieval examples of similarly large scale (non-local) systems in Western Europe.[5] Since the soil stratigraphy and archaeological finds in these drains did not always permit the determination of their age or use (continuously used channels were sometimes dredged, thus denying archaeologists of the stratigraphic context), Takács inferred their medieval (Árpádian age) origin from the match between

---

3   For a brief overview of this issue see: Laszlovszky 1999.
4   Takács 2003.
5   Bond 2007, Brown 2005 and Glick and Kirchner 2000.

the extensive network of surface traces and topographic data from perambulation charters, which mention these channels as landmarks on a number of occasions.

Another foothold on the chronology put forward by Takács was the hypothesis that the existence of a coordinating organization was inevitable for such extensive and complex systems to take shape. The author suggested that it was the hierarchically organized population of the royal estates (i.e. *comes, comes curialis, centuriones, decuriones*, and the servant folk) that formed the social basis for the construction of the channel network between the eleventh and thirteenth centuries. He argued that this basis disappeared as royal power weakened by the end of the Árpádian age, and concluded that the channels must have fallen out of use and gradually deteriorated during the fourteenth and fifteenth centuries.[6]

Apart from these landscape archaeological and topographical observations, there are very few explicit references to irrigation channels in late medieval documents (generally these are very late; i.e. dating from the late fifteenth and early sixteenth centuries), and these mostly concern legal conflicts between neighboring landowners, such as the flooding of another's land. The evidence suggests, however, that irrigation systems were still operating in that period, at least to a modest, local extent.

The combined study of landscape archaeological, cartographical and perambulation records may potentially reveal the existence of medieval irrigation and drainage systems in other regions as well. One of these could be, for example, Srijem, famous for its vineyards and orchards. Unfortunately, the topographical data preserved in local perambulation records is scarce, with large chronological and topographical gaps. None, for example, mention the large channels known from narrative sources to have been built in the Roman period, although the possibility that Roman drainage systems stayed in use through later periods cannot be ruled out. This particular problem highlights the importance of carrying out systematic archaeological surveys to gather data not only about medieval, but earlier, potentially Roman-period sites. Scientific methods of investigation can be also instrumental, not only for environmental reconstruction, but also for dating. To mention but one recent example, phytolith analysis of samples from boreholes drilled at several points at the above-mentioned Rábaköz drainage system has yielded evidence of regular maintenance, although chronological issues could not be clarified.[7]

---

6 On these social groups: Zsoldos 1999.
7 Persaits et al. 2010.

Apart from the drainage system demonstrated by Takács, another complex water management system was also present in medieval Hungary. This involved so-called *fok*s – channels characteristic of the flood plains of large meandering rivers (the Danube, the Tisza, and the Dráva). *Fok*s used to channel water from and to main rivers across levees, thereby connecting backwaters and oxbow lakes. *Fok*s appear as historical hydrological toponyms on maps and in documents from the eighteenth and nineteenth centuries. In some cases, they are also recorded in medieval charters,[8] mentioned as *ostium* and *brachium*. They were natural breaks in the levees, but partly also manmade features through which flood water entered the flood plain, filling it from bottom to top, and then flowing out when the river receded. As well as taming the destructive power of the floods, the *fok*s were used to maintain oxbow lakes used as fisheries, and also facilitated irrigation of neighboring pastures and fields.[9] As with the drainage systems of the Rábaköz, there has been much dispute about the *fok*s concerning how these inlets were actually used to regulate water, whether they were originally natural or artificial, what the extent of artificial intervention was, and how the whole system functioned exactly.[10]

Fishing

Medieval narrative sources attest to the country's exceptionally rich endowment of fish and game. Although fishing must have played a significant economic and nutritional role, it is very difficult to know the economic role of fishponds and river fisheries in general.[11] There are a few informative documents that contain quantitative data, but local conditions might have varied

---

8   For example, concerning the *fok*s of the River Dráva, see: Vajda 2001.
9   Andrásfalvy 1989.
10 Different viewpoints – primarily based on the works of Bertalan Andrásfalvy (Andrásfalvy 1973, 1975, 1976), Zsigmond Károlyi, Woldemár Lászlóffy and Antal András Deák – have been recently summarized in Fodor 2001. For the application of geomorphological and pedological methods in identifying the system of *fok*s: Lóczy 2007. Methods based on geomorphological criteria for identifying artificial water channels have been discussed more extensively by Rhodes 2007.
11 E.g. *Pars Danubialis irrigatur per medium ab illo famoso fluio qui dicitur Danubius qui est de maioribus totius mundi, fertilissimus in omni genere piscium et currit uersus orientem. Irrigatur et aliis fluuiis qui sunt fere eque magni ut Danubius, uidelicet Draua, Zaica, Tiscia, Vag, Culpa, Raba, Anrad, Bega, Lobret, Lucarta. Omnia hec flumina sunt naualia et multum fertilia in piscibus sicut et in husonibus qui sunt maximi et delicatissimi pisces, sturionibus, luciis et aliis piscibus sicut barbatis et cetera –* Górka (ed.) 1916, 47. (from ca. 1300).

greatly, thus such documents cannot be used to draw general conclusions.[12] Most of the knowledge we have is derived from early sixteenth-century financial accounts that give some information about expenses and incomes related to the management of certain fishponds and fisheries. In some fortunate cases, such accounts cover several consecutive years and are thus more representative in financial terms. Only fisheries that generated higher income have left us with records of this kind – for instance, fish weirs (i.e. the fish traps of river fisheries called *szégye*, where the catch was mostly sturgeon, the most expensive of fish). Accounts for the *szégye* fisheries in the neighboring villages of Kolárovo and Nesvady on the Danube, owned by the archbishopric of Esztergom, record the number of sturgeon caught in the late sixteenth century (1578, 1581, and 1594).[13] These averaged 150–160 a year, and the fish fetched 6–8 florins each. The accounts also record the names of customers, who included baronial families, tenant peasants of nearby market towns, burghers of the free royal town of Bratislava, and agents of the imperial court in Vienna. The latter regularly bought large quantities, up to 50–60 at a time.

The available documents rarely permit an assessment of the economic role of fishing lakes within a single estate. According to the accounts of the Ónod estate beside the River Tisza, fishing provided a considerable income (40–50 florins a year), commensurate with the sums brought in from the right to levy customs duty on the through-traffic of the ferry. As for types of fishing gear, the documents most frequently mention the *gyalom*, a kind of seine net used when fishing on mortlakes (e.g. along the Tisza), and fixed fish weirs, the *szégye*.[14] Lords were generally due half or a quarter of the income of the fishponds. This was usually collected from the fishermen in money, and more rarely, in kind. They could also charge for the use of gear (e.g. *szégye*, boats, etc.). The household accounts of the Ónod estate also recorded the expenses set against the incomes of the fisheries. These were sometimes very diverse: mostly food (even the purchase of fish!), but also salt, used to preserve the fish they caught.[15] The masters of the lord bought a variety of commercially available fish – species

---

12   For an early attempt to survey the written evidence, see: Degré 1939.

13   Takáts 1897. For similar *szégyés* on the Tisza owned by the bishopric of Eger: Sugár 1979. See also: Bartosiewicz 2008a and the study of László Bartosiewicz and his colleagues in the present volume.

14   Data about fisheries and fishing can be found in several accounts concerning different estates of the castle of Ónod: MNL OL DL 26 183 (1517), 26 194 (1518), 26 197 (1519), 26 204 (1519), 26 206 (1519), 26 212 (1519), 26 228 (1520) References to purchases of different types of fish can also be found in other accounts connected to customs duties. These accounts have been extensively discussed by Iványi 1906.

15   MNL OL DL 26 169 (1516), see also Iványi 1906, 14 and MNL OL DL 26 204 (1519).

mentioned in other sources of the time, and probably the most popular, include carp, sterlet (*Acipenser ruthenus*), sturgeon (*Acipenser huso*), burbot (*Lota lota*), and European wels (*Silurus glanis L.*). These were bought mostly from local fishermen, but sometimes also from the Pauline friary of Sajólád,[16] which neighbored the estate. On one occasion, sea fish (herring) was also purchased, but this might have been an exception, since it was noted that no other fish were available.[17] Herring, caught in the Baltic Sea and traded by Hanseatic towns, must have come into the country from Poland along the trade route through Košice. It is interesting that excavation of the nearby market town of Muhi has brought to light some barrel-lined wells whose interiors were made of wood from Polish-German territory, dated to the fourteenth century. The barrels were almost certainly originally used to transport herring.[18]

Land registers (*urbaria*) of secular or ecclesiastical estates[19] or other types of registers related to the economic administration of landed property (e.g. records of towns or chapters)[20] may also provide useful data, although less systematically or comprehensively than account books. For instance, chapter registers can include entries about the redistribution of incomes among the members of the chapter from year to year, some of which concern fishponds and lakes, although they do not address managerial-administrative issues. There is also much to be learned from references to fishponds and fisheries in lawsuits or land transactions. For instance, estimated damages were recorded after acts of might, often as much as 100–200 florins for fishing out a lake. To put this in context, if the total annual value of such fishing out of a lake was this much, the census of a few fishponds (representing a landowner's income as a lump sum from fishing) could have equaled the census income collected from a minor market town (a few hundred florins). With this in mind, it is not surprising to witness many references to the construction of ponds during the fourteenth and fifteenth centuries. As for the Kingdom of Hungary, there is no comprehensive survey to indicate this trend, but similar tendencies have been observed in Bohemia.[21] The payback time for building a fishpond could be as little as a year or two, although the construction costs varied according to the natural conditions and individual requirements. The initial choice of

---

16   MNL OL DL 26 193 (1518).
17   Mentioned by Iványi 1906, 27. See MNL OL DL 26 193 (1518).
18   For written evidence concerning the herring trade, see: Gulyás 2014b, 108.
19   E.g. Kredics and Solymosi (eds.) 1993.
20   E.g. Solymosi (ed.) 2002. For a brief overview of potential sources of economic administration – including *urbaria* type land registers and others –, see Szabó 2003.
21   Přikryl 2004.

a site for a pond had to be made very carefully to ensure it could be kept and maintained efficiently. On the other hand, maintenance costs – unlike those of mills, with their complex mechanisms – were usually negligible, the work mostly being assigned to tenants, or sometimes to an appointed caretaker, so that money only had to be spent on purchasing or making fishing tackle and other equipment.

Distinctions among types of fishponds appear very rarely in documents, one case being the oxbow lakes referred to by the word still currently in use in Hungarian, *morotva* (*piscina seu morotva*), maintained by the *fok* canal system. Sometimes such names are indicative of the lake's artificial or natural origin, e.g. *Kengyel*, which refers to the curved shape typical of oxbow lakes, or *Ásvány/ Ásványtó*, which occurs quite often, and clearly denotes an artificial pond. Some Western European sources make a functional distinction between lakes for breeding and keeping fish (*vivarium* and *servatorium*),[22] but in Hungarian sources the small artificial ponds for keeping fish and large flood-plain lakes for breeding fish could be both referred to as *vivarium*.[23] It was probably only in the later medieval period that the word *vivarium* came to mean a certain type of fishpond (for breeding or storage) – the more systematic study of the use of this term is desirable. In any case, flood-plain lakes regulated by *fok*s were suitable for both keeping and breeding fish, and where necessary there were other ponds for storing them.[24]

Documents frequently refer to fishponds and lakes as being large or small (*magna* or *parva*). This may be more informative than it first appears, because according to István Werbőczy's *Tripartitum*, an overview of the medieval customary law of Hungary compiled in 1517, the size of fishponds is one potential criterion for their valuation and classification of type. According to Werbőczy, a pond's value depended on two things: its size, and whether it periodically dried out or had a permanent water supply.[25] This typology can most probably

---

22 Aston 1988.
23 The *vivarium* may appear as a constructed pond: MNL OL DL 36 400 (1524): *unum vivarium sive piscinulam ad conservationem piscium construi fecit* (emphasis mine). However, in the donation charter (1138) of the collegiate chapter of Dömös, it suggests a natural origin: *Iuxta villam Tapai est vivarium, quod dicitur Citei/Etei, in quo vivario tertiam partem debent habere cives Cerugdienses, si claudere voluerint cum Demesiensibus exitus et reditus faucis vivarii, si claudere noluerint nullam partem habebit.* – Fejér (ed.) 1829–1844, II, 103.
24 For an overview see: Zatykó 2011.
25 See Bak et al. (eds.) 1992–2012, V, 220–221. (I, no. 133/40) *Item piscina effluens, et non deficiens ad m(arcam) 10. Non effluens autem, et tempore siccatis deficiens ad m(arcam) 5.* and *Piscina magna cum clausura existens Gyalmostho, vel etiam Morothwa dicta, necnon alia*

be traced back to a book which enjoyed popularity as a manual of economics in the fourteenth and fifteenth centuries, the *Ruralia Commoda*.[26] This was written by the thirteenth-century scholar Pietro de' Crescenzi, who also distinguished "large" and "small" fishponds, and classified them further according to whether they have a permanent water supply. Small artificial fishponds, as described in the book, had to be completely surrounded with stones, branches or wood to protect them from the ravages of predators like otters, and their beds had to be dug as deep as possible. Small ponds that were constantly refreshed were suitable for *cavidanii, scardinae*, and *barbii* – i.e. chub (*Squalius cephalis*), rudd (*Scardinius erythropthalmus*), and barbel (*Barbus barbus*) – and other small fish, and even for trout, whereas those which had no water inflow or were marshy because of clayey soil were better suited to tench, eels and several other small fish. Large fishponds on wet, marshy land were home to all kinds of fish, but in smaller ponds there were some kinds of fish it was inadvisable to keep, such as pike (*Esox Lucius*) which would eat smaller fish. The major difference between these fishponds and lakes was connected to the method of fishing, and thus the potential revenue, because larger equipment such as weirs and large seine nets could only be used on larger lakes and rivers.

Besides the systematic study of documents, topographical research and landscape archaeology can also tell us a lot about fishponds. In fact, for small ecclesiastical or secular estates, these methods provide the only data, as there are no written sources, or very few.[27] Typological classifications based on field observations concerning forms and shapes can help distinguish, for example, between all-purpose and special-function fishponds.[28] The latter include systems of multiple ponds which, according to sixteenth- and seventeenth-century fishing literature, served to separate younger and older fish, and to drain water from the pond beds and periodically dry them out. Typically, these involved a system of stepped weirs across a valley, of which traces are still perceptible on several – mainly monastic – estates. Another special type are those small fishponds that also involved the construction of a dam across a valley, which are characteristically found beside Pauline friaries (*see* Fig. 10.1). Some

---

piscatura Danubialis vel Thicalis, sive Zawe, aut Drawe Thanya nuncupata, si habet deputantum proventum annalem, decies tantum aestimatur, quantum facit eius proventus annualis. Si vero computatum proventum non habet (prout nos generaliter utimur) aestimatur ad m(arcam) 50. Bak et al. (eds.) 1992–2012, V, 220–221. (I, no. 133/41).

26 See Petrus de Crescentiis 1998. Chap. 81: *De piscinis et piscibus includendis*.
27 E.g. Belényesy 2004.
28 Aston 1988. See also the other studies in the same volume.

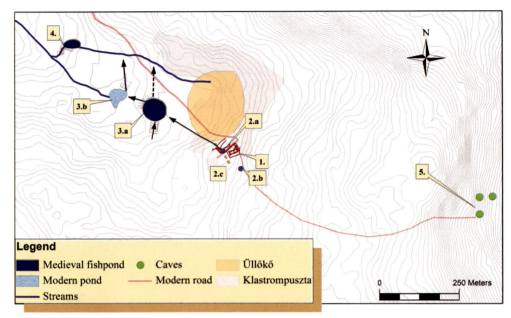

FIGURE 10.1　*Medieval fishponds of the Pauline monastery of the Holy Cross in the Pilis (after Zsuzsa Pető).*

of these were presumably too small for fish breeding, and must have been used for storing fish and storing and supplying water.

Hydropower – Mills

Literature on the harnessing of water energy in the Middle Ages is chiefly concerned with dating the appearance of vertical water-wheel mills, one of the most important medieval technical inventions, as well as assessing their efficiency and power, estimating the revenue they provided, and establishing their numbers and geographical distribution.[29] Studies in engineering history originally considered the vertical-wheel mill to have appeared in Hungary in the twelfth century, casting doubt on the authenticity of some earlier charters, but the early eleventh century is now more widely accepted. Economic historians clearly link this structure to the system of management and organization

---

29　Most recently, Vajda 2005, Vajda 2016 and Vadas 2018, all with reference to further literature.

developed on the large estates of the Benedictine order and the bishoprics. László Makkai has drawn on Western European parallels to highlight the role of these ecclesiastical estates which were created in the eleventh and twelfth centuries, and explained the increasing number of mills as a response to the demands of these estates as they grew in size.[30] A similar phenomenon, however, is perceptible in small estates of the time, as an economic history study of northern France in the eleventh–thirteenth centuries has highlighted, and this may be explained through the competition of local landowners.[31] The industrial applications of mills is recorded for the first time in Hungary in the thirteenth century,[32] when an increasing number of records reflect the spread of water mills throughout the country. However, these more plentiful references may not be a completely reliable reflection of the spread of this technology, since this was a period when numbers of archival records multiplied due to their issuance by places of authentication, and many other sources.[33]

The efficiency of milling and the output of mills (primarily the province of engineering historians) was also addressed by Makkai. Using eleventh-century sources from England and Hungary, he showed that the capacity of mills did not diverge from the European average: one mill could supply about 250 people (30–40 families).[34] This estimate was based on censuses which included the numbers of both families and mills, while Makkai assumed that the capacity of mills was even, that estates were self-sustaining, and the mills did not produce a surplus. The fourteenth- and fifteenth-century sources provide a lot more details about milling, although making similar calculations would be highly problematic. It is not only that economic conditions had changed by that time (due to the increase in significance of the market economy, apparently changing the demand for milling), but the greater number of accounts and registers attest that the capacity of mills was influenced by a number of factors. The available accounts and registers of incomes and expenses usually cover periods of no longer than a few years. Most of them record annual outputs; some accounts only give the quantities of grain without calculating incomes or prices. However, they only occasionally mention other influential

---

30 Makkai 1974.
31 Van der Beek 2010. A similar process appears to have been documented in the middle of the thirteenth century in the Rábaköz region, where the number of mills had grown rapidly so that some of them were already unsustainable. Eventually, the palatine ordered them to be destroyed. Cf. MNL OL DL 317 (1247).
32 Heckenast 1965 and Teke 2003.
33 In connection with this issue, see Kőfalvi 2002, or Solymosi 2008.
34 Makkai 1995.

factors such as the type of mill (undershot, overshot, shipmills), the number of mill wheels or millstones, the type of grain, the type of flour, the cereal that was milled (which was subject to regional variation) and whether the mill was operating to full capacity. Taken together, these factors are an obstacle to evaluating the sparse and local data about capacity and income, and to drawing general conclusions about how the technology of milling improved with time.

The Ónod estate is an exceptionally well documented case, where – according to the accounts – the mills ground 50, 150 and 300 *cubuli* of grain in 1516, 1518, and 1519 (respectively), which earned between 15 and 90 florins.[35] These figures show that mills were probably a little more modest sources of income than fishponds. An estate with several mills did not necessarily collect more than 100 florins a year from them.[36] István Kenyeres' study also gives examples of the income derived from mills on secular estates. Depending on what other sources of income an estate had, mills accounted for a highly variable proportion of the total. The same was, of course, also true for ecclesiastical estates (of bishoprics, chapters, and monasteries). Erik Fügedi has shown from fifteenth-century account books that the archbishop of Esztergom had an average annual income of 10 florins per mill, a total of 140–170 florins; a very modest proportion of his annual total of more than 10,000 florins.[37] Mills may have accounted for a greater share of income on monastic and chapter estates and bishoprics with lower annual incomes, but there are only a few scattered records to demonstrate this. For example, in 1356 the Cistercian Abbey of Pilis (present-day Pilisszentkereszt) derived an income of only 40 florins from the wine tithe and the mills from a total income of 700 florins.[38] Moreover, the expenses listed against the income from the Ónod mills shows that these figures did not in any way represent clear profit; the same conclusion may be drawn from the 1524 *urbarium* of the bishopric of Veszprém, where bailiffs were paid out of income from mills.[39] The owner of a mill let to a tenant would in any case only receive a certain part of the income.[40] Mills also required greater

---

35 The accounts of the mill at Ónod: MNL OL DL 26 172 (1516), és DL 26 203 (1519), DL 26 214 (1519). The accounts of the mill at Bölcs: MNL OL DL 26 186 (1518) and DL 26 213 (1519).

36 See e.g. Holub 1963, 51. There is mention here of the Lendava estate of the Bánffy family, where the income from mills amounted to only 71 florins in the early years of the sixteenth century.

37 Fügedi 1981a.

38 Hervay 1984, 144. The biggest part of the income (400 florins) came from custom duties.

39 See Holub 1943 and Holub 1963.

40 Either administered in money or in kind, this proportion varies considerably, but it is usually one-third. See e.g. Holub 1963, 50.

expenditure on maintenance than fishponds: money was required to replace worn millstones, iron fittings and tools, and to repair timberwork and dams.[41]

Nonetheless, mill leases and income records from the late sixteenth century show the effects of the agricultural economic upturn: as cereal prices rose, so did the income from mills. Compared with the 1 florin for 3–4 *cubuli*[42] of wheat in the fourteenth and fifteenth centuries, account books for the mills of the town of Cluj,[43] and those for the Esztergom archbishopric's mills in Kremnica in the 1580s and 1590s[44] show 1 *cubulus* of wheat being sold for 1–3 florins. It was probably urban mills that profited from this situation most, because they usually had greater capacity (more wheels), and generated more income. The Cluj and Kremnica mills had annual incomes of between 200 and 500 florins.

With general economic development, the total number of mills probably increased as new mills were established. Using eighteenth century statistical data, Zs. Károlyi estimated the number of mills in medieval Hungary at between 5000 and 6000. Whether this refers only to the sixteenth or the fifteenth century, or even the earlier period is not clarified, and a systematic collection of medieval charter data would be desirable to verify this claim. The most interesting problem is determining regional differences among ecclesiastical and secular estates, as well as fluctuations in mill numbers.[45]

Estimates for the eleventh–thirteenth centuries are highly problematic, as data from charters are sparse and spatially fragmented, with no representative value. The large ecclesiastical estates, especially those in Transdanubia – the Benedictine Abbeys of Pannonhalma and Tihany, and the bishopric of Veszprém – are the best documented, where mills are mentioned in charters granting or confirming donations as early as the eleventh and twelfth centuries. However, the mills located within the monastic precincts, which sometimes had specialized industrial functions, are almost never mentioned and are only known from excavations.[46] The variation in size of estate,

---

41 Such data are mentioned by Holub 1963, 48 and Iványi 1906, 20. See also in Iványi (ed.) 1918 and Vadas 2013b.

42 The exact size of these cubic measures, as well as their proportions, is difficult to establish due to terminological diversity in different regions, and the scattered data. According to Bogdán 1991, a *cubulus* of grain was about 50–90 kilograms, and a *metreta* 40 kilograms. However, the *metreta* also appears as a synonym of the *quartalia*; i.e., one quarter of a cubulus. It is also confusing that measures may frequently appear in the sources under their vernacular names.

43 Novák 2001.

44 Acsády 1895.

45 An exemplary study of this issue is Langdon 1991. See also Langdon 2004.

46 Gerevich 1977.

method of cultivation and preferences among different monastic orders and different chapters may show up in the divergent number and location of mills. For instance, the relatively large Cistercian estates – granted by the king – usually had no more than about five to ten mills,[47] and smaller ones had even fewer. The largest and most prestigious Benedictine house, Pannonhalma, had 20 or 30, clearly distinguishing it from other houses of the order. The priory of Csorna (whose significance among Premonstratensian houses can be compared to that of Pannonhalma among the Benedictines) also stands out for the number of its mills – between fifteen and seventeen. This was no doubt because the estate specialized in the production of grain, which it even transported to Vienna using its own Danube-bound ship. The smaller Mendicant friaries usually had fewer mills, but still looked to them as a major source of income. In general, Dominican and Franciscan friaries, which mostly established themselves in towns, were less inclined to set up fishponds and mills than the Paulines. It appears that the site selection of Pauline monasteries was better aligned with hermitic ideals and economic activity that enabled self-sustenance, and they derived substantial income from the tenants of mills acquired in nearby market towns.[48] As landlords, seeing the opportunity to increase their income through serving the demand of bigger local populations, these urban properties were identified by these orders as a good investment.

As has already been underlined, we have a better appreciation of the management of the great estates of secular lords in the fifteenth and sixteenth centuries because a greater number of registers, accounts and *urbaria* survive from this period. Ferenc Maksay argued that mill numbers are good indicators of the rising prosperity of landowners' manors, which were expanding at that time.[49] On the Rechnitz–Schlaining estate,[50] for example, 20–25 out of 40 villages had mills. The number of mills increased in the second half of the sixteenth century and declined in the early seventeenth century, almost certainly because of the Ottoman-Habsburg Fifteen Years' War (1591–1606). The increase in the number of mill wheels, however, meant that the overall level of output was probably maintained. This again raises questions about the interpretation of quantitative data, demonstrating that the income from mills was not

---

47. Ferenczi 2006. The case study also demonstrates the close topographical relation between central places and mill sites.
48. Belényesy 2004 and Romhányi 2010b for the Paulines. Romhányi 2014, 129–151 for the Mendicant orders.
49. Maksay 1959.
50. For a brief introduction to its history, see Zimányi 1992. For the mills of the nearby estate of Körmend, see: Vadas 2013b.

necessarily proportional to the documented number of mills. Thus, if only mill numbers are known from *urbaria*, and no account books or income figures are available, supporting Maksay's conclusion is problematic. Another example is the twenty-seven-village estate of the castle of Gyula, where there were 12–14 mills in operation in the 1520s. In subsequent decades, there was an increase in the number of mills, too, but to a lesser extent.[51] Given the position of the estate on the frontiers of occupied territory, it must have been more seriously affected by military action during the sixteenth century.

In summary, changes in the documented number of mills do not necessarily signal economic growth or manorial activity. Thus, even when general economic trends (agricultural development, and the rise of the manorial serf-economy) suggest that the significance of the milling industry was increasing, assessment and evaluation of the differences between the development of estates is important for understanding divergent natural endowments and various political, social and economic factors. Landlords leased out their mills to tenants, and the construction of new mills could have involved a combined effort to share risks and costs, so that an increase in the productivity of an estate should not be interpreted as the straightforward intention of the landlord to increase manorial income. Mill tenants (wealthy peasants and townsfolk) could also benefit from the economic opportunity generated by a rise in market demand. On the other hand, mill rents could of course inflate together with grain prices: in addition to the miller's additional duties and services, annual rents were often – indeed, customarily – recorded as 1 florin per year in the fourteenth and fifteenth centuries, but went up to 3, 6 or even 8 florins in the sixteenth and seventeenth centuries, although instances of exceptionally high rents can be found at any time.

Topographical studies of mills and fishponds can also fill in some gaps in our knowledge of the settlement hierarchy of a single estate or region, since the geographical distribution of mills was often connected to estate centers, manors, villages of sizeable population, and market towns. From a topographical perspective, a mill beside the castle at the center of a large secular estate, as with a mill beside a monastery, was an almost ubiquitous feature. An impressive, if exceptional, example was Tata Castle, a favored royal residence in the fifteenth century: Antonio Bonfini, King Matthias's court historian, noted that it had no less than nine mills. The complex hydraulic system constructed between 1412 and 1424 probably made use of a fishpond and some mills originally established by the Benedictine Abbey in Tata. The drainage system was linked to the castle moat, supplying it with water. The moat – according to

---

51   Kiss 1978.

sixteenth-century data – was also used to store Danube sturgeon purchased for the royal court, proudly shown off to guests by King Matthias himself.[52] Mills near castles must have taken on greater importance in the sixteenth century, when the military-strategic role of such forts increased: as well as grinding grain, the mills had to serve as forges and gunpowder mills. During the fourteenth and fifteenth centuries, more mills appeared in the expanding market towns. Where there were also favorable natural features, such as thermal springs, mills were built in considerable numbers. Along a 15-kilometer-stretch of the River Tapolca, for example, in the market town of Pápa and its neighboring villages, there were 15–20 mills in the fifteenth and sixteenth centuries.[53] The hydrological resources in the vicinity of the royal seat of Buda – Alhévíz, Felhévíz and Óbuda – were taken advantage of by several ecclesiastical bodies, including the Hospitallers' convent in Óbuda, the Poor Clares of Óbuda, the Cistercian Abbey of Pilis, and the Premonstratensians of the Margaret Island, as well as the burghers of Óbuda.[54] Attempts by the municipal authorities of developing Western European towns – particularly wealthy trading towns with territorial authority – to redeem water-use rights and buy up mills in the thirteenth century (water use was subject to *regale*; i.e., the pre-emptive right of kings) had no echo in Hungary, where town councils did not seem to have comparable territorial influence. The ownership of mills in the vicinity of towns was usually mixed, but in the case of archiepiscopal seats and chapter houses, there was, indeed, a clear policy of acquiring and letting out as many mills as possible.

---

52   Fülöp 2009, 74–75. On the usage of moats for milling and fishing, see: Vadas 2015–2016.
53   Kubinyi 1994b.
54   For a detailed topographical analysis, see Kubinyi 1964c.

PART 3

Money, Incomes and Management

∴

CHAPTER 11

Royal Revenues in the Árpádian Age

Boglárka Weisz *

Royal revenues in the Árpádian age were gathered in the form of money, produce or labor. At different times during this period, one form or another tended to dominate, but never to the exclusion of the rest. Food tax was the main source of revenue for the crown in the eleventh and twelfth centuries, giving way to monetary taxation in the thirteenth century, although the enormous amount of products demanded by the royal court stopped the food tax from dying out. Árpádian kings enjoyed income from royal estates and royal prerogative. Both were in use from the beginning of the era, and until the thirteenth century the kings made no distinction between them and did not link royal expenditure to the origin of the revenue. A register of revenues from the time of King Béla III – the only document of its kind which survives from the Árpádian age – places revenue from these two forms side by side.[1] From the early thirteenth century on, certain revenues were distinguished, as either due to the royal chamber (*ad fiscum pertinentes*), or to the king as a landlord (*ad regem pertinencia*). This might primarily be explained by the practice that the *comes* (ispán – *comes parochianus*), who administered the collection of fiscal revenues within a county, received one-third of such incomes, whereas he had no share from seigneurial dues. The treasury was due the freemen's pennies (*liberi denarii*), the *pondus* and the *collecta*, all gathered by the collector of public taxes (*collector publicorum vectigalium*). The king also had revenues payable in kind: the "bucket tax" on vineyards (*chybriones*), the "pig tithe" paid by people who grazed their pigs in castle forests (*tributum porcorum*) and the "ox tax" (*boves*). These taxes were initially payable to the crown even on estates not owned by the king. Some other revenues changed in the course of the centuries, such as the *marturina* ("marten's fur"), which in many cases became a seigneurial due – because the king assigned it, at least partly, to the landowners –, and the *pondus*, which was re-imposed on the royal estates in the thirteenth century, and the king thereafter could collect it only as a landowner. Royal revenues of the Árpádian age can be classified into the following categories: 1. revenues

---

* The author is the leader of the Research Centre for the Humanities, Hungarian Academy of Sciences "Lendület" Medieval Hungarian Economic History Research Group (LP2015-4/2015).
1 On this see also the chapter by Balázs Nagy in the present volume.

from royal monopolies; 2. customs and tolls; 3. direct taxes; 4. other royal revenues; 5. revenues from royal estates.

Revenues from Royal Monopolies

Salt Monopoly
Salt mines passed into the hands of the Árpáds early in the period,[2] and kings were determined to safeguard their monopoly. The privileges granted in the second half of the thirteenth century to the towns which had grown up next to salt mines did not include ownership of the mines. All these towns got was the opportunity to extract salt for a specified period and sell it freely. There were two methods employed to supply the kingdom with royal salt during the Árpádian age: setting up royal salt depots, and apportioning salt to the ecclesiastical bodies which excavated it from the mines or the depots and then distributed it.[3] Under the Golden Bull of 1222,[4] royal salt depots could be established only in Szeged, Sălacea and the border marches.[5] Charters attest to royal salt depots in Sălacea, Szeged, Bratislava, Sopron, and Vasvár. The location of the depots show that the king was above all intent on controling foreign trade.

Mining of Precious Metal Ore
Until the Mongol invasion of 1241–1242, the mines were owned by the king, who enjoyed all of their income. A landowner who was granted title to an estate containing a mine was due one third of the ore from the mine. The settlement of miners from Czech and German lands in the period following the Mongol attack prompted a change in the revenue from mines. The miners were granted mining freedom, the right to work independently, with obligations only to give the king a certain part of the extracted metal, the *urbura*, representing an eighth of the yield in silver and a tenth of that in gold. Mine-owners included ecclesiastical and temporal landowners. There were three arrangements under which mines on private land could be worked: 1. the king acquired the land enclosing the mine from the landowner in exchange for other land, so that the mine became royal property; 2. the landowners worked the mines themselves, paying *urbura* to the king; 3. the landowner was relieved of possession

---

2 Szentpétery (ed.) 1937–1938, II, 489–490. On salt extraction and trade, see the chapters by Beatrix F. Romhányi and István Draskóczy.
3 Kubinyi 1988, 217.
4 Cf. Engel 2001, 93–95 and Zsoldos 2011.
5 Marsina (ed.) 1971–1987, I, 199–201.

of the land while the mine was worked, and compensated with one third of the *urbura*.[6]

Coinage Privileges

The minting of money was a royal privilege in the Árpádian age, held solely by the king and the princes. The issuers of coins had to cover the costs of refining silver and minting the coins, for which there were several methods: 1. if precious metal from commoners was minted, a certain percentage of the coins' value was deducted as expenses (the procedure might have been in practice in Hungary, although there is only one source that refers to it. According to a mid-eleventh-century decision by the Mainz scholar Jehuda ben Meir ha-Kohen, a Hungarian Jew requested and received permission from the queen to get his own silver minted into coins.[7]) 2. If the king had the coins minted from his own ore, profit was made by increasing the number of coins per unit weight, circulation being counted using the smaller number. For example, 300 or 360 denars could be minted from one pound of ore, but one pound was still calculated as 240 denars. 3. There was regular renewal of money (*renovatio monete*), whereby chamber money changers (called *nummularius* or *monetarius*) exchanged newly-minted coins for old or foreign coins, deducting the "chamber's profit" (*lucrum camarae*). The money had to be changed within a fixed period, usually the six weeks from Palm Sunday to St George's Day.[8]

The way money renewal was carried out went through some changes in the course of the Árpádian age. In the early period, it was done at fairs; however, royal money changers could not operate on certain ecclesiastical lands: for example, the inhabitants of the ecclesiastical estate of the bishopric of Pécs acquired the royal coins (*regni monetam*) by selling their wares at other county fairs (*in aliis provincialibus foris*).[9] As foreign coins and unminted silver were also in circulation during the Árpádian age, the king could only secure his revenue through a form of money changing that required everybody in the kingdom to change a specified sum. Under the laws of King Andrew III, the king issued the coins via four good men (*quatuor boni homines*) from each county and the *comes* of the county (*comes parochianus*),[10] who – by ancient custom (*secundum antiquam consuetudinem*) – discharged this duty at fairs and other places.[11] The procedure for changing money is also recorded in a royal

---

6 Weisz 2007a and Weisz 2013c, 221–222.
7 Spitzler and Komoróczy 2003, 109–110.
8 Hóman 1916, 415.
9 Kubinyi (ed.) 1997, 17 (1190). See also: Szentpétery and Borsa 1923–1987, no. 151.
10 Bak et al. (eds.) 1992–2012, I, 43.
11 Bak et al. (eds.) 1992–2012, I, 50.

instruction to Ung County in 1330, and probably reflects how it was done in the late thirteenth century. Before the annual money changing, a body of persons elected by the county assembly assessed how much the county could pay, and this determined the amounts people had to change. Subsequently, money was changed at a specific place and time: every tenant peasant (*iobagio*) bound to pay landlord's tribute of more than one mark had to pay half a *ferto*. The chamber count gave half a *ferto* of new denars in exchange for half a *ferto* of silver, weighed on the scales, but the same amount of new denars for old coins weighing nine pondus (half a *ferto* being six *pondus*).[12] There is evidence from the late thirteenth century that the nobles were responsible for payment of the chamber's profit (*iuxta regni consuetudinem ab antiquo approbatam*), and had to ensure payment within a certain time limit after it was levied.[13] Anybody who did not accept the coins had to pay a *collecta* of half a *ferto* for every tenement (*per singulas mansiones*).[14] This *collecta monetae, collecta lucri camerae* – levied to redeem unchanged money or as chamber profit – appeared in the early thirteenth century.[15]

Customs and Excise (*Tributum, Teloneum*)

Collection of Customs Duty and Royal Customs Policy

When King Stephen I laid down the first royal policy of customs and excise policy in Hungary, he was formalizing an already well-established practice of collecting revenue in this form.[16] King Coloman legislated that everyone selling their own wares or products at a market was obliged to pay duty in accordance with the law of St Stephen.[17] Otto of Freising's history of Emperor Frederick I, who traveled to Hungary, tells of the collection of duties in the kingdom being the sole privilege of the king in the early twelfth century.[18] The right to exact customs and excise duties was granted to others on a substantial scale from the time of King Andrew II. The various customs and excise duties were reviewed in the second half of the thirteenth century[19] and commodities liable to them

---

12   Cf. Hóman 1921, 258–259 and Engel 1999, 37–38.
13   Bak et al. (eds.) 1992–2012, I, 72.
14   Bak et al. (eds.) 1992–2012, I, 50.
15   Weisz 2012a.
16   Cf. Györffy 1983a, 52–53 and 108–110.
17   Bak et al. (eds.) 1992–2012, I, 27.
18   Otto of Freising, *Gesta Frederici imperatoris* in Waitz 1912.
19   Bak et al. (eds.) 1992–2012, I, 44.

were specified in writing. The king eventually relinquished his sole control of customs and excise, retaining two parts and granting the third part to the *comes*. This applied to customs duty on imports and duties payable on goods transported and sold inland. The *comes* received a smaller proportion – one quarter – of the customs duty on exports.[20]

Forms of Duty – Inland Duties: Passage

Road tolls (*tributum viae*) were paid by those traveling by land – on foot, horse or cart. To cross rivers or lakes they had to pay bridge tolls (*tributum pontis*) and ferry tolls (*tributum portus*). Those traveling up and down rivers paid shipping tolls (*tributum navigii*), or anchorage (*tributum in portu*) probably collected at harbors beside bridges and ferries, where bridge and ferry tolls were also collected from persons crossing the water. The ferrymen charged their passengers ferriage (*naulum*), out of which they paid a toll (*tributum nauli*) to the lord holding the right to the shipping toll. Since goods transported by land often had to cross rivers, this was a device by which lords could impose their right to exact the shipping toll on such goods. Tolls were also collected on timber floated down the river (*tributum lignorum*). This category of duties also included salt toll (*tributum salinarum*), which the sources mention as being payable by salt carriers, whether they transported the salt by land or water.

Forms of Duty – Inland Duties: Market Tolls

The other main category of inland duties was that of market tolls (*tributum fori*), payable by both buyers and sellers at markets. Sales from workshops were also taxed, and stallholders had to pay stallage. Excise payable on wine and other beverages sold in taverns should also be regarded as market duty. Closely connected was gate toll (*tributum portae*). It is possible that gate tolls were initially confined to certain items, like carts laden with timber, and extended only later when it was realized that market tolls, too, could be collected more simply and effectively if payment was demanded at the castle gate.

Forms of Duty – Customs Duties Collected at Border Gates

Travelers going into or out of the country had to pay customs duties at border gates. These duties are mainly mentioned in privileges granting exemption,[21]

---

20   Kubinyi (ed.) 1997, 51–52 (1255). See also: Szentpétery and Borsa 1923–1987, no. 1237. Cf. Weisz 2013b, 9–46.

21   E.g. Wagner et al. (eds.) 1955–1999, I, 107 (1225), Wagner et al. (eds.) 1955–1999, I, 129 (ca. 1230), Kubinyi (ed.) 1997, 30 (6 May 1237) and Marsina (ed.) 1971–1987, II, 89 (7 June 1243).

and so we know of only two specific border gates and the duties they collected. In 1274 King Ladislas IV granted a customs gate at Samobor to Ivan, *comes* of Oklics (Okič). The grant included the duties to be collected there and the adjacent village (*cum tributo porte prope ipsam villam in regni nostri confinio existentis*).[22] At Ždiar in Szepes County, customs duties were collected at the gate (*in porta*) on the road to Poland. In 1298, Bald, *comes* of Szepes, exempted the inhabitants of the nearby village of Őr, within the estate of Szepes Castle (now the area of Spišská Belá, Slovakia) from duties to defend the customs gate.[23] There is also sufficient surviving information to tell us what these customs duties were worth. In 1217, King Andrew II granted Venetian merchants entering the kingdom the right to pay one eightieth in general, and nothing at all on gold, pearls, precious stones, spices and silk fabric.[24] In 1336, King Charles I prescribed the routes that merchants from Hungary, Bohemia and other neighboring lands had to take through the country, and required them, upon entering the Kingdom of Hungary at Fehéregyháza (referred to as Újvár, and now Holič, Slovakia), to pay "eightieth" duty on their wares (*octuagesima de rebus mercimonialibus*).[25] Payment of the eightieth upon crossing the border did not exempt the merchants from the "thirtieth" (*tricesima*) and other excise duties collected in the interior of the country.

Forms of Duty – Thirtieth

The earliest records of places being established to collect the thirtieth – the Queen's revenue, but occasionally at the disposal of the king – appear during the reign of King Andrew II.[26] The towns where thirtieth was collected were Dubica, Zagreb, Győr, Hlohovec, Esztergom and Košice. Győr and Esztergom lay on the western trade route, Košice and Hlohovec on the north and northwestern routes, and Zagreb and Dubica on the south and south-western routes.[27] This means that all of the towns where thirtieth duty was collected

---

22 Fejér (ed.) 1829–1844, VII/5, 590 (1274), Smičiklas and Kostrenčić (eds.) 1904–1981, VI, 99–100. See also: Szentpétery and Borsa 1923–1987, no. 2565. A few years later, in 1281, half of the income was subdonated to the Cistercian Abbey next to Zagreb. Cf. Wenzel (ed.) 1860–1874, XII, 341.

23 The authenticity of the charter is, however, uncertain. Szentpétery and Borsa 1923–1987, no. 4183.

24 Fejér (ed.) 1829–1844, VII/4, 72–73.

25 Wenzel (ed.) 1874–1876, I, 343–345, Cf. Skorka 2013.

26 Zsoldos 2005, 83–84 and Pach 1990, 47.

27 Collection of the thirtieth at Trnava is first mentioned in the 1336 charter of Charles I, and it was most probably established then, in connection with the setting up of new transport

were on central transit-route points. The "thirtieth" – which was indeed set at one thirtieth of the value of goods during the Árpádian age – had to be paid at these places by merchants importing goods from outside the kingdom. The thirtieth was therefore an *ad valorem* duty, defined as 8/240 of the value of the merchandise,[28] or eight times the known customs rate during the Árpádian age. Although the towns where it was collected lay in the interior of the country rather than at the border, they were on routes preferred by foreign merchants as they traveled through the Kingdom of Hungary, thus the king was assured of receiving his duty on imports.

Forms of Duty – Direct Taxes: The Freemen's Pennies and the Pondus

Until the reign of King Coloman, freemen were obliged to pay the king 8 denars (*liberi denarii, vulgo fumarii*).[29] Coloman changed this arrangement so that 8 denars were still payable by freemen who lived on another person's land, although 4 denars of this could be redeemed by supplying the king with horses, carts or military service (*stipendium*). Freemen who lived on their own land were exempt from the tax.[30] In 1222, King Andrew II exempted church freemen from paying freemen's pennies,[31] and in the Golden Bull[32] he also exempted the "royal servants" (*serviens regis*) – freeman who provided military service to the kings.[33] The royal privileges record another form of tax payable by freemen besides the freemen's pennies: the *pondus*. This was equivalent to 5 or 6 denars.

Other Royal Revenues

Twentieth, Hundredth

The king was due twentieth and hundredth parts of the church tithe. It was King Stephen I who laid down the law of the church tithe: "Any man to whom God has given ten parts in a year shall give one part to God."[34] The twentieth was paid by everybody subject to the church tithe. We do not know when

---

routes. As there is no reference to the thirtieth collected at Hlohovec later than 1316, this could have been relocated to Trnava.
28 Cf. Weisz 2011.
29 Cf. Györffy 1994 and de Cevins 2004, 204.
30 Bak et al. (eds.) 1992–2012, I, 28.
31 Marsina (ed.) 1971–1987, I, 198.
32 Bak et al. (eds.) 1992–2012, I, 32.
33 Cf. Berend, Urbańczyk and Wiszewski 2013, 286–287.
34 Bak et al. (eds.) 1992–2012, I, 11.

payment of the twentieth started, but it is certain that King Béla II granted the revenues from the royal twentieth in the bishopric of Vác to St Margaret's Church in Dömös.[35] According to a charter issued by King Charles I in 1319, the "holy kings" and the prelates of the kingdom had decreed that the twentieth and hundredth parts of the church tithe were due to the king, and it was also "under royal authority and within royal powers" that the remainder, due to the church, was to be gathered.[36] The twentieth and hundredth could, however, be held by barons of the kingdom, or by *comites* or *vicecomites*,[37] either under special royal grant or by custom of their office (*ex speciali donacione regia aut ex consvetudine sui officii vel honoris*), but they were also required to have the authority and powers sufficient to gather the remainder of the tithe. This tells us that both the twentieth and the hundredth were defined on the church tithe, and not as revenue additional to the tithe. Secondly, the tithe was originally collected by the king or the royal apparatus, which is probably why he was due part of it for himself.[38]

Census

Communities bearing charters of privilege had to pay taxes to the king, and these were variously referred to as *collecta*, *census* or *terragium* (land tax). The king received revenue in kind – sheep or cattle – from the Székelys and the Vlachs; in the Vlachs' case, we know this was called the "fiftieth" tax (*quinquagesima*). The tax obligations of the Transylvanian Saxons were prescribed in the 1224 Andreanum: they had to pay 500 marks annually. The Saxons were already paying a separate tax to the sovereign before the Andreanum. This shows up firstly in a register from the period of King Béla III, which set the revenue from foreign settlers (*hospites*) in Transylvania at 15,000 marks, and secondly in the exemption of German-speakers – before the Andreanum was issued – from payment of the *collecta* imposed on other Saxons. The other group of Saxons,

---

35   Marsina (ed.) 1971–1987, I, 75.
36   Smičiklas and Kostrenčić (eds.) 1904–1981, VIII, 530.
37   The twentieth could be held by the *nádor* (*comes palatinus*), and the hundredth by the *ispán* of the county (*comes parochianus*) Cf. Fejér (ed.) 1829–1844, II, 256.
38   This can be also assumed from a privilege granted to the bishopric of Pécs by Béla III in 1190 (Fejér [ed.] 1829–1844, II, 255). King Béla forbade the *comes palatinus* and the *comes parochianus* to collect the twentieth as well as the hundredth, which he granted to the bishop. Thereby it was also mentioned that church officials may turn to the *decimatores* of the palatinus or comes for help while collecting tithes. When Charles I granted privileges to the town of Bardejov in 1320 (Fejér [ed.] 1829–1844, VIII/2, 253), he disposed that half of the tithes should be given to the parish priest, the other half to the king. This demonstrates that sharing of church tithes was in practice even later.

in the Spiš region, received a charter of privilege from King Stephen V in 1271. This required the Spiš Saxons to pay – on St Martin's Day – land tax (*racione terragii*) amounting to 300 marks of silver. In return, they were exempted from all other taxation imposed within the kingdom (*ab omnibus exaccionibus et collectis, dacis et vectigalibus*). Like communities with charters of privilege, those with settler status (*hospites*) also paid land tax (*terragium*). What distinguished the *terragium* and the *census* from previous taxes – the freemen's pennies and the *pondus* – was that collection of the taxes was not supervised by the *comes*'s regime. It was the king's or the lord treasurer's agent who delivered it to the treasury, meaning that the community itself guaranteed payment. This relieved the king from having to share the revenue with the *comes*. The entire sum flowed into the treasury, although the king must have made some payment to the tax collectors.

Collecta

An additional source of revenue for the king in the second part of twelfth century, was the *collecta*, a tax levied in money or kind. This *collecta* could be imposed on the whole kingdom or specific regions or counties. The *collecta* could be, but was not always, confined to certain sections of society. In the Golden Bull of 1222, King Andrew II pronounced that the *collecta* would not be collected on estates of royal *servientes*,[39] and followed this up in 1231 by confining the *collecta* to those subject to money tax (*census*) to the royal treasury (*qui fisco regio in debito censu tenentur*).[40] The nobles' exemption from payment of the *collecta* is also confirmed in later thirteenth-century laws,[41] and a law of 1298 also exempted people living on church estates (*populos ecclesiarum et monesteriorum*).[42] The king could levy *collecta* to provide chamber's profit (*ratione lucri camere*), or for various other reasons.[43]

Slavonia

A tax specific to the lands beyond the River Dráva – mostly comprising Slavonia, but also including the parts of Pozsega, Valkó and Baranya Counties on that side of the river –, was the *marturina*, known in Hungarian as *nyest*,

---

39   Bak et al. (eds.) 1992–2012, I, 32.
40   Bak et al. (eds.) 1992–2012, I, 37.
41   Bak et al. (eds.) 1992–2012, I, 40 and 43.
42   Bak et al. (eds.) 1992–2012, I, 51.
43   Cf. Eckhart 1908, 33–73.

meaning "beech marten". One source from 1300 states that *marturina* taxpayers (*marturinarius*) were those who in the past had given their lords the pelt of one beech marten a year.[44] By the reign of King Coloman, *marturina* was paid in money, equivalent to 12 Friesach denars per *mansio*.[45] This rate was gradually raised during the thirteenth century, but returned to 12 denars at the end and remained there in the fourteenth. The *pondus* was set at seven denars in Slavonia, and payable by all those who were bound to pay *marturina*. Both the *marturina* and the *pondus* were payable to the king or to the prince who ruled Slavonia, but were usually granted to landowners together with their estates, thus becoming a landowner's tax. In the fourteenth century, both taxes, where they were still owed to the king, were subsumed into the Ban's *honor*.

The *collecta* was levied under the heading of chamber's profit. King Béla IV set its amount in Slavonia as seven denars (*collectam septem denariorum, a tempore ipsius patris nostri editam et indictam ratione lucri camere*).[46] The seven-denar *collecta* was first imposed on the occasion of the wedding between Béla IV's son Prince Béla and Princess Kunigunda of Brandenburg in 1264 (i.e. as a special tax), but within a short time it became an annual tax in Slavonia, collected under the heading of chamber's profit.[47] Chamber's profit was the province of the king's *magister tavernicorum* in the thirteenth century, but was also acquired by the Ban in fourteenth century.[48]

---

44 Tkalčić (ed.) 1873–1874, I, 22.
45 Smičiklas and Kostrenčić (eds.) 1904–1981, III, 241. See also: Szentpétery and Borsa 1923–1987, no. 407.
46 Fejér (ed.) 1829–1844, V/1, 150 (1271). See also: Szentpétery and Borsa 1923–1987, no. 2130.
47 Smičiklas and Kostrenčić (eds.) 1904–1981, VI, 318 (1279).
48 Cf. Weisz 2015d.

CHAPTER 12

Seigneurial Dues and Taxation Principles in Late Medieval Hungary

Árpád Nógrády

There is a widespread assumption among Hungarian historians that medieval taxes, and particularly seigneurial dues, nearly always meant an oppressive burden on the peasantry. It is not a recent view. It was first formulated in modern historiography during the nineteenth century by Mihály Horváth, but the main points had long before been eloquently expressed, in the sixteenth century by Gáspár Heltai in his fable: *Egy nemesemberről meg az ördögről* ('On a nobleman and the devil').[1] The story is about a burgher of Cluj who, in league with the devil, perpetrates all kinds of maneuvers to squeeze wealth out of the people of the land. Heltai was pillorying the exploitation of large estates in response to the sixteenth-century price revolution, which had set off a boom in agriculture. His tale brings to life the landlord-controled taverns which watered the wine, the butchers selling poor-quality meat, the tenant peasants who had to pay taxes on the nobleman's produce, the lord's cattle trade, and everything by which the nobility of the time "filled their hats with money".

Although Heltai's charge-sheet on the world around him was drawn up after the battle of Mohács (1526), many items can definitely be applied to the late medieval period as well. For corroborating evidence we need to look no further than the amounts entered for wine sales in the Szapolyai family's accounts. In the castle estates of Tokaj, Tállya, Szárd, Regéc and Boldogkő (and some other estates) in 1517, the family's income from wine was an enormous 2928 florins, at a time when the 1-florin royal tax amounted "only" to 1382 florins.[2] Also relevant is an instruction given by Palatine Imre Perényi in which he required his *provisor* in Ónod to foist upon a stonemason working in the castle an elderly toothless ox from the *allodium*, clearly as part of the mason's pay.[3]

However true the observations in Heltai's fable and the figures in the Szapolyai accounts, they must be set against frequent references in medieval documents to well-off tenant peasants and relatively high peasant day-labor rates, prompting in the reader the suspicion that not all of the medieval tenant

---

1 Horváth 1868, 247–276 and Heltai 1978, 222–234.
2 MNL OL DL 26 161.
3 "qui fuit antiquus bos et carebat dentibus" – MNL OL DL 26 173.

peasantry could have lived "at the edge of utter ruination". It would therefore be very useful to determine the real magnitude of seigneurial dues and the principles by which they were levied.

The following analysis is a kind of snapshot, owing to the nature of the sources. We could hardly expect that seigneurial dues remained fixed throughout the kingdom over a period of several decades. Indeed, they were probably subject to changes from year to year, sometimes quite substantial. An illustration of what this could have meant is only available in an urban setting – for example, through the fluctuations in purchasing power of the Prešov *Stadtknechten* (urban servants who were in duty of the town's upkeep). An early accounts book from this town tells us, sometimes on a monthly basis, how the wages of town servants and the price of oats at the Prešov market varied over a period of eleven years, from 1443 to 1453. (The price of bread flour would of course be more relevant, but municipal accounts rarely recorded such figures at this time.) By comparing the two, we can identify the purchasing power of wages expressed in grain for a relatively long stretch of time.[4]

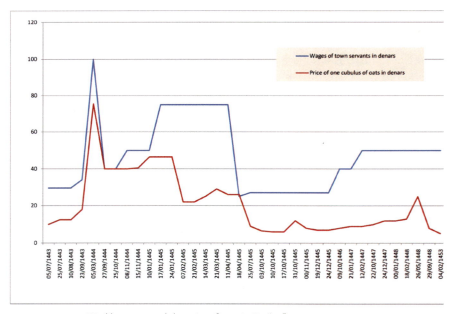

FIGURE 12.1   *Weekly wages and the price of oats in Prešov.*[5]

---

4   MNL OL DF 282 530. The rate of the denar fluctuated significantly in the period under study, thus the prices given in denar are better compared only within particular years.
5   In the cases marked with a star there is a one or two week gap between the wages and prices, and the dates always refer to the wages. 05/07/1443: 29.5 and 10; 25/07/1443: 29.5 and 12.5;

The table shows that town servants could buy nearly two *cubuli* of oats from their weekly wages in September 1443, and only one in the following year. This number was three and a half in autumn 1445, five in October 1446, and the same a year later. There followed a period of plenty for the *Stadtknechten* when the value of their pay in terms of grain rose steadily for five years and reached 6–8 *cubuli* in the autumn and winter months. These account entries may of course reflect only a few years of exceptionally good harvests, and the full picture must take account of the wide seasonal fluctuation in medieval grain prices.[6] Nonetheless, the figures show that even these darkest years of times of trouble included a period of prosperity.[7] The Prešov sources do not tell us when things took a turn for the worse.

There can be no doubt that such swings in income were also experienced by peasant households, but there is no way of proving it.

"Ordinary" Seigneurial Dues

The system of dues based on the independent peasant farm – what came to be known as the *sessio* – was first adopted in Hungary for guests (*hospites*) living on estates, and became general through the kingdom in the thirteenth century. It spread to the furthest points in the land under the Angevins (1308–1382). Tenant peasants (*iobagiones*) were assessed by unit of land, and their dues were set sometimes by contract, more usually by local common law. The predominant burden was payable in cash – the *census*. Its rate varied from county to county, from one area to another within a county, and even between

---

10/08/1443: 29.5 and 12.5; 23/09/1443: 34 and 18; 05/03/1444: 100 and 75.5; 27/09/1444: 40 and 40; 25/10/1444: 40 and 40; 08/11/1444: 50 and 40; 15/11/1444: 50 and 40.5; 10/01/1445: 50 and 46.5; 17/01/1445: 75 and 46.5; 24/01/1445: 75 and 46.5; 07/02/1445: 75 and 22; 21/02/1445: 75 and 22; 14/03/1445: 75 and 25; 21/03/1445: 75 and 29; 11/04/1445: 75 and 26*; 18/04/1445: 25 and 26; 25/07/1445: 27 and 9; 03/10/1445: 27 and 6.5; 10/10/1445: 27 and 6*; 17/10/1445: 27 and 6; 31/10/1445: 27 and 12; 00/11/1445: 27 and 8; 19/12/1445: 27 and 7; 24/12/1445: 27 and 7*; 09/10/1446: 40 and 8; 21/01/1447: 40 and 9; 12/02/1447: 50 and 9*; 22/10/1447: 50 and 10; 24/12/1447: 50 and 12; 00/01/1448: 50 and 12; 18/02/1448: 50 and 13; 26/05/1448: 50 and 25; 29/09/1448: 50 and 8*; 04/02/1453: 50 and 5.2.

6 Prices were lowest right after harvesting and in September, and then – at least in Prešov and its neighborhood – started to rise until the end of the year. During the first months of the year prices were stable, and from April–May they started to increase rapidly. In these times they were two or three times as much as prices at the market in September. See the data in two account books of the town of Prešov: MNL OL DF 282 535 and 282 538.

7 On the political situation in the first half of the 1440s, see e.g. Pálosfalvi 2000 and Pálosfalvi 2003.

neighboring villages. Its amount ranged from a few denars to two or three florins, averaging one gold florin over the kingdom. It was set according to the size of the holding, which varied from village to village. Rates therefore only applied to single villages, and so data on the *census*, despite appearing similar, are not directly comparable. Peasants paid dues under different headings, in accordance with the annual rhythm of agriculture, at times defined by common law. There were usually two installments, one paid in spring, typically on St George's Day (24 April) and the second in autumn, on St Michael's Day (29 September) or St Martin's Day (11 November). In addition to cash, the peasant paid his lord in produce and labor.

Dues payable in food were much less significant in the fifteenth century than they had been in the early Árpádian age. Peasants in many places redeemed them for cash, just as they did the fattened ox paid collectively by the village for the right to keep animals. The latter for the *iobagio* families living along the River Rába, for example, meant an annual payment of two or three denars, about the price of a hen.

Labor service under the unpaid labor system was insignificant at this time. Each peasant family had to give up at most two or three days' work a year (mostly mowing and carriage), and even this was not taken up on many estates. It was quite common for unpaid labor to resemble the modern concept of public works rather than enforced labor. The unpaid labor of a village thus might be expended on maintaining the village's own bridge, or cleaning out the mill race.

Neither is it easy to assess the form of seigneurial dues known as the "ninth". This was introduced by King Louis I in 1351, but was never universally collected – there are places where we find no trace of it. Elsewhere it was collected as prescribed, and other places it was nominally gathered, but in an amount that might more properly be called a "hundredth".[8]

Extraordinary Dues

In addition to the regular annual dues, landlords levied *taxa extraordinaria*. Extraordinary seigneurial dues differed from the ordinary cash levy, the *census*, in two major respects. First, the amount payable was not based on holdings but was proportional to the peasant's income, his "estimable wealth". Second, the

---

8 On the issue in general, see: Solymosi 1998 and Szabó 1975. Most recently, see: Nógrády 2015, 12–16.

lord – as is recorded in connection with a mortgaging as early as 1371 – could levy it, with or without proper grounds, as many times as he pleased.[9]

Known in German as *Steuer* and in Hungarian as *ostoradó* ("scourge tax"), the *taxa* became very widespread during the Sigismund period (1387–1437). István Szabó has made a very thorough study of the collection of this tax in the second half of the fifteenth century and the Jagiellonian period (1490–1526). First, through a (still-unique) analysis of one full *taxa* register (for the estate Duldumas–Korođ in 1469), he demonstrated the extremely complex hierarchy of peasant society at the time. Second, he found in documents for western Transdanubian estates (Sárvár, Kapuvár, Lockenhaus) and the Ónod estate evidence for the astonishingly high burden of dues paid by the peasantry. The amount levied in extraordinary dues was greater than the annual *census* by a factor of 25 at the Sárvár estate, 37 in Kapuvár, 18 in Sempte and 10–11 in Ónod. Szabó then drew the understandable inference that Hungarian landlords' increasingly-frequent imposition of the *taxa* brought peasants to the limit of their capacities by the eve of the battle of Mohács (1526): "even if the peasant farms were not faced with it every year, a single levy could eat up the fruits of the labor of several years, even decades".[10] Indeed, he saw the seigneurial *taxa* as indicative of a burden which, together with the law binding peasants to the soil, was a tragic symptom of Hungarian peasant society descending into crisis.[11]

The *taxa extraordinaria*, however, was not purely a product of the late medieval period. A royal charter of 1426 permitted it to be collected with annual regularity on the estates of the Bélháromkút Nunnery.[12] The exaction of the *taxa* in Sárvár and Kapuvár, a sum up to thirty times the *census*, although on average only 2–3 florins per taxable unit was not at all exceptional. No better evidence of this is a register of levies from 1425 showing extremely high amounts paid in dues by peasants in the early fifteenth century. The title of the register – *Registrum dicarum in Royche in anno vigesimo quinto* – is slightly misleading, the word *dica* suggesting a tax payable to the king, but the history of

---

9   *taxam, censum seu descensum toties quoties sibi placuerit iuste et iniuste iuxta libitum sue voluntatis recipiendi et extorquendi ... haberet facultatem* – MNL OL DL 5954, quoted by Mályusz 1965, 68.
10   Szabó 1975, 73–75.
11   Szabó 1975, 76.
12   *singulis annis in taxarum seu collectarum extraordinariarum ... prefato fratri Nicolao abbati debitam obedientiam exhibere, ymmo talismodo taxas pecuniarias per ipsum super vos imponendi sibi absque contradiccione et recalcitracione aliquali extradare et persolvere modis omnibus debeatis* – Nagy, Deák and Nagy (eds.) 1865–1891, II, 239–240.

the country as a whole[13] and local events lead us to the conclusion that this is in fact the earliest surviving register of seigneurial dues.[14] It concerns the area of Rovišće in Körös County, now in Croatia, which had changed from a small castle estate into a noble estate in the second half of the fourteenth century. It passed into private hands in 1393 at a stroke of King Sigismund's pen, the beneficiaries being Márton Ders of Szerdahely and his brother, members of a landowning family from Somogy County, who were thus raised to lords of the castle of Topolovac and owners of a famously wealthy estate.[15]

Early evidence of this wealth is the register itself, which stands out for several reasons. Only single names are entered on the register, and amounts less than one florin are stated in an accounting currency equivalent to one fortieth of the current denar, the *pensa*, which had been common for several centuries in Hungary but was already obsolete.[16] Most relevant to the present discussion are the strikingly high sums demanded from households. The 407 village and market-town peasants named on the register, on eight estates, paid amounts in *dica* totaling 1531 florins (i.e. they had to come up with an average of 4 florins each). The individual amounts vary around this very high average through an enormous range. The highest sum, 25 florins, was collected from six people. Exactly one hundred persons paid more than average, and fourteen paid no more than 40 denars, or 1/8 of a florin at the then-current rate (1 florin being equivalent to 300–320 denars).[17] These are impressive figures, unmatched by any others in medieval rural Hungary.

There are charters stating that two of the settlements listed, Rovišće and Virovitica, were market towns, even though the latter is first mentioned as an *oppidum* only in 1458 and sometimes occurs as a *possessio* even after that.[18] The

---

13   As is evident at first sight, this is not a *lucrum camarae* account and there is no information in the historiography that an extraordinary royal due was demanded in 1425. Mályusz 1984, passim.

14   MNL OL DL 25 929.

15   MNL OL DL 33 468.

16   On *pensa* see: Engel 1990, 75–78 and 91. The compiler of the register naturally counted in forints. The fact that *pensa* was an important element of the register as a counting unit might be attributed partly to the divisibility by twenty and forty of the golden florin – denar exchange rate and partly the setting of the lowest tax categories as 1/16 and 1/8 of the golden florin.

17   On the current rate, see: Mályusz 1984, 194 and Házi (ed.) 1921–1943, II/2, 340–342. In the town of Sopron in 1426, the rate was between 273 and 300 denars. The exact account for 1425 is not known to us.

18   As *oppidum*: MNL OL DL 15 272 and 15 274, as *possessio*: MNL OL DL 16 449 (1466) and 32 851 (1473).

remaining half-a-dozen settlements were villages of various sizes, although Zelán also had a customs place.[19] The main figures are shown in the following table:

TABLE 12.1 *Towns/villages, numbers of taxpayers, total dues collected and average dues (in florins)*

Settlement	Number of tax payers	Total collected dues (in florins)	Average dues (in florins)
Banicsevic	15	30.5	2.03
Besenevc	20	34.5	1.725
Dolné Zelenice	38	141.5	3.72
Dorozlouch	10	22.5	2.225
Stari Jankovci	48	278.8	5.8
Rovišće	192	738.5	3.84
Struga	11	36.5	3.32
Virovitica	73	249.0	3.41

Only the *oppidum* of Rovišće, with 192 taxpayers, seems to have had any significance in the county, and it is remarkable that the size of a village, to judge from the average dues, had no bearing on its taxable capacity. The reason for this must be that many *oppida* inhabitants were poor, so that well-off villages were just as important to landowners as sources of revenue as market towns.

The register gives us a cross section of the estate's micro-society, dividing the population into no less than twenty-eight "tax bands". Those at the top (25 florins) paid two hundred times as much as those at the bottom (40 denars), a much wider gap than is found in later documents of this kind.[20] A closer look at the percentage of *taxa*-payers in each band and the amount they paid reveals that the Szerdahelyis laid the lion's share of the burden on the shoulders of well-off tenant peasants. The six wealthiest *taxa* payers, paying 25 florins each, contributed nearly one tenth of the whole amount, the top

---

19 Zela appears as a customs post in 1476: MNL OL DL 33 392.
20 The difference is 400 times, as the lowest tax was 20 denars (that is, 1/15 to 1/16 of a golden forint). Only one of the taxpayers paid this amount of money, thus I thought it more realistic to calculate using 40 denars.

20 % brought in more than half, while those paying less than one florin – one seventh of the population of the estate – contributed only 5 % of the dues. The Rovišće *taxa* was thus clearly an income or wealth tax. We do not know the rate, unfortunately, but the amounts seem impossibly high.

By comparison, the day-rate for a town carpenter at this time (1426) was 20 Viennese denars in Sopron (i.e. 1/9 of a florin), and that of an unqualified laborer in the same town was 7–10 denars. This means that the lowest Rovišće *taxa* was equal to a day's wages for a town artisan and two–three days' wage for a *Knecht*, which does not seem unreasonable. But what can we make of a 5–6 florin *taxa*, by no means the highest amount levied, equivalent to a fifth of the Sopron carpenter's wages for the whole year? The very highest level is not worth comparing to urban artisan income at all; it is equivalent to the price of about a dozen oxen, or the cost of building a minor mill.[21]

Was this a special one-off levy, or were these sums due every year? How did it compare with the financial capacity of peasants and market-townspeople in the early fifteenth century? So high are these amounts – such as the average *taxa* of 6 florins for Stari Jankovci – that any suggestion of regular payment might seem unrealistic. Nonetheless, there are several direct written references to the owners of the estate, the Szerdahelyis, collecting extraordinary dues on an annual basis.

Our first source of information on this is a set of documents giving a very strong suggestion of what preceded the *dica* register. They tell the story of how the *iobagiones castri* of the former Rovišće *comitatus* carried on a long and bitter struggle against their landlords, the Szerdahelyis. The feud sheds light on several issues of social history, the details of which cannot be gone into here, but one bone of contention between the new landlord and the *iobagiones castri* was Márton's imposition of dues several times higher than those they had previously had to bear. The cash dues are described in some documents as *taxa* and others as *dica*. The Szerdahelyis demanded them from every one of their peasants, not only the *iobagiones castri*, and collected them with force if necessary. Not even the *oppidum* of Rovišće escaped this burden, although Ban Márton was prepared to make some concessions to his market town, and in compensation for the increased dues he assigned most fields of one castle estate and the wine hill of another *praedium* to the *civites* of the town. The town and the landlord having thus come to a settlement about the issue of seigneurial dues at the expense of the *iobagiones castri*, the shadow of conflict between them was lifted, and Márton even sought for his *civites* the right to hold

---

21   Wages: Házi (ed.) 1921–1943, II/2, 313. The cost of mill-construction (though from later times) is 28 florins: MNL OL DL 56 291.

an annual fair. The situation changed radically in 1417 when Márton fell into Ottoman captivity, and from then until 1421 a fierce struggle raged between the landowning family and the former *iobagiones castri*, a conflict eagerly joined by the market-townspeople in pursuit of their own ends. Peace was restored to the estate only in 1422 when the Szerdahelyis, by royal authorization, returned to the system of seigneurial dues designed by Márton, who had since died.[22]

The second report survives from somewhat later period, from 1503, and tells of the private war fought two years previously between János Ernuszt of Csáktornya and the family of Szerdahelyi Dersfis. In a large-scale act of might, Ernuszt captured an estate center called Topolovac (Zrinski Topolovac), installed himself in the estate, and started to enjoy its fruits as landlord. He did so in a somewhat peculiar manner. Although he plundered Topolovac in the customary fashion and emptied its fishponds, his men did not harass the peasant folk of the estate and did not rob travelers, nor did they loot the annual fair of Rovišće or the market of Keresztúr. They simply collected the customs duty and *tributum fori*, and, of course, the Szerdahelyis' usual dues. We know that Ernuszt gained possession of the St George's and St Michael's Day *census* and the 650-florin *taxa extraordinaria*, exacted on two occasions that year.[23]

Although the amount collected as *taxa* sixty-six years later was much less than the 1531 florins taken in the Sigismund-period, the Jagiello-period example does seem to show that the practice of collecting the *taxa extraordinaria* every year on the Szerdahelyis' Topolovac estates survived the struggle with the *iobagiones castri* and the Rovišće *oppidum*.

None of the documents, of course, prove directly and beyond doubt that the amounts entered in the 1425 register were collected at regular intervals. This is an unfortunate, but not completely unbridgeable gap. Since the basic question is the burden the *taxa* represented for the peasants of the estate, a quantitative determination of this burden will also address the question of regularity. But is such a quantitative determination possible?

Although medieval Hungary was a literate kingdom, no account or survey giving an itemized list of the entire income of a town or village has yet come to light, and nor is it likely to.[24] Nonetheless, there is one town for which we have an accurate record of annual income. This is the *oppidum* of Gönc in

---

22   Nógrády 2001, 73–82.
23   On the occupation of Topolovac and the damage it caused: MNL OL DL 21 225.
24   Similar registers of course were written, a register of this kind from the late fifteenth century being preserved in the archives of the Chapter of Zagreb. However, this does not come close to referring to all elements of the farming of the peasantry, and the measures are unknown. For these reasons, I rejected its use: MNL OL DF 256 598.

Abaúj County. According to a receipt, the town paid the so-called "seventh" tax, amounting to no less than 1000 florins in 1387.[25] This tax, introduced by King Sigismund to finance the war against the rebellious Horvátis, was levied on both peasants and townspeople. As its name implies, it had the fixed rate of one seventh of annual income.[26]

This means that the annual income of Gönc in 1387 was at least 7000 florins. In fact, it must have been much more than this because the people of Gönc had to supplement this amount in cash with 50 barrels of wine. The king waived this demand, however, and we omit it from the calculation. Another crucial item of information is the number of households in Gönc. This may be obtained from the chamber's profit survey of Abaúj County in 1427: Gönc, part of the Bebek family's estate since 1391, is recorded as having 191 taxpayers.[27]

The average annual income of a household in Gönc in the first year of Sigismund's reign was thus thirty-seven florins. A substantial sum, and perhaps most importantly, not the result of indirect calculation. This leaves us with the question of whether the financial position of a major wine-producing and trading town in Abaúj County (in northeast Hungary) can be projected to a Slavonian *oppidum* with about the same number of taxpayers. I consider that it may. Indeed, Rovišće also had a considerable wine trade, and to judge from customs and market revenues of more than 100 florins in 1501, and the records of wealthy merchants (sometimes robbed, other times giving out loans of up to 240 florins), it might have even been wealthier than Gönc.[28]

However shaky the basis of such a comparison, we can be fairly clear about the scale of incomes at the time, and see that the owner of the Slavonian estate may have been asking a lot, but not the impossible. The form of dues introduced by Ban Márton in the *oppidum* of Rovišće thus corresponds to an income tax of about 10 %, the rate being lower for the poorest and higher for the wealthiest. The Szerdahelyis most probably collected it every year at that time.

Gönc and Rovišće were of course both wealthy market towns. Their position cannot be generalized to the kingdom as a whole. Let us now look at the situation in simple peasant villages. It is in principle much more straightforward to determine the dues payable in a village where affairs were much simpler than in a market town: all we need is the value of agricultural production, the

---

25   On the 'seventh' tax of Gönc: Nagy et al. (ed.) 1872–1931, IV, 344.
26   Cf. Mályusz 1984, 30.
27   Engel 1989, 35.
28   On the customs: MNL OL DL 21 225, loans: MNL OL DL 99 628, the sack of the merchants of Rovišće in 1417: MNL OL DL 10 971 and in 1488: MNL OL DL 19 409, the occupation of the customs of Rovišće in 1464: MNL OL DL 16 401.

number of farms, and the amount paid in dues. Such is the state of sources for the medieval Kingdom of Hungary, however, that at least one of these is always absent. Neither is it possible to derive the total value of the agricultural output of medieval Hungarian villages via a statistical approach, because the number of sources on animal husbandry, especially the herding of large animals, is less than would be required for a reliable sample. Despite these factors, the task of reconstructing the rate of appropriation needs not be dismissed as hopeless if we are prepared to make a few compromises.

The accounts book of the Bratislava chapter,[29] although subject to these limitations, includes enough entries to permit an estimate to be made for the half-a-dozen estates of that ecclesiastical body: Jánovce (Körmösd in its medieval name), Farná and Tureň lying along the Čierna Voda River, Vlky, at the western end of Žitný ostrov, and Trhová Hradská and Topoľníky in the middle of the island. Two brief aggregate records of the villages' grain tithes have survived for 1474 and 1479. Additionally, and indeed almost uniquely, we know the number of taxpayers and the annual ordinary *census* of the villages, and also the amount of the *taxa extraordinaria* levied on their inhabitants.

Under the established custom of medieval Hungary, the collegiate chapter of the St Martin's Church in Bratislava received the full tithe from its estates.[30] The figures in the brief record of dues thus do not have to be supplemented with the part of the tithe due to the archbishop of Esztergom, and can be used directly to calculate the villages' grain production. There are of course plenty of unknown factors. Without knowing the yields, it has been necessary to work with threshing records and some accounting items from 1552, and to take the figure for the price of grain as the average on the Bratislava market rather than the prices it was sold at the villages.[31] The number of taxpayers has also been arrived at indirectly, because the chapter *Liber proventuum* is a book of accounts and not an *urbarium*. These limitations, however, add up to no greater a difficulty than is faced everywhere else in medieval Hungarian economic history, and in relative terms, the sources for these few villages are outstandingly informative.

They permit the conclusion that the cash dues on the chapter's estates did not constitute a heavy burden on the peasants there. The *census* was

---

29 MNL OL DF 281 414.
30 The account book of the chapter briefs us well. Holub 1929, 385. (The example of the diocese of Veszprém).
31 For threshing records: MNL OL MKA Regesta decimarum (E 159) Pozsony County, in 1552. Threshing counted with the gauge of Trnava informs us of a rounded off 3 gauge/shock (that is 1.5 gauge/shock of Bratislava) of harvest.

equivalent to 3–5 % of the pure grain income in nearly every case, inhabitants of three villages paying no more than 40 denars, and it seems that the chapter was also restrained in its application of the *taxa extraordinaria*. Such a light burden on the tenant peasants, relative to their income, is a remarkable phenomenon, one outstanding case being that of Trhová Hradská. This was clearly a wealthier village, and the chapter levied a higher amount – an average of more than two florins per holding. Nonetheless, these dues were only just over 10 % of the villagers' grain production, and since their income was boosted by animal husbandry, there is good reason to believe that the amount was equivalent to only 6–8 % of the village's total income. Although Trhová Hradská was indubitably a wealthy village, its inhabitants were unlikely to have been all that better off than those living in other villages of the Žitný ostrov. This may be inferred partly from indirect data, because there are signs – if fragmentary – of prosperity in nearly every village on the island. More useful than such indirect data, however, is an examination of three villages belonging to the Counts of Szentgyörgy, the native lords of Pozsony County. Two of these villages, Hviezdoslavov and Nové Košariská, seem to have been far from average. Their income from cereals probably resulted from record yields on an area of exceptional fertility. Nonetheless, they are relevant here for two reasons. The bounteous harvests – the average per household being equivalent to the extraordinary yield in the Žitný ostrov village of Trnávka in 1568[32] – show that the yields in one of the most fertile areas of the country at the peak of the sixteenth-century agricultural boom were not unusual, and had precedents going back at least a hundred years. Second, the figures for seigneurial dues, despite being drawn from only three villages, reveal the state of a late medieval large estate, and the burdens imposed on peasants in other western Hungarian estates are unlikely to have been substantially different. Much more likely to have varied are the economic conditions prevailing in areas where the fertility did not match that of Žitný ostrov.

"We give thanks that we have such a beneficent lord and live in God's breadbasket," is how the peasants of the Gyula estate of George, margrave of Brandenburg-Ansbach, paying average dues of 3 florins a year, summarized their state on the eve of the battle of Mohács.[33] The overall conclusion we can draw from the examples of Gönc, Rovišće and the Žitný ostrov villages is that seigneurial dues, even including the "notorious" *taxa extraordinaria*, and amounts of 2–4 florins per household, could not have deprived peasant farms

---

32   The settlement Vera Zimányi counted on an average harvest of about 153 quintal of wheat and oats. See: Pach (ed.) 1985, III/1, 341–342.
33   Wenzel (ed.) 1857, 45. Cf. Bácskai 1967, 441.

of more than a tenth of their annual income, and the voice of the Gyula peasants, satisfied with their lot, points to a similar situation. Set against this is a letter of the people (*tota communitas*) of Zselic, itemizing their complaints against their landlord in the summer of 1427.[34] These were: severe *taxa*, frequent carriage, obstruction of forest use and the withdrawal of a previously-permitted pasture. Their case was not isolated, but does not mean we have been misled by the sources. The complaints, as is clear from the Zselic letter, do no more than document anomalies in the system. Indeed, what outraged the people of Zselic was not the *taxa* itself. What they complained about was that their lord not only levied the *taxa* but – unlike his predecessor (father) – demanded it to the full extent; i.e. was attempting to exert his power without *consensus*.

Our understanding of medieval seigneurial dues must be guided by the general truism that taxation, however intimately it is bound up with the economy, is really a question of power. The peasant did not, at least in principle, pay dues to his lord in return for use of the land.

"We must serve the lords because they protect us,"[35] are words put into the mouths of peasants in the south German statute book, the *Schwabenspiegel*, in 1275. It was a widely-held principle that the landlord afforded protection to all inhabitants of his estate, including his tenant peasants, and was due advice and assistance (*consilium et auxilium*) from his subjects. The "advice" of the knight took the form of military service, and that of the peasant the payment of dues. (*Consilium* was the primary service, and automatically implied assistance.) Hungarian charters contain few such references, but one is a charter granting *hospes* privileges to the people of Bogdán in Veszprém County in 1275. The people of Bogdán would remain under the lordship of the new owner of the land, Saul's son Lőrinte, and would look to him for protection (*ab ipsoque sperantes protegi et ab omnibus defensari*); they would in principle pay their dues so that they could, under his protection, live on his land (*pro inhabitatione terre*).[36]

Enlightened by this, we may return to Gönc and the Žitný ostrov villages and compare their incomes with the taxes imposed in the period of Matthias's reign (1458–1490). Then, too, it seems that taxes rarely exceeded the 10 % limit. In Gönc, for example, the single payment of the one-florin *subsidium* took 2.8 % of income on average; in Hviezdoslavov the figure was about 1.5 % in 1474, and in Nové Košariská it was 2 %. Cases of more severe taxation did occur

---

34 Nagy, Nagy and Véghely (eds.) 1871–1931, XII, 124–126.
35 *Wir sullen den herrn darumbe dienen, daz si uns beschirmen* – quoted by Brunner 1942, 294.
36 Solymosi 1988, 230–231.

even here: the one-forint crown tax accounted for about 7 % of the cereals income in Vlky, for example. There can of course be no doubt that payment of the king's tax meant a considerably higher burden for a peasant family in Árva or Liptó Counties, with poor soil and limited cultivable areas, than for its counterpart on a farm in Žitný ostrov. Nonetheless, the case of Vlky seems to permit some generalization. The village's income from cereals was actually quite low, about 15 florins per holding, an amount equivalent to the harvest of about 15 acres (*hold*) at Bratislava prices. An income of one florin per hold does not seem to have been confined to Pozsony County. It must have been usual in Somogy, because the local peasants calculated the standing wheat at this rate.[37] Supplementing the income from crops were the returns on livestock and *viticulture*, suggesting that even the double or even triple levying of Matthias' *subsidium* cannot be regarded as a completely unrealistic tax,[38] although it was set according to the income of wealthier market towns and villages. To verify the scale of this estimate, we could draw on an example from contemporary France. In the most populous kingdom of medieval Europe, royal taxes accounted for 13 % of agricultural production in 1482, and 6.5 % in 1515.[39] This correspondence is not a mere coincidence. Late medieval Europe knew neither the modern state nor the tax burdens the Modern period were to bring.

The changes in the Modern period came first to the more fortunately-placed western half of the continent. The power of the nobles, who were increasingly unable to fulfill their old functions, was gradually subordinated to the crown. By depriving his subjects of the rightful use of force (reducing it to self-defense in the narrow sense), the king thus took over the protective function of noble estates, and turned the kingdom into a state. For the greater security and freedom from arbitrary interference that ensued, however, his people paid a high price. First of all, the enormous financial demand generated by a state which took on many more functions than the old *regnum* placed an unprecedented burden on its population. Secondly, as the direct political power of the great estates was curtailed, their income-generating capacity became the focus of interest for their owners, and the new profit-oriented administration brought for the peasantry an age of much more burdensome dues and rents. The world of medieval lords demanding only a small proportion of people's incomes had come to an end.

---

37   Závodszky (ed.) 1909–1922, II, 391 and 395.
38   Fügedi 1982, 503–504.
39   Le Roy Ladurie and Morineau 1977, I/2, 978–979. Very recently, the taxation of the royal towns in the Hungarian Kingdom was investigated by Neumann 2017.

CHAPTER 13

Minting, Financial Administration and Coin Circulation in Hungary in the Árpádian and Angevin Periods (1000–1387)

Csaba Tóth

The tradition established by monetary historians in the early nineteenth century divides Hungarian medieval coinage into two periods. Hungary started to mint its own coins around 1000, marking the start of a period which lasted until the turn of the thirteenth and fourteenth centuries. This covers all coins minted by the kings of the Árpádians until the dynasty died out in 1301 and extends into the short reigns of Wenceslas and Otto. The second period was the age from Charles I up to the death of John Szapolyai. This periodization is in harmony with international coinage systems, which are named after their main denomination. The denar period roughly corresponds to the Árpádian age, and the groat period to late medieval Hungary. This chapter traces the minting of coins through the Árpádian and Angevin periods. The Árpádian age is treated as a unit, even though by monetary history criteria – minting techniques, financial administration, the characteristics of images on coins – it could be divided into two periods, the first covering the eleventh and twelfth centuries, and the second, the thirteenth. The Angevin period is also an independent period in Hungarian monetary history, ending with Sigismund's ascent to the throne in 1387.

The first thing that must be said about Hungarian monetary history is that those engaged in its research stand somewhat apart from other historical disciplines. Alongside the very small number of "professional" numismatists, a large number of coin collectors, strictly "amateurs", have produced very substantial work of a greatly varying standard. Another feature is the uneven depth of treatment: some themes, like the beginnings of minting in Hungary, or the monetary reforms in the era of Charles I, have always attracted a lot of attention and have thus been thoroughly researched, while the whole of the twelfth and thirteenth centuries and – despite some developments in recent decades – the second half of the Angevin period have been somewhat neglected.

Sources

Although numismatics stands as an area of research of its own, the full depth of Hungarian monetary history only emerges from the joint use of documentary and material sources. The relative importance of different types of source naturally changes over time. Material sources are gradually overshadowed by written sources, but remain essential for the whole of the Middle Ages.

Material Sources

The primary material sources are the coins themselves, both those of unknown provenance held in collections and those from excavations, including hoards, fragmentary finds,[1] grave finds and sporadic finds. The other group comprises all materials related to the process of minting coins: dies, blanks, crucibles, remains of built structures related to minting (standing or excavated mints and their furniture), and a very small number of pictorial representations, all of foreign origin, and thus not covered here.

Catalogues of Coin Types

As source publications are for diplomacy, type catalogues – also known as coin corpuses –, are the basic reference books for descriptive numismatics. These contain an image and description of each coin, covering the main types and main variations of inscription, depiction and mint mark. Hungarian numismatics is well up to date in this field. Indeed, István Schönvisner had the benefit of much previous work when he produced the first general work on Hungarian numismatics in 1801,[2] which he followed up a few years later with a catalogue of the Széchényi coin collection in four volumes (three text, one illustrations), which formed the basis for the Coin Collection of the Hungarian National Museum.[3] József Weszerle produced a manuscript on numismatics based on an enormous study of material, but his early death prevented its publication. It remains in the Hungarian National Museum, and the engravings for the catalogue were published only in 1873.[4] Jakab Rupp, carrying on where Weszerle left off, studied a range of coin types wider than any before. His coin descriptions followed a rational scheme, and he attempted to find foreign precursors and parallels of the inscriptions and images on each type.

---

1 Some of the hoards can be regarded as fully recovered, while some are only parts of larger hoards, not fully recovered.
2 Schönvisner 1801.
3 Schönvisner 1807.
4 Weszerle 1873.

His catalogue appeared in two volumes, one on coins of the Árpádian dynasty (1841) and the other on late medieval coins (1846), with text in Hungarian and Latin.[5] These were the predecessors to the "the Corpus", the coin catalogue produced by László Réthy of the Hungarian National Museum. Its two volumes (following the same logic) form the basic reference that remains in use today.[6] New types continued to accumulate after the Corpus was published, and in 1979, Lajos Huszár produced a new compilation, this time in German.[7] This is distinguished by the inclusion of mint marks as well as types, and in a break from past catalogues presents the coins in chronological rather than typological order. Almost in parallel with this, Artúr Pohl published catalogues of mint marks on late medieval Hungarian coins, identifying each letter of each mint mark and attempting an interpretation.[8] Popular among both coin collectors and professional archaeologists is the *Magyar Éremhatározó* ('Hungarian Coin Guide'),[9] which has been printed in several editions, although its illustrations are drawings, which was a step backwards. It has the great advantage, however, of including coins from places outside Hungary, such as Slavonia. Also of great help to Hungarian research are foreign catalogues such as Ivan Rengjeo's on the denars of the bans of Slavonia,[10] and Austrian corpuses on Friesach and Vienna denars.[11] The latter are of particular interest not only because of the large numbers of Friesach and Vienna denars which turn up at Hungarian archaeological sites, but also because of the fact that they were also highly influential on Hungarian coinage in terms of appearance (motifs) and standard. Indeed, we know of Hungarian reproductions and counterfeits.

In the thirty years since publication of the *Münzkatalog*, the number of coin types has continued to proliferate, mainly because of coins that have turned up at the auctions that have become increasingly common since they started in the early 1990s, and partly because of the abrupt increase in the number of metal-detector users. These have combined to bring many new types and versions to light: at least three dozen new types from the late Árpádian and Angevin periods, and innumerable variations and hybrids of varying significance.[12] All of these finds are only now being entered into the history

---

5   Rupp 1841–1846.
6   Réthy 1899–1907.
7   Huszár 1979.
8   Pohl 1974 and Pohl 1982.
9   Unger 1960.
10 Rengjeo 1959.
11 Koch 1994.
12 See e.g. Tóth 2003–2004.

of the coinage. Related objects of study are the dies used for striking the coins, of which we have a total of four from the present periods of interest: one from the eleventh century, two from the twelfth and one from the fourteenth.[13] The only archaeologically excavated mint on the territory of modern Hungary is in Visegrád.[14]

Coin Finds

Hungary is up to date with corpuses, but lags behind its neighbors in the compilation of coin-find surveys. In recent decades, Austrian, Romanian, former Yugoslav and Slovak numismatists have produced important surveys.[15] In Hungary, however, with a few exceptions, it is customary only to publish compilations on hoard horizons related to short periods or to certain types of find.[16] Among the few exceptions are compilations by István Gedai of foreign coin hoards deposited in Hungary between the eleventh and thirteenth centuries[17] and occurrences of Árpádian-age bracteates. There are also some regional repertories, and compilations basically focused on other types of objects which use coins for dating. A refreshing exception is the compilation by Ernő Saltzer, although it can only be used with the corrections made by László Kovács.[18]

Written Sources

We have no written sources on the beginnings of Hungarian coinage, and almost none from the whole of the eleventh and twelfth centuries. The earliest sources referring to the use of coins are laws and ecclesiastical council resolutions from the reign of Stephen I, Ladislas I, Coloman and Andrew III, stipulating fines and blood money in various denominations.[19] A unique document is a set of accounts from the reign of Béla III listing the crown revenues, including the profit made on minting coins.[20] Most early references only indirectly involve minting, usually in some judicial context. Disputes as to the rightful recipient of tithes from minting, the profit from minting, recoinage, and the movements of money changers, especially in connection with exemptions

---

13   Gedai 1985–1986.
14   Tóth 2004.
15   Velter 2002, Mirnik 1981 and Hlinka et al. 1964–1978.
16   Tóth 2007.
17   Gedai 1969.
18   Saltzer 1996 and Kovács 2005–2006.
19   Cf. brief surveys by Huszár 1934, Huszár 1971–1972a, Gedai 1979.
20   Hóman 1916, 424–436 and Barta and Barta 1993. The authenticity of the source was long debated.

(e.g. the Andreanum) and diplomas throw light on financial administration, as do some data in the Golden Bull (1222) and the Treaty of Bereg (1233). There are also only scattered mentions of the persons in charge of financial administration and cases of counterfeiting. Various customs regulations also throw light on the circulation of money.

Registers of papal tithes, especially for the period between 1332 and 1337, and to a lesser extent for the thirteenth century and the 1370s, contain a wealth of information on monetary history.[21] The several dozen names of coins, the accounting currency and the long-unexplained coin values and exchange rates have caused much head-scratching for (economic) historians since their discovery. Some named coins can be identified with those in other written sources and with surviving coins themselves. Comparable with the papal tithe registers are the accounts of the Chapter of Transylvania (functioning in Alba Iulia), which unfortunately survive only for one year, 1331.

Minting orders and chamber leases, documents of a kind which have not survived at all from the previous period, are the most important sources for the monetary history of the Angevin period. The earliest source of this kind is an order to the Chapter of Alba Iulia, dated 6th January, 1323, which reports the minting of new coins of stable value. This document marks the start of Charles I's financial reform. It specifies the base of the coins and the rate of exchange and provides reliable information on how the administration of minting was to be reorganized. Similar to this is a decree of 1330, which survives in a copy sent to Ung County. It specifies the base of the denars to be issued that year and provides for the redemption of old denars and the administrative details of the exchange.

There are seven chamber leases surviving from the Angevin period (March 26, 1335: Kremnica chamber lease; March 25, 1336: Transylvania chamber lease; March 29, 1338: Smolník and Kremnica chamber lease; February 2, 1342: Pécs-Srijem chamber lease; 1344: Zagreb chamber lease (Ban's mint); and February 2, 1345: Pécs-Srijem chamber lease).[22] These comprise a category of their own, telling us the base of the currency at the time and the rent and the name of the chamber count, as well as throwing light on every aspect of each chamber and mint from the geographical extent of their powers in each county of the kingdom down to the tiniest detail of the inspection of the mint. Unfortunately, we know of such documents only from two decades, and there is no similar source of Hungarian monetary history before or since.

---

21 Fejérpataky (ed.) 1887.
22 Érdy 1870, Szekfű 1911, Hóman 1921, 258–259. Döry, Bónis and Bácskai (eds.) 1976, 77, 86–89, 90–94, 95–102, 107–115, 116–123 and 118–123.

The Emergence of Minting in Hungary

Hungarian numismatic research started in the eighteenth century with the collection and identification of the various types of coins. A series of catalogues, first of collections and later of types, laid the foundations for deeper research into monetary history, one of whose focal points was the beginnings of Hungarian coinage, a subject around which there is now an enormous body of literature.[23] Since there are no surviving written sources on this period, research has always relied on artifact studies. The coins of St Stephen,[24] with STEPHANVS REX on the obverse and REGIA CIVITAS on the reverse, were identified in the early 1700s. By the mid-twentieth century, almost every possible aspect had been covered in the literature,[25] but the debate flared up again in the 1960s, when Gyula László reviewed the subject,[26] followed by international scholars who attempted to link other types of coins to King Stephen.[27] This led to the curious state of affairs that these coins are regarded as Hungarian by the latter, and as foreign by Hungarians.[28]

The debate took on new momentum with the discovery of a hoard in Nagyharsány, Baranya County, in 1968. This included forty coins of a type that had formerly been regarded as modern forgeries or contemporary imitations. On the obverse is an arm holding a lance surrounded by the inscription LANCEA REGIS, and on the reverse a Carolingian church with the inscription REGIA CIVITAS. Investigation into the hoard showed conclusively that this was almost certainly Stephen I's first coin, and so the order of coins issued by the first Hungarian king had to be revised accordingly.

One unresolved question surrounds a golden coin weighing 4.5 grams (the weight of the classical antique solidus), thought to date from the eleventh century and possibly linked to the reign of Stephen I.[29] Three of these are definitely known, and a fourth has been published, but only a drawing; its location is as yet unknown. There is a front-facing haloed portrait on the obverse and reverse, with the inscriptions STEPHANVS REX and PANNONIA respectively. The present view is that the coin is medieval and not a modern fictive piece, although further information would be required to determine why and when

---

23 Gedai 1986. Cf. Kovács 1988.
24 Gedai 2001.
25 Hóman 1916 and Huszár 1938.
26 László 1962.
27 Hatz 1965, Gedai 2007, Turnwald 1965–1966, Turnwald 1967–1968 and Suchodolski 1990.
28 Huszár 1966.
29 Gedai 1999.

it was minted. It may not have been intended for circulation, and have been issued in connection with the cult of St Stephen which was evolving in Hungary.

What is still regarded as the core work on Árpádian-age minting is a great monograph by Bálint Hóman,[30] drawing on enormous range of sources, which covers the financial affairs and coinage of the Árpádian age and sets out the subsidiary topics pursued by research ever since. Apart from László Kovács's large-scale monograph on coinage and hoards from the period from Stephen I to Béla II,[31] there has been no major book on eleventh- and twelfth-century coinage since, although there have been studies of specific areas.

Coins and Minting Techniques in the Eleventh–Twelfth Centuries

Hungarian coins of the eleventh and twelfth centuries are linked by their special minting techniques and privy marks. The dies for early Hungarian coins were punched rather than engraved. This means that needle punches of various sizes were hammered on to the die to make the image and the legend; this technique gave way to engraving only during the reign of Andrew II. The other distinctive feature is the system of privy marks – auxiliary marks separate from the image and legend. These first appeared on coins minted during the reign of Andrew I and continued in use until the turn of the twelfth and thirteenth centuries, although they are also found in a degenerate form on coins from the early period of the reign of Andrew II. Each type has several dozen different privy marks, and some have several hundred. Various explanations for their use have been proposed, the most durable being that they were control marks used in the process of minting. Work has recently started on putting privy marks in order and publishing them.[32]

The copper coins issued during the reign of Béla III, a unique development in medieval Hungary, remain shrouded in mystery despite the series of research findings on them.[33] Copper coins basically fall into two types. "Byzantine" coins have two front-facing kings seated on thrones on the obverse and the seated figure of the Virgin Mary on the reverse. The legend is only a partial help in identifying the figures on the obverse: the figure marked REX BELA is clearly Béla III, but the other, marked REX SANCTUS, is probably one of the "sainted kings", perhaps Ladislas I, whom Béla III had canonized

---

30   Hóman 1916.
31   Kovács 1997.
32   Tóth 2006a.
33   Velter 1996 and Suchodolski 1999.

in 1192.[34] "Arabic" copper coins have an image that imitates kufic script, but is completely meaningless.[35]

Early Hungarian coins had very simple images. Initially, the principal motif was a cross with equal-length arms surrounded by a legend referring to the kingdom (REGIA CIVITAS, PANNONIA, PANNONIA TERRA). The first – somewhat schematic – royal portraits appeared during the reign of King Solomon, and nearly all subsequent monarchs had at least one type representing the king. At the turn of the eleventh and twelfth centuries, during the reign of Coloman, coins started to be minted with fundamentally different images. As the coins became smaller, the legends disappeared to be replaced by various non-figurative, mostly geometrical signs. The lack of an inscription prevents definite identification of the issuer, and the expression "anonymous denar" became common in the literature. Although every king from Coloman to Emeric had at least one coin type bearing his name, the vast majority of twelfth century coins are undatable anonymous denars.

Coins, Circulation of Money, and Minting in the Thirteenth Century

Minting technique and financial administration in the Árpádian age went through fundamental changes during the reign of Andrew II, and coins were minted with new kinds of images. Friesach denars – discussed below – were instrumental in the adoption of figurative representations. Royal portraits, buildings, ecclesiastical symbols, and real and mythical animal figures were joined by various heraldic elements: the shield with barry of eight first appeared during the reign of Andrew II, and the double cross in the first half of the thirteenth century.

Works on the monetary history of the thirteenth century in recent decades focused on the circulation of money, particularly the presence of foreign coins in the Carpathian Basin. Indeed most twelfth- and thirteenth-century hoards are of foreign coins, especially Friesach denars. These were originally very pure coins minted by the archbishop of Salzburg in the town of Friesach in Carinthia, starting in the middle of the twelfth century. Later, Friesach denars became a collective term for coins minted on the pattern of the originals by other secular and ecclesiastical minting authorities – the princes of Carinthia, the counts of Andeasch-Meran, the bishops of Bamberg, the patriarchs of

---

34   Ujszászi 2010.
35   On these, see: Nagy 2016, 53–57.

Aquileia, etc. – in mints spread around the territory of Carinthia and Krajina: Friesach, Sankt Veit, Ptuj, Rann, Gutenwert, Slovenj Gradec, Kostanjevica na Krki and others. This continued through the twelfth and thirteenth centuries and many copies – of variable quality – were produced by mints elsewhere, including Hungary. The importance of Friesach denars in contemporary Hungarian money circulation is borne out by written sources as well as coin hoards.[36] Their first appearance in Hungary may be dated to the late twelfth century, and their circulation reached a peak in the first half of the thirteenth. They do not appear in hoards following the Mongol invasion of 1241–1242.

The chronology of Friesach denars started with pioneering work by Arnold Luschin von Ebengreuth, which was later refined by Egon Baumgartner, Bernhard Koch, Heinz Winter and Herbert Ban to produce a very useful relative chronology, one that in several cases may be regarded as absolute. Their work largely relied on Friesach denar hordes found in Hungary.[37] By comparing the composition of finds with their chronology, it is possible to determine the end-date of a horde to within a five–ten-year interval, although Hungarian and Austrian numismatists do not always arrive at the same dates. György V. Székely, drawing mostly on earlier research by István Gedai,[38] has used this means to distinguish the find horizons of purely, or predominantly Friesach denar-containing coin hoards in Hungary.

Another focal point of study, involving several Croatian as well as Hungarian scholars, is the coinage of the bans of Slavonia.[39] The Bans of Slavonia started minting coins in the mid-thirteenth century and continued for about a hundred years, during which they made the first breach in the system of periodic recoinage. Both financial administration and taxation are inextricably linked with the concept of "chamber's profit" (*lucrum camerae*), a long-researched subject which still lacks a modern synthesis that brings together work on diverse sources. By contrast, there has been considerable progress in one area of financial control, the *pizetum* right. This right of the archbishop of Esztergom to supervise minting to prevent all kinds of abuse was earlier thought to date from the early eleventh century; it has now been discovered to have been granted only in the mid-thirteenth century. Since its establishment is almost certainly related to decrees against 'Ismaelite' (Muslim) and Jewish,

---

36   Gedai 1996.
37   von Ebengreuth 1922–1923, Baumgartner 1949, Baumgartner 1952, Ban 1992 and Winter 2002.
38   Gedai 1969.
39   V. Székely 1980 and Korčmaros 1997.

i.e. non-Christian chamber counts (tenants of the mint), it is inevitably linked to the issues of the "Hebrew-symbol coins" of the Árpádian kings.

Hebrew Letters on Hungarian Coins

Hungarian coins bore Latin inscriptions from the earliest times. Only in the nineteenth century did German-language, and during the 1848–1849 War of Independence, Hungarian-language legends appear. It is thus curious to find a group of thirteenth-century Hungarian coins bearing Hebrew letters (but not text). The Hebrew letters on Hungarian coins were noted in the nineteenth century by Sámuel Kohn in his history of the Jews, and in some type descriptions by László Réthy. Nonetheless, they only arose as a subject of research in the 1970s following the publication of a paper by Gyula Rádóczy drawing attention to them. Rádóczy systematically went through their various types, identified each Hebrew character, and attempted to link them with the initials of chamber counts known from written sources. He reached the conclusion that the 'alef' was linked with Altman, the 'chet' with Henoch, the 'ef' with Fredman, the 'teth' with Theka and the six-pointed star with Samuel. The investigation was quickly joined by Sándor Scheiber and Lóránt Nagy, the latter attempting to use Rádóczy's findings to date late Árpádian-age coins.[40] Later, several papers attempted to clarify the issue and determine the persons of Jewish birth who could be linked with the coins.[41] Still not published, however, is the best and most broadly-based treatment of the subject: László Vermes's dissertation,[42] which restated the problem and identified the tasks for further research.

The first and most important task is to identify the sound value of each character. This is not a straightforward matter, because one symbol can, by rotating it through 90 or 180 degrees, stand for more than one Hebrew character. Another issue is the chronological order of each coin. Research in Hungary has so far only managed to link coins bearing the name of a king with their reign, and has not produced a relative chronology of thirteenth-century coins. It is irresponsible to identify the Hebrew characters found on the coins with Jewish names (or their initials) known from written sources, or to date a particular coin purely from the mention of a name, because the written source could have been written several decades later than the coin was minted. There is a need

---

40   Nagy 1973–1974 and Scheiber 1973–1974.
41   Saltzer 1998, Guest 1998 and Guest 1999.
42   Vermes 1998.

to gather data from written sources on Jews involved in thirteenth-century Hungarian minting, and to identify what their activities were. Since most of these men of finance migrated to the Kingdom of Hungary from Austria (in fact, Vienna), much more data can be found on them there than from the few surviving Hungarian sources. It is not certain, however, that the Hebrew letters on the coins are personal initials in any case, let alone those of Jewish chamber counts.[43] Some other possibilities ought to be examined. The symbols might refer to the contemporary denomination of the coins (which does appear on them); i.e., they could be the Hebrew equivalent of the Latin words denar, *obulus, moneta*, etc., or they may refer to the place of issue (mint [?]). The latter deserves particular attention, because it was just at the time when Hungarian minting started to be decentralized – the early decades of Andrew II's rule –, that the Hebrew-character coins first appeared.

Coins and Minting in the Angevin Period

The Angevin period, or at least its first half, has attracted almost as much numismatic interest as the beginnings of Hungarian minting. It was a period which saw the proliferation of written sources directly concerned with minting – which are very rare for the whole of the Árpádian age – and the start of large-scale financial reforms, always the object of special attention among numismatists and economic historians. Denominations previously unseen in Hungarian minting began to appear: the gold florin[44] and the silver *grossi*,[45] and there was a complete reform of chamber administration, mining and taxation, putting them on a new legal footing. Chronological lists of Angevin-period coin types appear in two papers by Alfréd Schulek.[46] The first deals with Charles's coins, and the second the financial affairs of King Louis I and Queen Mary in connection with minting in Buda. The latter appeared alongside Henrik Horváth's art historical study on the development of coin design in the late medieval period, including the Angevin period.[47] Lajos Huszár's 1958 monograph on medieval minting in Buda surveyed the output of the Buda mint from its foundation in the thirteenth century, devoting a whole chapter

---

43 On Jewish chamber counts in the Árpádian age, see: Weisz 1999.
44 Gedai 1987, Hóman 1917, Huszár 1970–1972, Kováts 1922, Mályusz 1985, Probszt 1957 and Probszt 1963.
45 Huszár 1971–1972b.
46 Schulek 1926 and Schulek 1931–1932.
47 Horváth 1931–1932.

to a unique episode in Hungarian monetary history, the autonomous issue of coins in Buda during the Angevin period.[48] Bálint Hóman wrote an economic and monetary history of the reign of Charles I,[49] and findings by Ferenc Kováts on the circulation of money in fourteenth-century Hungary remain influential today.[50]

While the literature on the reforms of economic policy and minting by King Charles, who changed the face of medieval Hungarian coinage and issued the gold florin, is enough to fill a library, almost no attention has been paid to the financial affairs of his son Louis – as he was thought to have confirmed his father's measures. Bálint Hóman devoted a monograph to the financial affairs of Charles's reign, and not a single line to Louis's economic policy. Schulek was the first to produce a chronology of Louis's coins, but it was not on the same scale as his thorough study of Charles's finances. Lajos Huszár basically followed on from Schulek, and although he noticed the distinctive features of the two kings' coinage (the appearance of durable small coins, the change of the image on the gold florin, the revival and later ending of *grossi* minting and the Francesco Bernardi problem,[51] which greatly influences the chronology of coins), he did not properly incorporate them into his major study of the Buda mint. In the 1980s, historians also started to address the issue. The first was András Kubinyi, whose article on the history of the town that accommodated the most important mint of the late medieval and modern periods, Kremnica, covered the transformation of Angevin-period mint administration in the second half of the fourteenth century.[52] He devoted particular attention to Francesco Bernardi and his associates, the operations of the Szerecsen family, and explained the significance of the Pécs-Srijem chamber in terms of economic policy and demographics. He also pointed out the fundamental changes in Hungarian financial administration during the 1370s.

Kubinyi's student István Hermann expanded on this brief outline, focusing on the financial administration and circulation of the second half of the fourteenth century. He compiled an enormous database on mint personnel and documentary references to coinage types,[53] and this was drawn on by Pál Engel for his study of unsolved issues of the monetary history of the Angevin period.[54]

---

48   Huszár 1958.
49   Hóman 1921.
50   Kováts 1926.
51   Mályusz 1958.
52   Kubinyi 1981a.
53   Hermann 1984.
54   Engel 1990.

Engel practically rewrote the monetary history of the period, giving a new interpretation of issues like the recoinage system and the standard of each coin, and uncovering a previously-unknown double gold exchange rate (chamber-market). He also discussed details of various forms of accounting currency and how they evolved. The information he discovered was instrumental in reopening the debate about the chronology of Louis' and Mary's coinage.[55]

Gold Coins in the Angevin Period

Perhaps the most intriguing chapter of Angevin monetary history is the minting of gold coins on a scale that sets the country apart from the rest of Europe.[56] Many facets of this have been analyzed, although the change in the standard of the coinage has only come to light recently.[57]

It used to be a basic tenet of Hungarian monetary historiography that the standard of the gold florin was steady from the Angevin period onwards. Hungarian fourteenth-century sources are silent on the issue – except for the chamber leases from 1335 and 1336, when it was specified that Hungarian florins have to be minted *ad modum florenorum Florencie, de fino auro, sed aliquantulum ponderaciones –*,[58] and the first credible information on the standard of the Hungarian gold florin dates from the sixteenth century. This states that 69 florins were struck from one Buda mark (= 245.5378 grams) of 23 ¾ carat (= 989.58 %) purity gold, so that each coin had a raw weight of 3.5585 grams and a fine weight of 3.5214 grams. This figure is usually projected back to the medieval period.[59]

The constant standard of the Hungarian florin, having long been held as an unassailable principle, came under attack from scientific testing and the publication of previously unknown sources. The greatest upset was an assay of 141 Angevin-period gold florins (16 Charles I, 81 Louis I, 44 Mary) in the late 1990s. Charles's gold florins were found to have an average gold content of 994 ‰, the two extreme values being 997 ‰ and 990 ‰. This actually surpassed the 23 ¾ carats (989 ‰) extrapolated to the medieval period. Queen Mary's gold florins were of an even higher grade: the gold content was consistently high,

---

55 Tóth 2002.
56 Mályusz 1985 and Huszár 1970–1972.
57 Tóth 2003–2005.
58 Döry, Bónis and Bácskai (eds.) 1976, 86 and 91.
59 Hóman 1916, 98–99, Hóman 1921, 85–86 and Paulinyi 1937, 493 (published again in Paulinyi 2005, 171–182). Huszár 1958, 32 and Engel 1990, 43.

never below 994 ‰ and up to 998 ‰, with an average of 997 ‰. By contrast, the purity of Louis I's gold florins is widely variable. The earliest type from his reign, bearing a Florentine image (O: Florentine lily, R: St John the Baptist) was found to have an average purity of 990 ‰, with extreme values of 996 ‰ and 986 ‰. The downward trend continued with Louis's next florin, from the middle of his reign (O: Hungarian-Angevin shield, R: St John the Baptist): its purity averaged 987 ‰, with extreme values of 993 ‰ and 977 ‰. This was still only a hairsbreadth lower than the assumed 23 ¾ carats. A relatively "dramatic" debasement came with coins bearing St Ladislas on the reverse. In addition, the gold content of sub-types with different mint marks showed wide deviations. They had a fineness of 984 ‰ on average, but 980 ‰ in some subgroups, and even lower in certain specimens.

The measurements tell us that the standard of gold florins issued by Charles I, Louis I and Mary during the fourteenth century was not at all constant. Charles's and Mary's coins were effectively fine gold, as far as was technically possible, while those from Louis's reign were of fluctuating purity. Although the deterioration has only become apparent through modern scientific tests and only amounts to a few per cent, it would, given the very high value of gold, have been significant even in the Middle Ages. A half-carat difference must have been noticeable. The change is not detectable in Hungarian written sources, but recent research reveals it as having been a known fact in contemporary Italy.

The figures for Hungarian coins entered in some Italian merchants' reference books and account books bear out the scientific findings.[60] These frequently mention the Hungarian gold florin, which was of equal value to Florentine florins and Venetian ducats, and the description of the image struck on each variant allowed precise identification. It was crucial for merchants on the great money markets to be able to tell between coins of different forms and values issued by several dozen mints, and know for certain how much they were worth. They therefore had to know all of the identification marks and the exact exchange rate for each coin.

The sources usually give the purity of Hungarian gold florins in carats (24 carats = 1000 ‰), of which we present a few examples:

"Fiorini ungheri del giglio"	23 ¾ carat
(Hungarian florins with lily)"E quelli de giglio"	23 ¾ carat
(And those florins with lily)	
"Fiorini unghari di giglio e della mannaia"	23 ¾ carat

---

60   Oberländer-Târnoveanu 2003–2004.

(Hungarian florins with lily and battleaxe)
"Fiorini ungheri di Mannaia, e scudi"   23 ¼ carat
(Hungarian florins with battleaxe)
"Unghere della manaia e dello scudo"   23 ¼ carat
(Hungarian [florins] with battleaxe and shield)

These sources thus claim that Hungarian gold florins bearing a lily were 23 ¾ carat (989 ‰) gold, and those with axe and shield only 23 ¼ carat (968 ‰). It is easy to recognize from the descriptions of the Charles- and Louis-era gold florins having the Florentine lily on the obverse; the Hungarian florins with "battleaxe" and "shield" clearly refer to Louis's coins with a heraldic shield on the obverse and St Ladislas on the reverse. The axe mentioned in the description refers *pars pro toto* to the saint, as confirmed by another reference: *Fiorini d'Ongaria, [...] da l'altra parte santo Ladussalus con una mannaia in mano* ... ("Hungarian gold florins, [...] on whose other side is St Ladislas with an axe in his hand ..."). The contemporary source thus makes a precise distinction between the "lily" and "St Ladislas" florins and states the difference in their purity as half a carat. This would seem to clarify the matter, except that we know of no coins with both a lily and an axe (i.e. St Ladislas); for want of better explanation we must put this down to confusion. In other places, the sources hold the lily and John the Baptist florins to be equivalent to pure gold, and so were nominally regarded as fine gold.

The latest research has caused us to re-evaluate our view of the uniform standard of Angevin-period Hungarian gold florins. Both scientific tests and contemporary foreign written sources clearly indicate that the "St Ladislas" gold florin introduced by Louis I contained at least half a carat less pure gold than the florins struck earlier in his reign or during the reign of Charles I. The assays give us the further detail that the gold content was lower only in versions bearing certain mint-marks, and not in all coins of the type. It is interesting that Louis' last gold florin, also bearing St Ladislas, restored the almost pure-gold standard. Italian sources, understandably, do not distinguish between sub-types and mint marks, and hold these coins *en bloc* to be of poorer quality than the older ones.

We do not yet know the reason for the debasement of the coinage during Louis's reign, but it seems only to have been a brief interlude. It was certainly associated with the change in type of gold florins – the appearance of St Ladislas on the reverse. The change could hardly have been a secret among the men of finance of Western Europe, who immediately took note of the phenomenon and adjusted the exchange rate of the new coins. This could not have had a good effect on Hungarian gold's international reputation, and may explain why Louis's late florins were once again made of fine gold, a standard subsequently maintained by Mary.

Outlook

The precious metal content of post-Angevin Hungarian gold coins is also relevant here, because there is some scattered information about fluctuations in the standard of the coinage in the fifteenth and sixteenth centuries. Assays carried out in the nineteenth century by Carl Schalk showed that the standard of some gold florins from the reigns of Sigismund, Wladislas I and even Matthias fell short of 23 ¾ carats.[61] Suspicion of the debasement of Sigismund-era gold florins had already arisen from written sources such as the 1434–1435 accounts of the Kremnica chamber.[62] Catalan sources mention some early-fifteenth-century Hungarian coins which they record as being 22-carat ones.[63] Although none of the above examples suggest that the Hungarian gold florin ever severely deviated from its famed excellence, the standard was not quite as steady throughout the medieval period as previously thought. There was no spectacular debasement, only deviations of 1 or 2 %, equivalent to a quarter or half a carat, but the new data certainly inspire a rethinking of the monetary history of the period.

---

61   Schalk 1880, 194.
62   Paulinyi 1973.
63   Oberländer-Târnoveanu 2003–2004.

CHAPTER 14

Coinage and Financial Administration in Late Medieval Hungary (1387–1526)

Márton Gyöngyössy

This chapter is an overview of the monetary history of the "long fifteenth century". The subject divides into six main areas. For some of these, the discussion is traced back to the previous period in order to get a proper understanding of developments. The level of detail also varies, and is lower in areas where there has been relatively little research, such as the circulation of money. Indeed, some questions have been almost entirely neglected in the modern literature. The discussion relies on the same kinds of sources as Csaba Tóth's chapter on the monetary history of the previous period; i.e. a combination of numismatic studies and monetary history findings derived from written sources.

The Mint Chamber System

Starting in the reign of King Charles I, the person in effective charge of the kingdom's finances was the *magister tavernicorum*, who had control of crown property and headed financial administration (minting, salt and customs administration). As Bálint Hóman put it: "all the lines of control of the chamber ran to the *magister tavernicorum*, the highest central authority of royal financial administration. As an administrator, the *magister tavernicorum* had a network of officials who kept control of all the chambers. He also held full legal jurisdiction over everyone in his employ." His judicial powers also extended to the free royal towns and the Jews living in the country.[1]

Indeed, so far did the functions of the *magister tavernicorum* expand in politics, administration and the judiciary that a new office had to be established to manage the food tax revenues, control the royal treasury and take charge of minor affairs involving financial administration officials. This was the treasurer, an office which was initially subordinate to the *magister tavernicorum* but became increasingly important in its own right during the fourteenth century;

---

1 Hóman 1921, 40–45, 87, 193, 231, 245–250, Gyöngyössy 2013–2014, 129 and most recently Weisz 2016.

by the fifteenth, the treasurer had become the sole head of royal financial administration.[2]

King Charles I merged the mint and mining chambers in the mining regions to form a coherent system. This solved the problems of supplying precious metal to the mints in each mining region. After 1338, the chamber count in each mining chamber seat directed the combined mint and mining chamber. The chambers were leased to chamber counts contracted to the king under private law, and directly accountable to the monarch. The lease had a term of two years, which usually started from the Feast of the Purification (February 2nd), and sometimes from the Feast of the Annunciation (March 25th). From 1336, the lease stipulated that a chamber tenant who fulfilled his duties properly should have the right to extend his lease to the following year. The lease afforded the chamber count "the enjoyment of the income from changing money, the portal tax which replaced the compulsory renewal of money (*lucrum*), the precious metal ore monopoly and the *urbura*", as was shown by Bálint Hóman. As the head of the combined mint and mining chamber, the chamber count had an array of duties. He supervised the working of the mines, was responsible for collecting the *urbura*,[3] and held jurisdiction over mining affairs. He was also responsible for the working of the mint, for redeeming precious metal under the chamber monopoly, for refining the metal, and for minting coins. The mints (of which there were several in the territory of some chambers) operated under the chamber count's direct supervision, as did the ore refining and assaying workshops in the mining towns. He also performed some tax administration functions, collecting the portal tax and the tax imposed on towns in lieu of chamber's profit. His duties were therefore complex, mixing official administration with the rights and powers of commercial production. He bore full liability for all the official activity of chamber staff and held full administrative and judicial powers over those accountable to him. This meant that he had sole right to judge their legal disputes, although either party could appeal to the *magister tavernicorum*.[4]

The *magister tavernicorum* and the archbishop of Esztergom sent representatives to inspect the chamber counts, and to be present for the opening of the chest – locked with three keys and closed by the seals of these dignitaries – in which the minting dies and metal bars were kept. They also had to be personally present when the silver was cast and the coins struck, and every week

---

2 Kubinyi 1957, 25, Kubinyi 1980, 11–12, Kubinyi 1981a, Gyöngyössy 2013–2014, 132 and Weisz 2015c.
3 On the *urbura*, see: Weisz 2015b.
4 Hóman 1921, 197–224, Tóth 1999, 307–308 and Gyöngyössy 2013–2014, 130.

they had to check the fineness and weight of the minted coins. Their authority extended to every area of chamber administration and chamber works. Their pay had to be provided by the chamber count, and they also laid claim to a third of fines and penalties. These representatives were usually chosen from the landowning class.[5]

The combined financial administration led by the *magister tavernicorum* was abolished in the mid-fourteenth century and, as was shown by András Kubinyi, were "replaced ... by persons in direct contact with the monarch and managing each branch of royal revenue as tenants or officials" The powers of the mint-chamber counts also changed in the 1370s. They lost their tax collection powers, which passed to the newly-created offices of chamber's profit counts (whose territory was coterminous with that of the mint-chamber counts). In regions where there was no mining, the loss of the chamber's profit eventually led to the withering away of the office of chamber count, because of the difficulty of obtaining the requisite precious metal. The administrative separation of chamber's profit from minting did not take place until the reign of King Sigismund of Luxemburg, although the first certain information dates from exactly 1387.[6]

Although the sources usually mention chamber counts only by their title (*comes camerarum*), omitting the name of their chambers, it is reasonable to assume that the old system persisted, but minting was from time to time concentrated in the hands of a national chamber count. This probably favored foreign-based tenants, who thereby gained influence over minting and precious metal extraction throughout the kingdom. The chamber counts mentioned in written sources between 1387 and 1487 were all foreign. Although we do not know the rate of profit enjoyed by chamber tenants, they were clearly in continual receipt of – and could sell – enormous quantities of precious metal. Consequently, it was common for the tenant named in a chamber lease to be, in reality, an agent or member of a foreign group of financiers. In the years where there are records of a national chamber count, it is striking that only *urbura* counts are mentioned in local seats. At these times, the duties of the mining chamber probably separated from those of the mint chamber, and the latter similarly passed into the hands of a single person in the kingdom.[7]

Minting operated efficiently under the lease system, requiring only fine tuning through the means of control. An illustration of this can be found in *propositiones* for the royal council, drafted sometime between 1415 and 1417.

---

5 Hóman 1921, 225–228, Gyöngyössy 2002–2003 and Gyöngyössy 2013–2014, 130.
6 Kubinyi 1980, Kubinyi 1981a and Gyöngyössy 2013–2014, 130–131.
7 Gyöngyössy 2003, 13–14, Soós 2013–2014, 98–106 and Gyöngyössy 2015.

The person appointed as guard of the mint, according to the proposal, was to be a wealthy nobleman; his duties would be to receive weekly proofs of coins, keep the proofs under seal, and – together with officials of the archbishop of Esztergom and the king – examine the coins struck during the year. This proposal departed from the system introduced by King Charles I inasmuch as the new official would have sole responsibility for control of the mints, taking over from the *magister tavernicorum*'s deputy and the *pisetarius*, an official of the archbishop of Esztergom. In fact, fifteenth-century laws normally assigned control of the mints to the *magister tavernicorum*'s men, although András Kubinyi seems to have been correct in stating that the chief controller appointed by the king may have received the remuneration, but it was the local town councils, via their own appointees, which actually inspected the mints.[8]

Florin Outflow and Foreign Trade

The role of the gold florin in Hungarian medieval finances has become the most hotly disputed issue in the economic history of the period. One position, based on findings by Ferenc Kováts and Oszkár Paulinyi from their study of mid-fifteenth-century Bratislava customs registers, is that Hungary ran a foreign trade deficit. Medieval Hungary obtained a large part of its manufactures and textiles through Western imports, a fact clearly reflected in the customs registers. Entries for trade in the opposite direction, however, seem to suggest that Hungarian exports were insufficient to balance these imports. By extrapolating the figures to the kingdom as a whole, Kováts and Paulinyi calculated an annual deficit of 300,000 florins. This became the basis of their "rich land – poor country" theory: the medieval foreign trade deficit was covered by precious metal extraction and high-standard Hungarian florins.[9]

There are several flaws in this theory. Imports mainly comprised manufactures (broadcloth, spices, etc.), which Hungary attempted to counterbalance by the export of livestock, wine and copper. The country's industry was not developing satisfactorily, and foreigners provided much of the capital required for trade. Nonetheless, the foreign trade deficit demonstrated by the 1457/1458 Bratislava register (as found by Kováts) turned to a surplus in 1542. Using these and other figures, András Kubinyi proved that the Hungarian foreign trade

---

8   Kubinyi 1981a, Gyöngyössy 2003, 22 and Gyöngyössy 2013–2014, 131–132.
9   Gyöngyössy 2014. See also the introduction to the present volume.

deficit had almost certainly come to an end by the time of the battle of Mohács (1526).[10]

Elemér Mályusz has also challenged the applicability of the theory to the earlier years of the fifteenth century, on the basis of contemporary affairs. He arrived at a much lower figure than Paulinyi for the rate of issue of Hungarian florins, and showed their circulation in the West (e.g. Austria) to have been much more modest than Kováts and Paulinyi assumed. Even at that time, he argued, Hungarian livestock was the export commodity which balanced textile and spice imports from the West.[11]

The text of a 1427 decree by King Sigismund in which he took away from Queen Barbara of Cilli the "thirtieth" customs duty (an estimated annual revenue of 20,000 florins) and replaced it with the *urbura* of Kremnica, implies that about 200,000 gold florins were being struck each year. Oszkár Paulinyi put Hungarian gold extraction in the second half of the fifteenth century at 410–420,000 florins. By contrast, it is possible to determine that Hungary annually produced no more than 327,000 florins in the 1480s, and the rate almost certainly decreased in the early sixteenth century, to judge from the annual drop of about 10,000 florins in Kremnica. Since the crisis in precious metal mining was also perceptible elsewhere, it is unlikely that this shortfall could have been made up for by other centers.[12]

Nonetheless, the high esteem of the Hungarian florin abroad must have been significant. The success of King Matthias's monetary reform to a substantial degree lay in fixing the value of silver relative to gold. On the world market at that time, the value of gold and silver had a ratio of 1:12, but the reform set the ratio within Hungary (in coins, and neglecting the value of copper coins) at 1:8.38. The treasury thus revalued the silver denar and devalued the gold florin. János Ernuszt and his successors as treasurer attempted to stabilize the economy and financial affairs using the tools of monetary economic policy: they regulated the rate of coin issue. For example, after some fluctuation in the early 1480s, the minting of coins in Baia Mare was discontinued. The reform had a beneficial effect on the Hungarian economy: interest rates fell after 1470 (from 10 % to 4–5 %), and a sharp division emerged in foreign trade: imports were controlled by foreign financiers while exports remained in domestic hands. Hungarian traders amassed substantial fortunes from livestock exports, and there grew up a distinctive Hungarian class of market-town businessmen. The foreign merchants profited because the internationally-reputable florins

---

10   Kubinyi 1994c, 16–19.
11   Mályusz 1985 and Mályusz 1986.
12   Mályusz 1985, 31–33, Paulinyi 1972b, 595 and Gyöngyössy 2003, 62, 101, 111 and 119.

they received for their goods delivered them a good margin when they went home. In the other direction, Hungarian livestock traders coming home with silver coins after selling their herds abroad could exchange them for florins at a good rate. As foreign trade developed, the crown increased its revenues from customs duties and from taxes paid by towns involved in trade, and tax collection and taxation became easier. The long-term effects of this were very favorable for state finances. The fact that this exchange rate stood up for more than fifty years following the reform proves that János Ernuszt and his successors had a solid grasp of contemporary economic developments.[13]

The Standard of the Hungarian Florin

Hungarian monetary history research has always taken as axiomatic that the fineness of Hungarian florins and the statutory average weight did not change during the medieval period. Csaba Tóth has found, however, that there were fluctuations in the second half of the Angevin period. This prompts the question as to whether any change can be detected during the fifteenth century. Using the Kremnica chamber accounts, Oszkár Paulinyi has determined the fineness of King Sigismund of Luxemburg's gold coins as 23 ½ carats (979.16 ‰). His figures must be treated with caution, however: Carl Schalk's nineteenth-century measurements came up with similar but slightly higher gold content: the florins he measured had a fineness of 981 ‰.[14]

The earliest certain figure for the standard of florins comes from the *Ars cementi*, and coincides with those from the Bornemissza–Werner report of 1552. The fineness was determined as 23 ¾ carats from the 1564/1565 accounts of the Kremnica chamber. Schalk's measurements differ: he found the standard of florins to be 981 ‰ in Sigismund's reign, 984 ‰ in Wladislas I's, and 982 ‰ in Matthias's. János Buza has produced the most recent analysis of the standard of the florin, using sixteenth-century sources. He found a brief to an envoy of King Ferdinand I from 1533 stating that the fineness of the Hungarian florin was 23 ¾ carats (=989.6 ‰) and seventy-eight of them weighed one Vienna mark; i.e., the official average weight was 3.60 grams. This standard is slightly different from what other sources tell us. In addition, Emperor Frederick III ordered the minting of florins on the Hungarian model in 1481. This is the other extreme: eighty coins were to be minted from one Vienna mark of 23 ½ carat (979 ‰) gold, a statutory average weight of 3.5 grams. Research

---

13 Kubinyi 1992, Kubinyi 1998a, 112–117 and Gyöngyössy 2003, 53–54 and 58–60.
14 Paulinyi 1973, 83–84, Schalk 1880, 194 and Gyöngyössy 2008, 44–45.

in the nineteenth century found the statutory average weight of medieval Hungarian florins to be 3.5593 grams. Carl Schalk also measured the weight of thirty of Matthias's florins and found the average to be 3.53 grams. It is interesting that the result was similar for twenty-four of Sigismund's florins: 3.536 grams.[15]

The issue of the fineness of the Hungarian florin thus cannot be regarded as settled. A study of foreign sources could take us closer to a full picture. A few years ago, Ernest Oberländer-Târnoveanu collected information from several Italian, Catalan and French sources. Definite references to fifteenth-century Hungarian florins include: "The florins of Florence, Genoa, Pisa, Hungary, Siena and Bologna are of equal value to gold" (Florence, 1425), "the weight of the previously mentioned twelve types of florins of the Papal chamber, which are called Roman, Papal and eagle florins and florins of Florence, Genoa, Pisa, Hungary, Siena, Bologna, Lucca, Duchy of Milan and Venice, must be equal to the heavy Sienese standard, which ... is said to be twenty-three and a half grains" (Florence, 1425), "the Hungarian florins ... and their official fineness is 22 carats", (Catalonia, ca. 1405), "Hungarian ducat ... of 23 ¾ carat gold ...", "Ducats minted by ... Matthias ... of 23 ¾ carat gold," "another ducat ... of 23 ¾ carat gold," Ducat minted ... by Wladislas of 23 ¾ gold," "the ducat minted by this Wladislas ... of 23 ¾ carat gold" (Paris, before 1524).[16]

The Late Medieval Hungarian System of Mint Mark and Master's Mark

Late medieval Hungarian coins have been classified by Artúr Pohl using the marks they were struck with; i.e., the mint and master marks. These marks were used in controlling the mint. The distinctive late medieval Hungarian mint mark and master mark system first developed on the coins of King Sigismund's German-born chamber counts. The former personal marks gave way to a pair of letters. The first letter was usually the initial of the place of minting, and the second the initial letter of the (first) name of the person responsible for the mint; if the person concerned was a nobleman, the second letter could be replaced by his coat of arms. The mint mark system made Hungarian minting more controllable and transparent.

The earliest written mention of the system is in the chamber lease of captain-general Jan Jiškra, instructing the chamber tenants of Košice, Captain Pál

---

15   Buza 2002, 29–30, Gyöngyössy 2008, 44–45 and Lengyel 2013.
16   Oberländer-Târnoveanu 2003–2004, 49–52.

Modrár of Nagida and Ágoston Greniczer, former judge of Košice, to strike the mint mark (C = Cassovia) on one side of the cross on the obverse of the coins, and the sign of the chamber count on the other.[17]

King Ladislas V's decree on coinage issued in 1453 also clearly refers to the system when it mentions the "chamber count's letters" for gold florins, and the letters to be struck on silver coins (on each side of the cross): the initial letters of the town of Kremnica and the names of the chamber counts.[18]

Hans Dernschwam, the Fugger Company's factor in Hungary during the Jagiellonian period, in his memoirs written around 1563 described the late medieval Hungarian mint mark-master mark system: "The two letters struck on silver and gold coins in Hungary refer to the chamber where they were minted. The *K* and the *G* mean Kremnica and György Thurzó.... in Baia Mare, since Thurzó was chamber count there too, the letters *N* and *H* were struck on the coins, meaning Baia Mare [Nagi Bania] and János Thurzó.... In Sibiu in Transylvania, florins were struck with the letter H and the chamber count's coat of arms."[19]

The traditional Kremnica mint mark (*K–B*) of the Modern Times started in the first half of the sixteenth century and originated from the mint and master marks of Bernhard Beheim (Kremnitz–Bernhard). Later – after Beheim's fall – the mark gained a new meaning, and was looked on as the abbreviation first of Kremnitz–Bergstadt, and later Körmöcz-Bánya. Coins struck on Baia Mare coins also retained the *N–B* mint mark ("NAGI BANIA") throughout the early modern period. These letters are the precursors of the *BP* mint mark on today's coins.[20]

Crown Revenues and Profits on Minting

When King Ladislas V took over government of the kingdom after the resignation of Regent John Hunyadi (1446–1452), the king and his retinue commissioned the Austrian Ulrich Eizinger to report on the revenues of the Hungarian king. The Eizinger report is one of the main sources of monetary history of the era, and the information it contains about crown revenues extends to the reigns of previous kings. The figures for crown revenue from the mint and mining chambers also tell us about the volume of output. Eizinger's figures put

---

17   Huszár 1975–1976, 47.
18   Krizskó 1880, 31–32.
19   Ratkoš 1957, 472–473. The above quote has been translated by the author.
20   Huszár 1975, 165 fn. 271.

TABLE 14.1 *Ordinary revenues of the king of Hungary in the fifteenth century (in florins)*[a]
(*including copper)

	c. 1427		c. 1453		c. 1475	
Salt regale	100,000	32 %	125,000	52 %	80,000	13 %
Portal tax	88,000	28 %	40,000	16 %	385,000	61 %
Groups of special status	25,000	8 %	29,000	12 %	27,000	4 %
Mining (*) and minting	60,000	19 %	24,000	10 %	60,000	10 %
Customs	20,000	6 %	12,000	5 %	50,000	8 %
Towns and Jews	21,000	7 %	11,000	5 %	26,000	4 %
Total	314,000	100 %	241,000	100 %	628,000	100 %

a Bak 1987, Barta and Barta 1993, Draskóczy 2001a, Engel 1993, Fügedi 1982 and Kubinyi 1999a.

the total annual revenue of the chambers (*urbura*, precious metal redemption, minting) at 24,000 florins. This is a modest sum compared to what was to come, but there are clear political and economic reasons why it may be true: revenues were dented by the changeover of power and by the location of most mints in John Hunyadi's sphere of influence, so that the mints halted their operations except in Sibiu, where Hunyadi had coins struck in Ladislas V's name, but for his own profit. Even the Košice mint, run by Jiškra, did not operate for a few years (*see* Table 14.1).[21]

The profit on mining made up a small but rising proportion of the ordinary revenue (500,000–750,000 florins per year) of Matthias. From an assortment of contemporary sources (a report by Papal nuncio Hieronymus Landus, archbishop of Crete from 1462, and Francesco Fontana's account of crown revenues from 1475), cementation records from Baia Mare for the 1480s and 1490s, and the accounts of Peter Schaider, chamber count of Kremnica (1486–1492), we have relatively precise figures for the revenue from sovereign rights to minting and mining. In 1462, nuncio Landus put the revenue from minting and precious ore mining at 44,000 florins. Whereas Landus gave the same figure as Eizinger for the profit of the Kremnica chamber (12,000 florins), the profit of the other mints had, in the intervening ten years, increased by a factor of two or three. Unfortunately, Landus did not count the revenue of the Košice mint, but this sum can be inferred from the 1451 chamber lease to have been about 5000 florins. In May 1476, Francesco Fontana, the Hungarian king's ambassador

---

21 Bak 1987, 356–358, 380–384 and Draskóczy 2001a.

TABLE 14.2 *The profit from mint chambers in the first half of the fifteenth century*[a] (*florins*)
(**on the basis of the 1451 chamber lease*)

	Kremnica	Sibiu	Baia Mare	Košice	Buda	Total
c. 1453	12,000	2,000	6,000	2,000	2,000	24,000
c. 1462	12,000	6,000	20,000	(*)5,000	6,000	49,000
1480s	12,000	5,600	25,000	–	–	42,600

a Paulinyi 1936, Bak 1987, Kubinyi 1990, Gyöngyössy, 2003, 58–62 and Draskóczy 2010b.

to Pavia, delivered an account of his master's ordinary revenues, mentioning that 60,000 florins flowed into the treasury each year from the gold and silver mines. Fontana's figure most probably includes the profit on sale of copper (about 26,000 florins), so that the actual total would have been 34,000 florins. This shows a drop in revenue of 15,000 florins over fourteen years. We also have data on each chamber from the 1480s and 1490s, giving the total revenue of the three chambers working at the time as 43,000 florins. The figures show that after the great monetary reform, the chambers' yield severely declined, and then brought steady, slowly-growing and predictable income to the treasury, although the state of affairs of the early 1460s was never again attained (*see* Table 14.2).

Circulation of Money

King Sigismund of Luxemburg's ascent to the throne brought fundamental changes to the circulation of coins. The change shows up very clearly in a large number of hoards in village locations. Sigismund's silver coins were of varying standard, and since they were the medium of inland monetary transactions, this had implications for the circulation of money. His first denars were modeled on the *bardus* of the Angevin period, often referred to as accounting currency in charters from the late 1390s. Within a short time, however, Sigismund had recourse to debasement, and the standard of his silver denars steadily declined. The resulting uncertainty rendered their value unstable. By the end of the fourteenth century, the new royal denar was equivalent to three *parvi*, and one *bardus* was equivalent to two *parvi*. Commonly known as the *fillér*, the *parvus* was the lowest-standard and most-counterfeited coin. The Hungarian gold florin maintained its successful career as a means of payment, its value consistently equaling that of the Florentine florin and Venetian ducat, and surpassing that of the *Rhinegulden* (florins of the Rhine region). Since the stability of the florin benefited two key interest groups – the Hungarian magnates and foreign (Italian and south German) financiers – there could be no question of its debasement. But silver coins, the money of the lower nobility and townspeople, were viewed differently. In consequence, the silver coins' durability was a persistent problem during Sigismund's reign. The florin was used above all in the granting of pledges, payment papal taxes and conducting foreign trade with the West. The sources most frequently refer to it as *florenus*, but sometimes also as the "red florin". The Hungarian florin attained its true significance via Sigismund's reform of weights and measures.

The early fifteenth century saw the devaluation of silver coins to the benefit of gold. The florin rose to the value of a hundred and fifty denars. Twenty years would pass before the treasury restored the denar to its proper value relative to the florin. The withdrawal from circulation of *parvi* and the issue of new and again low-standard silver coins (the *quarting* and the *ducat*) devalued the smaller denominations even further.

After Sigismund's death, there was an even greater disturbance to the country's monetary affairs. After an unsuccessful attempt to settle monetary affairs by King Albert Habsburg, subsequent rulers were forced to give up on reform completely. Viennese coins circulated along the Austrian border; the first Ottoman coins appeared in the southern border region, and archaeological finds tell us they also reached the interior; Romanian coins seeped into Transylvania. The country thus became divided in terms of the money in circulation, and not only because of foreign currency. The legal rulers Wladislas I and John Hunyadi minted only some of the coins in circulation, the rest being issued by dowager Queen Elizabeth (and later captain-general Jan Jiškra), who controlled the mining regions of Upper and Lower Hungary. Baronial private coins minted under license appeared in the 1440s. This situation only started to be rectified in the 1460s.[22]

King Matthias's monetary reform was clearly a success in terms of circulation, because most hoards from the end of the medieval period comprise Hungarian denars. By the close of the Middle Ages, Hungarian coins had been asserted as almost the sole currency within the kingdom. Deviations from this show up in two sets of hoards where Hungarian denars were in the minority or hardly present at all. In West Hungarian finds there are large numbers of Austrian coins, which tallies with evidence from written sources: in 1495, for

---

22 Gyöngyössy 2016. On the monetary circulation in the first half of the fifteenth century: Huszár 1958, 76–80, Pohl 1967–1968, Tóth 2006b and Gyöngyössy 2003, 32–35.

example, crown tax collectors in Vas County received the tax in Austrian coins. Austrian coins were of a lower standard than current Hungarian coins, but they were the medium of exchange in trade between the Hungarian border lands and the neighboring Austrian provinces. In the Saxon region of Transylvania, hoards show a large proportion of *asperi*. Records show that, in the early sixteenth century, Transylvanian Saxons paid their taxes (partly) in *asperi*. The *asper* had an exchange rate set by royal decree: King Wladislas II ordered in 1505 that a good *asper* was worth two Hungarian denars. It was also in circulation: the Saxons were granted several royal charters permitting them to pay their tax in this currency. But the *asper* had problems of its own. The basic *asper* was of a high standard, but there were frequent occurrences of debased versions and even forgeries. For example, in 1505, Wladislas II instructed János Tárcai, *comes* of the Székelys, to arrest and punish forgers of coins operating in Transylvania. In another decree to the Transylvanian Saxons, the king had *asperi* withdrawn from circulation: the Sibiu chamber was to strike new coins from the good ones, and the bad ones were to be destroyed. At the same time, he permitted the townspeople of Sibiu and Braşov to continue using good *asperi* in trade with Wallachia. A minor contribution to Hungarian monetary circulation came from Aquileian coins struck in the early fifteenth century. These probably came into the country via cattle exports, because one of the main routes that opened up in the 1470 led through the Aquileia region. Their use in Hungary is interesting because they appeared in the country fifty years after they were issued.[23]

This relatively coherent state of the currency was maintained right up to 1526. Both hoards and written sources tell us that the predominant unit of currency for paying taxes and minor commercial transactions was the Hungarian royal denar, and even during the much-lamented period of the *moneta nova* reform there were many references to the "old" denars.

---

23   Gyöngyössy 2003, 205–215, Kubinyi 1998a, 116 (see also Kubinyi 1992), Gyöngyössy 2004a, 9–11, Gyöngyössy 2004b and Gyöngyössy 2004c, 329–330 and 335.

PART 4

Spheres of Production

∴

CHAPTER 15

The Ecclesiastic Economy in Medieval Hungary

Beatrix F. Romhányi

Although the relationship of the church to economic issues was controversial in the Middle Ages, economic activities were present in the life of different ecclesiastical institutions. While usury was condemned, the necessity of economic activity, including finance, was acknowledged. Conscious planning in estate management was practiced from very early in the monastic orders, and even theoretical discussion of the economy appeared as early as by the turn of the thirteenth and fourteenth centuries among the Franciscans.[1] When founding new institutions – monasteries, dioceses or parishes – a solid economic basis was required; even the economic interests of earlier institutions affected by the emergence of a new neighbor were taken into consideration.[2] Furthermore, written records on such issues often precede those kept by lay actors. Thus, the economy of church institutions, monastic or not, has raised the interest of medievalists at least from the late nineteenth century. Since written evidence survives in lesser amounts in Hungary, church records – usually better preserved – are considered even more important, not only for the research of ecclesiastic institutions, but also of the general economic history of the medieval period.

Bishops and Chapters

According to the tradition, King St Stephen founded ten dioceses, but only the existence of eight can be proven for the period of his reign (the archbishopric of Esztergom with its suffragan bishops of Eger, Győr, Veszprém, Pécs, and the archbishopric of Kalocsa with the bishoprics of Transylvania and Cenad). Vác and Oradea (transferred from Biharia) were in fact founded by the mid-eleventh century. Further changes of the diocesan structure happened around 1100 with the foundation of the bishoprics of Zagreb (around 1093) and Nitra

---

1 Cf. Todeschini 2009.
2 Cf. the foundation of the parish of Baratka in 1156 (Marsina [ed.] 1971–1987, I, 80). Similar situations occurred between monasteries, too: e.g. in Ilok between the Franciscan and the Austin friars (Kristó et al. [eds.] 1990–2015, XXVII, no. 770).

(around 1106). A last group of missionary dioceses was founded in the thirteenth century: Milcovul (1227), Srijem (1229), Belgrade (1290), and, for Bosnia, Đakovo (around 1200/1239), all of them being entrusted with promoting the mission among the orthodox and Bogomil population of the Balkans. However, most of these bishoprics lost their territories by the end of the fourteenth century and became titular. In some periods even Dalmatian dioceses, primarily Knin, Split and Zadar, were added to this list, but they never became integral parts of the Hungarian church.

Bishops had to share the estates and incomes of the diocese with chapters, both cathedral and collegiate. The first collegiate chapters were founded in the same period as the first bishoprics. The Holy Virgin's Chapter of Székesfehérvár (1018) and the St Peter's Chapter of Óbuda (around 1040) were important ecclesiastical institutions of the *medium regni*, but from the late eleventh century collegiate chapters were also founded in order to organize and control more remote areas (e.g. Titel, Bratislava and Spišská Kapitula). These institutions had landed property which they managed like monasteries.

In an economic sense, independent cathedral chapters emerged gradually, mainly in the twelfth century. The first evidence in medieval Hungary for the autonomy of a chapter is the division of tithe incomes between the archbishop of Esztergom and his cathedral chapter in 1156. From the twelfth century on, a third type of chapter also appeared, connected to the cathedral chapters. Although they were formally independent collegiate chapters, these colleges depended in fact on the provost of the cathedral: their deans were canons of the cathedral chapter and their economy was also controlled by the provost.

Sources and Incomes

Unlike some Western European dioceses, there are no comprehensive sources concerning any of the Hungarian dioceses until the end of the Middle Ages, and archival material is fragmentary and sporadic. Consequently, we cannot describe the economy of the bishoprics, chapters or parishes in its complexity, including estate management and its transformations. The only area for which we have more sources is incomes. Hints about church revenues, namely tithes, can be found in sources as early as the eleventh- and early-twelfth-century laws.[3] According to the decree of King Coloman, bishops received tithe from other royal revenues such as tolls and taxes as well.[4] The first comprehensive

---

3   Bak et al. (eds.) 1992–2012, I, 11 (St Step. II § 20), 59 (St Lad. I § 27 and 30) and 31 (Colom. § 66).
4   Bak et al. (eds.) 1992–2012, I, 27 (Colom. I § 25).

source on the incomes of the bishops is the income register of King Béla III from 1184, in which the king recorded the tithe paid after his revenues to the bishops.[5] The total sum was 24,100 marks, 23,200 paid in Hungary, and 900 in Dalmatia. Fifty years later, in 1233 King Andrew II had to issue the Oath of Bereg in which he also tried to regulate the rights of different churches regarding salt trading. However, since the text speaks only about a part of the salt transported from Transylvania, we cannot analyze the salt incomes of the bishops in their complexity. Certainly, bishops and chapters shipped and stored approximately 40 % of the salt transported on River Maros.[6]

The next summative source containing analyzable data was compiled in 1375, when papal tax collectors made the account of the tithe paid by the bishops.[7] Further data on fourteenth- and fifteenth-century incomes are provided by the documents of the Camera Apostolica.[8] The last medieval source is a report of the Venetian ambassador of 1525 (*see* Table 15.1).[9] According to these sources, the incomes of the bishops increased considerably in the Late Middle Ages, although we do not know the reasons behind the spectacular ups and downs reflected in the sums of the *commune servitium*.[10] However, on the level of the two church provinces (Esztergom and Kalocsa) these dramatic fluctuations are not identifiable. Due to economic and perhaps environmental transformations, the difference between the incomes of Esztergom and Kalocsa (~60:40 before 1400) decreased in the fifteenth century (~55:45) (*see* Fig. 15.1).

---

5   Forster (ed.) 1900, 140. This source has been analyzed in a larger context, involving royal revenues in Hungary until the reign of King Mathias, by János Barta Jr. and Gábor Barta (Barta and Barta 1993). However, their conclusions are questionable.
6   See the chapter on salt trade by Beatrix F. Romhányi.
7   Fejérpataky (ed.) 1887, 454–457.
8   Lukcsics et al. (eds.) 2014.
9   Mályusz 2007, 172.
10 The *commune servitium* was originally one third of the annual income, but according to recent research its rate was lower (a fifth or sixth) in the fifteenth century (cf. Fedeles 2014, 189–209, esp. 202). However, the rateable value was probably not total income, but earnings. Based on the entries recorded by the Venetian ambassador, one can guess that the tax due to the Camera Apostolica was around 10 % of total income. The diagram shows the incomes of the dioceses in this way from the fourteenth century. The sums recorded in the register of King Béla III were converted to florins, taking into account the difference between the twelfth- and the fourteenth century marks. Nevertheless, these data are but rough estimates.

TABLE 15.1 *Incomes of and taxes paid by the Hungarian bishops between 1184 and 1525 (The bishop of*

Diocese	1184 (florins)		1375 (florins)		commune servitium fourteenth c.	
	mark	%	florins	%	florins	%
ESZTERGOM	6000	25.9	3678	30.9	2000	12.8
Eger	3000	12.9	454	3.8	800	5.1
Győr	1000	4.3	365	3.1	800	5.1
Nitra	300	1.3	81	0.7	275	1.8
Pécs	1500	6.5	1825	15.3	3500	22.3
Vác	700	3.0	248	2.1	500	3.2
Veszprém	1700	7.3	518	4.4	900	5.7
Subtotal	**14,200**	**61.2**	**7167**	**60,2**	**8775**	**56.0**
KALOCSA	2500	10.8	650	5.5	2100	13.4
Cenad	2000	8.6	432	3.6	900	5.7
Transylvania	2000	8.6	2395	20.1	1500	9.6
Oradea	1000	4.3	503	4.2	2000	12.8
Zagreb	1500	6.5	751	6.3	400	2.6
Subtotal	**9000**	**38.8**	**4732**	**39.8**	**6900**	**44.0**
Total	***23,200***		***11,899***		***15,675***	

a The income of the bishop of Srijem (a suffragan of Kalocsa) was estimated by the Venetian otherwise it would be double. As a result of the former, 6000 florins were added to the larger sum perhaps because of the higher proportion of orthodox population (cf. Romhányi 2015, 28), or due recurring Ottoman raids.

Church incomes usually came from three sources: tithes, seigniorial incomes and extraordinary incomes. The internal structure of the incomes of the bishoprics is not known before the fifteenth century. The first and most important source was the tithe that was collected from grains, wine, sheep, and beehives, but in some cases also of pigs and beer. According to early modern urbaria, in some regions even poultry was talliable. Until the mid-twelfth century, the collection of tithe was the exclusive right of the bishops. The institutionalization of the chapters necessitated that canonical colleges obtain fixed incomes, too, but the solutions were different from diocese to diocese. In the Esztergom diocese the estates of the cathedral chapter were defined as early as in 1156, while in the Eger diocese the chapter received only a part of the wine tithe

Srijem is counted with Kalocsa, the bishop of Bosnia with Pécs)

	1420		late fifteenth c.		1525 maximum[a]		minimum	
	florins	%	florins	%	florins	%	florins	%
	4000	20.8	4000	18.6	35,000	15.9	35,000	16.9
	800	4.2	3000	13.9	22,000	10.6	22,000	10.0
	800	4.2	800	3.7	14,000	6.4	13,000	6.3
	275	1.4	275	1.3	4000	1.8	4000	1.9
	3500	18.2	3500	16.3	26,000	11.8	25,000	12.1
	500	2.6	500	2.3	5000	2.3	4000	1.9
	900	4.7	900	4.2	12,000	5.5	10,000	4.8
	10,775	55.9	12,975	60.3	118,000	53.6	113,000	54.6
	2100	10.9	2133	9.9	28,000	12.7	22,500	10.9
	900	4.7	900	4.2	3000	1,4	3000	1.4
	1500	7.8	1500	7.0	25,000	11,4	24,500	11.8
	2000	10.4	2000	9.3	26,000	11.8	26,000	12.6
	2000	10.4	2000	9.3	20,000	9.1	18,000	8.7
	8500	44.1	8533	39.7	102,000	46.4	94000	45.4
	19,375		21,508		220,000		207,000	

ambassador as 2500–3000 florins, remarking that was so low only because of the Ottoman wars, (22,000 florins) of the Kalocsa diocese. In the case of the Cenad bishopric, a similar remark is absent, to the fact that such decreases in income had become normal in the previous decades because of the

from the thirteenth century. Since the revenues from wine were rather high, they led to litigation in several cases (e.g. between the bishop and the cathedral chapter of Eger, and between the bishop of Veszprém and the parsons of Pest and Buda). The opportunity to pay the tithe in cash was given at least from 1290,[11] but this form of payment did not become general before the end of the Middle Ages. One of the most valuable sources of this period is the register of the Oradea diocese compiled in the time of Bishop Benedict, between 1291 and 1294, and preserved in the so-called Viennese Codex, which lists the grain

---

11 Marczali 1902, 189 (decree of King Andrew III, 1290, § 21).

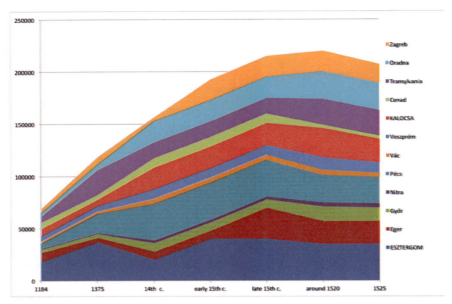

FIGURE 15.1   *Estimated incomes of the Hungarian dioceses between the end of the twelfth and the beginning of the sixteenth century (incomes in florins).*

tithes of bishops.[12] Although the actual value of this income cannot be calculated, the relative value of the settlements can be estimated. Furthermore, it offers an excellent overview of the cereal species produced in a significant part of the Great Hungarian Plain. The same source also contains a list of the yearly contribution of the diocesan priests from three archdeaconries.[13] From the fourteenth century, bishops sometimes rented out the collecting of the tithes, thereby receiving cash instead of payment in kind. Among ecclesiastic revenues, tithe income predominated until the end of the Middle Ages – or at least this can be concluded from the accounts of two bishops of Eger, Tamás Bakóc and Ippolito d'Este (1493–1497 and 1497–1520, respectively; *see* Table 15.2[14]), as well as of the *urbarium* of the Veszprém diocese of the year 1524, although tithe represented a much smaller proportion (~50 %) of the latter.[15] The accounts of archbishop Ippolito d'Este of Esztergom from the years 1488–1490[16] also prove

12   Jakubovich 1926.
13   Bunyitay 1883, 268–269.
14   Kandra (ed.) 1888 and E. Kovács (ed.) 1988.
15   Kredics and Solymosi (eds.) 1993.
16   Fügedi 1981a.

that the income structure of the different dioceses were fairly different (*see* Table 15.3). It is not only the *pisetum* – one part of the royal income derived from minting – which makes the difference, but also the significantly higher proportion of seigniorial and extraordinary incomes.

TABLE 15.2 *The incomes of two bishops of Eger, Tamás Bakóc and Ippolito d'Este (golden florins)*

	1493	%	1495	%	1503	%	1507	%
Tithes	18,256	87.6	19,621	66.6	15,265	92.7	14,884	93.0
Seigniorial incomes	1359	6.5	6,022	20.5	1052	6.4	750	4.7
Extraordinary incomes	1225	5.9	3,803	12.9	153	0.9	359	2.3
Total	20,840	100.0	29,446	100.0	16,470	100.0	15,993	100.0

TABLE 15.3 *The incomes of Ippolito d'Este, archbishop of Esztergom (golden florins)*

	1488	%	1489	%	1490	%
Tithes (*decimae maiores*)	5915	37.1	9648	43.3	5788	38.6
Seigniorial incomes	4544	28.5	4062	18.2	5103	34.0
Pisetum	2532	15.9	2967	13.3	1476	9.8
Extraordinary incomes	2959	18.6	5598	25.1	2638	17.6
Total	15,950	100.0	22275	100.0	15005	100.0

Since the right of the church to the tithe was based on the Old Testament (Gn 14:20), in principle it had to be paid by all the faithful, including the king and even members of the clergy as abbots or friars. However, exemption from taxation was granted to different social groups from the beginning of the fifteenth century. One of these were the nobles who fought against the Ottomans, the other were the Cumans and the Jazygians who farmed cattle on the Great Hungarian Plain. The latter ones paid a fixed sum instead which was called pecunia Christianitatis in early modern times.

It is more difficult to define the incomes of the parsons. The basis was the tithe of the parish, but only the priests of exempt churches could collect the whole sum, while the vast majority had to be content with a quarter or even a sixteenth part of it. The only medieval source on parishes that covers the whole territory of the kingdom is the papal tithe register of 1332–1337.[17] This contains 4066 parishes (those of the Győr diocese are missing from the list, as well as some smaller territories belonging to the Esztergom archbishopric). Until now, a complex quantitative analysis of the whole set of data has been lacking, the source mainly being used for the reconstruction of the parish system and the settlement network. However, it is clear that there were significant differences between the average incomes of the parsons in the different dioceses: while the average is around 14 *grossi* in the diocese of Oradea, it is only around 7 in the diocese of Esztergom. However, we do not know what lies behind these differences (demographic, economic or legal causes). According to these and some other data, the parsons of the towns and even of some market towns reached the income level of the canons, but most parish priests – together with the chaplains, rectors and other members of the lower clergy – had rather modest incomes.

Returning to the bishops, we should also outline in brief the two other income sources (seigniorial and extraordinary incomes). Extraordinary incomes were usually paid by the king as subsidy or salary for certain services and represented a very small part of revenues. Seigniorial incomes consisted of the regular feudal taxes, the most important of which was the ninth in Hungary after 1351. The size of the estates varied in the different dioceses. The archbishop of Esztergom owned dozens of villages all over his diocese (in Esztergom County alone he had 12). Similarly, the bishop of Eger counted as a rich landlord with his 71 villages recorded in a charter of King Béla IV of 1261. On the other hand, in the Late Middle Ages the cathedral chapter of the Transylvanian bishopric had more landed property than the bishop, who possessed only three villages and a number of manors, but this was exceptional. While the possessions of the bishops did not change considerably after 1300, the estates of the chapters grew in the fourteenth and fifteenth centuries with acquisitions and through last wills. In addition to these sources of income, another was their activity as places of authentication.

Beside villages and manors, the bishops owned other real estate, such as mills, fishponds and vineyards, and – in the Late Middle Ages – even urban plots and houses. From the late eleventh century they also received tolls – partially or totally – from the kings[18] and at least from the twelfth century on they took part in the salt trade. A special privilege of the Esztergom archbishop was the *pisetum*, first mentioned in 1211. This was 1/48 of all minted coins paid

---

17   Fejérpataky (ed.) 1887, 39–409.
18   For further data, see Weisz 2013b.

in exchange for preserving the minting tools.[19] Due to the estates and perhaps also to the higher proportion of cash income, the Hungarian prelates reached the standard of the aristocracy by the beginning of the thirteenth century. Still, according to the sources, the level of their revenue was around the European average.

Our knowledge of disbursements is even more fragmentary than of incomes. Certainly, bishops and chapters had to pay daily expenses, the costs of the liturgy, maintenance of buildings, salaries, prebends, etc. Furthermore, they financed arts, architecture and study at home or abroad. From the beginning of the fifteenth century, an extra item of disbursement appeared in their accounts: the expenses of defense against Ottoman expansion. According to the propositions of 1433, bishops were required to raise at least 5200 soldiers, while in the decree of 1498 this number decreased to 4850.[20] However, the proportion of church troops was about 1/7th of the total, and it should be stressed that this commitment significantly strained the budgets of the clergy. In many cases, their whole income would not have been enough to pay the troops throughout the year. Nevertheless, ecclesiastic landlords – not only bishops – did their best to respond to the military requirements of the kingdom.[21]

The Monastic Economy

Monastic estates formed a special category of ecclesiastical holdings in the Middle Ages. It was customary even early in the period for some abbeys and provostries to receive donations of land, large and small, and in return to provide a last resting place for the donor and his family, or at least help them on their way to everlasting life by prayer and the saying of mass. The monastic economy in the narrow sense thus means the running of estates by monastic (Benedictine, Cistercian, Premonstratensian, etc.) and eremitic (Carthusian, Pauline, and Augustine) orders and by communities of nuns. Even the mendicant orders, however, which had had no landed estates, engaged in some activities belonging to the monastic economy.

Although the estates granted to the medieval church were in principle inalienable, and the property of an extinct institution could only be passed on

---

19   Kollányi 1889.
20   Döry, Bónis and Bácskai (eds.) 1976, 405–424 and Bak et al. (eds.) 1992–2012, IV, 84–137. There are two versions of the propositions, the higher number is 5500. The total number of soldiers raised by ecclesiastic institutions (bishoprics and monasteries) was 5600 in 1433 and 5750 in 1498.
21   Kubinyi 2007.

to another church body, secular nobles regularly intervened in the economy of monastic estates throughout the period, first via the *Eigenkirche* system and later by seigneurial right, and often used estate revenues for their own purposes. These practices weighed most heavily on Benedictine abbeys, which lacked a central organization. The hierarchical structure of the reform orders founded after the turn of the eleventh and twelfth centuries gave them some protection from this kind of interference, although not complete immunity, at least during the Middle Ages.

Another point to consider is that the economic pursuits of individual orders went through changes with time. Over the centuries, the monastic economy had to adapt to economic developments in Europe and the changing environment in Hungary.

Sources, Research Issues and Methods

An overriding feature of sources on monasteries and friaries in Hungary is their concern with property and economic activity. Historians first noted this at the turn of the nineteenth and twentieth centuries, regretting the lack of the kind of sources on the internal life of monasteries that are well known in Western Europe. Nonetheless, it may be surprising to learn that there has as yet been no systematic analysis of the sources we do have. One reason is that there is hardly a single monastery whose documents have not suffered serious damage. Most of the surviving documents concern the estates themselves and the associated legal action and acts of violence committed against them. There are only a few scattered surviving account books, *urbaria* and other sources telling of economic affairs. The main sources are documents of monasteries which were places of authentication (*loca credibilia*).[22] Even though the *loca credibilia* documents of a monastery concern matters unrelated to the issuing institution itself, they sometimes contain information useful to the economic historian, mostly concerning income related to place-of-authentication

---

[22] The establishment of places of authentication (*loca credibilia*) is a particular element of Hungarian legal practice during the Middle Ages. In the twelfth and thirteenth centuries, several ecclesiastical institutions contributed to the handling of court cases, mainly concerning landed properties. The charters they had issued – and archived – had public authority. Primarily cathedral and collegiate chapters, Premonstratensian and Benedictine monasteries were active. In 1353, following a decree of King Louis I regulating their operation, a number of these places lost the right to issue charters. The ones that remained functioned until the early modern period. From the mid-sixteenth century, however, most of them functioned only as repositories and archives, but they were only closed down permanently during the nineteenth century when the institution of public notaries was organized. Cf. Rokolya 2008, esp. the article of T. Kőfalvi.

activity. There is also good evidence that Benedictine and Premonstratensian monasteries had a better chance of survival in the Late Middle Ages if they were also places of authentication, a function providing a more stable economic base and a healthy system of social contacts. The converse is also true: the monasteries permitted by King Louis I to continue as places of authentication were those whose large estates, and thus stable economies, made them less vulnerable to influence.

It is clear that such sources do not permit a coherent economic history of each monastery to be written. Studies most frequently involve the estate accounts, and sometimes the history of possession. Such work has been done for nearly every major monastery, mostly in the late nineteenth and early twentieth centuries by eminent religious order historians.[23] The *A Pannonhalmi Szent-Benedek-rend története* ('History of the Benedictine Order of Pannonhalma')[24] still stands as a model. These source publications, produced in the positivist spirit, are still one of the most important points of reference for historians.

Research was interrupted during the World War I and the following years, but there were further substantial developments from the mid-1920s onwards. Besides source publications,[25] there appeared the first attempt at a treatment of the monastic economy: Elek Kalász's book covered the estate affairs of the Cistercian monastery at Szentgotthárd and the economy of the wider order in Hungary.[26] The section on the estates is still useful, but the findings on the economy must be handled with care, because Kalász made up for the scarcity of Hungarian sources through the use of Western European (especially French) documents and the order's instructions concerning material affairs. We will return to these difficulties in the discussion of research today and its problems.

The post-war period, for well-known ideological reasons, brought about another gap in the writing of ecclesiastical history in general, including that of monastic estates and their economy. In the meantime, treatment of Western European sources continued steadily, and there were great steps forward in

---

23   Erdélyi and Sörös (eds.) 1902–1916 (concerning Benedictines), Békefi 1891, Békefi 1894, Békefi 1898 (concerning Cistercians). See also Fraknói 1879, Knauz 1890 and Dedek 1889. Dedek wrote the first comprehensive history of the Carthusians – although he did not always refer properly to the sources he used, these can be attested and identified based on known charters. A modern overview of the order's history has been published by Sarbak et al. 2004.
24   Erdélyi and Sörös (eds.) 1902–1916.
25   Lukcsics 1923, Mályusz 1925–1935, Borsa 1944–1946, Pataki 1942 and Szabó 1936.
26   Kalász 1932.

methodology. Monographs on the history of monastic orders written in the years following World War II only became available to Hungarian researchers after a considerable delay.[27]

One peculiarity of affairs in Hungary is that in the second half of the 1950s, research in this area was relieved of some official restrictions; it was mainly taken up by archaeologists and historic building researchers. The opening work in this period was a book by the Premonstratensian F. A. Oszvald on the Premonstratensian provostries of Árpádian-age Hungary.[28] In the decades which followed, archaeologists, art historians and architectural historians investigated a great many monasteries.[29] Although this research did not venture into issues of economic history, much of the data it produced on the history of construction and on the buildings themselves – especially (sadly, rarely-excavated) barns and outbuildings – has definite economic relevance. Work on publishing sources also revived at that time, if under peculiar circumstances: the Art History Research Group of the Hungarian Academy of Sciences published the medieval and early modern written documents of the Pauline order, under the title *Documenta Artis Paulinorum*, in three stencilled-manuscript volumes.[30] Another portion of the data was disseminated outside the sphere of ecclesiastical history, in books on the historical geography of the Árpádian age,[31] or in studies of economic, especially agricultural history.[32]

The next revival in ecclesiastical history started around 1980. The symbolic opening move was the publication of a book by the Benedictine monk Lajos J. Csóka on the history of the Benedictines in Hungary.[33] Although the subject was Hungarian, the place of publication was Munich. A similar route was followed a few years later by the repertory of documents of Cistercian abbeys in Hungary by the Cistercian F. Levente Hervay, which was published in Rome.[34] Reflecting the official thaw, there was an upsurge in ecclesiastical history publications, particularly by the Catholic Church. This was followed immediately after the political transition by the publication in Hungarian of Lajos Lékai's book, originally appearing in English, on the history of the Cistercian

---

27   Schmitz 1998, Schmitz 2006 and Lékai 1991 (based on the English version published in 1977).
28   Oszvald 1957.
29   Valter 1982a, Valter 1982b, Valter 1982c, Altmann 1994, H. Gyürky 1996 and Németh 1967.
30   Gyéressy and Hervay 1975–1978.
31   Györffy 1963–1998 and Mályusz 2007.
32   E.g. Belényesy 1956b and Sugár 1979.
33   Csóka 1980.
34   Hervay 1984.

order in Hungary, with an additional chapter by F. Levente Hervay.[35] In the same period, Zsuzsa Bándi produced two publications on Pauline documents from northeast Hungary and Szakácsi (Somogy County).[36]

The political transition heralded a resurgence in the writing of ecclesiastical history, also reflected in some major exhibitions and conferences. These large-scale ventures – partly by their nature – concentrated on buildings and physical relics, but all of the catalogues and conference proceedings included chapters on monastic estate management and related documents. Notable developments were maps showing the extent of monastic lands and the estates of the larger abbeys, the latter containing references to land use and management of property.[37] Éva Knapp introduced some new methodological features in her study of the Pécs episcopate's relationship with the Pauline friaries of Baranya.[38]

In the 1990s, a new generation of historians – to which the present author belongs – began to take up some previously neglected or forgotten areas of ecclesiastical history. Their work has included the modern historical treatment of Knights Hospitallers and other knight orders in Hungary,[39] new approaches to the minor mendicant orders,[40] the architectural and art historical analysis of monastic buildings,[41] the social situation and education of common priests and the middle clergy,[42] and increasingly, the monastic economy.[43] The latter subject has also taken on new currency in Western Europe, extending beyond the usual monastic context to embrace the mendicant orders. Furthermore, some international interest arose concerning East Central Europe, including Hungary, which resulted in publications by foreign, mainly German scholars.[44]

Besides the publications of documentary sources of specific orders, a great deal of information on monastic estates, some touching on their economic

---

35   Lékai 1977.
36   Bándi 1985 and Bándi 1987.
37   Takács (ed.) 1996, Takács (ed.) 2001, Hervay 1984 and Kollár (ed.) 2000.
38   Knapp 1994.
39   Hunyadi 2010, Kurecskó and Stossek 1998 and Stossek 2001.
40   Regényi 1998 and Romhányi 2005.
41   The results of this research were published in conference volumes and exhibition catalogues: Haris (ed.) 1994, Takács and Mikó (eds.) 1994, Takács (ed.) 1996 and Takács (ed.) 2001.
42   Köblös 1994, Koszta 2007, Erdélyi 2006 and Erdélyi 2015.
43   E.g. Romhányi 1998, Romhányi 2010b (partly in German: Romhányi 2010c), Romhányi 2010a, Romhányi 2014 and Ferenczi (in preparation). I am grateful to László Ferenczi for allowing me to consult his unpublished manuscript.
44   Weinrich 1999 and Elm 2000.

affairs, has become available in diverse source editions,[45] historical geographical surveys,[46] and – most recently – the digital version of the entire medieval document collection of the Hungarian National Archive. The latter is significant because it has put on to the internet fifteenth- and sixteenth-century documents which have hitherto hardly been accessible, even in printed form, creating new opportunities for research. The program has continued to open up access to the *Urbaria et Conscriptiones* documents. The importance of the latter sources, mostly from after 1526, cannot be emphasized enough, because they also contain information on medieval affairs, especially concerning the estates of mendicant houses.[47]

Finally, the results of archaeological research form a completely different category of sources, although we have already mentioned them in the discussion of historical studies. Archaeology has shed new light on the economy of specific monasteries and indeed of whole orders. Landscape archaeology, since its beginnings in England, has substantially revised our picture of the monastic landscape and the economic affairs that took place on it. The exploration of the land use of certain monasteries and the monastic topography of larger regions or the kingdom as a whole have shed light on economic issues such as the complementary exploitation of sources of income. Although these methods have appeared in Hungarian research in recent decades, they cannot be described as widespread. Archaeological excavations have traditionally concentrated on the complex of buildings comprising the monastery in the narrow sense, with the main emphasis being on the church. As a result, we only rarely find excavations of buildings concerned with agriculture and trade. Even rarer are surveys of other structures such as fishponds, millraces, irrigation systems, or traces of surrounding land use.[48] In the almost total absence of written information on these, the monastery activities they represent can only be studied by archaeological excavation or field survey, which underlines the importance of such work.

---

45 E.g. Nagy and Tasnádi Nagy (eds.) 1878–1920 and Kristó et al. (eds.) 1990–2015 or Mályusz et al. (eds.) 1951–2017.

46 Csánki and Fekete Nagy 1890–1944 and Györffy 1963–1998. An increasing number of topographical publications have appeared for smaller regions, partly from historians, partly from archaeologists, which are not listed here.

47 Both databases are available at: http://www.hungaricana.hu (last accessed: 26 August 2016).

48 Gerevich 1984, Valter 1981, Kovalovszki 1992, Miklós 1997b, Belényesy 2004, Benkő 2015, Ferenczi (in preparation) and volumes from the series: *Magyarország régészeti topográfiája* [Archaeological topography of medieval Hungary] (for this, see: http://ri.btk.mta.hu/hu/kiadvanyok/sorozatok/mrt-1966-2012 [last accessed: 20 August 2016]).

The work done to date – source publications, archaeological and historic-building research – has already produced a wealth of data. What have been lacking until very recently are studies that focus expressly on the monastic economy in Hungary. One reason for this is the methodological challenge arising from the unevenness of the source material. It is also true, however, and a sufficient explanation in itself for the decades following World War II, that the subject has aroused little interest. It was perhaps a little too materialistic for ecclesiastical historians, and too clerical for economic historians. A common feature of whatever studies have been published is that they present a static picture, a kind of snapshot of the holdings of one house or one order. Given the current state of research, this could hardly be otherwise, but we should be clear about where we stand. A fortunate development of recent years is the upsurge in research on land-use issues, with results that can supplement much of what we know about the monastic economy from written sources.

The Benedictine Economy

In terms of economic affairs, or more precisely land use and estate history, the Benedictines in Hungary have been studied longer and more thoroughly than any other religious order. This is not just because Benedictine abbeys were founded first (at the turn of the tenth and eleventh centuries) and the order remained the most widespread during the Árpádian age. The largest monasteries founded by the royal dynasty, such as Pannonhalma, Pécsvárad and Hronský Beňadik, were among the largest ecclesiastical landowners in Hungary until the end of the Middle Ages, and the evidence clearly demonstrates that they strove to apply the most advanced principles of agriculture. The most fully covered period of their history in this respect is the twelfth and thirteenth centuries, when they changed over from an economy based purely on transfers in kind (basically involving obligations of produce from various servant folk), to monetary transactions.[49]

Like the abbeys themselves, Árpádian-age Benedictine estates varied widely in size. Research is effectively restricted to the royal abbeys, the others only being referred to in one or two, mostly later, sources. From the findings on the most thoroughly-studied houses of Pannonhalma and Hronský Beňadik, we know that the estates of the great royal abbeys lay somewhat far from the abbeys themselves, in separate blocks, ensuring that the monks were

---

[49] Cf. the publications of László Erdélyi, Vilmos Fraknói, Nándor Knauz, or from the more recent literature those of László Solymosi: Solymosi 2009 and Solymosi 2016b.

supplied with food and raw materials throughout the year. One group of estates – usually the largest – lay around the abbey. Documents show that these lands, understandably, had a greater tendency to remain intact throughout the centuries than any of the others (as attested too, for example, by a comparison of the eleventh- and thirteenth-century censuses of the Pannonhalma estates).[50] The agriculture of the great abbeys in the eleventh and twelfth centuries was based on a system of servant villages. According to Albeus's survey of Pannonhalma Abbey around 1238, the abbey had more than ninety villages in ten counties, in which the population was recorded mostly by the service they provided rather than social standing (2243 households). The servant folk bore diverse obligations of service: stewards, plowmen, vineyardists, blacksmiths (who had the right to draw raw material each year from the royal iron stores in Vasvár), equerries, fishermen, bee-keepers and various church functionaries (*sanctiferi*, bell-ringers, *exequiatores*[51]). Some of the servant folk worked (at least partly) in the monastery, and they also provided most of the workers in the monastic workshops. About 26 % of the lands lay within a 25 kilometer radius of the abbey hill, and nearly half of the servant population lived there. There were two other major blocks of land apart from the central estate: one north of the Danube, Salaföld (Diakovce) and its environs, along the River Váh, and the other northwest of Pécs, the 300-household Zselicerdő. The other estates were widely scattered, and two of them were on the Great Hungarian Plain. Mills were recorded at twenty different places on the abbey estates, and constituted one of the major sources of income. Other notable possessions of the abbey during the Árpádian age were ferry tolls and market excise duties.[52]

This scattered estate structure in fact caused one of the greatest problems in the thirteenth century, particularly after the Mongol invasion of 1241–1242. Hronský Beňadik, for example, was obliged to enter a ten-year legal action to recover its remote estates beyond the River Tisza, a fight which it ultimately lost. In addition to agriculture, the Benedictine abbeys had possession of various tolls and customs duties from the late eleventh century (some of them donated by St Ladislas), and in the early thirteenth century had a very substantial share of the salt trade. The above-mentioned Oath of Bereg granted a share of the Transylvanian salt trade to the Benedictine abbeys beside the River Maros, and even to distant Pannonhalma and Pécsvárad Abbeys.

---

50   Solymosi 1996b.
51   *Exequiatores* (Hungian *torló* or *dusnok*, < Slavic *duša* = soul) were serves or freedmen given to the church and obliged to commemorate the late patrons with mass and anniversary feasts. http://lexikon.katolikus.hu/D/Dusnok.html (*last accessed: 31 August 2016*).
52   Solymosi 1996b.

The abbey estates introduced various agricultural improvements, and were also instrumental in the appearance and development of markets. There were even examples of market towns emerging in the direct vicinity of the abbeys (such as Pécsvárad and Báta). Unlike in some parts of Western Europe, however, the Benedictine abbeys did not in general become prime movers of urbanization.

In the years following the Mongol invasion, Benedictine estates – as with most others throughout the kingdom – went through a rapid process of change. The disappearance of servant villages obliged monasteries to convert obligations fulfilled in kind into cash dues, adapted as required to local economic conditions.[53] There was a further reorganization of monastic estates in the fourteenth and fifteenth centuries, but what this involved has not yet been the subject of any detailed study. This absence is down to the late medieval crises of the order: many of the abbeys founded in the Árpádian age were closed down in the fourteenth century, and most of the survivors were in the hands of commendators in the fifteenth. Historians of the order have tended to highlight the decline and to forget that the houses which remained, despite the obvious problems, were stable and – at least in economic terms – under control. We have evidence for this in Act XX of 1498, in which five monastic institutions were among the most important ecclesiastical organizations and three of these were Benedictine abbeys (Pannonhalma, Pécsvárad and Zobor, although the latter had already been merged with the diocese of Nitra). A line of research which started only recently is discovering that abbeys in different parts of the kingdom pursued different economic strategies.[54] Hronský Beňadik, for example, granted leases on about half of its lands, while Cluj-Mănăştur in Transylvania managed all of its own estates, and even its income from its vineyards was collected in kind. These differences clearly arose from regional variations in socio-economic conditions. Although the sources are still being studied, it is already quite clear that there was no such thing as "Benedictine estate management" in the late medieval period, and each abbey – as far as its surviving documents allow – has to be assessed separately. This is hardly surprising. The Benedictines had no central organization; attempts to establish a Hungarian congregation in the fourteenth century seem to have petered out by the fifteenth century. It was only through the work of Máté Tolnai, abbot of Pannonhalma in the early sixteenth century, that the Hungarian Benedictine congregation was set up in 1514, but that rather belongs to the history of the order in the early modern period.

---

53   Maksay 1972.
54   Keglevich 2012, Keglevich (ed.) 2014, Szabó 2012a and Szabó 2012b.

Monasteries of the Eastern rite (Basilite monasteries) also appeared in Hungary in the eleventh century, but most of them had closed or fallen into the hands of other, Western, religious orders by the early thirteenth. As a result, we know much less about their estates and how they ran them than we do for the Benedictines, but what data we do have suggests that their economic affairs were similar to those of the Benedictines in the Árpádian age. This emerges from the examples of Sremska Mitrovica and Visegrád.[55]

The Economy of Cistercian Monasteries

It was mentioned in the historiographic overview that the unevenness of sources in Hungary poses severe problems for methodology. It is quite certain that we cannot trace the formation and development of the economic affairs of the vast majority of individual monasteries. That is what led Elek Kalász to draw on foreign sources for his study of Szentgotthárd abbey, an approach which, although methodologically valid in principle, raises two serious concerns. First, he chose parallels far removed from Hungary in time and space (although distance seems the lesser problem in this case), and second, he considered only a small part of Hungarian sources. It is therefore worthwhile considering whether, by examining the sources concerning a single order's Hungarian monasteries, specifically the abbeys of the Cistercian order, and comparing the general picture we obtain with the practices of the same order in contemporary Europe, we might gain a more realistic view of the economic situation of abbeys in Hungary, and of the expectations and aims of the order.

With the exception of Cikádor Abbey, the Cistercian order settled in Hungary in the late twelfth century, and under somewhat unusual circumstances. King Béla III was the direct patron of five of the six abbeys founded in the final decade of the century, and gave his active support to the sixth. In a break from usual practice (also applying to the foundation of Cikádor) the parent abbey of the new foundations was not one of those in geographical proximity (such as Heiligenkreuz). The monks came directly from the Burgundian center of the order: to Igriş from Pontigny, to Zirc from Clairvaux, to Pilis (Pilisszentkereszt) from Acey, and to Szentgotthárd from Troisfontaines. The fifth royal foundation, Pásztó, was an affiliate of Pilis, and the only private foundation of the age, Klostermarienberg, was populated by monks from Heiligenkreuz. There was to be another directly Burgundian foundation in the Kingdom of Hungary. At Topusko in Slavonia, Andrew II founded an abbey with monks from Clairvaux.

---

55   Györffy 1959 and Györffy 1963–1998, IV.

This means that during the period of foundations, the Hungarian Cistercians had extremely close relations with the order's Burgundian center, and in 1183 Abbot Peter of Cîteaux himself traveled to the kingdom.

Secondly, the estates of these early foundations seem to have fallen somewhat short of the Cistercian expectations of the time. The *grangia* system was hardly established at all, there were very few *conversi* in Hungarian abbeys even in the earliest times, and a strikingly high number of estates provided direct cash income (tolls and customs duties, salt income). It is also remarkable that some Cistercian estates had possession of sources of income which in other European lands (England, France, Holy Roman Empire) provided substantial abbey revenue (sheep farming, vineyards, fishponds, metalwork, and even ore mining). The estate and revenue structure of abbeys established in the late twelfth and early thirteenth centuries thus more or less corresponded to the contemporary economic system recognizable in the order's other abbeys. Of course, it was not possible to exploit all of the opportunities. The ore deposits on the estates of Szentgotthárd abbey proved uneconomical to work after the ore mines in neighboring Styria opened at the turn of the twelfth and thirteenth centuries. Similarly, Klostermarienberg abbey failed to become a major sheep farming center because the quality of Hungarian wool could not compete with that from England and elsewhere. Among the estates which did prosper were those with vineyards. French monks must have brought with them the advanced viticulture techniques from their homeland, although these were already spreading in Hungary, partly via Wallonian viniculturists who settled in the kingdom around this time. As with the Benedictine abbeys, Cistercian estates were not arranged in a single block, although they were not as widely scattered or complex around the time of their foundation in the late twelfth century.

The central hierarchy of the order clearly took a close interest in the opportunities available. Although the grand chapters regularly issued orders against the spread of paid labor, the leasing of estates and the cash economy, the reality was different, as the Cistercian leaders well knew. For one thing, by acquiescing in the failure to recruit many *conversi* brothers in Hungary (the grand chapter granted permission in 1203 for the employment of paid laborers in abbeys in Bohemia, Poland and Hungary) they clearly had the advance of their order in mind, and they also soon had to face the fact that abbeys in Hungary had great trouble in recruiting monks. This can be clearly inferred from the number of French monks, who still formed a majority in the first third of the thirteenth century. Secondly, the estates acquired by royal donation were strikingly similar in character to those of contemporary Cistercian abbeys operating successfully elsewhere, complete with the cash transactions which were already prevalent in the late twelfth century. This situation quite definitely developed with the knowledge and consent of the order's leaders.

Archaeological findings can usefully complement what the documents tell us about the economics of Cistercian abbeys. This has been most useful for Pilis Abbey, and has helped in some respects for Pásztó and Topusko. Béla III founded an abbey in the middle of the royal forest of Pilis in the late twelfth century[56] which engaged in considerable industrial activity: glassmaking at its nearby grange (at Pomáz-Nagykovácsi-puszta),[57] while beside the abbey buildings there was a metallurgical operation in the late medieval period. The capacity of the latter is indicated by the meter-thick layer of slag excavated in the area of the forge, and by the rebuilding of the forge first after the monastery burned down in 1526, clearly trusting in its capability to provide income to restore the rest. In the area around the abbey, there were fishponds, mills and a quarry, and the brothers probably also engaged in forestry on their Pilis estates. At Pásztó, although the Cistercians took over a well-equipped glass house from the Benedictines, they only ran it for another fifty years. The building was not restored after its destruction during the Mongol invasion, possibly owing to the exhaustion of raw material, but there may also have been a lack of available expertise.[58]

Commercial activity emerges from the documentary records as being an area of intensive activity for the Cistercians. Topusko Abbey sold its products at market; Pilis abbey did the same via its house in Bratislava, and Petrovaradin abbey via its house in Buda. The produce was most often wine from the abbeys' vineyards, and they also sold other agricultural produce and sometimes craft products.

Pauline Estates

Another key research question regarding the monastic economy is how affairs changed with time. A good example is the economy of the Pauline order in the late medieval period, when existing estates started to be managed differently, and a new form of acquisition emerged. The Paulines started in very modest circumstances in the thirteenth century, in locations befitting a community of hermits, but were later recognized as an order and in the second half of the fourteenth century became increasingly active as part of the economy. Part

---

56   A similar process can be observed at Zirc, too. See: Szabó 2005.
57   Laszlovszky et al. 2014.
58   Valter 1994.

of the driving force for this was the multiplication of baronial donations after papal confirmation in 1308, although the salt allowance – allegedly granted by King Louis I and confirmed by several monarchs – also greatly contributed to the order's accumulation of wealth. At the end of the century, a new estate structure and system of estate management began to emerge. This was based partly on the cash income from urban houses, mills, various tolls and customs duties, wine trade, etc., partly on pledging the income from these, and there was also income from various dues. The privileged position of the Paulines' principal friary derived, in addition to its role within the order, from its proximity to the royal center of Buda (and to Pest). These economic developments may be seen as being behind the foundation of the short-lived friary at Kenderes on the Great Hungarian Plain in the fifteenth century, and the subsequent transfer of its lands to the Budaszentlőrinc friary, indirectly giving the order an opening into the growing cattle trade.[59]

It was largely from the nobility that the order drew its members until the end of the Middle Ages, although it also maintained intensive – largely economic – relations with the nearby (market) towns. Support from propertied townspeople is detectable, mainly in what in the Middle Ages was west Hungary (Sopron, Bratislava, Stadtschlaining), Slavonia (Zagreb, Dubica) and the Dalmatian coast (Zadar).

At the turn of the fifteenth and sixteenth centuries, the better-off houses of the Pauline order were becoming increasingly reliant on estates which provided cash income. The components of this economic system were all markedly present in the management of the order's Rome house in the sixteenth century. Such a form of management was quite widespread in Western Europe, already being known and exploited by the Benedictine and Cistercian abbeys in the thirteenth, and in some places even in the twelfth, centuries. In Hungary, however, it is in the late medieval economy of the Paulines that we can first detect such practices of estate management and capital investment, and although they were probably not on their own in this respect, we simply do not have enough knowledge about the late medieval management followed by the other orders.

There is another aspect of Pauline affairs which we should mention. It is clear from the surviving sixteenth-century *formularia* of the Pauline order, and also from a large number of late medieval last wills providing for pious donations, that the Paulines' estates and income, even with their relatively advanced management, could not cover the costs of maintaining the friaries and providing a living for the friars, a state of affairs more characteristic of mendicant

---

59   Romhányi 2010bc, 95–96.

orders. A substantial if occasional contribution to the economy of some friaries came from various feasts, and more constant revenue derived from places of pilgrimage (such as the grave of St Paul the Hermit in Budaszentlőrinc). The absence of sources precludes any estimate of this income, but its effect on construction is perceptible.

Mendicant Economy

The next area of discussion concerns the mendicant orders, specifically the two largest, the Dominicans and the Franciscans.[60] As noted in the introduction, the orders which did not originally possess land stood well apart from those which did in terms of how they made their living. The brothers in the early period lived entirely on donations, while sums received under various headings remained the principal income of friaries throughout the Middle Ages. The Dominicans, for example, were often the beneficiaries of landowners' wills, and thus received properties which could either be sold, or redeemed by the family heirs. It was also quite common for the sum payable in redemption to be defined in the will. The testator in such a case no doubt expected that his relatives would want to re-acquire the donated property, but would need time to obtain sufficient means.

Towards the end of the Middle Ages, however, Dominican and Franciscan friaries began to hold title to their own estates, mostly vineyards, orchards, small manorial farms and fishponds which all served the daily needs of the friars. In most cases, around the turn of the fourteenth and fifteenth centuries it is not clear whether the possession of an estate by a friary for a sustained period was due to unfortunate family circumstances or deliberate permanent donation. However, patrons of some friaries founded in the Conventual branch of the Franciscans at the end of the fourteenth century (Eisenstadt and Muraszemenye) provided an endowment of estates because they could not assure the friars of an appropriate mendicant environment. There were other Conventual Franciscan friaries with minor estates (e.g. Sopron, Nitra, Segesd, Futog, Bistriţa) which in part provided them cash income. Such were

---

60 For Western Europe, see Bériou and Chiffoleau (eds.) 2009. Although Austin Hermits and Carmelites were also categorized as mendicant, their friaries have never been inhibited from accepting smaller landed properties. Thus their economy was from the beginning of a dual nature: on the one hand, they used the incomes of their estates, while on the other – because of the small size of the estates – they always had to call upon the faithful. Therefore the friaries received certain districts for alms collecting as well (Elm 1977).

the mills of the Nitra and Sopron friaries, and the Buda house of the Segesd friars, on which we have data from 1433. This information purely concerns the fact of possession. For the Franciscans' economic affairs, we have even fewer references. The only source which is to any extent continuous comprises two account books for the Sopron friary, containing figures for two extended periods in the early sixteenth century (1518–1522 and 1524–1527). These tell us that the Hungarian Franciscans – like their fellows in Western Europe – arranged their estate affairs via secular procurators (*kirchvater, kirchmeister*) and did not seem to have great success in deriving a surplus from their estates. The Sopron example leads us to the conclusion that a large section of the friary's income came from the alms of the faithful, but it is not possible to determine the magnitude and composition of this (i.e. cash or donations in kind). This of course only concerned the Conventual branch of the order. The Observants stuck strictly to the ideal of poverty and consistently rejected possession of property – at least in Hungary.[61] The Observant vicariate probably obtained its living from three sources: income, partly in kind, from their mendicant district; regular or occasional donations from monarchs and barons; and via hermit-like houses. There is some meager documentary data surviving about the first two sources of income, but none at all on the third. Archaeology, however, has opened up the possibility of filling this gap in Hungary, as it has in other countries, such as France.[62] The support of monarchs and barons is also sometimes suggested by the location of the friary. In Visegrád, for example, the Observant friary founded by King Sigismund was built directly adjacent to the royal palace, and a major phase of construction started in the Franciscan friary in Buda after the royal palace was relocated from the north to the south side of Castle Hill, next to the friary. The amount of income some friaries received in kind may be inferred from the enormous cellars in some of them, such as Visegrád. Sometimes we can also infer the contribution a friary made to the economic development of the town or surrounding area, partly through its craft activity and partly by how it "generated business" (e.g. Târgu Mureş).[63]

---

61   Bosnian friaries had small properties due to their special conditions (fewer catholics, a small quantity of alms). I am grateful to Darko Karačić for the related information.
62   For data on alms-collecting districts, see Karácsonyi 1924. On royal and aristocratic donations, Entz 1996. In the case of some Observant Franciscan friaries it cannot be excluded that they served as food stores, while alms in a larger quantity could have been preserved for several friaries (e.g. Uzsa, Pula north of Lake Balaton). Similar features have been observed at the Collettan Franciscan friary at Mont Beuvray, Burgundy. All these issues have been treated in detail in Romhányi 2014 and Romhányi 2016.
63   Soós 2013.

Like the Franciscans, the Dominicans also became landowners in the late medieval period, although by a somewhat different route. Some Dominican friaries had already had minor properties in the fourteenth century, and Pope Martin V granted permission to possess these in 1425. Finally, Pope Sixtus IV, at the Dominicans' request, permitted the whole order to retain estates, thus abolishing the mendicant status of the order.[64] The decision was no doubt prompted by the economic changes of the fifteenth century, as the cash economy became more predominant and estates were increasingly put out to lease. Renunciation of landed property was not only justified on the grounds of poverty; land required regular management, and a large proportion of the income from it was in kind. This conflicted with the extremely high level of mobility attaching to the vocation of mendicant friars. From an early sixteenth-century source, for example, which lists the friars of the Dominicans' Transylvanian vicariate, including those of the Sighişoara friary, we know that the residents of each friary changed very rapidly.[65] Landed estates, based on peasant tenancies and transactions in kind, would have created bonds that were difficult to break. The rise of the cash economy clearly changed the situation sufficiently that the Dominican general considered it opportune to lift the ban. The order to a large extent maintained its contacts with society, and the resulting donations and legacies. This social support is reflected in the written sources and, for example, the gravestones in the Buda friary.[66]

Conditions in Hungary, of course, differed sharply from those in Western Europe, so that the Dominicans could not have lived from their cash income alone. From the data available, it seems that more than half of the friaries of the province had some kind of property, and in contrast with the Franciscans, it was those observant of the Dominican rule that tended to have the most diverse lands, most of them of course providing a living for the friars. These predominantly comprised farms, fishponds, vineyards, and sometimes revenue-generating mills.[67] Nonetheless, the available data suggests that if they were left an urban house in a will, they did not, or were not able to, keep it.[68] The order's largest estate was the abbey estate of Vértesszentkereszt, taken over from the Benedictines, for whom, even in that period of decline, it was a

---

64   Mortier 1909, 495.
65   Fabritius 1861, Ipolyi 1867, Lupescu-Makó 2001 and Romhányi 2004.
66   H. Gyürky 1984b, Lővei 1991 and Prajda 2011.
67   Romhányi 2010a.
68   Possession of urban houses was, for instance, also forbidden in German towns (e.g. Cologne).

very small possession.[69] Late medieval documents also reveal that regardless of permission the Dominicans frequently had no choice but to become holders of property, because the original owners were unable to redeem an estate passing to the friary by bequest or as a pledge against a loan, as happened with the village of Sülysáp (Dominicans of Lábatlan) and with an estate in Albeşti (Dominicans of Sighişoara).[70] Such data is informative of the kingdom's general economic condition as well as certain aspects of monastic economics. Slowness or failure to redeem an estate was most commonly the result of impecuniousness or liquidity problems.

Besides the two main mendicant orders, it is important to mention the hermits of the Augustinian order. Their documentary records have received somewhat less treatment, but the fragmentary picture which has emerged shows that several friaries possessed quite extensive properties (e.g. Sátoraljaújhely, Veľký Šariš, Hrabkov, and Osijek). Although the order's Ratisbon Constitutions of the late thirteenth century reflected the strict rule of poverty, several of its monasteries in Hungary had previously belonged to the Wilhelmite order, and no doubt retained the property they inherited along with them. In the late fifteenth century, Matthias' policy of supporting the reform of religious orders furnished the Augustinians with new estates, namely the abandoned Cistercian abbey of Ercsi (the Ercsi convent only started in the 1520s). At the current stage of exploring the sources, we only know of the existence of estates, and hardly anything about their composition or management.

Economic Affairs of Nunneries

Unlike certain regions of Western Europe, there were very few nuns' convents in Hungary. A large proportion of female communities were small Beguine (tertiary) groups who derived a living from their own work and through gifts of money and property from townspeople, often donated by the women joining them. Most of these small Beguine communities emerged right at the end of the medieval period, whereas there were some real nuns' convents from an early date. The most prominent of these, the Dominican convent on Margaret Island founded by King Béla IV in 1252 and the Poor Clares convent founded in Óbuda by Queen Elizabeth in 1331, were also among the largest ecclesiastical landowners in the kingdom. Court actions by the Margaret Island's convent give a good account of its land holdings. The structure of its estates hardly

---

69 Romhányi 2010a.
70 Romhányi 2010a.

changed from that of Árpádian-age nunneries, except perhaps a larger proportion of holdings providing income in cash, in line with the changes of the age. In addition to these, there were two convents founded in the eleventh century which had substantial property: the Convent of the Byzantine rite in Veszprémvölgy (that became Cistercian in the thirteenth century) and the Benedictine convent in Somlóvásárhely (that became Premonstratensian in the sixteenth century).

Estates provided the economic basis for convents of all orders, the differences only being in their extent. Convents' estates varied in size according to their founders (the king, or a town, sometimes others) and their later patrons (monarchs, barons or townspeople).

A thorough understanding and more penetrating analysis of the medieval monastic economy requires the historian to go beyond strictly medieval sources. It is essential to involve the largely unexplored documentary material of the early modern period, roughly up to Hungary's three-way split in the middle of the sixteenth century. This is because the running of medieval monasteries in the greater part of the kingdom did not come to an end with the battle of Mohács. The surviving monasteries kept control of their estates for several decades, although they undoubtedly had to face many difficulties (wartime destruction, acts of violence, religious tensions). The structure of their economy changed only gradually, over a long period. Fortunately, for the area of the kingdom which escaped occupation, there is a very large number of documents from this period, most of them completely untouched, *terra incognita*.

CHAPTER 16

The Urban Economy in Medieval Hungary

Katalin Szende*

There are innumerable paths that link every branch of the medieval economy – from mining to animal husbandry, or handicrafts to forestry – to towns. This is particularly true of trade, domestic and foreign. What follows is not an attempt to embrace this complex area in its entirety, and neither is this necessary, because many aspects are covered by chapters of this book that deal with specific branches of the economy. Instead, this article is written to indicate how the town, as a particular form of settlement and social structure, influenced and interlinked economic activities, and vice versa: how the local economy formed or transformed the countenance and people of Hungarian towns. Since this book contains another chapter devoted to market towns, the focus of attention here will be the free royal towns. Royal private towns, and towns owned by ecclesiastical or private landowners, could be the subject of another study.

The Context: Town and Economy

In the Middle Ages, towns did not form a homogeneous category.[1] Even if we look at the functional rather than the legal concept of the town (as indeed the economic approach would require) we have to contend with the fundamental rearrangement that occurred between early centers and later urban settlements. In the western half of Europe, this process took place in the eleventh and twelfth centuries; Hungary experienced it mainly in the second and third quarters of the thirteenth. A full analysis of the process is well beyond the scope of this study, but one can usefully focus on one of its major aspects. The clear winner in the transformation was the economy. The function of the early centers primarily involved control/administration and church/cultic activity, and it was to these that economic activities were connected, often in a loose spatial arrangement. By contrast, the new model of urbanization took its

---

* Principal investigator of the NKFI-funded project "Hungarian Atlas of Historic Towns" (K 116594) and member of the Research Centre for the Humanities, Hungarian Academy of Sciences "Lendulet" Medieval Hungarian Economic History Research Group (LP2015-4/2015).
1   Irsigler 2003. On Hungary: Kubinyi 2004c and Kubinyi 2006a.

direction from the economy, which was the driving force for settlement and determined how the other central functions arose.[2]

As the economy started to play a more prominent role in the formation of towns, the converse also applied: the towns which grew up after the middle of the thirteenth century attracted to themselves an increasingly diverse and substantial section of economic activity. We have insufficient sources to evaluate this tendency precisely, but it emerges indirectly from archaeological and written sources as one of the distinctive features of the late medieval period, and corresponds to what was happening elsewhere in Europe.[3] Progress was qualitative as well as quantitative, and can be traced in the "urbanization" of all three main sectors of the economy – production, distribution, and consumption.

In assessing the rise in the economic role of the towns, the urban economy as an overall framework must be distinguished from the economies of the towns themselves. For the former, the town was the scene of production, the interaction of buyers and sellers, and everyday consumption by the local and surrounding populations. Most research has dwelt on this side of the economy until now. The urban economy in the other sense meant the sum of economic activity engaged in by the town itself as a self-governing body and territorial unit. This activity was manifested at several levels. First, the privileges granted to the town – which were frequently expanded in line with its own purposes – and the by-laws it made under its own authority, influenced and guided the economy by administrative means. It was in a town's basic interests to secure the best possible conditions for its inhabitants and to obtain as much income as possible from outsiders not eligible to its benefits. A further purpose of these measures was to ensure supplies to the town, especially basic foodstuffs and fuel.[4] Second, by building and maintaining town walls, streets, marketplaces and other points of sale, public wells, water pipes and similar amenities, the town authorities put in place the infrastructure for economic activity.[5] Third, by running its own enterprises – manors, woods, vineyards, fishponds, lime and brick kilns, mills and other means of production appropriate to local natural endowments – and selling the products, towns were active agents in the local, regional and continental economy.[6]

---

2   Piekalski 2001 and Johanek 2006, on Hungary: Szűcs 1993, 223–276, Laszlovszky 1995, Kubinyi 1996a and Szende 2011b.
3   Perring 2002, 9–32 and 107–126 and Johanek 2011, 132–142.
4   Isenmann 2014, 986–994, Galloway, Keene and Murphy 1996 and Keene 1998.
5   Fouquet 1999, Paranko 2000, Végh 2011 and Piekalski 2014, 139–153.
6   E.g. Dirlmeier and Fouquet 1985.

The framework of the urban economy was not defined purely by the internal needs of the local community. All holders of power – the monarch, and ecclesiastical or secular landowners – could impose their own wishes. In so doing, the founding landowners were doing more than demonstrating their presence and providing themselves with a residential base. They wanted to use the towns' resources to reinforce their power in the economic field too. The most common and most lucrative of the means they employed to this end was the imposition of taxes and seigneurial dues, in regular and irregular forms. Less universal, but also delivering substantial sums, was the use of services available in the town (provision of food and accommodation, production and delivery of military supplies). In addition, there were some places, most of all the mining towns, where the owner of the town was himself an entrepreneur in control of production.[7]

Finally, any examination of the economic role of towns must also take into account the wider context: the links between town and country. These include relations with peasant communities near the town, the landlord of which was the town itself; villages that traded with the towns and were a source of new urban inhabitants; and the market towns and small towns in the town's hinterland. It was the very functional differentiation of these settlements that strengthened their interdependence and forged close links between them.[8] Going one step further, one encounters the question of economic relations between towns, and the urban network. Did these relations involve cooperation, coordinated action, hierarchical relations or competition? How intense were they, what was their geographical reach, and what inhibited their operation?

Sources and Studies

Sources on the economy of medieval Hungarian towns are at once abundant and scarce, full and fragmentary, encouraging and hopeless. In some towns diverse and informative written sources have been preserved; in others, only a single valuable set of sources, and in yet others only sporadic, fragmentary data, if any. Among the first group are the free royal towns of Upper Hungary and some mining towns,[9] the Transylvanian Saxon towns,[10] and, within the

---

7   Kaufhold and Reininghaus (eds.) 2004.
8   Perring 2002, 2–5, Epstein (ed.) 2001 and Denecke 1985.
9   Some source publications include: Iványi (ed.) 1910, Iványi (ed.) 1931–1932, Piirainen (ed.) 1983, Piirainen (ed.) 1986, Halaga (ed.) 1994 and Lacko and Mayerová 2016.
10 Quellen Hermannstadt, Quellen Kronstadt and Zimmermann et al. (eds.) 1892–1991.

territory of modern Hungary, Sopron.[11] The second category includes Buda, which despite the loss of its medieval archives has left us valuable sources such as the *Stadtrecht*, the guild book of the German butchers, and the wine tithe registers of 1505 and 1510.[12] We might also include here Cluj, which preserves a fine series of charters and documents that form a solid base with which to work.[13] The third group embraces the royal and market towns of the Great Hungarian Plain and even such major centers as Esztergom, Fehérvár and Pécs.

The unevenness of written source material has resulted in a picture of the medieval urban economy which, despite the best efforts of historians, is biased towards the better-represented towns. Research has built up a detailed account of the patterns of production and consumption and regional roles of these places, while the affairs of towns and market towns in the middle expanses of the kingdom largely remain obscure. This places all the more importance on archaeological excavations of areas of the country for which there are few written documents, which can to some extent compensate for the unevenness of sources.[14] Excavations and building archaeology research can localize buildings, roads, water pipes and similar structures that are mentioned in account books and other records, and establish their extent and phases of construction. They also reveal sources, and call attention to phenomena that are inaccessible by other means. Excavations can cover the early phases of urban development before written sources were produced on any scale, and establish data on aspects of the built-up area or surrounding fields which were ignored by documents even in later periods.[15] Also important as sources are objects that can help in the analysis of local production, imports, consumption patterns, and the link between town and country. Archaeological research in Hungary and the Carpathian Basin has extended to nearly every major royal and episcopal town in recent decades.[16] These all have made contributions to the study of the economy of the towns themselves and economic activity under their control.

Primary among written sources concerning the economy are the privilegial charters. As we have seen, towns formed and developed at the will of the monarch or ecclesiastical or secular landowners. The relationship between

---

11   Házi (ed.) 1921–1943, Mollay (ed.) 1993 and further volumes in the series *Quellen zur Geschichte der Stadt Ödenburg*.
12   Mollay (ed.) 1959, Kenyeres (ed.) 2008 and Szakály and Szűcs (eds.) 2005.
13   Jakab (ed.) 1870–1888.
14   Font and G. Sándor (eds.) 2000, Szende 2009a and Szende 2010 with further literature on the archaeological research of Hungarian towns.
15   Verhulst 1997, Szende 1998b and O'Keeffe and Yamin 2006.
16   See the various studies in Benkő and Kovács (eds.) 2010.

towns and the monarch was to a large extent determined by the privilegial charter. This, rather than a unilateral statement of royal grace, has been shown by recent research to have taken the form of a kind of contract between landowners and town-dwellers.[17] The economic aspects of town charters were systematically analyzed several decades ago in a classic study written by Erik Fügedi. This demonstrated that the charters defined the framework for the towns' operation both as a venue for economic activity and as an enterprise in itself.[18] The charters granted permission for weekly markets and annual fairs on specified days, the right to force road travelers to pass through the town, and the staple right.[19] Other rights in this context were linked with a provision often repeated in later town by-laws that outsiders could only sell in wholesale quantities.[20] From the point of view of town-dwellers, exemption from customs anywhere in the kingdom was the factor which most stimulated trade, and starting in the reign of Andrew II became an almost indispensable feature of *hospes* privileges, and through these, of town charters.[21] These sections of the charters were an attempt to strengthen the towns as trade centers at the expense of surrounding and more distant towns and villages.

The basis of the towns' own enterprises was a series of privileges transferring the king's rights as landlord over the town and fields around it, so that the land became the property of the community of burghers. Apart from some isolated cases, towns were also exempted from the unpaid labor, because they held the rights of landownership to their own land. The grant of title to the land or other revenues around the town was often confirmed by linking the

---

17   The texts of all privilegial charters issued to towns in medieval Hungary are not available in a common new critical edition. For the territories of modern Hungary and Romania until 1300, see Kubinyi (ed.) 1997 and Niedermaier (ed.) 2005 respectively; for present-day Slovakia until 1328, see Marsina (ed.) 1971–1987 and Juck (ed.) 1984. For parts of the Carpathian Basin in Ukraine, Serbia and Croatia only old source publications are at our disposal. On the thirteenth-century privileges, see Szende 2015a, and on the development in the first half of the fourteenth century: Szende 2016, 287–308.
18   Fügedi 1981b, 239–280 and Szende 2016, 324–335 and 529–533.
19   Weisz 2010b and Weisz 2012b. See also András Kubinyi's study on internal trade in the present volume.
20   Mollay (ed.) 1959, 93, 100–101, 121 and 194–197 (cap. 84, 104, 174 and 418–424), similarly in the privileges of Satu Mare in 1271: *nec extranei mercatores incidendo vendere possint pannos suos.* – Niedermaier (ed.) 2005, 49.
21   Szűcs 1993, 54, Zsoldos and Neumann 2010, 32–34, Weisz 2013b, 40–47 and gazetteer, passim.

privileges to the perambulation of the boundaries.[22] Land ownership by the townspeople paved the way for the free trade in urban real estate. This, apart from sale of communally-owned urban property, took the form of business transactions between private individuals. Since taxes and dues were linked to property ownership, however, the municipal authorities maintained strict control and administrative supervision over the sale of houses, gardens, vineyards and other properties.[23] Municipal ownership usually incorporated the fields and pastures around the town, and the woods, which were the source of timber, firewood and stone.[24] Wherever the economy of the town demanded, as in the case of mining towns, the woods under exploitation could extend beyond the land around the town. When the king made grants of his 'forest counties', the new owners often got into bitter disputes with the towns that had been using the forest.[25]

In return for the assignment of the land and the usufructory rights attached to it, the townspeople had to pay taxes. These included military support for the king and occasional royal "lodging" (*descensus*), but the charters show that the monarch looked to taxation on towns in cash as his principal source of revenue from these places. Several studies have highlighted the role of towns in crown taxation and budget policy (and the limitations of that role).[26] Much less remarked on, however, is that the benefits and obligations provided by the charters necessarily encouraged towns to carry on their own enterprises and keep municipal accounts in balance, and this also affected the self-governance, internal life and even layout of the towns.

The most revealing information about towns' economic affairs comes from the accounts and other statements kept by municipal clerks. The fixed system

---

22   The issue of landownership features prominently, e.g., in the privileges of Pest (Kubinyi [ed.] 1997, 39–41 and more recently in Nagy et al. [eds.] 2016, 557–558) and Győr (Kubinyi [ed.] 1997, 61–63). Boundary descriptions are added to the privileges of Banská Bystrica, 1255: Marsina (ed.) 1971–1987, II, 340–341, Nitra, 1248: Marsina (ed.) 1971–1987, II, 208–209, Hybe, 1265: Juck (ed.) 1984, 48–50, Kežmarok, 1269: Juck (ed.) 1984, 51–52, Satu Mare, 1271: Niedermaier (ed.) 2005, 49, to name just a few examples.

23   Kováts 1918a, Szende 1996 and Mollay (ed.) 1993.

24   E.g. Zvolen, 1243: *ligna autem infra metas terre ville eorum libere possint incidere et lapides recipere* – Marsina (ed.) 1971–1987, II, 94. In the privileges of Satu Mare, the king orders the *comes* of nearby Ugocsa County, that *eisdem sylvam de Erdeud statueret usui eorum sufficientem*, since the settlement does not have enough woods, see Niedermaier (ed.) 2005, 49.

25   Fügedi 1981b, 264–265, Magyar 1985, Halaga 1996 and Weisz 2013a, 304–305.

26   Kováts 1900, Kováts 1902b, Draskóczy 1993 and Kubinyi 2000a.

of these records makes it possible to trace changes in town income and expenditure from year to year. In both large and small towns, these account books were based on similar principles to those used everywhere in Europe.[27] The "income" column comprised taxes raised from the townspeople and various minor royal usufructory rights assigned to the towns (sale of wine and meat, use of woods), and the income of the municipal enterprises. In addition, there were sums from loans taken out by the town, the sale of movable and immovable property, and duties and fines. On the expenditure side, there was payment of regular and extraordinary crown taxes, the repair and maintenance of properties and communal roads, bridges and defenses carried out at municipal expense, the pay of municipal employees, sometimes maintenance of professional soldiers, banquets for high-placed visitors and their retinues, delegations and diplomatic gifts, and items related to the repayment of loans and collection of dues. Each volume contains several thousand items of economically-interpretable information. Such accounts have survived from medieval Sopron, Bratislava, Sibiu and Brașov, and from fragments from Bistriţa, Bardejov and Prešov, while there are some tax registers and other lists of assorted sizes from other towns in Upper Hungary and Transylvania.[28]

Some Elements of the Urban Economy

The Town as Entrepreneur – The Town as Builder
As we saw in connection with charters, if towns were to run municipal institutions and properties and bear the burdens imposed by their overlord (the

---

27 Arlinghaus 2006 and Isenmann 2014, 516–560.
28 Teutsch 1892, Kováts 1900 and Kováts 1918b. Main editions of account books: Fejérpataky 1885, Házi (ed.) 1921–1943, II/2–6, Iványi (ed.) 1910, passim, Iványi (ed.) 1931–1932, passim, Quellen Hermannstadt 1880 and Quellen Kronstadt 1886–1889. The account books of Bratislava until 1526 are available in the photo collection of the Hungarian National Archives State Archives (MNL OL) DF 277 059–277 133. See also the online version at http://archives.hungaricana.hu/en/charters/ (last accessed: 13 January 2018). Later volumes from the sixteenth century are available in: MNL OL Microfilm collection Box C 402. The account books of Bistriţa have been transcribed by András Péter Szabó and Zsolt Simon in a project coordinated by the Ungarisches Institut München: http://www.ungarisches-institut.de/forschungen/projekte/laufende-projekte/251-die-mittelalterlichen-rechnungsb%C3%BCcher-der-stadt-bistritz-in-siebenb%C3%BCrgen-2.html (last accessed: 13 January 2018).

king), they had to become engaged in active enterprise.[29] The account books tell us that the biggest drain on the annual budget nearly everywhere, apart from the payment of taxes, was the building and upkeep of infrastructure, particularly defensive works,[30] since participation in the defense of the town was the second-ranking obligation of townspeople (the first being taxation). As a criterion of urban status for a medieval settlement, defensive walls were as important at the time as they became in retrospect for historians seeking criteria of urban status. Although not absolutely essential for urban development, the town wall was an unmistakable manifestation of urbanity, and its image was often proudly included as a symbol on town seals and coats of arms. Taking over responsibility for the defense of their town from the overlord was a great qualitative leap for the burghers' community, but of course, also a financial burden. This burden was partly met from the escheated property of persons who died intestate. The charters of privileges of the most prominent towns, Buda (a charter of 1276 confirming previous privileges) and Košice (charter of 1347) assigned this property not to the crown, but one third to charitable purposes and two thirds to the construction of the town walls.[31] Since Buda's charter later became the model for towns throughout the kingdom, this provision became increasingly widespread. Later, as the custom of writing a last will spread, a sense of solidarity among the town community prompted townspeople to support the construction of the defenses of their own free will.[32] However, as the example of Prešov testifies, the most important input was the murage grant and other allowances provided by the king that made it possible to complete the circuit of the walls.[33]

The account books show that construction took up 12–20 % of total expenditure in some European towns during the fifteenth century.[34] The corresponding figure for Bratislava was 18.5 % in 1526/1527,[35] and for Brașov it varied between 5.9 and 25 % between 1521 and 1526, with an average of 14.6 %.[36] The workers included carpenters, masons, locksmiths, blacksmiths and carters,

---

29   Lederer 1934, Szűcs 1955, 198–254, Halaga 1983 and Gyarmati 2014.
30   Fouquet 1999, 17–80 and Sander-Berke 1997.
31   The confirmation of Buda's privileges, 1276: Kubinyi (ed.) 1997, 64–65, Košice, 1347: Juck (ed.) 1984, 147–149.
32   Szende 2004a.
33   Gulyás 2014a and Vadas 2015–2016.
34   In Nuremberg between 1430 and 1440 this proportion was 18 %; in Hamburg 19.3 %; in Schwäbisch Hall 13.1 %; in Basel 12 %. See Isenmann 2014, 518–523, Fouquet 1999, 309–332 and Figs 4–8.
35   Danninger 1907.
36   Simon 2006b, Table 21.

whose work can be traced from day to day via the accounts. The fifteenth-century accounts of Sopron tell us that tradesmen received weekly wages in the form of six day-wages paid as a lump sum; the number of craftsmen and the duration of their employment depended on the stage of the construction work.[37]

The cost of building materials fluctuated from year to year according to the work that was needed. In this respect, the woods granted in the charter were crucial for obtaining the timber and quarried stone needed for the maintenance of the town defenses and other public buildings. Other raw materials were produced by the towns themselves in lime and brick kilns. In Sopron, in addition to written records, much information has been obtained from a lime kiln uncovered in an archaeological excavation on the edge of the third quarter of the medieval suburbs, beside the bridge over the River Ikva, outside the house which now stands at number 4, Híd Street. Fragments of a jug found among the kiln debris dates the site to the middle of the fifteenth century.[38] Contemporary records do not reveal unambiguously whether the municipality operated these kilns. Both the account books and assembly minutes, however, do permit the inference that it was in Sopron's interest to monopolize the production and sale of lime. Lime kilns are mentioned in Dudlesz-dűlő (-field), lying about 5 kilometers north of the town, in the period between 1403 and 1437, which probably passed to the town from the Agendorfer family. Lime firing also started at the Felberbrunn-dűlő to the north-east of the town in the late 1430s, and to meet rising demand, larger-capacity kilns were built in Attengräben-dűlő along the Bratislava road in the 1470s.[39] Records which survive more or less continuously from 1498 onwards tell us the number and wages of people who worked in lime firing, and the costs of refurbishing the kilns and quarrying and transporting the limestone, their raw material. We also know that as well as meeting the town's own needs, the kilns supplied the surrounding villages. The market zone extended 15–20 kilometers to Eisenstadt and Marz in the north and at least 35–40 kilometers to Csepreg, Bük and Beled in the south-east (see Fig. 16.1). An interesting aspect of the town's trading policy was that buyers from outside Sopron had to pay one-and-a-half times

---

37 In Sopron, the following account books contain a large amount of data about building activities: Házi (ed.) 1921–1943, II/3, 1–18, 82–88, 148–195, 229–344 and 389–406, II/5, 47–65, 77–95, 118–138, 141–164, 205–241, 292–350 and 382–440.
38 Gömöri 1984.
39 Mollay 1992.

as much as local residents for the lime.[40] There were also means of lime provisioning: in Bardejov, particularly from the 1440s onwards, the town used the services of some well-to-do local entrepreneurs, whereas in Bratislava it was more reasonable to buy the lime from nearby producers in Lower Austria – for instance, in Hainburg.[41]

The other important locally produced building material was brick. Even towns quite well supplied with stone – such as Sopron – manufactured bricks because they were relatively cheap and easy to use. There is data about a brick kiln (*ziegeloffen*) and a kiln master (*ziegelmaister*) in Sopron in the early sixteenth century. The kiln master was usually a master mason, and he also supervised one of the lime kilns.[42] In the post-1528 account books, which were kept with greater regularity, the clerk set aside a separate expenditure column for the wages of the brick kiln master and the cost of running the kiln, and one income column for the return on selling bricks. The sixteenth-century accounts also included data on the types and quantities of bricks that were produced.[43]

For data on defensive works, we have to rely most of all on archaeological research,[44] because many aspects of construction were not recorded in the accounts. In particular, when the first walls were erected, municipal literacy had not reached the level of keeping regular accounts about such works. Excavations can also offer an explanation for the appearance of some costs at later periods: existence or demolition of old structures, earthmoving work, and the repair or conversion of parts of the wall system as military technology advanced.[45] Indeed, excavations and building archaeology can verify the existence of comprehensive defensive systems in towns where all of the written sources have been destroyed, such as in Székesfehérvár.[46] Building and reconstructing town walls also had its effect on the urban topography as a whole: walls determined the course of streets, as happened on the Castle Hill in Buda,[47] and they left their impressions on the orientation of streets when they were demolished, like the thirteenth-century Pest town wall. Archaeological research in the same town has also shown the rearrangements and expropriations

---

40 Házi (ed.) 1921–1943 II/5, 300, 332, 406–407 and 412, Mollay 1992, 164–167 and map on 152–153.
41 Gulyás 2009a [2012].
42 Mollay 1992, 164 and Házi (ed.) 1921–1943, II/5, 205 and 235.
43 MNL Győr-Moson-Sopron megye Soproni Levéltára (Archive of Győr-Moson-Sopron County, Sopron Town Archive), Kammeramtsrechnungen, series IV. 1009. Cf. Baraczka 1969.
44 Scholkmann 1997, VII–XI.
45 Holl 1981, 201–243.
46 Siklósi 1999, Farkas and Siklósi 2009.
47 Végh 2006–2008, I, 53–61 and Szende and Végh 2016, 269–275 (research by András Végh).

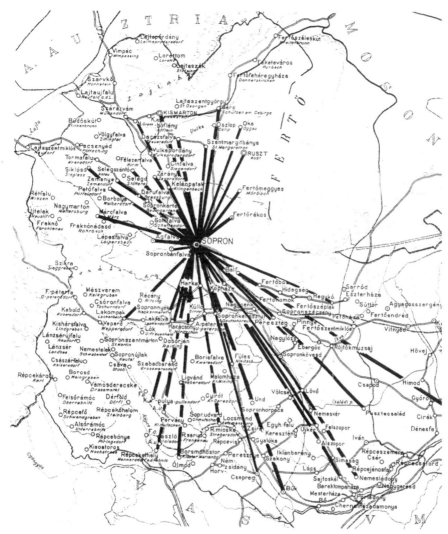

FIGURE 16.1   *The market zone of lime produced in the kilns run by the municipality of Sopron (after Mollay 1992).*

involved in laying out a new, outer wall in the early fifteenth century (*see* Fig. 16.2).[48] Archaeologists have attempted to estimate the quantity of stone used in building and the quantity of earth that had to be moved. Construction obviously entailed enormous costs, but we know from other sources that Pest was so wealthy it had enough left over to be able to assist the constantly

---

48   Irásné Melis 2004 and Kovács and Zádor 2015.

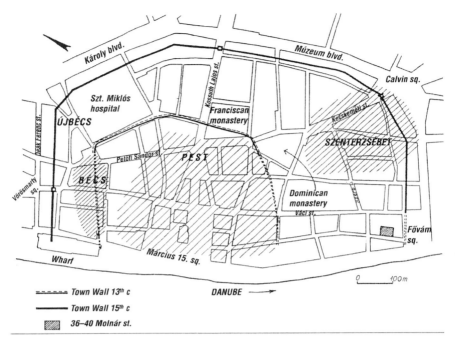

FIGURE 16.2 Layout of the new town wall of Pest in the late fifteenth century (after Irásné Melis 2004).

cash-strapped King Sigismund with the sum of 1000 florins, in return for which it asked for free appointment of judge and council.[49] This is an example of how closely interconnected are the issues of topographic development, the town economy, and municipal administration.

Defense works were the largest, but not the only item of municipal construction expenditure. Each town had to build and maintain at least one parish church, and occasionally extend it in order to house a growing population and to better express the prestige of the community. This was in turn a manifestation of autonomy, which had its own effects on the town economy. By European comparison, Hungarian towns were remarkably autonomous as regards advowson and other church patronage.[50] The rights came at a price: the town had to finance the priest and the church, which it did partly from community resources, although burghers' private donations also featured. A recent investigation into affairs in Bratislava has revealed the significance of these

49 Mollay (ed.) 1959, 204–205 (cap. 445) and Szende 2009b.
50 Kubinyi 1995a.

forms of support with unusual precision. The variation over time of sums left in wills for building or maintaining churches corresponds almost exactly with the phases of construction determined by archaeological excavation and historic buildings research in the city. The wording of the wills often indicates that a new construction project stimulated or redirected townspeople's propensity to make donations. The Bratislava example is a most convincing demonstration of the inseparable unity of private and public investment, both in this world and the other.[51] Data for other towns may not be sufficient to permit the use of such quantitative methods, but there is still much that can be learned from the joint study of written and architectural sources.

Town defenses and church buildings were accompanied by items of community-financed urban infrastructure which, although less ostentatious, similarly increased the town's attractiveness and widened its sources of revenue. The laying out, consolidation, surfacing and upkeep of roads, streets and squares were aspects of a town's economic life which have left traces susceptible to both archaeological and documentary research. There are already sufficient observations to form the basis of a comprehensive study. There have been investigations of water pipes, wells and cisterns, the upkeep and repair of which are the subject of frequent entries in municipal account books.[52] Studies of the marketplace, the principal scene of urban trading activity, yield further points of intersection between the work of archaeologists and economic historians.

Marketplaces and the Urban Economy

Topographical studies are an area of hitherto almost unexplored potential for finding out about the Hungarian urban economy.[53] Economic considerations were fundamental in the choice of a town's location, and its physical interior had an effect on the local economy. The prime movers in towns that were changing over from administrative-ecclesiastic centers to economic centers were the venues for the organized and controlled exchange of goods – the marketplaces. These were controlled and protected by the community, and as

---

51 Majorossy 2006, Ch III. 1. b., forthcoming in print by CEU Press in 2018.
52 Kubinyi 1981b, Nagy 2003, 358–359 and 368–369, Siklósi 2003, Piekalski 2014, 139–153 and Sowina 2016.
53 The currently running research project on the economic history of medieval Hungary led by Boglárka Weisz at the Institute of History of the Hungarian Academy of Sciences has extended its attention to this issue as well, see Weisz 2015a, 504–505.

municipal autonomy strengthened, they took on increasing importance in the structuring of the economy and of the urban space as a whole.[54] How is this reflected in the layouts of medieval Hungarian towns, and how were their marketplaces located, structured and supervised? The following examples give an indication of the potential and limitations of research in this area.

Óbuda is an "old type" of town, its original significance stemming from an ecclesiastical center, the Collegiate Chapter of St Peter, and an occasionally-used royal residence.[55] It also lay at a major Danube crossing-point, an advantage which led the Romans to set up the Aquincum military camp at almost the same place. The location and development of the town's medieval marketplace is therefore of particular significance. Like most of Óbuda's topographical features, repeated destruction and reconstruction have brought so many changes that we have to rely on archaeology alone for localization and investigation of the marketplace (see Fig. 16.3).[56] It was roughly triangular in shape, and lay to the south of the harbor, on a road to the ferry which was already in use in the eleventh or twelfth century. There were stone-built houses standing on both of the long sides of the square at the turn of the twelfth and thirteenth centuries, and a reconstruction of the plot system shows that the western side was probably lined with properties of equal size in an orderly row. Further topographical research is needed to determine whether these phenomena, which suggest planned development, date from the same time as the formation of the market or are related to later building around the square. Certainly, the road and the square were re-paved several times, and remained the only marketplace even after the town was divided between Queen Elizabeth and the St Peter chapter in 1355.

This is particularly interesting, because there were also two marketplaces in Veszprém, another town partially in the queen's possession from an earlier date. One market was held on Wednesdays and the other on Saturdays, and we know (from documentary analysis rather than archaeology) that they were certainly held in different places in 1318 (see Fig. 16.4). The Saturday market, which was more important, lay to the south of Castle Hill (Várhegy), on what is now Óváros Square, on land owned by the bishop of Veszprém. The lesser Wednesday market also had a topographically less central position: the Beszédkő Market on what is now Patak Square.[57]

---

54 On the legal and institutional framework of markets and fairs, see Tringli 2010, Kubinyi 2000b and Weisz 2012b.
55 Fügedi 1959.
56 Altmann and Bertalan 1991a, Altmann and Bertalan 1991b and Altmann 2004.
57 Solymosi 2000, 140–147.

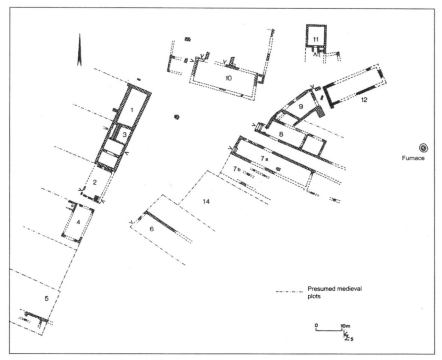

FIGURE 16.3   The marketplace of medieval Óbuda as reconstructed by archaeological research (after Altmann 2004).

Some elements of the marketplace of Győr have been determined from excavations on what is now Széchenyi Square, on the land (suburb) of the medieval chapter town. These have shown that remains of an Árpádian-age settlement were deliberately leveled on this site. The archaeological evidence clearly links this phenomenon to the town's charter of 1271, proving that the charter led to the restructuring of the town. The area maintained its market function continuously from the late thirteenth century, and was occupied by open-air stalls, tents, huts and little shops. To judge from the foundation trenches cut into the surface of the square for the sole timbers of the structures, and from their clay floors, these took up permanent positions at some points, and market infill was quite advanced by the end of the Middle Ages.[58] The area was only freed

58   Gabler, Szőnyi and Tomka 1990, 23–25, T. Szőnyi and Tomka 2002 and Bíró et al. 2010. Further research on the marketplace of Győr is part of the research project mentioned above – fn. 53, researcher: Ágnes Kolláth. See its first results in Kolláth and Tomka 2017.

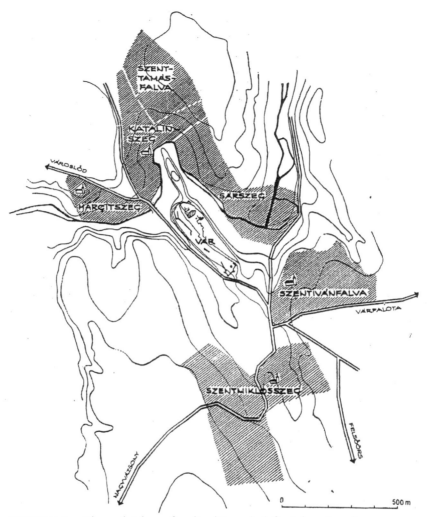

FIGURE 16.4   The marketplaces of medieval Veszprém (after Solymosi 2000).

up and cleared of the huts when Győr was made into a fortress town in the mid-sixteenth century, but the question of how much this restructuring contributed to the regular ground plan of the town is still open to discussion.[59]

Markets evolved with completely different morphological features in the towns of medieval north-east Hungary: Košice (see Fig. 16.5), Bardejov, Prešov and their smaller neighbors. These towns developed a spatial structure based on elongated marketplaces, widening in a spindle shape in the center, the

---

59   Gecsényi 1991 and Szende 2013a.

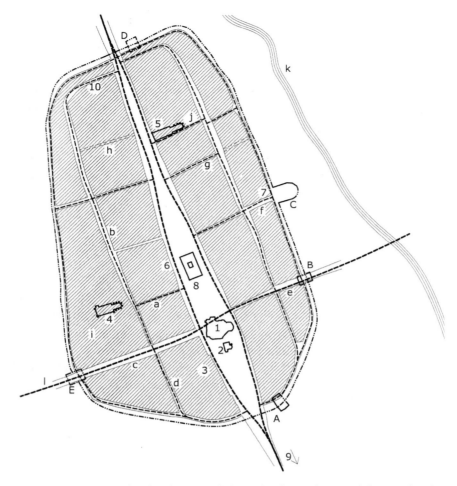

FIGURE 16.5   Layout of medieval Košice with the marketplace at the center (after Mencl 1938).

other streets of the town and the later ramparts also being arranged relative to these lines. The marketplace evolved when a section of the long-distance trading route, which was the foundation for the town's existence, was transformed into a built-up area, so that the spatial structure of the town itself confirmed its denizens' control over trade. At the center or one end of the marketplace was the town's (usually only) parish church, onto which other public buildings (town hall, school, separate chapels) were later built.[60]

---

60   Mencl 1938, with the town plans of the major towns, Urbanová 2003a and Urbanová 2003b.

In Trnava, the marketplaces reflect the two phases of the town's early development (*see* Fig. 16.6). The spindle-shaped marketplace in the east of the town was the venue of the early street market *Zumbothel* (Saturday-market), recorded in the place name and the 1238 charter. The marketplace in the west of the town took up an oblong area at the intersection of the east-west street running from the parish church to the Franciscan friary and the north-south street between the two town gates. This formed the center of a new district which was built up according to a plan, as encouraged by the town's charter.[61] West of this marketplace, on the other side of the street, also within the town wall, was the grain market, its separate location being a clear sign of differentiation by type of goods.

The same trend appeared even more strongly in the functional diversification of Sopron's marketplaces. The relatively small area of the town center, squeezed within a triple ring of walls that incorporated the Roman walls and isolated from the main through-routes, severely restricted its trade functions. As a comital castle during the Árpádian age, the inner town accommodated only the *Salzmarkt* (salt market) at the south-east corner, whose principal functions were storage and distribution rather than trade in the modern sense. The real marketplace lay outside the castle walls, where the intersecting trade routes to Vienna and Bratislava crossed the Ikva River.[62] The cereals, timber and livestock markets, whose locations are identified mostly from fifteenth-century data, occupied the eastern and western sections of the roads as they widened into squares outside the town's defensive trench. Within the walls, meat was sold on the site of the salt market and the area beside it, fish to the east of there, towards the Hátsókapu Gate (*Hindertor*), and poultry and vegetables in the eastern extension of Fő tér (*Fragnermarkt*). The area of Fő tér (*Platz*), and probably the triangular space south of the Franciscan friary, was where small but valuable goods – cloth, spices, jewelry and plate – were sold and was also the site of the annual fairs (*see* Fig. 16.7).[63]

The abundant written sources for Sopron tell us more than just the function of each marketplace. We can trace what opportunities were open to the town in the trading of goods, and how it profited from the trading facilities. First, there were regulations which governed the opening hours of marketplaces and

---

61 The 1238 charter: Marsina (ed.) 1971–1987, II, 30–31. On the town plan: Mencl 1938, 44–49 and Urbanová 2003a, Fig. 37.
62 Holl 1996–1997, 7–9 and Szende 1997.
63 Holl 1979, 130–132, Holl 1996–1997, 8–10, Jankó, Kücsán and Szende 2010, [study] 19–20, 23, [gazetteer] 72, [map] A.3.3.

THE URBAN ECONOMY IN MEDIEVAL HUNGARY 353

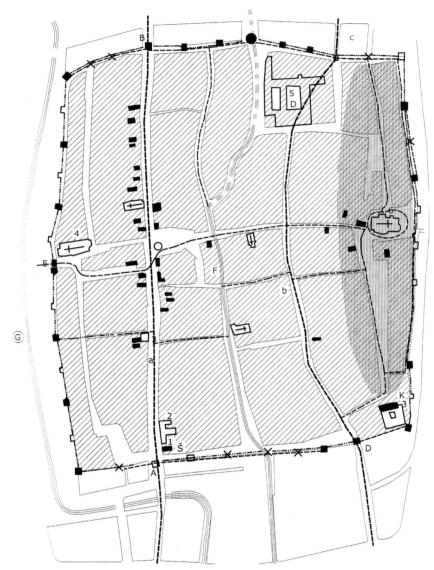

FIGURE 16.6   *The topography of medieval Trnava with the marketplaces (after Mencl 1938 and Urbanová 2003a).*

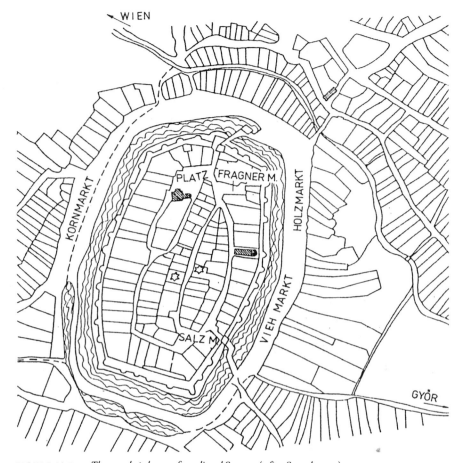

FIGURE 16.7   The marketplaces of medieval Sopron (after Szende 1997).

the persons permitted to use them,[64] and second, the town authorities derived revenue from rental of shops, particularly shambles. There were municipal traders' stalls in Sopron beside the Franciscan friary and between the Előkapu Gate (*Vordertor*) and the northern outer gate, both of which have been precisely located by archaeological excavations.[65] The municipal accounts have entries for 12 butchers' shops in the *Salzmarkt* (now Orsolya tér) in 1466, and 14 in 1490. The latter definitely involved stone, brick or timber structures, because the town authorities paid day-rates to masons and carpenters for their repair. The lease stipulated burgher status and guild membership, so that nobody

64   See the town statute of 1455 in Házi (ed.) 1921–1943, II/2, 176.
65   Jankó, Kücsán and Szende 2010, [gazetteer] 72.

from outside could rent the stalls or shops there. The place of the shambles was in all likelihood identical with the building of the modern-day Lábasház.[66]

The most highly differentiated market system in the kingdom was of course to be found in the late medieval capital city, Buda. There were two marketplaces on Castle Hill, the enormous, originally triangular St George's Market in the German district, in the middle of the plateau, and the approximately square-shaped Szombathely ("Saturday-place") in the Hungarian district in the north-east corner.[67] Apart from the morphological difference between the two squares, their size and place in the street system reflected the relative standing of the two main ethnic groups within the population. Topographical research has proved that both marketplaces occupied much larger areas when the town was first founded, and were gradually built on until, by the end of the fifteenth century, they were whittled down to the dimensions known from late medieval reconstructions (*see* Fig. 16.8).

The high level of specialization among marketplaces and other points of sale in Buda can be traced from three main sources: medieval street names (Kalmár utca [Retailer Street], Patikáros sor [Apothecary Row], Zsemlyeszék [Baker's shop], Mészárszék [Shambles], Elevenhalszer [Live-fishmongers' row], Tikszer [Poulterers' row], Nyirő utca [Cloth-shearer Street], Tej utca [Milk Street]); the topographical data from the tithe registers; and written regulations governing traders, above all the Buda *Stadtrecht*. From the work of several generations of historians we have a good picture of the marketplace layout, with the positions of stall-holders selling fruit, dried vegetables, cheese, chicken, game, fresh vegetables and salt, and the butchers' and bakers' shops.[68] Complementing the market system on Castle Hill were the produce markets in the suburbs (Búza utca [Wheat Street], Szénaszer [Hay row]), the Szentpétermártír and Zeiselbüchel markets, the slaughterhouse by the Danube,[69] the ware- and storehouse in the vicinity of the harbor,[70] and of course the markets and trading points of Pest. The annual fairs were held on Virgin Mary's Day in the Szentpétermártír district beside the castle, and on Whitsunday in Felhévíz.[71]

---

66 Holl 1996–1997, Appendix, 14. On the structure and layout of shambles, including the example of Sopron, see Benda 2012, 24–34.
67 Végh 2006–2008, I, 156–211 and 274–301, Benda 2011 and Benda 2016a.
68 Mollay (ed.) 1959, Végh 2006–2008, I, 72–87 and 108–122, Figs 47–48, Benda 2011, 261–263, Fig. 2, Benda 2012 and Benda 2016b.
69 Végh 2008. Butchers had different locations for residential, commercial and industrial (slaughtering) purposes, see Benda 2016b.
70 Benda 2012 and Benda 2016a.
71 Végh 2006–2008, I, 108–122. On the annual fairs see Szende 2017.

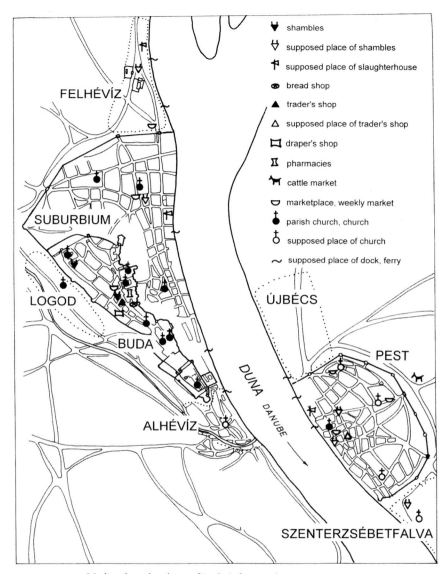

FIGURE 16.8   *Medieval marketplaces of Buda (after Benda 2016a).*

Even such a brief outline of the marketplaces demonstrates the need for a study of the functions of the infrastructure that links up topographical and economic-history research. How were the marketplaces and stalls located in relation to church buildings, ramparts and municipal buildings? How much was this influenced by deliberate planning? How central was the town market place? What measures did the town authorities take to regulate or change the positioning of markets? What direct and indirect revenue did the town obtain from maintaining places for trade, and what expenditure and obligations did this entail for the community? What other authorities (crown, secular landowners, church) had influence over what went on there and who profited from it? How were the marketplaces related to the presence and location of ethnic groups in the town (including Jews, not otherwise discussed here)? And what non-commercial functions did the marketplace have, such as the administration of justice and communication? Rather than formal typological groupings, a study of such and similar questions could lead to much better understanding of the structure and operation of towns, and useful comparisons to other places of selling in a European context.[72]

Balance: "To the Multiple Benefit of King and Country?"

The *arenga* of Körmend's charter of 1244 includes a statement characteristic of the time: *Cum constet evidenter ex fideli confluentium hospitum famulatu regi et regno multiplex commodum provenire* ...[73] ("it is clear that the gathering together of faithfully serving settlers provides multiple benefits for the king and the realm"). Were the king's expectations fulfilled? And were these expectations to the benefit of the towns themselves?

The word *commodum* meant, in addition to mere material gain, advantage, convenience, and favor. As we have seen in connection with building ramparts, these very costly constructions – as with the other community-maintained components of the urban space – meant much more to both the king and the town than the money it cost to build them. Nonetheless, it is mainly the pecuniary component of these questions that a study of the urban economy can address. Given the amount of data that is available, it is as difficult to draw up a balance of municipal accounts as it is to estimate the trade balance of the kingdom as a whole. Where this has been attempted, calculations show that the majority of urban revenue – regardless of its source – went (under various headings) to satisfy the needs of the king's treasury or army.[74] The pecuniary obligations often exceeded the towns' means, requiring them to take out loans, and in many cases causing permanent indebtedness. Municipal authorities

---

72 Calabi 2004.
73 Kubinyi (ed.) 1997, 38–39 and Kubinyi 1984a.
74 Kováts 1900, Kováts 1902b, Simon 2006a and Kubinyi 1993a.

took out the loans partly from their own burghers and partly from other individuals, both Christians and Jews.[75]

Some of the municipal enterprises also served to cover the towns' external liabilities, as touched on earlier. Others were set up to satisfy internal needs, but took advantage of the opportunities available to extend their reach beyond the town boundaries, as the example of the Sopron lime kilns shows. A similar situation existed with municipally-operated mills, omitted from this discussion for reasons of space.[76] Finally, towns had "enterprises" that concentrated on local needs and operated according to more than economic criteria, such as the maintenance of schools, almshouses and hospitals.[77] Experience in running such operations meant that when the Reformation came, the town was able to take over what had been church benefits and foundations, and usually managed them effectively.

In comparison with other forms of organization – above all, the estate economy of ecclesiastical or secular landowners – the position of the urban economy was at once much better and much worse. The main differences lay in the artificial inflation of resources with privileges and favors, and in the continual – regular and irregular – extraction of taxes. Part of this mutuality-based policy was the town's management of its land. The monarch renounced his direct title to the benefit of the townspeople in the hope that the more intensive utilization of the land would indirectly bring him higher revenue than would have been possible through putting it under direct cultivation. This resulted in the very strong interdependence of crown and town, in respect of which royal policy towards the towns can be set beside "municipal policy towards the crown", towns' relations to the monarchs. In the same way, private landowners had a role in stimulating the economy of their own towns, and in making use of urban revenue, similar to that of the king in relation to royal towns. Town and overlord were also closely interdependent. Nonetheless, it was certainly the king or the overlord who had the upper hand. In the long term, the undoubted dependence on crown economic policy inhibited the growth of towns and became even more restrictive in the centuries after the end of the Middle Ages.[78]

---

75   Pühringer 2003 and Boone, Davids and Janssens (eds.) 2003, with further references.
76   Vadas 2015–2016.
77   Majorossy and Szende 2008, 434–437.
78   Zimányi 1980, H. Németh 2008 and H. Németh 2011.

CHAPTER 17

The Medieval Market Town and Its Economy

István Petrovics

The Market Town in Historiography

Historians used to view the market town (*oppidum*) as an intermediate between a village and a real town, a form of urban settlement that had "frozen" at a certain stage of development and retained an essentially village character. Writing in 1927, Elemér Mályusz considered that *oppida* had acquired urban privileges without sufficient reason. He changed his view only in 1953, on discovering that fourteenth-century *oppida* were not a homogeneous set of village-like entities with urban privileges, but existed at different levels of urban development and were instrumental in leading the peasants towards an urban life. Jenő Szűcs continued to express reservations about market towns in 1955, seeing their spread and expansion as narrowing the market opportunities of "real towns" and ultimately contributing to a hypothesized halt in the development of Hungarian *civitates* in the late fifteenth century. By contrast, a positive evaluation of market towns emerged in works by István Szabó and György Székely in the early 1960s, and the clearest elucidation of their distinguishing features was produced by Vera Bácskai in her monograph of 1965. Erik Fügedi introduced some new ideas to the study of *oppida* in the 1970s. Most importantly, he stressed the role played by landowners in the granting of privileges to market towns and in their emergence as centers of seigneurial estates. He also proposed the following definition of the *oppidum*: "market towns in the fourteenth century were places whose economic, administrative and, to a limited extent, judicial functions had an urban character, but fell short of real towns in all of these respects. They occupied categories of their own between villages and towns."[1]

This brief survey indicates the problems that have arisen in studying the history of medieval market towns. The areas of dispute have been concerned less with the economy of the market town than its definition and the assessment of its historical role. Recently, however, historians seem to have reached a consensus even on the latter two questions. This has emerged to a large extent

---

1 Mályusz 1927, Mályusz 1953b, Szűcs 1955, Szabó 1960, Székely 1961, Bácskai 1965, Fügedi 1972a and Fügedi 1972b. See also Kubinyi 2000b, 8–10 and Bácskai 2002, 32–40.

from several major theoretical discussions and monographs on medieval market towns published in recent decades.[2]

The main problem with the definition was that the market town lacked even the kind of loose interpretation that István Werbőczy gave for the *civitas*, the "real town" in his Tripartitum, a compilation of the customary law of medieval Hungary completed in 1517: "A city in fact is a great number of houses and streets, necessary walls and fortifications, privileged for a good and honest life."[3]

The words denoting the market town – *oppidum* in Latin and *mezőváros* in Hungarian – presented problems of their own. Until the mid-fourteenth century, or more precisely, 1351, the terms *civitas* and *oppidum* were not sharply distinguished. A law of 1351 exempted inhabitants of the *civitas* (i.e., a town surrounded by a wall) from payment of the *nona*, or "ninth" tax.[4] Thereafter, *civitas* denoted a royal or episcopal town surrounded by a wall, and *oppidum* increasingly, if not exclusively, a town subject to the jurisdiction of the lord, and lacking a wall.[5] Some confusion arose from the word *mezőváros*, the Hungarian equivalent of *oppidum*. Since *mező* is the word for field, such a town was associated in the public mind with agriculture, and many historians made the same (erroneous) assumption. It is clear from early modern Hungarian vernacular sources that the significance of the prefix *mező* was as a distinction from the gated or enclosed town; it meant an "open" town, a town without a wall. So it

---

2   Bácskai 1967, Ladányi 1977, Mikó 1995, Szakály 1995a, esp. 9–32, Bácskai 1997, Kubinyi 1997b, Benkő, Demeter and Székely 1997, Petrovics 2001b, Blazovich 2002, Lengyel 2003, C. Tóth 2004, Gulyás 2009b, Petrovics 2009, Éder 2010 and Petrovics 2014.

3   *Est autem civitas, domorum et vicorum pluralitas, moeniis, et praesidiis circumcincta necessariis, ad bene, honesteque vivendum privilegiata* – Bak et al. (eds.) 1992–2012, V, 388–389.

4   *Preterea, ab omnibus jobagionibus nostris, aratoribus et vineas habentibus, in quibuslibet villis liberis ac etiam vduarnicalibus villis quocunque nomine vocatis ac reginalibus constitutis, exceptis civitatibus muratis, nonam partem omnium frugum suarum, et vinorum ipsorum exigi faciemus et domina regina exigi faciet, ac predicti barones et nobiles similiter ab omnibus aratoribus jobagionibus et vineas habentibus in quibuslibet possessionibus ipsorum existentibus nonam partem omnium frugum suarum et vinorum suorum eorum usibus exigant et recipiant* ("Furthermore, we and the lady queen will cause the ninth part of all their crops and vines to be exacted from all our tenant peasants holding plowlands and vineyards in any free village of ours of whatever kind and also in the *udvarnok* [bondsmen of royal estates] villages by whatever name they are known, and the villages of the queen, with the exception of the walled cities, and similarly the said barons and nobles should exact and take for their own use the ninth part of all their crops and vines from all tenant peasants holding plowlands and vineyards on any of their estates.") – Bak et al. (eds.) 1992–2012, II, 10–11.

5   Ladányi 1977, 6–14. See also: Kubinyi 1987, I, 235–236.

was not agriculture that gave the *mezőváros* its name, although agricultural activity undoubtedly played a prominent part in the lives of these towns.[6]

From the juridical point of view, the market town lacked the autonomy of the real town because it was under the jurisdiction of its seigneur – the king, the queen, the church or the lord. This judicial distinction has a bearing on the definition, because much of the historical literature still calls any town under seigneurial jurisdiction a market town. This is only correct in the broader sense of the word; i.e., by the criterion of jurisdiction rather than the possession of walls. Strictly, only unfortified *oppida* can be called market towns, and walled episcopal seats and walled towns under the control of the king, queen or secular landlord should more properly be termed seigneurial towns.[7]

Popular misconceptions regarding the number and location of market towns also persist today. Dezső Csánki produced what might be called the first "virtual list" of *civitates* and *oppida* in the Kingdom of Hungary. He put them in a combined category, and came up with an overall figure of between eight and nine hundred. This was later shown to be unrealistically high, because it included any village which held an annual fair and any settlement mentioned even once as being an *oppidum*.[8] In 1927, Elemér Mályusz put the number of market towns in Hungary at eight hundred; in 1961, Vera Bácskai produced an estimate of seven hundred and fifty market towns in the fifteenth century (omitting the areas of Transylvania, Slavonia and Croatia), and more recently, András Kubinyi proposed a number of around five hundred.[9] Given that there were only about two and a half dozen royal towns in the kingdom, even this lowest figure is striking evidence in support of a fact that historians only accepted after a long time, and with reservations: there were many more "towns" in Hungary than those legally designated as such. Seigneurial towns and some *oppida* should be included among them.[10] Even contemporaries considered *oppida* to be towns, as may be inferred from an anonymous account of the region from 1308, the *Descriptio Europae Orientalis*.[11] Added to this is the vernacular designation *mezőváros* in Hungarian, *mestečko* in Slovak; in Hungarian

---

6   Szakály 1995b, 13.
7   It was András Kubinyi who drew attention to this problem. Since the publication of his research results, the number of monographs and studies that use the appropriate terms when referring to the different types of towns has increased.
8   Csánki and Fekete Nagy 1890–1944. Unfortunately, we do not have any contemporary source that refers to what was conceived of as a market town in the Middle Ages.
9   Cf. Szakály 1995b, 13 fn. 25, Bácskai 1965, 14–16, Engel, Kubinyi and Kristó 1998, 280.
10   Engel, Kubinyi and Kristó 1998, 281. See also: Kubinyi 2000b, 5–12.
11   Górka (ed.) 1916, 1, 2–3, 43–45.

linguistic consciousness and Slovak historiography, they were definitely regarded as towns.[12]

The "only" question was how settlements qualifying economically as towns, but lacking the legal designation, could be distinguished from other seigneurial towns and *oppida*. Earlier attempts at making such a distinction restricted the study to single features (e.g. terminology, presence of mendicant friaries and hospitals, number of students at foreign universities). A much more comprehensive approach was taken by András Kubinyi, who borrowed the geographical method of central place theory and drew up a set of criteria (including administrative functions, number of guilds, transport intersections, markets and fairs) as the basis of a broad-based and much more reliable system.[13]

Of course, determining the centrality scores of settlements in the medieval Kingdom of Hungary between 1200 and 1250 tells us little by itself; what is needed is a categorization based on these scores. Kubinyi did this by adapting a Polish classification for the early sixteenth century. The resulting system divides central places into seven categories. The important central places for the present discussion are those which score at least 16 out of the maximum of 60 points. These fall into the following categories: 1. first-class (main) towns (at least 41 centrality points); 2. secondary towns (31–40); 3. smaller towns and market towns having major urban functions (21–30); and 4. market towns with medium urban functions (16–20). In terms of the urban economic functions they performed, the seigneurial towns and *oppida* in the second, third and fourth categories all qualify as medieval "towns". For the same reason, we may leave out the market towns in the fifth, sixth and seventh categories, although some of those in the fifth (transitional) category probably scored low only because of insufficient data.[14]

This gives a figure of one hundred and eighty to two hundred towns in the Kingdom of Hungary in the Late Middle Ages, and most of these – some one hundred and fifty – were *oppida* and seigneurial towns which did not have full civic freedoms. Plotted the *civitates*, together with the seigneurial towns and *oppida* which performed urban functions show a relatively even and hierarchical spatial pattern, convincingly refuting the old view of medieval Hungary as being "bereft of towns". It also refutes the view of the market town as a phenomenon confined to the Great Hungarian Plain, although the larger and wealthier market towns were indeed concentrated in that part of the kingdom

---

12 Engel, Kristó and Kubinyi 1998, 280, Bácskai 2002, 29–30.
13 See a presentation of earlier attempts: C. Tóth 2004, 589–590 and Kubinyi 2000b, 10–15.
14 Kubinyi 2000b, 15–16. For a critical analysis of Kubinyi's point system: Lakatos 2013, 18–25.

THE MEDIEVAL MARKET TOWN AND ITS ECONOMY

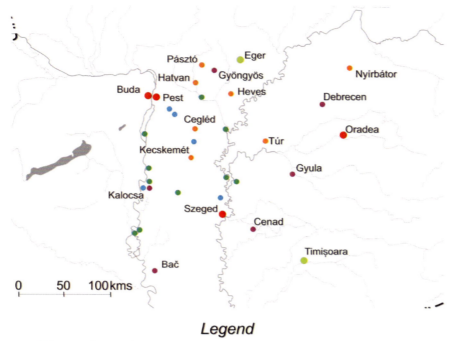

FIGURE 17.1 *Towns and market zones in the Great Hungarian Plain in the Late Middle Ages (after Sárosi 2016).*

(see Fig. 17.1). It also deserves mention here that comparative urban history studies have shown the market town to be more than a Hungarian phenomenon: it occurred in German-speaking areas, above all Austria, involving the word *Markt*.[15]

Research into market towns has hitherto concentrated on the core area of the Kingdom of Hungary. As yet, little is known of *oppida* in Croatia, Slavonia

---

15 Engel, Kristó and Kubinyi 1998, 280–281 and Kubinyi 2000b, 11, 15–101.

and Transylvania, owing to the preference of historians both in Hungary and neighboring countries for research into free royal towns rather than *oppida*.[16]

Alongside the issue of geographical distribution is that of the chronological variation of market towns. Vera Bácskai found that pre-1390 sources refer to a total of fifty market towns, usually using the words *civitas* and *oppidum* interchangeably. Their number increased by two hundred and forty-nine between 1391 and 1440 and by a further thirty-three before 1490. Another seventy-nine *oppida* appeared in charters by 1526.[17] Mályusz's work had the effect of concentrating attention on developments in the fourteenth century, and Bácskai's on those in the fifteenth century. The only detailed study of the sixteenth century was by György Székely, who examined the issue of market towns in the first two decades in his analysis of the causes of the peasant war of 1514 led by György Dózsa.[18] Recently, research chiefly by Ferenc Szakály has proved that the sixteenth century was also a unique and significant period in the development of market towns. Another clear result of research is that the real chronological divide for medieval market towns in Hungary is not 1526 or 1541, but rather the Fifteen Years' War (1591–1606).[19]

Economy of Market Towns

Investigation of the economic and agricultural life of market towns, despite the many results that have been achieved, suffers from a basic lack of accurate information. One reason for this is that the level of literacy in *oppida* fell far short of that in the free royal towns, especially the tavernical towns (those which appealed to the tavernical bench; i.e., the court led by the *magister*

---

16   Szakály 1995b, 13 and 19. On the problem of market towns in Székely Lands in Romania: Benkő, Demeter and Székely 1997. On the same issue in the Upper Hungarian territories (present-day Slovakia) in the early modern period, see: Lengyel 2003, 79–85.

17   Bácskai 1965, 15. It is a pity that unlike in the case of most *civitates* the letters of privileges of the *oppida* did not come down to us. Therefore the building up of chronology that lists the foundation and the multiplication of market towns can only be carried out based on the first mention of them as *oppida*. This is the right place to refer to the fact that most of the *oppida* in the fourteenth century were in the hands of the kings, while in the fifteenth century most of the new market towns gained their privileges from landlords. According to Vera Bácskai, at the end of the fifteenth century 80 % of the market towns belonged to landlords and 11 % to the Church. See: Bácskai 2002, 31.

18   Székely 1961.

19   Szakály 1995b, 14 and Blazovich 1996. See the Introduction and the different entries in the volume.

tavernicorum (the master of the treasury). Another is the catastrophic destruction of medieval sources, especially in the south of the kingdom. For market towns, the historian has no access to detailed information in municipal law books, account books, municipal accounts or tax registers, but has to be content with the often fragmentary or limited information available in *urbaria*, tithe registers and charters.[20] As Ferenc Szakály was the first to point out, the gaps left by the lack of Christian sources and the paucity of information they contain, especially as regards the late medieval period, can be filled from the Ottoman *tahrir defter*s, the sanjak tax censuses. These were produced for the specific reason of recording every inhabited and uninhabited district within each sanjak, and – in the inhabited settlements – every household and the income to be expected from it. Despite the mass of information available from both Hungarian and Ottoman tax censuses from between the first quarter and the end of the sixteenth century, Hungarian historians have until very recently shown almost no interest in them.[21]

Vera Bácskai's study of the market town economy reached the conclusion that craft industry and foreign trade should not be taken as the prime measures of urban development of medieval Hungarian settlements. In the conditions that prevailed in the kingdom, agricultural output and the internal trade of agricultural products[22] were also urbanizing forces. This is not to downgrade craft industry; indeed, Bácskai showed that the chief distinguishing feature of market towns was the interrelationship between commodity-producing agriculture and commodity-producing crafts, and market towns also played some part in foreign trade. The craft industries of *oppida*, however, were much less specialized than those of the free royal towns, and they were mainly geared to serving everyday local and village needs. Nonetheless, guilds were well established in market towns in the fifteenth century.[23]

---

20   Lakatos 2013.
21   Szakály 1995b, 14. Ferenc Maksay, for example, published in the form of tables the tax-registers of 48 counties of Hungary and the Partium (the latter roughly corresponds to Crişana and Maramureş in modern Romania) from the period between 1543 and 1561 (most of the data is from 1549). Maksay also drew attention to known market towns from county to county: Maksay 1990. For the Ottoman defters, see Engel 1996, Fodor 1997, Káldy-Nagy (ed.) 2000 and Vass 1979. For the tithe lists, see, for instance, Szabó 1954.
22   See the study of András Kubinyi in the present volume.
23   Bácskai 1965, 23–61 and Bácskai 2002, 35–37. It is worth drawing attention to the fact that few of the craftsmen of market towns seceded from the traditional forms of production. This might be the reason for the frequent presence of craftsmen in the local councils of market towns, unlike in the case of *civitates*. It was not rare that a half or third of the

Bácskai also found that there were market towns in Transdanubia and the Little Hungarian Plain in the early fifteenth century which accommodated 10–17 different crafts, and that in the mid-fifteenth century the momentum of development of craft industries shifted to *oppida* in the center of the kingdom and its eastern periphery. There were more than ten crafts in nine towns, and there are records from the early sixteenth century of more than twenty in Gyula (*see* Fig. 17.1). We also know that sixteen *oppida* acquired exemption from external customs duty, thirty-one *oppida* had exemption from internal customs duty throughout the kingdom, and several dozen others had exemption within one or more counties. Then there were several hundred *oppida* which held annual fairs in addition to their weekly markets.[24] These research results also convincingly prove that many market towns' trading activity – unlike their craft industry – went beyond their narrow market zones; i.e., was not confined to gathering surplus produce from the immediate environs.

Viticulture and animal husbandry have been clearly identified as central to the *oppidum* economy; arable produce was mainly consumed locally. Since vineyards and pastures did not form part of a tenant peasant's tenure, they were held on a freer basis than the land around the average village. Attempts to extend the town's plowland and pasture by leasing or forcibly occupying land were a general phenomenon among *oppida*, even those with extensive fields of their own. By the nature of the market town economy, the peasant-burghers of the *oppida* traded primarily in wine, livestock, animal produce and coarse woolen cloth.[25] Although they certainly had fewer merchants engaged in foreign trade and possibly less capital than their counterparts in the *civitates*, the differences between free royal towns and *oppida* seem to have been more quantitative than qualitative.[26]

Market towns in a strong economic position tended to pay their taxes and seigneurial dues in cash. Many of them paid their landlords in a lump sum, and others by census imposed per head or other services redeemed in cash. Inhabitants of poorer *oppida*, however, paid their dues in the same way as the *iobagiones*. Unlike villages, market towns – particularly the larger ones – usually had broad powers of self-government. The economic and legal privileges and various concessions had great attractive power for the peasants, who

---

sworn burghers (*iurati cives*) of the councils of the market towns – generally consisting of twelve, sometimes of six members – were from amongst them.

24 Bácskai 1965, 32–62 and Bácskai 2002, 36–37.
25 Székely 1961, 318–322, Mályusz 1986, Ember 1988, Bácskai 2002, 52–53 and Petrovics 2014, 284–291.
26 Székely 1961, 309–341 and Bácskai 2002, 46.

were very keen to move to market towns. By the end of the fifteenth century about one fifth of peasants are estimated to have lived in market towns. Another distinctive feature of the society of these towns was the large number of landless peasants (*inquilini*). It would be a mistake to regard *inquilini* as synonymous with "poor", because they also had the opportunity to rent land and engage in gainful activity other than agriculture.

Despite their flourishing economies, only a very few of the large market towns achieved full civic freedoms in the fifteenth and sixteenth centuries. The reasons for this unfortunate situation were mainly political. One was the common habit among late medieval sovereigns of mortgaging their towns and *oppida* for quick financial gain. This was not due to a lack of appreciation of the towns' importance, but because of the treasury's pressing need for finance to defend the kingdom against the Ottomans. Towns were also granted outright to ecclesiastical and secular landlords so as to secure their loyalty in the rendering of services required for defense of the realm and other political purposes.

At the turn of the fifteenth and sixteenth centuries, several factors combined to interrupt the development of towns and market towns in Hungary. One of the most important was the restructuring of internal political power following the death of King Matthias Corvinus. The lesser nobility used their new strength to force the passage of laws inhibiting central power and adversely affecting the towns. Act 47 of 1492, for example, required that *iobagiones* living on estates of the king, the queen, the barons and the nobles, except inhabitants of towns enclosed by a stone wall, were obliged to pay the ninth in produce. Under Article 49 of the same law, the tenant peasant had to pay the ninth on the lands not only held from their own chief landlord, but also on the fields which they leased from other landlords. This law adversely altered the relatively free conditions that had hitherto applied to possession of peasant and market-town land leases, and put *oppida* in a somewhat difficult position. Act 41 of 1498 withdrew the exemption on paying the ninth on rented land from inhabitants of *civitates*. This provision must have been difficult to enforce, however, because it had to be confirmed by Act 58 of 1514 and Act 27 of 1518. The 1498 law also set new rules for the tithe, one of which was that it should be paid in kind.[27]

These laws went a long way to tightening peasant bondage, and also created the opportunity for the lords, by obtaining some of the peasants' saleable produce, to get involved in the trade of agricultural produce. The clear proof of this is Act 35 of 1498, which informs us directly of trade by nobles. Another problem was the tying of the peasants to the soil following the above

---

27 Bak et al. (eds.) 1992–2012, IV, 24–27, 116–117, 202–203 and 230–231.

mentioned peasant war led by György Dózsa.²⁸ The nobility attempted to stop peasants moving to market towns by withdrawing their freedom of movement.

Recent research has discovered that these laws and measures were only partially put into practice. One reason for this was that some landowners still saw it as being to their advantage if their market towns continued to pay their dues in cash. The abolition of peasants' right of movement also proved unfeasible, because the nobles themselves were divided on the issue, and the flood of refugees from the southern parts of the country under Ottoman attack could hardly be stemmed by mere laws.

Further adding to the woes of the *oppida* at the turn of the fifteenth and sixteenth centuries was competition from 'real' towns. This was partly the result of the discovery of America in 1492, which shifted trade routes to the Atlantic and opened up a much wider world market than had been known in medieval times. The sixteenth century also brought an agricultural boom to Europe: the demographic explosion in the west of the continent greatly increased the demand for food, and food prices shot up. This permitted a considerable increase in the imports of broadcloth and manufactures in exchange for the grain, wine and livestock exported to Western Europe. One consequence was to dampen the development of craft industries in Hungarian *civitates*, already severely lagging behind their counterparts in Western European towns. The slump in craft industries, the fall-off in demand for Hungarian precious metals, and the unprecedented rise in the price of agricultural products turned the attention of even *civitas* burghers to viticulture and the wine trade, and to grain production.²⁹

Overall, despite their economic and judicial disadvantage relative to the *civitates*, and the shackles which new laws granting trade preferences to the nobles put on their development at the turn of the fifteenth and sixteenth centuries, market towns in Hungary came out of the medieval period resilient and capable of adapting to the prevailing circumstances.

---

28   Bak et al. (eds.) 1992–2012, IV, 110–113.
29   It is worth emphasizing that at the beginning of the sixteenth century 40 % of the burghers of Sopron owned plowland and 80 % of the whole population and two-thirds of the craftsmen had vineyards, despite the fact that traditional forms of production (except for, of course, wine production) has been wiped out. It is likely that the role of plowland grew in the case of towns in the borders of which cereals could have been cultivated. This claim is reinforced by the example of Prešov, where most of the burghers were also owners of plowland in the late sixteenth century. See: Bácskai 2002, 61.

CHAPTER 18

Crafts in Medieval Hungary

László Szende

> ... the pious devotion of the faithful neglect what the wise foresight of our predecessors has transmitted to our age; what God has given man as an inheritance, let man strive and work with all eagerness to attain.[1]

The Benedictine monk Theophilus Presbyter, who was active at the turn of the eleventh and twelfth centuries, gave this general appraisal of crafts in the introductory chapter of his book *Schedula diversarum artium*. He succinctly defined crafts as "the useful work of the hands". Historical research has of course gone somewhat beyond this, and through the work of several disciplines, employing various methodologies, we now have a complex view of the definition and socio-economic role of crafts. Ethnographers, historians and archaeologists have all brought their own individual methods to bear, but their results are best viewed side by side in a coordinated interdisciplinary approach, and further detail may be added to the picture by incorporating archaeometric analyses.[2] There has been a welcome increase in the number of craft-related studies and monographs in Hungary in recent decades, but most of these are published in Hungarian, and their findings have only indirectly been available to international research.[3]

The first and most fundamental problem is to find a precise definition of "crafts". Owing to methodological differences, a consensus has yet to emerge. The most recent review uses the following key concepts: independent productive activity, learned skills, fashioning by hand, and products made individually or at most in small series. To these may be added the technical term material

---

1 Theophilus 1986, 2.
2 See for instance the new results on iron smelting in the Árpádian age: Török 2010, Thiele, Török and Költő 2013.
3 On the different areas of craftmanship, see: Benkő and Kovács (eds.) 2010, II, 613–708. Gathering the prolific secondary literature is difficult. The most important works are available on the website of the Veszprém Regional Commission of the Hungarian Academy of Sciences (MTA VEAB): http://iparmuzeum.hu/sztkonyvtar.php (last accessed: 7 July 2016), while on the different find spots, see: Industrial Archaeological Cadastre database: https://sites.google.com/site/iparregeszetikateszter/Home (last accessed: 7 July 2016).

culture, since most of the objects made were used in everyday life. The skills craftsmen had to learn would also be a worthwhile area of study if there were sufficient usable sources. All we have to go on are late medieval or early modern guild charters which prescribed the "tricks of the trade" to be acquired by apprentices and journeymen before they could be admitted as masters. Neither do we know whether there existed in medieval Hungary any practical works of reference of the kind there were in the West – like Theophilus Presbyter's. Or to put the question differently: was there any need for a body of practical knowledge to be put in to writing? Since apprentices were trained on the job, the information was passed on verbally, thus searching for clues in written sources might be in vain.[4]

Sources on Crafts

Sources on medieval Hungarian crafts – written, archaeological and pictorial – are highly diverse, and there are also ethnographic analogies to draw on. Written sources present a highly variable picture,[5] and are much scarcer for the Árpádian age than for the Late Middle Ages. The important documents, above all ecclesiastical estate censuses, are those which made records of people who had trades or provided services.[6] Particularly notable are privilege charters of towns and villages, which started to become common in the thirteenth century. In many cases they granted permission for craftsmen to work there, and defined the rules governing markets and excise duties. Late medieval account books form a special group of sources, and call for special methods to extract information from them. Much useful information can be gained from analyzing urban wills,[7] which often mention craftsmen's tools. Town statutes are an important set of sources with many layers. The most thoroughly studied is the Law Code of Buda (*Ofner Stadtrecht*), many of whose articles govern the work of craftsmen.[8]

---

4 Heckenast 1996, 96.
5 See Kubinyi 1985.
6 In 1238, on the order of King Béla IV, Master Albeus conscripted the estates of the monastery of Pannonhalma: Erdélyi and Sörös (eds.) 1902–1916, I, 771–787 (no. 185). For an overview of the crafts: Erdélyi and Sörös (eds.) 1902–1916, I, 578 and Solymosi 1996b.
7 There were 224 (25.4 %) artisans or craftsmen in Bratislava, 80 (25.5 %) in Sopron and 37 (30.3 %) in Prešov among those who left behind testaments. The number of crafts: Bratislava – 39, Sopron – 23, Prešov – 21. See Szende 2001 and Majorossy and Szende (eds.) 2010–2014.
8 Mollay (ed.) 1959.

Narrative sources tend to be less than eloquent on the subject of crafts. The so-called Fourteenth-century Chronicle Composition mentions at one point that King Stephen I engaged stonemasons from Greece.[9] The Acephalus Codex devotes some lines to construction commissioned by Csanád Telegdi, archbishop of Esztergom, and mentions some of the work it involved.[10] From the hagiographic literature, there is a much-cited passage in the Greater Legend of St Gerhard in which he praises a woman working with a handmill.[11] Records of miracles also contain some information on craftsmen. One is a record from the canonization protocol of Margaret, daughter of Béla IV from 1276,[12] which mentions Beguine Méza, who spun gold, and Feka, a carpenter who lived under Buda Castle.[13] The account of miracles attributed to the intercession of St John Capistran tells the story of Benedek Molnár, a miller who suffered an occupational accident.[14]

As important as written sources are archaeological findings, especially for the period of the Conquest and foundation of the state.[15] It is almost solely through archaeological finds that we can reconstruct the crafts of the Hungarians when they arrived in the Carpathian Basin. They permit the fairly definite conclusion that the most distinctive crafts had developed before the Conquest, and craft industries corresponded to the lifestyle of the steppe. According to broad consensus in the literature based on the Hungarians' material-culture vocabulary, objects and tools implying the existence of handicrafts were present from the earliest times. The demand for tools of animal husbandry, fishing and cultivation, and for arms, horse gear and items of costume led to the emergence of specialized activities. Initially, these were pursued alongside agricultural work and warfare rather than on their own, but there is evidence of their existence in occupation names such as *vasverő* (smith), *ötvös* (goldsmith), *ács* (carpenter), *bocsár* (cooper), *fazekas* (potter), *fonó* (spinner), *szűcs* (furrier) and *tímár* (tanner). After settling in the Carpathian Basin, contacts with the Slavic population led to the adoption of many Slavic words: *kovács* (blacksmith), *csatár* (swordsmith), *taszár* (carpenter), *kádár* (cooper),

---

9   Szentpétery (ed.) 1937–1938, I, 317.
10   Szentpétery (ed.) 1937–1938, I, 492–493.
11   Szentpétery (ed.) 1937–1938, II, 475.
12   Laszlovszky 2010.
13   Csepregi, Klaniczay and Péterfi (eds.) 2018, 116–117 and 147–148.
14   Master Benedek "took an axe, got off one of the planks and started planning it, and see, a small string accidentally went into his the pinkie of his right hand" – the story is recorded by János Geszti, in his collection of miracles of St John Capistran. See Andrić 2000, 326–336.
15   Révész–Nepper 1996 and Fodor 2012.

takács (weaver), *gerencsér* (potter), and *esztergár* (woodturner). Toponyms that include names of trades are a special set of sources whose importance for research has long been recognized.[16] They can only be used, however, with the help of proper linguistic skills and archaeological methods.[17]

The blacksmith, nowadays denoted by the Slavic loan-word *kovács*, was known to the early Hungarians as a *vasverő*. It was a trade that required much skill and experience, and the blacksmith had to work in simple circumstances, being in constant motion with his forge. His products were chiefly tools, horse gear and weapons. The latter required great precision to make, so that the craftsmen who made them formed a separate class. The manufacture of one of the Hungarians' most important weapons, the recurve bow, can only be deduced from the methods known to have been available, because the only surviving remains (found in graves) are bone plates from the ends and on the grip. The drawn bow was carried in a separate quiver, whose exact shape has been reconstructed from finds in a grave in Karos.[18] Goldsmiths worked for the elite at the top of the social pyramid.[19] In the eighth and ninth centuries, Sogdian metal art, which followed the artistic traditions of the Persian Sassanids, clearly influenced the finest work of Hungarian goldsmiths, on cups, pouch plates and the decoration of plate disc hair ornaments (*see* Fig. 18.1).[20] The potters among the Hungarians arriving in the Carpathian Basin brought with them simple-shaped beakers and pots fired dark grey, and clay pots. Pots were made on simple hand-driven wheels, the walls built by the coiling technique.

Craft products which did not leave sufficient remains to be reconstructed from archaeological finds may be usefully approached via ethnographic analogies. Although the products of spinners, weavers and felt-makers decompose in the ground,[21] their work may be reconstructed from studies of peoples with similar material culture, as well as of goldwork and folk art. Felt plays an important part in the life of the steppe peoples, and the various stages of felt-making are useful areas of study. This wool material was used to make blankets, footwear, warm clothing and tent covers.

---

16 Takács 2012a, 48–49.
17 For instance, László Solymosi noted that from the 86 place names referring to crafts, formerly assumed to be of tenth-century origin, only 20 % appear in eleventh–twelfth-century sources, 68 % in forged or original charters of the next two centuries, and a further 12 % appear only after 1400. Solymosi 1972, 179.
18 Révész 1996, 105.
19 Révész 2014, 56–57.
20 Mesterházy 2014, 107.
21 Bollók et al. 2009.

CRAFTS IN MEDIEVAL HUNGARY 373

FIGURE 18.1   *Sabretache plate from Hlohovec (tenth century; Hungarian National Museum).*

Representations of crafts in pictorial sources can also be informative. There are many relevant sources of this type from the West, and some directly relating to Hungary, such as a miniature of the Hungarian Illuminated Chronicle showing Oradea Cathedral under construction.[22]

---

22   Budapest, Széchényi National Library, Clmae 404. f. 50r On building the church of Oradea and on the death of King Ladislas (099/86 Rubric): Wehli 2009, 136–137.

Principal Areas of Research

Several issues have opened up through investigations of the social position of craftsmen and women. In the eleventh and twelfth centuries, craftsmen were concentrated around forest estate centers, royal castle estate seats, *curiae* and *curtes* supplying the royal court, and royal and princely residences. The position within society of people engaged in craft work was generally among the servant folk, the *servi*.[23] It may be concluded from documents that there were distinctions among craftsmen even in the early Árpádian age, and further functional divisions among them. A key problem has been the determination of who the people engaged in crafts were. In the hunting and extensive animal husbandry that characterized the early Árpádian age, there were two levels of craft production. The first concerned simpler implements that the servant folk made for their own self-sufficiency, and the second was the work of craftsmen serving the demands of the landowning classes. The craft-making section of society paid dues to its overlords in two ways: working for a specified time or contributing specified products. Products of a fixed quantity were demanded from craftsmen who worked where they lived. The main evidence for this comes from ecclesiastic documents. The servant folk were divided into decades and centuries, each headed by an official (*decurio, centurio, ispán – comes*). Artisans are found to have become more significant in the thirteenth century, a process associated with privileges designed to build up the towns. Some of the free artisan population of privileged towns and villages were originally *hospites*.[24] Craftspeople formed the largest section of burghers. Many craftsmen also settled in the early towns, making goods for all kinds of purposes.[25]

The importance of the link between crafts and the royal, ecclesiastical and urban centers, and of its formative role, have long been noted by historians.[26] The medieval town in the legal sense appeared in Hungary at the turn of the twelfth and thirteenth centuries. Before this, some urban functions had been provided by "pre-urban" settlements, places with higher consumption

---

23 Solymosi 1993, 64–66.
24 Petrovics 2009, 67–73.
25 The town of Buda can be mentioned here as an example. It was founded by Béla IV following the Mongol invasion in 1241–1242. In 1255 there was a minting chamber here, which clearly underlines the status of the settlement. Besides coiners, a goldsmith was also employed, who assessed the refinement of silver. In 1292 a certain *Kunc examinator* was a member of the town council, who also appears in 1295 as *Kunc Prenner comes*. In ancient Steyr dialect, *Brenner* denoted a person "who is probing or examining the silver content of the new money". Kubinyi 1991f, 21, on the foundation of the town, see: Végh 2015, 12–15.
26 Szende and Németh 2014, 274–285.

demands than the average, and having in their area venues for the early exchange of goods. Early secular and ecclesiastical centers were served by workshops grouped in their direct vicinity (*suburbium*) or nearby, and in the case of monasteries sometime within the walls. Excavations (Sály–Lator,[27] Visegrád–Várkert,[28] Pásztó[29] or more recently Pomáz–Nagykovácsi-puszta[30]) have produced a variety of finds demonstrating the presence of working craftsmen. In towns and villages with charters, especially those granting trade and market-holding privileges, craftspeople were assured of a living.[31] This was especially true for royal centers where the largest orders came from the king and his court. The presence of the elite had a beneficial effect on crafts, including those whose products were luxury items (see Fig. 18.2).[32] From a social geographical point of view, craftspeople usually operated in the agglomeration area around these pre-urban centers.[33] Another type of settlement was the market place, which formed without the presence of an administrative center. Villages of craft-industry servant folks and ethnic groups engaged in trade grew up around these settlements. Market places however proved incapable of rapid development without the grant of privileges.

In major towns in the fifteenth century, when agriculture lost its primacy, the proportion of full-time artisans increased. They made up an expanding section of the urban population, their trades became increasingly differentiated, and purely urban industries emerged; the better-off towns even had a clockmaker. Most crafts were concerned with clothing, food and metal working. There was also increasing stratification by wealth: craftsmen in trades that produced luxury items (goldsmith, swordsmith) and some kinds of food, and some who were involved in the building industry could make a good living. Most artisans, however, belonged to the middle strata of urban society. Research apart from their social position also addressed the gender distributions in the different crafts, mostly analyzing the towns of Bratislava and Sopron.[34]

---

27 Mesterházy 1986.
28 Szőke 2000, 585–586.
29 The glassworks and the smithery were probably founded by the Benedictines, but the Cistercians kept on using them: Valter 1994, 393–398.
30 The glassworks was built in the former church building: Laszlovszky et al. 2014, 9–10.
31 Szende 2015a, 50–51.
32 In the thirteenth century, there are references to goldsmiths of "Latin" origin in Esztergom, as well as to a woman who was a gold-spinner. Zolnay 1965, 148–151.
33 An illustrative example is *Kovácsi* (the name refers to a blacksmith), a district lying southeast from the center of the archbishopric and royal town of Esztergom. Cf. Horváth 2000, 579.
34 Szende 1998a and Szende 1999.

FIGURE 18.2   The seal of the Latins of Esztergom (thirteenth century; Hungarian National Museum).

There are several interesting issues concerning the location of craftspeople in towns, well-illustrated by a case study of Sopron.[35] The interdependence of different trades made it practical to group them together, and this often influenced street names. Thus in Buda[36] there were streets called *Ötvösök* (goldsmiths) and *Posztómetők* (tailors), and in Víziváros beneath it streets called *Kerékgyártó* (wheelwright), *Mészárosok* (butchers) and *Halászok* (fishermen). In Bratislava there were streets called *Lakatos* (blacksmith) and *Késes* (knifemaker). Elsewhere, however, several different crafts could be located on the same street. In Király (king) Street in Cluj in 1453, the furrier, the joiner, the quiver-maker, the tailor, the carter, the harness-maker, the shoemaker and the fletcher all lived side by side. The proximity of the market may have been a major factor. Safety and hygiene could also have been considered when locating workshops. Smiths, tanners, cartwrights and wheelwrights were all to be found in the suburbs. Those plying the same trade in a town tended to pull together to create a monopoly. The guild was the body representing the interests of free craftsmen in a single trade in the same town. There were strict regulations governing the conditions for entering the guild and the tasks, rights and obligations of its members. The guild also filled the role of a religious association.

35   Holl 1979.
36   Bencze 1991, 334 and Benda 2016a.

Despite the substantial international and Hungarian literature on the history of medieval Hungarian guilds,[37] some issues require further research. One of these is the question of when guilds came into being. According to some historians, the first Hungarian guilds may have been set up by German *hospites*. Others see the Hungarian guilds as having developed out of religious brotherhoods. Then there is the view that some special activities performed in the town (military, defense) forged the guild into an organization. The economic boom of the mid-fourteenth century must have been a major factor in their creation. The meagre sources do permit the conclusion that the first guilds formed in about the middle of that century, although some trades may have had some kind of organization as early as the thirteenth. 1376 was an important year in the history of guilds, when Louis I issued a general decree for the seven Transylvanian Saxon districts (*szék*s).[38] The same year, privileges were granted to the butchers, bakers and shoemakers of Bratislava. The momentum of guild development continued into the fifteenth century.

Crafts were also involved in the development of market towns. The Hungarian word for these, *mezőváros*, means town "in the open", or unfortified. Most of them rose above the mass of villages in the fourteenth and fifteenth centuries. Referred to as *oppida* in the charters, only a few dozen could have borne the external features of a town. There were mainly economic reasons behind their creation, better transport having led to the formation of the market. Landlords also supported these settlements, it being in their interest to concentrate trade and crafts in a single center, but there was no move to establish "true" towns. Townspeople were largely granted a free hand in economic affairs, and could pursue trade in various ways, through which they accumulated wealth. Many of the market towns had the right to appoint their own judge, their forum of appeal had been the seigneurial seat. There have recently been great advances in the archaeological investigation of market towns. One of the main issues is whether archaeological techniques can serve to verify data in written sources. Excavation of craft workshops provides one of the criteria sets for studying the market town way of life.[39]

---

37 Interest in the subject is reflected as early as the beginning of the twentieth century, when Lajos Szádeczky published his findings together with a collection of archival sources. Cf. Szádeczky 1913 and Skorka 2012b.
38 Skorka 2012b, 58.
39 Laszlovszky et al. 2003, 369. The archaeological excavation of the medieval market town of Ete (in the area of Decs, Central-Hungary), which was deserted in the seventeenth century, brought promising results. See Miklós and Vizi 1994 and Miklós 2005.

Medieval villages, too, had their own craft industries. The people engaged in crafts, as we have seen, cannot be viewed as artisans completely divorced from agricultural activity. Social and economic developments took their effect here, too. The earlier group industries gave way, in villages, to peasant artisans who satisfied many of the needs of the locals. Smithies were of central importance,[40] while the development of pottery depended on sources of clay.

The Legacy of the Craftsmen

Excavations are a constant source of new additions to research collections, and work on these is constantly expanding our knowledge. The basis for the discussion of specific craft industries is the divisions in a Catalogue of Hungarian guilds, the *Céhkataszter*,[41] but there is space to cover only the main crafts in detail.

Food and Chemicals
There were various kinds of workshops that processed food. Written sources show sharp differences in the consumption habits of different sections of society. There were few changes in the way grain was processed. First, after it had been harvested, the grain had to be stored. Pits were mainly used for this in villages, although there were also above-ground stores. From there, the grain went to be milled. The simplest means was the hand mill. Contemporary representations and village excavations give us a fairly precise picture of mills, which are first mentioned in documents in the middle of the eleventh century.[42] The quern stone was usually mounted on a table-like structure and driven by an arm, of varying length, which fitted into a hole in the upper stone. The lower stone could have a larger diameter. The flour exited via a channel into some kind of storage vessel (wooden trough, basket) placed under the outflow. The millstones could be set to grind fine or coarse. In villages, the mills were located in various structures (reed huts, sunken buildings, barn-like structures). These could serve the needs of a small community.

There were of course mills with greater capacity. Millwrighting was a trade which passed from generation to generation. "Dry mills" were driven by men

---

40 The village of Sarvaly (Veszprém County) was deserted around 1530. The excavation recovered – inter alia – the remains of a smithy. Cf. Holl and Parádi 1982, 46–47.
41 Éri, Nagy and Nagybákay 1975, 134–140.
42 In 1061 "molarius cum mola" is mentioned in the foundation charter of the Benedictine abbey of Zselicszentjakab. Györffy (ed.) 1992, 173.

or animals. The Carpathian Basin abounds in rivers and streams whose speed of flow ideally suited them to driving water mills. The water was led into a separate channel and dammed, and the energy stored there released to turn the millwheel, which in turn drove the millstones. There were both undershot and overshot mills. Records of court actions have told us much about mill-building.[43]

Bread was baked in several different ways. There was the baking bell, set above the open fire on two or three stones. Most commonly, bread was baked in an oven built of clay, brick or stone. The base of the oven was plastered flat, and the bottom of its round mouth formed into a step. It was protected against the rain by a roof, open at one side to provide ventilation. Where demand was higher, there was a building – a bakery – for making bread. The products were large and small loaves, and wafers made on special iron plates. The wafer was unleavened flatbread baked from wheatflour and had a central place in liturgy, embodying the sacrament.

Meat was a major part of the medieval diet, and butchers were to be found nearly everywhere. The medieval Buda Butchers' Guild has left us a very good set of sources, much of its archive having survived.[44] A guild privilege issued by the Buda town council on 2 May 1481 contains an article which seems to link King Béla IV with a guild charter. It is unlikely that the butchers formed a guild as early as the thirteenth century, but they may have had some form of organization.[45] In the Law Code of Buda (Articles 105–107), the butchers rank highly, coming after the different categories of merchants, the minters of coins and the goldsmiths, and ahead of all other crafts.[46] Immediately after them in the ranking are trades associated with butchery: game traders, smoked meat traders, fishermen and fish traders.[47]

Chemical activities hardly show up among archaeological finds. The medieval refuse pit of a house in the Buda Castle District contained the remains of a round flask used for distillation.[48] The forecourt of Buda Palace yielded fragments of a distillation vessel made of green lead-glazed grey pottery.[49] The

43   Tringli 2001, 250–258.
44   In 1529 the German butchers of Buda transported some of their documents to the western confines of the country, among them an invaluable source, their guild book dating from 1520–1529. Kubinyi 2008, 100. For their archive, see: Kenyeres (ed.) 2008.
45   Kubinyi 2008, 89–91.
46   Mollay (ed.) 1959, 101–102 (cap. 105–106).
47   See the chapter by László Bartosiewicz and his colleagues in the present volume.
48   H. Gyürky 1982b.
49   Boldizsár 1984, 218–219.

fragments belonged to a tall, stone-shaped lid, on whose inner side liquid condensed and was collected in a trough and passed out through a sloping outflow tube. Its precise function is unknown, but it was probably part of a medicine-distillation apparatus, although it could also have been used for distilling alcohol.

Metallurgy, Metal Ware and Weapons

Iron emerges from both archaeological and written sources to have had a central place in the Árpádian-age economy, being the material for most everyday tools and implements and many kinds of weapons. Early medieval ironworks mostly used surface deposits of bog ore. Ironmaking forges were in operation in many parts of the country, particularly along the western border and in Borsod and Somogy Counties.[50] The distinctive type of bloomery found at Somogyfajsz may have come with the conquering Hungarians, because no similar design is known of in the Carpathian Basin in the ninth century.[51]

The bloomeries produced a loaf-shaped "bloom" which was only partly iron, and was passed to the forges to be wrought. The iron mined in the Transylvanian Ore Mountains and the Slovak Ore Mountains was supplied in the form of rods or rails. Since ore was expensive, iron waste and old iron implements were also melted down. Blacksmiths in villages, market towns and towns undertook different kinds of activities to suit local demands, but almost certainly used the same techniques. The village blacksmith did all kinds of metal work, and was also a healer of animals. His workshop had several kinds of implements and tools – punches, axes, swages and plate shears. There was usually a large and a small anvil in the smithy, and the hammer and tongs were the most universal among the blacksmith's tools. In towns, specialization set in as early as the thirteenth century: sources differentiate between armorers, spurriers, swordsmiths, cutlers, blacksmiths, nailsmiths, braziers and platesmiths. Iron agricultural implements followed developments in technology.[52]

Bronze, made by melting copper and tin together, could be formed into a great variety of objects. The various techniques and types have been thoroughly explored in the literature. Pectoral crosses, processional or altar crosses, cross bases, candlesticks, censers, lavabos, aquamaniles, fonts, mortars, bells and statues bear witness to the high level of expertise of Hungarian

---

50   Szegedy 1960, Nováki 1969 and Vastagh 1972.
51   The Somogyfajsz workshop was in fact a 6-by-8 meter pit with furnaces dug into its wall. Cf. Gömöri 1980.
52   Müller 1975 and Müller 1980.

craftsmen.[53] Casting varied according to whether simple or complex forms were required. The simpler molds were made of sand or clay, and sometimes carved negative stone molds. Relatively few molds have been found on the territory of medieval Hungary.[54] Bronze was melted in specially made furnaces which made use of natural features to provide a flow of air to make the fire hot.[55] The first relics of Hungarian bronze art are imitations of reliquary pectoral crosses imported from Byzantium. The complex form and pattern of the crosses was achieved by the lost wax method. Other pieces, especially those produced in series, do not display such craftsmanship. The casting of some corpuses, for example, was done without any attempt at artistry. Some items can be traced with high probability to the same workshop.

Bell-founding was a special trade, with mystical associations that no doubt derived from the extreme care required in making the mold and the arcane technological secrets involved in casting (*see* Fig. 18.3).[56] An important change in bell-founding appeared around 1200: a clay model bell was made and the outer mold formed around it and fired. The assembly was then taken apart and the mantle replaced over the core, leaving a precise gap into which the bronze was poured. It was difficult to make bells that were properly tuned to each other, and there was a constant search for techniques, molds and materials by which the sound of the bell could be improved.

FIGURE 18.3
Bell from Drăuşeni (fourteenth century; Hungarian National Museum).

---

53   Valter 1972, Lovag 1980 and Lovag 1999.
54   For a summary, see Ódor 1998.
55   E.g. the mouth of one in Visegrád-Várkert faced the Danube. Cf. Kovalovszki 1994–1995.
56   Benkő 2009.

Some workshops at this time were already fulfilling major orders. One of these was established by Konrád in Spišská Nová Ves in Upper Hungary. Traces of a large bell foundry in Visegrád, in the form of clay mantle fragments, have been found to the north-east of Solomon's Tower. The Spišská Nová Ves workshop was in operation until 1516, and had a monopoly on making bells and fonts for the Spiš area. The traditions of the workshop were carried on by successive generations who grew up there. The craftsmen developed their own distinctive decorative schemes. Patterns and letters carved from wood were either pressed into the clay mantle or cast in wax and affixed to the finished model.[57] Some of the craftsmen must have been illiterate, because there are cases where they mixed up the letters of inscriptions compiled by others. Other decorative elements made use of metal fittings for belts and clothing, and pilgrim's badges.[58]

Many craftsmen in Transylvania were Saxons, thus the effects of links to Germany must be taken into account. Bronze workers had a high social status and made a good living.[59] A good indication of their wealth is that they were among the major taxpayers and were able to send their children abroad to be educated. One of the foremost workshops was in Sibiu. Here, the work of bronze craftsmen can be traced from the late thirteenth century. The closure of their greatest competitor in Sighișoara around 1480 was a major boost to their business. This brought quite distant places (such as the Székely Lands) into their market range. In the second half of the fifteenth century, new foundries were set up in Bistrița and Brașov. The most famous workshop in Transylvania, however, was that of the Kolozsvári brothers, Márton and György, who learned their trade in Italy in the fourteenth century. Their sole surviving work is the statue of St George the Dragon-slayer in Prague.[60] They were renowned for their bronze statues of the sainted kings of Hungary (Stephen, Emeric and Ladislas), particularly an equestrian statue of St Ladislas erected in Oradea. The latter was smashed by the Ottomans in 1660.

Pewtering was a highly regarded trade in the Late Middle Ages. Since it was common to melt down medieval pewter objects, few of them survive nowadays. Most of the pewter wares mentioned in written sources (jugs and tankards, bowls and cups, plates, flasks, etc.) must have been made by local

---

57   It has been observed that certain motifs were used for centuries. E.g. the thirteenth century seal of Boleslav the Pious was kept at the monastery of St Andrew in Cracow, and its imprint was taken from here by Johannes Weygel, a master craftman of the workshop in Spišska Nova Ves. The motif first appeared in the fourteenth century, but it was also applied on a couple of bells which were produced in 1483 and 1500.
58   Benkő 2008.
59   Benkő 2005.
60   Marosi 1999.

craftsmen. Most pewter vessels were to be found in the households of well-to-do town dwellers.[61]

The goldsmithing characteristic of the Conquest-period Hungarians came to an end with the founding of the state, although some of its components survived in folk art. The destruction of objects is so complete that products of the eleventh century can only be reconstructed from written sources. Since goldsmiths worked with expensive material and had a high level of skill, they tended to be grouped around the major centers. The foremost of these in the Árpádian age was Esztergom, where the Mongol invasion of 1241–1242 "preserved" some of the workshop apparatus.[62] The metalware destroyed by the Mongols was replaced by imports from Limoges (see Fig. 18.4).[63] Craftsmen continued to supply the Hungarian political elite, and a workshop which operated in the court of Béla IV in the second half of the thirteenth century has been identified as the source of several surviving works. An outstanding relic of metal art from outside the centers is a drinking cup with a representation of the *Agnus Dei*, now held in the Hungarian National Museum (see Fig. 18.5).[64]

The display of power and wealth which became common in the fourteenth and fifteenth centuries increased the demand on craftsmen. Hungarian metalware of the time vied with what was being produced in Western Europe, and craftsmen made bold use of technical innovations and developed their own sets of motifs. Their work was definitely in the "art" category, and they energetically strove for perfection in every detail. There are several surviving pieces from the Angevin period, and some items of the Aachen Treasure are of outstanding significance for Hungarian metalware.[65] Intensifying foreign relations also took their effect on goldsmiths' work. Close Hungarian–Italian links led to the introduction of filigree enamel into Hungarian art in the early fifteenth century. The most outstanding surviving art objects of the time, the St Ladislas Herma and Suki Chalice of Győr, were made using this technique (see Fig. 18.6).[66] Gold and silverware, easily-movable pieces of very high value, were regarded as repositories of material security, to be hidden in case of war. Analysis of hoards according to various criteria can provide answers to many key questions.

---

61 Holl 1987.
62 Fettich 1968, 157–158 and Szende 2011b, 190–194.
63 Kovács 1968.
64 F. Vattai 1966.
65 Takács 2006.
66 The Hungarian King Ladislas I was canonized as a saint in 1192. His burial place, Oradea, became one of his cult centers. Cf. Kiss 2006.

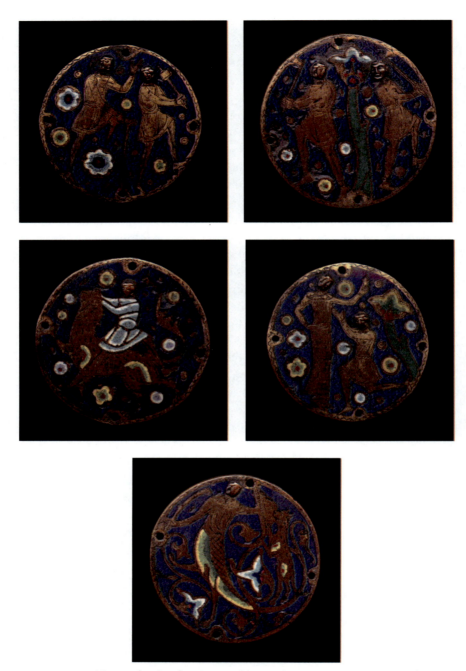

FIGURE 18.4   *Mounts of caskets from Limoges (thirteenth century; Hungarian National Museum).*

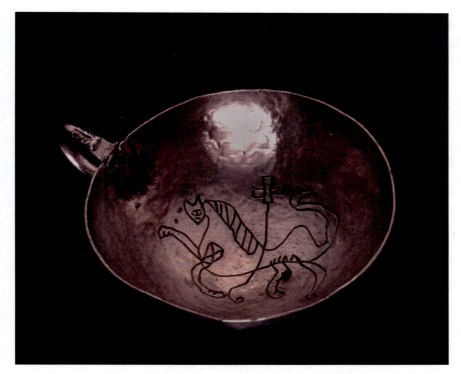

FIGURE 18.5   *Drinking cup with representation of the* Agnus Dei *(twelfth–thirteenth century; Hungarian National Museum).*

Leather-making and Leatherware

Animal hides were used for a wide range of purposes, but their preparation involved two principal techniques. The Hungarians may have brought one of these, alum tanning, when they came to the Carpathian Basin. Hair was removed by knife and then the hide was coated with alum and salt, and dried. Then it was coated with hot tallow and held above glowing embers. This caused the pores to open and be filled with tallow, giving the leather a white finish. Alum-tallow Hungarian leather was sought after throughout Europe and regarded as a special class of goods in the Middle Ages.[67] The other kind of tanning used, instead of minerals, vegetable extracts. The materials favored in Hungary were oak, pine and willow bark, horse chestnut wood, gall and Venetian sumac. In general, leather items only survive in very fortunate

---

67   Gáborján 1962.

FIGURE 18.6   *The Benedek Suki chalice (ca. 1440; Treasury of the Basilica of Esztergom).*

circumstances. A fifteenth-century shoemaker's workshop has been found in what was at that time a suburb of Pest (Molnár Street), and from the (dog) feces found in the pits it is easy to understand why the trade could not be carried on within the city walls.[68]

Textile and Garment Industries

The ancient ways of making textiles did not change during the Middle Ages. There were two main raw materials: animal (lamb's and sheep's wool) and vegetable (flax and hemp). The coarseness of Hungarian textiles restricted their use mainly to blankets and similar items; finer broadcloth was imported into the kingdom. The operations may be inferred from ethnographic analogies. Written sources show evidence of the diversity of the textile trade.[69]

Hungarian weaving developed at the end of the fourteenth century. King Sigismund recognized its significance, and attempted to make Košice a center of the weaving trade. In the fifteenth century, there was a great demand for peach-stone pattern linen, made by weaving with dyed yarn. The most popular motifs were various forms of rosette and star, animal figures set among floral decoration, birds, and stylized lettering (*see* Fig. 18.7).

Construction Materials, Building and Timber

The production of materials for building involved various technologies. Stone came largely from quarries, but re-using stone from abandoned buildings was also common. As with ore mines, the difficulty in studying medieval quarries is that later working removed all earlier traces. Nonetheless, there are a few fortunate cases where medieval traces have been found. A major factor in the location of quarries was the proximity of running water, which was almost essential for transport. The larger blocks were usually carved at the quarry. There were various carving techniques specific to different kinds of stone.[70] The stonemasons bore personal liability for their work, as recorded in masons' marks. Stones were fixed with mortar, which required lime. The first references to lime pits in Hungarian sources date from 1222. Burnt lime was transported by cart or made on the building site. Archaeologists have found

---

68 Irásné Melis and Vörös 1996, 226 and 242–243. Sopron may be a counter example, where remains of a workshop were found by one of the main streets of the town: Gömöri 2010, 211–213.
69 V. Ember 1981, 9–14.
70 Miklós 1985, 484–486.

FIGURE 18.7   Chausble of Košice (*fifteenth century; Hungarian National Museum*).

many lime kilns of different types.[71] Traces of brick making have been found in several places. In the Great Hungarian Plain, kilns were certainly built above ground.[72] A brick kiln excavated at Dombóvár-Szigeterdő has been dated to

---

71   Grated kilns, earth klins, kilns with fire-chanenel, kilns with two stoke-holes. Müller 1981, 58–63.
72   Jakab 2011, 138–142.

the Árpádian age.[73] Bricks from here were used to build a nearby thirteenth-century donjon.

Sometimes written sources also come to our aid here. A document issued by the Chapter of Veszprém on 5 May 1387 sets out an agreement between the abbess of the Veszprémvölgy Convent and a master mason named Konch.[74] This specifies in detail the work to be carried out and the number of buildings to be built. When Bratislava Castle was rebuilt in 1434, an account book recorded many details of the organization responsible for the work,[75] including a separate group charged with the administration. At the top of the hierarchy was György Rozgonyi, *ispán* of Pozsony County, but the works were supervised by János Kakas, the "agitator" (*sollicitator laborum*). He was assisted by a clerk, a tally-clerk, a lower-ranking foreman, and three workshop assistants. The tradesmen were supervised by Konrád Erlingi (*magister lapicidarum*). There were many trades – stone-breakers, carpenters, blacksmiths, coopers, rope-makers and painters – involved in the work. On average, two hundred and twenty to two hundred and forty people worked on the site.

The forests supplied ample material for the timber trades.[76] The carpenter had to have a wide range of skills. He put up wooden structures for buildings, scaffolding and roofs. He also made the log structures for wells and the wellheads.[77] Surviving wooden artifacts tell of diverse forms, progress in technique, and varying demands. Excavations in Buda Castle have turned up large numbers of wooden objects used in the kitchen: salt cellars, leavening troughs, wooden spoons, wooden plates and bowls, wooden stoppers, wooden flasks, and bellows.[78] Some of these were turned on a lathe, others are barrel-like products made with staves and hoops. A fine carved bookcase and the "Matthias stalls" at Bardejov are products of the advanced workshops which appeared in the late medieval period (*see* Fig. 18.8).[79] Foreign influences are perceptible in some workshops: just to give but one example, the altar maker Paul of Levoča in Spiš studied in the workshop of Veit Stoss in Cracow. Transylvanian Saxon furniture shows a direct link with contemporary south German and Tyrolean furniture.

Bone carvers used similar techniques, just different material, and it is possible they worked together with woodworkers in the same workshop. The

---

73   Miklós 2002.
74   Mályusz et al. (eds.) 1951–2017, I, no. 53.
75   Szűcs 1958 and Bischoff 2006.
76   Szabó 2005, 67–70.
77   Miklós 1997a.
78   Irásné Melis 1971–1972, 32–36 and Holl 2005a, 330–348.
79   Marosi 2009.

FIGURE 18.8   The Matthias stalls at Bardejov (from 1483; Hungarian National Museum).

Buda workshop stands out from the rest, and the site has been successfully excavated, yielding items related to various stages in the working process. Chessmen are characteristic finds of royal or baronial residences (Visegrád, Pomáz-Klissza, Diósgyőr, Nagyvázsony).[80] The fine proportions of bone artifacts were achieved on the lathe. The remains of semi-finished products found at Visegrád have further refined our picture of bone craftsmanship.[81] Bone-mounted belts occur quite frequently in medieval graves.[82]

80 Petényi 1994, 52–55.
81 Gróf and Gróh 2001.
82 K. Németh 2005, 287.

Glass was used both in construction and for household objects. The raw materials of glass were sand, sandstone powder and potash recovered from burnt beech wood, and were converted into glass products in the "glass house".[83] The materials were first put into the frit kiln at a relatively low temperature, melted in another kiln and cooled in a third. Glassblowers dipped a pipe into the liquid glass and blew it into vessels. There was a perceptible boom in the glass industry in Hungary in the fifteenth century. Until then any domestic initiatives had been swamped by the mass of imports, especially from Venice. As part of a policy of weakening his enemy economically, Sigismund attempted to keep Venetian goods out of the lands under his control. This opened up the market to domestic glass makers. Master glass makers also came from Italy: Antonius Italicus was working in Óbuda in 1438–1439. The court's demand for glassware was satisfied by the recently excavated glass house in Visegrád.[84] Venetian glass remained the standard to look up to: Buda excavations have discovered fragments of vessels that imitated Venetian forms.[85] The quality of products was very uneven, and those found outside the main centers are generally of much lower standard.

Other Crafts

Pottery is the subject of scattered mentions in written sources, but is a ubiquitous and often the dominant part of archaeological finds. Archaeologists have long perceived the methodological potential in these.[86] Because of the demand from every household, potteries were to be found in nearly every town and village. Although potters' basic ways of working did not fundamentally change for centuries, some technical innovations are perceptible in Hungary. There were two kinds of cooking vessel in the Árpádian age: ceramic and clay pots. The latter was hardly used anywhere outside of the Carpathian Basin. Its shape, with a rounded base, imitated the form of metal cooking pot.[87] There were clay flasks and bowls and small ceramic pots (beakers) for serving and consuming food. Until the early thirteenth century, pottery was generally a village handicraft.[88] Potters served the needs of their immediate locality, and did not compete with each other. The development of urban crafts changed this situation. Vessels thrown on fast, foot-driven wheels, made from new kinds

---

83   H. Gyürky 1986a.
84   Mészáros 2008 and Mészáros and Szőke 2008.
85   H. Gyürky 1974.
86   Takács 1986.
87   Takács 2012b, 234–241 and 269.
88   Takács 2007, 64–66.

of clay that fired to a light color, appeared on the market and led to the abandonment of the old techniques. Major technical changes in pottery started to appear in the fourteenth century. This was related to the higher standards and increasing volume demanded by the rising urban population that the coiling technique used in the Árpádian age could not satisfy. The change did not of course take place overnight, and the old techniques clearly persisted for a long time. The main innovation was the fast-turning heavy potter's wheel, mounted on a solidly-built structure standing on legs with a lower cylinder or batten. The rapid rotation resulted in a more regular shape and even wall thickness, with a smooth surface over the whole piece. Decoration became more sophisticated: designs scratched in erratic lines gave way to regular ribs, and the rim was formed into a pattern. Polychromatic glazes led to products of much higher aesthetic standard. By the fifteenth century, Hungarian potters were able to satisfy nearly every demand, as the wide diversity of finds bears out. Only highly durable cooking pots and special-function large storage vessels, crucibles and the different fine ceramics had to be imported.[89] Potters sometimes based their designs on the work of other crafts. In search of new forms, earthenware cups were made in imitation of contemporary metal and glass cups.

King Matthias's ambitious building projects required potters that could produce building ceramics, and some of them came from Italy. The Buda Majolica ware workshop[90] was founded by master Petrus Andreas from Faienza, yet his associates included Hungarian potters (see Fig. 18.9). The floor bricks, vessels and mixed-glaze stove tiles used to fit out the royal palace bear the traces of Italian technology. Some of the ornaments also followed Italian precursors, but the cups reflect the local Gothic style (in Buda).

Potters were also responsible for the main components of stove tiles, a means of heating which first appeared in the area of northern Switzerland and southern Germany in the twelfth century. Stoves walls were originally made of plate-like elements, later replaced by ceramic tiles. These were usually square or rectangular, and could be decorated. Tile stoves became very widespread. Comparative studies have distinguished workshops with their own formal vocabulary and different manufacturing techniques, and shown up their interactions.[91]

Crafts in medieval Hungary make up a very diverse picture, but with some remaining blank patches, owing to lack of sources. Craft industry was an organic part of everyday life, and the products and services of craftsmen were used

---

89 Holl 1990, 263–267.
90 Kovács 2008 and Fényes 2008.
91 Kocsis et al. 2003, 398–402.

FIGURE 18.9   *Majolica ware from the Buda workshop (ca. 1480–1490 Budapest History Museum).*

by every sector of society. Craft industries came under all kinds of influences, and wandering craftsmen accumulated diverse impressions. Chief among the formative influences were the customer base, social position and financial conditions.

CHAPTER 19

The Economy of Castle Estates in the Late Medieval Kingdom of Hungary

István Kenyeres

Period Boundaries and Scope of Research

In the thirteenth and fourteenth centuries, possession of castles became the key to power in the Kingdom of Hungary. The castle was more than just a military base; its lord had command of the surrounding estate, giving him judicial and seigneurial authority over the inhabitants. Castle estates were thus the basic sources of military and economic strength, and the ranking in the power elite enjoyed by prelates and nobles, and indeed by the king and queen themselves, ultimately derived from the number of castles and estates they held.[1] Of course, not every castle in the medieval Kingdom of Hungary was associated with an estate (border castles, later the southern defensive border forts, etc.) and not every estate had a castle at its center. The vast majority of settlements, however, were villages and market towns belonging to some castle estate. The main exceptions were free royal towns and towns or regions with other privileges. For the economic historian, castle estates offer a framework for macro-studies covering the majority of the kingdom's rural population.

Research Questions and Sources

The paucity of medieval sources on Hungary, especially sources useful for economic investigations, has hitherto largely restricted the discussion to the economy of ecclesiastical estates.[2] The relatively few studies of secular landlords' estates have focused on the numbers of estate centers, landlords' residences, manors and tenant peasants; the process of abandonment of villages; and the

---

1   Fügedi 1977, 14–15, Engel 2003a, 101–102, Engel 2003b, 162–172 and Engel 2001, 324–328.
2   A few important studies (with no claim to completeness): Holub 1943, Fügedi 1981a, Kalász 1932, Romhányi 2010a, Romhányi 2010b and Romhányi 2010d.

management of estates, particularly the role of landlords' retainers in estate administration.[3]

The prime sources for the economic history of castle estates are the inventories of income (*urbaria*) and account books (*regesta*). Supplementary sources include inventories of the movable property of castles, structures and manors (*inventaria*) and valuations (*aestimationes communis*),[4] which record the values of real estate and movable property as used by the courts. Good control sources are the state tax censuses: those for chamber's profit (*lucrum camarae*) and from the second half of the fifteenth century, the extraordinary war taxes and dues (*contributio, subsidium*) and the *dica*. The tithe (*decima*) registers also have copious data, but treated in isolation they can easily be misleading. The *urbaria* recorded all of the feudal duties such as those due to the landlord. They tell us the numbers of tenant peasant holdings and of landless tenants (owning no more than a house) and the dues extracted from them: the *census*, the dues payable in kind (*munera*) and the as-yet insignificant unpaid labor (*robot*).[5] Account books tell us even more about the estate economy. They cover all kinds of revenue, including such things as the *taxa extraordinaria* payable to the landlord, the dues payable by people in non-feudal bonds, such as the sheep dues of the Vlach shepherds, income from manors, trading activities, etc., customs duty income, other external income collected by the castles, such as the war tax in the Jagiellonian period, and sometimes income from tithes on which the landlord took a lease from the church. The other category of data essential for the study of the estate economy found in the account books is expenditure.

There exist some financial records which cover several estates owned by the same aristocratic family. Such are the account books for the northeast Hungarian estates of the Szapolyai family in the period 1517–1519,[6] and – from the post-Mohács period – for the Thurzó family's estates in what is now western Slovakia between 1543 and 1546.[7] These give a good insight into the economy of a group of large secular estates at the time, and the central administration and financial management of estates.

---

3 Sinkovics 1933, Kubinyi 1973a, Kubinyi 1986, Kubinyi 1989, Kubinyi 1991a, Kubinyi 1991b, Neumann 2003 and Kenyeres 2004.
4 Kubinyi 2001b.
5 For the terms, see Engel 2001, 224 and 274.
6 MNL OL DL 26 161.
7 MNL OL E 196 Archivum familiae Thurzo Fasc. 12. fol. 539–586 and 509–537.

Except for ecclesiastical estates, there are hardly any "classical" estate accounts and *urbaria* from the period before the battle of Mohács.[8] Even though economic literacy on estates expanded very quickly in Hungary from the late fifteenth century, there are only twenty-four–twenty-five estates or large estates for which *urbaria* or accounts survive from the period 1490–1530.[9] An even greater problem is that nearly all estate accounts dating from before 1526 are incomplete. In order to establish anything meaningful about the subject, we are therefore obliged to push the boundary of investigation to the end of the 1540s. No official instructions regarding estate administration have survived (neither were many of these written in the Middle Ages), but there are a great many documents, mainly private correspondence (*missilis*) which mention, or were issued by, estate office-bearers. These include specific orders and instructions and documents relating to the rendering of accounts or material liability relating to these. There are some estates for which we have official instructions from the post-Mohács period, but these only survive in any numbers from after 1550.[10]

The best documented private estates in the period immediately before and after the battle of Mohács are the Gyula and Hunedoara estates belonging to George, margrave of Brandenburg.[11] There are accounts for the Hunedoara estate from the periods 1511–1522 and 1530–1534,[12] and for the Gyula estate from between 1524 and 1528. It is also for Gyula that we have the only source that can really be interpreted as an official instruction.[13] The only other estate with

---

8   Edited sources concerning some important ecclesiastical estates: E. Kovács (ed.) 1992, Kredics and Solymosi (eds.) 1993, Kredics, Madarász and Solymosi (eds.) 1997 and Solymosi (ed.) 2002.

9   Kubinyi 1993b, 14, Szabó 1975, 22, 55–56 and 65. Some important source editions: Pataki 1973, Kovács 1998, Prickler 1998 and Nógrády (ed.) 2011.

10 Kenyeres (ed.) 2002. The earliest instructions in this volume are: Magyaróvár: 1532. I, 392–399, Šariš: 1540. II, 522–527, bishopric of Eger: 1546. I, 144–149, archbishopric of Esztergom: 1550. I, 207–214, Trenčín 1549. II, 743–748, Muráň: 1550. II, 476–480 and Szigetvár 1550. II, 641–646.

11 Records of these two estates are known from source editions (Veress 1938 and Pataki 1973), it should be noted, however, that in the Brandenburg Archives – Staatsarchiv Nürnberg Brandenburgisches Archiv, Brandenburger Literalien (copies of charters are to be found at MNL OL DF U 659) – a considerable amount of accounts survived as regards the Slavonian possessions of the margrave (Varaždin, Medvedgrad, Rakovec, Vrbovec, Krapina). See e.g. MNL OL DF 267 358, 267 359, 267 362 and 267 367.

12 Pataki 1973, 1–127.

13 Veress 1938, 87–91 (no. 119), 91–93 (no. 121), 94–95 (no. 122), 98–107 (no. 127), 114–116 (no. 137), 116–120 (no. 138) and 130–131 (no. 147).

a similar wealth of sources is Magyaróvár, a large tract of land covering most of Moson County which became the property of Queen Mary Habsburg, wife of King Louis II in 1522.[14] A very detailed *urbarium* survives from 1525,[15] and there are surviving accounts of the estate spanning the years 1531–1547.[16] The Magyaróvár estate accounts are practically the only set of sources which represent large estates in Hungary subsequent to 1526. It is also from here that we have the earliest official instructions, the first being from 1532.[17]

Economic Management of Castle Estates

Administration of large medieval estates was handled by the landlord's retainers.[18] At the top of the administrative organization were the castellan (*castellanus*), the steward (*provisor*, Hungarian *udvarbíró*) and the chief officer (*officialis*).[19] After these came the customs duty collectors, under-stewards, forest wardens, etc. The landlord's residence was the administrative center of the estate, and it was here that the office of steward first appeared with the Latin title *comes curiae, iudex curiae*, the origin of the Hungarian term *udvarbíró* (estate judge). In the fifteenth century, the Latin title gradually changed to *provisor curiae*, and then simply *provisor*. This word derives from the verb *provideo*, in the sense of arranging or obtaining something in advance, so that the *provisor* was basically somebody who provided or obtained something (usually food).[20] The Latin etymology well reflects the change in the duties of the title holder, because towards the end of the medieval period his responsibilities as a judge were overshadowed by his provisioning duties. The German-language title is also unusual, because before Mohács the term *Hofrichter* corresponded to *iudex curiae*, and had a different meaning than it had in German-speaking lands (where it usually referred to a judicial office in

---

14 For the estates and incomes of Mary of Hungary in Hungary, see Kenyeres 2007.
15 Országos Széchényi Könyvtár [National Széchényi Library], Kézirattár [Manuscript collection], Quart. Germ. 168 (MNL OL DF 290 627).
16 Vienna, Österreichisches Staatsarchiv (ÖStA), Haus-, Hof- und Staatsarchiv (HHStA), Belgien Manuscrits Divers (MD) no. 17 (3741), 18 (3742), 19 (3743).
17 Kenyeres (ed.) 2002, I, 392–399.
18 Sinkovics 1933, 6–30.
19 Szekfű 1912, 37–46, Bónis 2003, 181–185, Kubinyi 1973a, 3–44, Kubinyi 1986, 197–225 and Draskóczy 1989.
20 Finály 1884, 1611. Szenczi Molnár's dictionary refers to the word *provisor* with the meaning of *gondviselő* ('caretaker'). At the same time, in the Hungarian–Latin index *udvarbíró* translates as *provisor*. Cf. Szenci 1604.

the royal court). The equivalent of *udvarbíró* in Austro-German terminology was *Pfleger*, having the same meaning as *provisor*, suggesting that this is the origin of the word. Indeed the *Pfleger* did originally have a judicial function too, but in the late medieval period primarily performed administrative and estate-management duties.[21]

It seems that the economic affairs of the estate initially fell within the duties of the castellan.[22] It was in the late fourteenth, and even more so in the fifteenth century that stewards began to take on financial responsibilities. With no instructions to go on, the duties and powers of the medieval steward can only be discerned from estate documents (*urbaria*, account books) and *missiles*. The office first appeared in the landlord's residence on the estate (which may be what the terms *iudex curiae, provisor curiae* and *provisor curiae castri* refer to) and – drawing a parallel with the story of the office of *judex curiae regiae* (chief justice) – almost certainly involved duties as deputy in the landlord's powers as judge.[23] This judicial function, however, increasingly gave way to estate management and providing for the landlord's family and the numerous and assorted inhabitants of the castle. In the fifteenth century, the *provisor* of a large estate comprising several estates increasingly served in the lord's residence, while the castellans were located in the castles at the center of each estate. From the second half of the fifteenth century, we encounter the office of *provisor castri* in a specific estate, and with increasing frequency, it is held by the same person as the castellan. From the early sixteenth century, there were two castellans in the larger estates, one of which also held the office of *provisor*. In the system of estate administration which evolved by the late fifteenth or early sixteenth centuries, the *provisor* stood at the head of the estate's economic and administrative apparatus. He took in all of the income, arranged all of the administrative affairs and was also usually the treasurer. The castellan supervised the castles and the lands attaching to it. He also held jurisdiction over the people of the castle estate, and so was their judge. The castellans also commanded the castle's armed forces. By the end of the Middle Ages, the *udvarbíró*, despite the literal meaning of his title, rarely sat as judge over the people of the estate, and with very restricted competence. This function was usually performed by the castellan and the *officialis* in the lord's seat, or by the *udvarbíró* together with invited jurors.[24] The castellans and *udvarbíró*s were the landlord's closest retainers. The castellan's duties were primarily military,

---

21 Olberg 1984.
22 Bónis 2003, 181.
23 For the parallel between noble and royal estates, see Bónis 2003, 144 and 182.
24 Kubinyi 1964d, 69 and Varga 1958, 12–13 and 41–42.

and the *udvarbíró*'s economic, but the two areas were not clearly delineated. This is clear from the fact that the same retainer could serve as castellan and then *udvarbíró*, or even both at the same time. The primary qualification for the office was thus not expertise (in business, financial administration, farming, etc.), but loyalty to the lord of the estate.

No completely homogeneous system of estate administration emerged in the medieval period, and structures were strongly influenced by local conditions. Major factors were the size of the estate and the landlord's rank among the barons, dignitaries and prelates of the kingdom. Another defining characteristic was that a magnate who owned several estates supervised the economic affairs of his extensive lands in person or via one of his family members. In the system of criteria devised by András Kubinyi, one of the identifying marks of an aristocratic residence was that it was the administrative center of the magnate's estates. Thus the Újlakis governed their estate from Ilok, the Szapolyais from Trenčín and the Kanizsais from Sárvár.[25] We know that the member of the Szapolyai family who lived in the residence dealt with estate affairs with the counsel of local officials: castellans and *udvarbíró*s.[26] It was also the head of the Újlaki family who retained executive control, and if he died, the estates were managed by an appointed "regency council" headed by the castellan of Kaposújvár.[27]

From the early sixteenth century onwards, we also have some specific data on the administration of secular estates. Let us look at the example of the Gyula estate. There are documents which may be regarded as instructions: the *conventio* and *ordo* (decree) which George, margrave of Brandenburg, issued to the officers of the castle and estate.[28] Although the decree lumps together the duties for the castle's castellans and the *provisor curiae*, those assigned to the *provisor* can be clearly discerned, as can the apparatus for economic governance of the estate. The decree tells us that there were two castellans and one *provisor* at the head of the estate. In practice, one of the castellans was also the *provisor*. The *provisor* had to keep accounts of all items of income, large or small. He had to obtain a receipt for every item of expenditure and enclose it with the accounts. His duties for the manors were more than supervision. He had to "reform" them, increase cultivation on the estate, and buy calves and

---

25   Kubinyi 1989, 89 and Kubinyi 1991a, 215–216.
26   Kubinyi 1991a, 215–216 and Kenyeres 2004.
27   Kubinyi 1989, 89 and Kubinyi 1991a, 215–216.
28   Veress 1938, 77–79 (no. 104). See also Bónis 2003, 173–174, Szabó 1975, 60–61. See also the similar 'instruction' regarding the Slavonian possessions of the margrave issued in 1520. MNL OL DF 267 672.

bullocks and have them raised on the manors, all with a view to providing a surplus for the lord. The *provisor* also had to supervise the forests. The lord prescribed that the castle was always to be provisioned with food for one year. The castellans exercised jurisdiction over the estate villages, receiving fines up to one florin. Higher fines were collected by the *provisor* for the landlord. The *officiales*, known as *ispán*s (*officiales seu ispani possessionum*) were responsible for local administration. On several large estates, there was a division into areas known as *officiolatus* or *districtus*, under the supervision of *officiales*, *ispán*s or *kenéz*es. Returning to the Gyula decree, an interesting novelty was that the *notarius*, paid by the *provisor*, was replaced by an official who took an oath directly to the lord, from whom he received his pay. This was based on a German equivalent, the *Gegenschreiber* (controller).[29] The function of financial controller of the estate on the German model had therefore appeared in Gyula by the early sixteenth century, but seems to have been an exception, no such function being found on any other estate prior to Mohács. Gyula is also exceptional in several other respects, all deriving from the efforts of its German lord to transplant the Brandenburg model to his Hungarian estates. In the other estates, especially those of the magnates, some specialization was introduced into the administrative apparatus, the *provisor* being joined by the scribe (*scriba, notarius*), bailiff (*racionista*), estate attorney (*procurator*) and others, and there was increasing emphasis on the *provisor*'s obligation to render accounts.

The Economy of Castle Estates

Castle-estate economics embraces several different subject areas. Here we will examine the principal economic data of a few well-sourced estates. This basically involves drawing up the balance sheet for each estate based on its surviving account books. These, together with the *urbaria*, also contain a wealth of data that could be useful for agricultural history studies – output, peasant-landlord relations, etc. – and could make important contributions to research into castle construction and material culture in general.

We begin with the estates' cash income and expenditure. Although income in kind, chiefly in the form of grain – wheat, rye, oats, barley, spelt, etc. – and wine, and in some places pigs and sheep, was also very important, late

---

29 "Item. Quod notarius de hinc, qui antea habuit salarium a provisore curiae, deinceps a domino Ill[ustrissi]mo sallarium suum exspectet, et sit juratus domino Ill[ustrissi]mo, sicut consuetum est in Germania: Gegenschreiber." – Veress 1938, 79 (no. 104).

medieval account books did not usually record these two kinds of income together. Some separate records were kept for income in kind, but since much more weight was attached to the cash accounts at the time, it is no surprise that they survive in greater numbers. Why was this? Perhaps it is related to the increasing prevalence of the money economy at this time, as pointed out by István Szabó.[30] Since payments in kind were diminishing, there was less need for landlords to keep record of them. If cash transactions were indeed becoming more prevalent, however, we might wonder why – as András Kubinyi put it – "most of the estate's income went on management expenses" and "however large a baron's estates were, he could not be sure of an income that would pay the costs of presenting himself as an aristocrat."[31] Indeed, Kubinyi saw large estates as having been rescued from serious financial trouble only by the military reforms of 1498–1500, which officially granted landlords some of the state war tax,[32] and by the *taxa extraordinaria* (also the focus of more recent research) which the lords could impose at will.[33]

We will concentrate here on data for the above-mentioned three large estates: Gyula and Hunedoara, belonging to George of Brandenburg, and Queen Mary's estate of Magyaróvár. The economic geography of these three estates was widely divergent, and they were located in distant parts of the kingdom. Magyaróvár, in the Little Hungarian Plain, lay near the Austrian border in an area of free royal towns, and boasted fertile land, fishponds and extensive viticulture. Gyula was one of the largest estates on the Great Hungarian Plain, mainly in the central and southern parts of Békés County, along the Fehér-Körös, Fekete-Körös and Kondoros Rivers, and in the western corner of Zaránd County along the Fehér-Körös. It also had productive grain fields and pasture. The estate of Hunedoara in Transylvania lay in the counties of Hunyad and Temes, mostly in the eastern Apuseni Mountains but extending into the Transylvanian Ore Mountains and the Tisza–Maros–Danube Interfluve (Temesköz) area. It had less grain-growing land, but included the kingdom's foremost iron ore mining and iron works, and significant gold mining. These three estates also were also distinctively large for the Kingdom of Hungary: Magyaróvár had an area of 1115.79 square kilometers; Gyula 2232.6 square

---

30   Szabó 1975, 65.
31   Kubinyi 1993b, 15.
32   Engel 2001, 358, Kubinyi 1993b, 16. A detailed account of the reform: Kubinyi 1982 and Kubinyi 2000c.
33   Nógrády 1996 and Nógrády 2002.

kilometers, and Hunedoara 1611.1 square kilometers, so that together they covered nearly 5000 square kilometers (4959.49 square kilometers).[34]

We will examine how much cash the estates provided for their owners, how the income was distributed, and what it was spent on. The other main questions concern contributions in kind and other sources of income. We will consider how these related to each other and whether the money generated by the land went to boost the magnate's wealth or had to be spent on the estate's own expenses.

First, let us examine the cash income stated in the accounts from year to year:[35]

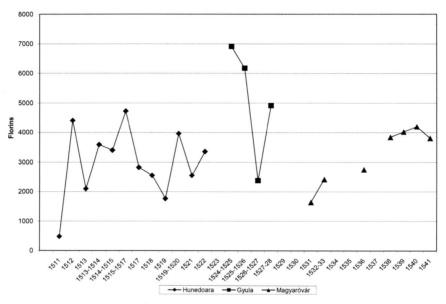

FIGURE 19.1   *Cash income from the Hunedoara, Gyula and Magyaróvár estates (1511–1541).*

---

34 Based on the map of Engel 2002.
35 The accounts of Hunedoara estate from 1518, 1521 and 1522: Pataki 1973, 42 and 47–48. Revenues from the years 1511 to 1523: Pataki 1973, LXXXIX. The accounts of Gyula estate from 1524 to 1527: Veress 1938, 116––121 (no. 138). In the case of Magyaróvár, the accounts from 1531, 1532–1533, and 1536: ÖStA HHStA Belgien MD 17 (3741).

The graph shows that the truly large estate of Hunedoara had a typical annual cash income of between 3000 and 4000 florins,[36] although there were wide fluctuations around this figure. Gyula's income was also highly variable, but in general the estate provided George of Brandenburg with 6000–7000 florins, more than twice the sum in Hunedoara. (We will return to the reasons for the dip in 1526/1527.) For Magyaróvár, we have data through the 1530s and up to 1541, showing that income there, in contrast to the other estates, increased steadily from between 1000 and 2000 florins at the beginning to 4000 florins.

Now we will look at the general conclusions that may be drawn from the structure of income in each estate.

TABLE 19.1 *Income of the Hunedoara estate (1518, 1521–1522)*

Income	1518	%	1521	%	1522	%
War dues	486	19.0	892	34.9	483	14.4
Extraordinary dues					900	26.9
Gold exchange	815	31.9	585	22.9	688	20.5
Census (on peasant holdings)	564	22.1	588.5	23.0	573	17.1
Fines		0.0		0.0	52	1.6
Mill income	28	1.1	20	0.8	38	1.1
Customs duty	35.5	1.4	15	0.6		
Redemption of pork and honey dues, table money	139.5	5.5	71	2.8	31	0.9
"Fiftieth" (tax on Romanians)	283	11.1				
Redemption of sheep dues and sale	72	2.8				
Income from mining and processing iron ore	131.7	5.2	381.8	15.0	585.7	17.5
Total	2554.7	100	2553.3	100.0	3350.7	100.0

36 The main currency of the period was the (golden) florin, and its change the denar (*denarius*). In the fifteenth century, 100 denars made a (golden) florin. From the end of the fifteenth century and in the sixteenth century the florin was used as an accounting currency of the treasure and the chamber, being the equivalent of 100 denars. The exchange rate of the golden florin was about 150–160 denars in the same period. Below we refer to the amounts in accounting currency, where a florin was worth 100 denars.

The table clearly shows which sources of income dominated in the Hunedoara estate. The largest items were the extraordinary dues levied by the landlord, and war dues. Taken together, these two made up 20–40 % of the total in the three years studied. The war dues included two separate categories of tax levied at the time. One was the army dues (*pecunia exercitualis*) collected from their own estates by those lords required by law to maintain their own militia (*banderium*),[37] and the royal war tax to be collected for the treasury on every estate, the *dica* (*contributio, subsidium*).[38] The margrave was permitted – as we will see – to collect both of these taxes for himself, but not every year. Out of the three years studied here, he could keep both of them only in 1521, which explains the higher figure for war dues in that year. A special source of income was gold exchange, granted to the lords of the Hunedoara estate in the fifteenth century.[39] This made up 20–30 % of the total. The census, in principle the main source of income due by right of title, was essentially constant at 560–580 florins, or 17–22 %. The other classic seigneurial dues were substantial only in 1518, and steadily declined in importance, giving way to the rising local phenomenon, iron ore working, from which the income recorded in the accounts went up from 5 % of the total at the beginning of the period to 15–17 % by the end. Being relatively poorly endowed with agricultural resources, Hunedoara had a special income structure, in which two local sources of income, gold exchange and iron ore working, were prominent, but even they were overshadowed by the state war tax collected by the landlord and the landlord's own extraordinary tax. Since we also have figures for these two sources of income (the two kinds of war dues and the extraordinary dues), it is interesting to examine them in detail:[40]

---

37   Engel 2001, 183.
38   For the terminology and concept, see Engel 2001, 358, Kubinyi 2000c, 401–407, Kubinyi 1994a, 290–291 and Kubinyi 1998b. In Hunedoara the royal *dica* was *taxa regia secundum constitucionem huius regni, dica regia, königs anschnit* and in 1521 *dica waywodalis*. The army dues *pecunia exercitualis* and *raißgelt* [i.e. Reisgeld], and the extraordinary dues are mentioned as *taxa extraordinaria* and *meins gnedigen herrn anschnitt*. Pataki 1973, 2–48.
39   Pataki 1992, 98.
40   For the data, see Pataki 1973, 2–4, 12–16, 25, 27–28 and 42–43.

TABLE 19.2 *War dues and extraordinary dues in Hunedoara (1512–1522)*

Year	Royal war tax	%	Army dues	%	War dues combined as %-age of total income	Extraordinary dues	%	Three categories combined as %-age of total income	Total income
1511/1512	300.3	4.3	315.6	4.5	8.8	683.39	9.8	18.6	6968.59
1513	815.15	27.6			27.6	448	15.2	42.8	2950.9
1514						1229	36.2	36.2	3393.79
1515	666.65	14.1	206.135	4.4	18.4			18.4	4731.54
1517						940	33.2	33.2	2827.79
1518	486	19.0			19.0			19.0	2554.7
1519						700	39.6	39.6	1768.51
1520	505	12.6			12.6	1000	25.0	37.7	3995.37
1521	392	15.4	500	19.6	34.9			34.9	2553.3
1522			483	14.4	14.4	900	26.9	41.3	3350.7

The figures show that taken together, war dues and extraordinary dues accounted on average for a third of the estate's income (32.2 %). The breakdown of the figures, however, also tells us that although extraordinary dues yielded larger sums, they were not usually levied at all if both categories of war dues were available (only in 1512 do all three occur together). It is also striking that royal *dica* was collected more often (seven times, the same number as *taxa extraordinaria*) than army dues (four times). Certainly it would appear that George of Brandenburg obtained the extra sums he wanted through a mutually-complementary combination of these three kinds of dues.

War dues were also the largest item in Gyula, where they similarly comprised both the royal *dica* and the army dues,[41] and added up to a third or a quarter of the estate's cash income in the two years under study. The *taxa*

---

41 According to the accounts from 1524–1525, 815.24 florins were collected in Békés, Zaránd and Arad Counties as royal *dica* (*ex dicis Regalibus*), and 985.71 florins in 1525 as army dues (*taxa exercitualis*). In 1525–1526, 1840 florins came in from Békés and Zaránd Counties as

TABLE 19.3 *Income of the Gyula estate (1524–1526)*

Income	1524/25	%	1525/26	%	1526/27	%
War dues	1800.95	26.1	1840	29.8	37	1.6
Extraordinary seigneurial dues	1412.25	20.4	2389	38.7	27	1.1
Census	348	5.0	847.5	13.7	705	29.6
Mill income	1848.26	26.7	599.5	9.7	473.25	19.9
Customs duties	173.42	2.5	84.6	1.4	115.045	4.8
Fines	338.01	4.9	300.73	4.9	258.41	10.9
Sale of grain (ninth)	781	11.3			627.5	26.4
Sale of other produce (fish, pork, hay, etc.)	151.67	2.2	114.75	1.9	89.52	3.8
Other seigneurial income (redemption of pig dues, inheritances, forestry income, etc.)	59.34	0.9	3.65	0.1	46.92	2.0
Total	6912.9	100	6179.73	100	2379.645	100
Total, less war dues	5111.95	73.9	4339.73	70.2	2342.645	98

extraordinaria, stated as dues (*taxa*) or aid (*subsidium*),[42] was also quite high in Gyula in these two years, especially in the year of the battle of Mohács (1526), when it made up nearly 40 % of the total. Together, these two sources (war dues and extraordinary dues) amounted to 47 % of income in one of the two years and 68 % in the other. The figures in the table also reveal why income dipped substantially in 1526/1527: that was when no war dues were collected. The following year, the margrave's officials collected the war tax levied by King John Szapolyai, once more significantly increasing cash income.[43] The

war tax, approved for the king – and at this time exceptionally also for the queen (*contributio Regalis et Reginalis Maiestatuum*). See Veress 1938, 98–99 and 117–118.

42 E.g. as *taxa pro Domino Illustrissimo* (1525), and also as *taxa subsidii Illustrissimi Domini* (1526).

43 According to the accounts from 1527–1528 (Veress 1938, 121) the castle had a total revenue of 4921 florins and 8 denars in cash, out of which 823.10 florins (16,7 %) was the *dica*, levied by King John Szapolyai and collected by the officials of the castle, and 1500 florins (30,5 %) was the extraordinary tax.

landlord's ordinary dues amounted to 41.3 % of the total in 1524/1525, 31.6 % in 1525/1526 and 69 % in 1526/1527. The dip in 1525/1526 was because the war dues and extraordinary dues were so high, and the peak in 1526/1527 was because they were absent. It is therefore reasonable to say that the total income from the lord's ordinary dues made up 30–40 % of the total. The census income, despite its apparent variability, was in fact about 700 florins each year. The reason for the smaller figure in the first year is that only the St George's Day (24 April) installment was stated in the accounts, and the other installment, payable on St Michael's Day (29 September), was omitted. A very substantial item was the mill income, especially in the first year, when the kingdom was still at peace. It then understandably diminished, but remained remarkably high in comparison with other estates. Also quite considerable was the landlord's commercial income, mainly from sale of grain acquired from the "ninth" (the lord's share of the harvest, actually one tenth), which was 13 % in 1524 and 33 % in 1525. These two sources of income (mill charges and grain sales) illustrate the grain-growing nature of a fertile tract of the Great Hungarian Plain. Arable farming remained important even as animal rearing grew, so that there was grain left over for sale even after the castle's own needs had been met. (By contrast, the Hunedoara estate used up all of its grain income.) Nonetheless, grain sales only made up 2 % of income in 1526/1527, probably because of the vicissitudes of the year of Mohács, and the increased military demand for grain.

TABLE 19.4 *Income of the Magyaróvár estate (1531–1536)*

Cash income	1531	%	1532–33	%	1536	%
Census	218.4	13.3	278.4	11.5	505.6	18.3
Customs and ferries	1113.6	67.9	653.6	27.0	1397.6	50.7
Pasture rent	81.6	5.0	38.4	1.6	115.2	4.2
Fishponds	4	0.2			35.2	1.3
Fines					56.8	2.1
Wine sales			380	15.7	302.4	11.0
Salt sales			653.2	27.0	133.6	4.8
Cowhide sales			79.6	3.3		
Sale of produce	205.6	12.5			211.2	7.7
Payments by landlord	16	1.0	336	13.9		
Total	1639.2	100	2419.2	100	2757.6	100

The most striking contrast we find in the Magyaróvár estate accounts for the first half of the 1530s is the absence of war dues and extraordinary dues. In fact we know that war tax was collected for Queen Mary (e.g. 349 florins in 1542), and by the castellan of Magyaróvár himself, but it was not stated among the estate income. Also remarkable is the magnitude of the customs income for the estate. The source of this was the cattle trade, for which the Magyaróvár estate was one of the main stations on the road to Vienna. Cattle not sold in Vienna was also rested and, if necessary, overwintered there, resulting in substantial grazing rent for the estate. Also in striking contrast with the two Brandenburg estates is the substantial income on seigneurial wine sales (*educillatio vinorum*). This was based on the estate's extensive vineyards around Lake Fertő (Neusiedler See) at Neusiedl am See and Rust, and substantial ninth dues payable on wine. There was also notable income from selling produce, which was in abundance. Income from grain included the tithes leased from the Győr chapter, and grain could be sold at good prices to merchants from Székesfehérvár and Pest. Then there was a somewhat exceptional source of income: salt. The salt trade had been a royal monopoly until Mohács, but in the new circumstances, the salt mines of Maramureş and Transylvania fell into the possession of John Szapolyai. As a result, Queen Mary, a devoted supporter of her brother Ferdinand I Habsburg (1526–1564) after Hungary split into two, could not get her hands on the salt from her east Hungarian mines (the Maramureş salt chamber in principle belonged to her). The solution was to set up a separate salt chamber and places for selling salt in Magyaróvár and the larger market towns, such as Neusiedl am See, and to bring salt down the Danube from Vienna.

Now we will examine estate expenditure. Expenditure accounts for Hunedoara are not available for all of the above years. For 1518, for example, only the total is known (2580 florins 12 denars).

About two thirds of the castle expenses in Hunedoara went towards the pay of the castellans, the garrison and the hussars. The latter, some of which were taken on for a year's service (*jargalás*) and others paid monthly, accounted for 20–30 % of the total. The castle's material expenses varied between 8 and 17 %, and iron working and gold exchange 8–13 %. It is interesting that the estate showed a substantial surplus in 1521 and in 1522 – if we take into account that the largest item of expenditure in 1522 was nearly 1300 florins sent to the margrave. The estate therefore yielded quite substantial sums for the landlord in some financial years. The account books of 1515–1517 show that George of Brandenburg had nearly 1800 florins (65 % of expenditure) sent to himself,

TABLE 19.5 *Expenditure of Hunedoara estate (1521–1522)*

Expenditure	1521	%	1522	%
Castellans' pay	440	21.5	440	13.6
Wine for castellans	80	3.9	95	2.9
Procurators' pay	24	1.2	24	0.7
Garrison	166	8.1	166	5.1
Hussars on annual service	114	5.6		0.0
Monthly-paid hussars	482.5	23.6	590	18.3
Other expenditure on castle	351.09	17.2	272.79	8.4
Kitchen expenditure	11	0.5	16	0.5
To cultivation of seigneurial vineyards	57	2.8	53	1.6
Wine purchase	48	2.3		0.0
Gold exchanges expenses	111	5.4	76	2.4
Iron working expenses	158.85	7.8	195.34	6.0
Money changing expenses			4.5	0.1
Sent to lord			1297.2	40.2
Total	2043.44	100	3229.83	100
Balance	+509.86	(25.0)	+120.87	(3.7)

mainly to Buda, and in general about 40 % of expenditure comprised sums sent to meet his needs.[44]

The table shows that in Gyula the pay of the castellans, the garrison, the castle folk and the craftsmen took up about 40 % of expenditure in the first two years, although the military expenditure for 1524/1525 also includes the county militia enlisted out of war dues. These expenses made up nearly 90 % of the total in 1526/1527, when there was no income from war dues. These figures therefore tell us that without war dues, even a major estate such as Gyula could run into economic troubles. At the same time it is notable that the estate could provide cash of up to 2000 florins for its owner if required, and in the year of the battle of Mohács, two thirds of its expenditure went to meet the needs of the margrave or on expenses he ordered, and not on the Gyula estate.

44 Pataki 1992, 100–101 and Pataki 1973, 14.

TABLE 19.6 *Gyula estate expenditure (1524–1527)*

Expenditure	1524/1525	%	1525/1526	%	1526/1527	%
Sent to lord	1900	33.2	296	4.0	250	10.5
Payments made by lord's command	50	0.9	4200	57.0	0	0.0
Soldiers' pay	1097.28	19.2	252	3.4	405	17.0
Castellans' pay	136	2.4	213.91	2.9	469.7	19.7
Retainers, castle folk, craftsmen	126.21	2.2	138	1.9	274.28	11.5
Wine bought for castle	628.9	11.0	1179.48	16.0	360.7	15.1
For castle needs	1397.72	24.4	1088.17	14.8	626.96	26.3
Arrears	386	6.7	5	0.1		
Total	5722.11	100	7372.56	100	2386.64	100
Balance	+1190.79		−1192.83		−7.0	

So George of Brandenburg could look to both Hunedoara and Gyula for substantial sums from year to year, if not both estates every year, and when he was in particular need, as in the year of Mohács, he could get his hands on larger sums than average.

It is striking that the Magyaróvár estate, despite being supported from Mary's other sources of income, ran a substantial deficit in these years. The largest expenditure items were pay and provisioning of castle personnel, accounting for nearly half of the total, but there were also major castle reinforcement works in 1532–1533 (11 %), in 1536 (22 %) and also later 1538 (10.5 %) and 1539 (15.4 %). The first signs of investments intended to raise estate income were emerging, however, in the form of expenditure on the salt trade and the seigneurial vineyards. It should be added that after the 1530s, the estate was able to finance the modest number of estate staff and soldiers, and even provided some surplus to be sent to the landlord, Queen Mary. Indeed, the Magyaróvár estate started to generate an increasing level of profit for its owner: Captain Ulrich Freiherr von Eitzing paid to Queen Mary's cashier the sum of 2305 florins in 1542/1543, although this included the war tax. The Magyaróvár estate contributed more than a third (38 %) of the 5963 florins which Queen Mary derived that year from what was one of her major sources of income, the Bratislava thirtieth customs duty.[45] The Castellan of Magyaróvár, Jacob von

---

45   Engel 2001, 156 and 226.

THE ECONOMY OF CASTLE ESTATES   411

TABLE 19.7 *Magyaróvár estate expenditure (1531–1536)*

Expenditure item	1531	%	1532–33	%	1536	%
Pay of castellan, garrison and craftsmen	612	35.2	1156.8	37.8	875.2	30.1
Provisioning expenses	194.4	11.2	524.8	17.1	661.6	22.8
Castle building			262.4	8.6	561.6	19.3
Travel and other administrative expenses	2.4	0.1	28	0.9	27.2	0.9
Other castle expenses	932	53.5	365.6	11.9		
Lord's vineyards			248	8.1	93.6	3.2
Salt trade costs			478.4	15.6	568.8	19.6
Pensions					117.6	4.0
Total	1740.8	100	3064	100	2905.6	100
Balance	−101.6		−644.8		−148	

Stamp, paid the Queen 500 florins from the castle's income in 1546, and 2000 florins in 1547.[46]

The other major question we have to address is income in kind. Unfortunately, the published accounts for Gyula do not reveal the estate's income in the form of grain, wine, etc., and out of the three years examined for Hunedoara, there are entries for income in kind only for 1518, and these are also very restricted. József Pataki has determined the value of the castle's income in kind for this period as between 1900 and 2100 florins,[47] so that of its almost 5000 florin annual income, cash contributions accounted for two thirds. For Gyula, the absence of other sources forces us to rely on the 1525 income assessment, which gives the enormous figure of 9802 florins for income in kind, of which the wine and pork ninths made up about 4000 each, the grain ninth about 1200 florins, and the produce of the manor only 566 florins. The assessment also states that the estate could make a further 6000 florins from the cattle and horse trade and

---

46   Based on the 1542–1550 accounts of Wolfgang Kremer, who was a (tax)collector (*Einnehmer*) of Queen Mary, and resided in Vienna. See ÖStA HHStA Belgien MD 15 (3739).

47   Pataki 1992, 95–96. Among the edited accounts, there are data on the *naturalia* type of revenues and their value. Cf. Pataki 1973, 1–127. Revenues from crops came close to those of the Gyula estate, but from wine, they were minimal.

TABLE 19.8 *Average income in cash and kind of the three estates (florins)*

Estate (year)	Cash (Florins)	%	Value of produce (Florins)	%	Total
Hunedoara (1518, 1521–1522)	2819.5	58.5	2000	41.5	4819.5
Gyula (1524–1527)	5157.4	34.5	9802	65.5	14959.4
Magyaróvár (1536–1539)	3536	49.4	3616.9	50.6	7152.9

sale of wine.[48] We have much more specific data for Magyaróvár. All grain and wine income is recorded from 1536 onwards, and even its distribution. We can even derive approximate figures for the value of local sales from their prices. The total annual income in kind adds up to between 2500 and 5000 florins, of which two thirds came from wine, although the estate also had very substantial income from grain.

Overall, the available data show income in kind to have made up a substantial proportion of the total. In large, agriculturally well-endowed late medieval estates, the value of produce received could be as much as the cash income. More detailed research would be needed to verify the general validity of the conclusions drawn from the surviving accounts of these three large estates.

To give an impression of what this might involve, we will finish off with a very brief look at some examples taken from the accounts of a medium-sized estate. We can get a clue to the preponderance of war dues and extraordinary dues from the example of the Lockenhaus estate in what is now Austria. There, war dues made up 38 % of income in 1524 and 28 % in 1526. Despite the decrease in relative terms, the latter sum is higher, because it included "army dues" (*pecunia exercitualis*) as well as royal war tax. The reason for the relative decrease was the substantial *taxa extraordinaria* levied in 1526, accounting for 49.5 % of cash income. Without that, war dues would have constituted 56 % of the income that year.[49] The two kinds of war dues made up 60 % of income

---

48   Veress 1938, 87–91 (no. 119). Estimations on the revenues seem to be overstated – even János Ahorn himself, the steward who compiled the register, estimated the total income of the Gyula estate at 11,520 florins; however, if one sums up all the entries he listed, the total would be 19,740 florins.

49   In 1524 the *dica* was 141 florins, and the total revenue was 368.71 florins. MNL OL DL 26 317. In 1526, 114 florins came in as *dica*, and 155 florins as *pecunia exercitualis*, thus, altogether

of George of Brandenburg' Krapina estate in Varasd County in 1516.[50] On the Ónod estate, 11 % of the annual income around 1518 came from war dues and 28 % from extraordinary dues.[51]

There were other ways of increasing cash income, such as the retail and wholesale trade of wine, and the sale of grain. In Lockenhaus, wine sales made up 35 % of income in 1524 and 11 % in 1526 (or 23 % without the *taxa extraordinaria*). In Ónod, retail sales of wine alone made up 30 % of income. Retail and wholesale wine sales were therefore also rising at a remarkable rate. Contributions in kind, especially wine, therefore had considerable value. At Lockenhaus, the 1526 wine accounts record income equivalent to 139 barrels, of which 78 barrels were from the tithes leased from the bishop of Győr (56 %). If we take an average price of 10 florins a barrel,[52] the Lockenhaus wine income was 1390 florins, equivalent to 146 % of annual cash income (942.06 florins). Even in 1524, when the tithes were not leased, the income the castle derived from the mere 35 barrels it sold was equivalent to 95 % of its cash income (368.71 florins). Grain also provided substantial income: the castle estate sold 870 *cubuli* of wheat and rye and 314.5 *cubuli* of oats in 1526. For want of better, we must use the 1536 Magyaróvár figures for the price per *cubulus* of wheat – approximately 46 denars; the price of oats may be taken as half of that, 23 denars. This puts a value of about 400 florins on the sales of wheat and 72 florins 33 denars on those of oats. The whole Lockenhaus grain income was therefore 472 florins 33 denars, so that in 1526, the ratio of cash and in-kind income at Lockenhaus was 1:2. At Ónod, however, using István Szabó's figures, the equivalent ratio was only 0.37. Neither of these figures seem to permit any new generalizations, but they reinforce the importance of contributions in kind.

Overall, it seems that in the period immediately prior to the battle of Mohács, large estates were indeed dependent on their ability to levy war dues, and the landlord could only meet his needs through imposing extraordinary

---

269 florins, whereas the extraordinary tax was 468.4 florins. In that year, the total revenue of the estate was 946.02 florins. MNL OL DL 26 355.

50 The total revenue of the estate was 333.54 florins, out of which 75 florins (22,5 %) was the *dica* (*Kriegsanschnitt*), and 124 florins (37,3 %) the war tax (*Raißsteuer*, i.e. *Reissteuer*). MNL OL DF 267 246.

51 Based on the figures of Szabó 1975, 64.

52 In 1524, 13.5 barrels of wine were sold for the price of 130 florins and 72 denars (i.e. for the average price of 9.68 florins per barrel) in Lockenhaus. MNL OL DL 26 317. For contemporary wine prices averaging around 10 florins per barrel, cf. Nógrády 2002, 453. In a 1528 damage assessment at Lockenhaus, two barrels of wine were bought for 12 florins on the estate (6 florins per barrel), yet it was sold for 9 florins per barrel. Maksay (ed.) 1959, 85 and 87. Thus, the sales price listed above of between 9 and 10 florins seems to be correct.

dues. Without these two sources of income, they would have faced bankruptcy. It is also clear that there were other ways of raising cash income, most notably sale of wine in taverns, wholesale trade of wine by the barrel, sales of grain in some places such as Magyaróvár and Gyula, and some more specialized sources, such as the salt trade in Magyaróvár. There were yet other ways of raising money, such as pledging the thirtieth customs duty, often managed by estate centers, as the Szapolyais did in the 1520s and the Thurzós for the local Trenčín thirtieth in the 1540s. An illustration of how substantial this could be is that 12 % of the Trenčín income was from the Trenčín and Kysucké Nové Mesto thirtieth.[53]

The main source of increasingly-important goods that could be sold for money was not the manorial farm, as Marxist historiography assumed,[54] but, as the example of the Lockenhaus estate showed, the tithe, which was leased by secular landowners from the second half of the fifteenth century onwards. The accounts of the archbishopric of Esztergom and of the bishopric of Eger show that the tithes were regularly let out in the late fifteenth century.[55] If the tithes had already been leased earlier, why does the income from them not appear in estate accounts before the 1520s and 1530s? There are several possible answers to this question, but the paucity of sources makes it difficult to choose between them. Certainly a single tenant often took out a lease on the tithes for the area of several counties. They were not necessarily the local landowner or magnate, but neither was the administration for all tithes in the tenancy necessarily conducted in a single estate, and it is particularly unlikely that a commoner tithe-tenant would have been able to do this.[56] Neither do we know how the tithe tenants sold the produce they collected. Before of the 1520s, there were few estates for which the landlord acquired the tithe tenancy.[57] This became more widespread in the first third of the sixteenth century, and magnates managed to acquire for their large estates tenancies on tithes not only for their own lands but also for parishes beyond them, so that one castle was collecting

---

53 Kenyeres 2004, 138 and Kenyeres 1997, 124–125.
54 Se e.g. Pach 1963, especially 151–159 and Pach 1964. Pach underlined both the establishment of manors and the increase of labor time. Indeed, there are several references to the establishment of manors from this period, yet this did not jumpstart an increase in revenues from the demesne.
55 E. Kovács (ed.) 1992 and Fügedi 1981a, 146–150.
56 Fügedi 1981a, 146.
57 See e.g. the accounts of the estate of Hornstein, dating from 1448, which shows that the collection of tithes (both of crops and wine) was administered by the estate. Tagányi 1895.

tithes from a larger area than its own estate. This might explain the increase in income, but another factor was the progressive nature of the tithe, so that the rising tithe revenue could partly have resulted from increasing agricultural output. Towards the end of the period, therefore, the tithe had an increasing role in providing income in kind, and indirectly it also had its effect on cash income, because it was the source of produce for wine sold in taverns, and for trade in wine and grain. By the middle of the sixteenth century, retailing wine and selling produce based on the tithes was the basis of the income of large estates, and displaced the extraordinary dues and war dues which were recovered by the king. A good illustration of these developments is that on the Šintava estate, 33.8 % of wine income originated from tithes in 1543, and in Hlohovec, they accounted for 32 % of wine income in 1542/1543, 41.7 % in 1544 and 56.6 % in 1545/1546. Also in Hlohovec, we know how much income came from the seigneurial vineyards in 1544, and it made up no more than 4.2 % of the total. On the Šintava estate, wine sold in the lord's taverns provided him with 38 % of his income between 1543 and 1546. In the same period, war dues provided only 12.4 %, and he only levied extraordinary dues once during the three years, when it made up 15 % of the annual income, and 2.8 % of the total over the period. At Hlohovec in the period 1542–1546, wine sold in taverns provided 59 % of cash income, war dues 14.2 %, and extraordinary dues, levied only twice there, a mere 3.2 %. By contrast, on the Trenčín estate, war dues accounted for 26 % and retail wine sales 22 %.[58] War dues completely disappeared as sources of estate income during the 1540s, because by the end of that decade Ferdinand I managed to recover control of their collection for the treasury.[59]

As regards the profitability of estates, the data presented here show that although operating expenses were indeed high, the very large estates were capable of occasionally providing their lords with sums of up to several thousand florins,[60] and the increasing income in kind presented lords with

---

58   MNL OL E 196 Archivum familiae Thurzo Fasc. 12. fol. 539–586 and 509–537. Kenyeres 2008, 397–400 and 456.
59   Kenyeres 2005, 123–124 and 136–137.
60   See the above-mentioned 1517–1519 accounts of the Szapolyai estates in the northeastern part of the Hungarian Kingdom (*see* fn. 6), according to which roughly 6000 florins (5948 florins) were sent either to the center of the Szapolyai estates in Trenčín, or immediately to the Szapolyai brothers to Buda, in addition to paying off local costs. Kenyeres 2008, 250–251. In a slightly different situation, in two years (between 1544 and 1546) 59 %

money-making opportunities through selling wine locally, and commercial sale of produce.[61]

(5937.8 florins) of the 10,048.5 florins received by the central cashier of the Thurzós came from the estates, i.e. Hlohovec, Šintava, Bojnice, Trenčín, Lindva and Nitra, and 34 % from leased thirtieth, foreign trade customs. See also fn. 7.

61   The growing significance of feudal dues in kind, seigneurial wine sales and commercial activities has already been emphasized by Pach. Pach 1963, 145–151. For a summary of the role of tithe leasing, and aristocrats interested in trade during the Jagiellonian period, see Kubinyi 1994a, 299–301 (with further secondary literature).

PART 5

Trade Relations

∴

CHAPTER 20

Domestic Trade in the Árpádian Age

Boglárka Weisz*

The main venue for buying and selling in the Middle Ages was the market, although "shops" did start to appear, at least in larger towns, from the early thirteenth century onwards. Markets continued to grow in number and significance in the thirteenth century as both production and population increased – i.e., driven by the interrelated growth of supply and demand.[1]

Types of Markets

Markets came into being in one of two ways: either by natural evolution, or being regulated into existence. For the former, the grant of market privileges merely represented the reinforcement of an existing activity. One type of the former were the markets which emerged in ecclesiastical and secular centers of administration, such as Kéménd in Baranya County, the center of the Baranya estate complex of the Óvári family, part of the Győr kindred, and Pécs, an ecclesiastical center having only an indirect connection with the great trade routes. The market at the county center of Bački Monoštor is mentioned in sources as early as the eleventh century, and the market town of Nógrád may also have been helped in the development of its market by virtue of being a county center. The connection between administrative centers and markets has prompted the proposition that every county center held a weekly market in the eleventh and twelfth centuries.[2] However, the converse was also true: places where fairs were held later became secular centers: it may be shown that the day of session of county law courts (*sedes judiciaria*, or just *sedria*)[3] was also the day of the weekly market of the town which held jurisdiction.[4]

---

* The author is the leader of the Research Centre for the Humanities, Hungarian Academy of Sciences "Lendulet" Medieval Hungarian Economic History Research Group (LP2015-4/2015).
1 Cf. Weisz 2012b. For population growth see also the contribution by András Kubinyi and József Laszlovszky on demographic issues in the present volume.
2 Fügedi 1961, 32 and Szende 2011c, 389–392.
3 Cf. in details: Engel 2001, 180.
4 Csukovits 1997, 377–378.

The remainder of the fairs developed under the influence of economic and geographical factors – transport intersections, river crossings, or boundaries between areas of countryside that supported the sale of different kinds of produce. To name but a few, these included Sîmbăteni in Arad County beside the River Maros, the main water transport route for salt; Osijek in Baranya County, the most important crossing-point of the River Dráva on one of the busiest military routes, also used as a pilgrims' route to Jerusalem; and Pásztó in Heves County, which lies where the hills rise out of the plain.

These two factors often acted together in the development of markets, as in the cases of two early episcopal cities founded by the Árpádians.[5] The town of Esztergom is discussed below, and Fehérvár, a royal center with prominent ecclesiastical institutions, was also located favorably for the development of its market: it lay on a road intersection where the Bakony Hills meet the Mezőföld (the western edges of the Great Hungarian Plain). These were joined in the mid-thirteenth century by the third royal town, Buda, whose market attained predominance almost at the same time. Its location beside the Danube and at a position in the road network was fundamental to the rise of both the town and its market.

The granting of market charters in the Árpádian age was a royal prerogative, and even an established market could not have operated for long without this form of support.

"Markets" in the Árpádian age mostly comprised weekly markets and annual fairs. Weekly markets were known by the terms *forum ebdomadale, forum sollempne,*[6] *forum generale,*[7] *forum commune,*[8] *forum comprovinciale* or *forum provinciale*;[9] annual fairs, linked to church holidays and usually lasting two weeks were referred to as *forum annuum, forum annuale, nundinae, congregatio* or *feria*.[10]

There was also a third category, the *forum cottidianum*, interpreted by historians as a "daily market". The places where it was permitted to trade every

---

5   On the sees in detail, cf. Engel 2001, 255–257.

6   For example, 1242: *Item statuimus, quod in eadem civitate forum sollempne duobus diebus in ebdomada, videlicet die Lune et die Jovis celebretur et preterea forum cottidianum cottidie habeatur* – Tkalčić (ed.) 1889, I, 17.

7   For example, 1307: forum generale, quod feria tercia celebratur – Sedlák (ed.) 1980–1987, I, 240 and Kristó et al. (eds.) 1990–2015, II, no. 277.

8   For example, 1427: *in foro conmuni eodem die* [feria quarta– BW] *in possessione Thapolcha vocata celebrato* – Erdélyi and Sörös (eds.) 1902–1916, VIII, 464.

9   For example, 1330: *villa ecclesie praefate Errad vocata feria tertia singulis ebdomadis imperpetuum forum conmune et provinciale possit celebrari* – MNL OL DF 200 402.

10   Cf. Engel 2001, 253.

day, however, usually involved wholesale operations rather than retail markets. The privilege granted by King Béla IV in 1244 to the Pest *hospes* specified that ships and ferries plying up and down the river had to stop and bring in their goods and carts and hold a market; as before, a market had to be held every day.[11] When a large number of the inhabitants of Pest moved to the Castle Hill of Buda at the news of another Mongol invasion and took their privileges with them,[12] the town of Buda started to exercise this staple right. Weekly markets were also established in Buda – on Saturday and Tuesday in 1320,[13] and on Wednesday, Friday and Saturday in the Late Middle Ages.[14] The town retained its staple right throughout the medieval period. This represented a way of tying wholesale trade to Buda, and in return the town had to enable incoming merchants to offer their goods for sale whenever they arrived; this was made plain in the 1244 charter stipulating the holding of a market every day. In 1271, King Stephen V's market charter for the *hospites* of Győr concerned not a market on a specified day but a *forum liberum*,[15] to be held every day both within and outside the castle, even where the *comes* of Győr and his officers had no jurisdiction. Markets held on Saturdays in the village of Győr continued to be the privilege of the *comes* of Győr.[16] The need for the *forum liberum*, which could be held on any day, arose because in the same charter Stephen V ordered merchants going to or from Austria to lay out their goods and offer them for sale[17] This they could only be expected to do if the means of selling goods was available to them at whatever time on whatever day they passed through. A weekly market on a fixed day (Friday) also later developed in Győr.[18] King Louis I similarly granted a daily market privilege to Košice in 1347 upon granting the staple right to the town.[19] Weekly markets were held in Košice on Thursday and Friday.[20] As in Győr and Buda, there is a clear link between daily

---

11 *Item naves et carine descendentes et ascendentes cum mercibus et curribus apud eos descendant et forum sicut prius habeant cottidianum* – Kubinyi (ed.) 1997, 40. Published most recently in: Nagy et al. (eds.) 2016, 557–558.
12 Fügedi 1961, 80–81 and Szűcs 1993, 55.
13 MNL OL DL 40 389. (Kristó et al. [eds.] 1990–2015, V, no. 852).
14 Mollay (ed.) 1959, 137 (cap. 227).
15 *Forum liberum* implied twofold liberty: first, freedom from toll on roads to and from the market, second, immunity from the jurisdiction of the *comes*.
16 *concessimus eisdem liberum forum tam in castro, quam exterius quotidiem celebrandum* – Kubinyi (ed.) 1997, 62.
17 Kubinyi (ed.) 1997, 63.
18 1361: Erdélyi and Sörös (eds.) 1902–1916, II, 474.
19 Juck (ed.) 1984, 148. Cf. Weisz 2013d.
20 1327: MNL OL DL 16 095 and 1342: MNL OL DL 103 170.

markets and the staple right; i.e. wholesale trading. It is almost certain that this form of trading, which mostly involved large amounts of goods, took place in market halls or similar suitable premises rather than marketplaces,[21] and it is conceivable that in the initial period before these buildings were erected, the exchange of goods occurred at marketplaces or even at merchants' lodgings.[22] The town of Košice also arises in connection with the issue of depots: in 1482, the town protested that, despite its privileges, nobles living around and in the county of Košice (*in illa provincia*) were setting up places for storing goods in their estates and villages – for example, collecting stocks of foreign wines and selling them.[23] This information may be sufficient grounds to deduce that when King Béla IV in 1239 granted the archiepiscopal city of Esztergom a weekly market from Friday midday to Saturday evening *cum foro quotidiano*,[24] the town's staple right – although held only by tradition – and the related trading may have been behind this. The situation may have been similar in Zagreb where in 1242 King Béla IV granted a daily market to the Zagreb *hospites* in addition to their weekly markets on Monday and Thursday.[25] Although there is no mention of a staple right in this charter, it does contain remarks about daily markets connected to foreign trade.

The Day of the Market

In the early eleventh century, markets were held on Sundays, in front of churches. This was acceptable to the ecclesiastical authorities because people coming to the market also came into the church. The charter of Pécsvárad Abbey, where it mentions a market held on Sundays beside the church of St Peter, may be referring to this period.[26] A few decades later, however, there was a move to have the market held at times other than Sundays and feast days; i.e., to separate churchgoing and trading. The latter was turning out to have a greater attraction, and discouraged people from going to church. The

---

21　In Košice, for instance, the market hall was a part of the town hall, cf. Szende 2008, 432.
22　The passage in the Buda customs register on the estimation at the residence of the merchants may refer to the latter. Kubinyi (ed.) 1997, 45.
23　*in villis et possessionibus ipsorum quedam loca depositionis instituissent et ad huiusmodi loca vina externa congererent et exinde ... venditioni exponerent* – MNL OL DF 271 438.
24　Kubinyi (ed.) 1997, 33.
25　*Item statuimus, quod in eadem ciuitate forum solempne duobus diebus in ebdomada videlicet die Lune et die Iouis celebretur, et preterea forum cottidianum cottidie habeatur* – Tkalčić (ed.) 1889, I, 17.
26　1015: Györffy (ed.) 1992, 72–80. (Szentpétery and Borsa 1923–1987, no. 6).

text of the Hungarian Illuminated Chronicle states that markets were moved to Saturday by King Béla I,[27] although historians now consider that King Géza I was responsible for this.[28] Records from Esztergom and Szigetfő provide evidence of markets being held on Saturdays even during the reign of King Stephen I.[29] Shifting the time of the market did not always go down well. King Ladislas I was forced to take action against Sunday markets. The king made a law ordering the horses of people going to market on Sundays and feast days to be confiscated, and traders' tents to be taken down.[30] Other days of the week were later added to Saturday on the calendar of markets, and in the twelfth and thirteenth centuries, markets could effectively be held on any day from Monday to Saturday. Weekly markets also appear in place names: it is a widely-shared view that where a day of the week forms part of a place name (e.g. Keddhely [Tuesday] or Szombathely [Saturday]), it refers to the day when a fair was held.[31] Charters started to grant Sunday markets again in the mid-fourteenth century,[32] Christianity having consolidated its position and there being a Sunday market day at annual fairs in any case.

Markets and Customs Duties

The collector of customs was responsible for guaranteeing the market as a place where trading could be conducted in peace, and the imposition of duty was an assurance to the customer that he was not buying stolen goods. Customs duties, initially due solely to the king, were later divided in proportions of two parts to the king and one to the *comes*. The royal customs grant concerned only the king's two-thirds share, although we know of cases when he also granted the *comes*'s share. By the grant of *forum liberum* in the thirteenth century, the king renounced both his own and the *comes*'s share of the customs. This may also have applied to newly-established customs stations, for which the sources make no mention of a share for the *comes*. The *comes* received a smaller share

---

27 Szentpétery (ed.) 1937–1938, I, 358.
28 Györffy 1983a, 335 and Jánosi 1996, 102.
29 Györffy 1983a, 335.
30 Sancti Ladislai regis decretorum liber primus 15–16. cc. (Bak et al. [eds.] 1992–2012, I, 58).
31 Cf. Major 1966 51–55, Szabó 1994 51–55 and Szabó 1998.
32 The royal donation also relates to the Sunday weekly market. For instance: Lél (Komárom County) – 1390: Mályusz et al. (eds.) 1951–2017, I, no. 1434, Kapušany (Sáros County) – 1418: Mályusz et al. (eds.) 1951–2017, VI, no. 1706, Egyedfalva (Bács County, south of present-day Mladenovo, Serbia) – 1462: MNL OL DL 15 714.

of the customs on goods intended for export (a quarter) than they did on imported goods or goods which were transported and sold in domestic trade.[33]

Customs also embraced stallage and gate tolls.[34] It is also possible to identify a whole category of customs-free markets, although it is also true that markets provided sources of revenue other than customs alone. Among these were the fines from the administration of justice in the market. Money changers were also present, but the king did not relinquish control of the profit from this, conceding at most that his money changers would not be present at a particular market,[35] or would perform their duties only together with the judge and the village elder.[36] Traders used their own weights and measures to dispense their wares, but had to have them calibrated when they came to the market. The municipal laws of Banská Štiavnica prescribed severe punishments for uncalibrated liquid measures and dry measures, yardsticks, scales and weights.[37] It is possible that traders had to pay a small sum to the calibrator for their services.

As with transit customs, the most primitive form of market customs was flat-rate duty. This was collected on each cart and packhorse brought into the market. The system became more sophisticated with the introduction of a customs tariff, which adjusted levels of duty to the type of merchandise, although collection was still based on carts and packhorses or smaller units of carriage (item, bolt, bushel, barrel, bundle). This is the procedure found most often in market customs regulations. The final stage of development was *ad valorem* duty, defined in proportion to the value of the merchandise, although the latter was left to the collector of customs to determine.

The sources record many different ways in which customs duty was collected. The Esztergom customs regulations specified the duty payable on each item, either by the trader or the customer, while the Buda and Gelnica

---

33   Cf. 1255: Kubinyi (eds.) 1997, 51–52 (Szentpétery and Borsa 1923–1987, no. 1237).
34   There are different views about the latter: some scholars regard it as a road toll (Eckhart 1908, 86) and others as market duty. Sólyom 1933, 11, Kubinyi 1964c, 112–113, Kubinyi 1973b, 46 and Weisz 2007c, 889–890. At border gates, there also was gate duty, but this was a customs duty on foreign trade. See also the other chapter by Boglárka Weisz in the present volume.
35   1190: Kubinyi (ed.) 1997, 14–19 (Szentpétery and Borsa 1923–1987, 151) and 1217: Tkalčić (ed.) 1873–1874, I, 44–46.
36   1255: Marsina 1971–1987, II, 344–345 (Szentpétery and Borsa 1923–1987, no. 1062).
37   *Wir wellen, das welich mensch, es say weib oder mon, das mit unrechter maas fwndnn wirt, sye sey trewg oder feuchtt, oder mit unrechter Elln, Waag oder gelött, der sol deu gesworenn ein marck gebnn, wirdet er zu dem anndernn mal begriffnn, so sol er czwu Marck gebnn, wirtt er zu dem drittnn mal daran begriffnn, so ist er bestanndnn mit der hannt, oder er löse sie mit zehnn Marknn, der gefallenn czwei tail dem Richtter und das dritte tail den Gesworenn, also verr mon in begenadnn wil* – Wenzel (ed.) 1860–1874, III, 209.

regulations required that both customer and seller pay duties, presumably at the market itself. The Esztergom tariff may have been the earlier procedure,[38] and may have required the seller to pay nothing except stallage to the holder of the market.

Market Wares

The endorsement on the deed of foundation of Tihany Abbey, dating from 1055, tells us that King Andrew I granted to the abbey the market customs (*mercati tributum*) of Veszprém "its part thereof, in cooking vessels, food, pails, and all ironmongery (tools)."[39] The articles of merchandise mentioned there well reflect the primitive barter which went on at markets in the early period, although these items, essential as they were to everyday life, also appear in later sources connected with markets.[40]

The sale of stolen goods is detectable from sources as a problem as early as the eleventh century, when internal trade was still in its infancy. Laws passed under the reigns of Kings Ladislas I and Coloman show this to have concerned mainly the trade of people and livestock. The laws treated slaves as chattel; buying and selling them was quite natural.[41] Slaves were also among the major articles of merchandise in foreign trade in the eleventh century. King Coloman attempted to restrict the export of Hungarian slaves so that slaves born in Hungary would boost the kingdom's economic strength.[42] Slaves were still being bought and sold at markets in the thirteenth century, as an entry in the Esztergom customs register attests.[43]

---

38 The customs tariff was written in 1288, but researchers have identified four chronological layers in it, the first from c. 1205–1235, a second from 1255, a third from 1284 and a fourth from 1288. Cf. Domanovszky 1916, 33–38, Hóman 1916, 531–534, Szűcs 1984, 7–8 and 26 fn. 112 and Weisz 2013b, 143–148.

39 Györffy (ed.) 1992, 149–152. (Szentpétery and Borsa 1923–1987, no. 12).

40 1209: Marsina 1971–1987, I, 123–124, Szentpétery and Borsa 1923–1987, no. 246 (Pečovská Nová Ves, Sáros County), 18 April 1288: Knauz et al. (eds.) 1874–1999, II, 236–241, Szentpétery and Borsa 1923–1987, no. 3483 (Esztergom, Esztergom County).

41 Sancti Ladislai regis decretorum liber primus 2., 10. cc. (Bak et al. [eds.] 1992–2012, I, 56 and 57) and Sancti Ladislai regis decretorum liber secundus 11. c. (Bak et al. [eds.] 1992–2012, I, 14), Colomanni regis decretorum liber primus 44. c. (Bak et al. [eds.] 1992–2012, I, 29).

42 Colomanni regis decretorum liber primus 77. c. (Bak et al. [eds.] 1992–2012, I, 32).

43 18 April 1288: Knauz et al. (eds.) 1874–1999, II, 236–241. (Szentpétery and Borsa 1923–1987, no. 3483).

Kings Ladislas I and Coloman restricted the export of oxen, important for farming, and horses, essential in warfare and travel.[44] The king retained a monopoly on the export of horses: they could be taken over the border only with his express permission.[45] Changes in livestock exports, however, may be observed during Coloman's reign. While the king retained monopoly on horse exports, traders were allowed to take cattle out of the country.[46] Restrictions on trading horses became even stricter, all mention of royal permission for export disappearing, and even inhabitants of the kingdom were banned from buying them.[47] The last time the horse appears in either domestic or foreign trade is in the thirteenth century.[48]

Oxen were widely traded in the thirteenth century, both for export and on domestic markets. The Győr customs rules made a distinction between the oxen driven by Germans and Hungarians: Germans paid five times as much as Hungarians, perhaps because they took their oxen abroad, whereas Hungarians sold theirs within the kingdom.

The animals traded in the Árpádian age, other than horses and oxen, included goats, lambs and pigs. There were also important fish markets in towns and villages beside rivers (those along Danube tributaries are well documented). The Esztergom customs regulations specifically mentioned sturgeon (*Acipenser sturio* and *Acipenser huso*) as being among the most valuable Danube fish, as well as the easier-to-catch pike and carp. The customs rate shows that sturgeon was the most expensive fish.[49] There were animal products as well as live animals on sale at markets: meat, fat tallow and hides (goat- sheep- cow- and rabbit-skin). Valuable furs (like squirrel) also appeared on market stalls, probably from the earliest times. Wax, of use in many areas of life, was another animal product often sold in markets.

---

44 Sancti Ladislai regis decretorum liber secundus 15. c. (Bak et al. [eds.] 1992–2012, I, 15).

45 Sancti Ladislai regis decretorum liber secundus 16–17. cc. (Bak et al. [eds.] 1992–2012, I, 15–16).

46 Colomanni regis decretorum liber primus 77. c. (Bak et al. [eds.] 1992–2012, I, 32).

47 Colomanni regis decretorum liber primus 76. c. (Bak et al. [eds.] 1992–2012, I, 31–32).

48 The duty regulations specifically mention the proportions due to the duty collector and the *comes*. They state that one-third of the duty on incoming goods was due to the *comes*, and two-thirds to the collector of customs. For outgoing goods, the respective proportions were one-fifth and four-fifths. The one third – two thirds division also applied to oxen driven by Hungarians, indicating that the oxen were sold domestically. Cf. Kubinyi (ed.) 1997, 51–52 (Szentpétery and Borsa 1923–1987, no. 1237).

49 On sturgeon fishing, see the chapter in this volume written by László Bartosiewicz and his colleagues.

Among the most sought-after commodities of the age were salt and wine. The only information we have on wine areas comes from the Esztergom customs regulations. These regarded wine from *Marchia* (Srijem) as being in a category of its own, distinguished from wine of any other origin – primarily that from Somogy, Zala Counties and Sokoró (the southeastern edges of the Little Hungarian Plain). The same regulations indicate that wine was also an export commodity.

A wide range of textile products were on sale at markets, both the cheaper kinds (grey cloth, German canvas) and the more expensive (scarlet, fustian, silk).[50] Distinctions among some items only appear in customs tariffs in the thirteenth century, presumably when there was an increase in both supply and demand. As well as the material itself, there were finished products on sale: gloves, clothes and hats.

Foods, like cheese, fruit, honey (essential for sweetening) and pepper (for both medicinal and culinary purposes), all featured in Árpádian-age markets. Pepper was just one of the spices which came to Hungary from abroad. Cereals – wheat, rye, barley and oats – were sold for both human and animal consumption.[51] Other crops were also present among market wares, like hops, used in the brewing of beer, and the tanning agent sumac. Hay for animals was also sold at markets, as were building timber and firewood.

Although the customs regulations also covered metals such as lead, copper, iron and silver, duty was charged only on silver (1/240th). It is interesting that gold, one of the main foreign trade commodities, does not appear on any customs regulations, and the other precious-metal ore, silver, appears only on the customs regulations of Buda and – slightly later – Gelnica. It may thus be inferred that precious metal ores were sold not at markets but through some other channel associated with the mines. Precious stones and pearls, however, appeared at markets as the wares of Venetian merchants. There were of course many other wares on sale, both everyday items and luxury products.

Royal Policy Towards Markets

Laws passed by King Ladislas I were the first expressions of the king's wish to make markets the sole arena for trading commodities. By doing so, he aimed to provide security for trade and enforce collection of market customs duties. Buying and selling were to be conducted solely at markets, and Ladislas

---

50   Cf. Pach 2003, 9–17.
51   On the wheat trade: Szűcs 1984.

I stipulated that, to protect customers, contracts were to be made in the presence of the judge, the collector of customs, and witnesses.[52] Ladislas's laws also tell us that it had already long been customary to make transactions before witnesses.[53] The presence of witnesses was probably needed because of the prevalence of theft at that time, and also to be able to settle any legal disputes that might arise in connection with transactions.

King Coloman extended Ladislas's laws to regulate trade between Jews and Christians. Coloman required that transactions be made in the presence of Christian and Jewish witnesses, and that the commodities and the witnesses' names be set down in a document to which both parties added their seals.[54] The law provided for a procedure similar to that of loan transactions, although the requirement for a sealed document for the latter was linked to a specified minimum amount.[55]

Coloman's laws are notable for not stipulating the openness of markets to transactions between Jews and Christians, and for replacing the role of the market judge and collector of customs by Christian and Jewish witnesses and a sealed document. It should be noted, however, that the main purpose of the *cartula sigillata* was to record the names of the witnesses and not to set in writing the transaction itself. The *cartula sigillata* was presumably used until the thirteenth century,[56] because the Jewish privilege of 1251 only mentions the mortgaged property in loan transactions,[57] even though the sealed document was already used in the mortgaging of estates.[58]

In addition to the laws of Kings Ladislas I and Coloman, there is indirect evidence that markets may have been open to both free and bonded people as early as the eleventh century, and certainly were in the twelfth.[59]

Royal policy made Esztergom the commercial center of the country up to the time of the Mongol invasion. Esztergom was a royal seat until the mid-thirteenth century, and remained a county seat and a center of the Hungarian church throughout the Middle Ages. Its geographical location at the confluence of the Danube and the River Hron also contributed to the city's emergence as

52 Sancti Ladislai regis decretorum liber secundus 7. c. (Bak et al. [eds.] 1992–2012, I, 14).
53 Sancti Ladislai regis decretorum liber tertius 11. c. (Bak et al. [eds.] 1992–2012, I, 20).
54 Capitula Colomanni regis de iudeis 4–7. cc. (Bak et al. [eds.] 1992–2012, I, 68).
55 For a loan transaction, only witnesses and an item pledged as security were required for an amount under three pensa, but the law required a loan of more than three pensa to be set down in writing (Bak et al. [eds.] 1992–2012, I, 68).
56 Cf. Kumorovitz 1980, 85–87.
57 1251: Friss (ed.) 1903, I, 27–28.
58 Friss (ed.) 1903, I, 30.
59 Kubinyi 1996c, 60–61 and Kubinyi 1996a, 39–42.

a focal point of long-distance trade. Its Castle Hill, rising above the natural crossing point, afforded control of both the waterways (Danube and Hron) and the roads. In the second half of the thirteenth century, Esztergom lost its dominance, and its market went down with it. The waning of the city's significance, like its emergence, was due to a combination of circumstances. Firstly, at the turn of the twelfth and thirteenth centuries, church influence halted urban development there. Secondly, after the Mongol invasion, King Béla IV moved the royal seat to Buda, which had a staple right, and this speeded the decline of Esztergom's market. Buda became the country's primary crossroad, a function already latent in its geographical location. Árpádian-age charters offer no clue as to what day the weekly market was held in Buda. In the early fourteenth century, markets were held on Tuesday and Saturday.[60] The Buda Law Code (*Ofner Stadtrecht*) mentioned a Saturday market held by custom (*von gewonhait*).[61] Other evidence for the Saturday market is the name "Saturday Gate". Erik Fügedi has placed the origin of this Saturday market to the second half of the twelfth century.[62] András Kubinyi traced the emergence of the Tuesday market to the period following 1255.[63] Buda acquired the privilege to hold an annual fair on the birthday of the Virgin Mary (8 September) in 1287.[64]

Closely linked with the markets was King Béla IV's customs policy, by which he attempted to systematize the customs in 1255. This was when the Buda and Győr customs tariffs were set, and the items on the Esztergom tariff adjusted.[65] Jenő Szűcs has proposed that Béla IV was attempting to draw off some of the profit from foreign trade and at the same time relieve the burden on domestic trade by the grant of customs exceptions,[66] but since the three customs tariffs issued during the reign of Béla IV all concerned customs posts where the right of collection was held by the church, they could not have boosted revenue to the royal treasury. The setting of customs tariffs was also primarily in the interests of the merchants rather than the collectors of customs. It may have been related to the appearance of a problem which was to become serious in the second half of the century: the collection of unjustified customs duty.

---

60   1320: MNL OL DL 40 389.
61   Mollay (ed.) 1959, 137 (cap. 227).
62   Fügedi 1961, 79.
63   Kubinyi 1972, 51.
64   Gárdonyi (ed.) 1936, I, 228–230. (Szentpétery and Borsa 1923–1987, no. 3449).
65   1255: Gárdonyi (ed.) 1936, I, 56–58, Szentpétery and Borsa 1923–1987, no. 1044 (Buda), 1255: Kubinyi (ed.) 1997, 51–52, Szentpétery and Borsa 1923–1987, no. 1237 (Győr), 18 April 1288: Knauz et al. (ed.) 1874–1999, II, 236–241, Szentpétery and Borsa 1923–1987, no. 3483 (Esztergom).
66   Szűcs 1993, 72.

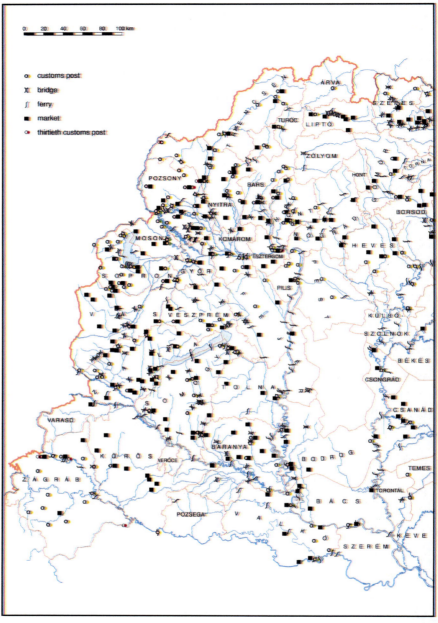

FIGURE 20.1 *Customs places, fords, markets and thirtieth customs places until the mid-fourteenth century (drawn by Béla Nagy).*

DOMESTIC TRADE IN THE ÁRPÁDIAN AGE

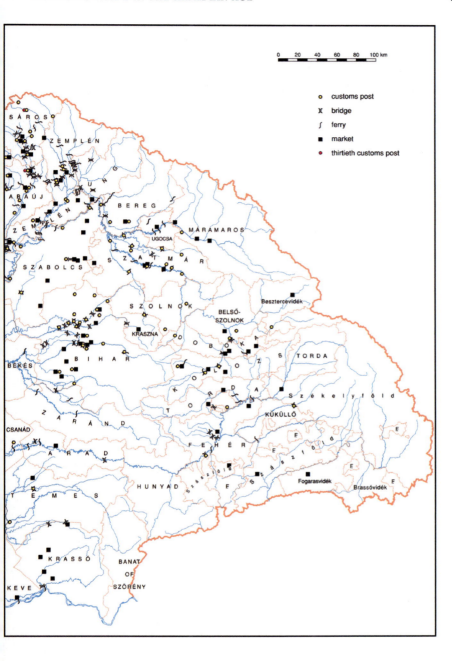

CHAPTER 21

Professional Merchants and the Institutions of Trade: Domestic Trade in Late Medieval Hungary*

András Kubinyi

Domestic trade was interlinked with every branch of economic life. Peasants sold their produce or animals for money, with which they bought manufactured goods; craftsmen bought food and raw materials, much of the latter from quarries or mines. The former is therefore covered in every branch of economic history to some extent, although rarely as a subject on its own.[1] Village and market-town histories also mention trade but rarely as primary goals of the studies.[2] Therefore, in this section the focus is on professional merchants and the institutions of trade in medieval Hungary.

Merchants by Vocation[3]

The most important professional merchants are listed in Act 1 of 1521. This regulation was set out – without much success[4] – to tax merchants (*mercatores*), retailers (*institores*), apothecaries (*apothecarii*), shearers (*pannicidae*), shopkeepers (*boltharii*) and other money-lenders (*foeneratores*) in free royal towns and other towns enclosed by walls the twentieth part of their goods. Since the *Corpus Juris* recorded this with the year 1522, some authors still date it a year later.[5] Article 10 of the Act provides differently for the tax on wholesale

---

* The chapter is a translation of an article by András Kubinyi published in 2008. Citations for works published after this date were added by the editors of the present volume.
1 Important exceptions are the recent works of Boglárka Weisz. See: Weisz 2010c, Weisz 2012b and Weisz 2013b.
2 Mályusz 1963, Szűcs 1955, Székely 1961, Pach 1963, Bácskai 1965 and Szabó 1969. On the archival sources of the topic, see: Solymosi 1978.
3 For a categorization of medieval merchants, see: Irsigler 1985, 385–397.
4 Bónis 1965, 93–102.
5 Kovachich 1818, I, 213, Nagy et al. (eds.) 1899, 790. Under the entry *institor* Harmatta et al. 1987–, V, 308 refers to Art. 6 of the *Corpus Juris Hungarici* under 1522. For the latest Latin-English bilingual edition, with a different numbering of the acts, see: Bak et al. (eds.) 1992–2012, IV, 236–239 (I. 5).

merchants and shearers (*mercatores, pannicidae*). Fifty denars had to be paid on every draft horse.[6] It is interesting that Article 4 set the basic tax on horses at only 5 denars,[7] so that the law was actually attempting – via the number of horses – to tax the merchants on their capital strength. The law thus acknowledged that merchants could live elsewhere than in towns, but assumed they operated primarily at fairs and markets and were thus keepers of horses and carts. Werbőczy, the editor of the customary law collection, also distinguished *mercatores* from *institores* in recognizing their right to create statutes.[8]

The most useful sources of distinctions among professional traders are to be found in urban records. Most important are statute books, accounts and minutes of meetings, but wills can also be useful.[9] Perhaps the most fruitful has been the Buda *Stadtrecht*.[10] Medieval towns wanted to grant retail trading rights, with privileges, to their own burghers, specifically to traders in certain goods and to craftsmen. Persons not specializing in a particular category of merchandise and non-locals could only trade wholesale, except at markets and fairs.[11] Wholesalers who supplied manufacturers or merchants can nonetheless be distinguished from dedicated retailers.[12] Their activities sometimes extended further afield, although they could sell retail too.[13] Finally, full-time merchants should be distinguished from occasional ones. Wholesalers commonly belonged among the latter.[14]

The Buda *Stadtrecht* afforded top positions to "shop men" (*gewelb herren*), whose retail activity was confined to silk. These were wholesalers, and it was mainly they who were referred to as merchants. The town council's 1421 resolution on trade, as copied into the Law Code, is concerned with members of three main commercial categories: merchants (*kaufleut*), retailers (*cramer*) and shearers (*gewant schnaider*). This resolution makes no separate mention of the *gewelb herren*, who were thus included under *kaufleut*.[15] Retail trade of cloth was the right of the shearers (*Gewandschneider, pannicida*), who sold their wares in storerooms – unlike the "shop men", who had vaulted shops – and

---

6   Kovachich 1818, II, 294.
7   Kovachich 1818, II, 292.
8   Bak et al. (eds.) 1992–2012, V, 378–379 (III/2, 7): *nec non mercatores ac institores* ...
9   On the latter, see: Szende 2004b, esp. 237–241.
10   Published by Mollay (ed.) 1959.
11   von Below 1926, 302–398.
12   Isenmann 1988, 248–249.
13   Isenmann 1988, 358–380.
14   von Below 1926, 357–358.
15   Mollay (ed.) 1959, 88 (cap. 70) – 1421. Mollay (ed.) 1959, 189 (cap. 404).

were thus also known as *kamerherren*. The Hungarian word for shop (*bolt*) is also derived from the vaulted room (*boltozott*).

The third category, retailers, sold certain spices and small quantities of other, mainly cheap goods, and only in stalls, never in their houses or in shops. Their Hungarian name *kalmár* is related to the German *Krämer*, which comes from *Kram* or stall.[16] Károly Mollay has distinguished three strata of merchant society in Sopron: wholesalers (*kaufman*), retailers (*kramer*) and small retailers (*ladner*). The wholesaler's *gwelb* was in his own house, and the retailers sold their wares beside the Franciscan Church in the main square (the same in Hungarian: Fő tér). The small retailers were mostly grocers.[17] The word used for retailers was *institor* (those who sell in an *instita*) or, in German, *krom* (*krame*) and hence in Hungarian, *kalmár*.[18] Stallholders were organized into guilds in the larger towns.[19]

The statute book also mentions apothecaries. The Latin word *apotecarius* – or *aromatarius*, as they were also called – means spice-seller. These merchants also sold medicines and many other goods, such as candles. They had trading houses (*domus apotecariorum*) in Óbuda and sometimes even in villages, such as Békásmegyer.[20] Then there were linen merchants,[21] fish-sellers, fodder and grain factors, oil-sellers, rag and bone men, grocers, etc., not to mention artisans who sold their own wares. The first four categories, however, were prominent, and some of their members were to be found among the city fathers.[22]

Merchants thus made up a broad spectrum of occupations in Hungarian medieval cities, and the 1521 Act implies that commerce was also a vocation for many people in market towns and even villages. Since the law sought to tax them on the number of draft horses they had, they probably went round regular markets and fairs. Various registers and records of acts of might also tell us about provincial merchants. Alongside the names of some tenant peasants (*iobagi*) included in registers, there are references to merchants. Charters related to acts of might or other judicial affairs give an account of market-town or village traders at work, sometimes telling us where they traveled, what goods they bought and sold, and what these were worth. Here we will

---

16   Mollay 1982, 336.
17   Mollay 1991, 9.
18   For the terms, see: Harmatta et al. 1987–
19   Mollay (ed.) 1959, 100 (cap. 104). On Sopron, see: Mollay 1991, 10–13. In Germany *Krämer* fell under guild-constraint. See: Isenmann 1988, 357. On the different spaces of trade in Buda, Óbuda and Pest, see: Benda 2009–2010, Benda 2012, Benda 2014a and Benda 2016a.
20   Kubinyi 1970, 65 and 70–74, Benda 2016a, 269–270.
21   Benda 2014b.
22   For details, see: Kubinyi 1973b, 51–54.

look at a few illustrative examples according to category. *Mercators*, it may be thought, lived only in towns. But in 1450, a village peasant (*iobagi*) from Zala County, Antal – a *mercator* – was robbed as he was taking his four-horse cart, laden with wares, to the Vásárhely fair.[23] The next reference is connected to the market town of Keve and a merchant from there who traded throughout the country. In 1508, a *mercator* called István Ötvös (meaning "Goldsmith"), made a promise on behalf of himself and his local associates Péter Markos and Lőrinc Garai that they would not harry members of the county landowning families Gyerőfi and Kemény. This was after the latter had extracted a payment of 12 gold florins from carters who were taking the merchants' goods to Oradea along back roads. The carters were also from Kolozs County.[24] This indicates that Keve merchants used local carriers to take goods bought in Transylvania to the Oradea fair. The former were probably known in Hungarian as *boltos* (shopkeepers), on the evidence of sources from elsewhere, including Pécs.[25]

There is also data on cloth merchants. A 1440 charter states that two bolts of broadcloth were impounded from Mihály, a *pannicida* of Bártfalva, at the Rokoszovo customs post in Ung County, as he was going to Maramureş.[26] What is interesting here is that Satu Barbă was a village that belonged to the Sólyomkő estate in Bihar County, and did not even hold a fair. It is possible that people with the Hungarian surname of Posztós (*posztó* = broadcloth) were also merchants, not weavers. Mihály Posztós, who was judge of Timişoara, may have been one of these.[27]

Most of the examples described here, although certainly not all, concern retailers in different locations, both town and village. We are fortunate to have the account book of a retailer – Paul Moritz[28] of Sopron – for the period 1520–1529, full of information about his wares and his commercial relations.[29] This wealthy Sopron retailer traded almost exactly the types and quantities of goods stipulated permissible for retailers by the Buda *Stadtrecht*.[30] These included fabrics, cloths, oil, spices, honey, wax, tallow, etc. Moritz clearly sold small quantities directly to the public. Research succeeded in demonstrating

23 MNL OL DL 93 200 (1451).
24 Jakó (ed.) 1990, II, no. 3477.
25 Petrovics 2001a, 179 and 183–185. On foreign ethnic groups in Pécs, see also: Petrovics 2009, 73–75.
26 C. Tóth (ed.) 2006, no. 40.
27 Petrovics 1996, 91–100. On new archaeological data for the trade of textiles and broadcloth, see: Mordovin 2013 and Mordovin 2014.
28 See fn. 17.
29 Published by Károly Mollay (ed.) 1994.
30 Mollay (ed.) 1959, 100 (cap. 104).

the boundaries of his market.³¹ His business extended into Austria, as far west as Mainburg, southwest of Sankt Pölten, as well as also to Neunkirch, Wiener Neustadt and Vienna, effectively covering the whole of Sopron County, part of Moson County and the northern part of Vas County, including Sárvár. His trading territory had a radius of about 100–110 kilometers. He often made loans, but also bought goods on credit.

Now for market-town and village traders. An *institor* from the market town of Turňa nad Bodvou was robbed at the Rudabánya "free market" – probably the weekly market. Sixteen new florins, 22 yards of canvas and 12 knives were taken from him.³² The next example permits some conclusions that go further. In 1498, the *universitas* of Nyírbátor made a written report to King Wladislas II regarding the legal dispute between Ferenc Harangi, *concivis* of Nyírbátor, and Jakab Trommellenk of Buda. This states that Harangi produced as a witness one certain János, *institor* and *concivis* of Kisvárda. (The Nyírbátor authorities therefore did not describe these two market-town residents as *iobagi*.) Under oath, the Kisvárda *institor* János stated that Harangi, but not his wife, had stayed with him. He did not know whether Harangi was engaged in transactions with, or was a business associate of, Tromellenk. There, Harangi had a visit from his brother Matthew, to whom he gave 75 florins, the purpose of which John did not know. Neither did he know whether the two brothers had any joint share in any transaction. Finally, the Nyírbátor *universitas* asked the king to dispense justice to Ferenc Harangi, Nyírbátor *concivis*.³³ The Kisvárda retailer János's claim to have no knowledge of the matters at issue is hardly credible. He must have had commercial contacts with the Harangi brothers if he was giving Ferenc accommodation. They, in turn, were probably associates of a Buda merchant, or at least that is what János had heard, otherwise he would not have mentioned the matter.

Perhaps the most interesting piece of information comes from an acts-of-might investigation of 1513. The record of the investigation gives details of the losses suffered by the victims, who were tenant peasants. Some of the robberies were committed in Szentpál, Zala County, where losses estimated at 111 florins and 92 denars were suffered by two *institors*, János and Pál Móróchelyi, who lived together, probably brothers. Of the 15 victims, only a furrier called Gergely had a comparable loss – 95 florins and 73 denars. The two retailers lost their household and agricultural implements and, it would seem, their entire stock-in-trade. This comprised hats and knives worth 60 florins and two bolts

---

31   Mollay 1991, 24–27 (map and short text).
32   Mályusz et al. (eds.) 1951–2017, V, no. 808.
33   MNL OL DL 20 752.

of fine linen, worth 10 florins. Their cash, however, must have been successfully hidden. The furrier was not so fortunate: the thieves got away with 60 florins cash (of which 21 were gold florins) and 26 sheepskin waistcoats (*pellicium*), each worth 1 florin, from his stock.[34]

There is a considerable body of data on retailers (*kalmár*), and the surname Kalmár is also found in registers, tax registers, *urbaria* and records of acts of might, in both towns and villages. Quantitative research and analysis of these, possibly by region, would be worthwhile.[35] It seems, however, that retailers, like most craftsmen in villages or market towns, also worked in agriculture, like the above-mentioned brothers of Szentpál.

None of this implies that trade was confined to a particular class of merchants. Indeed, the persons most prominently associated with commerce (in Buda, for example) were almost never called merchants.[36] In practice, trade was open to anybody – the craftsman, the landowner, or the peasant. The "merchants" discussed here are those who were generally regarded as making their living from trade. This did not exclude them from cultivating land. The number of agricultural implements owned by the Móróchelyi brothers suggests substantial farming activity. It is significant that many retailers were tenant peasants. Even professional merchants could have also had land – Paul Moritz had vineyards, for example.

Markets, Fairs, and other Factors Affecting Trade[37]

Medieval Fairs and Markets
Terminology

The words *mercatum* or *mercatus* in the Latin charters occur mainly in the first part of the Árpádian age.[38] Considering their affinity to the words *market*, *Markt* and *marché*, it is curious that they fell out of use in Hungarian Latin sources (an issue worth further investigation). The most common Latin term

---

34 Radvánszky and Závodszky (eds.) 1909–1922, II, 389–395.
35 Kredics and Solymosi (eds.) 1993, 70–72, 104, 25 and 39.
36 The most important businessmen in Buda and Pest were never called merchants. On them, see: Kubinyi 1994c.
37 With this title I follow the German economic historian Kellenbenz, who discussed markets under "Institutionen für den Handel". However, I refer here not only to markets, see: Kellenbenz 1991, 288 and following pages.
38 Györffy (ed.) 1992, 528. (Index based on the mentioned words) The first is from the appendix of the foundation charter of Tihany (1055); the second is from the foundation charter of Zselicszentjakab (1061): 152 and 172. On the early markets, see: Püspöki Nagy 1989.

in Hungary is *forum*, whose meaning is made clear when accompanied by an adjective (the same applies to *vásár* in Hungarian): *cottidianum* (*quotidianum*) thus corresponds to a daily market, *hebdomadale* to a weekly market and *annuale* to annual fair. There were some fairs for specific merchandise (e.g. *forum equorum*[39]), and some others which must be dealt with separately. A 1242 charter designated the weekly market as *forum sollempne*, but this occurs only rarely.[40] The word *sollempnis* basically means an annual or regular event, and so has a "festive" meaning.

A frequent term is *forum comprovinciale*, occasionally shortened to *provinciale*, and meaning "county fair". The term is used in references to the "three-fair auction", which involved a person whose goods were to be sold off being summoned to three consecutive such fairs or markets. The sources never state whether these were weekly or annual, and authors have interpreted this in both ways. The present author has determined that the term does in fact refer to the weekly market; the auctions were required to be carried out at county fairs near the land of the person summonsed.[41]

An apparent synonym for the *forum annuale* was *nundinae*, usually written in the plural. The two expressions were commonly used together, in the form *nundinae seu forum annuale*. In the thirteenth-century charters, the word *congregatio*, and even *feria* (feast) can be attested. A charter of 1287 granted permission for *nundinas seu ferias ac congregationem fori annui* in Buda.[42] The use of *congregatio* in this sense can also be found in some mid-fourteenth century charters.[43] An example from 1295 is a report about the robbery of ten carts being driven to the Whitsun *congregatio* in Budafelhévíz.[44]

Both weekly markets and annual fairs could be further qualified with the adjective *liberum*, and always were if granted by royal charter. Erik Fügedi has determined the meaning of *liberum*, working mainly on late Árpádian-age data: he claims this means that the king waived taxation and jurisdiction over a "free fair" in favor of the town.[45] This may have been characteristic of the era when towns were being founded, and "free fair" may later have meant something else. In Germany, for example, a free fair also meant one where an outsider could

---

39   In Michalovce. E. Kovács (ed.) 1992, 197.
40   On the word "forum", see: Harmatta et al. 1987–, IV, 135–136. On the names used to denote market, see the second contribution of Boglárka Weisz in the present volume.
41   Kubinyi 2000b, 32–35, Kubinyi 2001a, 53–60. Amongst others, Blazovich 2002 refers to markets.
42   Kubinyi (ed.) 1997, 83 and Fügedi 1981b, 247.
43   Harmatta et al. 1987–, II. Fasc. 2. 304.
44   Kubinyi 1972, 52.
45   Fügedi 1981b, 241–246.

trade without constraint, whether or not the prince had granted exemption from tax.[46] The form of the royal charter granting the free fair evolved gradually. In 1377, for example, Simontornya received a privilege for a *congregatio*, in which King Louis I exempted it, following the Buda model, from every jurisdiction held by magnate, noble or county. The period of the fair was set at 15 days. The king also assured the safe passage of wholesale and retail merchants and persons of any status, granted exemption from fair tax, and banned arrests for the duration of the fair.[47] In a 1501 charter of liberation granted for Varna *oppidum* in Trencsén County, King Wladislas II granted fairs for the feasts of Holy Trinity and St Michael and the days before and after, and a free weekly market on Mondays. The king assured every merchant, retailer, fair-goer and traveler that they and their wares enjoyed the king's special protection and defense for their safe passage there and back.[48] All privileges were granted on the condition that there should be no violation of the privileges of other fairs. The liberty of the fair was proclaimed by ringing a bell.[49] The term "free fair" was thus more complex than Fügedi's definition. In the late medieval period, permitting anybody to trade without constraint and affording protection to fair-goers were probably more important considerations. For the weekly markets and even annual fairs granted to many villages, however, the noble landowner could not waive his jurisdiction, and retained his customs rights at such times.

In other countries, there was, in addition to the daily, weekly and annual fair, the *Messe*, a word nowadays used for international fairs. Kellenbenz wrote on annual fairs whose reach went beyond the region, of which some became *Messen*, which were granted special privileges.[50] There are problems with this term, because such fairs were also referred to by the same Latin word as annual fairs (*nundinae*) and, in lasting at least 14 days, were similar to many Hungarian fairs.[51] In a study of the Lorraine-Luxembourg area there was only one fair found to qualify as a *Messe*, and so annual fairs were also included. The French use the word *foire* for *Messe* and annual fair, and *marché* for weekly and daily markets.[52] The issues has relevance to Hungary because Vienna is regarded by some as having been – if only for a brief period – the site of a *Messe*, and some

---

46 Isenmann 1988, 233.
47 MNL OL DL 6413.
48 The king informs: *universos et singulos mercatores, institores et forenses homines atque viatores quoslibet* – MNL OL A 57 Libri Regii. Vol. 6. 8. The letter of privilege of Wladislas II was transcribed by Matthias II.
49 Mollay (ed.) 1959, 160–161 (cap. 305).
50 Kellenbenz 1991, 229 and Irsigler 1985, 389–390 also discuss the *Messes* in detail.
51 Henn 1996, 205–206.
52 Pauly 1996, 105–107.

seek links between Passau, Linz, Vienna and Bratislava.[53] These links belong to the area of foreign trade and so their study falls outside the present subject of interest. The reason for mentioning *Messen* is that bills of exchange were frequently used in payment there instead of cash, and so they were closely associated with the infancy of the banking system.[54] There is very little data on the commercial use of bills of exchange in medieval Hungary.

Types of Fairs

No monograph has been written on the fairs of late medieval Hungary. The references given at the start of this paper, although containing a wealth of information,[55] do not give a full account. More has been written on the evolution and on the spatial system of fairs.[56] The difficulty is assembling data on all of the fairs, because sometimes some only have a single mention. An attempt at this by the present author through research of the central places has not resulted in a full collection.[57] The most important sources are the scattered surviving charters of royal fairs, but the extent to which the charters were realized in practice is not always known. Much can be learned from various account books: what the keeper of the accounts bought, and for how much, possibly from whom, and where. The customs statutes can be informative about the goods being traded, but are at most typical of the time they were issued. Perhaps most important are acts-of-might cases, because many fair-goers were attacked, and the transcripts can tell us where they came from, which fair they were going to, and with whom they did business. Finally, there are the three-fair auctions, from which the network of connected weekly markets can in principle be reconstructed. "In principle", because auctions did not take place at the site of every weekly market. This institution was abolished by a law of 1486.

Fairs offer a very broad topic of discussion, but lack of space requires us to concentrate on only two features of interest: the distance between fairs, and the goods sold at them. First of all, it is important to note that the sovereign always retained the right to grant both weekly markets and annual fairs. Less than half a dozen exceptions to this are known. This made sense in view of the basic principle that there should only be one market on any one day within a distance of twelve Hungarian miles (about 8000 meters). There were

---

53   Stoob 1996, 189–204.
54   North 1996, 223–238.
55   See fns 2 and 3, above.
56   Major 1966, 48–90 and Püspöki Nagy 1989.
57   Kubinyi 2000b, Kubinyi 2001a and Kubinyi 2005.

fairs that went on without the grant of royal privilege, mostly parish festivals.[58] There is no direct evidence of these in Hungary, although the Whitsun fair in Budafelhévíz must originally have been one.

Data on daily markets, as already mentioned, survives mainly from the Árpádian age.[59] This does not of course mean that there is no mention of them later.[60] They were essential features of larger villages and towns, and still are. They are probably mentioned less frequently because they did not receive the protection granted to the weekly and annual events.

Weekly markets were held at average distances of one or two days' travel, often at the stipulated two-mile *rasta* (rest) interval. By the Late Middle Ages, anybody could find a weekly market within one or two days' journey from where they lived, although people sometimes traveled further. Owing to church influence, it was rare, if not unknown, for weekly markets to be held on Fridays and Sundays. One calculation suggests that a person could travel 20 miles a day. If an individual wanted to get home the same day and spend a third of his time at the fair, then the distance between home and the market could be no more than one-third of 20 miles, i.e. 6.7 miles.[61] If we use the older 1523-meter London mile (rather than the modern 1609.35-meter mile), then the maximum distance between home and market would thus be 10158.4 meters, slightly more than a Hungarian mile. Of course, it was also possible to stay the night beside the market, and there are clues that the weekly market lasted from midday until next midday. The number of royal grants of weekly markets steadily increased. More than one annual fair could be held in one place, but only one *forum hebdomadale*, with very few exceptions.[62] Royal protection for weekly markets lasted three days.[63] This alone is evidence that not everybody came home from the market the same day.

A record of the layout of stalls at the weekly market in the village of Štvrtok na Ostrove in Pozsony County from 1333 tells us much about the wares on sale. There were stalls selling animals (cattle and horses), furs, skins, linen, broadcloth, imperishables and food; others assigned to coarse-cloth weavers, butchers, bakers, shearers and shoemakers; also wine sellers; carts from which grain,

---

58   In Austria, for example, there is a distinction between *rechte Markt* and the *Gaumarkt* – the latter lacking in privilege. See: Rausch 1996, 180.
59   Kubinyi (ed.) 1997, 33, 44, 62, 91, passim.
60   Mályusz et al. (eds.) 1951–2017, III, no. 1186. The daily market held in *Hétközhely* in Oradea is mentioned in 1411.
61   Pounds 1994, 358.
62   See also work by the present author referred to in fn. 56.
63   Mályusz 1953b, 130.

firewood, building timber, cartwheels, carts, crates and chests were sold; and finally, sellers of beans. The list indicates the location of stalls at the market: one side ended with the coarse-cloth weavers and the other started with the butchers.[64] The market must therefore have covered everybody's needs. The question remains, of course, as to how reliable this relatively early source is as a guide to later times, when there was a steep rise in the number of both weekly markets and annual fairs.

Some acts-of-might cases give specific examples of market trade. A peasant was robbed of two casks of wine and eight horses at the Saturday market in Nyírbátor in 1390. The horses may have been those drawing his carts.[65] In 1413, twenty peasant women were robbed as they traveled with their wares to the weekly market in Apát.[66] Data from 1415 about linen and knives being stolen from a Turňa retailer at the weekly market in Rudabánya have already been mentioned.[67] In 1417, four carts carrying grain and other goods and seven horses were stolen from peasants going to the Wednesday market in Kisvárda.[68] In 1418, a cask of wine worth 50 florins was stolen from a peasant at the Kálló market.[69] Peasants traveling to the Kálló Wednesday market in 1422 intending to sell eight smoked flitches of pork for 26 new florins were held up on the way.[70] An item from 1481 may or may not concern a weekly market. Peasants from Tăutelec (Bihar County), from the lands of the Csapis family of Eszeny, were driving pigs to be sold at the St Martin's Day fair in Kisvárda. On the day before the fair (7 November), the pigs were stolen and killed at Tiszaszentmárton, which lies 21.5 kilometers from Kisvárda as the crow flies.[71] In 1510, a peasant and his son were on their way to the weekly market in Páka, Zala County. They were attacked, battered, suffered losses of 60 florins, and a horse worth eight florins was stolen from them.[72] That the victims in these examples were all peasants is coincidental, although they do feature most commonly. The weekly markets were mostly devoted to agricultural produce, although some manufactured goods were also sold at them. It is characteristic that what was stolen from the Turňa retailer was similar to what the Szentpál retailers had in store.

---

64   Kristó et al. (eds.) 1990–2015, XVII, no. 345.
65   C. Tóth (ed.) 2005, no. 67.
66   Mályusz et al. (eds.) 1951–2017, IV, no. 236.
67   See fn. 31.
68   Mályusz et al. (eds.) 1951–2017, VI, no. 391.
69   Mályusz et al. (eds.) 1951–2017, VI, no. 1972. The acts of might took place at Lenten time, and during the market of Kálló, held on Saint George's day.
70   Mályusz et al. (eds.) 1951–2017, IX, no. 838.
71   C. Tóth (ed.) 2003, no. 640.
72   Kóta 1997, no. 627.

Things were different at the annual fairs. These were very rare throughout the Árpádian age, but afterwards more towns and villages were granted privileges, particularly during King Sigismund's reign, and in the later Middle Ages there were several fairs a year in some towns. Many villages also held annual fairs; some more than one. Most fair-goers came from within a radius of about 20 kilometers, although some traveled up to 60 kilometers.[73] The ordering of fairs (and *Messen*) – i.e., their arrangement in the calendar to permit traders to move on from one to the next – has been discussed in the international and the Hungarian literature.[74] Such a system can be verified for some cases,[75] but is unlikely to have been universally valid. Some fairs attracted people from long distances. Leaving aside Buda, which was worth visiting for commercial purposes at any time regardless of whether there was a fair, two towns stand out in this respect. One is Székesfehérvár, which had four fairs spread out over the year, and attracted people from as far away as Vienna and Braşov.[76] The other was Oradea, where a total of eleven fairs were held. In a tax case which started in Oradea in 1476, the Transylvania towns were joined by burghers of Pest, Székesfehérvár, Košice, Prešov, Bardejov, Levoča, Bratislava and Ráckeve in an action against the taxation rights of the local chapter.[77] Since the fairs in both of these cities attracted merchants from nearly every town in the kingdom, it would be worth examining their potential classification as *Messen*.

Fairs in other towns also attracted visitors from further than 60 kilometers. Several fair venues in the northern half of the Great Hungarian Plain had very long reaches. Oradea's was the longest, at 370 kilometers, Debrecen's was 350 kilometers and Tiszavarsány's 200 kilometers. In addition, Cluj attracted fair-goers from distances of up to 250 kilometers, and Mezőtúr from up to 130 kilometers.[78] It would be interesting to gather more data about the catchment areas of fairs and examine why some were larger than others. Four more examples of distances follow. In the central place system devised by the present author, the market town of Hatvan, on the border of Heves and Pest Counties, had 16 centrality points, which permits its categorization as a market town with intermediate urban functions. In 1444, men working for György Rozgonyi from Žitný ostrov, which is 170 kilometers distant from Hatvan as the crow flies, were attacked on their way home and robbed of the 200 oxen and 6 horses they

---

73 See also work by the present author referred to in fn. 56. Kubinyi 2004b, 277–284.
74 Fügedi 1981b, 248–249, Kellenbenz 1991, 229–230 and Pounds 1994, 359–363.
75 Kubinyi 2000b, 29–30 and Kubinyi 2001a, 55.
76 Kubinyi 2004b, 281–282.
77 Kubinyi 1963 190–199, Kubinyi 2000, 92. Most recently, see: Weisz 2014.
78 Kubinyi 2000b, 169–185.

had bought at the fair. In 1459, merchandise worth 500 gold florins was bought from residents of Kremnica and Zvolen. The distance was about 125 kilometers. In 1503, the steward of the bishopric of Eger bought sawn timber for building to the value of 7 florins 70 denars at the St Luke's Day fair at Gyöngyöspüspöki, some 46 kilometers from Eger in a straight line.[79] The market town of Muhi in Borsod County also has 15 centrality points. The earliest piece of data, from 1422, is not so interesting: a peasant was attacked on his way to the fair from Borsodgeszt, some 32 kilometers away. In 1425, however, nobles of Hodász (in Szatmár County, 80 kilometers from Muhi) sent their servants to buy weapons at the Muhi fair. The weapons were stolen from them on the way home. The steward of the Eger bishopric (45 kilometers distant) bought 16 draft oxen, horse gear and coarse linen there.[80] The market town of Michalovce in the Slovakian part of medieval Zemplén County has 19 centrality points, classing it as a market town with intermediate urban functions. It had two weekly markets and five fairs. In 1398, 3 bolts of cloth – Bohemian cloth and fine broadcloth – were stolen from a peasant on his way to the Michalovce fair from the market town of Vranov nad Topľou in Zemplén, 23.5 kilometers away. In 1416, tenant peasants of the noble family of Pazdics had 20 new florins stolen on their way home from the fair. The same year, duty was allegedly collected illegally from a potter's tenant peasants on the wares they had sold. The distance from Michalovce was only 6.5 kilometers. Neither was long distance involved in an acts-of-might case of 1417. Servants of Komoróc nobles were attacked on their 19-kilometer long journey home from the fair. In 1503, the steward of the Eger bishopric intended to buy horses at the horse fair in Michalovce, which is 145 kilometers in a straight line from Eger.[81] Szerencs, also in Zemplén, became an *oppidum* only immediately before the battle of Mohács, having been a village until then. It has only 10 centrality points, which classes it as an average market town or market town-like village. We have no information about its weekly market, but the single item about the annual fair is very important. According to a 1519 charter, a peasant from Tiszalúc sold four oxen on credit to a burgher of Cluj. Since the customer did not pay, the next year the seller arrested another Cluj burgher's merchandise at the Szerencs fair. It was customary for an unpaid debt to be collected from a resident of the same town as the debtor. Although we have no information about the place where the oxen were

---

79   1459: MNL OL DL 64 378 and 1503: E. Kovács (ed.) 1992, 199.
80   Central place: Kubinyi 1999b, 517, 1422: Mályusz et al. (eds.) 1951–2017, XI, no. 548. 1425: Borsa (ed.) 1993, Dancs no. 109 and 1501: E. Kovács (ed.) 1992, 114.
81   Kubinyi 2005, 29–30, 1398: C. Tóth (ed.) 2005, no. 260, 1416: Mályusz et al. (eds.) 1951–2017, V, no. 2355, 1417: Mályusz et al. (eds.) 1951–2017, VI, no. 431 and 1503: see above fn. 38.

sold, it is certain that people from Cluj brought goods to sell at the Szerencs fair, a distance of 230 kilometers.[82]

There are many other records providing information on goods sold at fairs and the losses suffered by victims of acts of might. Trade in foreign broadcloth, for example, was quite common. Some records of fair-goers who suffered losses follow: in 1431, men from Eisenstadt were robbed on their way to the St Stephen's Day fair in Székesfehérvár, with the loss of 1000 florins.[83] In 1447, wares of value 1035 florins were stolen from two residents of Székesfehérvár (one of whom was a tailor) at Tata. Here it may only be guessed that they were going to or from a market.[84]

Practically everything could be found at the weekly markets, and particularly at the annual fairs, including imported wares like broadcloth and knives. Secular and ecclesiastical lords, burghers of cities and market towns and village peasants were all represented as both customers and sellers. Transactions could be quite substantial: even village peasants often traded to the value of 20–100 florins. They were also more often attacked than nobles, and so there are more surviving records of crimes against them. Cases were pressed on their behalf by their landlords. There were considerable differences among fair venues. Most had only a small market range, some served a wider region, and a few traded in goods for the whole country. The trade and geographical range of a fair, however, did not always reflect the level of urban development of the venue. Whereas geography was most important in determining the significance of the fair, other criteria were involved in urban development.

Other Factors Affecting Domestic Trade

Besides the right to hold fairs, the king granted other privileges promoting trade, mostly to towns. One of these was the staple right. Merchants were required to stop in towns with such rights and offer their wares for sale to the locals. This was often connected to enforced routes, making it impossible for the former to avoid towns that held the staple right. Landowners also tried to prevent avoidance of their customs stations, but fair-goers often used back roads. As for royal revenue, Hungarian kings put most effort into maximizing levies from foreign trade, and so the subject is of lesser interest here. Some towns' staple right applied only to a small area, and thus served the interests of

---

82   Jakó (ed.) 1990, II, no. 3747.
83   Horváth (ed.) 2005, no. 37.
84   MNL OL DL 88 219.

the landowner as much as those of the town. One of these was the Nyírbátor staple right, the credibility of which has been disputed, although it definitely existed by 1512 at the latest and perhaps was mostly to the benefit of members of its landowners, the Bátori family.[85] Another regional privilege of this kind was held by Dolná Súča in Turóc County, originally granted by King Sigismund and confirmed by Kings Matthias, Ferdinand I and, in 1572, Maximilian II. This permitted a weekly market on Tuesdays and a staple right for Polish salt. The *magister tavernicorum* was obliged to seize the salt of violators of this order. Just like in the case of Nyírbátor, the staple right was also connected to the weekly market.[86]

Enforced routes were connected to customs duties imposed or permitted by the king, and also influenced trade. Unless the town itself held the right to collect duties, as was generally – but not always – the case for market duties, that influence was negative. Customs duty was collected in many forms in medieval Hungary. The thirtieth customs duty paid to the king had its effect primarily on foreign trade in the Late Middle Ages, and so is not of interest here.[87] In addition to this and the market duties, there were road, ferry and bridge duties. In principle, the holder of the right to collect customs duty had an obligation to safeguard passage. There are many charters to prove this. For instance, in 1441, King Wladislas I granted the lords of Michalovce customs rights in return for building a bridge over the River Laborec and an embankment to hold back the mud.[88]

In 1449, at the request of Hont County, the regent, John Hunyadi, ordered the provost of Šahy to build bridges over two rivers, in return for which every noble and merchant was obliged to go into Šahy and pay duty there.[89] Occasionally, a register was taken of each county's customs posts and the roads leading to them, and those held to be unlawful were closed.[90] Priests, nobles and burghers of towns and some market towns enjoyed exemption from duty, but this only applied to privately-held customs duties if the privileges of the town had been granted before the duty-collection right.[91] Merchants exempt from duty

85   On the territorially restricted stable right: Kubinyi 2000b, 24–25. The privilege of Nyírbátor: Balogh 1999, 107–131 and Draskóczy 2001b, 261–273.
86   MNL OL A 57 Libri Regii. Vol. 3. 1039–1040.
87   See: Pach 1990.
88   MNL OL DL 13 621.
89   MNL OL DL 14 315 and 16 755.
90   1405: Nógrád and Hont Counties, see: Mályusz et al. (eds.) 1951–2017, II/2, no. 1412. Pozsony and Moson Counties, see: Mályusz et al. (eds.) 1951–2017, III, no. 1584. Also see: Iványi 1905.
91   The frequent customs-related lawsuits are a consequence of this. Kubinyi 1963, 189–226.

could clearly sell their goods more cheaply or at a greater profit, which put traders from villages and smaller market towns in a weaker commercial position. The history of customs duties in Hungary in the late medieval period still lacks a modern treatment.[92]

Traders found ways of avoiding customs, non-locals got round restrictions on trading at times other than markets, and even those with insufficient capital managed to make up for it. The formation of merchant companies was common in medieval Europe. These could be set up for long periods or for a single transaction. In some countries, they were organized along family lines.[93] Although Article 16 of King Sigismund's 1405 "Urban Decree" forbade association with foreign merchants,[94] this could be got round by marriage or acquiring the rights of burgher in a Hungarian town.[95] Wealthier merchants, whether or not they belonged to a company, also kept employees. By the Late Middle Ages, the head of the company seldom actually went to a market, but managed the business from home.[96] He had agents operating on his behalf. German charters mention two categories of these. The *diener* kept accounts himself and could take money on his principal's behalf, while the *knecht* was more of a servant.[97]

Since no merchants' account books survive, except that kept by Paul Moritz, information can only be gleaned from municipal records, landowners' and municipal account books and records of acts-of-might cases. There are also some rare surviving records of accounts rendered between business associates or between the head of a company and his assistant. We have already seen some examples, such the assumed relationship between Jakab Trommelenk of Buda with Nyírbátor merchants. Some others may be mentioned. Košice's oldest municipal records contain several such references. Here we will look at two persons. In 1399, the company of Ulrich Kammerer of Nuremberg is mentioned in connection with the purchase of copper. His agents issued a document bearing the company's stamp.[98] In the other case, a document states that two bolts of cloth, one of long "Lemny" and one of Bohemian broadcloth, were taken from Lőrinc Torkos, a tenant peasant of the Perényi family, at the Kálló market

---

92   Sólyom 1933. For up to the Angevin period, see: Weisz 2013b.
93   See: Kellenbenz 1991, 231, Pounds 1994, 356–357 and Irsigler 1985, 391.
94   Döry, Bónis and Bácskai (eds.) 1976, 204–205.
95   Kubinyi 1994c, 26–39.
96   Pounds 1994, 356–357 and Isenmann 1988, 363–369.
97   Mollay 1991, 19.
98   Halaga (ed.) 1994, no. 2911. See most recently on the connections of German towns with Hungarian towns (mostly Buda): Draskóczy 2016c.

in 1398. The Košice municipal records for 1402 state that János Debreceni, son-in-law of Lőrinc Torkos of Patak (Sárospatak, then held by the Perényis), promised to pay 100 florins at the May Feast of the Holy Cross in Leles (where a fair was being held), on behalf of a resident of Levoča. Torkos is mentioned in the Košice municipal records in connection with loans totaling 634 florins, two concerning burghers of Cracow, and one in which the customer was Thomas Siebenlinder. In 1399, his house in the town (clearly Košice) was mortgaged against his debts. In 1401, his son John is mentioned as having debts of 153 florins. He may have been in business with his son and son-in-law. The point is that a market-town merchant, his son, and his son-in-law from Debrecen, had commercial dealings with merchants from Poland, Levoča and Sáros County, involving quite substantial sums. As a resident of Sárospatak, he also owned a house in Košice.[99]

Some examples of merchants' agents follow. In 1491, a Greek from Târgoviște, a man from Sibiu and a *Rác* (an ethnic Serbian) from Ráckeve called Keresztes met in front of a house in Cluj belonging to a burgher of Sibiu. As they spoke, it emerged that Keresztes was a retainer of the Haller family from Buda. Ruprecht Haller, a patrician from Nuremberg, was the son-in-law of a Buda judge (Johann Münzer) and himself a juror in Buda, later becoming a judge and a prominent merchant. Merchants from Ráckeve traded throughout the country, but the above information shows that some of them were certainly in the service of merchants based in the capital.[100] One curious affair: a retainer of the Pest burgher István Szép, Péter Bornemissza (probably actually Onwein) of Vienna (*de Wyenna*) lodged an action against the daughter of Matthias Eppel, a resident of Cluj, for breach of a marriage promise, but the action was mutually rescinded. What this tells us is that a Vienna merchant was in service with a Pest foreign-goods dealer, and went on his master's business to Transylvania, where he almost got married.[101]

Some accounts rendered: In 1483, Christopher Weiss, retainer (*diener*) of the Buda burgher Angelus (almost certainly Angelus Kanczlyr, brother-in-law of Tamás Bakóc and younger brother of the later Buda judge János), owed his master 200 florins and rendered accounts with him before a tribunal headed by the vice-judge. He also stated that he had not put his master in debt to anyone, and he had traded only with his money. He was to repay his debt by the next Lord's Day.[102] In 1491, the Buda Council engaged Buda jurors Ruprecht

---

99   C. Tóth (ed.) 2003, 45.
100 Jakó (ed.) 1990, II, no. 2750. On Haller: Kubinyi 1963–1964, 89–97.
101 Jakó (ed.) 1990, II, no. 3610.
102 Weiss' own promissory: MNL OL DF 242 948.

Haller and Hans Arnolt, and burgher Peter Edlasperger (otherwise Juncker, Buda customs officer) at the request of the widow of Buda burgher (and former judge) György Forster to review the accounts of the Košice burgher György Ferber. Forster had given merchandise to Ferber to sell. Forster's accounts were checked against the accounts of his former retainer János Mayerhofer. He owed more than 1100 florins, but at the request of the members of the tribunal, the widow waived part of that and claimed only 1100 florins. Ferber promised to settle the debt and named his father as guarantor.[103] In this case it is difficult to establish whether Ferber was a business associate or a commercial agent. The sum involved suggests the former. It is probable that such a distinction cannot always be made. Mayerhofer was presumably Forster's accountant. The city authorities took such matters very seriously and engaged reputable merchants to check the accounts of both debtors and creditors.

We can move on from this subject to touch on the written formulations of business life in the form of accounts. Trade in any substantial volume was impossible without business accounting. It should be mentioned, however, that double-entry bookkeeping, already common in Italy in the fourteenth century, had not yet spread to Hungary. Neither was it general practice in contemporary Germany.[104] Bills of exchange, used in lieu of cash from the twelfth century onwards, do not appear in the records of Hungarian merchants either.[105] Market halls, however, were set up in some towns. One was the *domus apotecariorum* in Óbuda, and Prešov also made revenue on its market hall.[106]

There is much else that has to be omitted owing to lack of space, or is still awaiting adequate research. Two examples of the latter, one relating to carriage: As we have seen, Act 10 of 1521 taxed full-time provincial merchants on the number of draft horses they had. It is unlikely that urban wholesale merchants kept as many horses as they needed, and they probably used peasant carriers. György Székely has treated this in more detail.[107] Earlier, I quoted a charter stating that peasant carriers from Kolozs County bore merchandise of Ráckeve merchants to Oradea. The 1481 guild charter of Oradea smiths, spurmakers and sword-makers mentions carters of Štítnik (in Gömör County) who sold ironmongery in Oradea. Since carters belonged to the same guild or similar association as smiths, they enjoyed some concessions at the time of

---

103   MNL OL DF 270 728.
104   See e.g. Isenmann 1988, 360–363.
105   Pounds 1994, 412–422 and North 1996, 223–238.
106   Fügedi 1981b, 244. See most recently: Benda 2016a, 269–270.
107   Székely 1961, 331–332.

the Whitsun fair.[108] This shows that the carriers themselves were involved in trade. River navigation must also be mentioned. Fair-goers from Pest and its suburb of Szentfalva went by boat to the Whitsun fair in Budafelhévíz. In 1524, 58 persons, most of them artisans, were examined, mostly about where their boats were tethered. Seven of those who made statements were women, two with their husbands, two spinsters and three widows.[109] Fair-going was a family event, but sometimes wives may have run the business.[110]

Research into prices and wages is needed. Medieval Sopron has been the subject of an excellent piece of work,[111] but Austrian money was in circulation there, and trade as well as the economy in general was under the influence of Hungary's western neighbor. The present author has gathered a large quantity of data from points scattered throughout the kingdom, but what is needed is a series of data from one place. There are considerable difficulties with establishing grain and wine prices because of fluctuations due to annual yields, and pre-harvest peaks. Some data have been established, however, for the building trades. Comparison with the south German lands shows wages to have been very similar. There was a difference in the cost of food and clothing. The former were lower in Hungary and the latter in the German lands. (Except for footwear, where prices in leather-rich Hungary were similar to those in Germany.) Accordingly, a better-off person in Hungary who could afford more and better-quality clothes had to spend more on provisions. Incidentally, the monthly salary of a Hungarian foot soldier was two florins, which means that it was possible to live from this amount.[112]

Late Medieval Domestic Trade: A Summary

The close spacing of fairs in the medieval kingdom of Hungary implies a high level of domestic trade. Agricultural produce, manufactures by Hungarian artisans, animals which were partly bred for export, and also merchandise brought in from abroad were all involved in this commerce. Not even village-dwellers, it seems, made everything for themselves. Much money was in circulation, which is understandable considering the taxes which had to be paid to the king and the landed gentry, and tithes which were often paid in money. A tenant peasant

---

108 Fejér, Rácz and Szász (eds.) 2003, no. 4.
109 MNL OL DL 32 685.
110 On the role of women: Szende 1993–1996, 171–190.
111 Dányi and Zimányi 1989.
112 Dirlmeier 1978. My analysis: Kubinyi 1991e, 24–26.

could only obtain this money by selling his produce. In practice, everybody from lord to peasant bought and sold. It should be borne in mind that commerce was not confined to the fairs; much went on in the merchants' premises or the artisans' workshops. The large quantity of merchandise which György Ferber of Košice received from György Forster of Buda, for example, was not sold at a fair, because he, as a Košice burgher, could trade freely.

There are three further issues to consider. Marxist historiography was intent on proving that the "feudal ruling class" suppressed peasants' market activity. To what extent is this true? What sources of income were available to the tenant peasantry? Is it possible to talk of a single national market in medieval Hungary?

Buying and selling in domestic trade was engaged in by practically the entire population of the country, including the secular and ecclesiastical lords, understanding the role of which was the subject of much effort by historians in the second half of the twentieth century. A wealth of source material has been unearthed, proving that the previously rare manorial system started to become widespread in the first half of the sixteenth century. This greatly increased landlords' interest in selling agricultural produce, and brought them up against competition from burghers of cities and market towns, and from peasants. It also explains the increasing number of laws against these sections of the population during the fifteenth and sixteenth centuries.[113] We should not, however, infer that no prelates, barons or nobles were involved in trade before that time. Although it was still a minority activity among them, there were both wealthier and poorer landowners who engaged in trade. Some joined up with professional merchants as sleeping partners, providing goods or money.[114] Others, however, traded directly themselves. A good example was Miklós Inárcsi, a man of letters and deputy to the Hungarian Diet for Pest County at the turn of the fifteenth and sixteenth centuries, who built up a flourishing trade in wine, cattle, cloth, building timber, etc. with effectively no capital, using a loan obtained when he was a retainer to the Losonci family.[115]

The writer of these lines has been intrigued by the question whether the income from a peasant plot can be used to determine the living standards of the peasantry. Was a patch of poor land, often just a fragment of a plot, enough to feed a family?[116] This question was behind a treatment, some years ago, of a

---

113   See e.g. Pach 1963, 135–317. Also: Draskóczy 1996a.
114   Engel, Kristó and Kubinyi 2003, 289.
115   Based on accounts between 1498 and 1503. MNL OL DL 104 071. See in detail the profit-margin of the different activities: Kubinyi 1984b, 23.
116   My pieces of work on everyday life are listed in: Kubinyi 2006b, 13 fn. 1.

register taken in Cesargrad in Varasd County in 1489, showing that the towns' fields were at most sufficient for feeding the inhabitants, but they also had vineyards, meadows, forests, fishing and mills. The annual customs revenue of the market town at the center of the estate was estimated at the very high figure of 200 florins. (The estate lay on the Austrian border.)[117] The question has also been examined by others, such as Árpád Nógrády.[118] Professional merchants, as we have seen, lived among village and market-town peasants, but they did not have a monopoly on trade. In cases of acts of might, peasant fair-goers usually suffered losses of between 20 and 100 florins, and sometimes more. In 1420, for example, a burgher of Rovišće in Körös County was robbed on his way home from the fair in Bélavár, Somogy County, of his six-horse cart, 30 bolts of broadcloth and 150 florins.[119]

Few records survive of tenant peasants' means in villages and market towns. When a village was robbed, it was not certain whether the well-hidden items were found. In a case of acts of might in Szentpál, although twenty-four persons in three villages suffered total losses of 300 florins, only four peasants lost their own money: the furrier had 60 florins stolen, but the sums taken from other three were 10 florins, 7 florins, and 75 denars respectively. The judge of Szentpál was beaten, but suffered no pecuniary loss. The judge of Nagyberény also got away with a loss of 6 florins 65 denars he was keeping in a purse, which was tax collected for the lord, László Kanizsai.[120] A fifteenth-century register of debtors published by István Draskóczy shows the significance of the circulation of money in rural areas. The Manini brothers, members of the salt chamber, registered the debts of 166 persons in sixty-seven towns and villages, mainly in the northeastern part of Transdanubia. The average figure was 10.82 florins per nobleman. Scholars had average debts of 15.75 florins, town and market-town burghers 10.57 florins, and villagers 4.61 florins.[121]

The present author knows only one source which gives the exact wealth of more than one member of the rural population. This is the record of a 1518 court case involving the Körmend Friary.[122] Unfortunately, only twelve witnesses stated their wealth in monetary terms. They included one rural parish priest (55 florins), two noblemen (100 and 50 florins), six burghers of Körmend

---

117 Kubinyi 2001b, 3–17.
118 See the contribution of Árpád Nógrády in the present volume.
119 Mályusz et al. (eds.) 1951–2017, VII, no. 2158.
120 Radvánszky and Závodszky (eds.) 1909–1922, II, 389–395.
121 Draskóczy 1996a, 93–112.
122 Erdélyi 2005, 212–213. The edition of the register: Erdélyi 2006, 49–193. Forty-nine witnesses were interrogated.

market town (2000, 300, 100, 100, 75 and 50 florins), and three village peasants (46, 16 and 10 florins). The wealthiest witness, with 2000 florins, was András Csuti, burgher of Körmend, who was a cattle trader.[123] These figures show that trade offered the way to quite substantial wealth, even for a person who did not live in a free royal town. They also reveal fairly narrow wealth gaps between village peasants, market-town dwellers, minor landed nobles, and priests. This explains the relatively substantial losses suffered by fair-goers in cases of acts of might: even peasants and market-town burghers could be moderately well off. Future research should devote more effort to understanding the wealth of people of different social stations. It should be remembered here that the criterion of poverty – and thus exemption from royal taxes – was possession of less than three florins.

Market towns were especially well-placed as regards circulation of trade. Recent historiography has tended to regard the *oppida* released from royal control (like Körmend), especially those acquired by ecclesiastical landlords, as having lost out under their new landlords. This was recently refuted by Norbert C. Tóth[124] as well as by Ján Lukačka, who argues that the new lords had no interest in curtailing the rights of their town.[125]

The extent to which the Kingdom of Hungary had a single market towards the end of the Middle Ages is yet be definitely decided. Over forty years ago, the present author concluded from a study of several customs cases that this could effectively be ruled out: there were smaller territorial units, and only the germs of a national market, whose development was mainly in the interest of the capital-city population.[126] The discussion of markets and fairs demonstrated that most of the annual fairs which had large geographical ranges attracted merchants from only certain parts of the country, but there were exceptions: the capital city Buda – which is not dealt with separately here – and the fairs of Oradea and Székesfehérvár. In principle, then, these three centers could have bound the whole country together. There is, however, another potential angle on the issue. The range of each fair venue may be determined from where fair-goers came from. We should also look at where else these people went. A merchant visiting one fair would also have visited several other rural centers, and so by linking up their places of origin it would be possible to determine a much larger market range. It is well known that merchants from the capital city (people from both Buda and Pest) made their appearance all over the kingdom.

---

123 Erdélyi 2015, 88–89.
124 C. Tóth 2004, 597.
125 Lukačka 2005, 129–130.
126 Kubinyi 1963, 189–226.

Curiously, traders from the market town of Ráckeve took their business everywhere from Transylvania to Styria (and obviously also to the Balkans).[127] The iron-mining towns of Gömör County had business relationships in several regions and in other countries.[128] Most of them had trading partners in towns and villages in modern Slovakia, Buda, and northern Transylvania. Family connections also offer a mirror on business relationships. The present author has published specific evidence of this among the burghers of late medieval Buda and Pest.[129] Recent research on other towns, such as István Petrovics's work on links between south Hungarian towns and Upper Hungary, supports this view.[130]

Although some annual fair venues may be identified as centers of commodity exchange in larger regions, more attention should be paid to towns and market towns from where merchants traveled to more than one regional center. It is not certain that these regional centers should be regarded as more important. Returning to our examples: the present author knows of instances of merchants from Hatvan or Muhi visiting other fairs. The lesson is that much more research is needed to determine the actual commercial centers. The national-market question is thus still very far from being answered.

---

127   Miskei 2003, 68–80.
128   Kollomann 2005, 117–122.
129   Kubinyi 1966, 227–291.
130   Petrovics 2005, 131–158.

CHAPTER 22

Import Objects as Sources of the Economic History of Medieval Hungary

István Feld

Economic historians have already explored most of the written sources on imports to the medieval Kingdom of Hungary, but none have yet attempted a comprehensive analysis of the still-tangible objects of these imports, the goods themselves. Since World War II, experts of medieval archaeology have brought to light great quantities of foreign-made luxuries and everyday personal objects in Hungary, and subjected finds of several types to – mostly typological – analysis. This mainly applies to items made of metal, glass and pottery, materials which could survive for centuries in the ground and various infill strata. Finds of textiles and other organic-material wares, such as the fourteenth-century Italian silk hangings found in a well near the buildings of the royal palace of Buda,[1] are extremely rare. Although many imported objects have been the focus of art history research, there have been hardly any comparative historical investigations aimed at imports as such.

This chapter reviews what is already known about imports, mainly object categories surviving in large quantities and thus attracting deeper research interest, and attempts to recommend future lines of investigation. The discussion inevitably reflects the state of research in archaeology, art history and history of craftsmanship. Consequently, it will not deal with weapon imports, despite their considerable economic significance, and also leaves out the rare category of bone and antler artefacts, as for instance the eleventh-century walrus-tusk crook, probably of Scandinavian origin, found in the Veszprémvölgy (presently part of Veszprém) Convent.[2] For reasons of space, the review will concern only research carried out within the present borders of Hungary.

By way of introduction, we will look at some fundamental issues. First of all, it is not always certain whether the arrival in Hungary of an object made abroad was an economic event at all; i.e., whether it came into the territory of the Kingdom of Hungary as a classical item of commerce. Many objects at

---

1 Nyékhelyi 2003.
2 Fülöp and Koppány 2004.

that time may have been made to order or brought in as gifts, or even as plunder. These considerations apply particularly to items in ecclesiastical or aristocratic collections; certainly some of the known foreign-made objects made of precious metal and weapons have never been in the ground.

Neither can we always be sure whether an object is foreign at all. It may be a domestic product following foreign patterns or displaying the effects of foreign workshops. This can also be important evidence for international connections, and is related to the question of immigration and the settlement of craftsmen and artists linked to specific ethnic groups. In the absence of explicit written sources, it is often not possible to decide beyond doubt whether we are looking at an import or a local imitation. The usual ways of studying medieval material culture and art – the collection and analysis of analogues and art-history style criticism – do not always give a useful basis in this area, and resources for high-cost material tests are scarce.[3]

Finally, there has been a tendency for archaeologists and art historians in Hungary to assume that an object's place of manufacture lies close to its find spot if there is no indisputable evidence of foreign origin. This means that the former have thought in terms of local production even when this is not the only available interpretation. Domestic crafts still attract much more interest from artisans concerned with material culture than imported wares.

Gold and Silverware

The introductory comments apply all the more strongly to objects of precious metals made in goldsmiths' workshops. These traditionally belong to art historians' territory, even though new additions nowadays come almost solely from archaeological discoveries and excavations. The archaeologists who actually find the gold and silverware only rarely publish about them, and so subsequent investigations are usually by art historians, or by archaeologists using art history approaches.

One such area has concentrated on analyzing objects of court pomp and church liturgy, particularly eleventh–twelfth-century items. It is common for these publications to state that the somewhat small number of imported items – Byzantine or Western – were made to royal commission or presented as gifts, and were not objects of economic or commercial history. A good illustration of the limited means of research in past decades is the study of a pearl-studded cloisonné enamel pendant found at the excavation of the royal palace

---

[3] Benkő 2005.

at Esztergom. This concluded that the pendant may have been Byzantine, but was more probably Byzantine-influenced local work from the late twelfth century.[4]

Even when art historians have touched on the trade in gold and silverware during the thirteenth century, they have usually seen it in terms of imports to the royal court, even though European commercial goldsmith centers had definitely been established by that time. Important examples are Hungarian trade with Venice, on which there are written records, and related items of gold and silverware, including some very significant reliquary crosses and female crowns that may be traced to Italy.[5]

Even research into the much greater quantities of fourteenth–fifteenth-century objects – liturgical pieces, jewelry, luxurious tableware (cutlery, silver cups and goblets, gilded or gold chalices and tankards)[6] – has not yet explicitly included trade among its primary objectives. In general, art historians researching medieval Hungary have primarily devoted themselves, using their own special style of critical methods, to the determination of local products and their features, at most referring to the influence of imported objects, or pattern-books.

Indeed, the rising domestic demand during this period may already have been largely satisfied by Hungarian-based goldsmiths, whose work is relatively well known from the written sources. Nonetheless, a systematic collection of written sources on the import of late medieval gold and silverware – a good example being Éva Kovács's investigations in France on the Matthias Calvary in Esztergom[7] – may be identified as an important line of future research for the assessment of trade in luxury goods. This is considerably helped by detailed catalogues, such as the Hungarian National Museum's liturgical gold and silverware collection catalogue produced by Judit H. Kolba in 2004.[8]

Bronze and Copper Work

The situation is similar for the increasing number of less prestigious (by virtue of the material) bronze and copper products found in recent archaeological

---

4 Kovács 1994.
5 Kovács 1971 and Kovács 1974.
6 Wetter 2011, Zsámbéki 1983 and Holl 2005a.
7 Kovács 1972, 120 and Kovács 1998.
8 Kolba 2004. On the archaeological finds connected to goldsmith work in medieval Buda see: Holl 1991.

excavations. Except for the period up to the thirteenth century, research into these has in the past been completely dominated by the art history approach. Some systematic work on late medieval objects has been done recently, however, principally on bells and church fonts, and for some museum catalogues.[9]

Not surprisingly, the issue of trade has been discussed in connection with processional and altar crosses, cross bases, candlesticks, censers, aquamaniles, and lavabos, rather than the Byzantine or Kievan type of bronze pectoral crosses[10] linked to pilgrimages to the Holy Land. Although previous research has not doubted the significance of the large number of bronze objects of twelfth century, mostly of liturgical function, which were brought into the country (in ways that are still largely unknown) from the Rhine-Maas region, Lorraine, Flanders, Swabia, Magdeburg and Nuremberg,[11] it has still primarily been concerned with determining the role of domestic bronze work and deciding which products were made in Hungary. For this, the style criticism method is increasingly being joined by material tests, although there is still considerable emphasis on the effects of foreign precursors and patterns, and on imitation and adoption of form. The limitations of research are indicated by a recent assessment of a cross recently found at an excavation in Balatonfüred,[12] displaying parallels with the Esztergom pendant. Byzantium was again identified as the place of manufacture, or the source of influence on a workshop or craftsman in Hungary.[13] A good example of linking find spot with place of manufacture concerns a distinctive group of aquamaniles representing mounted hunters, previously asserted to be of Hungarian origin, but found by more recent studies to be a somewhat more complex problem.[14]

There has been somewhat more research into enamel-decorated copper pieces – chiefly cladding and corpuses of wooden crosses, ciboria, reliquaries and lavabos – from Limoges, France, dated in the main to the thirteenth century. These are perhaps the most spectacular items in this group and were indisputably manufactured for trade. Having swept cast bronze work off the European market, they were imported into Hungary in large quantities, and domestic imitations further prove their popularity. Research interest arises from their abundance at archaeological sites, even excavations of small village churches. The current historical construction of the function of Limoges

---

9   Benkő 2002, Benkő 2010 and Lovag 1999.
10   Lovag 1971 and Lovag 1980.
11   Lovag 1979 and Lovag 1984.
12   Valter 1972.
13   Lovag 1994.
14   Lovag 1979, 24–26 and Benkő 2005.

IMPORT OBJECTS AS SOURCES OF THE ECONOMIC HISTORY 459

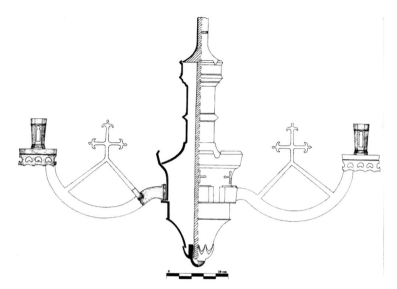

FIGURE 22.1   *Fragments of the chandelier of Ozora (kept in the Wosinsky Mór County Museum, Szekszárd).*

ware and the chronology of its importation into Hungary is that these objects were required in large quantities to meet the demands of reconstruction after the 1241–1242 Mongol invasion, but further and more precisely-investigated archaeological finds will probably modify this view. Although this gives us no better insight into the mode and route of imports, we can be sure that the majority of these relatively cheap, largely liturgical, items found their way to Hungary via trade.[15]

Late medieval imports from Western and Central Europe also included a "bulk goods" category which has been somewhat less researched. These are (mainly secular) bronze and copper vessels, mortars, candlesticks, chandeliers, metal fittings and "Nuremberg bowls" that survive in much larger quantities. A fifteenth-century chandelier reconstructed from fragments found in Ozora Castle,[16] proved partly by material test to have come from Nuremberg, shows the potential inherent in this kind of – very plentiful – archaeological material, and points the way forward for future studies (*see* Fig. 22.1.).

---

15   Kovács 1961 and Kovács 1968. Recent archaeological finds have already changed this dating and interpretation, see: Rosta 2013.
16   Gere 2003, 60–64.

There are also many objects held in museum collections whose publication could shed light on the volume and economic importance of imports relative to domestic production, and on the question of adoption of form. Comprehensive museum catalogues are an essential complement to the thorough assessment of new archaeological finds. A good example is Zsuzsa Lovag's 1999 work on the medieval bronze items in the Hungarian National Museum, which well reflects the current state of research. It includes a thorough discussion of twelfth–thirteenth-century, mainly Western European products, but devotes much less attention to late medieval items in the mass-market category which survive in greater quantities.[17]

Tinware

The extremely small number of tin products – bowls, plates, pitchers, jugs – which have been found in excavations and often in wells and rivers, or survive in collections, are insufficient to permit a judgment of their role and significance in everyday life in medieval Hungary. There are written sources, however, mainly from the Late Middle Ages, and Western European pictorial representations, which indicate quite widespread use, naturally varying between different sections of society.

A comprehensive analysis of medieval tinsmith work in Hungary by Imre Holl, involving a collection of objects has taken the study of this distinctive group of products beyond considerations of domestic manufacture alone. The author drew attention to data on the substantial import of tin items starting in the mid-fifteenth century and, on the basis of stamps on tin vessels bearing the mark of the maker and the town hallmark (sometimes even the intermediary craftsman), determined the origin of products from Hungary, Silesia (Wrocław, Nysa), Vienna, Salzburg and Nuremberg, most created in the early sixteenth century. Rejecting the view that the location of manufacture follows from the find spot, he proposed that tinsmiths in towns throughout Central Europe were, by the Late Middle Ages, producing similar products expressly for trade, products which satisfied the largely similar needs of households in each country. These hypotheses will stand or fall on further fortunate archaeological finds, the use of scientific methods, and of course the extension of the study to an international scale.[18]

---

17   Lovag 1999.
18   Holl 1987, Holl 1996 and Holl 2005a, 358–360.

Ironware

Ironware is the largest and perhaps most important category of medieval metal ware. Having relatively low artistic status, iron artifacts rarely feature in collections but do turn up in large numbers in excavations, presenting a costly exercise in restoration. As with tin objects, many pieces – especially tools – were observed quite early to bear the stamps of workshops or craftsmen, but these have not yet been subject to systematic research or comprehensively published. The only systematically collected and analyzed forgings are agricultural implements,[19] and there is hardly a single comprehensive publication or appraisal of major archaeological ironware finds in Hungary.[20]

Nonetheless, the importance of iron goods as import products is quite clear from the surviving fifteenth-century thirtieth customs registers. By quantity alone, the import of knives and knife blades in numbers approaching a million at Sopron and Bratislava shows that in terms of economic importance they far outstripped imports of precious metal-, bronze- or tinware (see Fig. 22.2).

Imre Holl was also the first to investigate archaeological finds to realize that the large number of stamped knives from the late medieval village of Sarvaly (a deserted settlement in the borders of Sümeg) excavated between 1969 and 1974 were in fact imports.[21] He then devoted a whole study to the late medieval craft specializations of knife-making, independently-working blade smiths and grinders, and the related trade in semi-finished products. From the maker's mark on the knife blades and often the hallmark based on the coat of arms of the country or town, he identified the knives found at Sarvaly and at many other Hungarian find spots as originating from the town of Steyr in Austria. He also identified products from Vienna and Nuremberg, and thus convincingly proved, in line with written sources, that complete knives and knife-blades were imported into Hungary, and also into Moldavia, on an enormous scale to meet the mass demand for cheap products, and their low prices meant that there was negligible domestic production.[22]

It is almost certain that comprehensive studies of other late medieval iron products bearing makers' marks would bear similarly significant results. Many shears and sickles found in Sarvaly have stamp marks, and the same is true for horseshoes from the Cistercian abbey at Pilisszentkereszt, for example.

---

19   Müller 1982 and Müller 2014.
20   Holl and Parádi 1982, 50–86 and Gere 2003.
21   Holl and Parádi 1982, 50–86.
22   Holl 1994–1995.

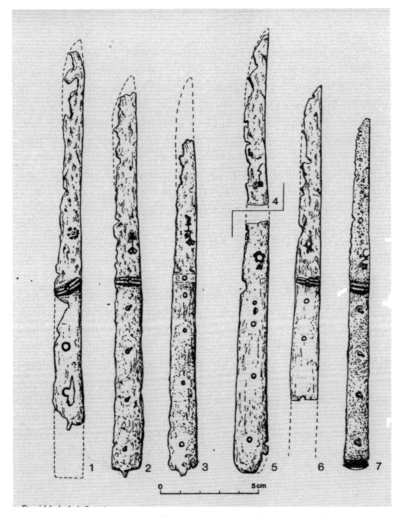

FIGURE 22.2A *Knives imported from Austria. Apart from their type the masters' signs also testify their origin (after Holl 1994–1995).*

This seems even more general in the case of hoes, axes, hatchets and adzes. This information has not yet been collated or subjected to a large-scale study. More attention also needs to be paid to preserving stamp marks by fast restoration. Most of these items may of course be local products of the substantial Hungarian iron industry, but evidence that at least some were of foreign origin

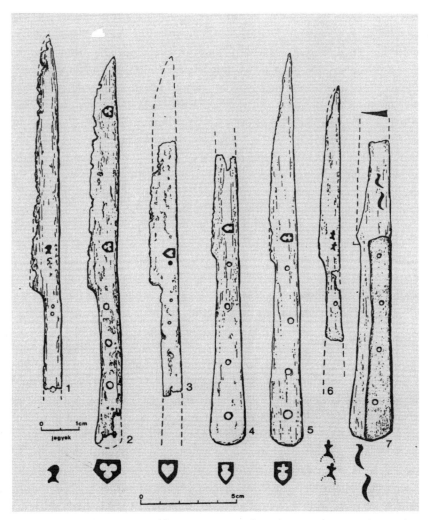

FIGURE 22.2B *Knives imported from Austria. Apart from their type the masters' signs also testify their origin (after Holl 1994–1995).*

comes from the late fifteenth-century thirtieth customs register of Sopron. Some – admittedly only a few – of its entries record the import of horseshoes, sickles and axes.[23]

---

23   Holl 2000, 39–47 and Benkő 2010.

Glassware

Glassware has yielded more information on imports than any other area of medieval archaeology. Until the 1970s, only a few fine goblets and cups surviving in collections, many of them originally produced to order, hinted at the significance of glassware in this period, particularly the glassware imported from Italy starting in the second half of the fifteenth century. Since then, research based on the special method of appraisal and reconstruction developed by Katalin H. Gyürky[24] has to a large extent traced the origin, range of types and chronology of glassware used in medieval Hungary. Some minor assistance in this has come from analysis of written sources, but much more significant is data provided by archaeological finds and the burgeoning research into glassware throughout Europe, followed by comprehensive publication of excavations, particularly the major royal seats.[25]

A striking result of recent glass research is that the earliest finds – some painted or ground-decoration cups traceable to Byzantine and Middle Eastern cultures and glass lamps and "goitred" bottles from around 1200 – cannot be proved to be commercial imports to the Hungarian Kingdom, although the possibility cannot be completely excluded. The literature links most of them with the crusade led by King Andrew II of Hungary.[26] From the mid-thirteenth century, however, there were demonstrable large-scale imports into the major towns in Hungary, and the several hundred glass vessel fragments found in the excavation of a Buda house almost certainly belonged to a merchant's stock. Imports were initially still from Byzantine lands, but increasingly from south and north Italy, and by the end of the century, mostly from the Venetian-held town of Murano, although the issue of origin is not completely closed. Glassware gradually became less of a luxury product. Gyürky considered glassware such as goitre neck bottles, "double cone" bottles (containing brandy, an increasingly popular beverage), prunt glasses, and enameled cups (many decorated with coats of arms) to have been imported initially by Ishmaelite merchants, and later by merchants from Dubrovnik, although some wares from the German lands were brought in by merchants from Regensburg and Vienna.[27]

By contrast, higher-quality Venetian glassware – which also included mold-blown, scalloped, "optically decorated" and some twisted-thread glasses and wine bottles, and more rarely chalices – supplied the needs of wealthier burghers and nobles in Hungary in the fourteenth century. Some types were

---

24 H. Gyürky 1982a.
25 H. Gyürky 1986b, H. Gyürky 1991 and Mester 1997.
26 H. Gyürky 1990, H. Gyürky 1991 and H. Gyürky 1999.
27 H. Gyürky 2003 and Holl 2005a, 348–350.

intended specifically for this country.[28] There is also more and more information on the manufacture of glass in Hungary, mostly of plain items like window panes, from the thirteenth–fourteenth centuries, involving craftsmen who had migrated from abroad. We also know of Hungarian assistants in Venetian glassworks, and it is also possible that the appellation *Glaser* and *vitripar* found in written sources from the fourteenth century onwards does not necessarily mean a local manufacturer. It could refer to the distributor of imported glass.[29]

The loss of Italian imports for a short period in the first half of the fifteenth century was partly made up for by poorer-quality Hungarian imitations of long-established Venetian vessel forms, but at a time when European glassmaking was booming, products of south German and Bohemian centers also appeared, although most of these cannot be definitely identified (*see* Fig. 22.3).[30]

The accession of Matthias Corvinus to the Hungarian throne set off the second age of Venetian glassware in Hungary. Hitherto less-popular vessel forms such as goblets and glasses with gilded and painted Renaissance ornamentation, and certain kinds of bowls and jugs, started to appear in royal and aristocratic centers and even in the houses of village nobles. More systematic research is required to determine which of these were imports from Northern and Western Europe, and in what proportions. Additionally, comparison with finds from Hungarian glassworks could positively identify which of them are domestic products, a classification hitherto made only on the criterion of poorer quality. Data on the trade and use of glassware in the Late Middle Ages also needs to be gathered systematically. Finally, economic historians would be interested in the extent and role of the medieval glass trade, an issue which could not, however, be satisfactorily addressed in a purely Hungarian context.[31]

Pottery

Fired clay objects account for the greatest number of finds in archaeological excavations, and are one of the main means of dating in this field. There is a long history of research into pottery, although in Hungary it gained momentum only after the large-scale excavation of the royal palace of Buda in 1945,

---

28 H. Gyürky 1984a.
29 H. Gyürky 1982b, 209 and H. Gyürky 1987, 67–68. On the issue of local glass production in medieval Hungary, see: Mester 2010 and Laszlovszky and Stark 2017.
30 H. Gyürky 1989.
31 H. Gyürky 1974, H. Gyürky 1990, 331–333 and Holl 2005a, 311–384. On more recent studies concerning the glass material from Bratislava see: Sedláčková et al. 2014 and Sedláčková et al. 2016.

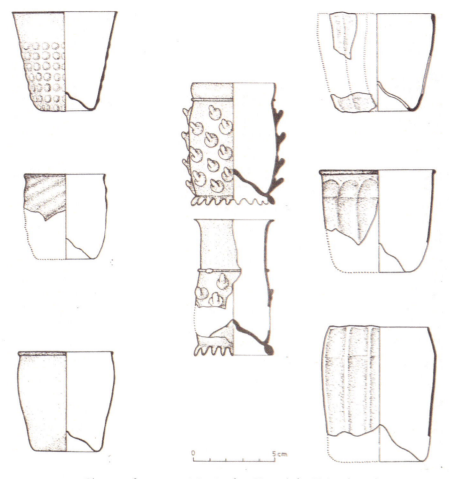

FIGURE 22.3   *Glassware fragments originating from Venice (after H. Gyürki 1989).*

which yielded an unprecedentedly rich array of pottery shards. This far surpassed the material in collections in terms of both quantity and quality, and included many foreign-made pottery items.

Stove-tiles

Our look at pottery imports will proceed from the complex to the simple, starting with stove-tiles. Through the seminal work by Imre Holl, comprising more than twenty internationally-oriented studies, there is probably more awareness of stove-tiles outside the country than any other area of Hungarian medieval archaeology. Also of great importance are the recent catalogues of pottery in the royal residences at Visegrád and Diósgyőr (presently part of Miskolc).

One thing made strikingly clear from this rich literature is the poverty of research into stove-tile decorations, even though the earliest occurrence of these in Central Europe is constantly being put back. Stove-tile decorations are the earliest and simplest stove elements, made in a way similar to pots. They appeared in large numbers in the fourteenth century and later retained the same basic forms. Analysis of changing types and regional differences has mainly been confined to the rural environment. There are some stove-tile decorations, however, which have long been identified – on the basis of their material and particularly the stamped impressions on them – as Austrian imports.[32] These are attributed particular significance in the spread of basic stove-tile types.

In other cases, researchers for some time tacitly assumed that the find spot coincided with the place of manufacture, and so the analyses of many fourteenth–fifteenth-century tiles, mainly found in royal residences, concluded that they were made in Hungary. Although no pottery workshops were found, this seemed self-evident from the royal coats of arms which frequently adorned Angevin- and Sigismund-period stoves.[33] The exclusively Hungarian origin initially suggested by Imre Holl for the "knight-figure stove" which undoubtedly represented the highest artistic standard during the fifteenth century – and was linked to the brief (1454–1457) stay in Buda by King Ladislas V – was gradually undermined by increasing numbers of original pieces found outside the Kingdom of Hungary.[34] This Hungarian-centered approach later changed fundamentally, especially in respect of the final third of the fifteenth century. Imre Holl has now determined many stoves imported into Hungary from the southern area of the German-speaking lands. We are thus now aware of a plain, unglazed Austrian set of tiles, the "Three Kings' Stove", probably made in Switzerland; a colored, mixed-glaze stove, or class of stove-tiles, from the Salzburg area; a similar stove that was certainly from Salzburg; and another from Regensburg.[35] Research has also identified stove-tile categories originating from Polish lands, although these mostly date from the first third of the sixteenth century.[36]

An important component of Holl's view, elaborated in several publications, is that these stoves, basically second-rank craft products whatever the undoubted artistic value of their decoration (coats of arms, figures and architectonic elements), were usually political symbols and should be identified above all as high-level gifts. He concluded from studies of several imported stoves that they

---

32 Holl 1963, 348 and Fig. 75, Holl 1974–1975, 135, 143 and Table 50.
33 Holl 1958 and Holl 1971.
34 Holl 1998a and Tamási 1995.
35 Holl 1980, Holl 1983, Holl 1998b and Holl 2001.
36 Holl 2004, 352–375.

came into the country as gifts for the monarch or his dignitaries, in connection with particular diplomatic-political events. The occurrence of components of the knight's figure stove in Austria can therefore be explained by the fact that the potter also worked for Emperor Frederick III Habsburg after the death of King Ladislas V. This logic would also explain why, in Bohemia, this type of stove has only been found in castles of nobles loyal to Ladislas V.[37] Imre Holl therefore does not look on ornate medieval tile stoves as normal commercial products. The types and motifs did not spread from one area to the other by migration of craftsmen, sale of molds, or copying of existing tiles. Finally, he attributes particular significance to royal workshops which in many cases provided tiles only to dignitaries particularly close to the king, although there is no written evidence for these, and they have not been identified in any other way. Nonetheless, this interpretation could be helpful in more accurately dating the Swiss, south German or Austrian stoves, wherever a category of tiles can be linked to a specific event or person.[38]

By contrast, there are written references to normal commercial imports of stove-tiles, if not in large quantities. Although the Bratislava thirtieth customs register does not give the place of origin of stove-tiles that came into the country in 1457/1458, there are records of imports of Austrian stoves in the case of the city of Bratislava and, in the mid-sixteenth century, Eger Castle, and there is similar information about Ónod Castle. It has not yet been possible to make more precise identification at the latter two sites, but Slovak research has attempted this for the Bratislava case. And in Buda, the simple stove-tile decoration types mentioned above, and grey, distinctive reduction-fired, unglazed tiles, also have Austrian origins.[39] The nature of the latter is somewhat less suggestive of expensive gifts.

Another task for research is to determine when and in what sections of society stove-tiles became trading commodities in Hungary. This must have been the case during the sixteenth century, as tile stoves gained in popularity, although there has been a suggestion that there were workshops supplying only certain noble estates.[40] There is also a need for an international-scale analysis to determine whether stove-tiles were indeed confined to a narrow social elite, and whether this follows from the representations of armorial bearings found on them. That would permit an answer to the question of whether this is just a misunderstanding of what was basically a commercial product, so that the

---

37 Holl 1998a.
38 Holl 1983.
39 Holl 1998b.
40 Simon 2000.

classification as prestigious gifts (something like goldsmiths' work) is just an artificial historical construct. This will obviously require publication of as many archaeological finds as possible, so that we can determine the chronology and spread of each type, and not least their relative proportions.

Vessels

There is a similar need for research on imports of pottery vessels, which basically comprise tableware. Imre Holl has published several research reports in this area too. German stoneware, mainly cups of distinctive decoration and form, appears to have been the most popular pottery imported from Western Europe. It became widespread in the fourteenth century. One type of stoneware was earlier attributed to Dreihausen was unearthed at Székesfehérvár. In recent research however it is referred to in the literature as the "Falke group" which does not anymore reflect on its place of origin.[41] Recently, Holl managed to distinguish Waldenburg pottery as being separate from Siegburg pottery, both having the same characteristic forms.[42] The highly individual salt-glazed pots from Loštice in Moravia have come to light in great numbers from recent excavations, and been subjected to intensive study in Hungary, mainly directed at determining their influence on domestic pottery.[43]

Stoneware was imported mainly because it could not be matched in quality by products of Hungarian potters (who became capable of making stoneware only in the last third of the fifteenth century), but the extent to which they counted as luxury products remains an open question. Imre Holl is quite definite in claiming that most of them came into the Hungarian Kingdom for the royal court and not as normal commercial products.[44] It is true that there are no known records of their being traded, but the social spread of their users and or market is unlikely to coincide with the geographical distribution shown on the published maps, which are unavoidably based on the locations of archaeological excavations.

Chinese porcelain, Middle Eastern, Anatolian and Persian faience ware, Spanish "Hispano-Moresque" and early Italian Majolica ware, partly Byzantine in style from the fourteenth–fifteenth centuries (mainly bowls and albarellos), are much rarer among medieval finds. In these cases, rarity value itself, besides high quality and artistic finish, could have been an important factor, although

---

41   Holl 1955, Holl 1990, 210–216 and Siklósi 1983.
42   Holl 2007.
43   Holl 1955 and Holl 1990, 227–239.
44   Holl 1990, 261–266. However, a more recent find came from a deserted medieval village site, see: Rácz and Laszlovszky 2005, 137–138, Fig. XXIX. 1.

several types of ware – above all the characteristically-shaped albarello – could even be classed as "packaging", often being used for storing and transporting spices, medicines and sweets. Direct trade, therefore, may have had a lesser role for such wares, especially in the early periods.[45]

Quite different conclusions offer themselves for late fifteenth and early sixteenth century Italian Majolica. As the plates produced in Faenza with the armorial bearings of King Matthias Corvinus prove, Majolica ware was frequently produced to order. It is also beyond doubt that many decorative wares came into the country as gifts. Research has distinguished several types of these. We know of albarellos, pitchers and jugs from Faenza and Florence from the closing decades of the fifteenth century, sgrafitto bowls made around 1500 in Bologna or Padua, and majolica ware made in the Casa Pirota workshop in Faenza and brought to Buda in the 1520s. It seems probable, although naturally difficult to determine from excavations of royal palaces or aristocratic castles, that at least some majolica pottery was accessible at town markets – naturally, for those who could pay for it.[46]

For more ordinary pottery, used also in the kitchen and for storage rather than solely for the table, as well as ceramic casting crucibles used by jewelers and glassmakers, there are written sources attesting to imports, if not on a mass scale. Here again we refer to the Bratislava thirtieth customs register of 1457–1458. Experts of research of medieval and early modern archaeology in Hungary are in almost full agreement that these involve "Austrian" or "Viennese" ceramics.[47]

It should be pointed out that imports of special types of Austrian-made pottery show up in the eleventh and twelfth centuries. These include the thick-walled, large, high graphite-content vessels (cooking and storage pots), of which a few have yet been found, in some (mostly larger) towns in north Hungary and the Buda area; they were almost certainly brought in by merchants.[48] The terms found in the written sources refer not to these but to largely reduction-fired vessels of characteristic forms which appear in the central and northwestern areas of the country from the second half of the thirteenth century, and a group of graphite-containing, very high-quality (high temperature resistant) wares, basically cylindrical-rim cooking pots and wide-mouthed jugs, and to a lesser extent bowls, found increasingly from the fifteenth century onwards. By virtue of their striking formal parallels, and particularly by the marks on

---

45 Holl 2005b and Holl 2007.
46 Bertalan 1991, Balla and Jékely 2008.
47 Holl 1955 and Holl 1963.
48 Altmann and Bertalan 1991a and Takács 1996b.

the pot rims, initially cut out but later stamped, these are considered by most researchers in this area to be products of pottery workshops in Vienna, Tulln and other Austrian and south German towns.[49]

Although there can be no doubt that large quantities of Austrian pottery were imported – the chief evidence being glazed table liquid containers with animal-head spouts and bucket handles[50] – there is increasing argument over the interpretation of these marks in Austrian, and to some extent in Slovak research. They may in fact indicate only a prescribed quality rather than the place of manufacture, so that the wares may not be linked to workshops in specific towns. It is therefore possible that a minor, or even a substantial, section of these wares were made in some of the larger towns in the northwest part of the medieval Kingdom of Hungary. Some of these may have been the work of German potters who settled because of the urban development in the thirteenth century and brought with them the pottery traditions of their former homes, although there are no written sources to back this up; others may have been copies of Austrian pottery. The main possibilities are Buda, Bratislava and Trnava, where no pottery products distinctive to the towns and differing from these groups of vessels have been positively identified from any time before the end of the medieval period. The very widespread occurrence of these wares and their high proportions show up very strongly in finds from the thirteenth–sixteenth centuries, and are undoubtedly of types which had a major influence on other products of Hungarian potters.[51]

Without further fortunate archaeological finds, most importantly of pottery workshops, it would be very useful to carry out a statistical analysis of finds and of the use of graphite to help decide what kind of economic-history phenomenon is involved. It is certainly unlikely that further research will establish a single clear-cut answer, because even proof of manufacture within Hungary would at most restrict the possibility to some popular vessel types, and not rule it out. Material tests could also be important here, because no graphite workings are known of in the territory of Hungary, although graphite itself may also have been imported. Maps of the distribution of pottery[52] products known as "Austrian" or "Viennese" clearly prove that Danube water transport was important in their trade, and tell us a lot about their market region, a no less important question and one to which research into the history of ceramics in Hungary has as yet devoted little attention. They do not, however, tell us where

---

49   Holl 1974–1975.
50   Holl 1966, 16–36.
51   Holl 2000, 31, Holl 2005b, 89–91 and Takács 1996b, 160 and 187.
52   Holl 1974–1975, Table 54.

the pottery was made. What is certain that graphite pottery ware – whether imports or domestic products – remains of considerable significance for historical research in Hungary.

Conclusions

This discussion, reflecting the state of research in Hungary, no doubt seems disproportionate and incomplete in many respects. This in itself indicates the tasks facing future research. The reader may also feel that the economic role of imports has been exaggerated in some product groups. The concentration on imports was an inevitable consequence of the choice of subject, since it was not possible in every case to compare imported wares with the products of local industry in terms of either quality or quantity. In drawing attention to this small segment of Hungarian medieval economic history, the aim has been to demonstrate the wealth of information inherent in fragmentary remnants of medieval glass and pottery from archaeological sites, the products of craftsmen in Hungary, Germany, Italy or even Spain. This is the kind of information which historians working purely from written sources may be less aware of. The striking fact that analysis of objects to some extent challenges the conclusions drawn from charters must surely be a spur to further work by economic historians and researchers into material culture.

CHAPTER 23

Foreign Trade of Medieval Hungary

Balázs Nagy

Sources on Medieval Foreign Trade

Reconstructing the foreign trade of a medieval country is a highly complex task. It involves determining the composition, quantity and value of goods imported and exported, and several other factors falling outside the scope of economic history in the narrow sense. Where sources permit, determination of the origin of goods imported and exported, and of the consumers of imported goods can also be informative. A completely credible account would require data of a type and character that medieval states did not produce even in places where more written sources are available than in Hungary. Hungary is particularly unfortunate in terms of surviving written sources, and research in coming years is unlikely to unearth many more domestic documents than we have at present. This enhances the importance of studies of known sources through new lines of enquiry or new methods.[1]

Most people living in medieval Hungary were peasants, who tilled the land and kept animals – the section of society that was entirely, or almost entirely, self-sufficient in both food and manufactures. This does not mean that the peasants lived in complete isolation from the exchange of goods provided by trade, or that they did not constitute a market for goods in trade. Nonetheless, this factor, which applies to medieval societies in general, largely determined the role of trade in economic life. The vast majority of goods and produce did not become commercial commodities but were consumed locally shortly after their production; only a minority went to market locally or in the region. Most goods that became commodities and changed hands via commercial channels went to market locally, or perhaps regionally, but certainly within the country.[2] Imports and exports made up the smallest portion of trade. One might then ask why economic historians anywhere should devote such attention to the history of trade in and out of Hungary. One reason is that such investigations can throw light on how a division of labor emerged among countries, and on the place of each country in that division of labor. The exploration of

---

[1] On the historiography of the medieval foreign trade of Hungary, see: Nagy 2012.
[2] See the chapters by Boglárka Weisz and András Kubinyi on internal trade.

channels of foreign trade reveal much more than the goods that left the country and those that came in. It can give an impression of the strength of international links, the emergence of the technical means of transport, and on the distribution of customs stations. Merchants did more than buy and sell goods, they brought into the country news, information, books and new trading techniques, and took them on to other areas. It was not uncommon for a merchant to settle in the country for a while, and to marry and establish family contacts, thus integrating deeply into the society of his new place of residence. These bonds of kinship then formed a basis for further trading links.[3]

Foreign trade, owing to the special nature of goods involved and their channels of movement, left more of a mark in medieval sources than other branches of the economy, such as agriculture. The customs duties levied on the traffic of goods in and out of the country formed a substantial proportion of sovereign revenues, and the customs registers recording them are particularly valuable as sources. Similarly, archaeologists take special interest in objects of foreign origin because, through identification by archaeological methods, such finds give a special perspective on mapping out medieval trade routes.

Historians also find themselves addressing questions to which written sources, and the data derived from them, do not give satisfactory answers. One of these is the proportion of foreign to domestic trade; another is the foreign trade balance. Despite the many uncertainties in this area, we know that internal trade differed from foreign trade in several respects: luxury items for a long time dominated in the composition of both exports and imports, and food, primary consumer articles and cheap goods only asserted themselves at a relatively late stage.

The history of Hungary's medieval foreign trade divides into clearly-distinguished chronological stages. In the Árpádian age up to the Mongol invasion of 1241–1242, almost nothing except luxury goods was either imported or exported. In this phase, the driving force of foreign trade was not the circulation of surplus agricultural and craft products, but the demand for luxury goods among the upper ranks of society. This picture is further confirmed by the nature of surviving sources. For the early period, we have to rely on scattered data in narrative sources to glean some details on foreign trade. These are of particular interest where archaeological finds can help to refine the picture. Only in very rare cases, however, do these sources permit quantitative or statistical findings, and only scattered mentions tell of goods that were exported or imported.

---

3 Arany 2006. See also the chapter by Krisztina Arany in the present volume on foreign (mostly Italian) merchants in Hungary. On Germans, see: Draskóczy 2016c.

It was not only the trauma of the Mongol invasion that set off a new era in the mid-thirteenth century. Opportunities began to open up for the mass import of relatively cheap goods, such as the foreign pottery and knives that appeared in Hungary at that time. The root cause was a boom in Hungary's precious-metal mining and, somewhat later, the incipient business of exporting livestock. These gave a broader section of the population the purchasing power to acquire "ordinary", less expensive imported items. Research into late medieval foreign trade also has a much wider base of material to work on. Written sources survive in much greater numbers, and the quality of data in charters, customs tariffs and, for the second half of the fifteenth century, foreign-trade customs-duty registers permit much more thorough reconstructions, if not sufficient to dispel every doubt. The mass occurrence of cheaper articles in archaeological finds is another important source of evidence. Further results for the late medieval period may be expected from systematic treatment of domestic and foreign archival material.

An understanding of Hungary's medieval foreign trade could fill out the picture that might be familiar from other – political- or social-history – analyses. Árpádian-age Hungary's links to international trade were relatively narrow and weak, but they extended in many directions, and those to the east – Constantinople and Kiev – were on an equal rank with those to the west. Late medieval Hungary was more firmly integrated into the European system of trading links, and its place in the international economic division of labor was among countries with links – either direct or through intermediaries – with nearly every significant economic region of Europe.

Early Foreign Trade of Hungary

The first appearance of Hungarian goods in international markets is known of through several items of information from around the same time.[4] The Russian chronicle *Povest' vremennyh let* states that in 969 Prince Sviatoslav of Kiev said to his mother, Princess Olga, that he was going to stay in Pereyaslavec in the Danube delta: "I do not care to remain in Kiev, but should prefer to live in Pereyaslavec on the Danube, since that is the center of my realm, where all riches are concentrated: gold, silks, wine, and various fruits from Greece, silver, and horses from Hungary and Bohemia, and from Russia furs, wax, honey, and slaves."[5] The Jewish traveler Ibrāhīm Ibn Ya'qūb, writing about

---

4 On early trade in general, see: Kubinyi 1996c, 60–65 and Kubinyi 1996a, 36–46, esp. 38–41.
5 Hazzard Cross and Sherbowitz-Wetzor 1953, 86.

Prague in 965, noted that Muslim, Jewish and Turkish (Hungarian) merchants from the land of the Turks (the Hungarians) arrived there with gold and Byzantine gold coins, and departed with "slaves, tin and various kinds of fur".[6] There were also links and trading relations with Nordic peoples. Scandinavian-made swords have been found in graves from the time of the Hungarian conquest, and Hungarian coins from the reign of Stephen I have turned up in Scandinavian lands.[7] These of course suggest more than just trading links. Weapons and money could have traveled far on marauding raids. Nonetheless, there are Hungarian conquest-period archaeological finds which do confirm trading links in various directions. Clear evidence of this comes from Byzantine objects and jewelry buried as grave goods.[8] The high-quality silver coins found in Hungary – *dirham*s – could not have been brought home from raiding expeditions. Unlike coins of western or southern origin, they are much more likely to have arrived in the course of trade.

These archaeological finds point to trading links with different destinations, but do not contradict other information on the Hungarian Kingdom's foreign relations in the second half of the tenth century. The sources tell of a double bond, east and west, but the goods suggest that trade was mainly with the East. The 969 Pereyaslavec mention is also one of the earliest records of Hungarian silver reaching a foreign market.[9] The abundance of silver in Hungary was also noted by a foreign traveler to the country. Abu-Hamid al-Garnati, who came to Hungary between 1150 and 1153, observed that its mountains "held much gold and silver".[10]

The armies of the Crusades passed through the country several times from the late eleventh century onwards, giving a substantial boost to foreign trade links and connecting the country into the system of European commercial relations. These campaigns brought to Hungary many people who would not have gone there otherwise. They discovered the goods produced in the kingdom and assessed which of them might be worth trading. In 1147, for example, Odo de Deogilo, chaplain to King Louis VII of France, quite openly considered the potential for trade when he noted that "the Danube, which follows a straight enough course and carries the wealth of many areas by ship to the

---

6   Blanchard 2001, 329. For the original text, see: Ibrāhīim Ibn Ya'qūb 1946, 146.
7   Györffy 1983a, 107–108.
8   Mesterházy 1990/1991 and Mesterházy 1993.
9   Györffy 1984a, 707–716, esp. 714–716.
10 Hrbek 1955, 208.

noble city of Esztergom".[11] There are also references to foreign trade in other reports of the Crusades. Emperor Frederick Barbarossa passed through Hungary in 1189 and met King Béla III in Esztergom. The Hungarian king presented the Holy Roman emperor with gifts that were almost certainly not made in the kingdom and must have got there via foreign merchants.[12] One was an ivory chair, whose raw material alone seems to identify it as a Byzantine import, and the scarlet-colored carpet and sumptuous quilt must have come from similar sources. The recorder of the imperial visit, Arnold of Lübeck, found the gifts particularly splendid. This may have been more than the customary politeness, and possibly implied that such goods, probably of eastern origin, were unusual or unfamiliar to an abbot from the northern German areas. Emperor Frederick also received from the king of Hungary a camel loaded with four precious gifts, and the king several times presented the crusading armies with gifts of flour and other food. These would of course have been needed by any army passing through the country, but the foreign image of Hungary became inextricably linked with abundance of food, a frequent theme in accounts by later travelers.

Among the commodities that made up early commercial traffic, slaves deserve a special mention. Abu-Hamid al-Garnati recorded the price of slaves in the mid-twelfth century.[13] A pretty slave girl fetched 10 denars. He bought for himself a concubine of his liking, who later bore him a child. During later campaigns, a slave-woman could be procured for 3 denars. The fall in price was no doubt due to abundance of supply. King Coloman's statutes promulgated at the turn of the eleventh and twelfth centuries prohibited Jews from selling Christian slaves.[14] He also prohibited Hungarian slaves being sold abroad, making an exception only for foreign-speaking slaves who had come to the kingdom from abroad. The horse was an important export item even in the early Árpádian age. Ladislas' statutes put restrictions on horses being taken for sale abroad and even to the border marches. Such was the importance of the horse as a commodity that the sovereign tried to regulate and restrict its

---

11 For the English text: Brundage 1976, 106. For the Latin text, see: *Danubio qui hanc satis in directum praeterfluit, et multarum regionum divitias nobili civitati Estrigim navigio invehit* – Waitz (ed.) 1882, 62.
12 Pertz (ed.) 1868, iv. 8 (De peregrinatione imperatoris), 129–130.
13 Hrbek 1955, 208–209.
14 *LXXIV. Nullus Judeus Christianum manicipium emere vel vendere audeat, aut in suo servitio tenere sinatur, nunc vero qui habet, si interea datis sibi induciis non vendat, amittat.* ("74. No Jew should dare to buy or sell Christian slaves, nor may he retain any in his service, and he shall lose those which he has now, if he does not sell them in the allotted time.") For the Latin text and the English translation, see: Bak et al. (eds.) 1992–2012, I, 30–31 (Coloman I. 74).

export.[15] Customs tariffs from the turn of the twelfth and thirteenth centuries in Hainburg, a town now in Austria near the Hungarian border, lists the goods carried up and down the Danube. It records grain, leather, timber, wine, wax, fish, copper and salt, among other things, as passing through the customs station. A similar customs tariff of Stein mentions, in addition to these, cattle, sheep, pigs, honey, and various metals: copper, tin, lead and iron.[16] These goods almost certainly came from Hungary, it being the only place from which such a combination of goods could have been carried along the Danube.

One document from the reign of Béla III, now held in Paris, tells of the crown revenues of early Hungary, including customs income from foreign trade.[17] Although some doubts have been expressed about its genuineness, the document gives a plausible account of the composition of revenues. Its figures tell us that the king's portion of customs, tolls and markets made up 18 % of his revenue. This included the trade of goods moving in and out of the country.

In the early period of Hungarian statehood, from the beginning up to the middle of the thirteenth century, the country's strongest foreign trade links to the west led through Vienna and Regensburg, and to the east towards the two Eastern European metropolises, Kiev and Constantinople. The Jewish traveler Benjamin of Tudela, mentions Hungarians as being among merchants who came to Constantinople in the period 1165–1173, along with Lombards, Italians, Spaniards and merchants from the East.[18] Regensburg had a special significance in trade in the East Central European region as early as the tenth century.[19] Lying on the Danube, it owed its economic rise to transit trade. Regensburg merchants were awarded privileges in Vienna in 1192, but that city was only one station on their eastward trade route, which took them all the way through Austria to Hungary. From there, they built up contacts all the way to the Russian lands. Among their most sought-after goods in the late twelfth and early thirteenth centuries were precious metals, especially silver. The staple right granted to Vienna in 1221 was aimed specifically at restricting Hungary's direct links with western markets and channeling its trade through the city's merchants. Vienna's staple right was renewed several times (1244, 1278, 1281),

---

15   Bak et al. (eds.) 1992–2012, I, 15 (Ladislas II. 15–17).
16   Knittler 1977–1978.
17   For the Latin text, see: Barta and Barta 1993, 443–444.
18   Spitzer and Komoróczy (eds.) 2003, 145–148.
19   Bosl 1966.

indicating that there was some obstruction and resistance to its enforcement. It only came into full effect in 1312.[20]

The Thirteenth-Century Transformation

Several factors combined in the sweeping changes to Hungary's foreign trade relations in the thirteenth century. 1204, the year the Crusaders occupied Constantinople, may be regarded as the start of a new era. The formation of the Latin Empire and the Byzantine restoration under the Palaiologos dynasty (1261) did not restore the former eastern metropolis to its key position in the long-distance trade across the Mediterranean and Eastern Europe. This was the period when Venice, having taken control of the Fourth Crusade which occupied Constantinople, seized the Byzantine sphere of operation and became the economic and commercial center of the region. No less influential was a military event some decades later. In 1240, Batu Khan and his Mongol army occupied Kiev. This eliminated another key point of Hungary's wider foreign economic environment. These circumstances caused Hungary to move from the western periphery of the Eastern European economic region to what Jenő Szűcs described as the zone of influence of the ascending West.[21]

An eloquent source on that transitional period is a list of goods which survives in Venice. It was written, probably around 1264, by somebody close to Stephen, junior king of Hungary.[22] László Zolnay has established that this text lists the goods delivered to the young king's court and the cash loans extended to him, possibly in the hope of later repayment. We do not know whether this part of the transaction was fulfilled; i.e., whether the merchant and court supplier, Syr Wullam, recovered the money he had invested. The composition and origin of the goods sold by Syr Wullam, however, are highly revealing. They are without exception foreign-made luxuries, most of them textiles, from two clearly-distinguishable geographical regions. Syr Wullam supplied scarlet textiles made in the East and brought to Europe through Byzantine and Italian intermediaries. This region provided the velvet and the silk, and the jewels and gems were also most probably oriental. The other major economic zone identifiable as a source of the goods in Syr Wullam's list was Flanders, whose textile

---

20   Szűcs 2002, 230.
21   Szűcs 2002, 224.
22   Huszti 1938, 737–770, Zolnay 1964, 79–114. Zolnay has published the text in question as well. On the later debates around this issue: Székely 1968, 3–31, esp. 4–6, Paulinyi 1972b, 581–585 and Szűcs 2002, 230–233.

industry was in the ascendant in Western Europe. The product featured was broadcloth, above all the highest-quality and most expensive variety, made in Ghent. Also characteristic of the Hungarian economy of the time is the way consignments were paid for: the list of goods mentions payment only in silver and salt. It was primarily by these two commodities that Hungary at that time could compensate imports, which were mostly luxury goods destined for consumption of persons close to the court.

An interesting point of comparison is a document written only slightly later, the end of the thirteenth century. It is a list of goods from various lands which were landed at Bruges,[23] and mentions articles from Hungary and the kingdoms surrounding it. Wax, gold and unminted silver came to Flanders from Hungary. Imports from Bohemia and Poland were very similar to those from Hungary, although Bohemia also sent tin, and Poland squirrel and other furs, and copper. We know from other sources, however, that Poland had no major exports of precious metals or copper at that time, and it is probable that these minerals also came from Hungary. They were almost certainly mined in northern Hungary, sent for processing north along the Vistula, and reached their destinations via the Baltic Sea and the North Sea. This would explain why they were regarded as being of Polish origin by the time they reached Flanders.[24]

There are also some clearly-identifiable objects belonging to the material culture of the Árpádian age which must have reached the country via foreign trade. Such were ecclesiastical and liturgical items, which reflect mission and church organization as well as trading links: Byzantine and Kievan pectoral crosses and bronze items from the Rhine-Maas region (aquamaniles, bronze bowls, etc.). In the mid-thirteenth century, following the Mongol invasion, large quantity of Limoges enamel crosses came into the country, together with objects made by similar techniques, making up for the losses suffered in the pillaging of churches and monasteries. Archaeological excavations have also established the arrival of an increasing number of glass items to satisfy demand among high-ranking households in the late Árpádian age. Most of these are of Venetian origin, although some of the earlier ones are oriental. Foreign-made pottery, by contrast, was not all for show. Excavations of settlements which had set out on the path of urban development have found many comparatively inexpensive items of tableware, used by lower-ranking sections of society: glazed pottery vessels, mainly Austrian-made, for storing beverages, indicating that imported goods of this kind were still largely owned by inhabitants.[25]

---

23   Höhlbaum and Kunze (eds.) 1876–1896, III, 419 fn. 1.
24   Halaga 1967.
25   On early trade in potteries, see e.g. Péterfi 2018. See in general the chapter by István Feld in the present volume.

Increasingly informative on Hungarian foreign trade from the thirteenth century onwards are customs registers, providing details not available anywhere else on both internal and external traffic. The thirtieth, which evolved into customs duty on foreign trade, was not collected at the country's border but at customs stations in the interior.[26] One of the most detailed customs tariffs was that of the Esztergom chapter. It went through several modifications during the thirteenth century, reaching its final form in 1288,[27] and preserves information going back to the early years of the century. The version from the reign of Andrew II mentions furs which merchants brought from Russia by wagon, and wine from Srijem and elsewhere, some of it brought by residents of Esztergom, and some of it carried on to foreign markets in Bohemia. Exported goods included cattle. Entries from the middle of the thirteenth century (1255) include a wide range of imported textiles: colored broadcloth, "scarlet" cloth, fustian (barchent) made of linen and wool, and German broadcloth. The same section also mentions the Venetians' merchandise, which was charged duty uniformly without further distinction. These rules reappear in a diploma issued by King Ladislas IV in 1288 in response to complaints by the Esztergom chapter that Buda and Pest merchants were avoiding Esztergom customs and preferring to take their goods west towards Győr. Ladislas prohibited the practice, and at the same time ordered merchants from Vienna, Regensburg and east of the Rhine to pay the same customs duty as merchants from beyond the Rhine and from France and Venice.

A good indicator of Esztergom's political and ecclesiastical significance, not to mention its wealth, is the information recorded in Master Roger's *Carmen miserabile* that there were wealthy Walloons and Lombards living in the city during the Mongol invasion, influential citizens, "almost the lords of the city". During the Mongol siege, when they realized they could not defend the lower city, "in the houses they burned immense amount of valuable cloth and garments, slaughtered the horses, buried gold and silver, and hid whatsoever goods they had before retiring to the palaces to defend themselves".[28] These luxury goods were almost certainly of foreign origin. The Walloon and

---

26   See the chapter by Boglárka Weisz in the present volume.
27   Domanovszky 1916. 2nd ed. Domanovszky 1979, 51–99, see esp. 70–77 and Weisz 2003, 973–981.
28   *Pannos de calore et vestes combusserunt in domibus infinitas, interfecerunt equos, aurum et argentum ad terram foderunt et, quicquid boni habuerunt, absconderunt et, ut se in palatiis deffenderent, in eadem se receperunt.* Master Roger's Epistle to the Sorrowful Lament upon the Destruction of the Kingdom of Hungary by the Tatars. cap. 39. For the English and the Latin text, see: Bak and Rady (eds.) 2010, 216–217.

Lombard inhabitants, speakers of Latin languages, grew wealthy above all through foreign trade.

Foreign relations remained important in Esztergom even after the invasion. In 1272, a Ghent merchant acquired title to one burgher's vineyard in lieu of repayment of debt. László Zolnay hypothesized that Rennerius's indebtedness could have been due to purchase of a large consignment of Ghent broadcloth, with the clear purpose of selling it in smaller amounts.[29]

The customs tariffs granted in 1209 and 1242 to Varaždin and Virovitica in present-day Croatia, lying slightly south of the River Dráva, list goods intended for German lands, most of all live animals (horses, oxen, pigs).[30]

Foreign goods attained increasing prominence on the Hungarian market after the thirteenth century. They were no longer exclusively confined to the prestige consumption of the royal court, and appeared on the market throughout the kingdom in increasing quantities. Good illustrations are the Ypres broadcloth registered at the customs station of Alsózsolca in Borsod County in 1329, and the Ypres, Tournai and Huy broadcloth at the customs station of Tileagd in Bihar County on its way to Transylvania in 1312.[31]

Broadcloth was one of the foremost commodities in medieval trade. From a modern viewpoint it is not immediately obvious why a fabric woven from wool and used mainly for upper garments should have had such significance in trade. The reason lies in the importance of clothing, and its material, color and style, as the expression of an individual's status in medieval society. Broadcloth was the material of upper garments throughout medieval Europe, regardless of climatic conditions. Its raw material – wool sheared from sheep – was available nearly everywhere, but its manufacture involved several phases (scouring, carding, combing, spinning, dyeing, weaving, fulling, etc.). Although it could be, and was produced as a home craft by the women of the community, a much different result could be achieved through specialization. This formed the basis of activity in regions which had access to the best quality raw material and could produce highly refined and thus very expensive broadcloth as luxury goods for export to distant destinations. Exports from different zones of the Western European broadcloth industry reached Central European and Hungarian markets at different periods. We have already seen that products of the broadcloth-weaving towns of Flanders – Ghent, Tournai, Ypres and Bruges – gradually made their appearance in Hungary in the thirteenth century. This cloth arrived in other Central European markets – Bohemia and

---

29   Zolnay 1964, 107–108 and Székely 1968, 4–6.
30   Kristó 1984, 1075–1076 and Szűcs 2002, 259 and 275.
31   Székely 1968, 7–9.

Moravia, Silesia and Poland – at about the same time. German towns, given their geographical advantage, provided most of the merchants who brought goods to Hungary from these distant lands. The same German towns produced broadcloth of their own, but given the activity of their merchants, they were presumably unable to match the quality of the Flemish product.[32]

Broadcloth weaving in the Low Countries, in Brabant, gathered momentum somewhat later, in the fourteenth century. Brabant broadcloth first appeared in Hungary in the second half of the fourteenth century, principally from Leuven, Mechelen, Herentals, Thienen, and of course Brussels. The early fifteenth-century statutes known as the *Ofner Stadtrecht* mention many of these, so that Brabant broadcloth had a presence in law as well as commercial transactions.[33]

Late Medieval Foreign Trade

Hungary's place in the European economic environment shifted decisively in the second half of the fourteenth century. The principal cause of this was the rise of precious metal production. Mining and precious metal production had started in the Árpádian age, some of it based on panning for gold, and Hungarian silver had already come to wider European attention, particularly in Italy. Fourteenth-century developments, however, dwarfed everything that had gone before. Between 1320 and 1350, Hungarian precious metal mining expanded several times over. This resulted from more effective exploitation of natural resources and deliberate measures by the crown to promote mining. Among the most important of these was the founding of mining towns and charters granting mining rights (e.g. to Kremnica in 1328) and the establishment of a new system of *urbura*.[34] By bringing in German miners from Kutná Hora in Bohemia and granting to the newly-founded mining towns the same rights that Kutná Hora enjoyed, the crown also played a part in providing appropriate technical knowledge and expertise for Hungarian mining. King Charles I permitted landowners to keep a prescribed part of the precious metals extracted on their estates. The system extended to the whole country in 1327 let the landowner keep title to the land where precious metals were found, and assigned to him a third of the king's *urbura*. The same system, however, made sale of precious metals a royal monopoly. This laid the foundations for the golden florin, minted after 1325 on the Florentine pattern. The mining

---

32 Endrei 1989, passim and esp. 123–132 and 233.
33 Mollay (ed.) 1959, 196–197 (cap. 424) and Székely 1968, 15–21.
34 See the chapter by Zoltán Batizi on mining.

industry, especially gold and silver mining, prospered in regions along the River Hron, in Spiš and in Transylvania. Quantitative data for mid-fourteenth century precious metal output cannot be determined precisely, but according to some estimates, Hungary's gold production constituted the majority of European production – possibly up to 90 %. An event that gives an impression of the abundance of Hungary's gold reserves was a journey to Italy by Queen Elizabeth, mother of Louis I in 1343: she took with her more than 6.5 tons of silver and 5 tons of gold, as well as a large quantity of minted coins. The sudden appearance on the market of so much precious metal and money had severe economic consequences.[35]

The rise of Hungarian precious metal mining coincided with similar developments in Bohemia. There, the mining towns of Kutná Hora, Jihlava and Havlíčkův Brod brought large amounts of silver to the surface. The minting of gold coins, too, started in Bohemia at the same time as in Hungary. The parallel late medieval development of these neighboring areas – Hungary and Bohemia – had a far-reaching influence on the economic and commercial character of the region.

The term "crisis" crops up frequently in international literature on the economic history of the fourteenth century. It was a period of phenomena which brought radical and sometimes traumatic changes. The sources tell of a famine which struck several regions at once between 1315 and 1317, with a severity that contemporaries claimed had not been seen "in living memory".[36] From the descriptions, it is clear that the cause was an accumulation of bad weather conditions. Although some Western sources suggest that Central Europe and Hungary were affected, with similarly devastating effects, the hypothesis is not fully supported by Hungarian documents. Then in the middle of the fourteenth century, Europe suffered the severest blow in its history, the Black Death. The epidemic of 1347–1351 killed about a third of the continent's population, and recurred in several waves later in the century. Historians now agree that the drop in population caused by the Black Death was geographically uneven, some regions suffering far worse than others. Erik Fügedi's study of the Black Death in Hungary published in 1992 found that "there is every sign that the plague took fewer victims in Hungary than in Western Europe".[37] He put forward several hypotheses for the causes, one of them involving Hungary's geographical location, lacking a busy sea port and not lying on any major trade route. Hungary's relatively low population density, and the characteristically small numbers of inhabitants in its towns and cities, also served as obstacles

---

35   Johannes de Thurocz 1985, 162–163, Hóman 1917, 225 and Paulinyi 1972b, 561–567.
36   Szántó 2005, 135–142. More recently: Vadas 2009, Vadas 2010 and Kiss, Piti and Sebők 2016.
37   Fügedi 1992, 30.

to the spread of the Black Death. Other possible explanations have been proposed for Hungary's escape from the worst effects of the plague. The parasite was less able to spread in areas of dry climate, and Fügedi also mentioned the possibility that people of blood group B, a large proportion of the fourteenth-century Hungarian population, had some resistance to infection. Although none of the many hypotheses has proved to be a final and satisfactory explanation, the fact that Hungary and some other Central European countries were spared the worst demographic consequences of the plague seems certain.

The catastrophe for the population of much of Western Europe, however, had deep economic effects. There are surviving sources on prices and wages in England, Italy and other areas. These show that the price of agricultural products and land rent remained relatively low and even decreased as the number of consumers and the number of inhabitants of the area fell, but the price of paid labor and the price of manufacture involving such labor increased. The plague was therefore instrumental in the emergence of crisis phenomena in some parts of Western Europe in the mid-fourteenth century, but it is not true to say that there was a general crisis in Western Europe. Some areas were devastated economically, but others were in a phase of buoyant prosperity. One of these was the sphere of interest of the Hanseatic towns; Nuremberg and the south German towns also strengthened their economic role and amassed capital at that time. The same occurred in Central Europe. Bohemia, Poland and Hungary experienced an economic boom not unrelated to the accumulation of capital from their burgeoning extraction of precious metals. As Jenő Szűcs put it, "Ultimately the salient point in the West's recovery was the fact that even before 1300 the whole structure's center of gravity shifted once and for all to the urban economy. The urban economy was the first of the forces affected (and the crisis affected all strata) to recover from the crisis. This it managed to do chiefly by discovering East Central Europe as the place where its market crisis could be solved and its demand for precious metals be fulfilled; the regions beyond the Elbe paid in the long run for the West's recovery from the crisis."[38] Accordingly, the changes occurring in the middle and late fourteenth century reinforced the division of labor among European economic regions and led to more intensive trading relations.

Several measures taken by Charles I tell us of the attention he paid to foreign trade relations. He granted free passage to foreign merchants traveling through the country, such as to that to the Venetian retailers (*institores*) crossing the River Sava in 1316, allowing them to travel freely throughout the kingdom if they paid the prescribed customs duties.[39] Two years later, Viennese

---

38   Szűcs 1983, 158.
39   Pach 1990, 54.

merchants received a free passage. The staple right which Vienna enjoyed to the full by that time, had a major effect on stimulating Western trading links. The main trading routes to the northwest were to Silesia via Žilina and to Bohemia and Moravia via Trnava and Holič; the northern route to Cracow in Poland led through Košice and the Spiš region.[40] There were also busy national highways (*magna via, strata publica*) in other directions important for trade. To the southwest, the *Via Latinorum*, the "Italians' road" passed through Körmend, another led to the southern counties via Baranya. Other roads went to Transylvania and the southeastern direction.[41] The latter were important land routes to the Levant. The spice trade involving Transylvanian trading towns such as Braşov and Sibiu satisfied the majority of the kingdom's total demand. This trade was to a large part compensated by manufactures, broadcloth and fine metal ware, some of them of Western origin, exported to Wallachia and Moldavia (*see* Fig. 23.1).[42]

Charles I's foreign policy and shifting alliances also affected the foreign trade interests of the kingdom. In the 1310s, the centerpiece of his diplomatic system was an alliance with Frederick Habsburg, prince of Austria, but this was subsequently downgraded as he sought connections with John of Luxemburg, king of Bohemia. A meeting in Trnava in 1327 resulted in a marriage pact between the two dynasties and a commitment to an alliance against the Habsburgs. Several diplomatic meetings were held in 1335, partly to discuss foreign trade matters. Emissaries of the Hungarian, Bohemian and Polish kings met in Trenčin in August, and the monarchs themselves came together in Visegrád on the banks of the Danube in early November. The agreement between Charles I, John of Luxemburg and Casimir III regulated traffic along the trading routes to the north-west. A separate treaty signed in January 1336 clarified the details of the route on the basis of statements by Trnava and Brno burghers who knew and used it.[43] The development of trade and the provision of satisfactory trading routes had thus become key issues of Central European politics by the middle of the fourteenth century. The many subsequent charters concerning the route to the northwest prove its importance for merchants from the two neighboring countries, as well as for those from many other, more distant lands. In 1344, merchants from Cologne and other Rhine towns, and from Huy on the Maas, received exemptions so that they would not have to pay higher customs duties

---

40   Pach 1990, 48.
41   Szűcs 2002, 232 and 265–266. On the trade routes and their transformations in the medieval period: Szende 2011b, and on the different routes: Szilágyi 2011 and Szilágyi 2014.
42   Pakucs-Willcocks 2007.
43   Skorka 2012a and Skorka 2013.

FOREIGN TRADE OF MEDIEVAL HUNGARY 487

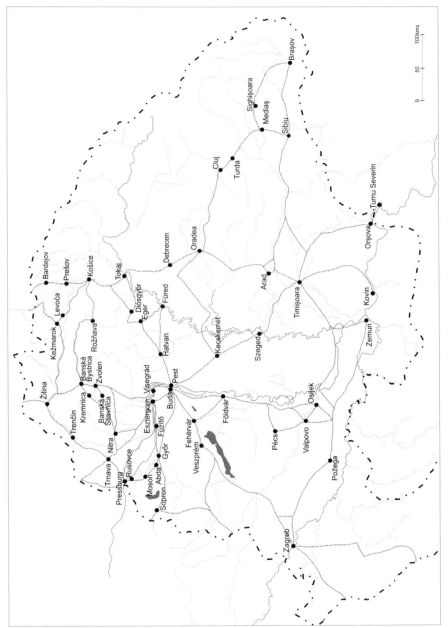

FIGURE 23.1 *Main trade routes in the late medieval Kingdom of Hungary (after Nagy et al. 2016).*

than the Bohemians and Moravians, and *institores* from Cologne were granted the same in 1345.[44]

We can build up a relatively precise picture of the composition of late medieval exports and imports from a surviving ledger of the Bratislava thirtieth customs duty for the years 1457 and 1458.[45] The thirtieth was originally paid on trade within the Hungarian Kingdom (*tributum fori*), but under King Charles I it became the source of crown revenue from foreign trade. Originally levied on exports, it was later also extended to imports. Paragraph 17 of the decree of 1405 defined the thirtieth as the general duty payable on goods taken across the border.[46] Initially, true to its name, it was set at 3.33 % of the value of the goods, but in the middle of the fifteenth century the rate was changed, so that the "thirtieth" offices actually levied a duty of one twentieth of the value. The thirtieth provided the king with much of his revenue.

The Bratislava thirtieth, and by implication the balance of trade in medieval and early modern Hungary, have been strenuously debated issues in Hungarian historiography for many years. The 1457–1458 customs register has preserved a very peculiar picture of the structure of trade, because it implies that imports accounted for 89 % of the total trade of goods.[47] It must be borne in mind, however, that the trade balance, whether in surplus or deficit, cannot be regarded as the only factor in a country's foreign trade.[48] Even less so than for a modern country, because the sources on this period are highly fragmentary. Thirtieth registers, the primary references, are not sufficiently reliable to permit a full reconstruction of the traffic of goods. A comparative analysis of thirtieth registers from other years, such as 1542, modifies the extremely negative figure for the foreign trade balance for the middle of the fifteenth century. A large part of Hungarian exports to the west comprised cattle on the hoof, for which customs duty was not, or not only, payable in Bratislava, so their value is presumably not entered into the Bratislava customs registers.

Precious metal mining retained its influence on trade, but the yield of Hungarian mines, having burgeoned in the middle decades of the fourteenth century, perceptibly stagnated, and started to decrease in the early fifteenth. Historians have come up with divergent estimates of precious metal yields, but the most accepted view for gold seems to be that from 3000 kilograms in the fourteenth century, the annual rate of extraction fell by half before the end of

---

44   Pach 1999, no. 159 and Nagy 1999, 349.
45   Kováts 1902a. See most recently, Nagy 2016 (with further literature).
46   Pach 1999, no. 224.
47   Draskóczy 1996b, 67.
48   Bak 1987.

the fifteenth. Silver extraction followed a similar course in this period, falling from an annual level of 10,000 kilograms in the late fourteenth century to half of that within a century.

It was just when precious metal production was in decline that the country's trade balance was increasingly influenced by other export items: livestock, particularly cattle, whose export was beginning and would later become big business, copper, other metals (iron) and wine.[49] Hungarian cattle found markets in Venice, the south German towns and Silesia. Cattle could be driven on the hoof to such relatively nearby places, but to counteract the loss of weight caused by the vicissitudes of the journey, they had to be fattened up again before being taken to market and slaughtered.[50] Hungarian cattle constituted a substantial part of the kingdom's foreign trade, and were also significant for the meat supply to some areas of Western Europe. When there was a downturn in the number of Hungarian cattle coming to market, the price of this meat rose in northern Italy, Nuremberg and Austria.[51]

The merchants involved in foreign trade fell into two principal groups: south Germans and Italians, above all those from Florence.[52] The foreign trade balance was almost certainly negative, i.e. imports surpassed exports. The goods at the top of the list of imports in terms of value were broadcloth and other textiles, followed by spices and metal implements. Knives constituted a segment of their own among late medieval Hungarian imports. Their manufacture involved expertise which was widespread in what is now Austria and southern Germany, and these areas supplied Hungarian markets in quantities of the order of millions.[53]

Our knowledge of large-volume craft imports comes from documents and from other material-culture sources, particularly archaeological excavations. A great many knives, most of all from nearby Austrian lands, have been found even in village sites, and their place of manufacture is often clearly identifiable from characteristic handle designs and hallmarks. The latter are also found on other metal and pottery wares, and can be used to trace the sources of imports. There is also information on large quantities of craft products being exported

---

49   For the wine trade: Kubinyi 1996c.
50   Blanchard 1986.
51   On the problem of cattle trade, Westermann 1979. In the volume, see amongst others the studies of Wolfgang von Stromer, Othmar Pickl and István N. Kiss.
52   On the role of the South-German merchant capital in Hungary and in the broader region, see: von Stromer 1970. For the presence of the Florentines: Teke 1995a, Teke 1995b and Teke 1996.
53   Kubinyi 1971b, 402–403.

from certain areas of Hungary. For example, the advanced craft industries of towns in Transylvania, especially Saxon towns, found markets in Moldavia. Saxon-town products, however, are less represented in archaeological finds.

The most abundant archaeological evidence of foreign trade certainly comes from pottery fragments, largely identified as Western imports. Stoneware, manufactured by special techniques in German potteries, spread throughout Europe. It was the material of tableware for high-ranking households (royal court, nobles, burghers), and its variety of forms and individual finishes also served as displays of position. Decorative pottery from Bohemia, the so-called "Loštice stoneware" filled a similar role. There was another category of foreign-made pottery, however, which found a place in less exalted households, even those of the urban poor, and the village population. The most distinctive examples of these are "Austrian ware" from several craft centers (e.g. Vienna and Tulln): cooking vessels whose high graphite content permitted them to withstand very high temperatures. These were marked on their rim, and made in a wide range of sizes. The same material was used to make graphite-containing crucibles essential for the work of goldsmiths and other metal workers.

The products of Austrian and German craft centers clearly came into the country in large quantities, and must have comprised more than just pottery, but unfortunately few other wares have survived at archaeological sites. We therefore have fewer of the pewter plates and bowls which were distinctive possessions of town households, and which must have come into the main Hungarian towns as articles of trade. Italian-made wares were present on markets alongside Western craft products, but relatively few have been identified among archaeological finds. The domestic glass industry produced relatively low quality ware, and so there was a constant demand for the finest-quality Venetian glassware. Towards the end of the medieval period, some products of Italian potteries also appeared, such as Majolica tableware.

The overall evidence is that Hungary was connected with European system of trade through a broad range of imports and exports, but its foreign trade continued to be fundamentally based on the export of agricultural products and the import of manufactures.

CHAPTER 24

Foreign Business Interests in Hungary in the Middle Ages

Krisztina Arany

Research on the operations of foreign men of business in medieval Hungary is encumbered by the scarcity of explicit written records. Whereas the keeping of accounts was customary as early as the twelfth century in the economically developed Mediterranean regions, particularly the Italian city-states, commercial transactions were seldom put on paper in Hungary.[1] Some contemporary documents and early sixteenth-century analogies, however, indicate that by the close of the Middle Ages, various kinds of transactions were registered in urban administration records, and some simple account books were also kept. A paragraph of the Buda *Stadtrecht* addressed the credibility of the account books kept by merchants in cases of legal claims.[2] Toll registers and guild books would also shed light on the range and quantity of goods appearing in the territory of the kingdom, had the majority of these sources not vanished irreversibly during the subsequent centuries.[3]

Long-distance trade, although it involved only a restricted circle of merchants and potential partners and clients, made up a considerable proportion of total trade by volume, and its few records still put it among the best-documented areas of the economy. Precious further evidence from archaeology also needs to be integrated into research. This can tell us about the variety of

---

1 A fifteenth-century Florentine businessman, Giovanni di Niccolo Falcucci, noted this in his tax declaration in 1427, offering a somewhat extreme picture: ... *E più ò debitori e creditori in Ungheria (...) Sono persone la maggiore parte non tenghono scritture né nulla, e chi à fare col loro e' domanda se n'à a stare al giuramento loro, a libri non danno fede ...* – Florence, Archivio di Stato di Firenze (ASF), Archivio del Catasto (Cat.) 53. 1096ᵛ.
2 Mollay (ed.) 1959, 182 (cap. 376). One surviving private business record is the account book by Paul Moritz, a Sopron retail-dealer: Mollay (ed.) 1994. According to the entries he kept more books, which did not come down to us: see Mollay (ed.) 1994, 9.
3 One surviving book of the Bratislava thirtieth customs from 1457–1458 should be listed here, see: Nagy 2016 (with further literature). For guild registers, see: Kenyeres (ed.) 2008.

long-distance trade goods present in the country, and urban topographical research can also provide information about long-distance trade with Hungarian towns.[4]

This analysis aims to give a general overview of several aspects of long-distance trade in medieval Hungary, relying mainly on the wealth of data concerning the activity of Italians in the kingdom, and comparing this with general features of Italian operations elsewhere in contemporary Europe. In Buda, the medieval capital of Hungary, south German merchants also had a prominent role in international trade, and this will be addressed by means of a comparative analysis of the strategies of these two ethnic groups.

Italian-Hungarian Financial and Business Relations

Italian merchants were present all over medieval Europe, trading in a wide range of goods, providing large loans, and holding key offices in financial administration in several lands.[5] The same patterns may be observed in their operations in Hungary, but in contrast with the long historiographic tradition on the activity of medieval Italian merchants elsewhere, Central Europe has until recently been a secondary target area, for a number of reasons.[6] The lag in urbanization and associated lower levels of consumer demand made the region less interesting, and any attempts at study have been discouraged by the lack of surviving homogeneous source material on this region even in the more fortunate Western European archives.

Research on the activities of Italians in Hungary up to the mid-fourteenth century has mainly concerned papal revenue collectors. Sienese and Florentine banking houses were among the first to appear regularly as collectors of papal revenues in Central Europe.[7] The houses of the Alfani, Acciaiuoli, Bardi, Mozzi, Frescobaldi and later on the Spini, del Bene and Medici of Florence managed the papal incomes in the region throughout the Middle Ages.[8] In

---

4   Holl 1990, 209–267, on Austrian knives in Hungary, see Holl 1982 as well as István Feld's contribution in the present volume. Végh 2006–2008, Laszlovszky 2009, 190, Benda 2009–2010, 93–104 and Benda 2016a.

5   On Florentines in England's, France's, Tyrol's, Poland's state finances, see: Goldthwaite 2009, 230–236. For analogies in Germany, see Weissen 2006, 368–369.

6   Braudel 1974, 2109–2110, de Roover 1999, 201–202, 448 fn. 25, Kellenbenz 1985, 333–357 and Dini 1995a, 632–655.

7   Fejérpataky 1887, 653.

8   On the Acciauoli, see: Fejérpataky (ed.) 1887, LXVII. On the Frescobaldi: Kristó et al. (eds.) 1990–2015, II, nos 679 (28 June 1309) and 694 (12 July 1309).

Hungary, however, they rarely established long-term commission agents until the Late Middle Ages.[9] The Pope also commissioned individual businessmen in Hungary, such as Francesco di Bernardo da Carmignano from the last decades of the fourteenth century, and Filippo di Giovanni del Bene.[10] Francesco di Bernardo established himself in Hungary and became a leading figure in the lucrative area of managing the ordinary royal revenues. For some years he also acted as an agent of Vieri di Cambio de' Medici's firm.[11] When Filippo del Bene came to Hungary in 1405, he first worked for the Spini banking house.[12] As early as 1410, however, he was operating in the region as *familiaris* of Pope John XXIII.[13] The Medici also had agents in neighboring areas, such as Poland.[14] Over a period of centuries, the sums collected in Central Europe were mainly transferred to Venice in form of precious metals. Venice played the role of intermediate banking center between Central Europe and regions of Europe such as Italy and the south German lands. From Venice, the sums were transferred by Venetian banking houses and Venetian branches of Florentine banking houses in the form of assignments. For the Florentines, participation in collecting papal revenues secured a precious knowledge of the business opportunities in various European regions and provided the financial basis for their Europe-wide banking and commercial transactions.[15]

In addition to its participation in the transfer of papal revenues, Venice soon became the most important commercial partner of the Kingdom of Hungary, despite somewhat fractious political relations due to both parties' ambitions regarding the Dalmatian territories and the Adriatic ports.[16] From 1105, Hungary controlled the northern part of Dalmatia with some of the Dalmatian port towns. This was before the Dalmatian cities' economic development started, and before the first mentions of Dalmatia's direct economic relations with the Kingdom of Hungary.[17] By dominating these territories, the Hungarian kings

---

9   Štefánik 2010, 79.
10 On Francesco di Bernardo da Carmignano, see: Trexler 1974, 79–80.
11 Melis 1962, 345 and 393.
12 ASF Signori, carteggi, missive-I. cancelleria Filza 26, 136^r–136^v.
13 Mályusz et al. (eds.) 1951–2017, II/2, no. 7968 (7 October 1410), IV, no. 357 (28 March 1413), IV, no. 399 (6 April 1413), IV, no. 437 (13 April 1413) and IV, no. 458 (17 April 1413).
14 In Poland, the overwhelming presence of Genoese in the thirteenth–fourteenth centuries is a clear indication of the importance of a different transcontinental trading route that linked Flanders with Eastern Europe, and the Genoese colonies at the Black Sea through Cracow. Sapori 1967, 149–176.
15 Dini 2001, 105–106.
16 Rady 2000, 90.
17 Engel 2001, 36.

were seeking to secure direct access to the Adriatic, one of their key political ambitions. The sea ports, particularly Senj and Zadar, were also a vital part of Venice's strategy of controlling some of the main overland trading routes to both the German territories and Central Europe.

Venetian-Hungarian Trade Contacts

Hungary's rich deposits of precious metals attracted foreign businessmen, among them Italians and south Germans, from the thirteenth century onwards.[18] Exports were of silver and copper, joined by gold after its discovery in the early fourteenth century. Some information is available on Italian presence in Hungarian towns even in the early period, although most comes from narrative sources.[19] Despite the constant conflict of interests, the intense commercial relations between Venice and Hungary were motivated by the Venetians' need for Hungarian copper and silver (later also gold) to supply the Levantine trade and the yearly *mude* (fleets directed to regions of high commercial priority for Venice, organized by the Venetian government) of the *Serenissima*. The agreement which King Andrew II of Hungary made with Venice in 1217 included measures regulating trade between the two states. Venetian merchants were exempted from import duties on for several luxury wares from Italy and the Levant, such as precious silk, species, precious stones, pearls and gold needed especially at the Hungarian royal court, but the exemption was not extended to the trade in silver. The text of the agreement is usually considered the first evidence of Venetian merchants' presence in Hungary during the Árpádian age.[20] Their activity in the kingdom in the following decades is recorded in Hungarian customs registers; accounts for Italian wares shipped via Venice to Junior King Stephen in 1264, and Venetian government decisions to provide compensation to its citizens who suffered losses in Hungary, by means of repercussions against Hungarian merchants in Venice.[21] As the entries in customs registers of Hungary (e.g. Esztergom customs) show, the main route for Venetian goods was initially through Austria, but as many Venetians established themselves in Senj, routes were established via Senj and Slavonia, and to a lesser degree through Zadar and Zagreb.[22]

---

18 Paulinyi 1972b, 561–608, Draskóczy 2004a, 61–77 and Štefánik 2004b, 210–226.
19 Nagy 2009, 169–178, here 175.
20 Teke 1979, 18.
21 Weisz 2003, 973–981 and Zolnay 1964, 79–114.
22 Glaser 1929, 138–167 and 257–285 and Teke 1979, 24–25.

In the first decades of the fourteenth century, however – after the sudden death of the last ruler of the Árpádian dynasty, King Andrew III, known as "the Venetian" because of his descent from the Venetian patrician family of Morosini on his mother's side – Venetian–Hungarian trade relations ceased somewhat abruptly, although Venetian goods were still available in Hungary, just as Hungarian precious metals and – from the mid-fourteenth century – Hungarian cattle found their way to Venice. This trade involved Florentine and south German middlemen (from the mid-fourteenth century onwards mostly from Nuremberg), and to a lesser extent other Viennese and Hungarian businessmen.[23] Thus indirect contacts were preserved. Some scholars consider that the invitations and safe-conduct guarantees the Hungarian king repeatedly offered Venetian merchants between the 1340s and 1360s refer to difficulties encountered by Venetians in the Dalmatian coastal territories, and far from indicating a strong presence of Venetian merchants in Hungary, actually imply their absence, since they are hardly mentioned in other records.[24] The decreasing presence of Venetian businessmen in the kingdom is usually explained by three major factors. The first was the Hungarian Angevins' policy on Dalmatia and its cities, leading to protracted military conflicts with Venice and increasing insecurity for Venetians within the kingdom.[25] Secondly, the monetary reforms introduced by King Charles I included a prohibition on the export of silver and gold bullion, contributing to the decline of direct economic relations.[26]

Finally, but equally importantly, Venice modified its economic strategy in the mid-thirteenth century. Through the *Fondaco dei Tedeschi* it began to rely on mediating foreign merchants for the silver and later copper it needed from Hungary for its Levantine trade, and precious metals also came in from the Serbian mines through merchants based in Dubrovnik.[27] Venice strove to concentrate long-distance trade and the exchange of Levantine goods and Western products on its own territory by means of the same *Fondaco dei Tedeschi*, by staple rights, and by its commercial fleet. Venetian businessmen were present in Western Europe, East–West trade being their main focus, but tended to avoid a personal presence in Central Europe until the end of the fifteenth century.

---

23 Štefánik 2004b, 212 and 220 and Štefánik 2010, 80. On cattle trade, see Blanchard 1986 and Engel 2001, 249.
24 Teke 1979, 30–31.
25 Pach 1975b, 105–119.
26 Engel 2001, 155–156.
27 Teke 1975, 143–152.

These factors contributed to the further decline in the Venetian–Hungarian relations in the early fifteenth century, culminating in open conflict between Venice and the Hungarian ruler Sigismund of Luxemburg in 1412. Sigismund imposed a trade embargo against Venice which lasted until 1433.[28] In the 1470s there was a revival in trade between Hungary and the *Serenissima*, mainly involving cattle.[29] The relations between the two states improved only under the reign of the Jagiellonian dynasty in Hungary. Through a treaty in 1501, Venice offered an annual subsidy to the Hungarian king.[30] Consequently, some Venetians, like the de la Seda brothers, reappeared in the kingdom and remained there until the early 1530s, due also to the role of Lodovico Gritti, natural son of the Venetian doge, Andrea Gritti, as governor of Buda (1529–1534).[31]

Trade Contacts of Hungary with Genoa and Florence

Genoa also supplied Levantine goods to the East Central European region through its Black Sea colonies. This is known from somewhat sparse evidence from the toll privileges of Sibiu, an important post on the transcontinental route passing through Transylvania.[32] There is also sporadic evidence on Italian businessmen from cities other than Florence and Venice, but except for the Genoese, no tendency of regular business activity on their part has yet been detected.

We have already seen that Florentine businessmen acted as papal tax collectors in Hungary. The role of Hungarian precious metal mines and the monetary reforms introduced by the Angevins were first assessed in the 1910s, when also the eventual motivations of Florentines to promote and support the ambitions of the Neapolitan Angevins in Hungary were addressed. The Florentines may have lent the Angevins financial support for accessing the Hungarian throne

---

28   Wolfgang von Stromer proposed the theory of a continental embargo to explain the shift in the main inland commercial routes involving opening of a new Levantine route. This was debated by Zsigmond Pál Pach. Von Stromer 1986, Pach 2007, 9–32 and Teke 1979, 35–36.
29   Kubinyi 1998a, 109–117, here 110–111. The little archaeological evidence about Venetian ducats confirms the scarcity of direct trade connections in the fourteenth–early fifteenth centuries, see Gyöngyössy 2008, 104–108.
30   Engel 2001, 360.
31   On Gritti, see Szakály 1995a.
32   Székely 1973, 37–57 and Pach 1975b.

so as to gain access to Hungarian gold production.[33] The Florentines' traditionally good relations with the Neapolitan Angevins, the wide-ranging privileges they enjoyed in Naples, and their role as close financial advisers to the Angevin kings, naturally support such a view of their ambitions.[34]

This view has been disputed, however, because in the first decade of the fourteenth century, struggling and threatened by anarchy, Hungary could hardly have been an attractive prospect for prospering Florence or Italian merchants in general.[35] There is in fact information on a few Italians, mainly of Florentine origin, becoming counts of mining and minting chambers, but the sources and the persons mentioned in them are isolated and scarce. The first appearance of Florentines in the territory of the Kingdom of Hungary in any significant numbers has recently been dated to the 1370s, at a time when the traditional Italian and Mediterranean markets for Florentine textiles were contracting.[36] After the economic depression of the mid-fourteenth century and the subsequent bankruptcies, Italian companies, particularly those based in Florence, quickly resumed their leading role in international commerce. Long-distance trade with traditional markets like England and Flanders, however, faced severe transport problems during the 1360s and 1370s[37] as a result of conflicts like the Florentines' war with Pisa (1356–1369). An emerging overproduction crisis, coupled with difficulties in reaching markets, intensified the general economic depression.[38] On top of all these troubles, Florence came into conflict with the papacy. The Florentines thus sought new, even if less prestigious, target areas for their wares.

Hungary also posed a transport problem for Florentine and other Italian merchants in the 1350s and 1360s because it was at war with Venice, which at that time controlled Zadar on the Adriatic coast. The Treaties of Zadar and Turin (1358, 1381) must therefore have been a further important factor behind the intensification of Italian long-distance trade with the interior regions of Hungary. The Dalmatian ports and some inland cities along the trade routes

---

33   Hóman 1917. On the role of the gold mines in Upper Hungary, see: Spufford 1989, 267–289 and Štefánik 2004a, 295–312.
34   Trexler 1974, 84–87, Abulafia 1981, 377–388 and Abulafia 1993, 418. Recently Goldthwaite 2009, 232.
35   Huszti 1941, 58–59 and Paulinyi 2005, 215–216.
36   Teke 1995a, 135–137.
37   Fryde 1983, 306–309 and Dini 1995b, 173.
38   Hoshino 2001, 67–73 and Dini 2001, 111–115.

also took an increasingly prominent role in Italian–Hungarian commercial exchange as intermediate centers.[39]

Information on Florentines in Hungary from the late Angevin period and the first decade of Sigismund's reign mainly concerns businessmen taking leases on "ordinary" royal revenues.[40] A company for the marketing of Hungarian copper was founded by the Florentine Vieri di Cambio dei Medici and partners between 1385 and 1387. The company of Vieri di Cambio did not get involved into the exploitation or refinement of the metal. They provided credits to small-scale local entrepreneurs in exchange for the copper, which they then sold.[41] They were followed in this business by two Nuremberg companies, Kammerer-Seiler and Flextorfer-Zenner, and – at the turn of the century – the Genoese company Gallici.[42] The same pattern is to be observed in the case of the customs on international trade (i.e. the thirtieth customs) and the minting and salt chambers, lucrative ventures for businessmen of both ethnic groups.[43] Italians and Germans in Buda also alternated as salt chamber counts, an area which they dominated from the close of the fourteenth century.[44] Some Florentine businessmen, such as Nofri di Bardo and his four sons, and Filippo Scolari, wielded great influence on the royal financial organization and opened up lucrative commercial channels for their countrymen in Hungary. Scolari held senior military offices, but was also involved in the management of the regalia income as count of the minting chamber (*comes pecuniae*) in 1398, and as count of the salt chambers (*comes salium*) he managed Hungarian salt mining chambers from 1401 to 1426. The influence he had on the Hungarian economy, and the extent of his own trading activities, have been the subject of recent detailed studies, as has the network of noble retainers he employed in the management of the salt chambers.[45] There is a theory that Italians wielding leases on the royal monopoly of precious metal mining at the turn of the fourteenth and fifteenth centuries were in competition with south Germans who sought the same positions.[46] Recently however, in the light of new findings, the image

---

39 Teke 1998, 233–243, Raukar 1995, 676 and Draskóczy 2004b, 287–288.
40 On the management of royal revenues, see Engel 2001, 153–155.
41 Paulinyi 1933, 34, Teke 1995a, 136. See also von Stromer 1985, 370–397.
42 Blanchard 2005, 1181.
43 Huszár 1958, 50, on the same see also von Stromer 1973/1975, 85–106 and Mályusz 1958, 301–309.
44 Draskóczy 2004b, 288–289.
45 Engel 1987, 53–89. See recently on Scolari also Prajda 2010a and Prajda 2010b.
46 von Stromer 1970 and von Stromer 1971, 79–87.

of a sharp conflict of interests between south Germans and Florentines has been revised, as we shall see in our discussion of affairs in Buda.[47]

In the course of the fifteenth century, the office-bearers and their relationships to the king changed fundamentally. The management of the royal revenues, particularly the salt chambers, were reorganized in the late 1420s.[48] Changes to the system of financial administration in King Matthias' reforms of 1467–1472 resulted in the previously honorary office of treasurer acquiring real competencies that included coordination and supervision of the officials of the royal chambers.[49] Consequently, lower members of the administration lost their direct accountability to the king. Moreover, the offices started to be filled by the emerging Hungarian educated elite, and most of the Florentines withdrew. At the turn of the fifteenth century, the great south German firms acquired the management of – indeed a monopoly in – mining.

In the end of the Middle Ages, the efficiency of the mining and minting chambers, the thirtieth customs, and particularly the formerly very lucrative salt chambers, was in decline. The chambers were pledged, leased or put under the administration of salaried office-holders, noble retainers of the royal treasurer.[50] At the turn of the fifteenth and sixteenth centuries, and particularly in the decades prior to the defeat at Mohács in 1526, these chambers were providing a relatively small profit to the royal treasury, but incurring high maintenance costs.[51]

The interests of medieval Florentine businessmen in Hungary were not restricted to the lease of royal revenues. Through their international contacts, they had a major share of the trade in luxury goods, particularly textiles, and they were also bankers. This is best studied through the role they played in Buda, evolving as the Hungarian royal seat and a commercial center lying at the intersection of significant trading routes.[52] In fact, Italian merchants based in Buda were able to supply the demand for luxury goods throughout Hungary in this period.[53] An example is the Florentine *accomandita* partnership founded by Lorenzo and Filippo Strozzi and Piero Pitti, which in its first phase operated only in Buda, with capital of 1900 florins, but in its second phase, although

---

47   Draskóczy 2001a, 158–159 and Arany 2006, 101–123.
48   Engel 2001, 224 and Kubinyi 2009a, I. 353.
49   Kubinyi 1957, 25.
50   Kubinyi 2009a, 353–354.
51   Draskóczy 2005, 83–117, esp. 83–91.
52   Nagy 1999, 347–356.
53   Kubinyi 2009d, 351.

still based in Buda, extended its activity to the whole kingdom, with capital of 3000 florins.[54]

Finally, the Florentines' reactions to local socio-economic conditions in the medieval town and royal residence of Buda and their movements within society, compared with the position of the local urban elite, particularly the section of south German origin, provides an insight into the character of Hungarian trade.

Italians and South Germans in Medieval Buda

The town of Buda was founded by King Béla IV in the mid-thirteenth century, after the Mongol invasion.[55] Most of its first settlers were of German origin, predominantly from Regensburg, and so only a minority of its inhabitants were Hungarian. The town had the same royal privileges as were granted to Pest, which lay opposite Buda on the left bank of the Danube. Pest was considered an important market town during the medieval period, whereas, by the fifteenth century, the majority of long-distance commercial transactions were being carried out in Buda, and Buda merchants definitely played a leading role in the kingdom's large-scale commerce, mainly due to the presence of the royal court.[56]

Buda had long been a notable center of long-distance trade, and enjoyed staple rights. By the fifteenth century, it had also developed into the permanent residence of the kings of Hungary. Royal urban policy and the gradual acquisition of central administrative and commercial functions turned Buda into one of the leading cities in Central Europe during the fifteenth century.[57] The urban administration and leadership of Buda at that time, as in most towns of the region, was largely composed of German burghers; although the surviving lists are incomplete, Germans clearly held the main urban offices and formed a large proportion of the medieval council.[58]

Under the Angevin dynasty, Buda gradually gained in importance in the fourteenth century, starting with the establishment of the minting chamber.

---

54   Dini 1995a, 639–640.
55   Végh 2009, 89–101 and Rady 1985.
56   Kubinyi 2009d, 351.
57   Kubinyi 1971b, 342–433. For other Hungarian towns, see Petrovics 2009, 67–87; on linguistic issues of multiethnic Hungarian towns, see Szende 2009b, 205–233.
58   On the role of Germans in Hungarian towns, see Kubinyi 1996b, 159–175 and recently: Draskóczy 2016c. For the lists see also Rady 1985, Appendix II, 169–176 and Végh 2008, 90.

This issued the Hungarian golden florin (from 1326), which was most probably based on the Florentine florin. The availability of leases on the minting and mining chambers attracted Italians, mainly Florentines, to the town. Another motivation was long-distance trade, in which Buda's patriciate had little interest, a fact generally explained by the ready supply of commercial goods secured by the town's staple rights.[59]

Sources show that the presence of Italians had, by the end of the fourteenth century, given rise to a *Vicus* or *Platea Italicorum* in Buda, as in other towns of the region.[60] Indeed, it was one of the town's principal streets. Research has clearly shown, however, that there were Italians living in other parts of the town, too, and most residents in the *Platea Italicorum* were Hungarians and some were actually Germans.[61]

In the second half of the fourteenth century, the Italians in Buda were mainly concerned with the trade of luxury goods, particularly textiles. The demand for these was further boosted by the establishment of the permanent royal residence there in the years 1405–1408.[62] Buda also became the center of royal administration and the location of the highest offices of the judiciary and financial administration. Being the judicial center of the kingdom meant at first the occasional, and later the regular appearance of landed aristocracy; while attending to their legal affairs in the town, they formed an additional market for goods imported by foreign merchants. This was further reinforced by the transfer of the diets to Buda and Pest, or sometimes the nearby field of Rákos.[63]

It is thus not surprising that the number of Italians arriving in Buda increased dramatically in the first half of the fifteenth century. Three Florentine companies set up in the town in the 1420s: the Carnesecchi-Fronte, the Melanesi and the Panciatichi,[64] making Buda the only Central European trading center with such an intensive Florentine presence.[65] Yet, at the end of the fourteenth century, they were joined by a new German elite (mainly from Nuremberg, although we find Buda burghers from Basel, Passau, Vienna and elsewhere), which fully integrated and displaced the earlier, fourteenth-century patriciate

---

59   Kubinyi 2009a, 96.
60   See Sapori 1967, 151.
61   Végh 2006–2008, I, 245–247.
62   Engel 2001, 241.
63   Kubinyi 1990, 79–81.
64   Based on the systematic research of the Florentine Catasto of 1427 and the medieval charter collections of Hungary, at present we know of 81 Florentine persons (43 families) operating in the territory of the kingdom of Hungary in the period 1371–1450. See Arany 2007, 483–549.
65   Arany 2008, 291–296.

from the leadership of the town. Although they were somewhat passive in long-distance trade, they were eager to use their high urban offices as an entry into Hungarian nobility.[66]

The theory of competition between south Germans and Italians in the region has mainly been applied to their relative situation in late medieval Buda, partly on the basis of the above mentioned Law Code of Buda compiled in the early fifteenth century. The Law Code made a clear distinction between long-distance merchants of foreign origin specializing particularly in luxury textiles, and local merchants, who mainly traded lesser-quality wool in the town and had citizenship of Buda.[67] The theory was further reinforced by the events of 1402–1403 leading to the expulsion of the Italian inhabitants of Buda and the seizure of their property,[68] interpreted as resulting from business competition among German and Italian merchants in the town.

More recent evidence, however, has required at least a partial revision of the idea of business competition, particularly in the context of Buda, because the two ethnic groups' commercial ambitions and the strategies they developed to attain them seem to have been mutually complementary rather than hostile.

The information gathered so far seems to indicate that, rather than competing with each other, the Italians and south Germans of Buda carved up the markets between them. The Germans mainly focused their activity on the sale of lower-value woolen cloth, even cloth from northern Italy (e.g. Verona), and left trade in luxury goods and prestigious textiles to the better-capitalized Italian merchants. The Florentines had access to a great many investors in their homeland through highly-developed banking facilities and the large business networks of which they were a part. They were also active in the provision of large loans to the crown and also to the members of the Hungarian aristocracy and foreigners visiting the Hungarian royal court.[69] Sources on their activity reveal occasional banking services – provision of assignments and bills of exchange – for prominent foreigners staying at court.

---

66   Southern Germans at that time already had a long tradition of commercial relation with Venetians through the Venetian Fondaco dei Tedeschi and Venetians operating in Nuremberg. The information available on the first Florentine businessman settled in the Southern German town, however, dates back to 1471. Direct and regular commercial relations were to be established in the subsequent decades. See Weissen 2003, 161–176, Guidi Bruscoli 2001, 359–394 and Goldthwaite 2009, 198.
67   Kubinyi 2009a, 88 and the contribution of András Kubinyi in the present volume.
68   Engel 2001, 262.
69   Arany 2006, 114–117.

Leases on royal monopolies were held by both Germans (Marcus of Nuremberg, Johann Siebenlinder and Michael Nadler, six times judge of Buda) and Italians (Francesco di Bernardo da Carmignano, Filippo di Stefano Scolari, Tommaso di Piero Melanesi, Filippo di Simone Capponi, Fronte di Piero Fronte) resident in Buda.[70] This is another area where the sources shed light on cooperation among members of these two ethnic groups. The Italians were still very much focusing on the sale of copper and salt and on the lease of the Slavonian customs duty levied on export (the so-called *thirtieth*). The latter was extremely important, as it afforded control of the main commercial routes between Italy and the Kingdom of Hungary. All the officials operating on this field were noble retainers to the king (*familiaris regis*). This position is usually viewed as a characteristically medieval feature of financial administration,[71] but of course it involved a personal relationship to King Sigismund. Out of twelve noble retainers to the king of Florentine origin, six certainly had citizenship of Buda.

According to the Law Code of Buda, the retail trade and shop keeping within the town was reserved for citizens of Buda, and there was a tax payable by holders of such rights.[72] This rule, which was probably in use several decades before the Law Code was written, caused wealthy foreign merchants, including most Italian and south German inhabitants of the town, to seek urban citizenship from the late fourteenth century onwards. A condition of citizenship was ownership of property, so that many of them had houses, gardens, vineyards or other land within the town walls. For example, at least thirty Florentine businessmen (in 25 families) were Buda citizens in the 1420s.

Buying and selling property may also have been an important business for the German elite of Buda. As these families frequently lacked the necessary capital for long distance trade with wool or cattle, their local property, including both mobile and immobile goods, may have also served as security for commercial operations. Although the medieval archives of Buda were destroyed, we can find plausible analogies in the *Verbotbuch* of Vienna, a town book, in which inalienability on properties of debtors was entered on behalf of their creditors. Such patterns are to be observed also in other Hungarian towns engaged in the same sort of trade, such as Bratislava, where Buda's German merchant elite had marriage and business alliances. The transactions were

---

70   Kubinyi 2009b, 492–498, Teke 1995a, 135 and 139 and Teke 1995b, 195.
71   Kubinyi 1957, 26.
72   On the conditions of trade in the town see Mollay (ed.) 1959, 87–88 (cap. 68), incl. the paragraphs on retail sale 91 (cap. 77), 92 (cap. 80–81) and 93 (cap. 84).

clearly entered into the towns' *Verbotbücher* in order to cover any eventual losses caused to the investors.[73]

The Germans tended to integrate into local urban community. It seems, however, to have been a somewhat peculiar integration, as they were not keen to marry into Buda's patrician families, either of the old German (Regensburg) stock or the developing Hungarian elite. They preferred family ties with members of the German elite in other Hungarian towns, particularly towns in their business network, such as Bratislava, or with German families in Vienna, Cracow and – most of all – their home town, Nuremberg. In contrast to their marriage policies, the members of the south German elite in Buda were very active politically. They had a strong presence on the town council and almost monopolized the office of town judge between 1403 and 1439.[74] This may appear contradictory, considering the usual interdependence of marriage alliances and urban status. But most of the families belonging to Buda's urban elite existed for no more than two or three generations. Two main factors contributing to this pattern have so far been identified: firstly, the laws of Buda granted equal inheritance rights to both male and female heirs and citizens' widows, and secondly, marrying one of these widows conferred urban citizenship, occasionally resulting in a wide age gap between the spouses.[75]

The south Germans had a continuous presence in Buda and in the economic life of the kingdom throughout the century, with a perceptible influx of newcomers to be observed in the 1470s. Later, south German trading houses such the as Welser and Fugger from Augsburg installed permanent agents in Buda.[76] These firms were sufficiently well capitalized to at last present real competition with the Italians. They first ousted the Italians from tithe collection in the Habsburg territories,[77] and then from the tenancy of mining chambers in Hungary. In 1494, by collaborating with entrepreneur János Thurzó, a burgher of Cracow, they obtained monopoly on the exploitation and sale of copper and silver.[78] The Germans of Buda also supplied the royal court, although to judge from the average value of consignments recorded in the court accounts,

---

73 Tózsa-Rigó 2008, 1135–1186, Tózsa-Rigó 2009, 95–120, Kubinyi 1963–1964, 80–128 and Kubinyi 1978, 67–88.
74 Kubinyi 2009b, 490.
75 Kubinyi 2009c, 513–570, esp. 517–520 and Szende 2009b, 206–207.
76 Buda burghers were representing Nuremberg firms (like Marcus of Nuremberg for the Flextorfer-Kegler-Kromer-Zenner firm) as early as the end of the fourteenth century, but did not focus their investments on the area. Blanchard 2007, 392.
77 Goldthwaite 2009, 198.
78 Kubinyi 2009d, 349, Engel 2001, 324 and Štefánik 2004a, 310.

they still had a lower volume of business than the Italians.[79] They continued to dominate the sale of cheaper cloth, however, both to office-bearers of the royal court and the townspeople of Buda. These activities came to an end with the Ottoman siege of Buda in 1529. Most of them were killed, and the remainder fled, causing an irreversible alteration in the town's economic and social structure.[80]

By contrast, neither the wealthy Italian merchants nor their agents, despite living and working in Buda for several decades, tended to marry into local urban community. Most of them had families in their homeland, and did not intend to settle permanently in Buda.[81] Neither did they directly participate in Buda's urban government, but tried instead to secure good relations with the leading local German and, later, Hungarian merchants.[82] In cases where they did make marriage alliances with local families, they usually chose spouses from the nobility. This often led to permanent settlement in Hungary and was most common among businessmen interested in taking leases on royal monopolies. Recently, the role of family and kinship in Florentine merchants' Hungarian business has been the subject of the same kind of detailed research as has been carried out for the German merchants. The records reveal some cases of complex strategy, such as that of the Melanesi brothers Simone, Tommaso and Giovanni, sons of Piero: Tommaso married into a noble kin group and Simone into a Buda family.[83] Their strategy also tells us about the utility of Buda citizenship, which the records show only Simone to have acquired, Tommaso defining himself as noble.[84] What they all disposed of (together with Giovanni, their third brother) was their close relation to King Sigismund as his noble retainers.[85] This is clear evidence, corroborated by the number of court-linked clients listed in their tax accounts, of the importance of admission to the king's service and of Buda as royal residence and administrative center. Buda's status as a wealthy town in its own right was of secondary importance.

The nature and intensity of the Florentines' presence in Buda changed in certain respects during the fifteenth century, partly owing to shifts in

---

79   Kubinyi 2009d, 338.
80   Zimányi 1987, 49.
81   Arany 2009, 133–140.
82   Kubinyi 1963–1964 94, fn. 96. On Francesco Bernardi also see Rady 1985, 89.
83   ASF Cat. 46. Tomo I. 654^r–655^v, Lukcsics (ed.) 1931 and Lukcsics (ed.) 1938, II, 253.
84   ASF Cat. 46. Tomo I. 655^v. On Simone and Tommaso see also Arany 2009, 135 and Kintzinger 2000, 444.
85   Kintzinger 2000, 444, on Giovanni see also: Commissioni 1869, II, 552–613 (no. 972), Lukcsics (ed.) 1931, 880 and 956.

international commercial trends, the increasing presence of south German capital in the region, and the general security of business ventures in the kingdom. Any interpretation of the presence and activity of the various ethnic groups living in Buda and the opportunities open to them must take into account the town's development as a royal residence and trading center, changes in the urban legal environment caused by the grant and withdrawal of staple rights, and the growth of the ethnic Hungarian community, which specialized mainly in the international cattle trade and secured parity in municipal leadership in 1439.[86] Finally, changes in the European trading and banking system influenced the activity of foreigners in Buda and throughout the kingdom. The changes in the Florentines' Central European activities which started in the 1450s have been described as a shift to "Renaissance" commerce, with a clear emphasis on marketing luxury goods to the royal court, and to the aristocracy, which was increasingly adopting the court's manner of display.[87]

The sources indicate a clear drop in number of new arrivals from Italy between about 1440 and 1480, although Italians who had settled in Buda and elsewhere in Hungary in the previous decades maintained their ongoing business. Following the restoration of stability under King Matthias and especially the arrival in Buda of his new wife Beatrice of Aragon and her Italian entourage in 1470, display of royal grandeur assumed a new scale, and the consumption of luxury goods increased accordingly. To meet the demand, Italian merchants, including several from Venice, reappeared in Buda.[88] Many of the Florentines supplying the Hungarian court in the late fifteenth century came from families which had also been present early in the century such as the Attavante, Cavalcanti, Strozzi, Albizzi, Pitti, Rucellai, Giugni, or the Viviani clans. This may be interpreted as the passing on of previous generations' experience and local knowledge.[89]

In contrast with the Sigismund period, very few of them were interested in leases on royal monopolies, the only exceptions being the management of the Slavonian toll of Zagreb, which was retained for a long time by the Florentine Domenico Giugni.[90] As in the reforms of 1458, the administration of royal

---

86 Kubinyi 2009b, 490.
87 Kellenbenz 1985, 333–357.
88 Balogh 1966 and Kubinyi 2009d, 342–343.
89 Arany 2007, MNL OL DL 37 684, 23 Nov 1493. (On-line: Rácz [ed.] 2010, accessible at: http://archives.hungaricana.hu/en/charters/ [last accessed: 15 July 2016]).
90 ASF Signori, Dieci di Balia, Otto di Pratica – legazioni e commissarie, missive responsive filza 77. c.129., 7. ottobre 1481. In 1495, another Italian, the Zagreb resident Giovanni Pastor, was appointed to the office of the collector of the thirtieth of Slavonia. Besides

monopolies was put in the care of the royal treasurer, and direct relations to the king diminished. Consequently, King Matthias had considerably fewer noble retainers of Italian origin than Sigismund. The need for foreign merchandise, however, prompted the king to grant Italian merchants the privilege to sell their luxury goods freely in the free royal town and royal seat of Buda, without having to procure urban citizenship. Besides the trade in luxury wares, Italians resumed their lending activity, mainly to members of the court. Their advantages over most south Germans in Buda included the use of sophisticated banking techniques and access to capital resources through an international business network, which reduced their exposure to commercial risk. These factors combined to shape the Italian merchants' general social standing among Buda's burgher community, as somewhat outsiders.

For their security, particularly in times of conflict with local community of the kind which occurred in 1496, they sought support from the Hungarian urban elite and their clients among the Hungarian lay and ecclesiastical aristocracy.[91] This is clearly demonstrated in an account book of Antonio di Pietro Bini which survives in the State Archives of Florence.[92] From the diaries of Marino Sanuto, we also know that there were conflicts between Hungarians and Venetians, and Florentines and Venetians.[93] In the years prior to the defeat of Mohács, Italians such as Niccolo Pitti were already leaving the kingdom, and some of those remaining in Buda until its Ottoman occupation faced bankruptcy, as befell the once-wealthy Florentine Felice di Stagio in 1525.[94]

Conclusions

Italian businessmen and firms, mainly from Florence and Venice, were active in the Kingdom of Hungary throughout the Middle Ages. Venetian merchants were dominant in the region up to the fourteenth century, while Florentines

---

this information we only know of one member of the Pitti family managing the Bratislava minting chamber (in cooperation with a Nuremberg burgher Jakob Fleischer). See MNL OL DF 241 269 (11 November 1524). In the record written by István Werbőczy, Pitti is mentioned as *mercator germanicus*. The same Niccolo Pitti has a tomb in St Stephen's cathedral in Vienna, where he must have moved, perhaps due to the Ottoman rule (he died in 1558); see Kassal-Mikula 1997, 50.

91   Kubinyi 2009d, 343 and Kubinyi 1963–1964, 94.
92   On Bini's partner, Ragione Buontempi, see Teke 2007, 967–990, Kubinyi 2009a, 100, Dini 1995a, 643 and Dini 1995b, 285.
93   Sanuto 1879–1903, XLII, 417–418.
94   Kubinyi 2009d, 340.

established an intensive presence in the first and the last decades of the fifteenth century. Their main fields of interest were trade in luxury goods, banking, and the lease of royal revenues.

There were some occasional conflicts among Italians and south Germans in Buda as they pursued lucrative business opportunities, but in general they seemed to have been content to divide the market between them and even – in areas requiring substantial capital and an extensive business network – to cooperate. Their activity definitely seems to have been of a complementary nature. The Italians faced more serious problems in times of conflicts involving Hungarian rulers, especially during the reign of Sigismund at the beginning of the century, and again in the 1490s, when their activity and privileges seriously hurt the commercial interests of the other leading ethnic groups in Buda.

While the south Germans in Buda tended to integrate into the urban elite, the Italians, even those who settled for long periods, remained separate. Cases of real integration were mainly confined to businessmen interested in the lease of royal monopolies, and they tended to find their way into the local nobility rather than the civic elite of Buda or the centers of mining and minting administration. Clearly it was Buda, gradually becoming established as the permanent seat of the royal court and central administration, which offered the most attractive business opportunities for foreign businessmen. At the end of the fifteenth century, the Italians working in Buda suffered a narrowing of their sphere of interests, again setting them apart from the south Germans, although there was still a substantial Italian community in the town at the turn of the century, and some of them remained until it was occupied by the Ottomans.[95]

---

95   Pickl 1971, 71–129.

Appendix

List of the Kings of Medieval Hungary

Árpádian Dynasty
Stephen I (Saint) 1000–1038
Peter Orseolo 1038–1041 and 1044–1046
Samuel Aba 1041–1044
Andrew I 1046–1060
Béla I 1060–1063
Salamon 1063–1074
Géza I 1074–1077
Ladislas I (Saint) 1077–1095
Coloman (the Learned) 1095–1116
Stephen II 1116–1131
Béla II (the Blind) 1131–1141
Géza II 1141–1162
Stephen III 1162–1172
Béla III 1172–1196
Emeric 1196–1204
Ladislas III 1204–1205
Andrew II 1205–1235
Béla IV 1235–1270
Stephen V 1270–1272
Ladislas IV (the Cuman) 1272–1290
Andrew III 1290–1301

Přemysl Dynasty
Wenceslas 1301–1305

Wittelsbach Dynasty
Otto 1305–1307

Angevin Dynasty
Charles I (Robert) 1301–1342
Louis I (the Great) 1342–1382
Mary 1382–1395
Charles II (the Short) 1385–1386

Luxemburg Dynasty
Sigismund 1387–1437

Habsburg Dynasty
Albert 1437–1439
Ladislas V (Posthumous) 1440–1457

Jagiellonian Dynasty
Wladislas I (Warnenczyk) 1440–1444

Hunyadi Dynasty
Matthias Corvinus 1458–1490

Jagiellonian Dynasty
Wladislas II 1490–1516
Louis II 1516–1526

Szapolyai Dynasty
John I 1526–1540
John II Sigismund 1540–1551 and 1556–70; Prince of Transylvania, 1570–1571

Habsburg Dynasty
Ferdinand I 1526–1564

List of References

Primary Sources

Anon. 1866, "A Bél-háromkúti apátság okmánytárának kiadatlan okmányai a XIII. századtól a XV. századig," [Unpublished documents from the archives of the Bél-Háromkút abbey from the 13th to the 15th centuries] *Archaeologiai Közlemények* 6, I–XXV.

Bak, J. M. and Rady, M. (eds.) 2010, Master Roger, *Epistle to the Sorrowful Lament Upon the Destruction of the Kingdom of Hungary by the Tatars* = *Miserabile Carmen Super Destructione Regni Hungarie Per Tartaros Facta* In Anonymus, *The Deeds of the Hungarians*, eds. M. Rady and L. Veszprémy and Master Roger, *Epistle to the Sorrowful Lament upon the Destruction of the Kingdom of Hungary by the Tatars* (Central European Medieval Texts, 5), eds. J. Bak, M. and M. Rady. Budapest: CEU Press.

Bak, J. M. et al. (eds.) 1992–2012, *Decreta regni mediaevalis Hungariae. The Laws of the Medieval Kingdom of Hungary*, I–V (The laws of East Central Europe; The laws of Hungary. Series 1). Budapest–New York–Salt Lake City–Los Angeles–Idyllwild: Charles Schlacks – Department of Medieval Studies, Central European University.

Balogh, I. 1999, "A Báthori család négy oklevele (1330–1332)," [Four charters of the Báthori family (1330–1332)] *Szabolcs-Szatmár-Beregi Levéltári Évkönyv* 13, 107–131.

Bándi, Zs. 1985 "Északkelet-magyarországi pálos kolostorok oklevelei," [Charters of the northeast Hungarian Pauline monasteries] *Borsodi Levéltári Évkönyv* 5, 557–725.

Bándi, Zs. 1986, "A szakácsi pálos kolostor középkori oklevelei," [Medieval charters of the Pauline monastery of Szakácsi] *Somogy Megye Múltjából* 17, 27–66.

Bél, M. 1764 [1984], *Tractatus de Rustica Hungarorum. A magyarországi halakról és azok halászatáról* [Hungarian country life: the fish of Hungary and their fishing] [Hungarian translation of the 1764 copy by Antal András Deák, 1984]. Budapest: Vízügyi Dokumentációs Szolgáltató Leányvállalat.

Borsa, I. (ed.) 1993, *Az Abaffy család levéltára 1247–1515. A Dancs család levéltára 1232–1525. A Hanvay család levéltára 1216–1525* [Cartulary of the Abaffy family 1247–1515, cartulary of the Dancs family 1232–1525, cartulary of the Hanvay family 1216–1525] (A Magyar Országos Levéltár Kiadványai, II/23), Budapest: Magyar Országos Levéltár.

Borsa, I. (ed.) 1944–1946, "A kaposszerdahelyi pálos kolostor középkori oklevelei. Regeszták," [Medieval charters of the Pauline monastery of Kaposszerdahely. Regestas] *Regnum Egyháztörténeti Évkönyv* 6, 40–58.

C. Tóth, N. (ed.) 2003, *Szabolcs megye hatóságának oklevelei II. (1387–1526)* [The charters of the authority of Szabolcs County, II (1387–1526)]. Budapest–Nyíregyháza: Jósa András Múzeum.

C. Tóth, N. (ed.) 2005, "A leleszi konvent országos levéltárában lévő Acta anni sorozat oklevelei," [The charters of the Acta anni series in the national archives of the convent of Leles] *A Nyíregyházi Jósa András Múzeum Évkönyve* 47, 235–343.

C. Tóth, N. (ed.) 2006, *Ugocsa megye hatóságának oklevelei (1290–1526)* [The charters of the authority of Ugocsa County (1290–1526)]. Budapest: MTA.

Csepregi, I., Klaniczay, G. and Péterfi, B. (eds.) 2018, *Legenda Vetus, Acta Processus Canonizationis et Miracula Sanctae Margaritae de Hungaria. The Oldest Legend, Acts of the Canonization Process, and Miracles of Saint Margaret of Hungary* (Central European Medieval Texts, 8). Budapest–New York: CEU Press.

Dernschwam, H. 1984, *Erdély, Besztercebánya, törökországi útinapló* [Transylvania, Banská Bystrica, diary of travels in the Ottoman Empire], ed. L. Tardy. Budapest: Európa.

Döry, F., Bónis, G. and Bácskai, V. (eds.) 1976, *Decreta Regni Hungariae. Gesetze und Verordnungen Ungarns 1301–1457* (Publicationes Archivi Nationalis Hungarici, II/11). Budapest: Akadémiai.

E. Kovács, P. (ed.) 1992, *Estei Hippolit püspök egri számadáskönyvei, 1500–1508* [Account books of Ippolito d'Este]. Eger: Heves Megyei Levéltár.

Erdélyi, G. (ed.) 2006, *The Register of a Convent Controversy (1517–1518). Pope Leo X, Cardinal Bakócz, the Augustinians, and the Observant Franciscans in Contest* (Collectanea Vaticana Hungariae. Classis, II/1). Budapest–Roma: Research Institute of Church History at P. Pázmány Catholic University.

Érszegi, G. and Solymosi, L. (eds.) 2010, *Supplementum ad Monumenta Civitatis Veszprimiensis (1000–1516)*. Veszprém: Veszprémi Érseki és Főkáptalani Levéltár.

Fejér T., Rácz E. and Szász, A. (eds.) 2003, *János Zsigmond királyi könyve 1569–1570* [The royal book of John Sigismund, 1569–1570] (Az erdélyi fejedelmek királyi könyvei, 1 = Erdélyi Történelmi Adatok, VII/1). Kolozsvár: Erdélyi Múzeum-Egyesület.

Fejér, G. (ed.) 1829–1844, *Codex diplomaticus Hungariae ecclesiasticus ac civilis*, I–XI. Budae: Typogr. reg. universit. hungaric.

Fejérpataky, L. (ed.) 1887, *Monumenta Vaticana Historiam regni Hungariae illustrantia. (Vatikáni magyar okirattár)* I/1. *Rationes collectorum pontificorum in Hungaria. (1281–1375)*. Budapest: Franklin.

Fejérpataky, L. 1885, *Magyarországi városok régi számadáskönyvei* [Old account books of Hungarian towns]. Budapest: MTA.

Fekete Nagy, A. and Makkai, L. (eds.) 1941, *Documenta historiam Valachorum in Hungaria illustrantia, usque ad annum 1400 p. Christum*. Budapest: Sárkány Ny.

Friss, Á. (ed.) 1903, *Magyar–zsidó oklevéltár*, I (1092–1539) [Hungarian–Jewish cartulary]. Budapest: Wodianer F. és Fia bizománya.

Gárdonyi, A. (ed.) 1936, *Budapest történetének okleveles emlékei*, I [Charters to the history of Budapest]. Budapest: Székesfőváros Kiadása.

Géresi, K. (ed.) 1882–1897, *A nagy-károlyi gróf Károlyi család oklevéltára*, I–V [Charters of the Károlyi family of Carei]. Budapest: Franklin.

Górka, O. (ed.) 1916, *Anonymi Descriptio Europae Orientalis: Imperium Constantinopolitanum, Albania, Serbia, Bulgaria, Ruthenia, Ungaria, Polonia, Bohemia anno MCCCVIII exarata*. Kraków: Sumptibus Academiae Litterarum.

Gyéressy, B. and Hervay, F. L. 1975–1978, *Documenta Artis Paulinorum*, I–III, ed. M. Tóth. Budapest: A Magyar Tudományos Akadémia Művészettörténeti Kutató Csoport.

Györffy, Gy. (ed.) 1992, *Diplomata Hungariae antiquissima (accedunt epistolae et acta ad historiam Hungariae pertinentia). I. (1000–1131)*. Budapest: Akadémiai.

Halaga, O. R. (ed.) 1994, *Acta iudiciaria civitatis Cassoviensis 1393–1405. Das älteste Kaschauer Stadtbuch* (Buchreihe der Südostdeutschen Historischen Kommission, 34). München: R. Oldenbourg.

Házi, J. (ed.) 1921–1943, *Sopron szabad királyi város története*, I/1–7, II/1–6 [The history of the free royal town of Sopron]. Sopron: Székely, Szabó és Társa Könyvnyomdája.

Házi, J. 1970, "Vas megyei középkori oklevelek. 11. közlemény," [Medieval charters of Vas County. Part 11] *Vasi Szemle* 24, 131–135.

Hazzard Cross, S. and Sherbowitz-Wetzor, O. P. 1953, *The Russian Primary Chronicle. Laurentian Text*. Cambridge: Mediaeval Academy of America.

Heltai, G. 1978, *A bölcs Esopusnak és másoknak fabulái és oktató beszédei valamint azoknak értelme* [The teaching and the meaning of the fables of Aesop the wise and others]. Budapest: Magvető.

Höhlbaum, K. and Kunze, K. (eds.) 1876–1896, *Hansische Urkundenbuch*, I–VI. Halle: Duncker et Humblot.

Horváth, R. (ed.) 2005, *Győr megye hatóságának oklevelei (1318–1525)* [The charters of the authority of Győr County (1318–1525)] (A Győri Egyházmegyei Levéltár Kiadványai. Források, tanulmányok, 1). Győr: Győri Egyházmegyei Levéltár.

Ibrāhīim Ibn Ya'qūb 1946, *Relatio Ibrahim ibn Jakub de Itinere Slavico, quae traditur apud Al-Bekri* In *Monumenta Poloniae Historica* NS, 1, ed. T. Kowalski, 161–172. Kraków: Nakł. Polskiej. Akad. Umiejetnosci.

Ila, B. and Borsa, I. (eds.) 1993, *Az Abaffy család levéltára 1247–1515. A Dancs család levéltára 1232–1525. A Hanvay család levéltára 1216–1525* [Archives of the Abaffy, Dancs and Hanvay families]. Budapest: Akadémiai.

Iványi, B. (ed.) 1910, *Bártfa szabad királyi város levéltára, 1319–1526* [The archives of the free royal town of Bardejov]. Budapest: MTA.

Iványi, B. (ed.) 1918, *A győri székeskáptalan régi számadáskönyvei* [The ancient accounts of the cathedral chapter of Győr]. Budapest: Stephaneum.

Iványi, B. (ed.) 1931–1932, *Eperjes szabad királyi város levéltára*, I–II [The archive of the free royal town of Prešov]. Szeged: Szeged Városi Nyomda és Könyvkiadó.

Jakab, E. (ed.) 1870–1888, *Oklevéltár Kolozsvár történetének. I. II., III. kötetéhez* [Cartulary to Vols I, II, and III of the History of Cluj]. Buda–Budapest: Magy. Kir. Egyetemi Könyvnyomda.

Jakó, Zs. (ed.) 1990, *A kolozsmonostori konvent jegyzőkönyvei (1289–1556)*, I–II [The protocols of the convent of Cluj-Mănăștur] (A Magyar Országos Levéltár Kiadványai, II/17). Budapest: Magyar Országos Levéltár.

Jakó, Zs. (ed.) 1997, *Erdélyi okmánytár I. 1023–1300* [Transylvanian cartulary]. Budapest: Magyar Országos Levéltár.

Johannes de Thurocz 1985, *Chronica Hungarorum*, eds. E. Galántai and Gy. Kristó. Budapest: Akadméiai.

Juck, Ľ. (ed.) 1984, *Výsady miest a mestečiek na Slovensku I (1238–1350)* [Privileges of towns and small towns in Slovakia]. Bratislava: Veda.

Káldy-Nagy, Gy. (ed.) 1985, *A budai szandzsák 1546–1590 évi összeírásai* [Account books of the Sandjak of Buda, 1546–1590]. Budapest: Pest Megyei Levéltár.

Káldy-Nagy, Gy. (ed.) 2000, *A csanádi szandzsák 1567. és 1579. évi összeírása* [The accounts of the sanjak of Cenad in 1567 and 1579] (Dél-Alföldi Évszázadok, 15). Szeged: Csongrád Megyei Levéltár.

Kandra, K. (ed.) 1888, *Bakócs-Codex vagy Bakócs Tamás egri püspök udvartartási számadó-könyve 1493–6. évekből* [Bakócs-codex aka the account book of the court of Tamás Bakóc, bishop of Eger] (Adatok az egri egyházmegye történelméhez, II/3). Eger: Szolcsányi Gyula Bizománya.

Karácsonyi, J. and Borovszky, S. (eds.) 1903, *Regestrum varadinense examinum ferri candentis ordine chronologico digestum, descripta effigie editionis a. 1550 illustratum*. Budapest: Typis Victoris Hornyánszky.

Keglevich, K. (ed.) 2014, *A garamszentbenedeki apátság 13. és 14. századi oklevelei (1225–1403)* (Capitulum, 9) [Charters of the abbey of Hronský Beňadik, 1225–1403]. Szeged: Szegedi Tudományegyetem, Történeti Intézet.

Kenyeres, I. (ed.) 2002, *XVI. századi uradalmi utasítások. Utasítások a kamarai uradalmak prefektusai, udvarbírái és ellenőrei részére*, I–II [16th-century instructions to the prefect, stewards, and controllers of estates of the royal chamber] (Fons Könyvek, 2). Budapest: Szentpétery Imre Történettudományi Alapítvány.

Kenyeres, I. (ed.) 2008, *Zunftbuch und Privilegien der Fleischer zu Ofen aus dem Mittelalter* (Quellen zur Budapester Geschichte im Mittelalter und in der Frühen Neuzeit, 1). Budapest: Budapest Főváros Levéltára – Budapesti Történeti Múzeum.

Knauz, F. et al. (eds.) 1874–1999, *Monumenta Ecclesiae Strigoniensis*, I–IV. Strigonium–Budapest: Horák–Argumentum.

Kondorné Látkóczki, E. (ed.) 1997, *Diplomata aetatis Arpadiana in archivo comitatus Hevesiensis conservata*. Eger: Heves Megyei Levéltár.

Kóta, P. 1997, *Középkori oklevelek Vas megyei levéltárakban. I. Regeszták a vasvári káptalan levéltárának okleveleiről (1130) 1212–1526* [Medieval charters in the archives of Vas county I. (1130) 1212–1356.]. Szombathely: Vas Megyei Levéltár.

Kovachich, J. N. 1818, *Sylloge Decretorum Comitialium Inclyti Regni Hungariae*, I. Pest: Typis et sumptibus Joannis Thomae Trattner.

Kredics, L. and Solymosi, L. (eds.) 1993, *A veszprémi püspökség 1524. évi urbáriuma / Urbarium episcopatus Vesprimiensis anno MDXXIV* (Új Történemi Tár, 4). Budapest: Akadémiai.

Kredics, L., Madarász, L. and Solymosi, L. (eds.) 1997, *A veszprémi káptalan számadáskönyve, 1495–1534: krónika, 1526–1558: javadalmasok és javadalmak, 1550, 1556. Liber divisorum capituli Vesprimiensis, 1495–1534: chronica, 1526–1558: beneficiati et beneficia, 1550, 1556* (Veszprém Megyei Levéltár Kiadványai, 13). Veszprém: Veszprém Megyei Levéltár.

Kristó, Gy. et al. (eds.) 1990–2015, *Anjou-kori oklevéltár. Documenta res Hungaricas tempore regum Andegavensium illustrantia*, I–XL. Budapest–Szeged: JATE – Csongrád Megyei Levéltár.

Kubinyi, A. (ed.) 1997, *Elenchus fontium historiae urbanae*, III/2. Budapest: Balassi.

Lukcsics, P. (ed.) 1931, *XV. századi pápák oklevelei. I. kötet, V. Márton pápa (1417–1431)* [Charters of 15th-century Popes, vol. 1. Pope Martin V (1417–1431)]. Budapest: MTA.

Lukcsics, P. (ed.) 1938, *XV. századi pápák oklevelei. II. kötet, IV. Jenő pápa (1431–1447) és V. Miklós pápa (1447–1455)*. [Charters of 15th-century Popes, vol. 2. Popes Eugene IV (1431–1447) and Nicholas V (1447–1455)]. Budapest: MTA.

Lukcsics, P. et al. (eds.) 2014, *The Documents of the Camera Apostolica about the Lands of the Hungarian Crown (1297–1536)* (Collectanea Vaticana Hungariae, I/9). Budapest–Rome: Bibliotheca Historiae Ecclesiasticae Universitatis Catholicae de Petro Pázmány Nuncupatae.

Lukinich, I. (ed.) 1937–1943, *A podmanini Podmaniczky-család oklevéltára*, I–V [Cartulary of the Podmaniczky family of Podmanin]. Budapest: MTA.

Madzsar, E. (ed.) 1938, *Legenda s. Gerhardi maior* In *Scriptores rerum Hungaricarum*, II, ed. E. Szentpétery, 461–506. Budapest: Typ. Reg. Univ. Litter. Hung.

Majorossy, J. and Szende, K. (eds.) 2010–2014, *Das Pressburger Protocollum Testamentorum 1410 (1427)-1529*, I–II (Österreichische Akademie der Wissenschaften, Philosophisch-Historische Klasse, Kommission für Rechtsgeschichte Österreichs, Fontes rerum Austriacarum, Dritte Abteilung: Fontes Iuris, 21/1–2). Wien–Köln–Weimar: Böhlau.

Maksay, F. (ed.) 1959, *Urbáriumok. XVI–XVII. század* [Urbaria from the 16th–17th centuries] (Magyar Országos Levéltár kiadványai, II. Forráskiadványok, 7). Budapest: Magyar Országos Levéltár.

Mályusz, E. 1925–1935, "A szlavóniai és horvátországi középkori pálos kolostorok oklevelei az Országos Levéltárban," [Charters of the Slavonian and Croatian medieval Pauline monasteries in the Hungarian National Archives] *Levéltári Közlemények* 3 [1925], 100–191, 5 [1927] 136–209, 6 [1928] 87–203, 7 [1929] 278–311, 8 [1930] 65–111, 9 [1931] 284–315, 10 [1932] 92–123 and 256–286, 11 [1933] 58–92, 12 [1934] 111–154, and 13 [1935] 236–252.

Mályusz, E. et al. (eds.) 1951–2017, *Zsigmondkori oklevéltár*, I–XIII [Sigismund-period cartulary] (A Magyar Országos Levéltár kiadványai, II. Forráskiadványok, 1, 3–4, 22, 25, 27, 32, 37, 39, 41, 43, 49, 52, 55). Budapest: Akadémiai – MOL.

Marsina, R. (ed.) 1971–1987, *Codex diplomaticus et epistolaris Slovaciae*, I–II. Bratislava: Academiae Scientiarum Slovacae.

Mollay, K. (ed.) 1959, *Ofner Stadtrecht. Eine deutschsprachige Rechtssammlung des 15. Jahrhunderts aus Ungarn* (Monumenta Historica Budapestinensia, 1). Budapest: Akadémiai.

Mollay, K. (ed.) 1993, *Első telekkönyv / Erstes Grundbuch* (Quellen zur Geschichte der Stadt Ödenburg, Reihe A 1). Sopron: Soproni Levéltár.

Mollay, K. (ed.) 1994, *Das Geschäftsbuch des Krämers Paul Moritz / Moritz Pál kalmár üzleti könyve (1520–1529)* (Quellen zur Geschichte der Stadt Ödenburg, B 1). Sopron: Soproni Levéltár.

Möller, J. 1984, *Az Europai Manufaktúrák' és Fábrikák Mesterség Míveik* [Manufactures and factories in Europe and their masterpieces]. Budapest: Állami Könyvterjesztő Vállalat.

Nagy, Gy. (ed.) 1887–1889, *A nagymihályi és sztárai gróf Sztáray család oklevéltára*, I–II [Cartulary of the Sztáray family of Nagymihály and Staré]. Budapest: Sztáray Antal.

Nagy, Gy. et al. (eds.) 1899, *Corpus Juris Hungarici. Magyar Törvénytár. 1000–1526. évi törvényczikkek* [Hungarian law-collection]. Budapest: Franklin.

Nagy, I. and Tasnádi Nagy, Gy. (eds.) 1878–1920, *Codex diplomaticus Hungaricus Andegavensis*, I–VII. Budapest: A M. Tud. Akadémia Könyvkiadó-hivatala.

Nagy, I., Deák, F. and Nagy, Gy. (eds.) 1865–1891, *Codex diplomaticus patrius*, I–VIII. Győr–Budapest: Sauervein Géza.

Nagy, I. and Véghely, D. (eds.) 1871–1931, *A zichi és vásonkeői gróf Zichy-család idősb ágának okmánytára. Codex diplomaticus domus senioris comitum Zichy de Zich et Vasonkeo*, I–XII. Pestini–Budapestini: Editio Societatis Histor. Hung.

Nagy, I., Véghely, D. and Nagy, Gy. (eds.) 1886–1890, *Zala vármegye története. Oklevéltár*, I–II [A history of Zala County. Cartulary]. Budapest: Zala vármegye közönsége.

Niedermaier, P. (ed.) 2005, *Elenchus Fontium Historiae Urbanae*, III/3. Bucureşti: Editura Academiei Române.

Nógrády, Á. (ed.) 2011, *Kanizsai László számadáskönyve* [The account book of László Kanizsai] (História könyvtár. Okmánytárak, 8). Budapest: História – MTA Történettudományi Intézete.

Pertz, G. H. (ed.) 1886, *Arnoldi Chronica Slavorum* In *Monumenta Germaniae Historica. Scriptores Rerum Germanicarum in usum Scholarum*, 14. Hannover: Hahn.

Pertz, G. H. (ed.) 1891, *Annales Fuldenses sive Annales Regni Francorum Orientalis* In *Monumenta Germaniae historica., Scriptores rerum Germanicarum*, 7. Hannover: Hahn.

Petrus de Crescentiis 1998, *Ruralia commoda: Das Wissen des vollkommenen Landwirts um 1300*, eds. W. Richter and R. Richter-Bergmeier. Heidelberg: Winter.

Piirainen, I. T. (ed.) 1983, *Das Stadt- und Bergrecht von Kremnica/Kremnitz*. Heidelberg: Winter.

Piirainen, I. T. (ed.) 1986, *Das Stadt- und Bergrecht von Banská Stiavnica/Schemnitz*. Oulu: Oulu Univ.

Quellen Hermannstadt 1880, *Quellen zur Geschichte Siebenbürgens aus sächsischen Archiven. Bd. 1. Rechnungen aus dem Archiv der Stadt Hermannstadt und der Sächsischen Nation, 1380–1516*. Hermannstadt: Michaelis.

Quellen Kronstadt 1886–1889, *Quellen zur Geschichte der Stadt Kronstadt. Bd. I. Rechnungen, 1503–1526.; Bd. II. Rechnungen, 1526–1540.; Bd. III. Rechnungen, 1541–1550*. Kronstadt: Commission bei H. Zeidner.

Rácz, Gy. (ed.) 2010, *Collectio Diplomatica Hungarica. A középkori Magyarország levéltári forrásainak adatbázisa* [Online (DL–DF 5.1)] [Database of Archival Documents of Medieval Hungary]. Budapest: Magyar Nemzeti Levéltár.

Radvánszky, B. and Závodszky, L. (eds.) 1906–1922, *A Héderváry család oklevéltára*, I–II [Cartulary of the Héderváry Family]. Budapest: Magyar Tudományos Akadémia.

Rady, M. and Veszprémy, L. (eds.) 2010, Anonymus *Gesta Hungarorum – The Deeds of the Hungarians* (Central European Medieval Texts, 5). Budapest–New York: CEU Press.

Ratkoš, P. 1957, "Hans Dernschwam: Memoriál fuggerovského faktora Jána Dernschwama o banskobystrických baniach a feudálnych rozbrojoch v mnohonárodnostnom Uhorsku pred tureckou okupáciou," [Hans Dernschwam: Memorandum of the Fugger Factor Hans Dernschwam on the mines of Banská Bystrica and feudal divisions in the multinational Hungary before the Turkish occupation] In *Dokumenty k baníckemu povstaniu na Slovensku (1525–1526)* [Documents on the mining towns' uprising in Slovakia (1525–1526)], ed. P. Ratkoš, 453–476. Bratislava: Vydavateľstvo Slovenskej Akadémie vied.

Sanuto, M. 1879–1903, *I Diarii di Marino Sanudo 1496–1533*, I–LVIII. Venezia: Visentini.

Schefer, Ch. (ed.) 1892, *Le voyage d Outremer de Bertrandon de la Brocquière*. Paris: Ernest Leroux.

Sedlák, V. (ed.) 1980–1987, *Regesta diplomatica nec non epistolaria Slovaciae*, I–II. Bratislavae: Sumptibus Academiae Scientiarum Slovacae.

Smičiklas, T. and Kostrenčić, M. (eds.) 1904–1981, *Codex diplomaticus regni Croatiae, Dalmatiae et Slavoniae*, I–XVII. Zagreb: Ex officina societatis typographicae.

Solymosi, L. (ed.) 2002, *Registrum capituli cathedralis ecclesiae Strigoniensis. Az esztergomi székeskáptalan jegyzőkönyve 1500–1502, 1507–1527*. Budapest: Argumentum.

Spitzer, S. and Komoróczy, G. (eds.) 2003, *Héber kútforrások. Magyarország és a magyarországi zsidóság történetéhez a kezdetektől 1686-ig* [Hebrew sources to the history of

Hungary and Hungarian Jewry form the beginnings to 1686] (Hungaria Judaica, 16). Budapest: MTA Judaisztikai Kutatócsoport.

Szabó, I. 1954, *Bács, Bodrog és Csongrád megye dézsmalajstromai 1522-ből* [The titheregisters of Bács, Bodrog and Csongrád Counties from 1522] (A Magyar Nyelvtudományi Társaság Kiadványai, 86). Budapest: Akadémiai.

Szakály, F. and Szűcs, J. (eds.) 2005, *Budai bortizedjegyzékek a 16. század első harmadából* (História Könyvtár, Okmánytárak, 4) [Wine tithe lists from Buda from the first third of the 16th century]. Budapest: História.

Szekfű, Gy. 1911, "Oklevelek I. Károly pénzverési reformjához," [Charters concerning the minting reform of Charles I] *Történelmi Tár* 12, 1–36.

Szentpétery, E. (ed.) 1937–1938, *Scriptores rerum Hungaricarum*, I–II. Budapest: Typ. Reg. Univ. Litter. Hung.

Szentpétery, I. and Borsa, I. (eds.) 1923–1987, *Az Árpád-házi királyok okleveleinek kritikai jegyzéke / Regesta regum stirpis Arpadianae critico diplomatica*, I–II. Budapest: Magyar Tudományos Akadémia.

Tagányi, K. (ed.) 1896, *Magyar Erdészeti Oklevéltár*, I–III [Cartulary of Hungarian Forestry]. Budapest: Országos Erdészeti Egyesület.

Theiner, A. (ed.) 1859, *Vetera Monumenta historica Hungariam sacram illustrantia*, I. Romae: Typ. Vaticanis.

Theophilus Presbyter 1986, *The Various Arts. De Diversis Artibus*, ed. C. R. Dodwell, Oxford: Clrendon.

Tkalčić, J. B. (ed.) 1873–1874, *Monumenta historica episcopatus Zagrabiensis*, I–II. Zagrabiae: Velocibus typis C. Albrecht.

Tkalčić, J. B. (ed.) 1889, *Monumenta historica liberae regiae civitatis Zagrabiae metropolis regni Dalmatiae, Croatiae et Slavoniae*, I. Zagrabiae: Velocibus typis C. Albrecht.

Tringli, I. (ed.) 2008, *A Perényi család levéltára 1222–1526* [Archives of the Perényi family, 1222–1526]. Budapest: Magyar Országos Levéltár – MTA Történettudományi Intézet.

Varga, E. (ed.) 1958, *Úriszék. XVI–XVII. századi perszövegek* [The manorial court. 16th–17th-century juridical texts]. Budapest: Akadémiai.

Vass, E. 1979, "A szegedi és csongrádi náhije 1548. évi török adóösszeírása," [The Ottoman tax-registers of the nahiye of Szeged and Csongrád from 1548] *Tanulmányok Csongrád megye történetéből* 3, 5–80.

Veress, E. 1938, *Gyula város oklevéltára, 1313–1800* [Archival records of the town of Gyula 1313– 1800]. Budapest: Gyula M. város kiadása.

Wagner H. et al. (eds.) 1955–1999, *Urkundenbuch des Burgenlandes und der angrenzenden Gebiete der Komitate Wieselburg, Ödenburg und Eisenburg*, I–V. Graz–Köln: Böhlau.

Waitz, G. H. (ed.) 1912, *Ottonis et Rahewini Gesta Friderici I. Imperatoris*. In *Monumenta Germaniae Historica. Rerum Germanicarum in Usum Scholarum Separatim Editi*, 46. Hannover: Hahn.

Waitz, G. H. (ed.) 1882, *Ex rerum Francogallicarum scriptoribus* in *Monumenta Germaniae Historica. Scriptores*, 26. Hannover: Hahn.

Weis, J. N. (ed.) 1856, *Urkunden des Cistercienser-Stiftes Heiligenkreuz im Wiener Walde*, I (Fontes rerum Austriacarum, 2/XI). Wien: K. K. Hof- und Staatsdr.

Wenzel, G. (ed.) 1857, *Magyar Történelmi Emlékek*, II/1 [Hungarian Historical records]. Pest.

Wenzel, G. (ed.) 1860–1874, *Árpádkori új okmánytár. Codex diplomaticus Arpadianus continuatus*, I–XII. Pest: MTA.

Wenzel, G. (ed.) 1874–1876, *Magyar diplomácziai emlékek az Anjou-korból. Acta extra Andegavensia*, I–III. Budapest: MTA.

Závodszky, G. (ed.) 1909–1922, *A Héderváry-család oklevéltára*, I–II [The cartulary of the Héderváry family]. Budapest: M. Tud. Akadémia.

Zimmermann, F. et al. (eds.) 1892–1991, *Urkundenbuch zur Geschichte der Deutschen in Siebenbürgen*, I–VII. Hermannstadt–Bukarest: Ausschuß des Vereins für Siebenbürgische Landeskunde–Michaelis–Verl. der Akad. d. Sozialist. Republik Rumänien–Böhlau.

Secondary Sources

Abulafia, D. 1981, "Southern Italy and the Florentine Economy, 1265–1370," *Economic History Review* 34, 377–388.

Abulafia, D. 1993, *Commerce and conquest in the Mediterranean 1100–1500* (Variorum). Aldershot: Ashgate.

Acsády, I. 1895, "Egy malom jövedelme, 1587–89," [Incomes of a mill from the years 1587–1589] *Magyar Gazdaságtörténelmi Szemle* 2, 134.

Acsády, I. 1906, *A magyar jobbágyság története* [History of Hungarian peasantry] (Magyar Közgazdasági könyvtár, 3). Budapest: Politzer-Féle Könyvkiadóvállalat.

Altmann, J. 1994, "Az óbudai és budavári ferences templom és kolostor kutatásai," [Research into the Franciscan church and friary of Óbuda and the Buda Castle] In *Koldulórendi építészet a középkori Magyarországon* [Mendicant architecture in medieval Hungary], ed. A. Haris, 143–148. Budapest: Országos Műemlékvédelmi Hivatal.

Altmann, J. 2004, "Piactér a középkori Óbudán," [Marketplace in medieval Óbuda] In *Változatok a történelemre. Tanulmányok Székely György tiszteletére* [Variations on history. Studies in honor of György Székely] (Monumenta historica Budapestinensia, 14), eds. B. Nagy and Gy. Erdei, 59–63. Budapest: Budapesti Történeti Múzeum–ELTE BTK Középkori és Kora Újkori Egyetemes Történeti Tanszék.

Altmann, J. and Bertalan, H. 1991a, "Óbuda vom 11. bis 13. Jahrhundert," In *Budapest im Mittelalter*, ed. G. Biegel, 113–131. Braunschweig: Braunschweigisches Landesmuseum.

Altmann, J. and Bertalan, H. 1991b, "Óbuda im Spätmittelalter," In *Budapest im Mittelalter*, ed. G. Biegel, 185–189. Braunschweig: Braunschweigisches Landesmuseum.

Andrásfalvy, B. 1973, *A Sárköz és a környező Duna-menti területek ősi ártéri gazdálkodása és vízhasználata a vízszabályozás előtt* [Die Wassernutzung im Sárköz und in den umgebenden Überschwemmungsgebieten der Donau – vor den Gewässerregulierungen] (Vízügyi Történeti Füzetek, 6). Budapest: Vízügyi Dokumentációs és Tájékoztató Iroda.

Andrásfalvy, B. 1975, *A Duna mente népeinek ártéri gazdálkodása Tolna és Baranya megyében az ármentesítés befejezéséig* [Floodplain management along the Danube in the counties of Tolna and Baranya before the water regulations]. Szekszárd: Tolna megyei Tanács Levéltára.

Andrásfalvy, B. 1976, "Fischerei und allgemeine Wirtschaft in den Überschwemmungsgebieten Ungarns," In *Studien zur europäischen traditionellen Fischerei*, ed. E. Solymos, 59–64. Baja: Türr István Múzeum.

Andrásfalvy, B. 1989, "Die traditionelle Bewirtschaftung der Überschwemmungsgebiete Ungarns: Volklstümliche Wassernutzung im Karpatenbecken," *Acta Ethnographica Hungarica* 35/1–2, 39–88.

Andrić, S. 2000, *The Miracles of St. John Capistran*. Budapest: CEU Press.

Arany, K. 2006, "Success and Failure – Two Florentine Merchant Families in Buda during the Reign of King Sigismund (1387–1437)," *Annual of Medieval Studies at CEU* 12, 101–123.

Arany, K. 2007, "Firenzei kereskedők, bankárok és hivatalviselők Magyarországon 1370–1450. Prozopográfiai adattár," [Florentine merchants, bankers and office holders bearers in Hungary, 1370–1450. Prosopoghraphic database] *Fons* 14, 483–549.

Arany, K. 2008, "Firenzei–magyar kereskedelmi kapcsolatok a 15. században," [Florentine-Hungarian commercial relations in the 15th century] In *Gazdaság és gazdálkodás a középkori Magyarországon: gazdaságtörténet, anyagi kultúra, régészet* [Economy and farming in medieval Hungary: economic history, material culture, archaeology], eds. A. Kubinyi, J. Laszlovszky and P. Szabó, 277–297. Budapest: Martin Opitz.

Arany, K. 2009, "Generations Abroad: Florentine Merchant Families in Hungary in the first Half of the Fifteenth Century," In *Generations in Towns: Succession and Success in Pre-Industrial Urban Societies*, eds. F.-E. Eliassen and K. Szende, 129–153. Cambridge: Cambridge Scholars.

Arlinghaus, F.-J., 2006, "Account Books," In *Transforming the Medieval World: Uses of Pragmatic Literacy in the Middle Ages*, eds. idem et al., 43–69. Turnhout: Brepols.

Aston, M. 1988, "Aspects of fishpond construction and maintenance in the 16th and 17th centuries," In *Medieval Fish, Fisheries and Fishponds in England* (BAR British Series, 18), ed. idem, 187–202. Oxford: B.A.R.

Aston, M. 2002, *Interpreting the Landscape. Landscape Archaeology and Local History*. London: Routledge.

Bácskai, V. 1965, *Magyar mezővárosok a XV. században* [Market towns in Hungary in the 15th century] (Értekezések a történeti tudományok köréből. Új sorozat, 37). Budapest: Akadémiai.

Bácskai, V. 1967, "A gyulai uradalom mezővárosai a XVI. században," [The market towns of the estate of Gyula in the 16th century] *Agrártörténeti Szemle* 9, 432–454.

Bácskai, V. 1997, "Város-e a mezőváros?," [Are market towns towns?] *Budapesti Könyvszemle* [*BUKSZ*] 9, 195–199.

Bácskai, V. 2002, *Városok Magyarországon az iparosodás előtt* [Towns in Hungary before the industrialization]. Budapest: Osiris.

Bak, J. 1964, "Zur Frühgeschichte ungarischer Landgemeinden," In *Die Anfänge der Landgemeinde und ihr Wesen* (Vorträge und Forschungen, 2), ed. T. Mayer, 404–417. Stuttgart: Jan Thorbecke.

Bak, J. 1987, "Monarchie im Wellental: Materielle Grundlagen des ungarischen Königtums im fünfzehnten Jahrhundert," In *Das spätmittelalterliche Königtum im europäischen Vergleich* (Vorträge und Forschungen, 32), ed. R. Schneider, 347–384. Sigmaringen: Thorbecke.

Bak, J. and Vadas, A. 2016, "Diets and Synods in Buda and Its Environs," In *Medieval Buda in Context* (Brill's Companions to European History, 10), eds. B. Nagy et al., 322–344. Leiden–Boston: Brill.

Balassa, I. 1973, *Az eke és szántás története Magyarországon* [History of plow and plowing in Hungary]. Budapest: Akadémiai.

Bálint, A. 1939, "A mezőkovácsházi középkori település emlékei," [The remains of the medieval settlement of Mezőkovácsháza] *Dolgozatok* 15, 146–160.

Bálint, Cs. 1980, "Természeti földrajzi tényezők a honfoglaló magyarok megtelepedésében," [The role of geographical constraints in the settlement of Magyars in the Conquest period] *Ethnographia* 91, 35–51.

Bálint, M. 2003, "Landscape Development and Soil Formation in the Danube-Tisza Interfluve," In *People and Nature in Historical Perspective* (CEU Medievalia, 5), eds. J. Laszlovszky and P. Szabó, 157–174. Budapest: CEU Press.

Bálint, M., Laszlovszky, J., Romhányi, B. and Takács, M. 2003, "Medieval Villages and Their Fields," In *Hungarian Archaeology at the Turn of the Millennium*, ed. Zs. Visy, 383–388. Budapest: Ministry of National Cultural Heritage – Teleki László Foundation.

Balla, G. and Jékely, Zs. (eds.) 2008, *The Dowry of Beatrice: Italian Maiolica Art and the Court of King Matthias. Exhibition catalogue*. Budapest: Museum of Applied Arts.

Balogh, J. 1966, *A művészet Mátyás király udvarában*, I–II [Art at King Matthias Corvinus' court]. Budapest: Akadémiai.

Bánffy, E. 2015, "The beginnings of salt exploitation in the Carpathian Basin (6th–5th millennium BC)," *Documenta Praehistorica* 42, 197–209.

Baraczka, I. 1969, "Az 1535/36. évi Sopron városi kamarai számadáskönyv néhány tanulsága," [Some conclusions based on the town accounts of Sopron in 1535/36] *Soproni Szemle* 23, 207–215.

Bárány, A., Papp, K. and Szálkai, T. (eds.) 2011, *Debrecen város 650 éves. Várostörténeti tanulmányok* [Debrecen is 650 years old. Studies in urban history] (Speculum Historiae Debreceniense, 7). Debrecen: Debreceni Egyetem Történelmi Intézet.

Baráth, A. C. 2015, "Archaeological and Pictorial Evidence for the Belt in Late Medieval Hungary," *Annual of Medieval Studies at CEU* 21, 64–84.

Bárczi, G. 1951, *A tihanyi apátság alapítólevele mint nyelvi emlék* [The foundation charter of the abbey of Tihany as a linguistic source]. Budapest: Akadémiai.

Bárczi, G., Benkő, L. and Berrár, J. 1978, *A magyar nyelv története* [A history of the Hungarian language]. Budapest: Tankönyvkiadó.

Barta, J. and Barta, G. 1993, "III. Béla király jövedelmei: megjegyzések középkori uralkodóink bevételeiről," [The incomes of Béla III. Notes to the income of medieval rulers of Hungary] *Századok* 127, 413–449.

Barta, J. and Barta, G. 1999, "Royal Finance in Medieval Hungary: the Revenues of King Béla III," In *Crises, Revolutions and Self-Sustained Growth. Essays in European Fiscal History 1130–1830*, eds. M. Ormrod, M. Bonney and R. Bonney, 22–37. Stamford: Shaun Tyas.

Bartels, Ch. and Slotta, R. 2012, *Der alteuropäische Bergbau: von den Anfängen bis zur Mitte des 18. Jahrhunderts*. Münster: Aschendorff.

Bartha, D. 2000, "Erdőterület-csökkenések, fafajváltozások a Kárpát-medencében," [The decline of wooded areas and the changes in tree species in the Carpathian Basin] In *Táj és történelem* [Landscape and history], ed. Á. Várkonyi, R., 11–24. Budapest: Osiris.

Bartosiewicz, L. 1993, "Late Medieval Lynx Skeleton from Hungary," In *Skeletons in Her Cupboard*, eds. A. T. Clason, S. Payne and H.-P. Uerpmann, 5–18. Oxford: Oxbow.

Bartosiewicz, L. 1994, "Árpád-kori állatcsontok a váci vár területéről," [Árpádian-age animal remains from the Vác castle] *Váci Könyvek* 7, 205–212.

Bartosiewicz, L. 1995a, *Animals in the Urban Landscape in the wake of the Middle Ages* (BAR International Series, 609). Oxford: B.A.R.

Bartosiewicz, L. 1995b, "Camel Remains from Hungary," In *Archaeozoology of the Near East II. Proceedings of the Second International Symposium on the Archaeozoology of Soutwestern Asia and Adjacent Areas*, eds. H. Buitenhuis and H.-P. Uerpmann, 119–125. Leiden: Backhuys.

Bartosiewicz, L. 1996a, "Közép- és török kori állatmaradványok Segesdről," [Medieval- and Ottoman-period animal bones from Segesd] *Somogyi Múzeumok Közleményei* 12, 183–222.

Bartosiewicz, L. 1996b, "Archaeozoological studies from the Hahót Basin, SW Hungary," *Antaeus* 25, 307–367.

Bartosiewicz, L. 1997, "A Székesfehérvár Bestiary. Animal bones from the excavations of the medieval city wall," *Alba Regia* 26, 133–167.

Bartosiewicz, L. 1998a, "Medieval animal bones from the castle of Váralja–Várfő (Western Hungary)," *A Wosinsky Mór Múzeum Évkönyve* 20, 157–172.

Bartosiewicz, L. 1998b, "Attitudes to pets in the ethnolinguistic record," In *Man and the Animal World. Studies in Memoriam Sándor Bökönyi*, eds. P. Anreiter, et al., 65–78. Budapest: Archaeolingua.

Bartosiewicz, L. 1999a, "Animal Husbandry and Medieval Settlement in Hungary: a Review," *Beiträge zur Mittelalterarchäologie in Österreich* 15, 139–155.

Bartosiewicz, L. 1999b, "Turkish Period bone finds and cattle trade in south-western Hungary," In *Historia animalium ex ossibus*, eds. C. Becker et al., 47–56. Rahden: Leidorf.

Bartosiewicz, L. 1999c, "The role of sheep versus goat in meat consumption at archaeological sites," In *Transhumant Pastoralism in Southern Europe*, eds. idem and H. J. Greenfield, 47–60. Budapest: Archaeolingua.

Bartosiewicz, L. 2001, "A leopard (*Panthera pardus* L. 1758) find from the Late Middle Ages in Hungary," In *Animals and Man in the Past*, eds. H. Buitenhuis and W. Prummel, 151–160. Groningen: A.R.C. Publications.

Bartosiewicz, L. 2002, "A török kori Bajcsavár állatai," [Animals of Ottoman-period Bajcsavár] In *Weitschawar / Bajcsa-Vár. Egy stájer erődítmény Magyarországon a 16. század második felében* [A Styrian fortification in Hungary in the second half of the 16th century], ed. Gy. Kovács, 89–100. Zalaegerszeg: Zala Megyei Múzeumok Igazgatósága.

Bartosiewicz, L. 2003a, "A millennium of migrations: Protohistoric mobile pastoralism in Hungary," *Bulletin of the Florida Museum of Natural History* 44, 101–130.

Bartosiewicz, L. 2003b, "Eat not this fish – a matter of scaling," In *Presencia de la arqueoictiología en México*, eds. A. F. Guzmán, Ó. J. Polaco and F. J. Aguilar, 19–26. México D. F.: Museo de Paleontología de Guadalajara "Federico A. Solórzano Barreto".

Bartosiewicz, L. 2004, "Data on the culture history of Crows (Corvidae) in the Hungarian Middle Ages," In *"Quasi liber et pictura." Tanulmányok Kubinyi András hetvenedik születésnapjára / Studies in Honour of András Kubinyi on His Seventieth Birthday*, ed. Gy. Kovács, 37–41. Budapest: ELTE Régészettudományi Intézet = Institute of Archaeological Sciences of Eötvös Loránd University.

Bartosiewicz, L. 2005, "Crane: food, pet and symbol," In *Feathers, Grit and Symbolism. Birds and Humans in the Ancient Old and New Worlds* (Documenta Archaeobiologiae, 3), eds. G. Grupe and J. Peters, 259–269. Rahden: Leidorf.

Bartosiewicz, L. 2006, "Are 'autochthonous' animal breeds living monuments?," In *Archaeological and Cultural Heritage Preservation within the Light of New Technologies*, eds. E. Jerem, Zs. Mester and R. Benczes, 33–47. Budapest: Archaeolingua.

Bartosiewicz, L. 2008a, "Sturgeon Fishing in the Middle and Lower Danube Region," In *The Iron Gates in Prehistory*, eds. C. Bonsall, V. Boroneanţ and I. Radovanović, 39–54. Oxford: Archaeopress.

Bartosiewicz, L. 2008b, "Szarvasagancsok," [Deer antlers] In *Régészeti nyomozások Magyarországon* [Archaeological investigations in Hungary], ed. G. Ilon, 31–39. Budapest: Martin Opitz.

Bartosiewicz, L. 2009, "Skin and Bones: Taphonomy of a Medieval Tannery in Hungary," *Journal of Taphonomy* 7/2–3, 95–111.

Bartosiewicz, L. 2011, "'Stone Dead': Dogs in a Medieval Sacral Space," In *The Ritual Killing and Burial of Animals: European Perspectives*, ed. A. Pluskowski, 220–229. Oxford: Oxbow.

Bartosiewicz, L. 2012, "Show me your hawk, I'll tell you who you are," In *A Bouquet of Archaeozoological Studies. Essays in Honour of Wietske Prummel*, eds. D. C. M. Raemaekers et al., 181–190. Groningen: University of Groningen Library.

Bartosiewicz, L. 2013a, *Shuffling Nags, Lame Ducks. The Archaeology of Animal Disease*. Oxford: Oxbow.

Bartosiewicz, L. 2013b, "Fishful thinking: aquatic animals in a late 17th century cookbook from Transylvania," In *Fish and Seafood: Anthropological Perspectives from the Past and the Present*, eds. A. Matalas and N. Xirotiris, 97–108. Heraklion: Mystis.

Bartosiewicz, L. 2016a, "Animal Remains from the Late Medieval Castellum of Őcsény-Oltovány, Southern Hungary," In *"per sylvam et per lacus nimios." The Medieval and Ottoman Period in Southern Transdanubia, Southwest Hungary: The Contribution of the Natural Sciences*, eds. Gy. Kovács and Cs. Zatykó, 153–176. Budapest: MTA BTK Régészeti Intézet.

Bartosiewicz, L. 2017, "Archaeology in Hungary 1948–1989," In *Archaeology of the Communist Era: A Political History of Archaeology of the 20th Century*, ed. L. R. Lozny, 195–233. London–Berlin: Springer.

Bartosiewicz, L. and Bonsall, C. 2008, "Complementary Taphonomies: Medieval sturgeons from Hungary," In *Archéologie du Poisson. 30 ans d'archéo-ichtyologie au CNRS. Hommage aux travaux de Jean Desse et Nathalie Desse-Berset. XXVIIIe rencontres internationales d'archéologie et d'histoire d'Antibes*, eds. Ph. Béarez, S. Grouard and B. Clavel, 35–45. Antibes: APDCA.

Bartosiewicz, L. and Choyke, A. M. 2002, "Archaeozoology in Hungary," *Archaeofauna* 11, 117–129.

Bartosiewicz, L. and Choyke, A. M. 2011, "Sarmatian and Early Medieval animal exploitation at the site of Endrőd 170," In *Archaeological Investigations in County Békés 1986–1992*, eds. A. H. Vaday, B. D. Jankovich and L. Kovács, 285–320. Budapest: Archaeolingua.

Bartosiewicz, L. and Gál, E. 2010, "Animal finds in the east and west," In *The Oxford Dictionary of the Middle Ages*, vol. I. A–C, ed. R. E. Bjork, 61–62. Oxford: Oxford University Press.

Bartosiewicz, L. and Gyöngyössy, M. 2006, "The Khan's mule," In *Horses and Humans: The Evolution of Human-Equine Relationships* (BAR International Series, 1560), eds. S. L. Olsen et al., 289–299. Oxford: B.A.R.

Bartosiewicz, L., Bonsall, C. and Şişu, V. 2008, "Sturgeon fishing along the Middle and Lower Danube," In *The Iron Gates in Prehistory. New perspectives* (BAR International Series, 1893), eds. C. Bonsall, V. Boroneanţ and I. Radovanović, 39–54. Oxford. B.A.R.

Bartosiewicz, L., Gyetvai, A. and Küchelmann, H.-Ch. 2010, "Beast in the feast," In *Bestial Mirrors* (ViaVIAS 03/2010), eds. M. Kucera and G.-K. Kunst, 85–99. Vienna: VIAS.

Bartosiewicz, L., Mérai, D. and Csippán, P. 2011, "Dig up-Dig in: Practice and Theory in Hungarian Archaeology," In *Comparative Archaeologies: A Sociological View of the Science of the Past*, ed. L. R. Lozny, 273–337. New York: Springer.

Bátky, Zs., Győrffy, I. and Viski, K. (eds.) 1934, *A magyarság néprajza*, I–IV [Ethnography of Hungary] Budapest: Király Magyar Egyetemi Nyomda.

Baumgartner, E. 1949, "Die Blütezeit der Friesacher Pfennige. Ein Beitrag zur Geschichte des innerösterreichischen Münzwesens im 13. Jahrhundert," *Numismatische Zeitschrift* 73, 75–106.

Baumgartner, E. 1952, "Die Frühzeit der Friesacher Pfennige," *Carinthia I* 142, 256–286.

Beke, Ö. 1913, "A -va, -ve és -ván, -vén képzőről," [About the suffixes -*va*, -*ve* and -*ván*, -*vén*] *Magyar Nyelvőr* 42, 193–199.

Békefi, R. 1891, *A pilisi apátság története 1184–1541* [History of the abbey of Pilisszentkerezt, 1184–1541]. Pécs: F. Pfeifer.

Békefi, R. 1894, *A cikádori apátság története* [History of the abbey of Cikádor]. Pécs: Taizs Nyomda.

Békefi, R. 1898, *A pásztói apátság története 1190–1702*, I [History of the abbey of Pásztó, 1190–1702]. Budapest: Hornyánszky.

Belényesyné Sárosi, E. 2013, *Landscapes and settlements in the Kecskemét Region, 1300–1700*. Unpublished PhD dissertation defended at CEU, Budapest.

Belényesy, K. 2004, *Pálos kolostorok az Abaúji-Hegyalján* [Pauline monasteries at Abaúj-Hegyalja] (Borsod-Abaúj-Zemplén megye régészeti emlékei, 3). Miskolc: Herman Ottó Múzeum.

Belényesy, M. 1948, *Adatok a tanyakialakulás kérdéséhez. (A "telek" és a magyar tanya középkori gyökerei)* [Data to the formation of isolated farmsteads (Medieval roots of the "telek" and the isolated farmsteads)]. Budapest: Néptudományi Intézet.

Belényesy, M. 1953, "A halászat a 14. században," [Fishing in the 14th century] *Ethnographia* 64, 148–162.

Belényesy, M. 1954, "Beszámoló az 'Anyagi kulturánk a XV. században' c. munkaközösség 1952/53. évi munkájáról," [Report of the working group called: Material culture in Hungary in the 15th century] *Ethnographia*, 65, 612–615.

Belényesy, M. 1954/1955, "A földművelés fejlődésének alapvető kérdései a XIV. században. I–II.," [Basic question of the development of agriculture in the 14th century, I–II] *Ethnographia* 65, 387–413 and 66, 57–93.

Belényesy, M. 1955, "Le serment sur la terre au moyen âge et ses traditions postérieures en Hongrie," *Acta Ethnographica Academiae Scientiarum Hungaricae* 4, 361–394.

Belényesy, M. 1955–1956, "Szőlő- és gyümölcstermesztésünk a XIV. században," [Viticulture and fruit production in 14th-century Hungary] *Néprajzi Értesítő* 37, 11–31.

Belényesy, M. 1955a, "Az erdei irtások parlaggazdálkodása," [The fallow economy of forest clearances] *Néprajzi Múzeum Adattárának Értesítője* no. 1–2, 60–62.

Belényesy, M. 1955b, "Le serment sur la terre au moyen âge et ses traditions postérieures en Hongrie," *Acta Ethnographica Academiae Scientiarum Hungaricae* 4, 361–394.

Belényesy, M. 1956a, "Az állattartás a XIV. században Magyarországon," [Animal husbandry in 14th-century Hungary] *Néprajzi Értesítő* 38, 23–59.

Belényesy, M. 1956b, "Angaben über die Verbreitung der Zwei- und Dreifelserwirtschaft im mittelalterlicher Ungarn," *Acta Ethnographica Academiae Scientiarum Hungaricae* 5, 183–188.

Belényesy, M. 1956c, "A földművelés Magyarországon a XIV. században," [Agriculture in 14th–century Hungary] *Századok* 90, 517–555.

Belényesy, M. 1958a, "Über den Brandfeldbau in Ungarn," *Ethnographisch-archeologische Forschungen* 4, 9–21.

Belényesy, M. 1958b, "Kerített település és gazdálkodás néhány zalai írtásos falunál egy 1460-as határjárás alapján," [Enclosed settlement and economy of some villages of Zala county in light of a perambulation from 1460] *Ethnographia*, 69, 117–138.

Belényesy, M. 1958c, "Der Ackerbau und seine Produkte in Ungarn in XIV. Jahrhundert," *Acta Ethnographica Academiae Scientiarum Hungaricae* 6, 265–321.

Belényesy, M. 1960a, "A permanens egymezős földhasználat és a két- és háromnyomásos rendszer kialakulása Magyarországon a középkorban," [The permanent one field land use and the formation of two- and three-field system in Hungary in the Middle Ages] *Ethnographia* 71, 81–106.

Belényesy, M. 1960b, "La culture permanente et l'evolution du système biennal et triennal en Hongrie medieval," *Ergon* 2, 311–326.

Belényesy, M. 1964, "A parlagrendszer XV. századi kiterjesztése Magyarországon," [Expansion of the fallow system in Hungary in the 15th century] *Ethnographia* 75, 321–346.

Belényesy, M. 1967, "La culture temporaire et ses variantes en Hongrie au XVe siècle," *Acta Ethnographica Academiae Scientiarum Hungaricae* 16, 1–34.

Belényesy, M. 1969, "Hufengrösse und Zugtierbestand der bäuerlichen Betriebe in Ungarn im 14–15. Jh.," In *Viehwirtschaft und Hirtenkultur: Ethnographische Studien*, ed. L. Földes, 460–502. Budapest: Akadémiai.

Belényesy, M. 2011, *Fejezetek a középkori anyagi kultúra történetéből*. I [Studies in the history of medieval material culture] (Documentatio Ethnographica, 26). Budapest: L'Harmattan.

Belényesy, M. 2012, *Fejezetek a középkori anyagi kultúra történetéből*. II [Studies in the history of medieval material culture] (Documentatio Ethnographica, 29). Budapest: L'Harmattan.

Bellon, T. 1996a, "Az alföldi mezővárosok fejlődésének gazdasági háttere," [The economic background of the development of market towns in the Great Hungarian Plain] *Ethnographia* 107, 85–101.

Bellon, T. 1996b, "Ártéri gazdálkodás az Alföldön az ármentesítések előtt," [Floodplain economy at the Great Hungarian Plain before the regulation works] In *A Kárpátmedence történeti földrajza* [Historical geography of the Carpathian Basin], ed. S. Frisnyák, 311–319. Nyíregyháza: Bessenyei György Tanárképző Főiskola Földrajz Tanszék.

Bencze, Z. 1991, "Die Handwerker und Kaufleute der Stadt Buda vom Anfang des 14. bis zum ersten Drittel des 16. Jahrhunderts," In *Budapest im Mittelalter*, ed. G. Biegel, 333–349. Braunschweig: Braunschweigisches Landesmuseum.

Benda, J. 2010, "A kereskedelem épületei a középkori Budán I. Kalmárboltok," [Commercial buildings in medieval Buda I. Retailers] *Budapest Régiségei* 42, 93–120.

Benda, J. 2011, "A piactól az árucsarnokig. Kereskedelmi célra készült épületek a középkori Budán," [From open markets to market halls. Buildings for trade in medieval Buda] *Történelmi Szemle* 53, 259–282.

Benda, J. 2012, "A kereskedelem épületei a középkori Budán, II. Mészárszékek háza, zsemleszékek háza, árucsarnok," [Commercial buildings in medieval Buda II. The house of butcheries, bakeries, market hall] *Tanulmányok Budapest Múltjából* 37, 7–42.

Benda, J. 2014a, "'Leugrok a sarki fűszereshez': Bolttípusok rövid kereskedelem- és építéstörténete a középkortól napjainkig," ["I'm going down to the grocer at the corner" – the short commercial and construction history of shop types from the Middle Ages to Modern Times] In *Középkori elemek a mai magyar anyagi kultúrában* [Medieval elements in present-day Hungarian material culture] (Életképek a Kárpát-medence anyagi kultúrája köréből, 1), eds. A. Báti and Zs. Csoma, 171–192. Budapest: Agroinform.

Benda, J. 2014b, "Posztókereskedelem és posztósboltok a későközépkori Budán," [Cloth trade and shops in late medieval Buda] In *A textilművesség évezredei a Kárpátmedencében* [Millennia of textile industry in the Carpathian Basin] (Az anyagi kultúra évezredei a Kárpát-medencében, 5), ed. J. Szulovszky, 27–42. Budapest: Plusz.

Benda, J. 2016a, "Merchants, Markets, and Shops in Late Medieval Buda, Pest and Óbuda," In *Medieval Buda in Context* (Brill's Companions to European History, 10), eds. B. Nagy et al., 255–277. Leiden–Boston: Brill.

Benda, J. 2016b, "Marhakereskedelem és mészárszékek a késő középkori Budán, Pesten, Óbudán," [Cattle trade and butchers' shops in late medieval Buda, Pest and Óbuda] In *Pénz, posztó, piac. Gazdaságtörténeti tanulmányok a magyar középkorról* [Cash, cloth, commerce. Studies in the economic history of medieval Hungary], ed. B. Weisz, 407–438. Budapest: MTA Bölcsészettudományi Kutatóközpont Történettudományi Intézet.

Bende, L. and Lőrinczy G. (eds.) 2000, *A középkori magyar agrárium* [Medieval Hungarian agriculture]. Ópusztaszer: Nemzeti Történelmi Emlékpark.

Benke, I. (ed.) 1996, *A magyar bányászat évezredes története* [A thousand years of mining in Hungary]. Budapest: Országos Magyar Bányászati és Kohászati Egyesület.

Benkő, E. 2002, *Erdély középkori harangjai és bronz keresztelőmedencéi* [Medieval bells and bronze baptismal fonts of Transylvania]. Budapest–Kolozsvár: Teleki László Alapítvány.

Benkő, E. 2005, "Mittelalterliche Bronzegegenstände aus Siebenbürgen. Probleme der Herkunftsbestimmung unter Berücksichtigung der Siebenbürger Sachsen," *Ungarn-Jahrbuch. Zeitschrift für interdisziplinäre Hungarologie* 27, 1–15.

Benkő, E. 2008, "Pilgerzeichenforschung und Pilgerzeichenüberlieferung in Ungarn und in Siebenbürgen," In *Das Zeichen am Hut im Mittelalter. Europäische Reisemarkierungen*, eds. H. Kühne, L. Lambacher and K. Vanja, 167–184. Frankfurt am Main: Lang.

Benkő, E. 2009, "Bronzeguß im mittelalterlichen Esztergom (Gran, Ungarn)," In *Varia Campanologiae Studia Cyclica* (Schriften aus dem Deutschen Glockenmuseum, 6), eds. K. Bund and R. Pfeiffer–Rupp, 73–80. Greifenstein: Glockenmuseum auf Burg Greifenstein.

Benkő, E. 2010, "Fémfeldolgozás a középkorban," [Metal processing in the Middle Ages] In *A középkor és a kora újkor régészete Magyarországon / Archaeology of the Middle Ages and the Early Modern Period in Hungary*, II, eds. E. Benkő and Gy. Kovács, 691–708. Budapest: MTA Régészeti Intézete.

Benkő, E. 2015, "Udvarházak és kolostorok a pilisi királyi erdőben," [Manor Houses and Cloisters in the Royal Forests of the Pilis Region] In *"In medio regni Hungariae." Régészeti, művészettörténeti és történeti kutatások az ország közepén / Arhaeological, art historical and historical researches 'in the middle of the kingdom'*, eds. E. Benkő and K. Orosz, 727–754. Budapest: MTA BTK Régészeti Intézete.

Benkő, E. and Kovács, Gy. (eds.) 2010, *A középkor és a kora újkor régészete Magyarországon / Archaeology of the Middle Ages and the Early Modern Period in Hungary*, I–II. Budapest: MTA Régészeti Intézete.

Benkő, E., Demeter, I. and Székely, A. 1997, *Középkori mezőváros a Székelyföldön* [Medieval market towns in the Székely Lands] (Erdélyi Tudományos Füzetek, 223). Kolozsvár: Erdélyi Múzeum Egyesület.

Benkő, L. (ed.) 1967–1984, *A magyar nyelv történeti-etimológiai szótára*, I–IV [A historical-etymological dictionary of the Hungarian language]. Budapest: Akadémiai.

Benkő, L. 1998, *Név és történelem. Tanulmányok az Árpád-korról* [Name and history. Studies on the Árpádian age]. Budapest: Akadémiai.

Berend, N. 2001, *At the Gate of Christendom. Jews, Muslims, and "Pagans" in Medieval Hungary, c. 1000 – c. 1301*. Cambridge: Cambridge University Press.

Berend, N., Urbańczyk, P. and Wiszewski, P. 2013. *Central Europe in the High Middle Ages: Bohemia, Hungary and Poland, c. 900–c. 1300*. Cambridge: Cambridge University Press.

Bériou, N. and Chiffoleau, J. (eds.) 2009, *Économie et religion. L'expérience des ordres mendiants (XIVe–XVe siècle)*. Lyon: Presses universitaires de Lyon.

Berrár, J. and Károly, S. (eds.) 1984, *Régi magyar glosszárium. Szótárak, szójegyzékek és glosszák egyesített szótára* [Old Hungarian glossary. United dictionary of dictionaries, glossaries and glosses]. Budapest: Akadémiai.

Bertalan, H. 1991, "Majolikafunde aus dem Königspalast von Buda," In *Budapest im Mittelalter. Katalog*, ed. G. Biegel, 288–291. Braunschweig: Braunschweigisches Landesmuseum.

Billamboz, A. 2003, "Tree Rings and Wetland Occupation in Southwest Germany between 2000 and 500 BC: Dendroarchaeology beyond Dating in Tribute to F.H. Schweingruber," *Tree-Ring Research* 59, 37–49.

Biller, A. Zs. 2007, "Vecsés környéki árpád-kori települések csontanyagának állattani vizsgálata," [The zoological study of osteological finds from the Vecsés area dated to the Árpádian age] *Archeometriai Műhely* no. 1, 45–54.

Bíró, Sz., Molnár, A., Szőnyi, E. and Tomka, P. 2010, "Régészeti kutatások a győri Széchenyi téren (2008–2009)," [Archaeological excavations at the Széchenyi Square in Győr]. In *Régészeti kutatások Magyarországon 2009* [Archaeological investigations in Hungary 2009], ed. J. Kisfaludy, 39–52. Budapest: Budapest: Kulturális Örökségvédelmi Hivatal.

Bischoff, F. 2006, "Französische und deutsche Bauhandwerker in Diensten Sigismunds von Luxemburg. Zur Identität des Preßburger Meisters Konrad von Erling," In *Sigismundus Rex et Imperator. Kunst und Kultur zur Zeit Sigismund von Luxemburg 1387–1437. Ausstellungskatalog*, ed. I. Takács, 246–250. Budapest–Mainz am Rhein: P. von Zabern.

Bishop, R. R., Church, M. J. and Rowley-Conwy, P. A. 2015, "Firewood, Food and Human Niche Construction: the Potential Role of Mesolithic Hunter–Gatherers in Actively Atructuring Scotland's Woodlands," *Quaternary Science Reviews* 108, 51–75.

Blanchard, I. 1986, "The Continental European Cattle Trades, 1400–1600," *The Economic History Review* NS 39, 427–460.

Blanchard, I. 2001, *Mining, Metallurgy and Minting in the Middle Ages*. Vol. 1. *Asiatic Supremacy, 425–1125*. Stuttgart: Steiner.

Blanchard, I. 2005, *Mining, Metallurgy, and Minting in the Middle Ages. Vol. 3. Continuing Afro-European Supremacy, 1250–1450* (*African Gold Production and the Second and Third European Silver Production Long-cycles*). Stuttgart: Steiner.

Blanchard, I. 2007, "Egyptian specie markets and the international gold crisis of the early fifteenth century," In *Money, Markets and Trade in Late Medieval Europe. Essays in Honour of John H. A. Munro*, eds. L. Armstrong, I. Elbl and M. M. Elbl, 383–410. Leiden: Brill.

Blazovich, L. 1996, *A Körös–Tisza–Maros-köz települései a középkorban* [The settlements of the Region between the Rivers Körös, Tisza and Maros in the Middle Ages] (Dél-Alföldi Évszázadok, 9). Szeged: Csongrád Megyei Levéltár.

Blazovich, L. 2002, *Városok az Alföldön a 14–16. században* [Cities in the Great Hungarian Plain in the 14th–16th centuries] (Dél-Alföldi Évszázadok, 17). Szeged: Csongrád Megyei Levéltár.

Bogdán, I. 1978, *Magyarországi hossz- és földmértékek a 16. század közepéig* [Hungarian system of measures of distance and lands until the 16th century]. Budapest: Akadémiai.

Bogdán, I. 1991, *Magyarországi űr-, térfogat, súly-, és darabmértékek 1874-ig* [Measurement units for space, volume, weight and piece in Hungary until 1874]. Budapest: Akadémiai.

Bognár, Sz. 2010, *A népi jogélet kutatása Magyarországon Tagányi Károly jogszokásgyűjtő programja* [The Study of Folk Law in Hungary. Károly Tagányi's Program on Collecting Living Legal Folks Customs]. Unpublished PhD-dissertation defended at ELTE, Budapest.

Bökönyi, S. 1974, *History of Domestic Animals in Central and Eastern Europe*. Budapest: Akadémiai.

Bökönyi, S. 1981, "Mende–Leányvár Árpád-kori – 13. századi – állatmaradványai," [Árpádian-age (13th century) animal bone finds of Mende-Leányvár] *Archaeologiai Értesítő* 108, 251–258.

Bökönyi, S. 1995, "The Development of Stockbreeding and Herding in Medieval Europe," In *Agriculture in the Middle Ages: Technology, Practice, and Representation*, ed. D. Sweeney, 41–61. Philadelphia: University of Pennsylvania Press.

Bökönyi, S. and Jánossy, D. 1965, "Szubfosszilis vadmadár-leletek Magyarországon," [Subfossile wild bird finds in Hungary] *Vertebrata Hungarica* 7, 85–99.

Boldizsár, P. 1984, "Egy 14. századi desztilláló készülék a királyi palota északi előudvarán folyó ásatások anyagából," [A 14th-century distillery from the excavations of the northern fore-court of the royal palace] *Budapest Régiségei* 26, 217–226.

Bolla, I. 1961, "A jobbágytelek kialakulásának kérdéséhez. A „curia" és „mansio" terminusok jelentésváltozása az Árpád-korban," [To the question of the formation of peasant estate. The changes of the meaning of the terms "curia" and "mansion" in the Árpádian period] *Annales Universitatis Scientiarum Budapestini Sectio Historica* 3, 97–120.

Bolla, I. 1980, "A középkori magyar hidak történetéhez," [To the history of medieval bridges in Hungary] In *Ünnepi tanulmányok Sinkovics István 70. születésnapjára, 1980. augusztus 19.* [Studies in honor of the 70th birthday of István Sinkovics, 19 August 1980], ed. I. Bertényi, 33–43. Budapest: [Eötvös Loránd Tudományegyetem].

Bolla, I. 1983, *A jogilag egységes jobbágyosztály kialakulása* [On the formation of legally unified peasantry in Hungary] (Értekezések a történeti tudományok köréből. Új sorozat, 100). Budapest: Akadémiai.

Bolla, I. 1998, *A jogilag egységes jobbágyságról Magyarországon* [On the legally equal peasantry in Hungary], ed. E. Ladányi. Budapest: Nap.

Bollók, Á. et al. 2009, "Textile Remnants in the Archaeological Heritage of the Carpathian Basin from the 10th–11th centuries," *Acta Archaeologica Academiae Scientiarum Hungaricae* 60, 147–221.

Bóna, I. 1987, "Dáciától Erdőelvéig. A népvándorlás kora Erdélyben (271–896)," [The Migration Period in Transylvania (271–896)] In *Erdély története*, I [History of Transylvania], eds. L. Makkai and A. Mócsy, 107–234. Budapest: Akadémiai.

Bóna, I. 2001, "Erdély a magyar honfoglalás és államalapítás korában," [Transylvania in the period of the Hungarian conquest] In *Erdély a keresztény Magyar Királyságban. Tanulmányok* [Transylvania in the Chrsitian Hungary. Studies] (Erdélyi Tudományos Füzetek, 231), 69–97. Kolozsvár: Erdélyi Múzeum-Egyesület.

Bond, C. J. 2007, "Canal Construction in the Early Middle Ages. An Introductory Review," In *Waterways and Canal Building in Medieval England*, ed. J. Blair, 153–206. Oxford: Oxford University Press.

Bónis, Gy. 1965, "Ständisches Finanzwesen in Ungarn im frühen 16. Jahrhundert," In *Nouvelles études historiques publiées à l'occasion du XIIe Congrès International des Sciences Historiques par la Commission Nationale des Historiens Hongrois*, I, eds. D. Csatári, L. Katus and Á. Rozsnyói, 93–102. Budapest: Akadémiai.

Bónis, Gy. 1972, *Középkori jogunk elemei* [Fundaments of Hungarian medieval law]. Budapest: Közgazdasági és Jogi Kiadó.

Bónis, Gy. 2003, *Hűbériség és rendiség a középkori magyar jogban* [Feudalism and corporatism in the medieval Hungarian laws]. Budapest: Közgazdasági és Jogi Könyvkiadó.

Boone, M., Davids, K. and Janssens, P. 2003, *Urban public debts, urban government and the market for annuities in Western Europe (14th–18th centuries)*. Turnhout: Brepols.

Borosy, A. and Laszlovszky J. 2006, "Magyarország, a Szentföld és a korai keresztes hadjáratok," [Hungary, the Holy Land and the early Crusades] In *Magyarország és a keresztes háborúk. Lovagrendek és emlékeik* [Hungary and the Crusades. Religious military orders and their heritage], eds. J. Laszlovszky, J. Majorossy and J. Zsellengér, 75–90. Máriabesnyő: Attraktor.

Bosl, K. 1966, *Die Sozialstruktur der mittelalterlichen Residenz- und Fernhandelsstadt Regensburg. Die Entwicklung ihres Bürgertums vom 9.–14. Jahrhundert* (Bayerische Akademie der Wissenschaften. Philosophisch-Historische Klasse, [NF] 63). München: Bayerische Akademie der Wissenschaften.

Braudel, F. 1974, "L'Italia fuori Italia. Due secoli e tre Italie," In *Storia d'Italia*, II/2, eds. R. Romano and C. Vivanti, 2089–2248. Torino: Einaudi.

Brázdil, R. et al. 2005, "Historical Climatology in Europe – The State of the Art," *Climatic Change* 70, 363–430.

Brown, G. 2005, "Irrigation of Water Meadows in England," In *Water Management in Medieval Rural Economy* (Ruralia, 5), ed. J. Klápště, 93–112. Prague: Institute of Archaeology.

Brundage, J. A. 1976, *The Crusades. A Documentary Survey*. Milwaukee: Marquette University Press.

Brunner, O. 1942, *Land und Herrschaft. Grundfragen der territorialen Verfassungsgeschichte Südostdeutschlands im Mittelalter*. Wien: Rohrer.

Bruscoli, F. G. 2001, "Drappi di seta e tele di lino tra Firenze e Norimberga nella prima metá del Cinquecento," *Archivio Storico Italiano* 159, 359–394.

Buczkó, K., Magyari, E. K., Bitušík, P. and Wacnik, A. 2009, "Review of Dated Late Quaternary Palaeolimnological Records in the Carpathian Region, East-Central Europe," In *Palaeolimnological Proxies as Tools of Environmental Reconstruction in Fresh Water*, eds. K. Buczkó et al., 3–28. Dordrecht: Springer.

Bunyitay, V. 1883, *A váradi püspökség története*, I [The history of the diocese of Oradea]. Nagyvárad: Franklin.

Bürgi, M. and Gimmi, U. 2007. "Three Objectives of Historical Ecology: the Case of Litter Collecting in Central European Forests," *Landscape Ecology* 22, 77–87.

Bürgi, M. and Stuber, M. 2013, "What, How, and Why? Collecting Traditional Knowledge on Forest Uses in Switzerland," In *Cultural Severance and the Environment: The Ending of Traditional and Customary Practice on Commons and Landscapes Managed in Common*, ed. I. D. Rotherham, 123–132. Dordrecht: Springer.

Buza, J. 2002, "Der Wechselkurs des ungarischen und türkischen Dukaten in der Mitte des 16. Jahrhunderts," In *Weltwirtschaft und Wirtschaftsordnung. Festschrift für Jürgen Schneider zum 65. Geburtstag*, eds. R. Gömmel and M. A. Denzel, 25–44. Stuttgart: Steiner.

Buzás, G., Laszlovszky, J. and Mészáros, O. 2014, "The Town: Administration, Inhabitants, Institutions," In *The Medieval Royal Town of Visegrád. Royal Centre, Urban Settlement, Churches*, eds. G. Buzás, J. Laszlovszky and O. Mészáros, 45–96. Budapest: Archaeolingua.

C. Tóth, N. 2004, "Szond. (Egy dél-alföldi mezőváros a középkorban)," [Szond. A medieval market town in the southern part of the Great Hungarian Plain] In *"Quasi liber et pictura." Tanulmányok Kubinyi András 70. születésnapjára / Studies in Honour of András Kubinyi on His Seventieth Birthday*, ed. Gy. Kovács, 589–600. Budapest: ELTE Régészettudományi Intézet = Institute of Archaeological Sciences of Eötvös Loránd University.

C. Tóth, N. 2016, "A Magyar Királyság 1522. évi költségvetése," [The budget of the Hungarian Kingdom in 1522] In *Pénz, posztó, piac. Gazdaságtörténeti tanulmányok a magyar középkorról* [Cash, cloth, commerce. Studies in the economic history of Hungary], ed. B. Weisz, 83–148. Budapest: Budapest: MTA Bölcsészettudományi Kutatóközpont Történettudományi Intézet.

C. Tóth, N. and Neumann, T. (eds.) 2015, *Keresztesekből lázadók: Tanulmányok 1514 Magyarországáról* [From crusaders to rebellers. Studies on Hungary in 1514]. Budapest: Budapest: MTA Bölcsészettudományi Kutatóközpont Történettudományi Intézet.

Calabi, D. 2004, *The Market and the City. Square, Street and Architecture in Early Modern Europe*. Aldershot: Ashgate.

Cappers, R. T. J. and Neef, R. 2012, *Handbook of Plant Palaeoecology*. Eelde: Barkhuis.

Carter, F. W. 1994, *Trade and Urban Development in Poland. An Economic Geography of Cracow, from its origins to 1795*. Cambridge: Cambridge University Press.

Choyke, A. M. and Kováts, I. 2010, "Tracing the Personal through Generations: Late Medieval and Ottoman Combs," In *Bestial Mirrors* (ViaVIAS 03/2010), eds. M. Kucera and G.-K. Kunst, 100–109. Vienna: VIAS.

Choyke, A. M., Lyublyanovics, K. and Bartosiewicz, L. 2005, "The various voices of Medieval animal bones," In *Animal Diversities* (Medium Aevum Quotidianum, Sonderband, 16), eds. G. Jaritz and A. Choyke, 23–49. Krems: Medium Aevum Quotidianum.

Commissioni 1869, *Commissioni di Rinaldo degli Albizzi per il comune di Firenze dal 1399–1433. Vol.2. 1424–1426* (Documenti di storia italiana). Firenze: Cellini.

Cooper, A. 2002, "The rise and fall of the Anglo-Saxon law of the highway," *The Haskins Society Journal: Studies in Medieval History* 12, 39–69.

Csalogovits, J. 1935, "Népi építkezés emlékei a tolnamegyei Sárközben," [Remains of vernacular architecture in the Sárköz region in Tolna county] *Néprajzi Értesítő* 27, 1–10.

Csalogovits, J. 1937, "Tolna vármegye Múzeumának második ásatása a török hódoltság alatt elpusztult Ete község helyén," [The second excavation of the Tolna County Museum in the village of Ete destroyed in the Ottoman Period] *Néprajzi Értesítő* 29, 321–333.

Csánki, D. and Fekete Nagy, Gy. 1890–1944, *Magyarország történelmi földrajza a Hunyadiak korában*, I–V [Historical geography of Hungary in the age of the Hundaydis]. Budapest: MTA.

Csippán, P. 2004, "13–14. századi állatcsontleletek a budai Szt. György tér délnyugati részéről," [13th–14th-century animal bones from the southwestern corner of the Szt. György Square] *Budapest Régiségei* 38, 201–206.

Csippán, P. 2009, "XVIII. századi szarvcsapleletek a budai Vízivárosból," [18th-century cattle horn core finds from the Víziváros district of Buda, Hungary] In *Csontvázak a szekrényből. Skeletons from the Cupboard*, eds. L. Bartosiewicz, E. Gál and I. Kováts, 195–201. Budapest: Martin Opitz.

Csippán, P. 2013, "Meat supplies of the markets of Medieval and Early Modern Age Debrecen (NE Hungary)," *Archeometriai Műhely* 10, 249–258.

Csóka, J. L. 1980, *Geschichte des benediktinischen Mönchtums in Ungarn*. München: Trofenik.

Csőre, P. 1980, *A magyar erdőgazdálkodás története. Középkor* [A history of Hungarian forestry. The Middle Ages]. Budapest: Akadémiai.

Csőre, P. 1994, *A magyar vadászat története* [History of hunting in Hungary]. Budapest: Mezőgazda.

Csukovits, E. 1997, "Sedriahelyek – megyeszékhelyek a középkorban," [Sedriahelyek – county centers in the Middle Ages] *Történelmi Szemle* 39, 363–386.

Csukovits, E. 2003, *Középkori magyar zarándokok* [Medieval Hungarian pilgrims]. Budapest: MTA Történettudományi Intézete.

Czuczor, G. and Fogarasi, J. (eds.) 1862–1874, *A magyar nyelv szótára*, I–VI [A dictionary of the Hungarian language]. Pest: Emich Gusztáv.

Danninger, J. 1907, *Pozsony szabad kir. város 1526–1527. évi számadáskönyve művelődéstörténeti szempontból* [The 1526–1527 account books of the free royal town of Bratislava as a source for cultural history]. Budapest: Stephaneum.

Dányi, D. and Zimányi, V. 1989, *Soproni árak és bérek a középkortól 1750–ig* [Prices and wages in Sopron from the Middle Ages to 1750]. Budapest: Akadémiai.

Daróczi-Szabó, L. 2004a, "Animal bones as indicators of kosher food refuse from 14th century AD Buda, Hungary," In *Behaviour Behind Bones. The Zooarchaeology of Ritual, Religion, Status and Identity*, eds. S. J. O'Day, W. Van Neer and A. Ervynck, 252–261. Oxford: Oxbow.

Daróczi-Szabó, L. 2004b, "Állatcsontok a Teleki Palota törökkori gödréből," [Animal remains from the Ottoman-era refuse pit of the Teleki Palace] *Budapest Régiségei* 38, 159–160.

Daróczi-Szabó, L. et al. 2014, "Recent Camel Finds from Hungary," *Anthropozoologica* 49/2, 162–302.

Daróczi-Szabó, M. 2006, "Variability in Medieval dogs from Hungary," In *Dogs and People in Social, Working, Economic or Symbolic Interaction*, eds. L. M. Snyder and E. A. Moore, 85–95. Oxford: Oxbow.

Daróczi-Szabó, M. 2009, "Szendrő–Felsővár kora újkori állatcsontjainak vizsgálata," [Early Modern Age animal remains from Szendrő–Felsővár] In *Csontvázak a szekrényből.* Skeletons from the Cupboard, eds. L. Bartosiewicz, E. Gál and I. Kováts, 151–171. Budapest: Martin Opitz.

Daróczi-Szabó, M. 2010, "Pets in pots: superstitious belief in a medieval Christian (12th–14th century) village in Hungary," In *Anthropological Approaches to Zooarchaeology: Complexity, Colonialism, and Animal Transformations*, eds. D. Campana et al., 211–215. Oxford: Oxbow.

Daróczi-Szabó, M. 2013, *Az Árpád-kori Kána falu állatcsontjainak vizsgálata* [The study of animal remains from the Árpádian-age village of Kána] Unpublished PhD-dissertation defended at the ELTE, Budapest.

de Cevins, M.-M. 2004, *Saint Étienne de Hongrie*. Paris: Fayard.

de Roover, R. 1999, *The Rise and Decline of the Medici Bank 1397–1494*. Washington: Northon Library.

Dedek, C. L. 1889, *A karthausiak Magyarországban* [Carthusians in Hungary]. Budapest: Wajdits N.

Degré, A. 1939, *Magyar halászati jog a középkorban* [Hungarian fishing rights in the Middle Ages]. Budapest: Sárkány Ny.

Denecke, D. 1985, "Beziehungen zwischen Stadt und Land in Nordwestdeutschland während des späten Mittelalters und der frühen Neuzeit. Historische Geographie Städtischer Zentralität," In *Stadt im Wandel. Kunst und Kultur des Bürgertums in Norddeutschland*, ed. C. Meckseper, 191–218. Stuttgart: Cantz.

Dini, B. 1995a, "L'economia fiorentina e l'Europa centro-orientale nelle fonti storiche," *Archivio Storico Italiano* 153, 632–655.

Dini, B. 1995b, *Saggi su una economia mondo: Firenze e l'Italia fra Mediterraneo ed Europa (secc. XIII–XVI)*. Firenze: Pacini.

Dini, B. 2001, *Manifattura, commercio e banca nella Firenze medievale*. Firenze: Nardini.

Dinnyés, et al. 1993, *Magyarország régészeti topográfiája 9. A Szobi és a Váci járás* [Archaeological topography of Hungary 9. The surroundings of Szob and Vác]. Budapest: Akadémiai.

Dirlmeier, U. 1978, *Untersuchungen zu Einkommensverhältnissen und Lebenshaltungskosten in oberdeutschen Städten des Spätmittelalters* (Abhandlungen der Heidelberger Akademie der Wissenschaften. Phil. – hist. Klasse, Jg. 1978. – 1. Abh.). Heidelberg: Winter.

Dirlmeier, U. and Fouquet, G. 1985, "Eigenbetriebe niedersächsischer Städte im Spätmittelalter," In *Stadt im Wandel. Kunst und Kultur des Bürgertums in Norddeutschland*, ed. C. Meckseper, 257–279. Stuttgart: Cantz.

Doboşi, A. 1951, "Exploatarea ocnelor de sare din Transilvania în evul mediu (sec. 14–16.)," [The exploitation of salt mines in Transylvania in the Middle Ages] *Studii şi cercetari de istorie medie* 2, 125–165.

Domanovszky, S. (ed.) 1939–1941, *Magyar Művelődéstörténet*, I–IV [History of Hungarian intellectual history]. Budapest: Magyar Történelmi Társulat.

Domanovszky, S. 1916, *A harmincadvám eredete* [The origin of the thirtieth customs] (Értekezések a történeti tudományok köréből, 24/4). Budapest: MTA.

Domanovszky, S. 1922, *A szepesi városok árumegállító joga* [The staple right of the cities of the Spiš region]. Budapest: MTA.

Domanovszky, S. 1938, "A mezőgazdaság Szent István korában," [Agriculture in the age of St Stephen] In *Emlékkönyv Szent István király halálának kilencszázadik évfordulóján*, II [Memorial book on the 900th jubilee of the death of King St Stephen], ed. J. Serédi, 311–333. Budapest: MTA.

Domanovszky, S. 1979, *Gazdaság és társadalom a középkorban* [Economy and society in the Middle Ages], ed. F. Glatz. Budapest: Gondolat.

Dordea, I. 2002, "Historiographie des Salzwesens in Rumänien," In *Festschrift Rudolf Palme zum 60. Geburtstag*, eds. W. Ingenhaeff, R. Staudinger and K. Ebert, 85–114. Innsbruck: Berenkamp.

Draskóczy, I. 1988, "András Kapy. Carrière d'un bourgeois de la capitale hongroise au début du 15ᵉ siècle," *Acta Historica Academiae Scientiarum Hungaricae* 34, 119–157.

Draskóczy, I. 1989, "Birtok és pénzügyigazgatás a Zsigmond-korban. (A Szentgyörgyi Vince-család)," [Estate organization and finances in the Sigismund-era (The Vince family of Szentgyörgy)] In *A Dunántúl településtörténete VII. Falvak, városok, puszták a Dunántúlon XI–XIX. század* [The settlement history of Transdanubia, VII. Villages, towns and barrens in Transdanubia, 9th–19th centuries], ed. B. Somfai, 87–93. Veszprém: MTA Pécsi és Veszprémi Akadémiai Bizottság.

Draskóczy, I. 1993, "A szászföldi adóztatás kérdéséhez," [To the question of the taxation of the Saxons in Transylvania] In *Perlekedő évszázadok. Tanulmányok Für Lajos történész 60. születésnapjára* [Centuries in debate. Studies in honor of the historian, Lajos Für's 60th birthday], ed. I. Horn, 81–100. Budapest: OMIKK Ny.

Draskóczy, I. 1994, "Olaszok a 15. századi Erdélyben," [Italians in 15th-century Transylvania] In *Scripta manent. Ünnepi tanulmányok a 60. életévét betöltött Gerics József professzor tiszteletére* [Studies in honor on József Gerics on his 60th birthday], ed. idem, 125–135. Budapest: [Eötvös Loránd Tudományegyetem Középkori és Kora-Újkori Magyar Történeti Tanszék].

Draskóczy, I. 1996a, "Adósjegyzék a 15. századból," [Debtor account from the 15th century] In *In memoriam Barta Gábor. Tanulmányok Barta Gábor emlékére* [Studies dedicated to the memory of Gábor Barta], ed. I. Lengvári, 93–112. Pécs: JPTE Továbbképző K. Irodája.

Draskóczy, I. 1996b, "A honfoglalástól a 16. századig," [From the Hungarian conquest to the 16th century] In *Magyarország gazdaságtörténete a honfoglalástól a 20. század közepéig* [Economic history of Hungary from the Hungarian conquest to the 20th century], ed. J. Honvári, 5–80. Budapest: Aula.

Draskóczy, I. 2001a, "Kamarai jövedelem és urbura a 15. század első felében," [Chamber revenues and *urbura* in the first half of the 15th century] In

Gazdaságtörténet – könyvtártörténet. Emlékkönyv Berlász Jenő 90. születésnapjára [Economic history – library history. Essays in honor of the 90th birthday of Jenő Berlász], ed. J. Buza, 147–165. Budapest: MTA Támogatott Kutatóhelyek Irodája.

Draskóczy, I. 2001b, "A nyírbátori oklevelek kérdőjelei. (Rendhagyó könyvismertetés)," [The problems of the charters of Nyírbátor (An exceptional book review)] *Levéltári Közlemények* 72, 261–273.

Draskóczy, I. 2002, "Forschungsprobleme in der ungarischen Salzgeschichte des Mittelalters," In *Investitionen im Salinenwesen und Salzbergbau: internationale Tagung am Lehrstuhl für Bauaufnahme und Baudenkmalpflege; globale Rahmenbedingungen, regionale Auswirkungen, verbliebene Monumente; gewidmet Rudolf Palme (1942–2002)*, 280–289. Weimar: Bauhaus-Univ. Weimar, Univ.-Verl.

Draskóczy, I. 2004a, "Der ungarische Goldgulden und seine Bedeutung im ungarischen Außenhandel des 14. und 15. Jahrhunderts," In *Der Tiroler Bergbau und die Depression der europäischen Montanwirtschaft im 14. und 15. Jahrhundert* (Veröffentlichungen des Südtiroler Landesarchivs, 16), eds. R. Tasser and E. Westermann, 61–77. Innsbruck–Wien–Bozen: Studien Verlag.

Draskóczy, I. 2004b, "A sóigazgatás 1397. esztendei reformjáról," [On the reform of salt administration in 1397] In *Változatok a történelemre. Tanulmányok Székely György tiszteletére* [Variations on history. Studies in honor of György Székely] (Monumenta historica Budapestinensia, 14), eds. B. Nagy and Gy. Erdei, 285–293. Budapest: Budapesti Történeti Múzeum–ELTE BTK Középkori és Kora Újkori Egyetemes Történeti Tanszék.

Draskóczy, I. 2004c, "Az erdélyi sókamarák ispánjai 1529–1535 (Az erdélyi sóbányák sorsa a Szapolyai korszakban)," [The counts of the salt chambers in Transylvania, 1529–1535 (The fate of the salt mines of Hungary in the Szapolyai Period] *Levéltári Közlemények* 75, 27–46.

Draskóczy, I. 2004d, "Erdély sótermelése az 1530-as években," [The salt production of Transylvania in the 1530s] In *Tanulmányok Szapolyai Jánosról és a kora újkori Erdélyről* [Studies on János Szapolyai and Early Modern Transylvania], eds. J. Balogh et al., 31–96. Miskolc: Miskolci Egyetem BTK.

Draskóczy, I. 2005, "Szempontok az erdélyi sóbányászat 15–16. századi történetéhez," [Notes on the history of the salt mining in Transylvania in the 15th–16th centuries] In *Studia professoris – professor studiorum. Tanulmányok Érszegi Géza hatvanadik születésnapjára* [Studies in honor of Géza Érszegi on the ocasion of his sixtieth birthday], eds. T. Almási, I. Draskóczy and É. Jancsó, 83–117. Budapest: Magyar Országos Levéltár.

Draskóczy, I. 2007, "Die demographische Lage des Sachsenlandes zu Beginn des 16. Jahrhunderts," In *Historische Demographie Ungarns (896–1996)* (Studien zur Geschichte Ungarns, 11), 94–134. Herne: G. Schäfer.

Draskóczy, I. 2008, *Magyarországi sóbányászat és sókereskedelem a késő középkorban* [Salt mining and salt trade in late medieval Hungary]. Unpublished Dissertation submitted to the Hungarian Academy of Sciences, Budapest.

Draskóczy, I. 2009, "A lengyel só a Magyar Királyságban a 15. század második felében és a 16. század elején," [Polish salt in the Hungarian Kingdom in the second half of the 15th and the beginning of the 16th centuries] In *Pénztörténet – gazdaságtörténet. Tanulmányok Buza János 70. születésnapjára* [Numismatics – economic history. Studies in honor of the 70th birthday of János Buza], eds. J. Bessenyei and I. Draskóczy, 111–124. Budapest–Miskolc: Mirio Kulturális Bt.

Draskóczy, I. 2010a, "15. századi olasz jelentés Erdély ásványi kincseiről," [15th-century Italian report on the mineral goods of Transylvania] In *Emlékkönyv ifj. Barta János 70. születésnapjára* [Studies in honor of the 70th birthday of János Bartha the younger], eds. I. Papp, J. Angi and L. Pallai, 49–59. Debrecen: Debreceni Egyetem Történeti Intézete.

Draskóczy, I. 2010b, "A 'Landus-jelentés' kéziratai," [Manuscripts of the 'Landus report'] In *"Fons, skepsis, lex." Ünnepi tanulmányok a 70 esztendős Makk Ferenc tiszteletére* [Studies in honor of the 70th birthday of Ferenc Makk], eds. T. Almási, É. Révész and Gy. Szabados, 85–94. Szeged: SZTE Történeti Segédtudományok Tanszék – Szegedi Középkorász Műhely.

Draskóczy, I. 2014, "A kősó bányászat átalakulása Erdélyben az Árpád-korban," In *Arcana tabularii. Tanulmányok Solymosi László tiszteletére*, II [Studies in honor of László Solymosi], eds. A. Bárány, G. Dreska and K. Szovák, 825– 835. Budapest–Debrecen: MTA.

Draskóczy, I. 2016a, "A Magyar Királyság kereskedelmére vonatkozó írott források a késő középkorból," [Late medieval sources on the trade of the Hungarian Kingdom] In *Művészet és mesterség. Tisztelgő kötet R. Várkonyi Ágnes emlékére*, II [Art and craft. Memorial volume in honor of Ágnes R. Várkonyi], eds. I. Horn et al., 41–62. Budapest: L'Harmattan.

Draskóczy, I. 2016b, "Highways between Buda and Kraków," In *On Common Path Budapest and Kraków in the Middle Ages. Exhibition Catalogue*, eds. J. Benda et al., 38–41. Budapest–Kraków: Budapest History Museum.

Draskóczy, I. 2016c, "Commercial Contacts of Buda along the Danube and Beyond," In *Medieval Buda in Context* (Brill's Companions to European History, 10), eds. B. Nagy et al., 278–299. Leiden–Boston: Brill.

Draskóczy, I. 2016d, "Belkereskedelem és sókamarák a 15. század második felében," [Interior trade and the salt chambers in the second half of the 15th century] In *Pénz, posztó, piac. Gazdaságtörténeti tanulmányok a magyar középkorról* [Cash, cloth, commerce. Studies in the economic history of medieval Hungary], ed. B. Weisz, 201–215. Budapest: MTA Bölcsészettudományi Kutatóközpont Történettudományi Intézet.

Dufraisse, A. 2008, "Firewood Management and Woodland Exploitation during the Late Neolithic at Lac de Chalain (Jura, France)," *Vegetation History and Archaeobotany* 17, 199–210.

Dyer, Ch. 1989, *Standards of Living in the Later Middle Ages: A Social Change in England, c. 1200–1520*. Cambridge: Cambridge University Press.

Dyer, Ch. 1994, *Everyday Life in Medieval England*. London: Continuum.

E. Kovács, P. 1998, "A grebeni uradalom 1522–es összeírása," [The 1522 conscription of the Greben estate] In *Tanulmányok Borsa Iván tiszteletére* [Studies in honor of Iván Borsa], ed. E. Csukovits, 131–171. Budapest: Magyar Országos Levéltár.

Eckhart, F. 1908, *A királyi adózás története Magyarországon 1323-ig* [The history of royal taxation in Hungary until 1323]. Budapest: Nyom. Réthy.

Éder, K. 2010, *Mezővárosi plébániatemplomok középkori városmentes tájakon* [Parish churches of market towns in town-free regions]. Unpublished PhD-dissertation defended at the Eötvös Loránd University, Budapest.

Elekes, L. 1964, *A középkori magyar állam története megalapításától mohácsi bukásáig* [History of the medieval Hungarian state from the foundation to the loss at Mohács]. Budapest: Kossuth.

Elm, K. (ed.) 2000, *Beiträge zur Geschichte des Paulinerordens*. Berlin: Duncker & Humblot.

Elm, K. (ed.) 1977, "Termineien und Hospize der westfälischen Augustiner-Eremitenklöster Osnabrück, Herford und Lippstadt," *Jahrbuch für westfälische Kirchengeschichte* 70, 1–49.

Ember, Gy. 1988, *Magyarország nyugati külkereskedelme a XVI. század közepén* [The foreign trade of Hungary towards Western Europe in the middle of the 16th century]. Budapest: Akadémiai.

Endrei, W. 1989, *Patyolat és posztó* [Cambric and blaize]. Budapest: Magvető.

Engel, J.-Ch. 1797–1801, *Geschichte des ungarischen Reiches und seiner Nebenländer*, I–III. Halle: Johann Jacob Gebauer.

Engel, P. 1985, "Ung megye településviszonyai és népessége a Zsigmond-korban," [Settlements and population of county Ung in the Sigismund period] *Századok* 119, 941–1005.

Engel, P. 1987, "Ozorai Pipo," [Pipo of Ozora] In *Ozorai Pipo emlékezete* [The memory of Pipo of Ozora], ed. F. Vadas, 53–88. Szekszárd: [Béri Balogh Múzeum].

Engel, P. 1989, *Kamarahaszna-összeírások 1427-ből* [Lucrum camarae inventories from 1427] (Új Történelmi Tár, 2). Budapest: Akadémiai.

Engel, P. 1990, "A 14. századi magyar pénztörténet néhány kérdése," [Some problems of 14th-century Hungarian monetary history] *Századok* 124, 25–93.

Engel, P. 1993, "A magyar királyság jövedelmei Zsigmond korában [Revenues of the Hungarian kingdom in the time of Sigismund]," In *A tudomány szolgálatában. Emlékkönyv Benda Kálmán 80. születésnapjára* [In the service of science. Memorial book on the 80th birthday of Kálmán Benda], ed. F. Glatz, 27–31. Budapest: MTA Történettudományi Intézete.

Engel, P. 1996, *A temesvári és moldovai szandzsák törökkori települései (1554–1579)* [The Settlements of the sanjaks of Timişoara and Moldova in the Ottoman Period (1554–1579)] (Dél-alföldi Évszázadok, 8). Szeged: Csongrád Megyei Levéltár.

Engel, P. 1998, *A nemesi társadalom a középkori Ung megyében* [Noble society in medieval county Ung]. Budapest: MTA Történettudományi Intézet.

Engel, P. 1999, "A 14. századi magyar pénztörténet néhány kérdése," [Some questions of the 14th-century Hungarian monetary history] *Századok* 124, 25–93.

Engel, P. 2000, "A török dúlások hatása a népességre: Valkó megye példája," [The impact of the Ottoman plunderings on the population of Valkó County] *Századok* 134, 267–321.

Engel, P. 2001, *The Realm of St Stephen. A History of Medieval Hungary 895–1526.* London–New York: I. B. Tauris.

Engel, P. 2002, *Magyarország a középkor végén.* CD-ROM [Hungary at the end of the Middle Ages]. Budapest: MTA Történettudományi Intézet.

Engel, P. 2003a, "Honor, vár, ispánság. Tanulmányok az Anjou-királyság kormányzati rendszeréről," [Honor, castle, comitatus. Studies on the government system of the Angevin rule] In idem, *Honor, vár, ispánság. Válogatott tanulmányok* [Honor, castle, comitatus. Selected studies], ed. E. Csukovits, 101–161. Budapest: Osiris.

Engel, P. 2003b, "Vár és hatalom. Az uralom territoriális alapjai Magyarországon," [Castle and power. The territorial background of rulership in Hungary] In idem, *Honor, vár, ispánság. Válogatott tanulmányok* [Honor, castle, comitatus. Selected studies], ed. E. Csukovits, 162–197. Budapest: Osiris.

Engel, P. 2007, "Probleme der historischen Demographie Ungarns in der Anjou- und Sigismundszeit," In *Historische Demographie Ungarns (896–1996)* (Studien zur Geschichte Ungarns, 11), 57–65. Herne: G. Schäfer.

Engel, P., Kristó, Gy. and Kubinyi, A. 2003, *Magyarország története 1301–1526* [The history of Hungary 1301–1526]. Budapest: Osiris.

Engel, P., Kubinyi, A. and Kristó, Gy. 1998, *Magyarország története 1301–1526* [A History of Hungary 1301–1526]. Budapest: Osiris.

Entz, G. 1958, *A gyulafehérvári székesegyház* [The cathedral of Alba Iulia]. Budapest: Akadémiai.

Entz, G. 1996, *Erdély építészete a 14–16. században* [Transylvanian architecture in the 14th–16th centuries]. Kolozsvár: Erdélyi Múzeum-Egyesület.

Epstein, S. (ed.), 2001, *Town and Country in Europe, 1300–1800.* Cambridge: Cambridge University Press.

Erdélyi, G. 2005, *Egy kolostorper története. Hatalom, vallás és mindennapok a középkor és az újkor határán* [History of a cloister trial. Power, religion and everyday life at the turning of the Middle Ages and the Modern Times] (Társadalom- és Művelődéstörténeti Tanulmányok, 38). Budapest: MTA Történettudományi Intézete.

Erdélyi, G. 2015, *A Cloister on Trial: Religious Culture and Everyday Life in Late Medieval Hungary*. Farnham: Ashgate.

Erdélyi, L. 1914/1915/1916, "Árpádkori társadalomtörténetünk legkritikusabb kérdései. 1–6.," [Critical questions of the social history of Árpádian-age Hungary] *Történelmi Szemle*, 3, 517–561; 4, 32–50, 202–226, 334–352, 481–514 and 5, 39–63.

Erdélyi, L. and Sörös, P. (eds.) 1902–1916, *A Pannonhalmi Szent-Benedek-Rend története*, I–XII/B [History of the Benedictine order of Pannonhalma]. Pannonhalma: Szent-Benedek-Rend–Stephaneum.

Erdődy, G. 1984, *Herman Ottó és a társadalmi–nemzeti felemelkedés ügye* [Ottó Herman and the issue of the social–national development]. Budapest: Stephaneum.

Érdy, J. 1870, "Róbert Károly (1308–1342) király 1335-dik évi érmelési szerződése," [The 1335 chamber lease contract of King Charles I (1308–1342)] *Archaeologiai Közlemények* 8, 154–157.

Éri, I., Nagy, L. and Nagybákay, P. 1975–1976, *A magyarországi céhes kézművesipar forrásanyagának katasztere*, I–II [Cadastre of sources of Hungarian guilds]. Budapest: Éri I.

Evans, J. and O'Connor, T. (eds.) 1999, *Environmental Archaeology*. Stroud: Sutton.

F. Vattai, E. 1966, "Die 'Agnus Dei-Schale' des Ungarischen Nationalmuseums," *Acta Historiae Artium Academiae Scientiarum Hungaricae* 12, 41–59.

Fabritius, K. 1861, "Zwei Funde in der ehemaligen Dominikanerkirche zu Schässburg," *Archiv des Vereins für siebenbürgische Landeskunde* 7, 1–40.

Facsar, G. 1973, "Agricultural-Botanical Analysis of the Medieval Grape Seeds from the Buda Castle Hill," *Mitteilungen des Archäologischen Institut der Ungarischen Akademie der Wissenschaft* 4, 157–174.

Fancsalszky, G. 2003, "Germán népek a Kárpát-medencében a Kr. u. I. évezredben," [Germanic peoples in the Carpathian Basin in the 1st millennium AD] *A Békés Megyei Múzeumok Közleményei* 24–25, 255–271.

Fara, A. 2010, *La formazione di un'economia di frontiera. La Transilvania tra il XII e il XIV secolo*. Napoli: Editoriale Scientifica.

Fara, A. 2015a, "An Outline of Livestock Production and Cattle Trade from Hungary to Western Europe in Late Middle Ages and Early Modern Period (XIVth–XVIth centuries)," *Crisia* 45, 87–95.

Fara, A. 2015b, "Il commercio di bestiame ungherese verso la Penisola italiana tra tardo Medioevo e prima Età moderna (XIV–XVI secolo)," *Mélanges de l'École française de Rome – Moyen Âge* 127/2. Online document: https://mefrm.revues.org/2709 (last accessed: 27 April 2016).

Farkas, Z. and Siklósi, Gy. 2009, "A város topográfiai fejlődése a kezdetektől a török korig," [Topographical development of the town from its beginnings up to the Ottoman period]. In *Székesfehérvár. Magyarország műemlékei* [Székesfehérvár. The monuments of Hungary], ed. G. A. Entz, 31–58. Budapest: Osiris.

Fedeles, T. 2014, "A Camera Apostolica és a magyar egyházi javadalmak a konciliarizmus időszakában," [The Camera Apostolica and Hungarian church stalls in the period of conciliarism] In *"Causa unionis, causa fidei, causa reformationis in capite et membris." Tanulmányok a konstanzi zsinat 600. évfordulója alkalmából* [Studies on the 600th anniversary of the Council of Constance], eds. A. Bárány and L. Pósán, 189–209. Debrecen: Print-Art.

Fejérpataky, L. 1887, "Pápai adószedők Magyarországon a XIII–XIV. században," [Collectors of Papal revenues in Hungary in the 13th–14th centuries] *Századok* 21, 493–517 and 589–609.

Fél, E. and Hofer, T. 1974, *Geräte der Átányer Bauern*. Budapest–Kopenhagen: [National Museum].

Fél, E. and Hofer, T. 1997, *Arányok és mértékek a paraszti gazdálkodásban* [Proportions and measures in peasant economy]. Budapest: Balassi.

Feld, I. 2004, "Buda (Ofen) und Sopron (Ödenburg), die Meilensteine der ungarischen städtischen Hausforschung," *Jahrbuch für Hausforschung* 47, 9–38.

Felde, V. A. et al. 2014, "The Relationship between Vegetation Composition, Vegetation Zones and Modern Pollen Assemblages in Setesdal, Southern Norway," *Holocene* 24, 985–1001.

Fényes, G., 2008, "Maiolica Floor Tiles from Buda Palace," In *Matthias Corvinus, the King. Tradition and Renewal in the Hungarian Royal Court, 1458–1490. Exhibition catalogue*, eds. P. Farbaky et al., 354–356. Budapest: Budapest History Museum.

Ferenczi, L. (in preparation), *Management of Monastic Landscapes. A Spatial Analysis of the Economy of Cistercian Monasteries in Medieval Hungary*. PhD thesis to be presented at the Medieval Studies Doctoral Program at CEU, Budapest.

Ferenczi, L. 2006, "Estate structure and development of the Topusko (Toplica) abbey – case study of a medieval Cistercian monastery," *Annual of Medieval Studies at CEU* 12, 83–100.

Fettich, N. 1968, "Ötvösmester hagyatéka Esztergomban a tatárjárás korából," [Inheritance of a smith at Esztergom from the age of the Mongol invasion] *A Komárom-Esztergom Megyei Múzeumok Közleményei* 1, 157–196.

Filep, A. 2006, "Gondolatok a néprajzi, népi építkezési kutatás és a régészet, építészettörténet együttműködéséről," [Thoughts on the collaboration of ethnography, study of vernacular architecture and architectural history] *Studia Caroliensia* no. 3–4 [Testis temporum, vita memoriae. Ünnepi tanulmányok Pálóczi Horváth András 65. születésnapjára (Studies in honor of the 65th birthday of András Pálóczi Horváth)], 401–418.

Finály, H. 1884, *A latin nyelv szótára* [Dictionary of the Latin language]. Budapest: Franklin.

Firbas, F. 1949–1952, *Spät- und nacheiszeitliche Waldgeschichte Mitteleuropas nördlich der Alpen*. Jena: G. Fischer.

Fodor, I. 1998, "The culture of Conquering Hungarians," In *Tender Meat under the Saddle* (Medium Aevum Quotidianum. Sonderband, 7), ed. J. Laszlovszky, 5–31. Krems: Medium Aevum Quotidianum.

Fodor, I. 2012, "Hungarian crafts in the 9th and 10th centuries," In *The History of Handicraft in Hungary*, ed. J. Szulovszky, 15–36. Budapest: Hungarian Chamber of Commerce and Industry.

Fodor, P. 1997, "Lippa és Radna városok a 16. századi török adóösszeírásokban," [The towns of Lipova and Rodna in 16th century Ottoman tax-registers] *Történelmi Szemle* 39, 313–334.

Fodor, Z. 2001, "Az ártéri gazdálkodást tárgyaló elméletek és alkalmazhatóságuk a magyarországi Tisza-szakasz kéziratos térképein szereplő fokok alapján," [The channels named "fok" and fok-husbanding along the banks of the Hungarian section of the Tisza River], *Agrártörténeti Szemle* 43, 87–149. [A shortened English version is available at: http://hej.sze.hu/ENV/ENV-020905-A/env020905a.pdf (last accessed: 14 October 2016)].

Font, M. and G. Sándor, M. (eds.) 2000, *Mittelalterliche Häuser und Strassen in Mitteleuropa*. Budapest–Pécs: Instituti Archaeologici Academiae Scientiarum Hungaricae.

Forster, Gy. (ed.) 1900, *III. Béla magyar király emlékezete* [The memory of King Béla III]. Budapest: Hornyánszky.

Foster, D. R. and Aber, J. D. 2004, *Forests in Time: The Environmental Consequences of 1,000 years of Change in New England*. New Haven: Yale University Press.

Fouquet, G. 1999, *Bauen für die Stadt. Finanzen, Organisation und Arbeit in Kommunalen Baubetrieben des Spätmittelalters* (Städteforschung Reiche A, 48). Köln–Weimar–Wien: Böhlau.

Fraknói, V. 1879, *A szekszárdi apátság története* [History of the abbey of Szekszárd]. Budapest: Franklin.

Fryde, E. B. 1983, "Italian Maritime Trade with Medieval England (c. 1270 – c. 1530)," In idem, *Studies in Medieval Trade and Finance*, 291–307. London: Hambledon.

Fügedi, E. 1953, "'Németjogú' falvak települése a szlovák és német nyelvterületen," [To the foundation of villages of German right in Slovak and German speaking areas] In *Tanulmányok a parasztság történetéhez Magyarországon a 14. században* [Studies in the history of peasantry in 14th-century Hungary], ed. Gy. Székely, 225–239. Budapest: Akadémiai.

Fügedi, E. 1957/1958, "Középkori várostörténetünk statisztikai forrásai," [Statistical sources of medieval urban history of Hungary] *Történeti Statisztikai Közlemények* 1/1, 43–85, 1/2–4, 16–75 and 2/1–2, 33–46.

Fügedi, E. 1959, "Topográfia és városi fejlődés a középkori Óbudán," [Topography and urban development in medieval Óbuda] *Tanulmányok Budapest Múltjából* 13, 7–56.

Fügedi, E. 1961, "Középkori magyar városprivilégiumok," [Medieval Hungarian urban privileges] *Tanulmányok Budapest Múltjából* 14, 17–107.

Fügedi, E. 1969, "Pour une analyse démographique de la Hongrie medieval," *Annales. Historie, Sceinces Sociales* 24, 1299–1312.

Fügedi, E. 1972a, "Die Ausbreitung der städtischen Lebensform: Ungarns oppida im XIV. Jahrhundert," In *Stadt und Stadtherr im 14. Jahrhundert*, ed. W. Rausch, 165–192. Linz: Österreichischer Arbeitkreis für Stadtgeschichtsforschung.

Fügedi, E. 1972b, "Mezővárosaink kialakulása a XIV. században," [The formation of market towns in Hungary in the 14th century] *Történelmi Szemle* 15, 321–342.

Fügedi, E. 1975, "Das mittelalterliche Königreich Ungarn als Gastland," In *Die deutsche Ostsiedlung des Mittelalters als Problem der europäischen Geschichte* (Vorträge und Forschungen, 18), ed. W. Schlesinger, 471–507. Sigmaringen: Jan Thorbecke.

Fügedi, E. 1977, *Vár és társadalom a 13–14. századi Magyarországon* [Castle and society in 13th–14th-century Hungary] (Értekezések a történeti tudományok köréből. Új sorozat, 82). Budapest: Akadémiai.

Fügedi, E. 1981a, "Az esztergomi érsekség gazdálkodása a XV. század végén," [The economy of the archbishopric of Esztergom at the end of the 15th century] In idem, *Kolduló barátok, polgárok, nemesek. Tanulmányok a magyar középkorról* [Mendicant, burghers, nobles. Studies on Hungarian Middle Ages], 114–237. Budapest: Magvető.

Fügedi, E. 1981b, "Középkori magyar városprivilégiumok," [Medieval Hungarian urban privileges] In idem, *Kolduló barátok, polgárok, nemesek. Tanulmányok a magyar középkorról* [Mendicant, burghers, nobles. Studies on Hungarian Middle Ages], 238–310 and 493–509. Budapest: Magvető.

Fügedi, E. 1981c, "Mezővárosaink kialakulása a XIV. században," [The development of our market towns in the 14th century] In idem, *Kolduló barátok, polgárok, nemesek. Tanulmányok a magyar középkorról* [Mendicant, burghers, nobles. Studies on Hungarian Middle Ages], 336–363. Budapest: Magvető.

Fügedi, E. 1982, "Mátyás király jövedelme 1475-ben," [Revenues of Matthias Corvinus in 1475] *Századok* 116, 484–506.

Fügedi, E. 1986, *Castle and Society in Medieval Hungary (1000–1437)* (Studia historica Academiae Scientiarum Hungaricae, 187). Budapest: Akadémiai.

Fügedi, E. 1992, *A középkori Magyarország történeti demográfiája* [Historical demography of medieval Hungary] (Népességtudományi Kutató Intézet: Történeti Demográfiai Füzetek, 10). Budapest: Központi Statisztikai Hivatal.

Fülöp, A. and Koppány, A. 2004, "A Crosier from the Territory of the Veszprémvölgy Convent," *Acta Archaeologica Academiae Scientiarum Hungaricae* 55, 115–135.

Fülöp, É. M. 2009, "'… A tenger a mi istenünknek ama nagy halastava …' Viza, a királyi hal," ['…the sea in the great fish pond of our God …' sturgeon, the royal fish] *Komárom-Esztergom Megyei Múzeumok Közleményei* 15, 71–82.

Füzes, E. 1984, *A gabona tárolása a magyar parasztgazdaságokban* [The storage of grain in Hungarian peasant households]. Budapest: Akadémiai.

Füzes, M. 1972, "Előzetes jelentés az 1967. évi pogányszentpéteri ásatás XVI. század eleji gabonaleletéről," [Preliminary report of the early-16th-century grain finds of the 1967–excavation at Pogányszentpéter] In *A nagykanizsai Thury György Múzeum jubileumi évkönyve 1919–1969* [Jubilee volume of the Thury György Museum at Nagykanizsa], 285–290. Nagykanizsa: Thúry György Múzeum.

G. Sándor, M. 1960, "Adatok az eszterga magyarországi történetéhez," [To the history of lathe in Hungary] *Történelmi Szemle* 3, 141–148.

G. Sándor, M. 1963, "Középkori csontmegmunkáló műhely a budai várpalotában," [Medieval bone manufacturing workshop at the Buda Palace] *Budapest Régiségei* 20, 107–124.

Gabler, D., Szőnyi, E. and Tomka, P. 1990, "The Settlement History of Győr (Arrabona) in the Roman Period and in the Middle Ages," In *Towns in Medieval Hungary*, ed. L. Gerevich, 9–25. Budapest: Akadémiai.

Gáborján, A. 1962, "A magyar módra való bőrkészítés problématikája," [Problem of processing leather in a Hungarian manner] *Néprajzi Értesítő* 44, 97–140.

Gál, E. 2002, "Madárleletek a bajcsai várból," [Bird bones from Bajcsa castle] In *Weitschawar / Bajcsa-Vár. Egy stájer erődítmény Magyarországon a 16. század második felében* [A Styrian fortification in Hungary in the second half of the 16th century], ed. Gy. Kovács, 101–105. Zalaegerszeg: Zala Megyei Múzeumok Igazgatósága.

Gál, E. 2004, "Murga-Schanz 13. századi földvár állatcsontleletei," [Animal bone remains from the 13th century Murga-Schanz hillfort] *A Wosinsky Mór Múzeum Évkönyve* 26, 245–258.

Gál, E. 2005, "New data on bird bone artefacts from Hungary and Romania," In *From Hooves to Horns, from Mollusc to Mammoth. Manufacture and Use of Bone Artefacts from Prehistoric Times to the Present* (Muinasaja Teadus, 15), eds. H. Luik et al., 325–338. Tallinn: Tallinn Book Printers.

Gál, E. 2007, "Bird bone remains from the archaeological sites around the Lake Balaton in the context of Central Transdanubia," In *Environmental Archaeology in Transdanubia* (Varia archaeologica Hungarica, 20), eds. I. Juhász, P. Sümegi and Cs. Zatykó, 79–96. Budapest: Archaeological Institute of the Hungarian Academy of Sciences.

Gál, E. 2010a, "Animal remains from the multi-period site of Hajdúnánás–Fürjhalomdűlő. Part II. Finds From the Árpád Period (10th–13th centuries)," *Acta Archaeologica Academiae Scientiarum Hungaricae* 61, 426–444.

Gál, E. 2010b, "The fowl in the feast," In *Bestial Mirrors* (ViaVIAS 03/2010), eds. M. Kucera and G.-K. Kunst, 100–109. Vienna: VIAS.

Gál, E. 2012, "Possible evidence for hawking from a 16th century Styrian Castle (Bajcsa, Hungary)," In *A Bouquet of Archaeozoological Studies. Essays in Honour of*

Wietske Prummel, eds. D. C. M. Raemaekers et al., 170–177. Groningen: University of Groningen Library.

Gál, E. 2015, "'Fine feathers make fine birds': the exploitation of wild birds in medieval Hungary," *Antaeus* 33, 345–368.

Gál, E. and Bartosiewicz, L. 2016, "Animal Remains from the Ottoman-Turkish Palisaded Fort at Barcs, Southwest Hungary," In *"per sylvam et per lacus nimios." The Medieval and Ottoman Period in Southern Transdanubia, Southwest Hungary: the Contribution of the Natural Sciences*, eds. Gy. Kovács and Cs. Zatykó, 181–253. Budapest: MTA BTK Régészeti Intézet.

Gál, E. and Kovács, Gy. 2011, "A walrus-tusk belt plaque from an Ottoman-Turkish castle at Barcs, Hungary," *Antiquity Project Gallery*. Online document: http://antiquity.ac.uk/projgall/gal329/ (last accessed: 1 August 2016).

Gál, E. et al. 2010, "Evidence of the crested form of domestic hen (*Gallus gallus* f. *domestica*) from three post-Medieval sites in Hungary," *Journal of Archaeological Science* 37, 1065–1072.

Gáll, E. 2013, *Az Erdélyi-medence, a Partium és a Bánság 10–11. századi temetői, szórvány és kincsleletei*, I–II [10th–11th-century burial sites, stray finds and treasures in the Transylvanian Basin, the Partium and the Banat]. Szeged: Szegedi Tudományegyetem Régészeti Tanszék.

Galloway, J., Keene, D. and Murphy, M. 1996, "Fuelling the City: Production and Distribution of Firewood and Fuel in London's Region, 1290–1400," *The Economic History Review* NS 49, 447–472.

Găzdac, C. and Cociş, S. 2004, *Vlpia Traiana Sarmizegetusa*. Cluj-Napoca: Mega.

Gecsényi, L. 1991, "A 16–17. századi magyarországi városfejlődés kérdéséhez (Az erődváros megjelenése)," [Issues of urban development in Hungary in the 16th–17th centuries. The appearance of the fortress towns] In *Unger Mátyás emlékkönyv* [Studies in the memory of Mátyás Unger], eds. P. Kovács, E., J. Kalmár and L. Molnár, V., 145–158. Budapest: MTA Történettudományi Intézet.

Gedai, I. 1969, "Fremde Münzen im Karpatenbecken aus den 11–13. Jahrhunderten," *Acta Archaeologica Academiae Scientiarum Hungaricae* 21, 105–148.

Gedai, I. 1979, "Die Münzprägung des ungarischen Mittelalters," *Numismatische Vorlesungen* 2, 1–12.

Gedai, I. 1985–1986, "A Magyar Nemzeti Múzeum verőszerszám gyűjteménye I.," [The collection of dies in the Hungarian National Museum, Part I] *Numizmatikai Közlöny* 84–85, 47–55.

Gedai, I. 1986, *A magyar pénzverés kezdete* [The beginnings of Hungarian minting]. Budapest: Akadémiai.

Gedai, I. 1987, "Die Rolle der Ungarischen Goldmünzen im Mittelalter," *Haller Münzblätter* 4, 274–283.

Gedai, I. 1996, "Friesach Denars and their Historical Background in the Hungarian Kingdom," In *Die Friesacher Münze im Alpen-Adria-Raum. Akten der Friesacher Sommerakademie Friesach (Kärnten), 14. bis 18. September 1992*, ed. M. J. Wenninger, 191–207. Graz: Akademische Druck- und Verlagsanstalt.

Gedai, I. 1999, "King Saint Stephen's Gold Coinage," *Numismatica e antichità classica* 28, 311–346.

Gedai, I. 2001, "Saint Stephen's Coins," *Numizmatikai Közlöny* 100–101, 35–44.

Gedai, I. 2007, "Where was the (P)'RESLAVVA CIV'(ITAS) Coin Minted?," *Sborník Národního Muzea v Praze A* 61, 25–31.

Gere, L. 2003, *Késő középkori és kora újkori fémleletek az ozorai várkastélyból* [Late medieval and Early Modern metal finds from the castle of Ozora]. Budapest: Magyar Nemzeti Múzeum.

Gerevich, L. 1966, *A budai vár feltárása* [Excavation of the Buda Castle]. Budapest: Akadémiai.

Gerevich, L. 1977, "Pilis Abbey, a Cultural Center," *Acta Archaeologica Academiae Scientiarum Hungaricae* 29, 155–198.

Gerevich, L. 1984, *A pilisi ciszterci apátság* [The Cistercian abbey of Pilisszentkereszt]. Szentendre: Pest Megyei Múzeumok Igazgatósága.

Gillis, J. R. 2012, *The Human Shore. Seacoasts in History*. Chicago–London: University of Chicago Press.

Glaser, L. 1929, "A Dunántúl középkori úthálózata," [The medieval route-system of the Transdanubia] *Századok* 63, 138–167 and 257–285.

Glaser, L. 1939, "Az Alföld régi vízrajza és a települések," [The ancient hydrography of the Great Hungarian Plain and the settlements] *Földrajzi Közlemények* 67, 297–307.

Glick, T. F. and Kirchner, H. 2000, "Hydraulic Systems and Technologies of Islamic Spain: History and Archaeology," In *Working with Water in Medieval Europe. Technology and Resource-Use*, ed. P. Squatriti, 267–329. Leiden–London–Köln: Brill.

Göckenjan, H. 1972, *Hilfsvölker und Grenzwächter im mittelalterlichen Ungarn*. Wiesbaden: F. Steiner.

Goda, K. and Majorossy, J. 2008, "Städtische Selbstverwaltung und Schriftproduktion im spätmittelalterlichen Königreich Ungarn: Eine Quellenkunde für Ödenburg und Preßburg," *Pro Civitate Austriae* NS 13, 62–100.

Goldthwaite, R. A. 2009, *The Economy of Renaissance Florence*. Baltimore: Johns Hopkins University Press.

Gömöri, J. (ed.) 1981, *Iparrégészeti kutatások Magyarországon. Égetőkemencék régészeti és interdiszciplináris kutatása* = *Research in industrial archeology in Hungary: Archeological and interdisciplinary researches on kilns and furnaces*. Veszprém: MTA Veszprémi Akadémiai Bizottságának Történelmi Szakbizottsága.

Gömöri, J. (ed.) 1984, *Iparrégészeti és archaeometriai kutatások Magyarországon = Research in Industrial Archaeology and Archaeometry in Hungary*. Veszprém: MTA Veszprémi Akadémiai Bizottságának Történelmi Szakbizottsága.

Gömöri, J. (ed.) 1999, *Traditions and Innovations in the Early Medieval Iron Production*. Veszprém: Dunaferr-Somogyország Archeometallurgiai Alapítvány – MTA VEAB Iparrégészeti és Archeometriai Munkabizottság.

Gömöri, J. (ed.) 2007, *Az erdő és a fa régészete és néprajza (kézművesipar-történeti megközelítésben)* [Archaeology and Ethnography of Forest and Wood (in Approximation of Handicraft History)]. Sopron: MTA VEAB Soproni Tudós Társasága.

Gömöri, J. 1977, "Számszeríjhoz tartozó csontfaragványok. Adatok a számszeríj történetéhez Sopronban," [Cross-bow bone fittings. Data to the history of cross-bows in Sopron] *Soproni Szemle* 31, 140–149.

Gömöri, J. 1980, "Frühmittelalterliche Eisenschmelzöfen von Tarjánpuszta und Nemeskér," *Acta Archaeologica Academiae Scientiarum Hungaricae* 32, 317–343.

Gömöri, J. 1984, "Középkori mészégető kemence Sopronban," [Medieval lime kiln in Sopron] In *Iparrégészet / Industrial Archaeology*, II, ed. idem, 249–262. Veszprém: MTA VEAB.

Gömöri, J. 2010, "Két középkori tímárműhely régészeti maradványai," [Archaeological Remains of Two Medieval Tanning Workshop from Sopron] In *Csont és bőr. Az állati eredetű nyersanyagok feldolgozásának története, régészete és néprajza* [Bone and leathe. History, archaeology and ethnography of crafts utilizing raw materials from animals], eds. J. Gömöri and A. Körösi, 205–213. Budapest: Line Design.

Gömöri, J. and Körösi, A. (ed.) 2010, *Csont és bőr. Állati eredetű nyersanyagok feldolgozásának története, régészete és néprajza* [Bone and leathe. History, archaeology and ethnography of crafts utilizing raw materials from animals]. Budapest: Line Design.

Granasztói, Gy. 2012, *A városi élet keretei a feudális kori Magyarországon. Kassa társadalma a 16. század derekán* [The settings of urban life in feudal Hungary. Society of Košice in the mid-16th century]. Budapest: Korall.

Gróf, P. and Gróh, D. 2001, "The Remains of Medieval Bone Carvings from Visegrád," In *Crafting Bone. Skeletal Technologies through Time and Space Proceedings of the 2nd meeting of the (ICAZ) Worked Bone Research Group, Budapest, 31 August – 5 September 1999*, eds. A. M. Choyke and L. Bartosiewicz, 281–285. Oxford: Archaeopress.

Gróf, P. and Gróh, D. 2004, "Játékkocka és rózsafüzér. A középkori csontmegmunkálás emlékei Visegrádon," [Dice and rosary. Remains of medieval bone working in Visegrád] In *Játszani jó! Történelmi barangolás a játékok birodalmában* [Playing is great! Historical ambulations in the empire of toys], eds. E. Matuz, D. and A. Ridovics, 83–95. Budapest: Budapesti Történeti Múzeum – Magyar Nemzeti Múzeum.

Grynaeus, A. and Grynaeus, T. 2001. "The Geobotany of Medieval Hungary: A Preliminary Report," *Medium Aevum Quotidianum* 44, 78–93.

Guerin, S. M. 2010, "Avorio d'ogni ragione: the supply of elephant ivory to northern Europe in the Gothic Era," *Journal of Medieval History* 36, 156–174.

Guest, E. 1998, "Héber betűjelek Árpád-házi királyok pénzein," [Hebrew letters on the coins of Árpádian kings] *Az Érem* 1, 6–11.

Guest, E. 1999, "Fe vagy pe?," ['Fe' or 'Pe'?] *Éremtani Lapok* 54/2, 13.

Gulyás, L. Sz. 2009a [2012], "Mészégetők és a mész forgalma a Mohács előtti Magyarországon," [Lime burning and trade in lime in Hungary before 1526]. In *Történeti tanulmányok [A Debreceni Egyetem Történelmi Intézetének kiadványa] 17* [Studies in history. Publication of the Institute of History at the University of Debrecen], 99–122. Debrecen: Debreceni Egyetem Történelmi Intézet.

Gulyás, L. Sz. 2009b, "Elite Citizens in the Market-towns of the Late Medieval Hegyalja Region," In *Matthias and his Legacy: Cultural and Political Encounters between East and West* (Speculum historiae Debreceniense, 1), eds. A. Bárány and A. Györkös, 227–242. Debrecen: University of Debrecen Department of History.

Gulyás, L. Sz. 2014a, "Városfalépítés a középkori Eperjesen," [Building of town walls in medieval Prešov] In *Falak és választóvonalak a történelemben* [Walls and dividing lines in history] eds. A. Buhály, G. Reszlet and Gy. Szoboszlay, 127–142. Nyíregyháza: Nyíregyházi Főiskola Történettudományi és Filozófia Intézet.

Gulyás, L. Sz. 2014b, "Vásári forgalom és vásározók a középkori Észak–Alföld és peremvidéke mezővárosaiban," [Market traffic and market-men in the market towns of the Northern Great Hungarian Plain and its margins] In *Piacok a társadalomban és a történelemben* [Markets in society in and history] (Rendi társadalom – polgári társadalom, 26), eds. K. Halmos, Zs. Kiss and J. Klement, 103–114. Budapest: Hajnal István Kör – Társadalomtörténeti Egyesület.

Gulyás, L. Sz. 2015, "A jobbágyság szabad költözése a középkorvégi Felső-Tisza-vidéken," [The free migration of peasantry in Upper-Tisza Region at the end of the Middle Ages] *Szabolcs-Szatmár-Beregi Szemle* 50, 49–59.

Gündisch, G. 1987, "Die Siebenbürgische Unternehmung der Fugger 1528–1531," In idem, *Aus Geschichte und Kultur der Siebenbürger Sachsen*, 149–166. Köln–Wien: Böhlau.

Gyarmati, S. 2014, "The Great Linen Register of Bardejov (Bártfa)," *Annual of Medieval Studies at CEU* 20, 113–132.

Gyöngyössy, M. 2002–2003, "Kiszorult-e az 'érsek embere' a pénzverésből a XV. században? Adalék a pisetumjog 'hanyatlásához'," [Was the 'man of the bishop' deprived of the right of coinage in the 15th century? Notes on the 'decline' of pisetum-right] *A Debreceni Déri Múzeum Évkönyve* 76, 109–116.

Gyöngyössy, M. 2003, *Pénzgazdálkodás és monetáris politika a késő középkori Magyarországon* [Finances and monetary politics in late medieval Hungary]. Budapest: Gondolat.

Gyöngyössy, M. 2004a, *Altin, akcse, mangir ... Oszmán pénzek forgalma a kora újkori Magyarországon* [Altın, akche, mangır ... Circulation of Ottoman coins in early modern Hungary]. Budapest: Martin Opitz.

Gyöngyössy, M. 2004b, "Münzen des 15. Jahrhunderts aus Aquileia im mittelalterlichen ungarischen Geldumlauf," *Acta Archaeologica Academiae Scientiarum Hungaricae* 55, 137–159.

Gyöngyössy, M. 2004c, "Nyugat-Magyarország kora újkori pénzforgalma," [Der frühneuzeitliche Geldverkehr in Westungarn] *Soproni Szemle* 58, 329–352.

Gyöngyössy, M. 2008, *Florenus Hungaricalis. Aranypénzverés a középkori Magyarországon* [Coinage of golden florins in medieval Hungary]. Budapest: Martin Opitz.

Gyöngyössy, M. 2013–2014, "A középkori magyar pénzverés területi szakigazgatási szervei. A pénzverőkamara-rendszer fejlődésének vázlata," [Die territoriale Verwaltung der mittelalterlichen Münzprägung in Ungarn. Ein Abriß der Entwicklung des Münzkammersystems] *Numizmatikai Közlöny* 112–113, 125–152.

Gyöngyössy, M. 2014, "'Gazdag föld – szegény ország': magyarországi aranytermelés és aranypénzverés Luxemburgi Zsigmond korában," ['Rich soil – poor country': Hungarian gold production and coinage in the time of Sigismund] In *"Causa unionis, causa fidei, causa reformationis in capite et membris." Tanulmányok a konstanzi zsinat 600. évfordulója alkalmából* [Studies on the 600th anniversary of the council of Constance], eds. A. Bárány and L. Pósán, 255–268. Debrecen: Print-Art.

Gyöngyössy, M. 2015, "Város és pénzverde a késő középkori Magyarországon," [Stadt und Münzanstalt im spätmittelalterlichen Ungarn] *Budapest Régiségei* 48, 139–168.

Gyöngyössy, M. 2016, "Főúri pénzverési jogosultak a 15. századi Magyarországon," [Aristocrats with minting rights in 15th-century Hungary] *Századok* 150, 341–368.

Györffy, Gy. 1959, "Das Güterverzeichnis des griechischen Klosters zu Szávaszentdemeter (Sremska Mitrovica) aus dem 12. Jahrhundert," *Studia Slavica* 5, 9–74.

Györffy, Gy. 1960, "Einwohnerzahl und bevölkerungsdichte in Ungarn bis zum Anfang des XIV. Jahrhundert," In *Études historiques publiées par la Comission Nationale des Historiens Hongrois*, 163–193. Budapest: Akadémiai.

Györffy, Gy. 1963–1998, *Az Árpád-kori Magyarország történeti földrajza*, I–IV [Historical geography of Hungary in the Árpádian age]. Budapest: Akadémiai.

Györffy, Gy. 1972, "Az Árpádkori szolgálónépek kérdéséhez," [To the question of servant folks in the Árpadián age] *Történelmi Szemle* 15, 261–320.

Györffy, Gy. 1975, "Budapest története az Árpád-korban," [History of Budapest in the Árpádian age] In *Budapest története az őskortól az Árpád-kor végéig* [History of Budapest until the end of the Árpádian age], ed. L. Gerevich, 219–349. Budapest: Akadémiai.

Györffy, Gy. 1983a, *István király és műve* [King Stephen and his legacy]. Budapest: Akadémiai.

Györffy, Gy. 1983b, *Wirtschaft und Gesellschaft der Ungarn um die Jahrtausendwende* (Studia historica Academiae Scientiarum Hungaricae, 186). Budapest: Akadémiai.

Györffy, Gy. 1984a, "A kalandozások kora," [The age of Hungarian raids] In *Magyarország története, előzmények és magyar történet 1242–ig*, I [History of Hungary: beginnings and the history until 1241], ed. Gy. Székely, 651–716. Budapest: Akadémiai.

Györffy, Gy. 1984b, "A pápai tizedlajstromok demográfiai értékelésének kérdéséhez," [To the problem of the demographic evaluation of the Papal tithe lists] In *Mályusz Elemér emlékkönyv* [Elemér Mályusz memorial volume], eds. É. Balázs, H., E. Fügedi and F. Maksay, 141–157. Budapest: Akadémiai.

Györffy, Gy. 1994, *King Saint Stephen of Hungary*. Boulder: Columbia University Press.

Gyulai, F. 2010, *Archaeobotany in Hungary. Seed, Fruit, Food and Beverage Remains in the Carpathian Basin from the Neolithic to the Late Middle Ages*. Budapest: Archaeolingua.

Gyulai, F. et al. 2009, "Domestication Events of Grape (*Vitis vinifera*) from Antiquity and the Middle Ages in Hungary from Growers' Viewpoint," *Hungarian Agricultural Research* 3–4, 8–12.

H. Gyürky, K. 1971, "Glasfunde aus dem 13. und 14. Jahrhundert im mittelalterlichen Dominikanerkloster von Buda," *Acta Archaeologica Academiae Scientiarum Hungarica* 23, 199–220.

H. Gyürky, K. 1974, "Venezianische und türkische Importartikel im Fundmaterial von Buda aus der ersten Hälfte des 16. Jahrhunderts," *Acta Archaeologica Academiae Scientiarium Hungariae* 21, 413–423.

H. Gyürky, K. 1981, *Das mittelalterliche Dominikanerkloster in Buda*. Budapest: Akadémiai.

H. Gyürky, K. 1982a, "Középkori üvegleletek Budáról. Rekonstrukciós módszerek," [Medieval glass finds from Buda. Reconstruction methods] *Communicationes Archaeologicae Hungariae 1982*, 153–166.

H. Gyürky, K. 1982b, "Forschungen auf dem Gebiete des mittelalterlichen Buda. Ein unbekanntes Wohnhaus und der Ursprung eines Destiller-Kolbens," *Acta Archaeologica Academiae Scientiarium Hungariae* 34, 177–212.

H. Gyürky, K. 1984a, "A 14. század üvegtípusai a budai régészeti leletanyagban," [Typology of 14th-century glass finds at the excavation material from Buda], *Budapest Régiségei* 26, 49–62.

H. Gyürky, K. 1984b, "Feliratos *sírkő* 1289-es évszámmal a *budai domonkos* kolostorból," [Epigraphic tombstone with the date 1289 from the Dominican friary of Buda] *Budapest Régiségei* 26, 247–252.

H. Gyürky, K. 1986a, "The Use of Glass in medieval Hungary," *Journal of Glass Studies* 28, 70–81.

H. Gyürky, K. 1986b, *Az üveg. Katalógus* [The glass finds. Catalogue]. Budapest: Budapesti Történeti Múzeum.

H. Gyürky, K. 1987, "Mittealterliche Glasfunde aus dem Vorhof des königlichen. Palastes von Buda," *Acta Archaeologica Academiae Scientiarium Hungariae* 39, 47–68.

H. Gyürky, K. 1989, "A magyarországi üvegművesség fellendülése a 15. század közepén," [The expansion of glass craftsmanship in Hungary in the mid-15th century] *Communicationes Archaeologicae Hungariae 1989*, 209–219.

H. Gyürky, K. 1990, "Das Glas im mittelalterlichen Ungarn im Spiegel der Ausgrabungen," In *Annales du 11ᵉ congres de l'Association Internationale pour le Histoire du Verre. Bâle, 29 aout–3 septembre 1988*, ed. A. von Saldem, 329–334. Amsterdam: Association internationale pour l'histoire du verre.

H. Gyürky, K. 1991, *Üvegek a középkori Magyarországon* [Glasses in medieval Hungary] (BTM Műhely, 3). Budapest: Budapesti Történeti Múzeum.

H. Gyürky, K. 1996, *A Buda melletti kánai apátság feltárása* [Excavation of the Kána abbey near Buda]. Budapest: Akadémiai.

H. Gyürky, K. 1999, "Szíriai festett üvegpohár töredékei a budai palotából," [Bruchstück eines bemalten syrischen Glasbecher aus der königlichen Burg von Buda] *Budapest Régiségei* 33, 325–330.

H. Gyürky, K. 2003, "A Budapest I. Fortuna u. 18. számú lakóház régészeti kutatásából származó üvegleletek," [Glass finds from the archaeological excavations at 18 Fortuna Street in Buda Castle] *Budapest Régiségei* 37, 13–28.

H. Kolba, J. 2004, *Liturgische Goldschmiedearbeiten im Ungarischen Nationalmuseum* (Catalogi Musei Nationalis Hungarici. Series Mediaevalis et Moderna, 1). Budapest: Magyar Nemzeti Múzeum.

H. Németh, I. 2008, "Die finanziellen Auswirkungen der osmanischen Expansion auf die Städteentwicklung in Ungarn. Die Steuerlasten der ungarischen königlichen Freistädte im 16. und 17. Jahrhundert," In *La fiscalità nell'economia europea secc. XIII–XVIII – Fiscal Systems in the European Economy from the 13th to the 18th Century*, ed. S. Cavaciocchi, 771–780. Firenze: Firenze University Press.

H. Németh, I. 2011, "Städtepolitik und Wirtschaftspolitik in Ungarn in der Frühen Neuzeit," In *Geteilt – Vereinigt Beiträge zur Geschichte des Königreichs Ungarn in der Frühneuzeit (16.–18. Jahrhundert)*, 1, eds. K. Csaplár-Degovics and I. Fazekas, 329–355. Berlin: Osteuropa-Zentrum.

Halaga, O. R. 1967, "Kaufleute und Handelsgüter der Hanse im Karpatengebiet," *Hansische Geschichtsblätter* 85, 59–84.

Halaga, O. R. 1975, *Košice – Balt. Výroba a obchod v styku východoslovenských miest s Pruskom (1275–1526)* [Košice–Balt: Production and Trade in the Contact Points with East Prussia from 1275 to 1526]. Košice: Vychodoslovenské vyd.

Halaga, O. R. 1983, "A Mercantilist Initiative to Compete with Venice: Kaschau's Fustian Monopoly (1411)," *Journal of European Economic History* 12, 407–437.

Halaga, O. R. 1996, "Wald- und Felddomänen der Ostslowakischen Städte als Grundlage ihres Montanhandels," In *Bergbaureviere als Verbrauchszentren*, ed. E. Westermann. 249–274. Stuttgart: Franz Steiner.

Haneca, K., Van Acker, J. and Beeckman, H. 2005, "Growth Trends Reveal the Forest Structure during Roman and Medieval Times in Western Europe: a Comparison between Archaeological and Actual Oak Ring Series (*Quercus robur* and *Quercus petraea*)," *Annals of Forest Science* 62, 797–805.

Haris, A. (ed.) 1994, *Koldulórendi építészet a középkori Magyarországon* [Mendicant architecture in medieval Hungary]. Budapest: Országos Műemlékvédelmi Hivatal.

Harmatta, J. et al. (eds.) 1987–, *Lexicon Latinitatis medii aevi Hungariae*, I–V. Budapest: Akadémiai.

Hartyányi, B. 1981–1983, "Kora Árpád-korból származó búza a Hont-i ispánsági várból," [Wheat seeds from the early-Árpádian-age ispán's castle at Hont] *Magyar Mezőgazdasági Múzeum Közelményei 1981–1983*, 95–113.

Hatz, V. 1965. "/B/RESLAVVA CIV/ITAS/ Zum beginn der ungarischen Münzprägung," In *Dona Numismatica. Walter Hävernick zum 23. Januar 1965 dargebracht*, eds. P. Berghaus and G. Hatz, 79–85. Hamburg: Lütcke und Wulff.

Heckenast, G. 1965, "Die Verbreitung des Wasserradantriebs im Eisenhüttenwesen in Ungarn," In *Nouvelles études historiques publiées à l' occasion du XIIe Congrès International des Sciences Historiques par la Commission Nationale des Historiens Hongrois*, eds. D. Csatári, L. Katus and Á. Katus, 159–179. Budapest: Akadémiai.

Heckenast, G. 1991, *A magyarországi vaskohászat története a feudalizmus korában* [History of siderurgy in Hungary in the age of feudalism]. Budapest: Akadémiai.

Heckenast, G. 1995, "Zur Geschichte des Technologietransfers von Deutschland nach Ungarn im Eisenhüttenwesen 14. bis 18. Jahrhundert," In *Technologietransfer und Wissenschaftsaustausch zwischen Ungarn und Deutschland*, eds. H. Fischer and F. Szabadváry, 59–69. München: Oldenbourg.

Heckenast, G. 1996, "Kézművesképzés a középkori Magyarországon," [Education of craftsmen in medieval Hungary] In *A magyar iskola első évszázadai 996–1526* [First centuries of education in Hungary, 996–1526], eds. K. Szende and P. Szabó, 93–96. Győr: Xántus János Múzeum.

Heckenast, G. et al. 1968, *A magyarországi vaskohászat története a korai középkorban* [The history of iron smelting in Hungary in the Early Modern period]. Budapest: Akadémiai.

Hegyi, I. 1978, *A népi erdőkiélés történeti formái (Az Északkeleti-Bakony erdőgazdálkodása az utolsó kétszáz évben)* [Historical forms of peasant forest clearance (Forestry in the northeast Bakony in the last two hundred years)]. Budapest: Akadémiai.

Henn, V. 1996, "Missglückte Messegründungen des 14. und 15. Jahrhunderts," In *Europäische Messen und Märktesysteme in Mittelalter und Neuzeit* (Städteforschung, A 39), eds. P. Johanek and H. Stoob, 205–222. Köln–Weimar–Wien: Böhlau.

Herman, O. 1887, *A magyar halászat könyve*, I–II [Book of Hungarian fishing]. Budapest: Természettudományi Társulat.

Herman, O. 1902, "Ironga, szánkó, kece," [Runner, sled, dragnet] *Természettudományi Közlöny* 7, 18–26.
Herman, O. 1914, *A magyarok nagy ősfoglalkozása* [Traditional labor of the Hungarians]. Budapest: Hornyánszky.
Hermann, I. 1984, *Finanzadministration in der zweiten Hälfte des 14. Jahrhunderts in Ungarn* (Dissertationes Archaeologicae Ser. II/13). Budapest: Hornyánszky.
Hervay, F. L. 1984, *Repertorium historicum Ordinis Cisterciensis in Hungaria*. Roma: Editions Cisterciensis.
Hindle, B. P. 1993, *Roads, Tracks, and Their Interpretation*. London: Batsford.
Hlinka, J. et al. 1964–1978, *Nalezy Minci na Slovensku*, I–III [Coin finds in Slovakia]. Bratislava: Veda.
Hocquet, J.-C. 1988, "Handel, Steuer(system) und Verbrauch in Verona vom 13. bis zum 16. Jahrhundert," In *Stadt und Salz* (Beiträge zur Geschichte der Städte Mitteleuropas, 10), ed. W. Rausch, 19–44. Linz: Österreichischer Arbeitskreis für Stadtgeschichtsforschung.
Hoffmann, I. 2010, *A tihanyi alapítólevél mint helynévtörténeti forrás* [The foundation charter of Tihany as a source for placename history]. Debrecen: Debreceni Egyetemi Kiadó.
Hoffmann, R. 2000, "Medieval Fishing," In *Working with Water in Medieval Europe. Technology and Resource-Use*, ed. P. Squatriti, 331–393. Leiden–London–Köln: Brill.
Hoffmann, R. 2014, *An Environmental History of Medieval Europe*. Cambridge: Cambridge University Press.
Hoffmann, T. 1968, "Vor- und frühgeschichte der ungarischen Landwirtschaft," *Agrártörténeti Szemle* 10 (Supplementum), 1–35.
Holl, I. 1955, "Külföldi kerámia Magyarországon a XIII–XVI. században," [Foreign ceramics in Hungary in the 13th–16th centuries] *Budapest Régiségei* 16, 147–197.
Holl, I. 1958, "Középkori kályhacsempék Magyarországon, I.," [Medieval stove-tiles in Hungary] *Budapest Régiségei* 18, 211–300.
Holl, I. 1963, "Középkori cserépedények a budai várpalotából," [Medieval stove-vessels from the Palace of Buda] *Budapest Régiségei* 20, 340–365.
Holl, I. 1966, *Mittelalterliche Funde aus einem Brunnen von Buda*. Budapest: Akadémiai.
Holl, I. 1972, "Középkori kályhacsempék Magyarországon, II.," [Medieval stove-tiles in Hungary] *Budapest Régiségei* 22, 173–192.
Holl, I. 1974–1975, "Zur mittelalterlichen Schwarzhafnerkeramik mit Werkstattmarken," *Mitteilungen des Archäologischen Instituts der Ungarischen Akademie der Wissenschaften* 5, 130–147.
Holl, I. 1979, "Sopron (Ödenburg) im Mittelalter: achäologisch-stadtgeschichtlichen Studie," *Acta Archaeologica Academiae Scientiarum Hungaricae* 31, 105–145.
Holl, I. 1980, "Regensburgi középkori kályhacsempék," [Medieval stove-tiles from Regensburg in Hungary] *Archaeologiai Értesítő* 107, 20–43.

Holl, I. 1982, "Feuerwaffen und Stadtmauern. Angaben zur Entwicklung der Wehrarchitektur des 15. Jahrhunderts," *Acta Archaeologica Academiae Scientiarum Hungaricae* 33, 201–243.

Holl, I. 1983, "Középkori kályhacsempék Magyarországon, III.," [Medieval stove-tiles in Hungary] *Archaeologiai Értesítő* 110, 201–230.

Holl, I. 1987, "Zinn im spätmittelalterlichen Ungarn, I.," *Acta Archaeologica Academiae Scientiarium Hungariae* 39, 313–335.

Holl, I. 1990, "Ausländische Keramikfunde in Ungarn (14–15. Jahrhundert)," *Acta Archaeologica Academiae Scientiarum Hungaricae* 42, 209–267.

Holl, I. 1991, "Goldschmiede in Buda. Handwerk und Topographie," *Beiträge zur Mittealterarchäologie in Österreich* 7, 79–91.

Holl, I. 1994–1995, "A középkori késes mesterség. Régészeti adatok az ausztriai és nürnbergi kések elterjedéséhez," [Medieval knife making. Archaeological data to the spread of Austrian and Nuremberger knives in Hungary] *Archaeologiai Értesítő* 121–122, 159–188.

Holl, I. 1996, "Zinn im spätmittelalterlichen Ungarn, II," *Acta Archaeologica Academiae Scientiarum Hungaricae* 48, 241–260.

Holl, I. 1996–1997, "Marktplätze und Handwerker – Entwicklungstendenzen in Sopron im Spätmittelalter," *Archaeologiai Értesítő* 123/4, 7–15.

Holl, I. 1998a, "Spätgotische Ofenkacheln. Werke einer mitteleuropäischen Ofenhafnerwerkstatt," *Acta Archaeologica Academiae Scientiarium Hungariae* 50, 139–214.

Holl, I. 1998b, "Középkori kályhacsempék Magyarországon, VI.," [Medieval stove-tiles in Hungary] *Budapest Régiségei* 32, 291–308.

Holl, I. 2000, *Funde aus dem Zisterzienserkloster von Pilis* (Varia Archaeologica Hungarica, 11). Budapest: Instituti Archaeologici Academiae Scientiarum Hungaricae.

Holl, I. 2001, "Spätgotische Öfen aus Österreich," *Acta Archaeologica Academiae Scientiarium Hungariae* 52, 353–414.

Holl, I. 2004, "Ungarisch-polnische Beziehungen aufgrund der Ofenkacheln," *Acta Archaeologica Academiae Scientiarium Hungariae* 53, 333–375.

Holl, I. 2005a, "Tischgerät im spätmittelalterlichen Buda," *Acta Archaeologica Academiae Scientiarium Hungariae* 56, 361–370.

Holl, I. 2005b, *Fundkomplexe des 15–17. Jahrhunderts aus dem Burgpalast von Buda* (Varia Archaeologica Hungarica, 17). Budapest: Archäologisches Institut der Ungarischen Akademie der Wissenschaften.

Holl, I. 2006, "Persische Fayancewaren im ungarischen Fundmaterial (15–17. Jh.)," *Acta Archaeologica Academiae Scientiarium Hungaria* 57, 475–510.

Holl, I. 2007, "Külföldi kerámia Magyarországon III. (14–17. század)," [Foreign ceramics in Hungary (14th–17th centuries)] *Budapest Régiségei* 40, 253–294.

Holl, I. and Parádi, N. 1982, *Das mittelalterliche Dorf Sarvaly*. Budapest: Akadémiai.

Holt, R. 1988, *The Mills of Medieval England*. Oxford: Blackwell.

Holub, J. 1929, *Zala megye története a középkorban* [The history of Zala County in the Middle Ages]. Pécs: [Egyetemi Nyomda].

Holub, J. 1943, *Egy dunántúli egyházi nagybirtok élete a középkor végén* [Life on a large ecclesiastical estate in Transdanubia at the end of the Middle Ages] (Pannónia Könyvtár, 62). Pécs: Pécsi Egyetemi Könyvkiadó.

Holub, J. 1963, *Zala megye középkori vízrajza* [Medieval hydrography of Zala County]. Zalaegerszeg: Zala Megye Tanácsa.

Hölzl, R. 2010. "Historicizing Sustainability: German Scientific Forestry in the Eighteenth and Nineteenth Centuries," *Science as Culture* 19, 431–460.

Hóman, B. 1916, *Magyar pénztörténet 1000–1325* [Hungarian monetary history, 1000–1325]. Budapest: M. T. Akadémia.

Hóman, B. 1917, "A XIV. századi aranyválság," [The 14th-century gold crisis] In *Emlékkönyv Fejérpataky László életének hatvanadik évfordulója ünnepére* [Memorial volume in honor of the 60th birthday of László Fejérpataky], ed. I. Szentpétery, 212–242. Budapest: Franklin.

Hóman, B. 1921, *A magyar királyság pénzügyei és gazdaságpolitikája Károly Róbert korában* [Monetary issues and economic policy of the Hungarian Kingdom during the reign of Charles I]. Budapest: Budavári Tudományos Társaság.

Homza, M. and Sroka, S. A. 2009, *Historia Scepusii* [The history of Spiš region]. Bratislava: Instytut Historii Uniwersytetu Jagiellońskiego.

Horváth, A. 2000, "Hazai újholocén klíma és kömyezetváltozások vizsgálata régészeti adatok segítségével," [Neo-holocene climatic and environmental changes in light of archaeological data] *Földrajzi Közlemények* 48, 149–158.

Horváth, F. and Viczián, 1. 2004, "Brigetio (Ószőny) – Azaum (Almásfüzitő) limesszakaszának római kori emlékei a terület geomorfológiai viszonyainak tükrében," [The Roman monuments of the Brigetio – Azaum section of the limes in light of the geomorphological situation of the area] In *A táj változásai a Kárpát-medencében, Víz a tájban* [Landscape changes in the Carpathian Basin. Water in the landscape], ed. Gy. Füleky, 223–227. Gödöllő: Környezetkímélő Agrokémiáért Alapítvány.

Horváth, H. 1931–1932, "A budai pénzverde művészettörténete a késői középkorban," [History of art at the mint of Buda in the Late Middle Ages] *Numizmatikai Közlöny* 30–31, 14–39.

Horváth, I. 2000, "Gran (Esztergom) zur Zeit Stephans des Heiligen," In *Europas Mitte um 1000*, II, eds. A. Wieczorek and H–M. Hinz, 576–580. Stuttgart: Theiss.

Horváth, M. 1868, "Az 1514–diki pórlázadás, annak okai és következményei," [The peasant uprising of 1514 and its consequences] In *Horváth Mihály kisebb történelmi munkái*, I [The minor historical works of Mihály Horváth], 247–276. Pest: Ráth Mór.

LIST OF REFERENCES

Hoshino, H. 2001, "La crisi del Trecento e Firenze," In idem, *Industria tessile e commercio internazionale nella Firenze del Tardo Medioevo* (Biblioteca storica toscana, 39), eds. F. Franceschi and S. Tognetti, 67–73. Firenze: Leo S. Olschki.

Hóvári, J. 1989, "Az erdélyi só a török Szendrőben, 1514–1516," [Transylvania salt in Smederevo, 1514–1516] In *Gazdaság, társadalom, történetírás. Emlékkönyv Pach Zsigmond Pál 70. születésnapjára* [Economy, society, historiography. Studies in honor of Pál Zsigmond Pach on his 70th birthday], ed. F. Glatz, 41–61. Budapest: Magyar Tudományoss Akadémia.

Hrbek, I. 1955, "Ein arabischer Bericht über Ungarn," *Acta Orientalia Academiae Scientiarum Hungaricae* 5, 205–230.

Hunyadi, Zs. 1999, "'... scripta manent' Archival and Manuscript Resources in Hungary," *Annual of Medieval Studies at CEU* 5, 231–240.

Hunyadi, Zs. 2010, *The Hospitallers in the Medieval Kingdom of Hungary, c. 1150–1387* (CEU Medievalia, 13). Budapest: CEU Press.

Huszár, L. 1934, "Le vicende della moneta ungherese dal 1000 al 1325," *Rivista Internazionale di Scienze Sociali 1934*, 426–431.

Huszár, L. 1938, "Szent István pénzei," [Coins of St Stephen] In *Szent István-emlékkönyv*, I [Saint Stephen memorial volume], ed. J. Serédi, 335–364. Budapest: MTA.

Huszár, L. 1958, *A budai pénzverés története a középkorban* [The history of minting at Buda in the Middle Ages] (Budapest Várostörténeti Monográfiái, 20). Budapest: Akadémiai.

Huszár, L. 1965–1966, "Bemerkungen zur Frage der ersten ungarischen Oboltyp.," *Numizmatikai Közlöny* 64–65, 29–31.

Huszár, L. 1970–1972, "Der ungarische Goldgulden im mittelalterlichen Münzverkehr," *Hamburger Beiträge zur Numismatik* 24–26, 71–88.

Huszár, L. 1971–1972a, "A középkori magyar pénztörténet okleveles forrásai I. rész," [Medieval documentary sources on Hungarian monetary history] *Numizmatikai Közlöny* 70–71, 39–49.

Huszár, L. 1971–1972b, "Der Beginn der Goldgulden- und Groschenprägung in Ungarn," *Numismaticky Sbornik* 12, 177–184.

Huszár, L. 1975, *Corpus Nummorum Hungariae, Vol. III/1: Habsburg-házi királyok pénzei 1526–1657* [Coins of the Habsburg kings 1526–1657)]. Budapest: MTA.

Huszár, L. 1975–1976, "A középkori magyar pénztörténet okleveles forrásai, II. rész," [Documentary sources on Hungarian medieval monetary history] *Numizmatikai Közlöny* 74–75, 37–50.

Huszár, L. 1979, *Münzkatalog Ungarn von 1000 bis Heute*. Budapest–München: Battenberg.

Huszti, D. 1938, "IV. Béla olaszországi vásárlásai," [The purchases of Béla IV in Italy] *Közgazdasági Szemle* 62, 737–770.

Huszti, D. 1941, *Olasz–magyar kereskedelmi kapcsolatok a középkorban* [Italian–Hungarian trade connections in the Middle Ages]. Budapest: MTA.

Ihrig, D., Károlyi, Zs., Károlyi, Z. and Vázsonyi, Á. 1973, *A magyar vízszabályozás története* [The history of water management in Hungary]. Budapest: Országos Vízügyi Hivatal.

Ipolyi, A. 1867, "Adalékok a magyar domonkosok történetéhez," [Contributions to the history of Dominicans in Hungary] *Magyar Sion* 5, 481–497, 590–609, 662–673 and 769–776.

Irásné Melis, K. 1971–1972, "A budai Várnegyed XIV–XV. századi faanyagú régészeti leletei," [Archaeological wooden finds from the Castle District of Buda from the 14th and 15th centuries] *Technikatörténeti Szemle* 6, 29–38.

Irásné Melis, K. 2004, "Archaeological Traces of the Last Medieval Town Planning in Pest," In *"Quasi liber et pictura." Tanulmányok Kubinyi András hetvenedik születésnapjára / Studies in Honour of András Kubinyi on His Seventieth Birthday*, ed. Gy. Kovács, 235–243. Budapest: ELTE Régészettudományi Intézet = Institute of Archaeological Sciences of Eötvös Loránd University.

Irásné Melis, K. and Vörös, I. 1996, "Középkori lakóházak és egy XV. századi vargaműhely régészeti kutatása a pesti Belvárosban," [Archaeological research of medieval dwelling houses and a tannery from the 15th-century in the downtown of Pest] *Communicationes Archaeologicae Hungariae 1996*, 237–245.

Irsigler, F. 1985, "Kaufmannstypen im Mittelalter," In *Stadt im Wandel. Kunst und Kultur des Bürgertums in Norddeutschland 1150–1650. Landesausstellung Niedersachsen 1985* (Ausstellungskatalog, 3), ed. C. Meckseper, 385–397. Stuttgart–Bad Cannstadt: Ed. Cantz.

Irsigler, F. 2003, *Was machte eine mittelalterliche Siedlung zur Stadt?* (Universität des Saarlandes. Universitätsreden, 51). Saarbrücken: Universität des Saarlandes.

Isenmann, E. 1988, *Die deutsche Stadt im Spätmittelalter 1250–1500. Stadtgestalt, Recht, Stadtregiment, Kirche, Gesellschaft, Wirtschaft.* Stuttgart: Ulmer.

Isenmann, E. 2014[2], *Die deutsche Stadt im Spätmittelalter 1150–1550 Stadtgestalt, Recht, Verfassung, Stadtregiment, Kirche, Gesellschaft, Wirtschaft.* Köln–Weimar–Wien: Böhlau.

Iványi, B. 1905, "Bihar és Bars vármegyék vámhelyei a középkorban," [The customs places of Bihar and Bars Counties in the Middle Ages] *Magyar Gazdaságtörténelmi Szemle* 12, 81–125.

Iványi, B. 1906, "A tiszaluczi vám bevételei és azok felhasználása 1516–1520-ig," [The accounts of custom revenues and expenses at Tiszalucz from 1516–1520] *Magyar Gazdaságtörténelmi Szemle* 13, 1–55.

Iványi, B. 1911, "Két középkori sóbánya statutum," [Two medieval salt statutes] *Századok* 45, 187–195.

Jakab, A. 2011, "Téglaégető kemencék a középkori Magyarországon," [Brick kilns on the territory of Medieval Hungary] *A Jósa András Múzeum Évkönyve* 53, 131–160.

Jakó, Zs. 1958, "Újabb adatok Dés város legrégibb kiváltságleveleinek kritikájához," [New data to the critics of the oldest privilege of Dej] *Studia Universitatum Babeş et Bolyai* [Series 4, fasciculus 2, Historia] 3/8, 35–52.

Jakubovich, E. 1926, "A váradi püspökség XIII. századi tizedjegyzéke," [The 13th-century tithe list of the diocese of Oradea], *Magyar Nyelv* 22, 220–223, 298–301 and 357–363.

Jamrichová, E. et al. 2013, "Continuity and Change in the Vegetation of a Central European Pakwood," *Holocene* 23, 46–56.

Jankó, F., Kücsán, J. and Szende, K. 2010, "The Historical Topography of Sopron," and "Topographical Gazetteer," In *Sopron* (Hungarian Atlas of Historic Towns, 1), eds. iidem, 5–55 and 61–83. Sopron: Soproni Levéltár – Soproni Múzeum.

Jánosi, M. 1996, *Törvényalkotás Magyarországon a korai Árpád-korban* [Legislation in early-Árpádian-age Hungary]. Szeged: Szegedi Középkorász Műhely.

Jánossy, D. 1985, "Wildvogelreste aus archäologischen Grabungen in Ungarn (Neolithicum bis Mittelalter)," *Fragmenta Mineralogica Palaeontologica* 12, 67–103.

Johanek, P. 2006, "Frühe Zentren – werdende Städte," In *Vom Umbruch zur Erneuerung*, eds. J. Jarnut and M. Wemhoff, 511–538. München: Wilhelm Fink.

Johanek, P. 2011, "Stadtgründung und Stadtwerdung im Blick der Stadtgeschichtsforschung," In *Stadtgründung und Stadtwerdung: Beiträge von Archäologie und Stadtgeschichtsforschung* (Beiträge zur Geschichte der Städte Mitteleuropas, 22), ed. F. Opll, 127–160. Linz: Arbeitskreis für Stadtgeschichtsforschung.

Juhász, I., Sümegi, P. and Zatykó, Cs. (eds.) 2007, *Environmental Archaeology in Transdanubia* (Varia archaeologica Hungarica, 20). Budapest: Archaeological Institute of the Hungarian Academy of Sciences.

K. Csilléry, K. 1982, *A magyar népi lakáskultúra kialakulásának kezdetei* [Beginnings of the formation of Hungarian folk furnishing]. Budapest: Akadémiai.

K. Németh, A. 2005, "Csontosövek a középkori Magyarországon," [Bone-mounted belts from the medieval Hungary] In *"... a halál árnyékának völgyében járok". A középkori templom körüli temetők kutatása* ["I am walking in the valley of the shadow of death ..." Research of medieval churchyards] (Opuscula Hungarica, 6), eds. Á. Ritoók and E. Simonyi, 275–288. Budapest: Magyar Nemzeti Múzeum.

K. Németh, A. 2014, "Adatok Tolna megye középkori útjainak kutatásához," [Data to the study of the medieval roads of Tolna County] In *A múltnak kútja. Fiatal középkoros régészek V. konferenciájának tanulmánykötete / The Fountain of the Past: Study Volume of the Fifth Conference of Young Medieval Archaeologists*, ed. Á. T. Rácz, 177–408 and 457. Szentendre: Ferenczy Múzeum.

K. Németh, A. 2015, *A középkori Tolna megye templomai* [The churches of Tolna County]. Szekszárd: IDResearch – Publikon.

Kachelmann, J. 1870, *Das Alter und Schicksale des ungarischen, zunächst schemnitzer Bergbaues nebst einer Erklärung des Landes*. Bratislava: Wigand.

Kalász, E. 1932, *A szentgotthárdi apátság birtokviszonyai és a ciszterci gazdálkodás a középkorban* [Cistercian economy and the estates of Szentgotthárd Abbey in the Middle Ages] (Tanulmányok a magyar mezőgazdaság történetéhez, 5). Budapest: Szerzői kiadás.

Karácsonyi, J. 1922–1924, *Szent Ferencz rendjének története Magyarországon 1711–ig*, I–II [History of the order of St Francis in Hungary until 1711]. Budapest: A Magyar Tud. Akadémia.

Kassal-Mikula, R. 1997, *850 Jahre St. Stephan: Symbol un Mitte in Wien 1147–1997*. Wien: Museen der Stadt Wien.

Katona Kiss, A. 2009, "A Kárpát-medencei bolgár térhódítás a 9. században. Történeti észrevételek a régészet tükrében," [The Bulgarian presence in the 9th-century Carpathian Basin. Historical remarks based on archaeology] *A Wosinszky Mór Múzeum Évkönyve* 31, 37–56.

Kaufhold, K.-H. and Reininghaus, W. (eds.) 2004, *Stadt und Bergbau* (Städteforschung, A 64). Köln–Weimar–Wien: Böhlau.

Kázmér, M. 1970, *A 'falu' a magyar helynevekben, XIII–XIX. század* [The 'village' in Hungarian settlement names, 13th–19th centuries]. Budapest: Akadémiai.

Keene, D. 1998, *Feeding Medieval European Cities, 600–1500*. Online document: http://sas-space.sas.ac.uk/4640/1/Feeding_Medieval_European_Cities,_600–1500_by_Derek_Keene_Institute_of_Historical_Research.pdf (last accessed: 10 July 2016).

Keene, D. 2006, "Sites of desire: shops, selds and wardrobes in London and other English cities, 1100–1550," In *Buyers and Sellers Retail circuits and practices in medieval and early modern Europe*, eds. B. Blondé et al., 125–153. Turnhout: Brepols.

Keglevich, K. 2012, *A garamszentbenedeki apátság története az Árpád- és az Anjou-korban, 1075–1403* [History of the abbey of Hronský Beňadik, 1075–1403] (Capitulum, 8). Szeged: Szegedi Tudományegyetem Törteneti Intézet.

Kellenbenz, H. 1985, "Gli operatori economici italiani nell'Europa centrale ed orientale," In *Aspetti della vita economica medievale. Atti del Convegno di Studi nel X. anniversario della morte di Federigo Melis*, ed. B. Dini, 333–357. Firenze: Universita degli studi di Firenze, Istituto di storia economica.

Kellenbenz, H. 1991, *Die Wiege der Moderne. Wirtschaft und Gesellschaft Europas 1350–1650*. Stuttgart: Klett-Cotta.

Kenyeres, I. 1997, "Egy nagybirtok igazgatása és gazdálkodása a 16. században. A trencséni várbirtok 1543 és 1564 között," [Administration and farming of a great estate in the 16th century. The estate of Trenčin castle, 1543–1564] *Levéltári Közlemények* 68, 99–142.

Kenyeres, I. 2004, "A Szapolyai család és Trencsén," [The Szapolyai family and Trenčin] In *Tanulmányok Szapolyai Jánosról és a kora újkori Erdélyről* [Studies on John Szapolyai and Early Modern Transylvania] (Studia Miskolciensia, 5), eds. J. Bessenyei, Z. Horváth and P. Tóth, 135–145. Miskolc: Miskolci Egyetem BTK.

Kenyeres, I. 2005, "Die Einkünfte und Reformen der Finanzverwaltung Ferdinands I. in Ungarn," In *Kaiser Ferdinand I. Ein mitteleuropäischer Herrscher*, eds. M. Fuchs, T. Oborni and G. Újváry, 111–146. Münster: Aschendorff.

Kenyeres, I. 2007, "Verwaltung und Erträge von Königin Marias ungarischen Besitzungen in den Jahren 1522 bis 1548," In *Maria von Ungarn (1505–1558). Eine Renaissancefürstin*, eds. M. Fuchs and O. Réthelyi, 179–207. Münster: Aschendorff.

Kenyeres, I. 2008, *Uradalmak és végvárak. A kamarai birtokok és a törökellenes határvédelem a 16. századi Magyar Királyságban* [Estates of the royal chamber and the organization of border defense against the Ottoman Turks in the 16th-century Hungarian Kingdom] (Habsburg Történeti Monográfiák, 2). Budapest: ÚJ Mandátum.

Kenyeres, I. 2012, "A bányakamarák szerepe a Magyar Királyság jövedelmeiben a 15–16. században," [The role of mining chambers in the incomes of the Hungarian Kingdom in 15th–16th centuries] In *Tiszteletkör. Történeti tanulmányok Draskóczy István egyetemi tanár 60. születésnapjára* [Lap of honor. Studies in honor of Professor István Draskóczy on his 60th birthday], eds. G. Mikó, B. Péterfi and A. Vadas, 177–188. Budapest: ELTE Eötvös Kiadó.

Keyser, R. 2009, "The Transformation of Traditional Woodland Management: Commercial Sylviculture in Medieval Champagne," *French Historical Studies* 32, 353–384.

Khin, A. 1957, *A magyar vizák története* [The history of Hungarian sturgeons] (Mezőgazdasági Múzeum Füzetei, 2). Budapest: Magyar Nemzeti Múzeum – Történeti Múzeum.

Kintzinger, M. 2000, *Westbindungen im spätmittelalterlichen Europa: auswärtige Politik zwischen dem Reich, Frankreich, Burgund und England in der Regierungszeit Kaiser Sigmunds*. Stuttgart: Jan Thorbecke.

Kiss, A. 1978, "A gyulai várbirtok malmainak története," [History of the mills on the estate of Gyula castle] *Békés Megyei Múzeumok Közleményei* 5, 269–291.

Kiss, A. 1996, "Some weather events from the fourteenth century (1338–1358), I.," *Acta Climatologica Universitatis Szegediensis* 30, 61–69.

Kiss, A. 1997–1998, "Changing Environmental Conditions and the Waterlevel of Lake Fertő (Neusiedlersee) before the Drainage Works (13th–18th centuries)," *Annual of Medieval Studies at CEU* 5, 241–248.

Kiss, A. 2001, "Hydrology and Environment in the Southern Basin of Lake Fertő/Neusiedler Lake in the Late Middle Ages," *Medium Aevum Quotidianum* 44, 61–77.

Kiss, A. 2009a, "Historical climatology in Hungary: Role of documentary evidence in the study of past climates and hydrometeorological extremes," *Időjárás* 113, 315–339.

Kiss, A. 2009b, "'Rivulus namque, qui dicitur Fuk, fluens de prefato lacu' Fok, Sár, Foksár," In *Antropogén ökológiai változások a Kárpát-medencében* [Anthropogenic ecological changes in the Carpathian Basin], eds. B. Andrásfalvy and Gy. Vargyas, 49–63. Budapest: PTE Néprajz–Kulturális Antropológia Tanszék.

Kiss, A. 2009c, "Floods and weather in 1342 and 1343 in the Carpathian Basin," *Journal of Environmental Geography* 2/3–4, 37–47.

Kiss, A. 2011, *Floods and Long-Term Water-Level Changes in Medieval Hungary*. Unpublished PhD-dissertation defended at CEU, Budapest–Szeged.

Kiss, A. 2012, "Időjárás, környezeti problémák és az 1340-es évek elejének tatár hadjáratai," [Weather, environmental problems and the Mongol military campaigns in the early 1340s] *Hadtörténelmi Közlemények* 125, 483–506.

Kiss, A. 2018, *Floods and Long-Term Water-Level Changes in Medieval Hungary*. Berlin: Springer (in press)

Kiss, A. and Laszlovszky, J. 2013, "14th–16th-Century Danube Floods and Long-Term Water-Level Changes in Archaeological and Sedimentary Evidence in the Western and Central Carpathian Basin: an Overview with Documentary Comparison," *Journal of Environmental Geography* 6/3–4, 1–11.

Kiss, A. and Nikolic, Z. 2015, "Droughts, Dry Spells and Low Water Levels in Medieval Hungary (and Croatia) I: The Great Droughts of 1362, 1474, 1479, 1494 and 1507," *Journal of Environmental Geography* 8/1–2, 11–22.

Kiss, A. and Piti, F., 2005, "A fertői fok," [The *fok* of Fertő] *Soproni Szemle* 59, 164–184.

Kiss, A., Piti, F. and Sebők, F. 2016, "Rossz termések, élelmiszerhiány, drágaság, (éh)ínség – és feltételezhető okaik a 14. századi Magyarországon," [Bad harvests, food shortage and famine and their possible reasons in 14th-century Hungary] In *Magyar Gazdaságtörténeti Évkönyv 2016. Válság – kereskedelem* [Hungarian economic history yearbook, 2016. Crisis – trade], eds. Gy. Kövér, Á. Pogány and B. Weisz, 23–79. Budapest: MTA BTK Történettudományi Intézet.

Kiss, E. 2006, "Die Anfänge des Drahtemails," In *Sigismundus Rex et Imperator. Kunst und Kultur zur Zeit Sigismund von Luxemburg 1387–1437. Auststellungskatalog*, ed. I. Takács, 279–283. Budapest–Mainz am Rhein: P. von Zabern.

Kiss, G., and Tóth, E. 1996, "Adatok a nyugat-dunántúli korai magyar gyepű topográfiájához," [Data to the topography of the early Hungarian *gyepű* in Western Transdanubia] In *Magyarok térben és időben* [Hungarians in space and time], eds. É. M. Fülöp and J. Cseh, K., 105–123. Tata: Komárom-Esztergom Megyei Önkormányzat Múzeumainak Igazgatósága.

Kiss, L. 1997, *Földrajzi nevek etimológiai szótára*, I–II [Etimological dictionary of place-names]. Budapest: Akadémiai.

Kiss, L. 1997b, "Korai magyar helységnévtípusok," [Early Hungarian settlement name types] In *Honfoglalás és nyelvészet* [Hungarian conquest and linguistics], ed. L. Kovács and L. Veszprémy, 177–187. Budapest: Balassi.

Knapp, É. 1994, "Pálos gazdálkodás a középkori Baranya megyében," [Pauline farming in medieval Barnya County] In *Varia Paulina. Pálos rendtörténeti tanulmányok*, I [Studies in the history of the Pauline order], ed. G. Sarbak, 81–100. Csorna: Stylus.

Knauz, N. 1865, "A magyar érsek- és püspökségek jövedelmei," [Incomes of the Hungarian archbishoprics and bishoprics] *Magyar Sion* 3, 552–559.

Knauz, N. 1890, *A Garam-melletti Szent-Benedeki apátság* [History of the Benedictien abbey of Hronský Beňadik]. Budapest: Esztergomi Főkáptalan.

Kniezsa, I. 1938, "Magyarország népei a XI. században," [Peoples of Hungary in the 11th century] In *Emlékkönyv Szent István király halálának kilencszázadik évfordulóján*, II [Jubilee volume in the memory of the 900th anniversary of the death of St Stephen], ed. J. Serédi, 368–472. Budapest: MTA.

Knittler, H. 1977–1978, "Zum ältesten Steiner Zolltarif. Eine handelsgeschichtliche Untersuchung," *Mitteilungen des Kremser Stadtarchivs* 17–18, 27–75.

Köblös, J. 1994, *Az egyházi középréteg Mátyás és a Jagellók korában. (A budai, fehérvári, győri és pozsonyi káptalan adattárával)* [Ecclesiastic middle class in the Matthias and Jagiellonian periods. (With the archontology of the Buda, Székesfehérvár, Győr and Bratislava chapters)]. Budapest: MTA Történettudományi Intézet.

Koch, B. 1994, *Corpus Nummorum Austriacorum I. Mittelalter.* Wien: Kunsthistorisches Museum, Bundessammlung von Medaillen, Münzen und Geldzeichen.

Kocsis, E. et al. 2003, "Medieval Material Culture – Medieval Archaeology," In *Hungarian Archaeology at the Turn of The Millennium*, ed. Zs. Visy, 397–404. Budapest: Ministry of National Cultural Heritage – Teleki László Foundation.

Kocsis, Gy. 1993, "Az érsekújvári hídvámjegyzék. Adatok a 16. század végi élőállat kivitelről," [Bridge customs of Nové Zámky. Data on animal export from the late 16th century] *Bács-Kiskun Megye Múltjából* 12, 287–359.

Kőfalvi, I. 1980, "Kőfaragókról és kőbányákról," [On stone-cutters and stone mines] *Építés–Építészettudomány* 12, 241–282.

Kőfalvi, T. 2002, "Places of Authenticaton (loca credibilia)," *Chronica* 2, 27–38.

Kollányi, F. 1889, *Az esztergomi érsekség pizetum-joga* [The pisetum right of the archbishopric of Esztergom]. Budapest: Athenaeum.

Kollár, T. (ed.) 2000, *A középkori Dél-Alföld és Szer* [Medieval Southern Great Hungarian Plain and Szer]. Szeged: Csongrád Megyei Levéltár.

Kolláth, Á. and Tomka, G. 2017, "A győri Széchenyi-tér topográfiája. Az Árpád-kortól az újkor kezdetéig," [The topography of the Széchenyi Square at Győr from the Árpádian age to the beginning of modern times] In *Hatalom, adó, jog. Gazdaságtörténeti tanulmányok a magyar középkorról* [Power, tax, law. Studies on the economic history of medieval Hungary], eds. B. Weisz and I. Kádas, 551–570. Budapest: MTA BTK.

Kollmann, Ö. L. 2005, "Az észak-gömöri központi helyek középkori és kora újkori fejlődése," [The development of the central places of the northern Gömör County in the Middle Ages and the early modern period] In *Bártfától Pozsonyig. Városok a 13–17. században* [From Bardejov to Bratislava. Cities in the 13th–17th century] (Társadalom- és Művelődéstörténeti Tanulmányok, 35), eds. E. Csukovits and T. Lengyel, 47–122. Budapest: MTA Történettudományi Intézet.

Kolossváry, Sz. (ed.) 1975, *Az erdőgazdálkodás története Magyarországon* [A history of forestry in Hungary]. Budapest: Akadémiai.

Korčmaros, L. 1997, "Slavonski banovci bibliografija," [Slavonian banal bibliography] *Numismatičke vijesti* 39, 117–137.

Körmendy, A. 1995, *Melioratio Terrae. Vergleichende Untersuchungen über die Siedlungsbewegung im östlichen Mitteleuropa im 13.–14. Jahrhundert*. Poznan: Wydawn. Poznańskiego Towarzystwa przyjaciół nauk.

Kőrösi, A. 2009, "Árpád-kori falu állatcsontleletei Gyálon (3. lelőhely)," [Faunal remains from the 11th–13th century Árpád Period settlement of Gyál (Site no. 3)] In *Csontvázak a szekrényből. Skeletons from the Cupboard*, eds. L. Bartosiewicz, E. Gál and I. Kováts, 131–145. Budapest: Martin Opitz.

Kósa, L. 2001, *A magyar néprajz tudománytörténete* [History of Hungarian ethnography]. Budapest: Gondolat.

Kósa, L., Keve, A. and Farkas, Gy. 1971, *Herman Ottó* [Ottó Herman]. Budapest: Akadémiai.

Koszta, L. 2007, *Írásbeliség és egyházszervezet. Fejezetek a középkori magyar egyház történetéből* [Literacy and ecclesiastical organization. Chapters of the medieval Hungarian church history]. Szeged: Szegedi Középkorász Műhely.

Kovács, É. 1961, "Croix limousines en Hongrie," *Acta Historiae Artium Academiae Scientiarium Hungariae* 7, 155–158.

Kovács, É. 1968, *Limoges champlevé enamels in Hungary*. Budapest: Corvina.

Kovács, É. 1971, "Über einige Probleme des Krakauer Kronkreuzes," *Acta Historiae Artium Academiae Scientiarium Hungariae* 17, 231–268.

Kovács, É. 1972, "Késő középkori francia inventáriumok magyar vonatkozásai," [Hungarian references in late medieval French inventories] *Művészettörténeti Értesítő* 21, 120–123.

Kovács, É. 1974, *Romanesque Goldsmiths' Art in Hungary*. Budapest: Corvina.

Kovács, É. 1994, "Gehänge," In *Pannonia Regia. Művészet a Dunántúlon, 1000–1541. Katalógus* [Art in the Transdanubia. Catalogue], eds. I. Takács and Á. Mikó, 212 and 569. Budapest: Magyar Nemzeti Galéria.

Kovács, É. 1998, *Species modus ordo. Válogatott tanulmányok* [Selected studies]. Budapest: Szent István Társulat.

Kovács, E. 2005, "Remains of the bone working in Medieval Buda," In *From Hooves to Horns, from Mollusc to Mammoth. Manufacture and Use of Bone Artefacts from Prehistoric Times to the Present* (Muinasaja Teadus, 15), eds. H. Luik et al., 309–316. Tallinn: Tallinn Book Printers.

Kovács, E. 2008, "Maiolica Ceramics from Buda – the Buda Maiolica Workshop," In *Matthias Corvinus, the King. Tradition and Renewal in the Hungarian Royal Court, 1458–1490. Exhibition Catalogue*, eds. P. Farbaky et al., 351–353. Budapest: Budapest History Museum.

Kovács, E. and Zádor, J. 2015, "Adatok a középkori Pest városfejlődéséhez. A régészeti kutatások újabb eredményei," [The rise of Pest in the Middle Ages. Recent archaeological findings] In *"In medio regni Hungariae." Régészeti, művészettörténeti és történeti kutatások "az ország közepén"* [Archaeological, art historical and historical researches 'in the middle of the kingdom'], eds. E. Benkő and K. Orosz, 561–576. Budapest: MTA BTK Régészeti Intézete.

Kovács, Gy. and Zatykó, Cs. (eds.) 2016, *"per sylvam et per lacus nimios" The Medieval and Ottoman Period in Southern Transdanubia, Southwest Hungary: The Contribution of the Natural Sciences*. Budapest: MTA BTK Régészeti Intézet.

Kovács, L. 1988, "Bemerkungen zur Arbeit von István Gedai: A magyar pénzverés kezdete," [Der Anfang der ungarischen Münzprägung] *Acta Archaeologica Academiae Scientiarum Hungaricae* 40, 275–300.

Kovács, L. 1997, *A kora Árpád-kori magyar pénzverésről. Érmetani és régészeti tanulmányok a Kárpát-medence I. (Szent) István és II. (Vak) Béla uralkodása közötti időszakának (1000–1141) érméiről* [On early-Árpádian age coinage. Numismatic and archaeological studies on the coins of the Carpathian Basin of the period between the reign of St Stephen and Béla II (1000–1141)] (Varia Archaeologica Hungarica, 7). Budapest: MTA Régészeti Intézet.

Kovács, L. 2005–2006, "Megjegyzések Saltzer Ernő kincskataszterének korai, 1000–1141 közötti keltezésű leletekre vonatkozó címszavaihoz," [Bemerkungen zu den Schlagworten bezüglich der zwischen 1000 und 1141 datierten Münzfunde des Schatzkatasters von Ernő Saltzer] *Numizmatikai Közlöny* 104–105, 31–56.

Kovalovszki, J. (ed.) 1986, *A magyar falu régésze. Méri István 1911–1976* [Archaeologist of Hungarian villages. István Méri (1911–1976)] (Ceglédi füzetek, 23), ed. J. Kovalovszki. Cegléd: Ceglédi Kossuth Múzeum.

Kovalovszki, J. 1992, "A pálos remeték Szent Kereszt-kolostora. (Méri István ásatása Klastrompusztán)" [The Holy Cross-monastery of the Pauline Hermits. The excavations of István Méri in Klastrompuszta] *Communicationes Archaeologicae Hungariae* 1992, 173–207.

Kovalovszki, J. 1994–1995, "Bronzeschmelzofen und Gießerei aus der Arpadenzeit (Visegrád, Feldebrő)," *Communicationes Archaeologicae Hungariae* 1994–1995, 225–254.

Kováts, F. 1900, *Városi adózás a középkorban* [Urban taxation in the Middle Ages]. Pozsony: Angermayer.

Kováts, F. 1902a, *Nyugatmagyarország áruforgalma a XV. században a pozsonyi harminczadkönyv alapján: történet-statisztikai tanulmány* [Trade of Western-Hungary in the 15th century in light of the thirtieth custom's register of Bratislava: a study in historical statistics] (Társadalom és Gazdaságtörténeti Kutatások, 1). Budapest: Politzer.

Kováts, F. 1902b, "Pozsony városának háztartása a XV. században," [Financial balance of Bratislava in the 15th century] *Magyar Gazdaságtörténelmi Szemle* 9, 433–466.

Kováts, F. 1918a, *Preßburger Grundbuchführung und Liegenschaftsrecht im Spätmittelalter*. Weimar: Hof-Buchdruckerei.

Kováts, F. 1918b, *A pozsonyi városgazdaság a középkor végén* [The economy of Bratislava at the end of the Middle Ages]. Pozsony: Eder István.

Kováts, F. 1922, "A magyar arany világtörténeti jelentősége és kereskedelmi összeköttetéseink a nyugattal a középkorban," [The world historical importance of Hungarian gold and the Hungarian trade relations with the West in the Middle Ages] *Történelmi Szemle* 11, 104–143.

Kováts, F. 1926, "Magyar pénzforgalom az Anjouk korában," [Circulation of currency in Hungary in the Angevin period] *Numizmatikai Közlöny* 25, 90–109.

Kováts, I. 2005, "Finds of worked bone and antler from the Royal Palace of Visegrád," In *From Hooves to Horns, from Mollusc to Mammoth. Manufacture and Use of Bone Artefacts from Prehistoric Times to the Present* (Muinasaja Teadus, 15), eds. H. Luik et al., 293–304. Tallinn: Tallinn Book Printers.

Kövér, Gy. 2013, "A Magyar Gazdaságtörténeti Szemle (1894–1906) gazdaságtörténete – intézményi megközelítés és historiográfia," [The economic history of the Hungarian Review of Economic History (1894–1906): an institutional approach and historiography] *Történelmi Szemle* 55, 201–224.

Kristó, Gy. 2003, *Early Transylvania (895–1324)*. Budapest: Lucidus.

Kristó, Gy. 2007, "Die Bevölkerungszahl Ungarns in der Arpadenzeit," In *Historische Demographie Ungarns (896–1996)* (Studien zur Geschichte Ungarns, 11), 49–56. Herne: G. Schäfer.

Kristó, Gy. 2008, *Nichtungarische Völker im mittelalterlichen Ungarn*. (Studien zur Geschichte Ungarns, 13). Herne: G. Schäfer.

Kristó, Gy., Makk, F. and Szegfű, Gy., 1973–1974, "Adatok 'korai' helyneveink ismeretéhez," [Data on the history of 'early' placenames] *Acta Universitatis Szegediensis: Acta historica* 44, 3–96 and 48, 3–55.

Krizskó, P. 1880, *A körmöczi régi kamara és grófjai* [The chamber of Kremnica and its chamberlains] (Értekezések a történelmi tudományok köréből, 8). Budapest: A. M. Tud. Akadémia Könyvkiadó-Hivatala.

Kropf, L. 1899, "Dárius király Erdélyben," [King Darius in Transylvania] *Századok* 33, 97–107.

Kubinyi, A. (ed.) 1998, *König und Volk im spätmittelalterlichen Königreich Ungarn. Städteentwicklung, Alltagsleben und Regierung im mittelalterlichen Königreich Ungarn* (Studien zur Geschichte Ungarns, 1). Herne: G. Schäfer.

Kubinyi, A. 1957, "A kincstári személyzet a XV. század második felében," [The personell of the treasury in the second half of the 15th century] *Tanulmányok Budapest Múltjából* 12, 25–49.

Kubinyi, A. 1963, "A városi rend kialakulásának gazdasági feltételei és a főváros kereskedelme a XV. század végén," [The economic conditions of the formation of urban order and the commerce of the capital at the end of 15th century] *Tanulmányok Budapest Múltjából* 15, 189–226.

Kubinyi, A. 1963–1964, "Die Nürnberger Haller in Ofen. Ein Beitrag zur Geschichte des Südosthandels im Spätmittelalter," *Mitteilungen des Vereins für Geschichte der Stadt Nürnberg* 52, 89–97.

Kubinyi, A. 1964a, "A mezőgazdaság történetéhez a Mohács előtti Budán (Gallinczer Lénárt számadáskönyve)," [To the agriculture of Buda before the battle of Mohács. The account book of Lénárt Gallinczer] *Agrártörténeti Szemle* 6, 371–404.

Kubinyi, A. 1964b, "L'agriculture à Buda et à Pest à la rencontre du XVe et du XVIe siècle," *Agrártörténeti Szemle* 6 (Supplementum), 1–21.

Kubinyi, A. 1964c, "Budafelhévíz topográfiája és gazdasági fejlődése," [The topographical development and economy of Budafelhévíz] *Tanulmányok Budapest Múltjából* 16, 85–180.

Kubinyi, A. 1964d, "A budai vár udvarbírói hivatala 1458–1541," [The office of the steward (*iudex curiae*) at Buda 1458–1541] *Levéltári Közlemények* 35, 67–96.

Kubinyi, A. 1966, "Budai és pesti polgárok családi összeköttetései a Jagelló-korban," [The family connection of the burghers of Buda and Pest in the Jagiellonian period] *Levéltári Közlemények* 37, 227–291.

Kubinyi, A. 1970, "Az egészségügyi foglalkozásúak társadalmi és gazdasági helyzete Budán a XV–XVI. század fordulóján," [Social and economic status of medical workmen at the turn of 15th–16th century in Buda] *Orvostörténeti Közlemények* 54–56, 63–81.

Kubinyi, A. 1971a, "A középkori magyarországi városhálózat hierarchikus térbeli rendjének kérdéséhez," [To the spatial hierarchy of the urban network of medieval Hungary] *Településtudományi közlemények* 23, 58–78.

Kubinyi, A. 1971b, "Die Städte Ofen und Pest und der Fernhandel am Ende des 15. und am Anfang des 16. Jahrhunderts," In *Der Außenhandel Ostmitteleuropas 1450–1650: Die ostmitteleuropäischen Volkswirtschaften in ihren Beziehungen zu Mitteleuropa*, ed. I. Bog, 342–433. Köln: Böhlau.

Kubinyi, A. 1972, *Die Anfänge Ofens* (Osteuropastudien der Hochschulen des Landes Hessen. Reihe I. Giessener Abhanndlungen zur Agrar- und Wirtschaftsforschung des europäischen Ostens, 60). Berlin: Duncker und Humblot.

Kubinyi, A. 1973a, "A kaposújvári uradalom és a Somogy megyei familiárisok szerepe Újlaki Miklós birtokpolitikájában. Adatok a XV. századi feudális nagybirtok hatalmi politikájához," [The role of the estate of Kaposújvár and the *familiares* of County Somogy in the estate policy of Miklós Újlaki] *Somogy Megye Múltjából* 4, 3–44.

Kubinyi, A. 1973b, "Budapest története a későbbi középkorban Buda elestéig (1541–ig)," [The history of late medieval Budapest until the fall of Buda in 1541] In *Budapest története II. Budapest története a későbbi középkorban és a török hódoltság idején* [The history of Budapest II. The history of Budapest in the late medieval period and during the Ottoman times], eds. L. Gerevich and D. Kosáry, 7–240. Budapest: Akadémiai.

Kubinyi, A. 1978, "Die Pemfflinger in Wien und Buda," *Jahrbuch des Vereines für Geschichte der Stadt Wien* 34, 67–88.

Kubinyi, A. 1980, "A középkori körmöcbányai pénzverés és történelmi jelentősége," [Die Kremnitzer Münzprägung im Mittelalter und deren geschichtliche Bedeutung] In *Emlékezés a 650 éves Körmöcbányára. A Magyar Numizmatikai Társulat ünnepi ülése a Magyar Tudományos Akadémián 1978. október 26–án Körmöcbánya várossá nyilvánításának 650. évfordulója alkalmából* [Erinnerung an das 650 jährige Kremnitz. Die feierliche Sitzung der Ungarischen Numismatischen Gesellschaft in der Ungarischen Akademie der Wissenschaften am 26. Oktober 1978 gelegentlich des 650. jährigen Jubiläums der Erhebung von Kremnitz zur Stadt], ed. I. Gedai, 9–39. Budapest: Magyar Numizmatikai Társulat.

Kubinyi, A. 1981a, "Die Kremnitzer Münzprägung im Mittelalter und deren geschichtliche Bedeutung," *Helvetische Münzenzeitung* 15/9, 385–388.

Kubinyi, A. 1981b, "Städtische Wasserversorgungsprobleme im mittelalterlichen Ungarn," In *Städtische Versorgung und Entsorgung im Wandel der Geschichte* (Stadt in der Geschichte, 8), ed. J. Sydow, 180–190. Sigmaringen: Thorbecke.

Kubinyi, A. 1982, "The Road to Defeat: Hungarian Politics and Defense in the Jagiellonian Period," In *From Hunyadi to Rákóczi. War and Society in Late Medieval and Early Modern Hungary* (War and Society in Eastern Central Europe, 3 = Eastern European Monographs, 104), eds. J. Bak, M. and B. Király, K., 159–178. Boulder: Columbia University Press.

Kubinyi, A. 1984a, "A királyi várospolitika tükröződése a magyar királyi oklevelek arengáiban," [The reflection of royal urban policy in the arengas of Hungarian royal charters] In *Eszmetörténeti tanulmányok a magyar középkorról* [Studies on intellectual history in medieval Hungary], ed. Gy. Székely, 275–291. Budapest: Akadémiai.

Kubinyi, A. 1984b, "A középbirtokos nemesség Mohács előestéjén," [The middle-landlords before Mohács] In *Magyarország társadalma a török kiűzésének idején* [Hungarian society at the period of the expell of Ottomans] (Discussiones Neogradienses, 1), ed. F. Szvircsek, 5–24. Salgótarján: Nógrád Megyei Múzeumok Igazgatósága.

Kubinyi, A. 1984c, "Bäuerlicher Alltag im spätmittelalterlichen Ungarn," In *Bäuerliche Sachkultur des Spätmittelalters: internationaler Kongreß Krems an der Donau 21. bis 24. Sept. 1982* (Veröffentlichungen des Instituts für Mittelalterliche Realienkunde Österreichs, 4 = Sitzungsberichte. Akademie der Wissenschaften in Wien, Philosophisch-Historische Klasse, 439), 235–264. Wien: Verlag der Österreichischen Akademie der Wissenschaften.

Kubinyi, A. 1985, "Die Rolle der Archäologie und der Urkunden bei der Erforschung des Alltagslebens im Spätmittelalter," In *Études historiques hongroises 1985 publiées á l'occasion du Congrès International des Sciences Historiques*, I, eds. F. Glatz and E. Pamlényi, 615–644. Budapest: Akadémiai.

Kubinyi, A. 1986a, "A nagybirtok és jobbágyai a középkor végén az 1478-as Garai–Szécsi birtokfelosztás alapján," [The grand estate and its tenant peasants at the end of the Middle Ages as reflected by the Garai–Szécsi estate division in 1478] *Veszprém Megyei Múzeumok Közleményei* 18, 197–225.

Kubinyi, A. 1987, "Zsigmond király és a városok," [King Sigismund and the towns] In *Művészet Zsigmond király korában*, I [Art in the age of King Sigismund], eds. L. Beke, M. Marosi and T. Wehli, 235–245. Budapest: Akadémiai.

Kubinyi, A. 1988, "Königliches Salzmonopol und die Städte des Königreichs Ungarn im Mittelalter," In *Stadt und Salz* (Beiträge zur Geschichte der Städte Mitteleuropas, 10), ed. W. Rausch, 233–246. Linz: Österreichischer Arbeitskreis für Stadtgeschichtsforschung.

Kubinyi, A. 1989, "Főúri rezidenciák a középkor végén," [Residential places of the aristocracy at the end of the Middle Ages]," In *A Dunántúl településtörténete VII. Falvak, városok, puszták a Dunántúlon XI–XIX. század* [The settlement history of Transdanubia, VII. Villages, towns and barrens in Transdanubia, 9th–19th centuries], ed. B. Somfai, 87–93. Veszprém: MTA Pécsi és Veszprémi Akadémiai Bizottság.

Kubinyi, A. 1990, "A Mátyás-kori államszervezet," [The state organisation during the reign of King Matthias] In *Hunyadi Mátyás. Emlékkönyv Mátyás király halálának 500. évfordulójára* [Matthias Corvinus. Essays in memory of the 500th anniversary of King Matthias's death], eds. Gy. Rázsó and L. Molnár, v., 53–147. Budapest: Zrínyi.

Kubinyi, A. 1991a, "Nagybirtok és főúri rezidencia Magyarországon a XV. század közepétől Mohácsig," [Grate estates and aristocratic residences in Hungary from the mid-15th century until the defeat at Mohács] *A Tapolcai Városi Múzeum Közleményei* 2, 211–228.

Kubinyi, A. 1991b, "Residenz- und Herrschaftsbildung in Ungarn in der zweiten Hälfte des 15. Jahrhunderts und am Beginn des 16. Jahrhunderts," In *Fürstliche Residenzen im spätmittelalterliche Europa* (Vorträge und Forschungen, 36), eds. H. Patz and W. Paravicini, 421–462. Stuttgart: Thorbecke.

Kubinyi, A. 1991c, "Költözés, helyváltoztatás, utazás a későközépkori Magyarországon. (A horizontális mobilitás kérdései)," [Migration, mobility, and travel in late medieval Hungary (The questions of horizontal mobility)] *A Tapolcai Városi Múzeum Közleményei* 2, 229–241.

Kubinyi, A. 1991d, "Die königlich-ungarischen Salzordnungen des Mittelalters," In *Das Salz in der Rechts- und Handelsgeschichte*, eds. J.-C. Hocquet and R. Palme, 261–270. Innsbruck–Schwaz: Berenkamp.

Kubinyi, A. 1991e, "A későközépkori magyarországi városi fejlődés vitás kérdései," [The debated problems of late medieval Hungarian urban development] In *Régészet és várostörténet. Tudományos konferencia* [Archaeology and urban history. Scientific conference] (Dunántúli Dolgozatok [C] Történettudományi Sorozat, 3), ed. Á. Uherkovich, 15–31. Pécs: Janus Pannonius Múzeum.

Kubinyi, A. 1991f, "Buda – Die mittelalterliche Hauptstadt Ungarns," In *Budapest im Mittelalter*, ed. G. Biegel, 15–41. Braunschweig: Braunschweigisches Landesmuseum.

Kubinyi, A. 1992, "Wirtschaftsgeschichtliche Probleme in den Beziehungen Ungarns zum Westen am Ende des Mittelalters," In *Westmitteleuropa – Ostmitteleuropa. Vergleiche und Beziehungen. Festschrift für Ferdinand Seibt zum 65. Geburtstag* (Veröffentlichungen des Collegium Carolinum, 70), eds. W. Eberhard et al., 165–174. München: Oldenbourg.

Kubinyi, A. 1993a, "Városaink háborús terhei Mátyás alatt," [Military burdens on Hungarian towns under Matthias Corvinus] In *Házi Jenő emlékkönyv* [Studies in memory of Jenő Házi], eds. É. Turbuly and P. Dominkovits, 155–167. Sopron: Soproni Levéltár.

Kubinyi, A. 1993b, *Változások a középkor végi Magyarországon* [Changes in late medieval Hungary] (História Könyvtár. Előadások a történettudomány műhelyeiből, 2). Budapest: MTA Történettudományi Intézet.

Kubinyi, A. 1994a, "A Jagelló-kori Magyarország történeti vázlata," [A historical sketch of Jagiellonian Hungary] *Századok* 128, 288–319.

Kubinyi, A. 1994b, "A középkori Pápa," [Medieval Pápa] In *Tanulmányok Pápa város történetéből* [Studies in the history of Pápa], ed. idem, 75–105. Pápa: Pápa Város Önkormányzata.

Kubinyi, A. 1994c, "Buda és Pest szerepe a távolsági kereskedelemben a 15–16. század fordulóján," [The role of Buda and Pest in long-distance trade at the turn of the 15th and 16th centuries] *Történelmi Szemle* 36, 1–52.

Kubinyi, A. 1995a, "Stadt und Kirche in Ungarn im Mittelalter," In *Stadt und Kirche* (Beiträge zur Geschichte der Städte Mitteleuropas, 13), ed. F.-H. Hye, 179–198. Linz: Österreichischer Arbeitskreis für Stadtgeschichtsforschung.

Kubinyi, A. 1995b, "A magyarországi zsidóság története a középkorban," [History of Hungarian Jewry in the Middle Ages] *Soproni Szemle* 49, 2–27.

Kubinyi, A. 1996a "A magyar várostörténet első fejezete," [First chapter of Hungarian urban development] In *Társadalomtörténeti tanulmányok* [Studies in social history] (Studia Miskolciensia, 2), ed. Cs. Fazekas, 36–46. Miskolc: Bíbor.

Kubinyi, A. 1996b, "Deutsche und Nicht-Deutsche in den Städten des mittelalterlichen ungarischen Königreiches," In *Verfestigung und Änderung der ethnischen Strukturen im pannonischen Raum im Spätmittelalter* (Internationales Kulturhistorisches Symposion Mogersdorf, 25), ed. R. Widder, 145–177. Eisenstadt. Amt der Burgenländischen Landesregierung.

Kubinyi, A. 1996c, "A korai Árpád-kor gazdasági fejlődésének kérdőjelei," [Quesitons of the development of early Árpádian-age economy] *Valóság* 39/3, 60–65.

Kubinyi, A. 1996d, "Weinbau und Weinhandel in den ungarischen Städten im Spätmittelalter und in der frühen Neuzeit," In *Stadt und Wein* (Beiträge zur Geschichte der Städte Mitteleuropas, 14), ed. F. Opll, 67–84. Linz: Österreichischer Arbeitskreis für Stadtgeschichtsforschung.

Kubinyi, A. 1997a, "A magyar királyság népessége a 15. század végén," [Population of the kingdom of Hungary at the end of the 15th century] In *Magyarország történeti demográfiája 896–1995* [A Historical demography of Hungary 896–1995], ed. J. Kovacsics, 93–110. Budapest: MTA Demográfiai Bizottság.

Kubinyi, A. 1997b, "Polgárság a mezővárosban a középkor és az újkor határán," [Burghers in the market towns at the turn of the Middle Ages and the early modern period] *Budapesti Könyvszemle [BUKSZ]* 9, 186–190.

Kubinyi, A. 1998a, "A későközépkori magyar-nyugati kereskedelmi kapcsolatok kérdése," [Questions of the Hungarian–Western trade connections in the Late Middle Ages] In *R. Várkonyi Ágnes emlékkönyv születésének 70. évfordulója ünnepére* [Essays in honor of the 70th birthday of Ágnes R. Várkonyi], ed. P. Tusor, 109–117. Budapest: ELTE BTK.

Kubinyi, A. 1998b, "Historische Skizze Ungarns in der Jagiellonenzeit," In idem, *König und Volk im spätmittelalterlichen Ungarn. Städteentwicklung, Alltagsleben und Regierung im mittelalterlichen Königreich Ungarn* (Studien zur Geschichte Ungarns, 1), ed. T. Schäfer, 322–368. Herne: T. Schäfer.

Kubinyi, A. 1999a, "Die Staatsorganisation der Matthiaszeit," In idem, *Matthias Corvinus. Die Regierung eines Königreichs in Ostmitteleuropa 1458–1490* (Studien zur Geschichte Ungarns, 2), 5–96. Herne: T. Schäfer.

Kubinyi, A. 1999b, "Központi helyek a középkor végi Abaúj, Borsod, Heves és Torna megyékben," [Central places in late medieval Abaúj, Borsod, Heves and Torna counties] *A Herman Ottó Múzeum Évkönyve* 37, 499–518.

Kubinyi, A. 2000a, "König Sigismund und das ungarische Städtewesen," In *Das Zeitalter König Sigmunds in Ungarn und im Deutschen Reich*, eds. T. Schmidt and P. Gunst, 109–120. Debrecen: Universität Debrecen, Institut für Geschichtswissenschaften.

Kubinyi, A. 2000b, *Városfejlődés és vásárhálózat a középkori Alföldön és az Alföld szélén* [Urban development and the network of markets in the Great Hungarian Plain and its periphery in the Middle Ages] (Dél-alföldi Évszázadok, 14). Szeged: Csongrád Megyei Levéltár.

Kubinyi, A. 2000c, "Politika és honvédelem a Jagellók Magyarországában," [Politics and defense policy in Jagiellonian Hungary] *Hadtörténelmi Közlemények* 111, 397–416.

Kubinyi, A. 2001a, "Vásárok a középkori Zala megyében," [Markets in medieval Zala county] In *Zala megye ezer éve. Tanulmánykötet a magyar államalapítás millenniumának tiszteletére* [A millennium of Zala county. Collected essay in honor of the millennium of the Hungarian state formation], ed. L. Kostyál, 53–60. [Zalaegerszeg]: Zala Megyei Múzeumok Igazgatósága.

Kubinyi, A. 2001b, "A császárvári uradalom közbecsü összeírása 1489-ből," [The land estimation of the Cesargrad estate] *Történelmi Szemle* 43, 3–17.

Kubinyi, A. 2003–2004, "Tárcai János, az utolsó székelyispán (Genealógiai és prozopográfiai tanulmány)," [János Tárcai, the last count of Seclers (Genealogical a prosopographical study] *Mediaevalia Transilvanica* 7–8, 117–138.

Kubinyi, A. 2004a, "Hungary's Power Factions and the Turkish Threat in the Jagiellonian Period (1490–1526)," In *Fight Against the Turk in Central-Europe in the First Half of the 16th Century*, ed. I. Zombori, 117–145. Budapest: METEM.

Kubinyi, A. 2004b, "Székesfehérvár helye a késő középkori Magyarország városhálózatában, valamint Fejér vármegye központi helyei között," [The place of Székesfehérvár in the urban network of late medieval Hungary and among the central places of Fejér County] In *Változatok a történelemre. Tanulmányok Székely György tiszteletére* [Versions of history. Studies in honor of György Székely] (Monumenta Historica Budapestinensia, 14), eds. Gy. Erdei and B. Nagy, 277–284. Budapest: Budapesti Történeti Múzeum – ELTE BTK Középkori és Kora Újkori Egyetemes Történeti Tanszék.

Kubinyi, A. 2004c, "Városhálózat a késő középkori Kárpát-medencében," [Urban network in the Carpathian Basin in the Late Middle Ages] *Történelmi Szemle* 46, 1–30.

Kubinyi, A. 2005, "Városhálózat a késő középkori Kárpát-medencében," [Urban network in late medical Carpathian Basin] In *Bártfától Pozsonyig. Városok a 13–17. században* [From Bardejov to Bratislava. Cities in the 13th–17th century] (Társadalom- és Művelődéstörténeti Tanulmányok, 35), eds. E. Csukovits and T. Lengyel, 9–36. Budapest: MTA Történettudományi Intézet.

Kubinyi, A. 2006a, "'Szabad királyi város'–'Királyi szabad város'?," ["Free royal town" – "royal free town"?] *Urbs. Magyar Várostörténeti Évkönyv* 1, 51–61.

Kubinyi, A. 2006b, "Okleveles adatok a késő középkor mindennapi életéről," [Charter data to the everyday life of the late medieval period] *Borsod-Abaúj-Zemplén megye. Levéltári Évkönyv* 14, 13–22.

Kubinyi, A. 2007, "Politika és honvédelem a Jagellók Magyarországában," [Policy and national defense in the Jagiellonian Hungary] In idem, *Nándorfehérvártól Mohácsig. A Mátyás és Jagelló-kor hadtörténete* [From Belgrade to Mohács. Military history in the period of King Mathias and the Jagiellonians], 216–232. Budapest: Argumentum.

Kubinyi, A. 2008, "Die Fleischerzunft zu Ofen im Mittelalter," In *Zunftbuch und Privilegien der Fleischer zu Ofen aus dem Mittelalter* (Quellen zur Budapester Geschichte im Mittelalter und in der Frühen Neuzeit, 1), ed. I. Kenyeres, 87–138. Budapest: Budapest Főváros Levéltára – Budapesti Történeti Múzeum.

Kubinyi, A. 2009a, "Buda kezdetei," [The beginnings of Buda] In idem, *Tanulmányok Budapest középkori történetéről*, I [Studies on the medieval history of Budapest], eds. I. Kenyeres, P. Kis and Cs. Sasfi, 43–100. Budapest: Budapest Főváros Levéltára.

Kubinyi, A. 2009b, "A budai német patriciátus társadalmi helyzete családi összeköttetései tükrében a 13. századtól a 15. század második feléig," [The social status of the Geman patriciate of Buda as reflected in their family connections from the thirteenth until the second half of the 15th century] In idem, *Tanulmányok Budapest középkori történetéről*, II [Studies on the medieval history of Budapest], eds. I. Kenyeres, P. Kis and Cs. Sasfi, 457–512. Budapest: Budapest Főváros Levéltára.

Kubinyi, A. 2009c, "Budai és pesti polgárok családi összeköttetései a Jagelló-korban," [Family alliances of Buda and Pest burghers in the Jagiellonian period] In idem, *Tanulmányok Budapest középkori történetéről*, II [Studies on the medieval history of Budapest], eds. I. Kenyeres, P. Kis and Cs. Sasfi, 513–570. Budapest: Budapest Főváros Levéltára.

Kubinyi, A. 2009d, "Budai kereskedők udvari szállításai a Jagelló-korban," [Court supply of Buda merchants in the Jagiellonian period] In idem, *Tanulmányok Budapest középkori történetéről*, I [Studies on the medieval history of Budapest], eds. I. Kenyeres, P. Kis and Cs. Sasfi, 337–359. Budapest: Budapest Főváros Levéltára.

Kubinyi, A. and Laszlovszky, J. (eds.) 1991, *Alltag und materielle Kultur im mittelalterlichen Ungarn*. Special issue of: *Medieum Aevum Quotidianum* 22.

Kubinyi, A. and Laszlovszky, J. 2008, "Völker und Kulturen im mittelalterlichen Ungarn," In *Kontinuitäten und Brüche: Zuwanderer und Alteingesessene von 500 bis 1500* (Wieser Enzyklopädie des europäischen Ostens, 12), eds. K. Kaser, D. Gramshammer-Hohl, M. J. Piskorski and E. Vogel, 397–403. Klagenfurt: Wieser.

Kubinyi, A., Laszlovszky, J. and Szabó, P. (eds.) 2008, *Gazdaság és gazdálkodás a középkori Magyarországon: gazdaságtörténet, anyagi kultúra, régészet* [Economy and farming in medieval Hungary: economic history, material culture, archaeology]. Budapest: Martin Opitz.

Kumorovitz, L. B. 1980, "Szent László vásártörvénye és Kálmán király pecsétes cartulája," [The market decree of St Ladislas and the bulla of King Coloman] In *Athleta Patriae. Tanulmányok Szent László történetéhez* [Studies to the history of St Ladislas], ed. L. Mezey, 85–109. Budapest: Szent István Társulat.

Kurecskó, M. and Stossek, B. 2006, "A Szent Sír Kanonokrend Magyarországon," [The Order of the Holy Sepulchre in Hungary] In *Magyarország és a keresztes háborúk. Lovagrendek és emlékeik* [Hungary and the crusades. Chivalric orders and their monuments], eds. J. Laszlovszky, J. Majorossy and J. Zsengellér, 211–222. Máriabesnyő: Attraktor.

Kvassay, J. and Vörös, I. 2010, "Az Árpád-kori Kolon falu kovácsműhelyének archaeozoológiai bizonyítékai," [Archaeozoological evidence of a blacksmith's workshop from Árpádian-age Kolon village] In *Csont és bőr. Az állati eredetű nyersanyagok feldolgozásának története, régészete és néprajza* [Bone and leathe. History, archaeology and ethnography of crafts utilizing raw materials from animals], eds. J. Gömöri and A. Kőrösi, 127–141. Budapest: Line Design.

Lacko, M. and Mayerová, E., 2016, *Das älteste Stadtbuch von Schmöllnitz 1410–1735. Eine Quelle zu den mitteleuropäischen Verflechtungen*. [Bratislava]: Slovenská spoločnosť pre sociálne a hospodárske dejiny.

Laczlavik, Gy. 2004, "Várday Pál esztergomi érsek, királyi helytartó pályafutásának kezdete," [The beginning of the career of Pál Várday, archbishop of Esztergom, royal lieutenant] *Levéltári Közlemények* 75, 3–43.

Ladányi, E. 1977, "Libera villa, civitas, oppidum. Terminologische Fragen in der ungarischen Städteentwicklung," *Annales Universitatis Scientiarum Budapestinensis de Rolando Eötvös Nominatae. Sectio Historica* 18, 3–43.

Lakatos, B. 2013, *Hivatali írásbeliség és ügyintézés a késő középkori magyarországi mezővárosokban, okleveleik tükrében* [Official local written culture and administration in late medieval Hungarian market towns, in the mirror of their charters]. Unpublished PhD-dissertation. defended at ELTE, Budapest.

Langdon, J. 1991, "Water-mills and windmills in the West Midlands, 1086–1500," *The Economic History Review* 44, 424–444.

Langdon, J. 2004, *Mills in the Medieval Economy. England 1300–1540*. Oxford: Oxford University Press.

Langó, P. 2005, "Archaeological research on the conquering Hungarians: A review," In *Research on the Prehistory of the Hungarians: a Review*, ed. B. G. Mende, 175–340. Budapest: Archeological Institut of the HAS.

László, A. 1977, "Anfänge der Benutzung und der Bearbeitung des Eisens auf dem Gebiete Rumäniens," *Acta Archaeologica Academiae Scientiarum Hungaricae* 9, 53–75.

László, Gy. 1944, *A honfoglaló magyar nép élete* [Life of Conquest-age Hungarians]. Kolozsvár: Magyar Élet.

László, Gy. 1962, "Die Anfänge der ungarischen Münzprägung," *Annales Universitatis Scientiarum Budapestiensis de Rolando Eötvös Nominatae. Sectio Historica* 4, 27–53.

Laszlovszky, J. 1986, "Einzelhofsiedlungen in der Arpadenzeit: Arpadenzeitliche Siedlung auf der Mark von Kengyel," *Acta Archaeologica Academiae Scientiarum Hungaricae* 38, 227–257.

Laszlovszky, J. 1991, "Social Stratification and Material Culture in 10th–14th Century Hungary," *Medium Aevum Quotidianum* 22, 32–68.

Laszlovszky, J. 1994, "'Per tot discrimina rerum' Zur Interpretation von Umweltveränderungen im mittelalterlichen Ungarn," In *Umweltbewältigung. (Die historische Perspektive*), eds. G. Jaritz and V. Winiwarter, 37–55. Bielefeld: Verlag für Regionalgeschichte.

Laszlovszky, J. 1995, "Frühstädtische Siedlungsentwicklung in Ungarn," In *Burg, Burgstadt, Stadt. Zur Genese mittelalterlicher nichtagrarischer Zentren in Ostmitteleuropa*, ed. H. Brachmann, 307–316. Berlin: Akademie Verlag.

Laszlovszky, J. 1999, "Field Systems in Medieval Hungary," In *The Man of Many Devices Who Wandered Full Many Ways ... Festschrift in Honor of János Bak*, eds. B. Nagy and M. Sebők, 432–444. Budapest–New York: CEU Press.

Laszlovszky, J. 2003, "Space and Place, Object and Text: Human-Nature Interaction and Topographical studies," In *People and Nature in Historical Perspective* (CEU Medievalia, 5), eds. idem and P. Szabó, 81–105. Budapest: CEU Press.

Laszlovszky, J. 2004, "Középkori kolostorok a tájban, középkori kolostortájak," [Medieval Monasteries in the Landscape, Medieval Monastic Landscapes] In *"Quasi liber et pictura." Tanulmányok Kubinyi András hetvenedik születésnapjára / Studies in Honour of András Kubinyi on His Seventieth Birthday*, ed. Gy. Kovács, 337–349. Budapest: ELTE Régészettudományi Intézet = Institute of Archaeological Sciences of Eötvös Loránd University.

Laszlovszky, J. 2009, "Crown, Gown and Town: Zones of Royal, Ecclesiastical and Civic Interaction in Medieval Buda and Visegrad," In *Segregation–Integration–Assimilation. Religious and Ethnic Groups in the Medieval Towns of Central and Eastern Europe*, eds. D. Keene, B. Nagy and K. Szende, 179–203. Farnham–Burlington: Ashgate.

Laszlovszky, J. 2010, "Fama sanctitatis and the Emergence of St. Margaret's Cult in the Rural Countryside. The Canonization Process and Social Mobility in Thirteenth-Century Hungary," In *Promoting the Saints. Cults and Their Contexts from Late Antiquity until the Early Modern Period. Essays in Honor of Gábor Klaniczay for His 60th Birthday*, eds. O. Gecser et al., 103–123. Budapest–New York: CEU Press.

Laszlovszky, J., Mérai, D., Szabó, B. and Varga, M. 2014, "The 'Glass Church' in the Pilis Mountains. The Long and Complex History of an Árpád Period Village Church," *Hungarian Archaeology* no. 4, 1–11. Online document: http://www.hungarianarchaeology.hu/wp-content/uploads/2015/ 01/Laszlovszky_ E14 T.pdf (last accessed: 7 October 2016).

Laszlovszky, J., Miklós, Zs., Romhányi, B. and Szende, K. 2003, "The Archaeology of Hungary's Medieval Towns," In *Hungarian Archaeology at the Turn of the Millennium*, eds. Zs. Visy and M. Nagy, 364–372. Budapest: Ministry of National Cultural Heritage – Teleki László Foundation.

Laszlovszky, J. and Stark, K. 2017, "Medieval Glass Production at Pomáz-Nagykovácsi: The Finds and Heritage Interpretation of an Archaeological Site," *Annual of Medieval Studies at CEU* 23, 239–264.

Laszlovszky, J., Pow, S. and Pusztai, T. 2016, "Reconstructing the Battle of Muhi and the Mongol Invasion of Hungary in 1241: New Archaeological and Historical Approaches," *Hungarian Archaeology* no. 4, 1–10.

Le Roy Ladurie, E. and Morineau, M. 1977, *Histoire economique et sociale de la France*, I/2. Paris: Presses universitaires de France.

Lederer, E. 1934, "Bártfa város vászonszövő üzeme a XV. században," [The manufacture of linen-weavers in Bardejov in the 15th century] *A Bécsi Magyar Történeti Intézet Évkönyve*, 150–158. Budapest.

Lederer, E. 1959, *A feudalizmus kialakulása Magyarországon* [The formation of feudalism in Hungary]. Budapest: Akadémiai.

Lékai, L. J. 1977, *The Cistercians: Ideals and Reality*. Kent: Kent State University.

Lengyel, A. 2013, *Gold Book 1325–1540. Hungarian Medieval Coinage*. Budapest: Hungarian National Museum – Pannonia Terra Numizmatika.

Lengyel, T. 2003, "A koraújkori mezővárosok kutatásának problémái Szlovákiában," [The problems of the study of early modern market towns in Slovakia] In *Várostörténet, helytörténet. Elmélet és módszertan* [Urban history, local history. Theory and practice] (Tanulmányok Pécs történetéből, 14), ed. J. Vonyó, 79–85. Pécs: Pécs Története Alapítvány.

Lichtenstein, L. and Tugya, B. 2009, "Adatok a XII. század végi Orosháza iparához. Egy csontmegmunkáló műhely hulladékanyaga," [Data on the late-12th-century bone industry of Orosháza. Bone manufacturing refuse from a workshop] In *Csontvázak a szekrényből. Skeletons from the Cupboard*, eds. L. Bartosiewicz, E. Gál and I. Kováts, 251–263. Budapest: Martin Opitz.

Lóczy, D. 2007, "The changing geomorphology of Danubian floodplains in Hungary," *Hrvatski Geografski Glaznik* 69/2, 5–20.

Lovag, Zs. 1971, "Byzantine Type Reliquary Pectoral Crosses in the Hungarian National Museum," *Folia Archaeologica* 22, 143–164.

Lovag, Zs. 1979, *Mittelalterliche Bronzekunst in Ungarn*. Budapest: Corvina.

Lovag, Zs. 1980, "Bronzene Pektoralkreuze aus der Arpadenzeit," *Acta Archaeologica Academiae Scientiarum Hungaricae* 32, 363–372.

Lovag, Zs. 1984, *Aquamanilék* [Aquamaniles]. Budapest: Múzsák Közmüvelödési Kiadó.

Lovag, Zs. 1994, "Vortragekreuz," In *Pannonia Regia. Művészet a Dunántúlon, 1000–1541. Katalógus* [Pannonia regia. Art in the Transdanubia. Catalogue], eds. I. Takács and Á. Mikó, 198–199 and 568. Budapest: Magyar Nemzeti Galéria.

Lovag, Zs. 1999, *Mittelalterliche Bronzegegenstände des Ungarischen Nationalmuseums*. Budapest: Fekete Sas.

Lővei, P. 1991, "Mittelalterliche Grabdenkmäler in Buda," In *Budapest im Mittelalter*, ed. G. Biegel, 353–354. Braunschweig: Braunschweigisches Landesmuseum.

Lukačka, J. 2005, "Költöző polgárok a középkorban. A polgárság mobilitása a mai Szlovákia délnyugati területén, a Dunántúlon és Alsó-Ausztriában," [Moving burghers in the Middle Ages. The mobility of burghers in the southwestern part of present-day Slovakia, Transdanubia and Lower-Austria] In *Bártfától Pozsonyig. Városok a 13–17. századba*n [From Bardejov to Bratislava. Cities in the 13th–17th century] (Társadalom- és Művelődéstörténeti Tanulmányok, 35), eds. E. Csukovits and T. Lengyel, 123–130. Budapest: MTA Történettudományi Intézet.

Lukcsics, P. 1923, *A vásárhelyi apácák története* [History of the nuns of Vásárhely]. Veszprém: Egyházmegyei Könyvnyomda.

Lupescu Makó, M. 2001, "'*Item lego*.' Gifts for the soul in late medieval Transylvania," *Annual of Medieval Studies at the CEU* 7, 161–185.

Lyublyanovics, K. 2008. *Before the cattle trade. Animals and people in Muhi, a medieval Hungarian village*. Unpublished MA-Thesis defended at CEU, Budapest.

Lyublyanovics, K. 2015, *The Socio-Economic Integration of Cumans in Medieval Hungary. An Archaeozoological Approach*. Unpublished PhD-dissertation defended at CEU, Budapest.

Lyublyanovics, K. 2016, "A kunok állattartása," [Cuman animal husbandry] In *Török nyelvű népek a középkori Magyar Királyságban* [Turkic-speaking peoples in the medieval Kingdom of Hungary] (Altajisztikai Tankönyvtár, 6), eds. Sz. Kovács and I. Zimonyi, 137–143. Szeged: SZTE Altajisztikai Tanszék.

Lyublyanovics, K. 2017, *New Home, New Herds: Cuman Integration and Animal Husbandry in Medieval Hungary from an Archaeozoological Perspective* (Central European Archaeological Heritage Series, 10). Oxford: Archaeopress.

MacGregor, A. 1985, *Bone, Antler, Ivory and Horn. The Technology of Skeletal Materials since the Roman Period*. London–Sidney: Croom Helm.

Magyar, E. 1983, *A feudalizmus kori erdőgazdálkodás az alsó-magyarországi bányavárosokban (1255–1747)* [Woodland management in Lower-Hungarian mining towns during the feudal period (1255–1747)]. Budapest: Akadémiai.

Major, J. 1966, "A magyar városok és városhálózat kialakulásának kezdetei," [Hungarian cities and the beginnings of the formation of urban network] *Településtudományi Közlemények* 18, 48–90.

Majorossy, J. 2006, *Church in Town: Urban Religious Life in Late Medieval Pressburg in the Mirror of Last Wills*, PhD-dissertation defended at CEU, Budapest. Forthcoming in print by CEU press in 2018.

Majorossy, J. and Szende, K. 2008, "Hospitals in Medieval and Early Modern Hungary," In *Europäisches Spitalwesen. Institutionelle Fürsorge in Mittelalter und Früher Neuzeit* (Mitteilungen des Instituts für Österreichische Geschichtsforschung, Ergänzungsband, 51), eds. M. Scheutz et al., 409–454. Wien–München: Oldenbourg.

Majorossy, J. and Szende, K. 2012, "Libri civitatum. Városkönyvek a középkori Magyar Királyság közigazgatásában," [Town books in the administration of medieval Hungary] In *Tiszteletkör: Történeti tanulmányok Draskóczy István egyetemi tanár 60. születésnapjára* [Lap of honor. Studies in honor of Professor István Draskóczy on his 60th birthday], eds. G. Mikó, B. Péterfi and A. Vadas, 319–330. Budapest: ELTE Eötvös Kiadó.

Makkai, L. 1957, "A mezővárosi földhasználat kialakulásának kérdései (A „telkes" és „kertes" földhasználat a XIII–XV. században)," [Questions of the medieval land-use patterns of market towns (The "telek" and "kert" based land-use in the 13th–15th centuries)] In *Emlékkönyv Kelemen Lajos születésének nyolcvanadik évfordulójára* [Memorial volume in honor of the 80th birthday of Lajos Kelemen], eds. A. Bodor et al., 463–478. Bucharest: Tudományos.

Makkai, L. 1961, "A magyar városfejlődés történetének vázlata," [An Outline of the Development of Hungarian Towns] In *Vidéki városaink* [Countryside towns in Hungary], ed. J. Borsos, 25–76. Budapest: Közgazdasági és Jogi Kiadó.

Makkai, L. 1971, "Der ungarische Viehhandel 1550–1650," In *Der Außenhandel Ostmitteleuropas 1450–1650: Die ostmitteleuropäischen Volkswirtschaften in ihren Beziehungen zu Mitteleuropa*, ed. I. Bog, 483–506. Köln: Böhlau.

Makkai, L. 1974, "Östliches Erbe und westliche Leihe in der ungarischen Landwirtschaft der frühfeudalen Zeit, 10–13. Jahrhundert," *Agrártörténeti Szemle* 16 (Supplementum), 1–53.

Makkai, L. 1988, "Hungary in the Middle Ages," In *One Thousand Years: A Consice History of Hungary*, ed. P. Hanák, 9–65. Budapest: Corvina.

Makkai, L. 1995, "A malom mint a középkori Európa erő- és munkagépe," [The mill, as the prime mover of medieval Europe] In *Műszaki innovációk sorsa Magyarországon (malomipar-vaskohászat-textilipar)* [Technological innovations in Hungary (milling – iron-smelting – textile industry)], ed. W. Endrei, 29–35. Budapest: Akadémiai.

Maksay, F. (ed.) 1990, *Magyarország birtokviszonyai a 16. század közepén* [The estate-structure of Hungary in the middle of the 16th century] (A Magyar Országos Levéltár kiadványai. II. Forráskiadványok, 16). Budapest: Magyar ORszágos Levéltár.

Maksay, F. 1957, "Urbáriumok," [Terriers] In *A történeti statisztika forrásai* [Sources of historical statistics], ed. J. Kovacsics, 119–144. Budapest: Közgazdasági és Jogi Könyvkiadó.

Maksay, F. 1962, "Gabonatermesztés Nyugatmagyarországon a XV–XVI. század fordulóján," [Grain production in western Hungary at the turn of the 15th century] *Agrártörténeti Szemle* 4, 14–24.

Maksay, F. 1971, *A középkori magyar falu településrendje* [The structure of villages in medieval Hungary]. Budapest: Akadémiai.

Maksay, F. 1972, "Benedekrendi gazdálkodás Tihanyban a XIII–XIV. századi strukrúraváltás idején," [Benedictine farming at Tihany in the time of the 13th–14th-century structural changes] *Somogy Megye Múltjából* 3, 1–47.

Maksay, F. 1975, "Umwandlung der ungarischen Siedlungs- und Agrarstruktur (13.–14. Jahrhundert)," *Zeitschrift für Agrargeschichte und Agrarsoziologie* 23, 154–164.

Maksay, F. 1978, "Das Agrarsiedlungssystem des mittelalterlichen Ungarn," *Acta Historica Academiae Scientiarum Hungaricae* 24, 83–108.

Mályusz, E. 1927, "Geschichte des Bürgertums in Ungarn," *Vierteljahrschrift für Sozial- und Wissenschaftgeschichte* 20, 356–407.

Mályusz, E. 1953a, "Az egyházi tizedkizsákmányolás," [Ecclesiastical tithe exploitation] In *Tanulmányok a parasztság történetéhez Magyarországon a 14. században* [Studies in the history of peasantry in 14th-century Hungary], ed. Gy. Székely, 320–333. Budapest: Akadémiai.

Mályusz, E. 1953b, "A mezővárosi fejlődés," [Market-town development] In *Tanulmányok a parasztság történetéhez Magyarországon a 14. században* [Studies in the history of peasantry in 14th-century Hungary], ed. Gy. Székely, 128–191. Budapest: Akadémiai.

Mályusz, E. 1958, "Az izmaelita pénzverőjegyek kérdéséhez," [On the problem of ismaelite mint marks] *Budapest Régiségei* 18, 301–309.

Mályusz, E. 1965, "Les débuts de vote de la taxe par les ordres dans la Hongrie féodale," In *Nouvelles Études Historiques publiées à l'occasion du XIIe Congrés International des Sciences Historiques par la Commission Nationale des Historiens Hongrois*, I, eds. D. Csatári, L. Katus and Á. Rozsnyói, 55–82. Budapest: Akadémiai.

Mályusz, E. 1984, *Zsigmond király uralma Magyarországon* [The reign of King Sigismund in Hungary]. Budapest: Gondolat.

Mályusz, E. 1985, "Der ungarische Goldgulden in Mitteleuropa zu Beginn des 15. Jahrhunderts," In *Études historique hongroises publiées à l'occasion du XVIe Congrès international des sciences historiques par la Comité national des historiens hongrois*, eds. D. Kosáry et al., 21–35. Budapest: Akadémiai.

Mályusz, E. 1986, "Bajorországi állatkivitelünk a XIV–XV. században," [Hungarian livestock export to Bavaria in the 14th–15th centuries] *Agrártörténeti Szemle* 28, 1–33.

Mályusz, E. 2007^2, *Egyházi társadalom a középkori Magyarországon* [Ecclesiastical society in medieval Hungary]. Budapest: Műszaki.

Mandelló, Gy. 1903, *Adalék a középkori munkabérek történetéhez* [To the history of wages in the Middle Ages] (Társadalom- és Gazdaságtörténeti Kutatások, 2). Budapest: Politzer és Fia.

Marczali, H. 1902, *A magyar történet kútfőinek kézikönyve* [Handbook of the sources of Hungarian history]. Budapest: Athenaeum Nyomda.

Marosi, E. 1999, "Probleme der Prager St. Georg-Statue aus dem Jahre 1373. The Question of the Prague Statue of St. George from 1373," *Časopis Ústavu Dějin Umění Akademie Věd České Republiky* 47, 389–399.

Marosi, E. 2009, "Stall from the Saint Aegidius parish church in Bártfa/Bardejov," In *On the Stage of Europe. The Millennial Contribution of Hungary to the Idea of European Community*, ed. idem, 75–77. Budapest: Research Institute for Art History of the Hungarian Academy of Sciences – Balassi.

Marton, T. and Serlegi, G. 2007, "Balatonlelle–Kenderföld," In *Gördülő idő. Régészeti feltárások az M7-es autópálya Somogy megyei szakaszán Zamárdi és Ordacsehi között* [Rolling time. Archaeological excavations at Somogy County-section of highway M7 between Zamárdi and Ordacsehi], eds. K. Belényesy et al., 139–146. Budapest– Kaposvár: Somogy Megyei Múzeumok Igazgatósága.

Máté, G. 2014, "A helyi úthálózat kutatásának néprajzi és településtörténeti kérdései," [The ethnographic and settlement-historical aspects of the research on the local networks of roads] *Etnographia* 125, 571–589.

Matolcsi, J. 1970, "Historische Erforschung der Körpergröße des Rindes auf Grund von ungarischem Knochenmaterial," *Zeitschrift für Tierzüchtung und Züchtungsbiologie* 87/2, 89–137.

Matolcsi, J. 1975a, "Sarud–Pócstöltés Árpád-kori állatcsont-leleteinek vizsgálata," [Studying the animal bone finds from the Árpádian-age settlement of Sarud– Pócstöltés] *Az Egri Múzeum Évkönyve* 13, 69–79.

Matolcsi, J. 1975b, *A háziállatok eredete* [The origins of domestic animals]. Budapest: Mezőgazdasági.

Matolcsi, J. 1977, "A budai királyi palota északi előudvarában feltárt XIV–XV. századi állatcsontok," [14th–15th-century animal bones unearthed at the northern forecourt of the royal palace of Buda] *Budapest Régiségei* 24, 179–198.

Matolcsi, J. 1981, "Mittelalterliche Tierknochen aus dem Dominikanerkloster in Buda," *Fontes Archaeologici Hungariae 1981*, 203–254.

Matolcsi, J. 1982a, *Állattartás őseink korában* [Animal keeping in the time of the ancestors of the Hungarians]. Budapest: Gondolat.

Matolcsi, J. 1982b, "Tierknochenfunde von Sarvaly aus dem 15.–16. Jahrhundert," In I. Holl and N. Parádi, *Das mittelalterliche Dorf Sarvaly*, 230–253. Budapest: Akadémiai.

Matschinegg, I. and Müller, A, 1990, "Migration – Wanderung – Mobilität in Spätmittelalter und in der Frühneuzeit. Eine Auswahlbibliographie," *Medium Aevum Quotidianum* 21, 7–92.

Mátyás, B. 2014, "Az Árpád-kori magyarországi muszlimok eredete," [Origin of Árpádian-age Muslims in Hungary] *Fons* 21, 315–329.

Melis, F. 1962, *Aspetti della vita economica medievale: studi nell'archivio Datini di Prato*, I. Firenze: Monte dei Paschi di Siena.

Mencl, V. 1938, *Středověká městá na Slovensku* [Medieval towns in Slovakia]. Bratislava: Universum.

Mendöl, T. 1963, *Általános településföldrajz* [Settlement geography]. Budapest: Akadémiai.

Méri, I. 1948, *A magyar nép régészeti emlékeinek kutatása (X–XVI. század)* [Research of the archaeological monuments of the Hungarians (10th–16th centuries)]. Budapest: Stephaneum.

Méri, I. 1954/1956, "Beszámoló a Tiszalök-rázompusztai és a Túrkeve-mórici ásatások eredményéről. I–II.," [Report of the excavations at Tiszalök-Rázompuszta and Túrkeve-Móric] *Archaeologiai Értesítő* 79, 49–65 and 81, 138–152.

Méri, I. 1962, "Az árkok szerepe Árpád–kori falvainkban," [Angaben zur Siedlungsform der Arpadenzeitlichen ungarischen Dörfer] *Archaeologiai Értesítő* 89, 211–218.

Méri, I. 1964, *Árpád-kori népi építkezésünk feltárt emlékei Orosháza határában* [The excavated remains of Árpádian-age vernacular architecture of Hungarians in the borders of Orosháza] (Régészeti füzetek Ser. II, 12). Budapest: Magyar Nemzeti Múzeum.

Méri, I. 1969–1970, "Árpád–kori falusi gabonaörlő és kenyérsütő berendezések," [Árpádian-age quern stones and ovens] *Magyar mezőgazdasági Múzeum Közleményei 1969–1970*, 69–84.

Mester, E. 1997, *Középkori üvegek* [Medieval glass finds] (Visegrád Régészeti Monográfiái, 2). Visegrád: MNM Mátyás Király Múzeuma.

Mester, E. 2010, "Üvegművesség a középkorban és a kora újkorban," [Glass art in the Middle Ages and the Early Modern period] In *A középkor es a kora újkor régészete Magyarországon / Archaeology of the Middle Ages and the Early Modern Period in Hungary*, II, eds. E. Benkő and Gy. Kovács, 643–674. Budapest: MTA Régészeti Intézete.

Mesterházy, K. 1986, "Az Örsúr nemzetség Váralja faluja," [The Örsúr clan's village: Váralja] In *Falvak, mezővárosok az Alföldön* [Villages and market towns at the Great Hungarian Plain] (Az Arany János Múzeum Közleményei, 4), eds. L. Novák and L. Selmeczi, 85–104. Nagykőrös: Arany János Múzeum.

Mesterházy, K. 1990/1991, "Bizánci és balkáni eredetű tárgyak a 10–11. századi magyar sírleletekben," [Objects Byzantine and Balkan origin in 10th–11th century Hungarian burials] *Folia Archaeologica* 41, 87–115 and 42, 145–177.

Mesterházy, K. 1993, "Régészeti adatok Magyarország 10–11. századi kereskedelméhez," [Archaeological data to the trade of Hungary in the 10th–11th centuries] *Századok* 127, 450–468.

Mesterházy, K. 2014, "Lotus bud and palmette," In L. Révész, *The Era of the Hungarian conquest. Permanent Exhibition of the Hungarian National Museum*, 107–109. Budapest: Hungarian National Museum.

Mészáros, L. 1979, "Kecskemét gazdasági élete és népe a 16. század közepén," [Economic life in the town of Kecskemét in the mid-16th century] *Bács-Kiskun Megye Múltjából* 2, 58–286.

Mészáros, O. 2008, "Archaeological Remains of the Medieval Glass Workshop in the 15th-Century Royal Residence Visegrád, Hungary," In *Glashüttenlandschaft Europa. Beiträge zum 3. Internationalen Glassymposium in Heigenbrücken/Spessart*, eds. H. Flachenecker, G. Himmelsbach and P. Steppuhn, 168–172. Regensburg: Schnell & Steiner.

Mészáros, O. and Serlegi, G. 2011, "The Impact of Environmental Change on Medieval Settlement Structure in Transdanubia," *Acta Archaeologica Academiae Scientiarum Hungaricae* 62, 199–219.

Mészáros, O. and Szőke, M. 2008, "The Fifteenth-Century Glass Workshop in Visegrád," In *Matthias Corvinus, the King. Tradition and Renewal in the Hungarian Royal Court,*

1458–1490. Exhibition catalogue, eds. P. Farbaky et al., 345–347. Budapest: Budapest History Museum.

Mészöly, G. 1908. "A -vány, -vény képző eredete," [The origins of the suffix *-vány, -vény*] *Magyar Nyelv* 4, 410–414.

Mezey, L. 1979, *Deákság és Európa. Irodalmi műveltségünk alapvetésének vázlata* [Students and Europe. An outline of the foundation of our literary culture]. Budapest: Akadémiai.

Mező, A. 1996, *A templomcím a magyar helységnevekben (11–15. század)* [Church names in Hungarian placenames]. Budapest: Magyar Egyháztörténeti Enciklopédia Munkaközösség.

Miklós, Zs. 1985, "Középkori épület és kőbánya a nagymarosi Malom-völgyben," [Medieval house and stone quarry in the Malom valley at Nagymaros] *Studia Comitatensia* 17, 479–498.

Miklós, Zs. 1997a, "Die Holzfunde aus dem Brunnen des Spätmittelalterlichen Paulinerklosters von Márianosztra-Toronyalja," *Acta Archaeologica Academiae Scientiarum Hungaricae* 49, 103–138.

Miklós, Zs. 1997b, "Falvak, várak, kolostorok a Dél-Börzsönyben," [Villages, castles, monasteries in the southern Börzsöny] *Váci Könyvek* 8, 7–154.

Miklós, Zs. 2002, "Dombóvár, Szigeterdő – Medieval Brick-kiln," In *Archaeological Investigations in Hungary 1999*, ed. E. Marton, 155–163. Budapest: Kulturális Örökségvédelmi Hivatal.

Miklós, Zs. 2005, "Spätmittelalterliches Eisendepot aus dem mittelalterlichen Marktflecken Decs-Ete," *Acta Archaeologica Academiae Scientiarum Hungaricae* 56, 279–310.

Miklós, Zs. and Vizi, M. 1994, "Beiträge zur Siedlunggeschichte des mittelalterlichen Marktflecksen Ete," *Acta Archaeologica Academiae Scientiarum Hungaricae* 53, 195–253.

Mikó, Zs. (ed.) 1995, *Mezőváros – kisváros. A Hajnal István Kör keszthelyi konferenciája, 1990. június 23–25*. [Market town – small town. The conference of the István Hajnal circle in Keszthely, 23–25 June 1990] (Rendi társadalom – polgári társadalom, 4). Debrecen: Csokonai.

Mirnik, I. A. 1981, *Coin Hoards in Yugoslavia* (BAR International Series, 95). Oxford: B.A.R.

Miskei, A. 2003, *Ráckeve története I. Ráckeve története a kezdetektől 1848-ig* [The history of Ráckeve I. Ráckeve from its beginnings to 1848]. Ráckeve: Ráckeve Város Önkormányzata.

Mollay, K. 1982, *Német-magyar nyelvi érintkezések a XVI. század végéig* [German-Hungarian linguistic connections until the end of the 16th century] (Nyelvészeti Tanulmányok, 23). Budapest: Akadémiai.

Mollay, K. 1990, "Magyarország nyugati külkereskedelme a 16. század közepén," [The Western trade of Hungary at the middle of the 16th century] *Soproni Szemle* 44, 228–248.

Mollay, K. 1991, "Kereskedők, kalmárok, árusok Moritz Pál Kalmár (1511–1530.)," [Dealers, Merchants and sellers. Paul Moritz merchant (1511–1530)] *Soproni Szemle* 45, 1–32.

Mollay, K. 1992. "A Tómalom középkori előzményei," [The medieval predecessors of the Teichmühle] *Soproni Szemle* 46, 150–167.

Mordovin, M. 2006, "The Building History of Zalavár-Récéskút Church," *Annual of Medieval Studies at CEU* 12, 9–32.

Mordovin, M. 2013, "A 15–17. századi távolsági textilkereskedelem régészeti emlékei Pápán," [Archaeological remains of 15th–17th-century long-distance textile trade at Pápa] In *Fiatal középkoros régészek IV. konferenciájának tanulmánykötete* [Study volume of the 4th conference of young medieval archaeologists], ed. M. Varga, 267–282. Kaposvár: Rippl-Rónai Megyei Hatókörű Városi Múzeum.

Mordovin, M. 2014, "Late Medieval and Early Modern Cloth Seals in the Collection of the Hungarian National Museum," *Archaeologiai Értesítő* 139, 193–237.

Mortier, R. P. 1909, *Histoire des maîtres généraux de l'Ordre des Frères Prêcheurs, IV, 1400–1486*. Paris: Picard.

Mravcsik, Z. et al. 2015, "Digital seed morphometry for genotype identification – case study of seeds of excavated (15th century Hungary) and current vinegrape (Vitis v. vinifera) varieties," *Acta Botanica Hungarica* 57, 169–182.

Müller, R. 1975, "Die Datierung der mittelalterlichen Eisengerätenfunde in Ungarn," *Acta Archaeologica Academiae Scientiarum Hungaricae* 27, 59–102.

Müller, R. 1980, "Die bosnische Sense," *Acta Archaeologica Academiae Scientiarum Hungaricae* 32, 437–442.

Müller, R. 1981, "Mészégető kemencék Magyarországon. On lime kilns fount in Hungary," In *Iparrégészeti kutatások Magyarországon (Égetőkemencék régészeti és interdiszciplináris kutatása)* [Industrial archaeological research in Hungary (Archaeological and interdisciplinary study of kilns)], ed. J. Gömöri, 55–65. Veszprém: MTA, Veszprémi Akadémiai Bizottságának Történelmi Szakbizottsága.

Müller, R. 1982, *A mezőgazdasági vaseszközök fejlődése Magyarországon a késővaskortól a törökkor végéig*, I–II [Die Entwicklung der eisernen Agrargeräte in Ungarn von der Späteisenzeit bis zum Ende der Türkenherrschaft] (Zalai Gyűjtemény, 19). Zalaegerszeg: Zala Megyei Levéltár.

Müller, R. 2014, "A középkor agrotechnikája a vaseszközök alapján," [Agricultural techniques in the Middle Ages in the light of iron tools] *Ethnographia* 125 (2014): 1–19.

Nagy, Á. 2003, "Brunnen und Zisternen im mittelalterlichen Ungarn," *Antaeus* 26, 343–371.

Nagy, B. (ed.) 2003, *Tatárjárás* [Mongol invasion]. Budapest: Osiris.

Nagy, B. 1999, "Transcontinental Trade from East-Central Europe to Western Europe (Fourteenth and Fifteenth centuries)," In *The Man of Many Devices Who Wandered Full Many Ways ... Festschrift in Honor of János M. Bak*, eds. idem and M. Sebők, 347–356. Budapest: CEU Press.

Nagy, B. 2009, "The Towns of Medieval Hungary in the Reports of Contemporary Travellers," In *Segregation-Integration-Assimilation: Religious and Ethnic Groups in the Medieval Towns of Central and Eastern Europe*, eds. D. Keene, B. Nagy, and K. Szende, 169–178. Farnham–Burlington: Ashgate.

Nagy, B. 2012, "The Study of Medieval Foreign Trade of Hungary: A Historiographical Overview," In *Cities – Coins – Commerce. Essays presented to Ian Blanchard on the Occassion of his 70th Birthday*, ed. Ph. R. Rössner, 65–75. Stuttgart: Franz Steiner.

Nagy, B. 2016, "Old Interpretations and New Approaches: The 1457–1458 Thirtieth Customs Registers of Bratislava," In *Money and Finance in Central Europe during the Later Middle Ages*, ed. R. Zaoral, 192–201. Basingstoke: Palgrave.

Nagy, B. et al. (eds.) 2016, *Medieval Buda in Context* (Brills's Companions to European History, 10). Leiden–Boston: Brill.

Nagy, B., Rady, M., Szende, K. and Vadas, A. 2016, "Introduction," In *Medieval Buda in Context* (Brill's Companions to European History, 10), eds. Balázs Nagy et al., 1–21. Leiden–Boston: Brill.

Nagy, L. [Without date], *A dunai árvizek és árterületek Budapest környékén az őskortól a magyar honfoglalás idejéig* (Manuscript) [The role Danube-floods in the surroundings of Buda from Pre-history to the Hungarian Conquest] Budapest Történeti Múzeum (Budapest History Museum), Régészeti Adattár (Collection of Archaeological Documentations), H. no. 206-79.

Nagy, L. 1973–1974, "Adatok a késő Árpád-kori pénzek kormeghatározásához," [Data on the dating coins from the late Árpádian age] *Numizmatikai Közlöny* 72–73, 43–47.

Nagy, P. T. 2016, "'Islamic' Artefacts in Hungary from the Reign of Béla III (1172–1196): Two Case Studies," *Annual of Medieval Studies at CEU* 22, 49–61.

Nagy, Z. and Szulovszky, J. (ed.) 2009, *A vasművesség évezredei a Kárpát-medencében* [Millennia of iron working in the Carpathian Basin]. Szombathely: MTA VEAB Kézművesipar-Történeti Munkabizottsága.

Németh, P. 1967, "Szabolcs és Szatmár megyék Árpád-kori (XI–XIII. századi) földvárai és monostorai," [Árpádian-age earthen castles and monasteries of Szabolcs and Szatmár Counties (11th–13th centuries)] *A Nyíregyházi Jósa András Múzeum Évkönyve* 10, 91–102.

Neumann, T. 2003, "Telekpusztásodás a késő középkori Magyarországon," [Plot-abandonement in late medieval Hungary] *Századok* 137, 849–884.

Neumann, T. 2017, "'Minden időkben kegyelmes uratok kívánunk lenni ...' A királyi városok adóztatása a 15. század végén," ['we plan to be your humble lords at all time ...' Taxation of royal towns at the end of the 15th century] In *Hatalom, adó, jog. Gazdaságtörténeti tanulmányok a magyar középkorról* [Power, tax, law. Studies on the economic history of medieval Hungary], eds. B. Weisz and I. Kádas, 13–106. Budapest: MTA BTK Történettudományi Intézet.

Niedermaier, P. 1997/1998/1999–2000, "Ortschaften des Siebenbürgischen Salzbergbaus im Mittelalter, I–III," *Forschungen zur Volks- und Landeskunde* 40, 118–145; 41, 9–20 and 42, 85–105.

Nógrády, Á. 1996, "Taxa – extraordinaria? Széljegyzetek Kanizsai László kapuvári-sárvári számadáskönyvének margójára," [Taxa – extraordinaria? Notes to the account book of Kapuvár–Sárvár of László Kanizsai] In *In memoriam Barta Gábor. Tanulmányok Barta Gábor emlékére* [Studies dedicated to the memory of Gábor Barta], ed. I. Lengvári, 125–149. Pécs: JPTE Továbbképző K. Irodája.

Nógrády, Á. 1998, "A paraszti napszámbér vásárlóértéke a középkor végi Magyarországon," [Purschasing value of peasant day-wages in late medieval Hungary] In *Szabó István emlékkönyv* [Memorial volume of István Szabó] ed. I. Rácz, 105–123. Debrecen: Kossuth Egyetemi Kiadó.

Nógrády, Á. 2001, "Paraszti telekhasználat és földbérlet a Kanizsaiak Sopron-környéki birtokain. (Csepreg 1522. évi összeírásai és a nagycenki Jankó István vagyona)," [Peasant ground use and land lease in the estates of the Kanizsai family around Sopron (The inventories of Csepreg in 1522 and the wealth of István Jankó of Nagycenk] *Soproni Szemle* 55, 361–368.

Nógrády, Á. 2002, "A földesúri pénzjáradék nagysága és adóterhe a késő középkori Magyarországon," [The amount and tax of feudal money dues in late medieval Hungary] *Századok* 136, 451–468.

Nógrády, Á. 2015, "Az elakadt fejlődés," [Hindered development] In *Keresztesekből lázadók. Tanulmányok 1514 Magyarországáról* [From crusaders to rebellers. Studies on Hungary in 1514], eds. N. C. Tóth and T. Neumann, 11–30. Budapest: MTA BTK Történettudományi Intézet.

North, M. 1996, "Von den Warenmessen zu den Wechselmessen. Grundlagen des europäischen Zahlungsverkehr in Spätmittelalter und Früher Neuzeit," In *Europäische Messen und Märktesysteme in Mittelalter und Neuzeit* (Städteforschung, A 39), eds. P. Johanek and H. Stoob, 223–238. Köln–Weimar–Wien: Böhlau.

Novák, K. I. 2001, "Kolozsvár város malmai a XVI. század végi számadások tükrében," [Urban mills of Cluj in the light of late 16th-century accounts] In *Areopolisz. Történelmi és társadalomtudományi tanulmányok* [Areopolis. Studies in history and social sciences], eds. G. M. Hermann and A. L. Róth, 84–91. Székelyudvarhely: Litera.

Nováki, Gy. 1969, "Archäologishe Denkmäler der Eisenverhüttung in Nordostungarn aus dem X.–XII. Jahrhundert," *Acta Archaeologica Academiae Scientiarum Hungaricae* 21, 299–331.

Nováki, Gy. 1984–1985, "Szántóföldek maradványai a XIV–XVI. századból a Sümeg-Sarvalyi erdőben," [Remains of fields from the 14th–16th centuries in forest at Sümeg-Sarvaly] *Magyar Mezőgazdasági Múzeum Közleményei 1984–1985*, 19–32.

Nyári, D. et al. 2006, "Az emberi tevékenység tájformáló hatása: futóhomok mozgások a történelmi időkben Apostag környékén," [Landcape changes induced by human activity: sand movement in historical times in the surroundings of Apostag] In *A táj változásai a Kárpát-medencében. Település a tájban* [Landscape changes in the Carpathian Basin. Settlements in the landscape], ed. Gy. Füleky, 170–176. Gödöllő: Környezetkímélő Agrokémiáért Alapítvány.

Nyári, D., Kiss, T. and Sipos, Gy. 2007, "Investigation of Holocene blown-sand movement based on archaeological findings and OSL dating, Danube-Tisza Interfluve, Hungary," *Journal of Maps* 3, 46–57.

Nyékhelyi, D. 2003, *Középkori kútlelet a budavári Szent György téren* [Medieval finds at the well of Szent György Square at Buda]. Budapest: Budapesti Történeti Múzeum.

O'Keeffe, T. and Yamin, R. 2006, "Urban Historical Archaeology," In *The Cambridge Companion to Historical Archaeology*, eds. D. Hicks and M. C. Beaudry, 87–103. Cambridge: Cambridge University Press.

Oberländer-Târnoveanu, E. 2003–2004, "A 13–16. századi magyar pénzverés emlékei nyugaton I. Korabeli itáliai, francia és katalán források," [Traces of 13th–16th-century Hungarian minting in the West. Part I. Contemporary Italian, French and Catalonian sources] *Numizmatikai Közlöny* 102–103, 45–56.

Ódor, J. G. 1998, "Anjou-kori öntőforma Majsról. (Adatok a 13–15. századi viselet történetéhez," [Casting mould from Majs from the Angevin period] *Communicationes Archaeologicae Hungariae 1998*, 123–137.

Ohler, N. 1989, *The Medieval Traveller*. Woodbridge: Boydell.

Olberg, G. 1984, "Pfleger," In *Handwörterbuch zur deutschen Rechtsgeschichte*, III, eds. A. Erler and E. Kaufmann, 1730–1733. Berlin: E. Schmidt.

Opll, F. 1996, "Jahrmarkt oder Messe? Überlegungen zur spätmittelalterlichen Handelsgeschichte Wiens," In *Europäische Messen und Märktesysteme in Mittelalter und Neuzeit* (Städteforschung, A 39), eds. P. Johanek and H. Stoob, 189–204. Köln–Weimar–Wien: Böhlau.

Ortvay, T. 1882, *Magyarország régi vízrajza a XIII. század végéig*, I–II [Old hydrograph of Hungary until the end of the 13th century]. Budapest: Akadémia.

Ortvay, T. 1891–1892, *Magyarország egyházi földleírása a XIV. század elején*, I–III [Ecclesiastical conscription of the lands of Hungary at the beginning of the 14th century]. Budapest: Franklin.

Oszvald, F. A. 1957, "Adatok a magyarországi premontreiek Árpád-kori történetéhez," [Data to the Árpádian-age history of Premonstratensians in Hungary] *Művészettörténeti Értesítő* 6, 231–254.

Out, W. A. 2010, "Firewood Collection Strategies at Dutch Wetland Sites in the Process of Neolithisation," *Holocene* 20, 191–204.

P. Hartyányi, B. and Nováki, Gy. 1967–1968, "Növényi mag- és termés leletek Magyarországon az újkőkortól a XVIII. századig. I.," [Plant seed and fruit remains in Hungary from the Neolithic to the 18th century] *Magyar Mezőgazdasági Múzeum Közleményei 1967–1968*, 5–58.

P. Hartyányi, B. and Nováki, Gy. 1973–1974, "Növényi mag- és termés leletek Magyarországon az újkőkortól a XVIII. századig. II.," [Plant seed and fruit remains in Hungary from the Neolithic to the 18th century] *Magyar Mezőgazdasági Múzeum Közleményei 1973– 1974*, 23–73.

Pach, Zs. P. (ed.) 1985, *Magyarország története*, III/1–2 (1526–1686) [The history of Hungary]. Budapest: Akadémiai.

Pach, Zs. P. 1963, *Nyugat-európai és magyarországi agrárfejlődés a XV–XVI. században* [Western Europe and the Hungarian agrarian development in the 15th–16th centuries]. Budapest: Kossuth.

Pach, Zs. P. 1964, *Die ungarische Agrarentwicklung im XVI–XVII. Jahrhundert: Abbiegung vom westeuropäischen Entwicklungsgang*. Budapest: Akadémiai.

Pach, Zs. P. 1972, "Egy évszázados történészvitáról: áthaladt-e a levantei kereskedelem útja a középkori Magyarországon?," [About a century-long debate of historians: did the Levantine trade route cross medieval Hungary?] *Századok* 106, 849–888.

Pach, Zs. P. 1975a, "A levantei kereskedelem erdélyi útvonala I. Lajos és Zsigmond korában," [The Transylvanian route of the Levantine trade during the reign of Louis I and Sigismund] *Századok* 109, 3–31.

Pach, Zs. P. 1975b, "La politica commerciale di Luigi d'Angió e il traffico delle 'mercanzie marittime' dopo la pace di Zara," In *Rapporti Veneto-Ungheresi all'Epoca del Rinascimento*, ed. T. Klaniczay, 105–119. Budapest: Akadémiai.

Pach, Zs. P. 1975c, *Levantine Trade and Hungary in the Middle Ages. Theses, Controversies, Arguments* (Studia historica Academiae scientiarum Hungaricae, 97). Budapest: Akadémiai.

Pach, Zs. P. 1990, *A harmincadvám eredete* [The origin of the thirtieth customs]. Budapest: Akadémiai.

Pach, Zs. P. 1991, "A közép-kelet-európai régió az újkor kezdetén," [East Central Europe and the beginning of the Modern times] *Budapesti Könyvszemle [BUKSZ]* 3, 351–361.

Pach, Zs. P. 1999, "A harmincadvám az Anjou-korban és a 14–15. század fordulóján," [The thirtieth-toll in the Angevin Period and at the turn of the 14th and 15th centuries] *Történelmi Szemle* 41, 231–277.

Pach, Zs. P. 2003, "Színesposztó és szürkeposztó a 13. századi Magyarországon," [Dyed cloth and grey cloth in 13th-century Hungary] In idem, *Szürkeposztó, szűrposztó, szűr. Fejezetek a magyarországi szövőipar történetéből* [Grey cloth, dyed cloth, cheap cloth. On the history of Hungarian textile industry], 9–17. Budapest: MTA Történettudományi Intézet.

Pach, Zs. P. 2007, "Hungary and the Levantine trade in the 14th–17th centuries," *Acta Orientalia Academiae Scientiarum Hungaricae* 60, 9–32.

Pais, D. 1933. "Hetevény," [Hetevény] *Magyar Nyelv* 29, 37–42.
Pakucs-Willcocks, M. 2007, *Sibiu – Hermannstadt. Oriental trade in Sixteenth Century Transylvania* (Städteforschung, A 73). Köln: Böhlau.
Paládi Kovács, A. 1979, *A magyar parasztság rétgazdálkodása* [Pasture economy of the Hungarians]. Budapest: Akadémiai.
Pálóczi Horváth, A. (ed.) 1996, *Élet egy középkori faluban. (25 év régészeti kutatása a 900 éves Szentkirályon)* [Life in a medieval village (25 years of archaeological research at the 900-year-old Szentkirály)]. Budapest: Magyar Mezőgazdasági Múzeum.
Pálóczi Horváth, A. 1980, "Le costume coman au Moyen âge," *Acta Archaeologica Academiae Scientiarum Hungaricae* 32, 403–427.
Pálóczi Horváth, A. 1989, *Pechenegs, Cumans, Iasians. Steppe Peoples in Medieval Hungary*. Budapest: Corvina.
Pálóczi Horváth, A. 1993, "A környezeti régészet szerepe Magyarországon a középkor kutatásában," [The role of environmental archaeology in Hungary in the study of the medieval period] In *Európa híres kertje. Történeti ökológiai tanulmányok Magyarországról* [The famous garden of Europe. Studies in environmental history from Hungary], eds. L. Kósa and Á. Várkonyi, R., 44–66. Budapest: Orpheusz.
Pálóczi Horváth, A. 1997, "The reconstruction of a Medieval (15th Century) House at Szentkirály. (Middle Hungary)," In *Zivot v archeologii Stredovëku. Das Leben in der Archäologie des Mittelalters. Life in the archaeology of the Middle Ages. La vie vue par l'archéologie médiévale. Sborník príspëvku vënovaných Miroslavu Richterovi (29. 5. 1932) a Zdenku Smetánkovi (21. 10. 1931). Festschrift für – Papers in honour of – Mélanges offerts à Miroslav Richter – Zdenek Smetánka*, eds. J. Kubková, J. Klápšte and M. Jezek, 507–513. Praha: Archeologický ústav Akademie vëd České republiky.
Pálóczi Horváth, A. 1998, "Variations morphologiques des villages désertés en Hongrie et la société rurale du moyen âge," In *Ruralia II. (Conference Ruralia II. – Spa, 1–7 September 1997)*, eds. J. Fridrich et al., 192–204. Prague: Institute of Archaeology.
Pálóczi Horváth, A. 2000a, "A Magyar Királyság mezőgazdasága a késő középkorban (A 13. századtól a mohácsi vészig)," [Agriculture of the Hungarian Kingdom in the Late Middle Ages (from the 13th to the battle of Mohács] In *A magyar mezőgazdaság 1000 éve. Rövid áttekintés* [1000 years of Hungarian agriculture. A short overview], ed. S. Oroszi, 23–46. Budapest: Magyar Mezőgazdasági Múzeum.
Pálóczi Horváth, A. 2000b, "Données démographiques sur la structure de l'habitat rural médiéval en Hongrie," In *Ruralia III. (Conference Ruralia III – Maynooth, 3rd–9th September 1999)*, ed. J. Klápšte, 60–68. Prague: Institute of Archaeology.
Pálóczi Horváth, A. 2002a, "Development of the Late – Medieval House in Hungary," In *The rural house from the Migration Period to the oldest still standing buildings. (Ruralia IV. 8–13th September 2001, Bad Bederkesa)*, ed. J. Klápšte, 308–319. Prague: Institute of Archaeology.
Pálóczi Horváth, A. 2002b, "La maison rurale de la Grande Plaine hongroise au bas Moyen Âge," In *Centre – Region – Periphery. Medieval Europe Basel 2002. 3rd*

International Conference of Medieval and Later Archaeology. Preprinted Papers I., eds. G. Helmig, B. Scholkmann and M. Untermann, 196–202. Hertingen–Basel: Folio Verlag – Archäologische Bodenforschung Basel-Stadt.

Pálóczi Horváth, A. 2002c, "A késő középkori Szentkirály határhasználata és gazdálkodása," [The borders and the economy of Szentkirály in the late medieval period] In *Gazdálkodás az Alföldön: földművelés* [Farming on the Great Hungarian Plain: agriculture] (Acta Musei de János Arany Nominati, 9), ed. L. Novák, 53–68. Nagykőrös: Arany János Múzeum.

Pálóczi Horváth, A. 2003, "A késő középkori népi építészet régészeti kutatásának újabb eredményei," [New archaeological results of late medieval vernacular architecture] In *Népi építészet a Kárpát-medencében a honfoglalástól a tizennyolcadik századig* [Vernacular architecture in the Carpathian Basin from the Conquest Period to the 18th century] (A Jász-Nagykun-Szolnok Megyei Múzeumok Közleményei, 58), eds. M. Cseri and J. Tárnoki, 221–260. Szentendre–Szolnok: Szentendrei Szabadtéri Néprajzi Múzeum – Damjanich János Múzeum.

Pálóczi Horváth, A. 2005, "The Archaeological Material of the Households of the Village of Szentkirály," In *Arts and Crafts in Medieval Rural Environment. L' artisanat rural dans le monde médiéval. Handwerk im mittelalterlichen ländlichen Raum.* (Ruralia VI. The Jean Marie Pesez Conferences on Medieval Rural archaeology. 22nd-29th September 2005, Szentendre – Dobogókő [Hungary]), 29–30. Turnhout: Brepols.

Pálóczi Horváth, A. 2014, *Keleti népek a középkori Magyarországon. Besenyők, úzok, kunok és jászok művelődéstörténeti emlékei* [Peoples of eastern origin in Medieval Hungary. The cultural heritage of Pechenegs, Uzes, Cumans and the Jász] (Studia ad Archaeologiam Pazmaniensiae, 2). Budapest–Piliscsaba: PPKE Bölcsészet- és Társadalomtudományi Kar, Régészeti Tanszék.

Pálosfalvi, T. 2000, "Cilleiek és Tallóciak: küzdelem Szlavóniáért (1440–1448)," [Cillis and Tallócis: struggles for Slavonia (1440–1448)] *Századok* 134, 45–98.

Pálosfalvi, T. 2003, "A Rozgonyiak és a polgárháború," [The Rozgonyis and the civil war] *Századok* 137, 897–928.

Papp, L. 1931, "Ásatások a XVI. században elpusztult Kecskemét-vidéki falvak helyén," [Excavations at the site of the villages around Kecskemét abandoned in the 16th century] *Néprajzi Értesítő* 23, 137–152.

Paranko, R. 2000, "Standards of Living, Order, and Prestige: Public Facilities in Early Fifteenth-Century Lviv (Lemberg)," *Medium Aevum Quotidianum* 42, 7–51.

Parrotta, J. A. and Trosper, R. L. (eds.) 2012, *Traditional Forest-Related Knowledge: Sustaining Communities, Ecosystems and Biocultural Diversity.* Dordrecht: Springer.

Pataki, J. 1973, *Domeniul Hunedoara la începutul secolului al XVI-lea. Studiu si documente.* [The great estate of Hunedoara at the beginning of the 16th century. Studies and documents] (Bibioteca istorică, 39). Bucureşti: Ed. Acad. Republicii Socialiste România.

Pataki, J. 1992, "A vajdahunyadi váruradalom a XVI. század első évtizedeiben," [The castle estate of Hunedoara in the first decades of the 16th century] *Erdélyi Múzeum* 44, 90–101.

Pataki, V. 1942, "A péterváradi ciszterciek a középkori Kelenföldön," [Cistercians of Petrovaradin in medieval Kelenföld] In *A Ciszterci Rend Budapesti Szent Imre Gimnáziumának Évkönyve az 1941–42. iskolai évről* [Yearbook of the St Emeric High School of the Cistercian Order on the year 1941/1942], 26–34. Budapest: Élet Ny.

Paulinyi, O. 1924, "A sóregále kialakulása Magyarországon," [the formation of salt regale in Hungary] *Századok* 58, 627–647.

Paulinyi, O. 1933, "A középkori magyar réztermelés gazdasági jelentősége," [Copper mining and its economic role in medieval Hungary] In *Emlékkönyv Károlyi Árpád születése nyolcvanadik fordulójának ünnepére* [Studies in honor of Árpád Károlyi on the 80th anniversary of his birth], 402–439. Budapest: Sárkány Ny.

Paulinyi, O. 1936, "Magyarország aranytermelése a XV. század végén és a XVI. század derekán," [The gold production of Hungary at the turn of the 15th and 16th centuries] *A Gróf Klebelsberg Kunó Magyar Történetkutató Intézet Évkönyve* 6, 32–142.

Paulinyi, O. 1937, "A magyar aranymonopólium jövedelme a középkorban," [The incomes from the monopoly on gold in Hungary in the Middle Ages] In *Emlékkönyv Domanovszky Sándor születése hatvanadik fordulójának ünnepére, 1937. május 27.* [Memorial volume on in honor of the 60th birthday of the birth of Sándor Domanovszky, 27 May 1937], ed. I. Bakács, 488–503. Budapest: Egyetemi Nyomda.

Paulinyi, O. 1965, "Die Edelmetallproduktion der niederungarischen Bergstädte, besonders jene von Schemnitz, in der Mitte des XVI. Jahrhunderts," In *Nouvelles études historiques publiées à l' occasion du XIIe Congrès International des Sciences Historiques par la Commission Nationale des Historiens Hongrois*, eds. D. Csatári, L. Katus and Á. Katus, 181–196. Budapest: Akadémiai.

Paulinyi, O. 1966, *A vállalkozás kezdeti formái a feudáliskori nemesércbányászatban* [The initial forms of enterprising in feudal-time precious metal mining] (Értekezések a történeti tudományok köréből, 40). Budapest: Akadémiai.

Paulinyi, O. 1972, "Nemesfémtermelésünk és országos gazdaságunk általános alakulása a bontakozó és a kifejlett feudalizmus korszakában (1000–1526). (Gazdag föld– szegény ország)," [Unsere Edelmetallproduktion und die allgemeine Gestaltung der Wirtschaft unseres Landes zur Zeit des sich entfaltenden und entwickelten Feudalismus (1000–1526) Reicher Boden, armes Land] *Századok* 106, 561–605.

Paulinyi, O. 1972a, "Mohács előtti nemesfémtermelésünk és gazdaságunk," [Hungary's economy and precious metal production prior to the battle of Mohács (1526)] *Századok* 106, 561–608.

Paulinyi, O. 1972b, "Nemesfémtermelésünk és országos gazdaságunk általános alakulása a bontakozó és a kifejlett feudalizmus korszakában (1000–1526)," [Hungarian precious metal production and the formation of the country's economic conditions in the period of early and high feudalism, 1000–1526, Rich Land – Poor Country] *Századok* 106, 561–608. (2nd ed.: Paulinyi, O. 2005, *Gazdag föld – szegény ország, Tanulmányok a magyarországi bányaművelés múltjából* [Rich soil – poor country. Studies in the history of the mining in Hungary], eds. J. Buza and I. Draskóczy, 183–227. Budapest: Budapesti Corvinus Egyetem.)

Paulinyi, O. 1973, "A körmöcbányai kamara 1434–1435. évi számadása (Műhelybeszámoló)," [The account book of the Kremnica chamber from the year 1434–1435 (Report on the workshop)] In *A Magyar Numizmatikai Társulat Évkönyve 1972* [Yearbook of the Hungarian Numismatic Association, 1972], ed. L. Zombori, 79–94. Budapest: Magyar Numizmatikai Társulat.

Paulinyi, O. 1977, "Nemesfém monopólium és technológia," [Prescious metal monopol and technology] *A Magyar Tudományos Akadémia Filozófiai és Történettudományok Osztályának Közleményei* 26/1–2, 251–278.

Paulinyi, O. 1980, *Der erste Anlauf zur Zentralisation der Berggerichtsbarkeit in Ungarn Aus der Vorgeschichte der Maximilianischen Bergordnung* (Studia Historica Academiae Scientiarum Hungaricae, 141). Budapest: Akadémiai.

Paulinyi, O. 1981, "The Crown Monopoly of the Refining Metallurgy of Precious Metals and the Technology of the Cameral Refineries in Hungary and Transylvania in the Period of Advanced and Late Feudalism 1325–1700," In *Precious Metals in the Age of Expansion*, ed. H. Kellenbenz, 27–39. Stuttgart: Klett-Cotta.

Paulinyi, O. 2005, *Gazdag föld – szegény ország, Tanulmányok a magyarországi bányaművelés múltjából* [Rich soil – poor country. Studies in the history of the mining in Hungary], eds. J. Buza and I. Draskóczy. Budapest: Budapesti Corvinus Egyetem.

Pauly, M. 1996, "Foires luxembourgeoises et lorraines avant 1600," In *Europäische Messen und Märktesysteme in Mittelalter und Neuzeit* (Städteforschung, A 39), eds. P. Johanek, and H. Stoob, 105–141. Köln–Weimar–Wien: Böhlau.

Perring, D. (ed.) 2002, *Town and Country in England. Frameworks for Archaeological Research* (CBA Research Report, 134). York: B.A.R.

Persaits, G., Páll, D. G., Sümegi, P., and Takács, K. 2010, "Fitolitelemzéssel kiegészített régészeti geológiai vizsgálatok egy középkori csatornarendszerben (Tököz, Magyarország)," [A geoarchaeological study of a medieval hydraulic system (Tököz, Hungary) supplemented by phytolith analysis]. In *Medencefejlődés és geológiai erőforrások* [Basin formation and geological resources], ed. E. Pál-Molnár, 124–125. Szeged: GeoLitera.

Petényi, S. 1994, *Games and Toys in Medieval and Early Modern Hungary* (Medium Aevum Quotidianum, Sonderband III/1). Krems: Medium Aevum Quotidianum.

Péterfi, B. 2018, "The Hayday and Fate of an Early Trade Center. Graphite Pottery at Early Óbuda," In *Medieval Networks in East Central Europe: Commerce, Contacts, Communication*, eds. B. Nagy, F. Schmieder and A. Vadas. New York: Routledge (in press).

Pető, Zs. 2015, "Medieval Pauline Monastic Space in a Royal Forest: Spatial Analysis in the Pilis," *Annual of Medieval Studies at CEU* 21, 243–264.

Petrovics, I. 1996, "Egy 14. századi temesvári bíró, Posztós Mihály," [A 14th-century judge in Timişoara, Mihály Posztós] *Acta Universitatis Szegediensis de Attila József Nominatae. Acta Historica* 103, 91–100.

Petrovics, I. 2001a, "A középkori Pécs polgárai," [The burhers of medieval Pécs] In *Pécs szerepe a Mohács előtti Magyarországon* [The role of Mohács in Hungary before the battle of Mohács] (Tanulmányok Pécs történetéből, 9), ed. M. Font, 163–196. Pécs: Pécs Története Alapítvány.

Petrovics, I. 2001b, "Urban Development in the Danube–Tisa–Mureş Region in the Middle Ages," *Analele Banatului. Serie nouă. Archeologie-Istorie* 9, 389–400.

Petrovics, I. 2005, "Dél-dunántúli és dél-alföldi városok kapcsolata Felső-Magyarországgal a középkorban," [The connections of the towns of the Southern Transdanubia and Southern Great Hungarian Plain with the Upper Hungary in the Middle Ages] In *Bártfától Pozsonyig. Városok a 13–17. században* [From Bardejov to Bratislava. Cities in the 13th–17th century] (Társadalom- és Művelődéstörténeti Tanulmányok, 35), eds. E. Csukovits and T. Lengyel, 131–158. Budapest: MTA Történettudományi Intézet.

Petrovics, I. 2009, "Foreign Ethnic Groups in the Towns of Southern Hungary," In *Segregation–Integration–Assimilation. Religious and Ethnic Groups in the Medieval Towns of Central and Eastern Europe*, eds. D. Keene, B. Nagy and K. Szende, 67–88. Farnham–Burlington: Ashgate.

Petrovics, I. 2014, "From Misunderstanding to Appropriate Interpretation: Market Towns in Medieval Hungary with Special Reference to the Great Hungarian Plain," In *Offene Landschaften*, eds. O. Heinrich-Tamáska et al, 271–296. Bonn: Selbstverlag ARKUM e.V.

Pfister, Ch. 2010, "The vulnerability of past societies to climatic variation: a new focus for historical climatology in the twenty-first century," *Climatic Change* 100, 25–31.

Piasecki, P. 1987, *Das deutsche Salinenwesen, 1550–1650*. Idstein: Schulz-Kirchner-Verl.

Pickl, O. 1971, "Die Auswirkungen der Türkenkriege auf den Handel zwischen Ungarn und Italien im 16. Jahrhundert," In *Die wirtschaftlichen Auswirkungen der Türkenkriege. Die Vorträge des I. Internationalen Grazer Symposiums zur Wirtschafts- und Sozialgeschichte*, ed. idem, 71–129. Graz: Selbstverlag der Lehrkanzel für Wirtschafts- und Sozialgeschichte der Universität.

Pickl, O. 1979, "Der Viehhandel von Ungarn nach Oberitalien vom 14. bis zum 17. Jahrhundert," In *Internationaler Ochsenhandel (1350–1750). Akten des 7th International Economic History Congress, Edinburgh, 1978*, ed. E. Westermann, 39–81. Stuttgart: Klett-Cotta.

Piekalski, J. 2001, *Von Köln nach Krakau. Der topographische Wandel früher Städte* (Zeitschrift für Archäologie des Mittelalters, Beiheft, 13). Bonn: Habelt.

Piekalski, J. 2014, *Prague, Wrocław and Krakow: Public and Private Space at the Time of the Medieval Transition*. Wrocław: University, Institute of Archaeology.

Pinke, Zs. 2011, "Adatok és következtetések a középkori Hortobágy-Sárrét demográfiájához (1300–1350)," [Data and conclusions for the medieval demography of the Hortobágy-Sárrét (1300–1350)] In *Környezettörténet 2: Környezeti események a honfoglalástól napjainkig történeti és természettudományi források tükrében* [Environmental History 2: Environmental Events from the Hungarian Conquest to Nowadays in the Mirror of Written and Natural Sources], ed. M. Kázmér, 80–117. Budapest: Hantken.

Pinke, Zs. 2015, *Alkalmazkodás és felemelkedés – modernizáció és leszakadás: Kis jégkorszaki kihívások és társadalmi válaszok a Tiszántúlon* [Adaptation and Rise – Modernization and Decline: Little Ice Age Challenges and Social Responses on the Trans-Tisza Region (Hungary)]. Unpublished PhD dissertation defended at the University of Pécs.

Pinke, Zs. and Szabó, B. 2010, "Analysis of the map of the Ministry of Agriculture: Water Covered Areas and Wetlands in the Carpathian Basin before the Commencement of Flood Protection and Draining," In *2. Nemzetközi és 8. Országos Interdiszciplináris Grastyán konferencia előadásai* [Proceedings of the 2nd international and 8th national Grastyán conference], eds. V. Rab and M. Szappanyos, 207–217. Pécs: PTE Grastyán Endre Szakkollégium.

Pinke, Zs. et al. 2017, "Zonal assessment of environmental driven settlement abandonment in the medieval Trans-Tisza region, Central Europe," *Quaternary Science Reviews* 157, 98–113.

Pinke, Zs., Ferenczi, L., Gábris, Gy. and Nagy, B. 2016, "Settlement patterns as indicators of water level rising? Case study on the wetlands of the Great Hungarian Plain," *Quaternary International* 415, 204–215.

Piotrowicz, J. 1991, "Die mittelalterichen Ordinationen und Regelungen der Herrscher von Polen für die Krakauer Salinen," In *Das Salz in der Rechts- und Handelsgeschichte*, ed. J.-C. Hocquet and R. Palme, 271–278. Schwaz: Berenkamp.

Pohl, A. 1967–1968, "Zsigmond király pénzverése (1387–1437)," [Coinage under King Sigismund] *Numizmatikai Közlöny* 66–67, 46–48.

Pohl, A. 1974, *Ungarische Goldgulden des Mittelalters (1325–1541)*. Graz: Akademische Druck- u. Verlagsanstalt.

Pohl, A. 1982, *Münzzeichen und Meisterzeichen auf ungarischen Münzen des Mittelalters 1300–1540*. Graz–Budapest: Akademische Druck- u. Verlagsanstalt.

Pounds, N. J. G. 1994^2, *An Economic History of Medieval Europe*. London–New York: Routledge.

Prajda, K. 2010a, "The Florentine Scolari Family at the Court of Sigismund of Luxemburg in Buda," *Journal of Early Modern History* 14, 513–533.

Prajda, K. 2010b, "Levelező üzletemberek. Firenzeiek a Zsigmond-korban," [Men of letters, men of business. Florentines in the Kingdom of Hungary during the reign of Sigismund] *Századok* 144, 301–335.

Prajda, K. 2011, "Egy firenzei sírköve a középkori Budán: Bene di Jacopo del Bene szerencsétlenül végződött követjárása," [The tombstone of a Florentine at medieval Buda: the unfortunate embassage of Bene di Jacopo del Bene] In *"és az oszlopok tetején liliomok formáltattak vala" – Tanulmányok Bibó István 70. születésnapjára* ["and lilies were formed on the top of the columns ..." Studies in honor of István Bibó on his 70th birthday], ed. Á. Tóth, 29–35. Budapest: CentrArt Egyesület.

Prickler, L. 1998, *Das älteste Urbar der Grafschaft Forchtenstein von 1500/1510* (Burgenländische Forschungen Heft, 77). Eisenstadt: Amt der Burgenländischen Landesregierung.

Přikryl, I. 2004, "Historický vývoj našeho rybníkářství a rybničních ekosystémů," [Historical fishponds and fishpond ecosystems] *Veronica* 1, 7–10.

Princz, Gy. Cholnoky, J., Teleki, P. and Bartucz, L. (eds.) 1936–1938, *Magyar földrajz* [Hungarian geography]. Budapest: Királyi Magyar Egyetemi Nyomda.

Priskin, K. 2006, "A csengelei kun vezér lovának genetikai vizsgálata," [The genetic investigation of the Cuman nobleman's horse from Csengele] *Folia Archaeologica* 52, 217–219.

Probszt, G. 1957, "Der Siegeszug des ungarischen Goldes im Mitteralter," *Der Anschnitt* 9, 4–11.

Probszt, G. 1963, "Die Rolle des ungarischen Goldguldens in der österreichischen Wirtschaft des Mitteralters," *Südostforschungen* 22, 234–258.

Pühringer, A. 2003, "Kleine Städte – grosse Schulden? Zur frühneizeitlichen Finanzstruktur der landesfürstlichen Städte ob und unter der Enns," *Pro Civitate Austriae* NS 8, 3–38.

Püspöki Nagy, P. 1989, *Piacok és vásárok kezdetei Magyarországon 1000–1301 négy kötetben. I. Az Árpád-kori vásártartás írott emlékei és azok kritikája az államszervezéstől a tatárjárásig* [The beginnings of markets and fair sin Hungary from 1000 to 1301 in four volumes. I. The written evidence and its critics of markets in the Árpádian Period until the Mongol invasion]. Bratislava: Madách.

Pusztai, T. 2013, "A tapolcai bencés apátság építéstörténete," [The construction history of the Benedictine abbey of Tapolca] *A Herman Ottó Múzeum Évkönyve* 52, 149–170.

R. Várkonyi, Á. and Kósa, L. (eds.) 1993, *Európa híres kertje. Történeti ökológiai tanulmányok Magyarországról* [The famous garden of Europe: historical ecological essays on Hungary]. Budapest: Orpheusz.

Rabb, P. 2006, "Natural conditions in the Carpathian Basin of the Middle Ages," *Periodica Polytechnica* 38/2, 47–59.

LIST OF REFERENCES

Rackham, O. 1975, *Hayley Wood: Its History and Ecology*. London: Dent.
Rackham, O. 1976, *Trees and Woodland in the British Landscape*. London: Phoenix Press.
Rackham, O. 1979, "Neolithic Woodland Management in the Somerset Levels: Sweet Track I," *Somerset Levels Papers* 5, 59–61.
Rackham, O. 2003², *Ancient Woodland*. Dalbeattie: Castlepoint Press.
Rácz, L. 2008, "Éghajlati változások a Kárpát-medencében a középkor idején," [Climate changes in the Carpathian Basin during the Middle Ages] In *Gazdaság és gazdálkodás a középkori Magyarországon. Gazdaságtörténet, anyagi kultúra, régészet* [Economy and farming in medieval Hungary. Economic history, material culture, archaeology], eds. A. Kubinyi, J. Laszlovszky and P. Szabó, 21–35. Budapest: Martin Opitz.
Rácz, M. and Laszlovszky, J. 2005, *Monostorossáp, egy Tisza menti középkori falu* [Monostorossáp, a deserted medieval village and its landscape] (Dissertationes Pannonicae, III/7] Budapest: ELTE Régészettudományi Intézet.
Rady, M. 1985, *Medieval Buda. A Study of Municipal Government and Jurisdiction in the Kingdom of Hungary* (Eastern European Monographs, 182). New York: Columbia University Press.
Rady, M. 2000, *Nobility, Land and Service in Medieval Hungary*. New York: Palgrave.
Raukar, T. 1995, "I fiorentini in Dalmazia nel secolo XIV," *Archivio Storico Italiano* 153, 657–680.
Rausch, W. 1996, "Jahrmärkte, Messen und Stadtenrwicklung in den habsburgischen Ländern Österreichs," In *Europäische Messen und Märktesysteme in Mittelalter und Neuzeit* (Städteforschung, A 39) eds. P. Johanek and H. Stoob, 171–187. Köln–Weimar–Wien: Böhlau.
Regényi, K. 1998, "Karmeliták a középkori Magyarországon," [Carmelites in medieval Hungary] In *Capitulum*, I, ed. L. Koszta, 67–82. Szeged: Szegedi Középkorász Műhely.
Rengjeo, I. 1959, *Corpus der mittelalterlichen Münzen von Kroatien, Dalmatien und Bosnien*. Graz: Akad. Dr. u. Verl.-Anst.
Réthy, L. 1899–1907, *Corpus Nummorum Hungariae, Magyar Egyetemes Éremtár, Vol. I: Árpádházi királyok kora, Vol. II: Vegyesházi királyok kora* [Hungarian coinage. Vol. 1. Age of the Árpádian kings. Vol. 2. Age of kings of mixed dynasties]. Budapest: Akadémiai.
Révész, L. 1996, "Karos-Eperjesszög. Cemeteries I–III.," In *The Ancient Hungarians. Exhibition Catalogue*, eds. I. Fodor et al., 105. Budapest: Magyar Nemzeti Múzeum.
Révész, L. 2014, *The Era of the Hungarian Conquest. Permanent Exhibition of the Hungarian National Museum*. Budapest: Hungarian National Museum.
Révész, L. and Nepper, M. I. 1996, "The Archaeological Heritage of the Ancient Hungarians," In *The Ancient Hungarians. Exhibition Catalogue*, eds. I. Fodor et al., 37–56. Budapest: Budapest: Hungarian National Museum.

Rhodes, E. 2007, "Identifying Human Modification of River Channels," In *Waterways and Canal Building in Medieval England*, ed. J. Blair, 133–152. Oxford: Oxford University Press.

Ringer, I. et al. 2010, "17. századi bőrfeldolgozó műhely maradványa Sárospatakon," [Remains of a 17th-century hide production workshop in Sárospatak] In *Csont és bőr. Az állati eredetű nyersanyagok feldolgozásának története, régészete és néprajza* [Bone and leather. History, archaeology and ethnography of crafts utilizing raw materials from animals], eds. J. Gömöri and A. Kőrösi, 215–228. Budapest: Line Design.

Ritoók, Á. 2007, "Medieval settlement history of the Little Balaton region," In *Environmental Archaeology in Transdanubia* (Varia Archaeologica Hungarica, 20), eds. I. Juhász, P. Sümegi and Cs. Zatkyó, 156–162. Budapest: Archaeological Institute of the Hungarian Academy of Sciences.

Romhányi, B. 1994, "The Role of the Cistercians in Medieval Hungary: Political Activity or Internal Colonization?," *Annual of Medieval Studies at the CEU 1993–1994*, 180–204.

Romhányi, B. 1998, "L'ordre paulinien et l'innovation agraire en Hongrie (XIV–XVe siecles)," In *L'innovation technique au Moyen Age. Actes du VIe Congres International d'archéologie medieval*, ed. P. Beck, 46–48. Paris: Ed. Errance.

Romhányi, B. 2004, "Egy régi-új forrás az erdélyi domonkosok történetéhez," [An old-new source to the history of Dominicans in Transylvania], *Communicationes Archaeologicae Hungariae 2004*, 235–247.

Romhányi, B. 2005, "Ágostonrendi remeték a középkori Magyarországon," [Austin Hermits in medieval Hungary] *Aetas* 20/4, 91–101.

Romhányi, B. 2007, "Pálos gazdálkodás a 15–16. században," [Pauline farming in 15th–16th century] *Századok* 141, 299–351.

Romhányi, B. 2010a, "Domonkos kolostorok birtokai a késő középkorban," [Estates of Dominican friaries in the late Middle ages] *Századok* 144, 395–410.

Romhányi, B. 2010b, *A lelkiek a földiek nélkül nem tarthatók fenn ... Pálos gazdálkodás a középkori Magyarországon*. [The spiritual cannot be kept up without the earthly. Pauline farming in medieval Hungary]. Budapest: Gondolat.

Romhányi, B. 2010c, "Die Wirtschaftstätigkeit der ungarischen Pauliner im Spätmittelalter (15–16. Jh.)," In *Der Paulinerorden. Geschichte – Geist – Kultur*, ed. G. Sarbak, 129–200. Budapest: Szent István Társulat.

Romhányi, B. 2010d, "Les moines et l'économie en Hongrie à la fin du Moyen Âge," In *L'Europe centrale au seuil de la modérnité. Mutations sociales, religieuses et culturelles. Autriche, Bohême, Hongrie et Pologne, fin du XVe–milieu du XVIe siècle*, ed. M.-M. de Cevins, 141–150. Rennes: Presses Universitaires de Rennes.

Romhányi, B. 2014, *Koldulló barátok, gazdálkodó szerzetesek. Koldulórendi gazdálkodás a késő középkori Magyarországon* [Mendicant brothers, farming monks. Mendicant economy in late medieval Hungary] Dissertation submitted to the Hungarian

Academy of Sciences, Budapest. Online document: http://real-d.mtak.hu/688/7/dc_702_13_doktori_mu.pdf (last accessed: 22 October 2016).

Romhányi, B. 2015, "Kolostorhálózat – településhálózat – népesség. A középkori Magyar Királyság demográfiai helyzetének változásaihoz," [Monastic network – settlement system – population. On the demographic changes of the medieval Hungarian Kingdom] *Történelmi Szemle* 57, 1–49.

Romhányi, B. 2016, "Quête et collecte des aumônes chez les frères mendiants de Hongrie à la fin du moyen âge," *Moyen Âge* 2, 301–323.

Rosta, Sz. 2013, "Egy elfeledett nemzetségi monostor," [A forgotten kindred monastery] In *Régészeti kalandozások. A régészet legújabb hazai eredményei* [Archaeological inquiries. The most recent results of Hungarian archaeology], ed. G. M. Nagy, 7–9. [Budapest]: Forster Gyula Nemzeti Örökséggazdálkodási és Szolgáltatási Központ.

Rosta, Sz. 2014, *A Kiskunsági Homokhátság 13–16. századi településtörténete* [History of the settlement of the Sand Ridges of Kiskunság between the 13th and the 16th century]. Unpublished PhD dissertation defended at ELTE, Budapest.

Rosta, Sz. and V. Székely, Gy. (eds.) 2014, *"Carmen Miserabile." A tatárjárás magyarországi emlékei. Tanulmányok. Pálóczi Horváth András 70. születésnapja tiszteletére* [The monuments of the Mongol invasion in Hungary. Studies in honor of András Pálóczi Horváth on the occasion of his 70th birthday]. Kecskemét: Kecskeméti Katona József Múzeum.

Rózsa, Z., Balázs, J., Csányi, V. and Tugya, B. 2014, "Árpád Period Muslim Settlement and Cemetery in Orosháza," *Hungarian Archaeology* no. 3, 1–7.

Rózsa, Z. and Tugya, B. 2012, "Kik voltak az első Orosháza lakói?," [Who were the first inhabitants of Orosháza?] *Mozaikok Orosháza és vidéke múltjából* 6, 17–31.

Rupp, J. 1841–1846, *Numi Hungariae hactenus cogniti, quos delineatos, ac e monumentis historico-numariis exhibet. I. (Periodus Arpadiana) II. (Periodus mixta)*. Pest: Typis Regiae Universitatis Hungaricae.

Russell, E. W. B. 1998, *People and the Land through Time: Linking Ecology and History*. New Haven: Yale University Press.

Rusu, A. A. and Toda, O. "Archaeological Evidence for Historical Navigation on the Mureş (Maros) River. Enquiries Based on a Medieval Boat Imprint from Bizere Abbey (Romania)," *Acta Archaeologica Academiae Scientiarum Hungaricae* 65, 139–154.

Sági, K. 1968a, "A Balaton vízállástendenciái 1863-ig a történeti és kartográfiai adatok tükrében," [The water-level fluctuations of the Balaton until 1863 in light of historical and cartographic data] *Veszprém Megyei Múzeumok Közleményei* 7, 441–462.

Sági, K. 1968b, "A Balaton szerepe Fenékpuszta, Keszthely és Zalavár IV–IX. századi történetének alakulásában," [The role of the Balaton in the 4th–9th-century history of Fenékpuszta, Keszthely and Zalavár] *Antik Tanulmányok* 15, 15–46.

Saltzer, E. 1996, *A történelmi Magyarország területén fellelt 156 árpádházi éremkincslelet összefüggő áttekintése* [A survey of 156 Árpádian-age coin hoards found in the area of historic Hungary]. Budapest: Tipográfiai Kft.

Saltzer, E. 1998, "Nem thet, hanem alef [Not teth, but aleph]," *Éremtani Lapok* 48/2, 21.

Sander-Berke, A. 1997, "Stadtmauer und Stadtrechnung. Schriftliche Quellen des Spätmittelalters zu dem technischen Voraussetzungen des städtischen Befestigungsbaus," In *Die Befestigung der mittelalterlichen Stadt* (Städteforschung, A 45), eds. G. Isenberg and B. Scholkmann, 33–44. Köln–Weimar–Wien: Böhlau.

Sapori, A. 1967, "Gli italiani in Polonia fino a tutto il Quattrocento," *Studi di Storia Economica* 3, 149–176.

Sarbak, G., Romhányi, B. and Csengel, P. 2004, "'Domus Lapidis Refugii,' 'Vallis S. Anthonii,' 'Vallis Auxilii,' 'Vallis S. Michaelis,' 'Ercsi,' and 'Váradhegyfok,'" In *Monasticon Cartusiense*, II (Analecta Cartusiana 185/2), eds. J. Hogg and G. Schlegel, 61–76, 88–94, 102–113, 149–150 and 152–153. Salzburg: Inst. für Anglistik und Amerikanistik, Univ. Salzburg.

Sárosi, E. 2016, *Deserting Villages – Emerging Market Towns. Settlement dynamics and land management in the Great Hungarian Palin 1300–1700* (Archaeolingua, Series Minor, 39). Budapest: Archaeolingua.

Schalk, C. 1880, "Der Münzfuss der Wiener Pfennige in den Jahren 1424 bis 1480," *Numismatische Zeitschrift* 12, 186–282.

Scheiber, S. 1973–1974, "A héber betűjeles Árpád-házi pénzekhez," [Notes on the Árpádian coins with Hebrew letters] *Numizmatikai Közlöny* 72–73, 91.

Schmidt, F. A. 1934, *Chronologisch-systematische Sammlung der Berggesetze der österreichischen Monarchie. Zweite Abteilung. Chronologisch-systematische Sammlung der Berggesetze der Königreiche: Ungarn, Kroatien, Dalmatien, Slavonien und des Großfürstenthumes Siebenbürgen*, III. Wien: K. K. Hofe U. Staats- Aerarial Druckerrey.

Schmitz, Ph. 1998, *A bencések civilizációs tevékenysége a XII.-től a XX. századig*, I–II [Cultural activities of the Benedictines from the 12th to the 20th century]. Pannonhalma: Pannonhalmi Főapátság.

Schmitz, Ph. 2006, *A bencések civilizációs tevékenysége a kezdetektől a XII. századig* [Cultural activities of the Benedictines from the beginnings to the 12th century]. Panonhalma: Pannonhalmi Főapátság.

Scholkmann, B. 1997, "Die Befestigung der mittelalterlichen Stadt als Forschungsproblem der Mittelalterarchäologie," In *Die Befestigung der mittelalterlichen Stadt* (Städteforschung, A 45), eds. G. Isenberg and B. Scholkmann, VII–XI. Köln–Weimar–Wien: Böhlau.

Schönvisner, I. 1801, *Notitia Hungaricae rei numariae ab origine ad praesens tempus*. Buda: Typ. Universitatis.

Schönvisner, I. 1807, *Catalogus numorum Hungariae ac Transilvaniae Instituti Nationalis Széchényiani*, I–IV (*I.: Numi Hungariae, II.: Numi Transilvaniae, III.: Numi miscellanei, IV.: Tabulae numismaticae pro catalogo numorum Hungariae ac Transilvaniae Instituti Nationalis Széchényiani*. Pest: Typis Matthiae Trattner.

Schulek, A. 1926, "Vegyesházi királyaink pénzei és korrendjük. I. Károly Róbert," [Coins and their chronology during the period of the mixed dynasties I. – Charles I] *Numizmatikai Közlöny* 25, 138–195.

Schulek, A. 1931–1932, "Vegyesházi királyaink pénzei és korrendjük II. A budai pénzverés Károly Róberttől Zsigmondig," [Coins and their chronology during the period of the mixed dynasties II. Minting in Buda from the time of Charles I until Sigismund] *Numizmatikai Közlöny* 30–31, 48–70.

Sedláčková, H., Rohanová, D., Lesák, B. and Šimončičová-Koóšová, P. 2014, "Medieval Glass from Bratislava (ca 1200–1450) in the Context of Contemporaneous Glass Production and Trade Contacts," *Památky Archeologické* 105, 215–264.

Sedláčková, H., Rohanová, D., Lesák, B. and Šimončičová Koóšová, P. 2016, "Late Gothic and Early Renaissance Glass from Bratislava, ca. 1450–1550," *Památky Archeologické* 108, 353–394.

Serlegi, G. 2007, "A balatonkeresztúri 'vízmérce'. Környezetrégészeti információk a Balaton déli partjának római kori történetéhez," [The 'water gauge' of Balatonkeresztúr. Environmental archaeological data on the Roman Period history of the southern shore of Lake Balaton] In *FiRKák I. Fiatal Római Koros Kutatók I. konferenciakötete* [Proceedings of the first meeting of Young Researchers of the Roman Times], ed. Sz. Bíró, 297–317. Győr: Győr-Moson-Sopron Megyei Múzeumok Igazgatósága.

Serlegi, G. 2009, "The Waterlogged Century," In *Ex Officina ... Studia in honorem Dénes Gabler*, ed. Sz. Bíró, 501–514. Győr: Mursella Régészeti Egyesület.

Siklósi, Gy. 1983, "Dreihausener Pokal von Székesfehérvár," *Alba Regia* 20, 153–168.

Siklósi, Gy. 1999, *Die mittelalterlichen Wehranlagen, Burg- und Stadtmauern von Székesfehérvár*. Budapest: Archäol. Inst. der UAW.

Siklósi, Gy. 2003, "Die Wasserversorgung und das Kanalsystem im mittelalterlichen Székesfehérvár (Stuhlweissenburg)," *Antaeus* 26, 217–244.

Simon, Z. 2000, *A füzéri vár a 16–17. században* [The Füzér Castle in the 16th–17th century]. Miskolc.

Simon, Zs. 2006a, "A baricsi és kölpényi harmincadok a 16. század elején," [The thirtieth of Baric and Kulpin in the beginning of the 16th century] *Századok* 140, 815–882.

Simon, Zs. 2006b, *The Finances of Brașov at the Beginning of the Sixteenth Century*, MA Thesis defended at CEU, Budapest.

Simon, Zs. 2009, "The Trade of Hungary with Wallachia and Moldavia during the reign of Matthias Corvinus," In *Matthias and his Legacy: Cultural and Political Encounters between East and West* (Speculum historiae Debreceniense, 1), eds. A. Bárány and A. Györkös, 243–261. Debrecen: University of Debrecen Department of History.

Simon, Zs. 2010, "Verzeichnis der Schuldner der Thorenburger Salzkammer aus den ersten Jahrzehnten des 16. Jahrhunderts," *Zeitschrift für Siebenbürgische Landeskunde* 33/2, 141–160.

Simon, Zs. 2014, *A Magyarország és az Oszmán Birodalom közötti kereskedelem a 16. század elején* [Trade between Hungary and Ottoman Empire in the early 16th century]. Cluj: Mega.

Simonyi, Zs. 1881, "A magyar gyakorító és mozzanatos igék képzése," [Forming iterative and momentaneous verbs in Hungarian] *Nyelvtudományi Közlemények* 16, 237–269.

Sinkovics, I. 1933, *A magyar nagybirtok élete a XV. század elején* [Life of the Hungarian great estate complexes at the beginning of the 15th century] (Tanulmányok a magyar mezőgazdaság történetéhez, 8). Budapest: Szerzői kiadás.

Skoflek, I. 1985, "Mag- és termésleletek Sarvalyról a XVI. századból," [Seed and crop finds from Sarvaly from the 16th century] *Magyar Mezőgazdasági Múzeum Közleményei 1985*, 33–44.

Skoflek, I. and Hortobágyi, I. 1973, "Medieval Seed and Fruit Finds from the Castle Hills of Buda," *Mitteilungen des Archäologischen Institut der Ungarischen Akademie der Wissenschaft* 4, 135–156.

Skorka, R. 2012a, "A bécsi lerakat Magyarországra vezető kiskapui," [Legal loopholes in the staple of Vienna] *Történelmi Szemle* 54, 1–17.

Skorka, R. 2012b, "The Evolution of the Guild System," In *The History of Handicraft in Hungary*, ed. J. Szulovszky, 53–67. Budapest: Hungarian Chamber of Commerce and Industry.

Skorka, R. 2013, "A csökkentett vámtarifájú út kialakulása I. Károly uralkodása alatt," [The formation of the road with reduced customs duties during the reign of King Charles I] *Történelmi Szemle* 55, 451–470.

Sófalvi, A. 2005, *Sóvidék a középkorban. Fejezetek a székelység középkori történelméből* [Salt region in the Middle Ages. Studies in the history of Seclers in the Middle Ages]. Székelyudvarhely: Haáz Rezső Múzeum.

Solymosi, L. 1972, "Árpád-kori helyneveink felhasználásáról," [On the usage of Árpádian-age placenames] *Magyar Nyelv* 68, 179–190.

Solymosi, L. 1978, "A helytörténet fontosabb középkori forrásainak kutatása és hasznosítása," [The most important suorces and their use of medieval local history] *Történelmi Szemle* 18, 123–155.

Solymosi, L. 1984, "Veszprém megye 1488. évi adólajstroma és az Ernuszt-féle megyei adószámadások," [the tax list of Veszprém county from 1488 and the county accounts of Ernuszt] In *Tanulmányok Veszprém megye múltjából* [Studies on the past of Veszprém county] (Veszprém Megyei Levéltár kiadványai, 3), ed. L. Kredics, 121–239. Veszprém: Veszprém Megyei Levéltár.

Solymosi, L. 1985, "Az Ernuszt-féle számadáskönyv és a középkor végi népességszám. (A középkori megyei adószámadások forrásértéke)," [The account book of Ernuszt and the late medieval population (The source value of medieval county accounts)] *Történelmi Szemle* 28, 414–436.

Solymosi, L. 1990, "A szőlő utáni adózás első korszaka," [The first period of the taxation of vineyards in Hungary] *Agrártörténeti Szemle* 32, 22–50.

Solymosi, L. 1993, "Gesellschaftsstruktur zur Zeit des Königs István der Heiligen," In *Gizella és kora. Felolvasóülések az Árpád-korból*, 1 [Queen Gizella and her Age. Colloquia on the Árpádian age], ed. Zs. V. Fodor, 59–69. Veszprém: Laczkó Dezső Múzeum.

Solymosi, L. 1996a, "A szőlő utáni adózás új rendszere a 13–14. századi Magyarországon," [New system of taxation of vineyards in 13th–14th-century Hungary] *Történelmi Szemle* 38, 1–43.

Solymosi, L. 1996b, "Albeus mester összírása és a pannonhalmi apátság tatárjárás előtti birtokállománya," [Conscription of the estates of the abbey of Pannonhalma before the Mongol invasion by Master Albeus] In *Mons Sacer 996–1996. Pannonhalma 1000 éve*, I [Thousand years of Pannonhalma], ed. I. Takács, 515–526 and 616–617. Pannonhalma: Pannonhalmi Főapátság.

Solymosi, L. 1998, *A földesúri járadékok új rendszere a 13. századi Magyarországon* [New system of seigneurial dues in 13th-century Hungary]. Debrecen: Argumentum.

Solymosi, L. 2000, "Veszprém korai történetének néhány kérdése," [Some questions on Veszprém's early history] In *Válaszúton. Pogányság – kereszténység, kelet – nyugat* [On the crossroads. Paganism – Christianity, East – West], ed. L. Kredics, 129–157. Veszprém: MTA Veszprémi Területi Bizottsága.

Solymosi, L. 2001, "Liberty and Servitude in the Age of Saint Stephen," In *Saint Stephen and His Country. A Newborn Kingdom in Central Europe: Hungary. Essays on Saint Stephen and his Age*, ed. A. Zsoldos, 69–80. Budapest: Lucidus.

Solymosi, L. 2008, "Die Entwicklung der Schriftlichkeit im Königreich Ungarn vom 11. bis zum 13. Jahrhundert," In *Schriftkultur Donau und Adria bis zum 13. Jahrhundert: Akten der Akademie Friesach "Stadt und Kultur im Mittelalter". Friesach, 11–15. September 2002*, eds. R. Härtel et al., 483–526. Klagenfurt: Wieser.

Solymosi, L. 2009, "Bortizedfizetés sátornál," [Vine-tenth and the tent] In *Pénztörténet, gazdaságtörténet: tanulmányok Buza János 70. születésnapjára* [Monetary history, economic history. Studies in honor of János Buza on his 70th birthday], eds. J. Bessenyei and I. Draskóczy, 313–321. Budapest–Miskolc. Mirio Kulturális Bt.

Solymosi, L. 2016a, "Kereskedelemmel kapcsolatos források az Árpád-kori Magyarországon," [Sources on trade in Árpádian-age Hungary] In *Művészet és mesterség. Tisztelgő kötet R. Várkonyi Ágnes emlékére*, II [Art and craft. Memorial volume in honor of Ágnes R. Várkonyi], eds. I. Horn et al., 33–39. Budapest: L'Harmattan.

Solymosi, L. 2016b, "Szent István és a pannonhalmi apátság somogyi tizedjoga," [St Stephen and the tithe right of the abbey of Pannonhalma in Somogy County] In *Episcopus, Archiabbas Benedictinus, Historicus Ecclesiae. Tanulmányok Várszegi Asztrik 70. születésnapjára* [Stuies in honor of the 70th birthday of Asztrik Várszegi], eds. Á. Somorjai and I. Zombori, 11–23. Budapest: METEM.

Sólyom, J. 1933, *A magyar vámügy fejlődése 1519-ig* [The development of Hungarian customs until 1519]. Budapest: M. Kir. Vámszaki Tisztviselők Otthona.

Soós, F. 2013–2014, "A középkori Magyarország gazdasági- és pénzügyigazgatási tisztségviselői," [Die Offiziere der Wirtschafts- und Finanzverwaltung im mittelalterlichen Ungarn] *Numizmatikai Közlöny* 112–113, 81–123.

Soós, Z. 2013, "Les Mendiants dans l'économie de la Transylvanie médiévale : l'exemple des franciscains de Marosvásárhely (Târgu Mureş)," *Études Franciscaines* NS 6/1, 57–82.

Sowina, U. 2016, *Water, Towns and People. Polish Lands against a European Background until the Mid-16th Century*, Frankfurt am Main: Peter Lang.

Spufford, P. 1989, *Money and its Use in Medieval Europe*. Cambridge: Cambridge University Press.

Štefánik, M. 2004a, "Die Anfänge der slowakischen Bergstädte. Das Beispiel Neusohl," In *Stadt und Bergbau* (Städteforschung, A 64), eds. K. H. Kaufhold and P. Johanek, 295–312. Köln–Weimar–Wien: Böhlau.

Štefánik, M. 2004b, "Kupfer aus dem ungarischen Königreich im Spiegel der venezianischen Senatsprotokollen im 14. Jahrhundert," In *Der Tiroler Bergbau und die Depression der europäischen Montanwirtschaft im 14. und 15. Jahrhundert* (Veröffentlichungen des Südtiroler Landesarchivs, 16), eds. R. Tasser and E. Westermann, 210–226. Innsbruck–Wien–Bozen: StudienVerlag.

Štefánik, M. 2010, "Metals and power: European importance of export of metals from the territory of Slovakia in 14th and 15th century. The interest of Italian businessmen in the field of competence of Kremnica Chamber under rule of the House of Anjou and Sigismund of Luxembourg," In *Historiography in Motion: Slovak Contributions to the 21st International Congress of Historical Sciences* (CD-ROM), eds. R. Holec and R. Kožiak, 77–97. Banská Bystrica: Institut of History of Slovak Academy of Sciences – State Scientific Library.

Štefánik, M. 2012, "Italian Involvement in Metal Mining in the central Slovakian Region, from the Thirteenth Century to the Reign of King Sigismund of Hungary," *I Tatti Studies* 14/15, 11–46.

Stibrányi, M. 2008, "A Sárvíz középkori településhálózatának vázlata, avagy a templom és a hozzá vezető út," [An outline of the medieval settlement system of the Sárvíz, or the church and the road leading to it] *Alba Regia* 37, 189–196.

Stoob, H. 1996, "Vorwort," In *Europäische Messen und Märktesysteme in Mittelalter und Neuzeit* (Städteforschung, A 39), eds. P. Johanek and H. Stoob, VII–XII. Köln–Weimar–Wien: Böhlau.

Stossek, B. 2001, "Maisons et possessions des Templiers en Hongrie," In *The Crusades and the Military Orders: Expanding the Frontiers of Medieval Latin Christianity* (CEU Medievalia, 1), eds. Zs. Hunyadi and J. Laszlovszky, 245–251. Budapest: CEU Press.

Strieder, J. 1933, "Ein Bericht des Fuggerschen Faktors Hans Dernschwam über den Siebenbürger Salzbergbau um 1528," *Ungarische Jahrbücher* 13, 268–276.

Suchodolski, S. 1990, "Noch einmal über die Anfänge der ungarischen Münzprägung," *Wiadomości Numizmatyczne* 34, 164–176.

Suchodolski, S. 1999, "East or West? Concerning the Iconographic Patterns of the Hungarian Copper Coins of the So-Called Byzantine Type," In *Emlékkönyv Bíró-Sey Katalin és Gedai István 65. születésnapjára* [Memorial volume in honor of the 65th birthday of Katalin Bíró-Sey and István Gedai], eds. K. Bertók and M. Torbágyi, 267–273. Budapest: Argumentum – Ungarische Numismatische Gesellschaft – Ungarisches Nationalmuseum Münzenkabinett.

Sugár, I. 1979, "Az egri püspökség és káptalan vizafogó szegyéi a Tiszán," [The sturgeon catches of the bishopric and the chapter of Eger at the Tisza] *Archívum. A Heves Megyei Levéltár közleményei* 9, 5–33.

Sugita, S. 2007, "Theory of Quantitative Reconstruction of Vegetation I: Pollen from Large Sites Reveals regional Vegetation Composition," *Holocene* 17, 229–241.

Sümegi, P. and Törőcsik, T. 2007, "Hazánk növényzete az éghajlatváltozások türkében," [Hungary's vegetation in light climate changes] *Természet Világa* 138, 292–295.

Szabó, D. 1936, "A dömösi prépostság adománylevele," [The donation charter of the collegiate chapter of Dömös] *Magyar Nyelv* 32, 54–57 and 130–135.

Szabó, G. F. 1994, "A hét napjai a helységnevekben," [The days of the week in Hungarian placenames] *Névtani Értesítő* 16, 51–55.

Szabó, G. F. 1998, *A vásározás emlékei középkori helységneveinkben* [The remains of markets in medieval placenames]. Nyíregyháza: Bessenyei György Könyvkiadó.

Szabó, I. 1938, "Hanyatló jobbágyság a középkor végén," [Peasantry in decline at the end of the Middle Ages] *Századok* 72, 40–59.

Szabó, I. 1948. "A parasztság társadalmi rétegei a középkor végén," [The social stratification of peasantry at the end of the Middle Ages] In idem, *Tanulmányok a magyar parasztság történetéből* [Studies in the history of Hungarian peasantry], 5–30. Budapest: Teleki Pál Tudományos Intézet.

Szabó, I. 1960, "La repartition de la population de Hongrie entre les bourgades et les villages dans les années 1449–1526," In *Études historiques publiées par la Comission Nationale des Historiens Hongrois*, 359–385. Budapest: Akadémiai.

Szabó, I. 1963, "A prédium. Vizsgálódások a korai magyar gazdaság- és településtörténelem körében," [the praedium. Studies in the early economic and settlement history of early Hungarians] *Agrártörténeti Szemle* 5, 1–49 and 301–337.

Szabó, I. 1969, *A középkori magyar falu* [Villages in medieval Hungary]. Budapest: Akadémiai.

Szabó, I. 1971, *A falurendszer kialakulása Magyarországon (X–XV. század)* [The formation of the village system in Hungary (10th–15th century)]. Budapest: Akadémiai.

Szabó, I. 1975, *A magyar mezőgazdaság története a XIV. századtól az 1530–as évekig* [The history of Hungarian agriculture from the 14th century to the 1530s] (Agrártörténeti tanulmányok, 2). Budapest: Akadémiai.

Szabó, K. 1938, *Az alföldi magyar nép művelődéstörténeti emlékei* [Cultural historical monuments of the Hungarians of the Great Hungarian Plain] (Bibliotheca Humanitatis Historica, 3). Budapest: Országos Magyar Történeti Múzeum.

Szabó, N. Gy. 2012a "A kolozsmonostori apátság XV. századi szőlőtized jegyzékei," [Vine-tithe registers of the abbey of Cluj-Mănăştur from the 15th century] *Fons* 19, 463–493.

Szabó, N. Gy. 2012b, *A kolozsmonostori bencés apátság gazdálkodása a késő középkorban* [Farming of the Benedictine abbey of Cluj-Mănăştur in the Late Middle Ages]. PhD-dissertation defended at the University of Debrecen.

Szabó, P. 2002, "Medieval Trees and Modern Ecology: How to Handle Written Sources," *Medium Aevum Quotidianum* 46, 7–25.

Szabó, P. 2003. "Sources for the Historian of Medieval Woodland," In *People and Nature in Historical Perspective* (CEU Medievalia, 5), eds. J. Laszlovszky and P. Szabó, 265–288. Budapest: CEU Press.

Szabó, P. 2005, *Woodland and Forests in Medieval Hungary* (BAR Series, 1348 = Archaeolingua Central European Series, 2) Oxford: B.A.R.

Szabó, P. 2010, "Ancient Woodland Boundaries in Europe," *Journal of Historical Geography* 36, 205–214.

Szabó, P. 2013, "Rethinking Pannage: Historical Interactions between Oak and Swine," In *Trees, Forested Landscapes and Grazing Animals: A European Perspective on Woodlands and Grazed Treescapes*, ed. I. D. Rotherham, 51–61. London–New York: Routledge.

Szabó, P. 2015, "Historical Ecology: Past, Present and Future," *Biological Reviews* 90, 997–1014.

Szádeczky, L. (ed.) 1913, *Iparfejlődés és a czéhek története Magyarországon okirattárral (1307–1848)*, I–II [Industrial development and the history of guilds in Hungary – with documents (1307–1848)]. Budapest: Ranschburg Gusztáv Könyvkereskedése.

Szakács, B. Zs. (ed.) 2001, *Guide to Visual Resources of Medieval East-Central Europe* (CEU Medievalia, 2). Budapest: CEU Press.

Szakály, F. 1995a, *Lodovico Gritti in Hungary 1529–1534. A Historical Insight into the Beginnings of Turco-Habsburgian Rivalry*. Budapest: Akadémiai.

Szakály, F. 1995b, *Mezőváros és reformáció. Tanulmányok a korai magyar polgárosodás kérdéséhez* [Market towns and reformation. Studies to the question of the formation of Hungarian bourgeoisie] (Humanizmus és reformáció, 23). Budapest: Balassi.

Szamota, I. and Zolnai, Gy. (eds.) 1902–1906, *Magyar oklevél-szótár* [Hungarian charter dictionary]. Budapest: Hornyánszky Viktor.

Szántó, R. 2005a, "Az 1315–17. évi éhínség," [The famine of 1315–1317] In *Medievisztikai tanulmányok. (A IV. Medievisztikai PhD-konferencia, 2005. június 9–10. előadásai.)* [Studies in medieval history. The papers presented at the 4th conference of medieval history in Szeged 9–10 June 2005], eds. Sz. Marton and É. Teiszler, 135–142. Szeged: Szegedi Középkorász Műhely.

Szántó, R. 2005b, "Természeti katasztrófa és éhínség 1315–1317-ben," [Natural disaster and famine in 1315–1317] *Világtörténet* 27/1–2, 50–64.

Szántó, R. 2007, "Környezeti változások Európában a 14. század első évtizedeiben," [Environmental changes in Europe in the first decades of the 14th century] In *Középkortörténeti tanulmányok 5. Az V. Medievisztikai PhD-konferencia előadásai* [Studies in medieval history v], eds. É. Révész and M. Halmágyi, 159–164. Szeged: Szeged: Szegedi Középkorász Műhely.

Szegedy, E. 1960, "Beiträge zur Metalltechnik der IX–XI. Jahrhunderte in Ungarn," *Acta Archaeologica Academiae Scientiarum Hungaricae* 12, 299–330.

Székely, Gy. 1953, "A földközösség és szerepe az osztályharcban," [Common lands and its role in class struggle] In *Tanulmányok a parasztság történetéhez Magyarországon a 14. században* [Studies in the history of peasantry in 14th-century Hungary], ed. Gy. Székely, 80–103. Budapest: Akadémiai.

Székely, Gy. 1961, "Vidéki termelőágak és az árukereskedelem a XV–XVI. században," [Rural systems of production and merchandizing in 15th–16th-century Hungary] *Agrártörténeti Szemle* 3, 309–343.

Székely, Gy. 1964, "Wallons et italiens en Europe Centrale aux XIe–XVIe siècles," *Annales Universitatis Scientiarum Budapestinensis de Rolando Eötvös nominatae. Sectio Historica* 6, 3–71.

Székely, Gy. 1968, "A németalföldi és angol posztó fajtáinak elterjedése a XIII–XVII. századi Közép-Európában," [The spread of the baize of the Low Countries and England in Central Europe in the 13th–17th centuries] *Századok* 102, 3–31.

Székely, Gy. 1973, "Les facteurs économiques et politiques dans les rapports de la Hongrie et de Venise l'époque de Sigismond," In *Venezia e l'Ungheria nel Rinascimento. Atti del I convegno studi italo ungheresi)*, ed. V. Branca, 37–57. Firenze: L. S. Olschki.

Székely, Gy. 1974, "A mezővárosi fejlődés kérdései a XVII. század végéig," [Questions of the development of market towns until the late 17th century] *A Debreceni Déri Múzeum Évkönyve* 55, 347–368.

Szekfű, Gy. 1912, *Serviensek és familiárisok. Vázlat a középkori magyar alkotmány- és közigazgatástörténet köréből* [*Servientes* and *familiares*. A sketch in Hungarian constitutional and governmental history] (Értekezések a történeti tudományok köréből, XXIII/3). Budapest: Akadémia.

Szenci [Szenczi], M. A. 1604, *Dictionarium Latinoungaricum*. Nürnberg: Elia Huttero.

Szende, K. 1993–1996, "The Other Half of the Town. Women in Private, Professional and Public Life in Two Towns of Late Medieval Western Hungary," *East Central Europe* 20–23, 171–190.

Szende, K. 1996, "Some Aspects of Urban Landownership in Western Hungary," In *Power, Profit and Urban Land. Landownership in Medieval and Early Modern Northern European Towns*, eds. F.-E. Eliassen and G. A. Ersland, 141–166. Aldershot: Ashgate.

Szende, K. 1997, "Sopron: a West-Hungarian Merchant Town on the Crossroad between East and West," *Scripta Mercaturae* no. 2, 29–49.

Szende, K. 1998a, "'mit Irer trewn Arbait geholffen' Frauen und Handwerk in mittelalterlichen Testamenten," In *"'Was nützt die Schusterin dem Schmied?". Frauen und Handwerk vor der Industrialisierung*, ed. K. Simon-Muscheid, 85–97. Frankfurt am Main: Campus-Verlag.

Szende, K. 1998b, "Medieval Archaeology and Urban History in Some European Countries," In *Urban History. The Norwegian Tradition in a European Context*, ed. S. Supphellen, 111–131. Trondheim: Department of History, Norwegian Univ. of Science and Technology.

Szende, K. 1999, "Craftsmen's Widows in Late Medieval Sopron," In *Women in Towns: the Social Position of Urban Women in a Historical Context*, eds. M. Hietala and L. Nilsson, 13–23. Stockholm: Stads- och Kommunhistoriska Inst., Historiska Inst.

Szende, K. 2001, "Testaments and Testimonies. Orality and Literacy in Composing Last Wills in Late Medieval Hungary," In *Oral History of the Middle Ages. The Spoken Word in Context* (Medium Aevum Quotidianum. Sonderband, 12), ed. G. Jaritz, 49–66. Krems: Medium Aevum Quotidianum.

Szende, K. 2002, "Egy győri úr Sopronban. Alföldy Bálint királyi harmincados (†1493)," [A gentleman from Győr in Sopron. Bálint Alföldy royal tax collector] *Fons* 9, 29–60.

Szende, K. 2004a, "'Gemainer Stadt Nutz, Ehren und Gefallen ...' The Expression of Civic Consciousness in Late Medieval Testaments," In *"Quasi liber et pictura." Tanulmányok Kubinyi András 70. születésnapjára / Studies in Honour of András Kubinyi on His Seventieth Birthday*, ed. Gy. Kovács, 494–501. Budapest: ELTE Régészettudományi Intézet = Institute of Archaeological Sciences of Eötvös Loránd University.

Szende, K. 2004b, *Otthon a városban. Társadalom és anyagi kultúra a középkori Sopronban, Pozsonyban és Eperjesen* [At home in the town. Society and material culture in late medieval Sopron, Bratislava and Prešov] (Társadalom és Művelődéstörténeti Tanulmányok, 32). Budapest: MTA Történettudományi Intézet.

Szende, K. 2008, "Városi gazdálkodás a középkori Magyarországon," [Urban economy in medieval Hungary] In *Gazdaság és gazdálkodás a középkori Magyarországon Gazdaságtörténet, anyagi kultúra, régészet* [Economy and farming in medieval Hungary. Economic history, material culture, archaeology], eds. A. Kubinyi, J. Laszlovszky, and P. Szabó, 413–446. Budapest: Martin Opitz.

Szende, K. 2009a, "Geschichte und Archäologie bei der Erforschung der mittelalterlichen Stadtentwicklung in Ungarn – Die Ebenen der Zusammenarbeit," In *Geschichte und Archäologie: Disziplinäre Interferenzen*, eds. A. Baeriswyl, M. Stercken and D. Wild, 193–202. Zürich: Chronos.

Szende, K. 2009b, "Integration through Language: the Multilingual Character of Late Medieval Hungarian Towns," In *Segregation–Integration–Assimilation. Religious and Ethnic Groups in the Medieval Towns of Central and Eastern Europe*, eds. D. Keene, B. Nagy and K. Szende, 205–233. Farnham–Burlington: Ashgate.

Szende, K. 2010, "A Kárpát-medence középkori városainak régészeti kutatása az elmúlt két évtizedben," [Archaeological research into medieval towns in the Carpathian Basin since 1990] In *A középkor és a kora újkor régészete Magyarországon / Archaeology of the Middle Ages and the Early Modern Period in Hungary*, I, eds. E. Benkő and Gy. Kovács, 141–172. Budapest: MTA Régészeti Intézete.

Szende, K. 2011a, "A magyar városok kiváltságolásának kezdetei," [The beginnings of privileging the Hungarian towns] In *Debrecen város 650 éves. Várostörténeti tanulmányok* [The town of Debrecen in 650 years old. Studies in the history of the town] (Speculum Historiae Debreceniense, 7), eds. A. Bárány, K. Papp and T. Szálkai, 31–57. Debrecen: Debreceni Egyetem Történelmi Intézet.

Szende, K. 2011b, "Towns along the way. Changing patterns of long-distance trade and the urban network of medieval Hungary," In *Towns and Communication. Volume 2: Communication between Towns. Proceedings of the Meetings of the International Commission for the History of Towns (ICHT)*, eds. H. Houben and K. Toomaspoeg, 161–225. Lecce: Congedo.

Szende, K. 2011c, "Von der Gespanschaftsburg zur Stadt: Warum, wie -- oder warum nicht? Ein möglicher Weg der Stadtentwicklung im mitteralterlichen Ungarn," In *Stadtgründung und Stadtwerdung. Beiträge von Archäologie und Stadtgeschichtsforschung* (Beiträge zur Geschichte der Städte Mitteleuropas, 22), ed. F. Opll, 375–405. Linz: Österr. Arbeitskreis für Stadtgeschichtsforschung.

Szende, K. 2013a, "How Far Back? Challenges and Limitations of Cadastral Maps for the Study of Urban Form in Hungarian Towns," In *Städteatlanten. Vier Jahrzehnte Atlasarbeit in Europa* (Städteforschung, A 80), ed. W. Ehbrecht, 153–190. Köln–Wien: Böhlau.

Szende, K. 2013b, "Urban Literacy in the Carpathian Basin: Questions, Results, Perspectives," In *New Approaches to Medieval Urban Literacy*, eds. G. Declercq et al., 23–33. Brussels: Université Libre de Bruxelles.

Szende, K. 2014, "Laws, Loans, Literates: Trust in writing in the context of Jewish-Christian contacts in medieval Hungary," In *Religious Cohabitation in Medieval Towns*, eds. S. Bosselier and J. Tolan, 243–271. Turnhout: Brepols.

Szende, K. 2015a, "Power and Identity. Royal privileges to the towns of medieval Hungary in the thirteenth century," In *Urban Liberties and Citizenship from the Middle Ages up to Now* (Beiträge zur Landes- und Kulturgeschichte, 9), eds. M. Pauly and A. Lee, 27–67. Trier: Porta Alba.

Szende, K. 2015b, "Scapegoats or competitors? The expulsion of Jews from Hungarian towns on the aftermath of the battle of Mohács (1526)," In *Expulsion and Diaspora Formation: Religious and Ethnic Identities in Flux from Antiquity to the Seventeenth Century*, ed. J. Tolan, 51–83. Turnhout: Brepols.

Szende, K. 2016, "Mennyit ér a kiváltság? Városprivilégiumok kibocsátása és rendelkezéseik betartása I. Károly alatt," [What is the privilege worth? Issuing and handling town privileges in Hungary during the reign of Charles I] In *Pénz, posztó, piac. Gazdaságtörténeti tanulmányok a magyar középkorról* [Money, cloth, market. Studies in the economic history of medieval Hungary], ed. B. Weisz, 285–339. Budapest: MTA BTK Történettudományi Intézet.

Szende, K. 2017, "Nundinae seu forum annuale. Sokadalomtartási engedélyek Nagy Lajos várospolitikájában," [Nundinae seu forum annuale. Grants to hold annual fairs in the urban policy of Louis the Great] In *Hatalom, adó, jog. Gazdaságtörténeti tanulmányok a magyar középkorról* [Power, tax, law. Studies on the economic history of medieval Hungary], eds. B. Weisz and I. Kádas, 231–261. Budapest: MTA BTK Történettudományi Intézet.

Szende, K. and Németh, I. 2014, "Research on the Towns of Medieval and Early Modern Hungary since 1989," *Vana Tallinn* 25, 266–294.

Szende, K. and Végh, A. 2015, "Royal Power and Urban Space in Medieval Hungary," In *Lords and Towns in Medieval Europe. The European Historic Towns Atlas Project*, eds. A. Simms and H. B. Clarke, 255–286. Farnham: Ashgate.

Szilágyi, M. 2011, *Árpád Period Communication Networks: Road Systems in Western Transdanubia*. PhD dissertation defended at CEU, Budapest.

Szilágyi, M. 2013, "Városok, utak, kereskedelem. Az úthálózat szerepe Vas megye városi fejlődésében a 13–14. században," [Towns, roads, trade. Role of road network in the urban development of the towns in Vas County in the 13th–14th centuries] *Savaria* 36, 203–221.

Szilágyi, M. 2014, *On the Road: The History and Archaeology of Medieval Communication Networks in East-Central Europe* (Archaeolingua Series Minor, 35). Budapest: Archaeolingua.

Szily, K. 1919, "A -mán és -ván képző történetéhez," [On the history of the suffixes -mán and -ván] *Magyar Nyelv* 15, 92–95.

Szögi, L. 1995, *Régi magyar egyetemek emlékezete 1367–1777* [The memory of old Hungarian universities 1367–1777]. Budapest: Eötvös Loránd Tudományegyetem.

Szőke, M. 2000, "Die mittelalterliche Burg von Visegrád," In *Europas Mitte um 1000*, II, eds. A. Wieczorek and H-M. Hinz, 584–587. Stuttgart: Theiss.

Szőke, M. 2015, *A garamszentbenedeki apátság alapítólevelének nyelvtörténeti vizsgálata* [Linguistic historical study of the foundation charter of the abbey of Hronský Beňadik] (A Magyar Névarchívum Kiadványai, 33). Debrecen: Debreceni Egyetemi Kiadó.

Szőnyi, E. T. and Tomka, P. 2002, "Győr, Széchenyi tér," [Győr, Széchenyi Square] In *Archaeological research in Hungary in 1999*, ed. E. Marton, 206–208. Budapest: Kulturális Örökségvédelmi Hivatal.

Szűcs, J. 1955, *Városok és kézművesség a XV. századi Magyarországon* [Towns and craftsmanship in 15th-century Hungary]. Budapest: Művelt Nép.

Szűcs, J. 1958, "A középkori építészet munkaszervezetének kérdéséhez," [To the question of labor organization in the Middle Ages] *Budapest Régiségei* 18, 313–363.

Szűcs, J. 1963, "Städtewesen in Ungarn im 15.–17. Jahrhundert," In *Renaissance und Reformation in Polen und Ungarn 1450–1650*, eds. Gy. Székely et al., 97–164. Budapest: Akadémiai.

Szűcs, J. 1981, "Megosztott parasztság – egységesülő jobbágyság. A paraszti társadalom átalakulása a 13. században, I–II.," [Divided peasantry – unifying peasantry. Transformation of peasant society in the 13th century] *Századok* 115, 3–65 and 263–319.

Szűcs, J. 1983, "The Three Historical Regions of Europe. An Outline," *Acta Historica Academiae Scientiarum Hungaricae*, 29, 131–184. 2nd ed.: Szűcs, J. 1988, In *Civil Society and the State: New European Perspectives*, ed. J. Keane, 291–332. London: Univ. of Westminster Press.

Szűcs, J. 1984, "A gabona árforradalma a 13. században," [The revolution of grain prices in the 13th century] *Történelmi Szemle* 27, 5–33.

Szűcs, J. 1993, *Az utolsó Árpádok* [The last Árpádians] (História könyvtár. Monográfiák 1). Budapest: MTA Történettudományi Intézet.

Szűcs, J. 2002^2, *Az utolsó Árpádok* [The last Árpádians]. Budapest: Osiris.

Szulovszky, J. (ed.) 2012, *The history of Handicraft in Hungary*. Budapest: Hungarian Chamber of Commerce and Industry.

T. Németh, G. 2013, "Angaben zum spätbronzezeitlichen Salzverkehr," In *Bronze Age Crafts and Craftsmen in the Carpathian Basin. Proceedings of the International Colloquium from Târgu Mureș, 5–7 October 2012*, eds. R. Botond, R. E. Németh and S. Berecki, 57–64. Târgu Mureș: Mega.

Tack, G., van den Bemt, P. and Hermy, M. 1993, *Bossen van Vlaanderen. Een historische ecologie* [Flemish woods: A historical ecology]. Leuven: Davidsfonds.

Tagányi, K. 1893, "A magyar gazdaság-történet főbb forrásai," [Main sources of Hungarian economic history] *Századok* 27, 915–919.

Tagányi, K. 1894, "A földközösség története Magyarországon," [History of common field system in Hungary] *Magyar Gazdaságtörténelmi Szemle* 1, 199–238.

Tagányi, K. 1895, "Szarvkő várának bevételei és kiadásai 1448-ból," [Incomes and expenditure of Hornstein castle in 1448] *Magyar Gazdaságtörténelmi Szemle* 2, 213–214.

Tagányi, K. 1916, "Felelet Erdélyi Lászlónak 'Árpádkori történetünk legkritikusabb kérdéseire'," [Answer to László Erdélyi's "Critical questions of the social history of Árpádian-age Hungary"] *Történelmi Szemle* 5, 296–320, 409–448 and 543–608.

Takács, I. 1996a, "Horse skulls on display: archaeological evidence of a widespread custom from Hungary," *Acta Archaeologica Academiae Scientiarum Hungaricae* 48, 317–320.

Takács, I. (ed.) 1996, *Mons Sacer 996–1996. Pannonhalma 1000 éve*, I–III [1000 years of Pannonhalma Abbey]. Pannonhalma: Pannonhalmi Főapátság.

Takács, I. (ed.) 2001, *Paradisum plantavit. Bencés monostorok a középkori Magyarországon* [Benedictine monasteries in medieval Hungary]. Pannonhalma: Pannonhalmi Bencés Főapátság.

Takács, I. 2006, "Königshof und Hofkunst in Ungarn in der späten Anjouzeit," In *Sigismundus Rex et Imperator. Kunst und Kultur zur Zeit Sigismund von Luxemburg 1387–1437. Auststellungskatalog*, ed. I. Takács, 68–86. Budapest–Mainz am Rhein: P. von Zabern.

Takács, I. and Mikó, Á. (eds.) 1994, *Pannonia Regia. Művészet a Dunántúlon 1000–1541. Katalógus* [Art and architecture in Transdanubia. Catalogue]. Budapest: Magyar Nemzeti Galéria.

Takács, K. 2003, "Medieval Hydraulic Systems in Hungary: Written Sources, Archaeology and Interpretation," In *People and Nature in Historical Perspective* (CEU Medievalia, 5), eds. J. Laszlovszky and P. Szabó, 289–312. Budapest: CEU Press.

Takács, L. 1972, "Sensesicheln in Ungarn," In *Getreidebau in Ost- und Mitteleuropa*, ed. I. Balassa, 561–582. Budapest: Akadémiai.

Takács, L. 1978, *Egy irtásfalu földművelése* [Farming of a clearance village]. Budapest: Akadémiai.

Takács, L. 1980, *Irtásgazdálkodásunk emlékei (Irtásföldek, irtásmódok)* [Remains of clearance farming in Hungary (clearances, clearance techniques)]. Budapest: Akadémiai.

Takács, L. 1987. *Határjelek, határjárás a feudális kor végén Magyarországon* [Boundary marks and perambulations at the end of the feudal period in Hungary]. Budapest: Akadémiai.

Takács, M. 1986, *Die arpadenzeitlichen Tonkessel in Karpatenbecken* (Varia Archaeologia, 1). Budapest: Magyar Tudomány Akadémia.

Takács, M. 1996b, "Formschatz und Chronologie der Tongefässe des 10–14. Jhs der Kleinen Tiefebene," *Acta Archaeologica Academiae Scientiarium Hungariae* 48, 135–196.

Takács, M. 2001, "Az Árpád-kori köznépi lakóház kutatása, különös tekintettel az 1990-es évekre," [Study of Árpádian-age vernacular architecture with special regard to the

1990s] In *Népi építészet a Kárpát-medencében a honfoglalástól a tizennyolcadik századig* [Vernacular architecture in the Carpathian Basin from the Conquest Period to the 18th century] (A Jász-Nagykun-Szolnok Megyei Múzeumok Közleményei, 58), eds. M. Cseri and J. Tárnoki, 7–54. Szentendre–Szolnok: Szentendrei Szabadtéri Néprajzi Múzeum – Damjanich János Múzeum.

Takács, M. 2007, "Handwerkliche Produktion in den dörflichen Siedlungen im árpádenzeitlichen Ungarn (10.–13. Jahrhundert)," In *Arts and crafts in medieval rural environment. Ruralia VI,* eds. J. Klápště and P. Sommer, 53–70. Turnhout: Brepols.

Takács, M. 2010, "Árpád-kori falusias települések kutatása Magyarországon 1990 és 2005 között," [Research of the Árpádian-age, village-like settlements in Hungary between 1990 and 2005] In *A középkor és a kora újkor régészete Magyarországon / Archaeology of the Middle Ages and the Early Modern Period in Hungary,* 1, eds. E. Benkő and Gy. Kovács, 1–67. Budapest: MTA Régészeti Intézete.

Takács, M. 2012a, "Crafts in the Árpád-era," In *The History of Handicraft in Hungary,* ed. J. Szulovszky, 37–51. Budapest: Hungarian Chamber of Commerce and Industry.

Takács, M. 2012b, "A korongolt, korai Árpád-kori cserépbográcsok formai sajátságairól," [About the formal characteristics of the Árpádian age wheel-throw clay cauldrons] In *Hadak útján 20. Népvándorláskor Fiatal Kutatóinak XX. Összejövetelének konferenciakötete* [On the path of wars. Proceedings of the 20th conference of young scholars working on the age of Migrations], ed. Zs. Petkes, 229–269. Budapest: Magyar Nemzeti Múzeum.

Takács, M. 2013, "Die Frage der Herrschaft in der mittelalterlichen Siedlungsarchäologie Ungarns. Überblick über eine selten analysierte Problematik in drei zeitlichen Abschnitten" In *Hierarchies in rural settlements (Ruralia, 9),* ed. J. Klápště, 407–422. Turnhout: Brepols.

Takács, M. 2014, "Die ungarische Staatsgründung als Modellwechsel und/oder möglicher Akkukturationsprozess," In *Akkulturation im Mittelalter* (Vorträge und Forschungen, 78), ed. R. Härtel, 165–205. Sigmaringen. Thorbecke.

Takács, M. 2016, "The archaeological investigation of medieval agrarian tools and techniques in Hungary – an overview of some rarely quoted analyses," In *Agrarian Technology in the Medieval Landscape Agrartechnik in mittelalterlichen Landschaften. Technologie agraire dans le paysage médiéval. 9th–15th September 2013 Smolenice, Slovakia* (Ruralia, 10), ed. J. Klápště, 385–394. Turnhout: Brepols.

Takáts, S. 1897, "A komáromi vizahalászat a 16. században," [The fishing of great sturgeon at Komárom in the 16th century] *Magyar Gazdaságtörténelmi Szemle* 4, 425–445 and 485–509.

Takáts, S. 1927, *Szegény magyarok* [Poor Hungarians]. Budapest: Genius.

Tálasi, I. 1965a, "Az anyagi kultúra vizsgálatának tíz éve (1945–1955)," [The first ten year of the study of material culture (1945–1955)] *Ethnographia* 66, 5–56.

Tálasi, I. 1965b, "Die materielle Kultur des ungarischen Volkes in Europa (Im Spiegel der sukzessiven Forschungen)," In *Europa et Hungaria. Congressus Ethnographicus in Hungaria*, eds. Gy. Ortutay and T. Bodrogi, 27–57. Budapest: Akadémiai.

Tamási, J. 1995, *Verwandte Typen im schweizerischen und ungarischen Kachelfundmaterial in der 2. H. des 15. Jahrhunderts*. Budapest: Akadémiai.

Teiszler, É. 2007. "A felvidéki soltészfalvakról," [On the villages founded in by organized settlers in Upper Hungary (Slovakia)] *Acta Universitatis Szegediensis, Acta Historica* 127, 39–45.

Teke, Zs. 1975, "Rapporti commerciali tra Ungheria e Venezia nel secolo XV," In *Rapporti Veneto-Ungheresi all'Epoca del Rinascimento*, ed. T. Klaniczay, 143–152. Budapest: Akadémiai.

Teke, Zs. 1979, *Velencei–magyar kereskedelmi kapcsolatok a XIII–XV. században* [Venetian–Hungarian trade relations in the 13th–15th centuries]. Budapest: Akadémiai.

Teke, Zs. 1995a, "Firenzei üzletemberek Magyarországon 1373–1403," [Florentine businessmen in Hungary 1373–1403] *Történelmi Szemle* 37, 129–151.

Teke, Zs. 1995b, "Firenzei kereskedőtársaságok, kereskedők Magyarországon Zsigmond uralmának megszilárdulása után 1404–1437," [Florentine commercial companies, merchants in Hungary after the stabilization of the reign of Sigismund 1404–1437)] *Századok* 129, 195–214.

Teke, Zs. 1995c, "Operatori economici fiorentini in Ungheria nel tardo Trecento e primo Quattrocento," *Archivio Strico Italiano* 153, 697–707.

Teke, Zs. 1996, "Firenzei üzletemberek Magyarországon a XIV. század végén és a XV. század elején," [Florentine merchants in Hungary in the late 14th and 15th century] In *A gazdaságtörténet kihívásai: Tanulmányok Berend T. Iván 65. születésnapjára* [The challenges of economic history. Studies in honor of the 65th birthday of Iván Berend T.], eds. J. Buza, T. Csató and S. Gyimesi, 21–28. Budapest: Budapesti Közgazdaságtudományi Egyetem Gasdaságtörténeti Tanszéke – MTA-BKE Közép- és Kelet-Európa Története Kutatócsoport.

Teke, Zs. 1998, "Zsigmond és a dalmát városok 1387–1413," [Sigismund and the Dalmatian Towns 1387–1413] In *Tanulmányok Borsa Iván tiszteletére* [Studies in honor of Iván Borsa], ed. E. Csukovits, 233–243. Budapest: Magyar Országos Levéltár.

Teke, Zs. 2003, "L'energia idraulica nella siderurgia medievale," In *Economia e energia, secc. XIII–XVIII: atti della XXXIV Settimana di Studi Istituto Internazionale di Storia Economica*, ed. S. Cavaciocchi, 335–340. Firenze: Le Monnier.

Teke, Zs. 2007, "Egy firenzei kereskedő a Jagelló-korban: Raggione Bontempi 1488–1528," [A Florentine merchant in the Jagiellonian period: Raggione Buontempi 1488–1528] *Századok* 141, 967–990.

Teutsch, F. 1892, "Der städtische Haushalt Kronstadts am Anfang des 16. Jahrhunderts," *Korrespondenzblatt des Vereins für siebenbürgische Landeskunde* 15, 1–38.

Thiele, Á., Török, B., and Költő, L. 2013, "A foszfor szerepe a vas somogyi archeometallurgiájában. – Avar és Árpád-kori vaskohászatból származó somogyi salakok SEM-EDS vizsgálata," [The role of phosphorus in the archaeometallurgy of iron: SEM-EDS analysis on slag samples from Avar- and Árpádian-age bloomery workshops of Somogy County] *Archeometriai Műhely* 10, 12–22. Online document: http://www.ace.hu/am/index.html (last accessed: 10 July 2016).

Thoroczkay, G. 2012, "A dömösi prépostság története alapításától I. Károly uralkodásának végéig," [The history of the collegiate chapter of Dömös from its foundation till the end of the reign of King Charles I] *Fons* 19, 37–55.

Timár, G. 2003, *Geológiai folyamatok hatása a Tisza alföldi szakaszának medermorfológiájára* [The impact of the geological processes of the river-bed morphology of the Great Hungarian Plain section of the Tisza]. PhD dissertation defended at ELTE, Budapest.

Tóber, M. 2012, "Mennyiben tükrözi Bertrandon de la Brocquiére útleírása a középkori Homokhátság természeti viszonyait?," [To what extent does Bertrandon de la Brocquiére's description reflect medieval environmental conditions in Homokhátság?] In *A táj változásai a Kárpát-medencében. Történelmi emlékek a tájban* [Landscape changes in the Carpathian Basin. Historical monuments in the landscape], ed. Gy. Füleky, 309–314. Gödöllő: Környezetkímélő Agrokémiáért Alapítvány.

Toda, O. 2014, "Archaeological Evidence for Historical Navigation on the Mureș River. Enquiries Based on a Medieval Boat Imprint from Bizere Abbey (Romania)," *Acta Archaeologica Academiae Scientiarum Hungaricae* 65/1, 139–154.

Todeschini, G. 2009, *Franciscan Wealth. From Voluntary Poverty to Market Society*. New York: St. Bonaventure University.

Torma, A. 2003, "Paleoethnobotanical Assemblages from Medieval Wells in Hungary," *Anteus* 26, 245–254.

Torma, I. 1986, "Mittelalterliche Ackerfeld-Spuren im Wald von Tamási (Komitat Tolna)," *Acta Archaeologica Academiae Scientiarum Hungaricae* 38, 227–255.

Török, B. 2010, "Árpád-kori vaskohászati műhelyek metallurgiája a műszaki vizsgálatok tükrében," [Metallurgy of Árpádian-age iron smitheries in light of technological investigations] *Gesta* 9, 227–232.

Tóth, A. et al. 2010, "In the light of the crescent moon," In *Integrating Zooarchaeology and Paleoethnobotany: A Consideration of Issues, Methods, and Cases*, eds. A. M. VanDerwarker and T. M. Peres, 245–286. New York–Berlin: Springer.

Tóth, Cs. 1999, "Pénzverdék az Anjou-kori Magyarországon," [Mint chambers in Hungary in the Angevin period] In *Emlékkönyv Bíró-Sey Katalin és Gedai István 65. születésnapjára* [Memorial volume on the 65th birthday of Katalin Bíró-Sey and István Gedai], eds. K. Bertók and M. Torbágyi, 307–314. Budapest: Argumentum – Ungarische Numismatische Gesellschaft – Ungarisches Nationalmuseum Münzenkabinett.

Tóth, Cs. 2001–2002, "Der Sarachen-Denar," *Folia Archaeologica* 49–50, 349–366.

Tóth, Cs. 2002, "Mária királynő dénárjainak korrendje," [Chronology of the denars of Queen Mary] *Az Érem* 2, 7–12.

Tóth, Cs. 2003–2004, "Unpublizierte Anjou-zeitliche Münzen im Ungarischen Nationalmuseum," *Folia Archaeologica* 51, 175–182.

Tóth, Cs. 2003–2005, "Contributions to the Study of the Alloy Standards of the Hungarian Gold Coins Struck during the Angevin Period," *Cercetări numismatice* 9–11, 199–207.

Tóth, Cs. 2004, "Mints of medieval Visegrád," In *"Quasi liber et pictura" Tanulmányok Kubinyi András hetvenedik születésnapjára / Studies in Honour of András Kubinyi on His Seventieth Birthday*, ed. Gy. Kovács, 571–573. Budapest: ELTE Régészettudományi Intézet = Institute of Archaeological Sciences of Eötvös Loránd University.

Tóth, Cs. 2006a, "Control Mark System of the Early Hungarian Coinage," *Numizmatika* 21, 174–178.

Tóth, Cs. 2006b, "Die ungarische Münzprägung unter Sigismund von Luxemburg," In *Sigismundus Rex et Imperator. Kunst und Kultur zur Zeit Sigismunds von Luxemburg*, ed. I. Takács, 170–172. Budapest–Mainz am Rhein: P. von Zabern.

Tóth, Cs. 2007, "A tatárjárás korának pénzekkel keltezett kincsleletei," [Hoards dated with coins from the time of the Mongol invasion] In *A tatárjárás* [The Mongol invasion], eds. É. Garam and Á. Ritoók, 79–90. Budapest: Magyar Nemzeti Múzeum.

Tóth, J. A. 2009, "La Drava (Hongrie), un fleuve inconnu," *Dossiers d'Archéologie* 331/1, 46–49.

Tóth, J. A. 2010, "Adatok a kora újkori közép-Duna-medencei hajók régészetéhez," [Data on the Archaeology of Early Modern Age Ships in the Middle Danube Basin Region] In *A középkor és a kora újkor régészete Magyarországon / Archaeology of the Middle Ages and the Early Modern Period in Hungary*, II, eds. E. Benkő and Gy. Kovács, 871–884. Budapest: MTA Régészeti Intézete.

Tózsa-Rigó, A. 2008, "A pozsonyi Tiltáskönyv (1538–1566) információs bázisa. (Különös tekintettel a pozsonyi felső- és középréteg városon túlnyúló kapcsolatrendszerére)," [The set of data in the Bratislava "Verbotsbuch," 1538–1566. (With special regard to the relationships of the high and middle class burghers of Bratislava outside the town)] *Századok* 142, 1135–1186.

Tózsa-Rigó, A. 2009, "Die Rolle des Donauhandels im Nürnberger Wirtschaftsleben. Beziehungen zwischen den Wirtschaftseliten Pressburgs und Nürnbergs im 16. Jahrhundert," *Jahrbuch für fränkische Landesforschung* 69, 95–120.

Trexler, R. T. 1974, *Spiritual Power: Republican Florence Under Interdict*. Leiden: Brill.

Tringli, I. 2001, "A magyar szokásjog a malomépítésről," [Hungarian customary law on mill construction] In *Analecta Mediaevalia. I. Tanulmányok a középkorról* [Studies in medieval history], ed. T. Neumann, 251–268. Budapest: Argumentum.

Tringli, I. 2010, "Vásártér és vásári jog a középkori Magyarországon," [Marketplace and market rights in medieval Hungary] *Századok* 144, 1291–1344.

Tringli, I. 2014, "Mittäter oder Anstifter? Die Rolle der Helfer bei den Fehdehandlungen im spätmittelalterlichen Ungarn," In *Fehdehandeln und Fehdegruppen im spätmittelalterlichen und frühneuzeitlichen Europa*, eds. M. Prange and Ch. Reinle, 163–194. Göttingen: V & R Unipress.

Tugya, B. 2014, "Késő Árpád-kori állatcsontleletek Kiskunfélegyháza, Amler-bánya lelőhelyről," [Late-Árpádian-age animal bone finds from Kiskunfélegyháza, Amlerbánya] *Archeologica Cumanica* 3, 387–397.

Turner, N. J., Davidson-Hunt, I. J. and O'Flaherty, M. 2003, "Living on the Edge: Ecological and Cultural Edges as Sources of Diversity for Social-Ecological Resilience," *Human Ecology* 31, 439–461.

Turnwald, Ch. 1965–1966, "Denare von ältesten Oboltyp," *Numizmatikai Közlöny* 64–65, 19–27.

Turnwald, Ch. 1967–1968, "Noch zum Münzwesen Stephans I," *Numizmatikai Közlöny* 66–67, 23–27.

Twigg, J. 2012, "Animal remains from Visegrád-Lower Castle from the 16–17th century," *Acta Archaeologica Academiae Scientiarum Hungaricae* 63, 197–220.

Ujszászi, R. 2010, *A XII. századi magyar rézpénzek* [12th-century Hungarian copper coins]. Budapest: Magyar Éremgyűjtők Egyesülete.

Unger, E. 1960, *Magyar éremhatározó. I–II: Középkor. III–V: Újkor.* [Hungarian Numismatic Catalogue I–II: Middle Ages III–V: Modern Age]. Budapest: Magyar Éremgyűjtők Egyesülete.

Urbanová, N. 2003a, "Základy stredovekých miest – urbanistická štruktúra," [The foundations of medieval towns – urban topography] In *Gotika. Dejiny slovenského výtvarného umenia* [Gothic. History of Slovak art], ed. D. Buran, 71–85. Bratislava: Slovenská Národná Galéria.

Urbanová, N. 2003b, "Premeny miest v neskorom stredoveku," [Changes in towns in the Late Middle Ages] In *Gotika. Dejiny slovenského výtvarného umenia* [Gothic. History of Slovak art], ed. D. Buran, 277–284. Bratislava: Slovenská Národná Galéria.

V. Ember, M. 1981, *Old Textiles* (*The treasures of the Hungarian National Museum*). Budapest: Corvina.

V. Székely, Gy. 1980, *Slawonische Banalmünzpragung* (Dissertationes Archaeologicae Ser. II/8). Budapest: Editio Instituti archaeologici universitatis de Rolando Eötvös nominatae.

Vadas, A. 2009, "Documentary Evidence on the Weather Conditions and a Possible Crisis in 1315–1317: Case Study from the Carpathian Basin," *Journal of Environmental Geography* 2/3–4, 23–29.

Vadas, A. 2010, *Weather Anomalies and Climatic Change in Late Medieval Hungary: Weather events in the 1310s in the Hungarian Kingdom*. Saarbrücken: VDM Verlag.

Vadas, A. 2011a, "Late Medieval Environmental Changes of the Southern Great Hungarian Plain – A Case Study," *Annual of the Medieval Studies at CEU* 17, 41–60.

Vadas, A. 2011b, "Floods in the Hungarian Kingdom as Reflected in Private Letters (1541–1650) – Sources and Possibilities," In *Anuarul Scolii Doctorale. "Istorie. Civilizaţie. Cultură" V*, ed. N. Toader, 77–101. Cluj-Napoca: Universitatea Babeş-Bolyai Facultatea de Istorie şi Filosofie.

Vadas, A. 2013a, "Long-Term Perspectives on River Floods. The Dominican Nunnery on Margaret Island (Budapest) and the Danube River," *Interdisciplinaria Archaeologica* 4/1, 73–82.

Vadas, A. 2013b, *Körmend és a vizek. Egy település és környezete a kora újkorban* [Körmend and the waters. A settlement and its environment in the early modern period]. Budapest: ELTE Történelemtudományok Doktori Iskola.

Vadas, A. 2015–2016, "Városárkok és vízgazdálkodás a késő-középkori Közép-Európa városaiban," [Urban moats and water management in the towns of Central Europe in the Late Middle Ages]. *Urbs Magyar Várostörténeti Évkönyv* 10–11, 323–353.

Vadas, A. 2018, "Technologies on the Road between West and East The Spread of Water Mills and the Christianization of East Central Europe," In *Medieval Networks in East Central Europe: Commerce, Contacts, Communication*, eds. B. Nagy, F. Schmieder and A. Vadas. New York: Routledge (in press).

Vadas, A. and Rácz, L. 2013, "Climatic Changes in the Carpathian Basin during the Middle Ages – The State of Research," *Global Environment* 12, 198–227.

Vajda, T. 2001, "Adatok a Dráva menti középkori fokgazdálkodásról," [Data on the medieval fok system by the River Dráva] In *Tanulmányok a középkorról: a II. Medievisztikai PhD-konferencia, Szeged, 2001. április 3., előadásai* [Studies in medieval history. Proceeding of the 2nd PhD conference in medievistics, Szeged 3 April, 2001], eds. B. Weisz, L. Balogh and J. Szarka, 125–137. Szeged: Szegedi Középkorász Műhely.

Vajda, T. 2005, "Okleveles adatok Árpád-kori vízimalmainkról," [Charter data on Árpádian- period mills] In *Medievisztikai tanulmányok: a IV. Medievisztikai PhD-konferencia (Szeged, 2005. június 9–10.) előadásai* [Studies in medieval history. Proceeding of the 4th PhD conference in medievistics, Szeged 9–10 June, 2005], eds. Sz. Marton and É. Teiszler, 193–220. Szeged: Szegedi Középkorász Műhely.

Vajda, T. 2016, "Korai bencés apátságaink vízimalmaink: a szerzetesek szerepe a technikai fejlődésben," [Water mills of the early Benedictine abbey of Hungary and their role in technological development] In *Episcopus, Archiabbas Benedictinus, Historicus Ecclesiae. Tanulmányok Várszegi Asztrik 70. születésnapjára* [Studies in honor of Asztrik Várszegi on the occasion of his 70th birthday] (METEM Könyvek, 85), eds. Á. Somorjai OSB and I. Zombori, 25–45. Budapest: METEM.

Valter, I. 1972, "La croix processionale de Balatonfüred," *Acta Archaeologica Academiae Scientiarium Hungariae* 24, 215–232.

Valter, I. 1982a, "Das Zisterzienserkloster Pásztó: Geschichte und neue archäologische Forschungsergebnisse," *Analecta Cisteriensia* 38, 129–138.

Valter, I. 1982b, "Die archäologische Erschließung des ungarischen Zisterzienserklosters Szentgotthárd," *Analecta Cisteriensia* 38, 139–152.

Valter, I. 1982c, "Die archäologische Erschließung des Zisterzienserklosters Bélaspátfalva," *Analecta Cisteriensia* 38, 153–165.

Valter, I. 1994, "Quelques établissements proto-industriels en Hongrie," In *L'espace cistercien*, ed. L. Pressouyre, 391–400. Paris: Comité des travaux historiques et scientifiques.

Van der Beek, K. 2010, "Political fragmentation, competition, and investment decisions: the medieval grinding industry in Ponthieu, France, 1150–1250," *The Economic History Review* 63, 667–684.

Vardy, S. B. 1975, "The Hungarian Economic History School: its Birth and Development," *Journal of European Economic History* 4, 121–136.

Vargha, M. 2015, *Objects in Hoards and in Burial contexts during the Mongol Invasion of Central-Eastern Europe*. Oxford: Archaeopress.

Vastagh, G. 1972, "Metallurgische Folgerungen aus den Ausgrabungsfunden der Eisenverhüttung des XI–XII. Jhs," *Acta Archaeologica Academiae Scientiarum Hungaricae* 24, 241–260.

Végh, A. 2006, "The Remains of the First Jewish Quarter of Buda in the Light of Recent Excavations," In *Régészeti kutatások Magyarországon 2005* [Archaeological Excavations in Hungary 2005], ed. J. Kisfaludi, 125–148. Budapest: Kulturális Örökségvédelmi Hivatal.

Végh, A. 2006–2008, *Buda város középkori helyrajza*, I–II [The medieval topography of Buda] (Monumenta Historica Budapestinensia, 15–16). Budapest: Budapesti Történeti Múzeum.

Végh, A. 2008, "Topographische Bezüge des Zunftbuches der deutschen Fleischer zu Ofen," In *Zunftbuch und Privilegien der Fleischer zu Ofen aus dem Mittelalter* (Quellen zur Budapester Geschichte im Mittelalter und in der Frühen Neuzeit, 1), ed. I. Kenyeres, 139–158. Budapest: Budapest Főváros Levéltára – Budapesti Történeti Múzeum.

Végh, A. 2009, "Buda: The Multi-ethnic Capital of Medieval Hungary," In *Segregation–Integration–Assimilation. Religious and Ethnic Groups in the Medieval Towns of Central and Eastern Europe*, eds. D. Keene, B. Nagy and K. Szende, 89–99. Farnham–Burlington: Ashgate.

Végh, A. 2011, "Kutak, vízművek. Kiegészítés Buda város középkori helyrajzához," [Wells, waterworks. Complementary data on Buda's medieval topography] In *"Fél évszázad terepen" Tanulmánykötet Torma István tiszteletére 70. születésnapja alkalmából* [Half a century of fieldwork. Studies in honor of István Torma], eds. K. Kővári and Zs. Miklós, 327–332. Budapest: MTA Régészeti Intézete.

Végh, A. 2015, *Buda, I. kötet, 1686–ig / Part I. to 1686.* (Magyar Várostörténeti Atlasz, 4 = Hungarian Atlas of Historic Towns, 4). Budapest: MTA Történettudományi Intézet.

Vékony, G. 2004, "Sókereskedelem a Kárpát-medencében az Árpád-kor előtt," [Salt trade in the Carpathian Basin before the Árpádian age] In *"Quasi liber et pictura"*

Tanulmányok Kubinyi András 70. születésnapjára / Studies in Honour of András Kubinyi on His Seventieth Birthday, ed. Gy. Kovács, 655–661. Budapest: ELTE Régészettudományi Intézet = Institute of Archaeological Sciences of Eötvös Loránd University.

Velter, A.-M. 1996, "Die Kupferstück von Bela III. – Kriegsprägung oder ein Ausrichtungsversuch auf byzantinischen Wahrungssystem?," In *Proceedings of the International Historical Conference 900 Years from Saint Ladislas' Death, June 16–18. 1995*, ed. A. Săşianu-Gheorghe, 54–62. Oradea: Pelikan.

Velter, A.-M. 2002, *Transilvania în secolele V–XII. Interpretari istorico-politice şi economice pe baza descoperirilor monetare din bazinul Carpatic, secolele V–XII* [Transylvania in the 5th–12th centuries. Historical-political and economic interpretations based on coin finds in the Carpathian Basin, 5th–12th centuries]. Bucureşti: Paideia.

Verhulst, A. 1997, "Medieval Socio-economic Historiography in Western Europe: towards an Integrated Approach," *Journal of Medieval History* 23, 89–101.

Vermes, L. 1998, *Héber betűs pénzveretek Budán a XIII. században* [Coin finds with Hebrew inscriptions in 13th-century Buda]. Unpublished MA thesis defended at ELTE, Budapest.

Viczián, I. and Zatykó, Cs. 2011, "Geomorphology and environmental history in the Drava valley, near Berzence," *Hungarian Geographical Bulletin* 60, 357–377.

Viczián, I. et al. 2014, "Environmental Reconstruction of the Area of Roman Brigetio (Komárom, Hungary)," *Studia Geomorphologica Carpatho-Balcanica* 47, 95–105.

Viczián, I., Havas Z., Szeberényi, J. and Balogh, J. 2015, "Az Óbudai-sziget környezettörténete," [Environmental history of the Óbudai Island] In *Ökonómia és ökológia: Tanulmányok az ókori gazdaságtörténet és történeti földrajz köréből* [Economy and ecology. Studies in Ancient economic history and historical geography] (Ókor-Történet-Írás, 3), eds. Z. Csabai et al., 327–344. Pécs: Pécsi Tudományegyetem Ókortörténeti Tanszék – L'Harmattan.

Virág, Á. 1998, "A siófoki római kori zsilip hipotézisének története," [The history of the hypothesis of the Roman sluice at Siófok] *Vízügyi Közlemények* 80, 604–623.

Virág, Á. 2005, *A Sió és a Balaton közös története (1055–2005)* [The common history of the Balaton and Siófok, 1055 to 2005]. Budapest: [Közlekedési Dokumentáció Kft.].

von Alberti, H.-J. 1957, *Mass und Gewicht*. Berlin: Akademie-Verlag.

von Below, G. 1926, *Probleme der Wirtschaftsgeschichte. Eine Einführung in das Studium der Wirtschaftsgeschichte. Zweite Auflage*. Tübingen: Mohr.

von Ebengreuth, A. L. 1922–1923, "Friesacher Pfennige, Beiträge zu ihrer Münzgeschichte und zur Kenntnis ihrer Gepräge," *Numismatische Zeitschrift* 55, 89–118 and 56, 33–144.

von Stromer, W. 1970, *Oberdeutsche Hochfinanz 1350–1450*, I–III (Vierteljahrschrift für Sozial- und Wirtschaftsgeschichte Beihefte, 55–57). Wiesbaden: Steiner.

von Stromer, W. 1971, "Das Zusammenspiel oberdeutscher und Florentiner Geldleute bei der Finanzierung von König Ruprechts Italienfeldzug 1401/02," In *Öffentliche Finanzen und privates Kapital im späten Mittelalter und in der ersten Hälfte des 19. Jahrhunderts. Bericht über die 3. Arbeitstagung der Gesellschaft für Sozial- und Wirtschaftsgeschichte in Mannheim am 9. und 10. April 1969* (Forschungen zur Sozial- und Wirtschaftsgeschichte, 16), ed. H. Kellembenz, 50–86. Stuttgart: G. Fisher.

von Stromer, W. 1973/1975, "Die Ausländischen Kammergrafen der Stephanskrone unter den Königen aus den Häusern Anjou, Luxemburg und Habsburg. Exponenten des Großkapitals," *Hamburger Beiträge zur Numismatik* 27–29, 85–106.

von Stromer, W. 1985, "Medici–Unternehmen in den Karpatenländern. Versuche zur Beherschung des Weltmarkts für Buntmetalle," In *Aspetti della vita economica medievale. Atti del Convegno di Studi nel X. anniversario della morte di Federigo Melis*, ed. B. Dini, 370–397. Firenze: Universita degli studi di Firenze, Istituto di storia economica.

von Stromer, W. 1986, "Die Kontinentalsperre Kaiser Sigismunds gegen Venedig 1412–1433 und die Verlagerung der interkontinentalen Transportwege," In *Atti della Quinta Settimana di Studio (4–10 maggio 1973). Trasporti e sviluppo economico, secoli XIII–XVIII*, ed. A. V. Marx, 1418–1433. Firenze: Le Monnier.

Vörös, I. 1986, "Egy XV. századi ház állatcsontlelete Vácott," [Animal bones from a 15th-century house at Vác] *Archaeologiai Értesítő* 113, 255–256.

Vörös, I. 1988, "Középkori agancs lőportartók az ugodi várból," [Medieval gunpowder holders made of horns from the castle of Ugod] *Acta Musei Papensis* 1, 131–135.

Vörös, I. 1990a, "Szabolcs ispánsági székhely Árpád-kori állatcsontleletei," [Árpádian-age animal bones from Szabolcs] *A Nyíregyházi Jósa András Múzeum évkönyve* 27–29, 165–188.

Vörös, I. 1990b, "Kutyaáldozatok és kutyatemetkezések a középkori Magyarországon I.," [Dog sacrifices and dog burials in medieval Hungary] *Folia Archaeologica* 41, 117–146.

Vörös, I. 1991. Kutyaáldozatok és kutyatemetkezések a középkori Magyarországon II/3. Per canem jurare," [Dog sacrifices and dog burials in medieval Hungary, II/3] *Folia Archaeologica* 42, 179–196.

Vörös, I. 2000, "Adatok az Árpád-kori állattartás történetéhez," [Data to the history of Árpádian-age animal husbandry] In *A középkori magyar agrárium* [Medieval Hungarian agriculture], eds. L. Bende and G. Lőrinczy, 71–111. Ópusztaszer: Nemzeti Történelmi Emlékpark.

Vörös, I. 2003, "Sixteenth and Seventeenth Century Animal Bone finds in Hungary," In *Archaeology of the Ottoman Period in Hungary* (Opuscula Hungarica, 3), eds. I. Gerelyes and Gy. Kovács, 339–352. Budapest: Magyar Nemzeti Múzeum.

Vörös, I. 2004, "A középkori Csőt falu állatcsontleletei," [Animal bone finds of the medieval village of Csőt] *Communicationes Archaeologicae Hungariae 2004*, 223–234.

Vörös, I. 2006, "Ló az Árpád-kori Magyarországon," [The horse in Árpádian-age Hungary] *Folia Archaeologica* 52, 163–216.

Vörös, I. 2009, "Adatok a Dunakanyar régió Árpád-kori állattartásához," [Data to the animal husbandry of the region of the Danube Bend in the Árpádian age] In *Csontvázak a szekrényből. Skeletons from the Cupboard*, eds. L. Bartosiewicz, E. Gál and I. Kováts, 131–145. Budapest: Martin Opitz.

Wehli, T. 2009, "The Illuminated Chronicle from the point of view of illuminations," In *The Book of the Illuminated Chronicle*, eds. L. Veszprémy, T. Wehli and J. Hapák, 37–193. Budapest: Kossuth.

Weinrich, L. (ed.) 1999, *Hungarici monasterii ordinis sancti Pauli primi heremitae de Urbe Roma instrumenta et priorum registra*. Roma–Budapest: Római Magyar Akadémia.

Weissen, K. 2003, "I mercanti italiani e le fiere in Europa centrale alla fine del Medioevo e agli inizi dell'etá moderna," In *La pratica dello scambio: Sistemi di fiere, mercanti e cittá in Europa (1409–1700)*, ed. P. Lanaro, 161–176. Venezia: Marsilio.

Weissen, K. 2006, "Florentiner Kaufleute in Deutschland," In *Zwischen Maas und Rhein. Beziehungen, Begegnungen und Konflikte in einem europäischen Kernraum von der Spätantike bis zum 19. Jahrhundert. Versuch einer Bilanz*, ed. F. Irsigler, 363–401. Trier: Kliomedia.

Weisz, B. (ed.) 2016, *Pénz, posztó, piac. Gazdaságtörténeti tanulmányok a magyar középkorról* [Cash, Cloth, Commerce. Studies in the economic history of Hungary]. Budapest: MTA BTK Történettudományi Intézet.

Weisz, B. 1999, "Zsidó kamaraispánok az Árpád-korban," [Jewish chamber counts in the Árpádian age] In *Tanulmányok a középkori magyar történelemről* [Studies in the history of medieval Hungary], eds. S. Homonnai, F. Piti and I. Tóth, 151–161. Szeged: Szegedi Középkorász Műhely.

Weisz, B. 2003, "Az esztergomi vám Árpád-kori története," [The Esztergom customs in the Árpádian age] *Századok* 137, 973–981.

Weisz, B. 2007a, "A nemesércbányákból származó királyi jövedelmek az Árpád-korban," [Royal incomes from ore mining in the Árpádian age] In *Középkortörténeti tanulmányok V. Az V. Medievisztikai PhD-konferencia előadásai* [Studies in medieval history, 5. Proceedings of the 5th PhD conference in medievistics], eds. É. Révész and M. Halmágyi, 247–259. Szeged: Szegedi Középkorász Műhely.

Weisz, B. 2007b, "Megjegyzések az Árpád-kori sóvámolás és -kereskedelem történetéhez," [Notes to the history of Árpádian age salt taxation and trade] *Acta Universitatis Szegediensis. Acta Historica* 125, 43–58.

Weisz, B. 2007c, "Vásártartás az Árpád-korban," [Markets in the Árpádian period] *Századok* 141, 879–942.

Weisz, B. 2010a, "Kamaraispánok az Árpád-korban," [Chamber counts in the Árpádian age] *Turul* 83, 79–87.

Weisz, B. 2010b, "Vásárok a középkorban," [Markets in the Middle Ages] *Századok* 144, 1397–1454.
Weisz, B. 2011, "Az Árpád-kori harmincadvám," [The thirtieth customs duty in the Árpádian age] In *Erősségénél fogva várépítésre való... Tanulmányok a 70 éves Németh Péter tiszteletére* [Proper for castle building for its strength. Studies in honor of Péter Németh on his 70th birthday], eds. J. Cabello and N. C. Tóth, 267–278. Nyíregyháza: Szabolcs-Szatmár-Bereg Megyei Önkormányzat Múzeumok Igazgatósága.
Weisz, B. 2012a, "A kamara haszna okán szedett collecta," [The collecta gathered by reason of the chamber's profit] In *"Köztes-Európa" vonzásában. Ünnepi tanulmányok Font Márta tiszteletére* [In the attraction of "Zwischeneuropa" Studies in honor of Márta Font], eds. D. Bagi, T. Fedeles and G. Kiss, 547–558. Pécs: Kronosz.
Weisz, B. 2012b, *Vásárok és lerakatok a középkori Magyar Királyságban* [Markets and staples in the Medieval Kingdom of Hungary]. Budapest: MTA BTK Történettudományi Intézet.
Weisz, B. 2013a, "Mining Town Privileges in Angevin Hungary," *Hungarian Historical Review* 2, 288–312.
Weisz, B. 2013b, *A királyketteje és az ispán harmada. Vámok és vámszedés Magyarországon a középkor első felében* [The king's half and the *comes*'s third. Customs and customs duties in Hungary in the first half of the Middle Ages]. Budapest: MTA BTK Történettudományi Intézet.
Weisz, B. 2013c, "Entrate reali e politica economica nell'età di Carlo I.," In *L'Ungheria angioina*, ed. E. Csukovits, 205–236. Roma: Viella.
Weisz, B. 2013d, "The Legal Background of the Trade Life of Košice in the Middle Ages," In *Košice in the Coordinates of European History*, eds. M. Hajduová and M. Bartoš, 94–111. Košice: The city of Košice – Košice City Archives.
Weisz, B. 2014, "A 15. századi váradi vámper Árpád-kori gyökerei," [Árpádian-age origin of the Oradea custom case] In *Nagyvárad és Bihar a korai középkorban* [Oradea and Bihar County in the early medieval period] (Tanulmányok Biharország történetéről, 1), ed. A. Zsoldos, 147–165. Nagyvárad: Varadinum Kulturális Alapítvány.
Weisz, B. 2015a, "A magyar gazdaság mozgatórugói a középkorban. Az MTA BTK Lendület Középkori Magyar Gazdaságtörténet Kutatócsoport programja," [The driving forces of the Hungarian economy in the Middle Ages. The program of the "Impetus" Research Group on Hungarian Economic History] *Történelmi Szemle* 57, 487–506.
Weisz, B. 2015b, "Az urbura," [The *urbura*] *Bányászattörténeti Közlemények* 19, 3–23.
Weisz, B. 2015c, "Ki volt az első kincstartó? A kincstartói hivatal története a 14. században," [Who was the first treasurer? The history of the office of the treasury in the 14th century] *Történelmi Szemle* 57, 527–540.

Weisz, B. 2015d, "Királyi adózás Szlavóniában az Árpád-kortól az Anjou-kor első feléig," [Royal Taxes in Slavonia from the Árpádian Age to the first half of the Angevin period] In *A horvát–magyar együttélés fordulópontjai. Intézmények, társadalom, gazdaság, kultúra* [Turning points of Croatian–Hungarian coexistence – institutions, society, economy], eds. J. Turkalj and D. Karbić, 285–293. Budapest: MTA Bölcsészettudományi Kutatóközpont Történettudományi Intézet – Horvát Történettudományi Intézet.

Weisz, B. 2016, "A tárnokmester jogköre az Anjou-korban," [The jurisdiction of *magister tavernicorum* in the Angevin period] In *Pénz, posztó, piac. Gazdaságtörténeti tanulmányok a magyar középkorról* [Cash, cloth, commerce. Studies in the economic history of medieval Hungary], ed. eadem, 181–200. Budapest: MTA Bölcsészettudományi Kutatóközpont Történettudományi Intézet.

Wenzel, G. 1879, *A magyar bányajog rendszere* [The system of Hungarian mining rights]. Budapest: Athenaeum.

Wenzel, G. 1880, *Magyarország bányászatának kritikai története* [Critical history of mining in Hungary]. Budapest: MTA.

Westermann, E. 1979, *Internationaler Ochsenhandel (1350–1750). Akten des 7th International Economic History Congress Edinburgh 1978* (Beiträge zur Wirtschaftsgeschichte, 9). [Stuttgart]: Klett-Cotta.

Weszerle, J. 1873, *Hátrahagyott érmészeti táblái* [His numismatic catalogues]. Pest: Athenaeum.

Weszerle, J. 1911, *Weszerle József hátrahagyott érmészeti táblái*, I [The numismatic tables of József Weszerle]. Budapest: Athenaeum.

Wetter, E. 2011, *Objekt, Überlieferung und Narrativ. Spätmittelalterliche Goldschmiedekunst im historischen Königreich Ungarn* (Studia Jagellonica Lipsiensia, 8). Ostfildern: Jan Thorbecke.

Wikander, Ö. 1985, "Mill-channels, weirs and ponds. The environment of ancient water-mills," *Opuscula Romana* 15, 149–154.

Willis, K. J., Rudner, E. and Sümegi, P. 2000, "The Full-Glacial Forests of Central and Southeastern Europe," *Quaternary Research* 53, 203–213.

Winter, H. 2002, "Die Frühzeit des friesacher Pfennigs. Die numismatische Evidenz," In *Die Frühzeit des Friesacher Pfennigs (etwa 1125/30–etwa 1166)*, eds. M. Alram, R. Härtel and M. Schreiner, 135–466. Wien: Österreichische Akademie der Wissenschaften.

Witthöft, H. 1976, "Struktur und Kapazität der Lüneburger Saline seit dem 12. Jahrhundert," *Vierteljahrschrift für Sozial- und Wirtschaftsgeschichte* 63, 1–117.

Wollmann, V. 1995, "Steinsalzbergbau in Siebenbürgen und im südlichen Karpatenraum," *Der Anschnitt* 47, 135–147.

Wyrozumski, J. 1968, *Państwowa gospodarka solna w Polsce do schyłku XIV wieku* [Salt management in Poland until the late 14th century]. Kraków: Nakładem Uniwersytetu Jagiellońskiego.

Wyrozumski, J. 1989, "Salzhandel im mittelalterlichen Polen," In *Salz – Arbeit – Technik. Produktion und Distribution in Mittelalter und Früher Neuzeit*, ed. Ch. Lamschus, 271–280. Lüneburg: Deutsches Salzmuseum.

Zatykó, Cs. 2003, "Medieval Villages and Their Landscape: Methods of Reconstruction," In *People and Nature in Historical Perspective* (CEU Medievalia, 5), eds. J. Laszlovszky and P. Szabó, 343–375. Budapest: CEU Press.

Zatykó, Cs. 2007, "Medieval settlement history of the Baláta Lake and its environs," In *Environmental Archaeology in Transdanubia* (Varia Archaeologica Hungarica, 20), eds. I. Juhász, P. Sümegi and Cs. Zatykó, 257–264. Budapest: Archaeological Institute of the Hungarian Academy of Sciences.

Zatykó, Cs. 2011, "Aspects of fishing in medieval Hungary," In *Ruralia VIII: Processing, Storage, Distribution of Food – Food in the Medieval Rural Environment*, eds. J. Klápště and P. Sommer, 399–408. Turnhout: Brepols.

Zatykó, Cs. 2015, "People beyond landscapes: past, present and future of Hungarian landscape archaeology," *Antaeus: Communicationes ex Instituto Archaeologico Academiae Scientiarum Hungaricae* 33, 369–388.

Zimányi, V. 1972, "Velence szarvasmarhaimportja az 1624–1647–es években," [Cattle import of Venice between 1624 and 1647] *Agrártörténeti Szemle* 14, 387– 397.

Zimányi, V. 1976, *Magyarország az európai gazdaságban 1600–1650* [Hungary in the European economy between 1600–1650] (Értekezések a Történeti Tudományok Köréből, 80). Budapest: Akadémiai.

Zimányi, V. 1980, "Die wirtschaftliche und soziale Entwicklung der Städte Ungarns im 16. Jahrhundert," In *Die Stadt an der Schwelle zur Neuzeit*, ed. W. Rausch, 129–141. Linz: Donau.

Zimányi, V. 1987, *Economy and Society in Sixteenth and Seventeenth Century Hungary (1526–1650)*. Budapest: Akadémiai.

Zimányi, V. 1992, "Sozial- und Wirtschaftsentwicklung in den Herrschaften Rechnitz und Schlaining an der Wende vom 15. zum 16. Jahrhundert," In *Andreas Baumkircher: Erben und Nachfolger: Symposium im Rahmen der "Schlaininger Gespräche" vom 20.–24. September 1989 auf Burg Schlaining* Wissenschaftliche Arbeiten aus dem Burgenland, 88), eds. U. Döcker and R. Kropf, 201–214. Eisenstadt: Burgenländisches Landesmuseum.

Zimonyi, I. and Kovács, Sz. (eds.) 2016, *Török nyelvű népek a középkori Magyar Királyságban* [Turkic speaking people in the medieval Kingdom of Hungary] (Altajisztikai Tankönyvtár; 6.). Szeged: SZTE Altajisztikai Tanszék.

Zolnay, L. 1964, "István ifjabb király számadása 1264-ből," [Accounts of Junior King Stephen from 1264] *Budapest Régiségei* 21, 79–114.

Zolnay, L. 1965, "Pénzverők és ötvösök a románkori Esztergomban," [Moneyers and goldsmiths in Romanesque Esztergom] *Archaeologiai Értesítő* 92, 148–162.

Zolnay, L. 1971, *Vadászatok a régi Magyarországon* [Hunting in old Hungary]. Budapest: Natura.

Zólyomi, B. 1952, "Magyarország növénytakarójának fejlődéstörténete az utolsó jégkorszaktól," [The development of Hungary's vegetation from the end of the last ice age] *MTA Biológiai Osztályának Közleményei* 1, 491–527.

Zólyomi, B. 1980, "Landwirtschaftliche Kultur und Wandlung der vegetation im Holozän am Balaton," *Phytocoenologia* 7, 121–126.

Zsámbéki, M. 1983, "14–15. századi magyarországi kincsleletek," [14th–15th-century treasure hoards in Hungary] *Művészettörténeti Értesítő* 32, 105–128.

Zsámboki, L. 1982a, "Magyarország ércbányászata a honfoglalástól az I. világháború végéig. (Topográfiai és gazdasági áttekintés.)," [Ore mining in Hungary from the Hungarian Conquest to the end of World War I (Topographic and economic overview] In *Közlemények a magyarországi ásványi nyersanyagok történetéből*, I [Studies in the history of mineral raw materials in Hungary] ed. idem, 13–48. Miskolc: Nehézipari Műszaki Egyetem.

Zsámboki, L. 1982b, "Az országos bányajog és bányaigazgatás fejlődési iránya Magyarországon a Honfoglalástól az I. világháború végéig," [Mining rights and the administration of mines in Hungary from the Hungarian Conquest to the end of World War I] In *Közlemények a magyarországi ásványi nyersanyagok történetéből*, I [Studies in the history of mineral raw materials in Hungary] ed. idem, 167–196. Miskolc: Nehézipari Műszaki Egyetem.

Zsámboki, L. 2005, *Selmeci ezüst, körmöci arany. Válogatott tanulmányok a szerző születésének 70. évfordulója tiszteletére* [Silver of Štiavnica, gold of Kremnica. Collected essays in honor of the seventieth birthday of the author]. Rudabánya–Miskolc: Érc- és Ásványbányászati Múzeum.

Zsidi, P. 2007, "Duna szerepe Aquincum topográfiájában," [The role of the Danube in the topography of Aquincum] *Budapest Régiségei* 41, 57–83.

Zsoldos, A. 1999, *A szent király szabadjai. Fejezetek a várjobbágyság történetéből* [The freefolks of the holy king. Chapters from the history of royal castle servants] (Társadalom- és művelődéstörténeti tanulmányok, 26). Budapest: MTA Történettudományi Intézet.

Zsoldos, A. 2005, *Az Árpádok és asszonyaik* [The Árpáds and their wives] (Társadalom- és művelődéstörténeti tanulmányok, 36). Budapest: MTA Történettudományi Intézet.

Zsoldos, A. 2007, *Családi ügy. IV. Béla és István ifjabb király viszálya az 1260-as években* [Family business. The conflict between Béla IV and Stephen junior king in the 1260s]. Budapest: MTA Történettudományi Intézet – História.

Zsoldos, A. 2011, "II. András Aranybullája," [The Golden Bull of Andrew II] *Történelmi Szemle* 53, 1–38.

Zsoldos, A. and Neumann, T. 2010, *Székesfehérvár középkori kiváltságai* [The medieval privileges of Székesfehérvár]. Székesfehérvár: Székesfehérvár Megyei Jogú Város Levéltára.

Index of Geographic Names

Aachen 65, 383
Abaúj County 77, 274, 300
Abrud (Abrudbánya, Altenburg) 166, 173
Acey (part of present-day Vitreux) 326
Adriatic Sea 210, 493–494, 497
Africa 147
Alba Iulia (Gyulafehérvár, Weissenburg) 9, 184, 198, 283
Albeşti see Albeştii Bistriţei
Albeştii Bistriţei (Kisfehéregyház, Fehéregyház) 205
Alhévíz (part of present-day Budapest) 252
Almás see Almásfüzítő
Almásfüzítő 168
Alps (mountains) 182
Alsózsolca 140, 482
Amsterdam 142
Apahida (Apahida, Apáthida) 73, 183
Apáthida see Apahida
Apáti see Zalaapáti
Apsa (part of present-day Türje) 68
Aquileia 287, 306
Aquitaine 182
Arad (Arad) 184, 188, 193–195, 198
Arad County 68, 420
Arieş (Aranyos; river) 169
Árpás 76
Árva County 278
Asszonyfa see Ostffyasszonyfa
Augsburg 504
Austria 21, 63, 71, 129, 132–133, 144, 168–169, 171, 175, 209, 217, 281–282, 287, 289, 299, 302, 305–306, 363, 401, 412, 421, 435, 441, 450, 461–462, 467–468, 470–471, 478, 480, 489–490, 492, 494

Bač (Bács) 198, 202–203
Bački Monoštor (Monostorszeg) 419
Badacsonytomaj 68
Baia de Arieş (Aranyosbánya) 173
Baia Mare (Nagybánya) 172–173, 299, 302–304
Baj 124, 151, 156
Bajcsavár (Bajcsa; part of present-day Nagykanizsa) 136, 142, 152, 156, 162

Bakony (mountains) 420
Bakonybél 169, 186–187, 189, 198, 207
Balaton (lake) 41–42, 68, 74, 331
Balatonfüred 458
Balatonkeresztúr 135
Balkans 33, 58, 67, 206, 209, 217, 310, 454
Baltic Sea 243, 480
Bamberg 286
Banská Bystrica (Besztercebánya, Neusohl) 144, 170, 175, 179, 340
Banská Štiavnica (Selmecbánya, Schemnitz) 168–169, 173, 176, 179–180, 424
Baranya County 68, 77, 263, 284, 321, 419–420, 486
Baranyavár see Duldumas
Barcelona 182
Barcs 148, 152, 156
Bardejov (Bártfa, Bartfeld) 8, 262, 341, 344, 350, 389–390, 443
Barlabáshida (part of present-day Pakod) 73
Barnag 236
Bârsa (Barca; river) 69
Basel 342, 501
Báta see Bátaszék
Bátaszék 325
Béc (part of present-day Letenye) 236
Bečej (Becse) 76
Bega (Béga; river) 241
Békásmegyer (part of present-day Budapest) 141, 434
Békés 152, 156
Békés County 401, 405
Bélavár 452
Beled 343
Belgrade (Nándorfehérvár, Beograd) 215, 310
Bélháromkút (part of present-day Bélapátfalva) 269
Benepuszta (part of present-day Kecskemét) 114
Bereg (forest) 200
Bereg County 75
Beuvray (mountain) 331
Bihar County 68, 73, 177, 435, 442, 482
Biharia (Bihar) 309
Biscay (region) 182

Bistriţa (Beszterce, Nösen)   183, 330, 341, 382
Bizere (part of present-day Vladimirescu)
   187–188, 192, 199
Black Sea   139, 167, 182, 493, 496
Bochnia   182, 208
Bőd (part of present-day Csongrád)   186
Bodrog (river)   62, 74
Bodrog County   230
Bodrogu Vechi (Óbodrog)   199
Bohemia   174, 243, 260, 327, 444, 447, 465,
   468, 475, 480–486, 488, 490
Boldogkő see Boldogkőváralja
Boldogkőváralja   265
Bologna   65, 301, 470
Bonţida (Bonchida, Bonisbruck)   73
Borsod County   70, 230, 380, 444, 482
Borsodgeszt   444
Bosnia   182, 310, 313, 331
Brabant (region)   483
Braşov (Brassó, Kronstadt)   31, 306, 341–342,
   382, 443, 486
Bratislava (Pozsony, Pressburg)   8, 9, 20, 29,
   85, 144, 184, 189, 209, 211, 217, 242, 256,
   275, 278, 298, 310, 328–329, 341–344,
   346–347, 352, 370, 375–377, 389, 410,
   440, 443, 461, 465, 468, 470–471, 488,
   491, 503–504, 507
Brezno (Breznóbánya, Bries)   175
Brittany (region)   182
Brno (Brünn)   486
Bruges   480, 482
Brussels   483
Buda (part of present-day Budapest)   27–28,
   61–62, 67–68, 85, 102, 109, 124, 126–128,
   132, 135, 137–138, 140–142, 144, 147,
   151–152, 156, 158, 162, 164, 170, 175, 188,
   195, 202, 209, 215, 226, 252, 289–291,
   304, 313, 328–329, 331–332, 338, 342,
   344, 355–356, 370–371, 374, 376, 379,
   389–393, 409, 415, 420–422, 424, 427,
   429, 433–439, 443, 447–449, 451,
   453–455, 457, 464–465, 467–468,
   470–471, 481, 491–492, 496, 498–508
Budafelhévíz (part of present-day Budapest)
   252, 355, 438, 441, 450
Budaszentlőrinc (part of present-day
   Budapest)   329–330
Bük   343

Bulci (Bulcs)   199
Bulgaria   67
Burgundy   331
Burul (part of present-day Zalavár)   74
Byzantium   31, 147, 285, 381, 456–458, 464,
   476–477, 479

Camargue (region)   182
Câmpia Turzii (Aranyosgyéres, Gieresch)
   183
Carinthia   286–287
Carpathian Basin   3, 12, 24, 30, 36, 39–41,
   45–46, 50, 56, 63, 82–83, 85–86, 90–92,
   99, 114, 117, 120, 126, 133–134, 138,
   166–168, 173, 177, 183–184, 205, 219, 223,
   225–227, 236–237, 286, 338–339,
   371–372, 379–380, 385, 391
Cârţa (Csíkkarcafalva)   199
Catalonia   182, 301
Cegléd   98, 129
Cenad (Csanád)   194, 199, 203–204, 309,
   312–313
Central Europe   10, 31, 45, 56, 65, 166, 172, 219,
   227, 459–460, 467, 482, 484–486,
   492–495, 500–501, 506
Cesargrad (Császárvár; part of present-day
   Klanjec)   225, 452
Chornotysiv (Feketeardó, Ardó)   75
Čierna Voda (river)   275
Cikádor (part of present-day Bátaszék)   326
Cinobaňa (Szinóbánya, Frauenberg)   170
Clairvaux   326
Cluj (Kolozsvár, Klausenburg)   171, 184, 236,
   249, 265, 338, 376, 443–445, 448
Cluj-Mănăştur (Kolozsmonostor; part of
   present-day Cluj)   68, 73, 325
Cojocna (Kolozsakna, Salzgrub)   183, 205
Cologne (Köln)   332, 486, 488
Constance (Konstanz)   144
Constantinople (Istanbul)   475, 478–479
Coştiui (Rónaszék)   183
Cracow (Kraków)   208, 382, 389, 448, 486,
   493, 504
Crimea (peninsula)   182
Crişana (Körösvidék; region)   365
Cristuru Secuiesc (Székelykeresztúr)   165
Croatia   210, 270, 287, 339, 361, 363, 482
Csanád County   74

INDEX OF GEOGRAPHIC NAMES 627

Csátalja 150, 154
Csatár 150, 154, 167
Csehimindszent 70
Csengele 127, 135, 160
Csepel (part of present-day Budapest) 138, 160
Csepel Island 74
Csepreg 343
Csitár 167
Csongrád 120, 150, 154, 185–186
Csongrád County 76
Csorna 250
Csőt (part of present-day Budapest) 73, 121, 150, 154
Czech Republic 166
Czechoslovakia 21, 24, 27

Dacia (province) 166, 183
Đakovo (Diakovár, Djakowar) 310
Dalmatia 182, 310–311, 329, 493, 495, 497
Danube (river) 45, 67–68, 74, 139–142, 187, 209, 241–242, 250, 252, 324, 348, 355, 381, 408, 420, 426, 428–429, 471, 475–476, 478, 486, 500
Danube Bend Gorge (Dunakanyar; region) 141
Danube–Tisza Interfluve (Duna–Tisza–köze; region) 84–85, 100
Debrecen 122, 129, 150, 154, 216–217, 443, 448
Decs 377
Dej (Dés, Burglos) 171, 183, 213–214, 216
Denmark 148
Diakovce (Deáki) 324
Diósgyőr (part of present-day Miskolc) 144, 390, 466
Doboka County 73
Dobšiná (Dobsina, Dobschau) 177
Dolná Súča (Alsószúcs) 446
Dolné Zelenice (Zela, Alsózélle) 271
Dombóvár 388
Dömös 186–187, 192, 197–199, 244, 262
Dorozlouch (part of present-day Turnašica) 271
Dráva (river) 85, 148, 192, 241, 245, 263, 420, 482
Dravce (Szepesdaróc, Drautz) 72
Droitwitch (part of present-day Droitwitch Spa) 182
Dubica 260, 329

Dubrovnik 464, 495
Duldumas (Baranyavár) 269
Dunaföldvár 141
Dunaszekcső 77

East Central Europe 87, 321, 478, 485, 496
East European Plain 91
Eger (Erlau) 139–140, 207, 224, 242, 309, 312–316, 396, 414, 444, 468
Eisenstadt (Kismarton) 330, 343, 445
Elbe (Labe; river) 29, 485
Endrőd 150, 154
England 65, 148, 175, 182, 220, 222, 247, 322, 327, 485, 492, 497
Ercsi 199, 333
Érd 152, 156, 163
Esztergom (Gran) 68, 76, 89, 121, 124, 141, 150, 154, 162, 168–170, 187, 189, 198, 200, 242, 248–249, 260, 275, 287, 296, 298, 309–312, 314–316, 338, 371, 375–376, 383, 386, 396, 414, 420, 422–429, 457, 477, 481–482, 494
Ete (part of present-day Decs) 377

Faenza 470
Fancsika (part of present-day Debrecen) 122
Farná (Farnad) 275
Fehér County 71
Fehéregyháza (part of present-day Budapest) 260
Fehér-Körös (Crişul Alb; river) 401
Fehérvár *see* Székesfehérvár
Fejér County 70, 73
Fekete-Körös (Crişul Negru; river) 177, 401
Felhévíz *see* Budafelhévíz
Fertő (Neusiedler See; lake) 41–42, 74, 408
Fertőrákos (Rákos) 71
Flanders 458, 479–480, 482, 493, 497
Florence (Firenze) 301, 470, 489, 492, 496–497, 507
Földvár *see* Dunaföldvár
Fonyód 151, 156
France 65, 147, 247, 278, 327, 331, 457–458, 481, 492
Friesach 264, 281, 286, 287
Fruška Gora (mountains) 68
Füle 70
Füzitő *see* Almásfüzítő

Gamás 66, 223
Gelnica (Gölnicbánya, Göllnitz) 177, 424, 427
Genoa (Genova) 301, 496
Germany 109, 129, 147–148, 172, 182, 382, 392, 434, 438, 449, 450, 472, 489, 492
Ghent (Gent) 480, 482
Gömör County 68, 449, 454
Gönc 273–274, 276–277
Gortva (Gortvakisfalud) 68
Great Hungarian Plain (Alföld; region) 40, 42, 44, 46–47, 53, 58–59, 63, 83–84, 88, 90, 101, 107, 109–110, 112, 120–121, 129, 131, 214, 225–226, 237, 314–315, 324, 329, 338, 362–363, 388, 401, 407, 420, 443
Greater Cumania (Nagykunság; region) 120
Greece 371, 475
Gutenwert see Otok
Gyál 120, 150, 154
Gyelid (part of present-day Arad) 199
Gyöngyöspüspöki (part of present-day Gyöngyös) 444
Győr (Raab) 140, 209, 260, 309, 312, 316, 340, 349–350, 383, 408, 413, 421, 426, 429, 481
Győr County 68, 73, 76
Gyula 152, 156, 163, 251, 276–277, 366, 396, 399–403, 405–406, 409–412, 414
Gyulakeszi 232

Hahót 121, 151, 154
Hainburg 344, 478
Hajdúnánás 120, 150, 154
Halle an der Saale 182
Halogy 77
Hamburg 342
Hatvan 443, 454
Havlíčkův Brod 484
Hegyalja (region) 85
Hegyeshalom 77
Heiligenkreuz im Wienerwald 188–189, 191, 198, 326
Herentals 483
Heves 129
Heves County 73, 226, 420, 443
Hídvég see Rábahídvég
Hlohovec (Galgóc, Freistadt) 260–261, 373, 415–416
Hodász 444
Hódmezővásárhely 129, 150, 154

Hodosmonostor see Bodrogu Vechi
Hodruš (Hodrushámor) 179
Holíč (Holics) 260, 486
Hollókő 146
Holy Land 67, 458
Holy Roman Empire 172, 327
Homokrév see Mokrin
Hont County 76, 232, 446
Hortobágy (region) 84
Hrabkov (Harapkó) 333
Hron (Garam; river) 175–177, 179–180, 428, 484
Hronský Beňadik (Garamszentbenedek, Sankt Benedikt) 169, 186–187, 189, 323–325
Hunedoara (Vajdahunyad, Eisenmarkt) 396, 401–405, 407–412
Hunyad County 177, 401
Hurhida see Úrhida
Huy 482, 486
Hviezdoslavov (Vörösmajor) 276–277

Iberian Peninsula 65
Igriş (Egres) 193–194, 199, 326
Ikva (river) 343, 352
Illmitz (Illmic) 74
Ilok (Újlak) 309, 399
Iron Gates Gorge (Vaskapu, Porţile de Fier, Đerdapska klisura) 141–142
Irshava (Makszemháza, Ilosva) 75
Italy 32, 62, 65, 109, 129, 147, 180, 182, 292, 382, 391–392, 449, 457, 464, 472, 483–485, 489, 493–494, 502–503, 506
Izsó (part of present-day Kötegyán) 199

Jánovce (Dunajánosháza, Jánosháza) 275
Jasov (Jászó) 170, 173
Jászberény 129
Jerusalem 65, 67, 420
Jihlava (Iglau) 484

Kálló see Nagykálló
Kállósemjén 232
Kalocsa 198, 309, 311–313
Kána (part of present-day Budapest) 122, 128, 150, 154
Kapuvár 269
Karcag 150, 154
Kardoskút 150, 154, 161

INDEX OF GEOGRAPHIC NAMES 629

Karos 372
Kaszaper 193
Kazinc (part of present-day Kazincbarcika) 167
Kecskemét 23, 84, 114, 129
Kéménd *see* Máriakéménd
Kenderes 329
Kenéz *see* Kenézmonostora
Kenézhida 73
Kenézmonostora (part of present-day Nădlac) 199
Kesztölc 69
Keve *see* Ráckeve
Khust (Huszt) 215
Kiev (Kyiv) 67, 475, 478–480
Kis-Balaton *see* Little Balaton
Kiskunfélegyháza 150, 154
Kiskunhalas 129
Kisnána (Nána) 187
Kisvárda 436, 442
Kisvásárhely 435
Klostermarienberg (Borsmonostor) 189, 194, 197–198, 326–327
Knin 310
Kőhídpordány (part of present-day Wulkaprodersdorf) 71
Kolárovo (Gúta, Guta) 242
Kolozs County 68, 73, 435, 449
Komárno 141
Komárom County 76, 226, 423
Komoróc (part of present-day Palad' Komarivtsi) 444
Kondoros (river) 401
Kopács (part of present-day Csempeszkopács) 230
Kőrév (part of present-day Tokaj) 74
Korođ (Kórógy)
Körös (river) 84
Körös County 270, 452
Košice (Kassa, Kaschau) 8, 144, 209, 211, 243, 260, 301–304, 342, 350–351, 387–388, 421–422, 443, 447–449, 451, 486
Kostanjevica na Krki (Landstraß) 287
Kőszeg 151, 156
Kovácsi (part of present-day Esztergom) 5, 167–169, 375
Kövesd *see* Sopronkövesd
Kovin (Keve) 209
Krajina (region) 287

Kraków *see* Cracow
Krapina (Korpona) 396, 413
Kremnica (Körmöcbánya, Kremnitz) 170, 176, 178, 249, 283, 290, 294, 299–300, 302–304, 444, 483
Kukeč (Újkökényes, Kükecs) 230
Kutná Hora (Kuttenberg) 483–484
Kysucké Nové Mesto (Kiszucaújhely) 414

Laborec (Laborc; river) 446
Lajosmizse 150, 154
Landstraß *see* Kostanjevica na Krki
Leányfalu (part of present-day Nagyvázsony) 70
Lébény 73, 75
Leles (Lelesz) 72, 448
Lendava (Alsólendva) 248
Leuven 483
Levoča (Lőcse, Leutschau) 389, 443, 448
Limoges 383–384, 458, 480
Linz 440
Liptó County 278
Little Balaton (lake) 41, 84
Lockenhaus (Léka) 269, 412–414
Lórév 75
Lorraine (region) 439, 458
Loštice (Loschitz) 469, 490
Low Countries 483
Lower Austria 188, 344
Lower Danube 142, 209
Ľubietová (Libetbánya, Libethen) 175
Lucca 301
Lüneburg 182, 195
Luxembourg (region) 439

Maas (river) 458, 480, 486
Magdeburg 458
Magyaróvár (part of present-day Mosonmagyaróvár) 396–397, 401–403, 407–408, 410–414
Mainburg 436
Mainz 257
Makszemháza *see* Irshava
Mallorca (island) 182
Maramureş (Máramaros; region) 68, 182–184, 205, 208–2010, 213–216, 365, 408, 435
Margaret Island (Margit-sziget; part of present-day Budapest) 189, 252, 333

Máriakéménd   419
Maros (Mureş; river)   84, 185–188, 190, 192,
   194–195, 208, 214, 311, 324, 401, 420
Maros (region)   185
Marz (Márcfalva)   343
Mauruchhida *see* Mórichida
Mechelen   483
Mecsek (mountains)   170
Medzev (Mecenzéf)   177
Megyer *see* Békásmegyer
Mende   151, 156
Meseş (Meszes)   187, 189, 194, 196, 208
Mezőföld (region)   420
Mezőtúr   129, 443
Mezőzombor (Zombor)   70
Michalovce (Nagymihály)   438, 444, 446
Middle East   147–148, 464, 469
Milan (Milano)   301
Milcovul (Milkó)   310
Mindszent *see* Csehimindszent
Mirşid (Nyirsid)   187
Miskolc   144, 466
Mokrin (Homokrév)   74
Moldavia   31, 461, 486, 490
Moravia   129, 184, 235, 469, 483, 486, 488
Mórichida   73
Moson County   75, 77, 397, 436, 446
Muhi   59, 101, 128, 153, 158, 165, 243, 444, 454
Murano   464
Muraszemenye (Szemenye)   75, 330
Murga   151, 156

Nagyberény   452
Nagybörzsöny   178
Nagyharsány   284
Nagykálló   442, 447
Nagykanizsa   136, 152, 156
Nagykőrös   129
Nagykovácsi   328, 375
Nagymaros (Maros)   141
Nagyszakácsi (Szakácsi)   321
Nagyvázsony   150, 154, 390
Nána *see* Kisnána
Naples (Napoli)   497
Nesvady (Naszvad)   242
Neunkirch   436
Nick   70
Nitra (Nyitra, Neutra)   73, 188, 192, 198, 210,
   309, 312, 325, 330–331, 340, 416

Nógrád   419
Nógrád County   69, 74, 170, 446
North Hungarian Mountains (Északi-
   középhegység)   83, 88, 108, 141, 210
North Sea   133, 480
Norway   148
Novaj   77
Nové Košariská (Misérd)   276–277
Nuremberg (Nürnberg)   342, 447–448,
   458–461, 485, 489, 495, 498, 501–504,
   507
Nyárád   70
Nyárhíd (part of present-day Nové Zámky)
   71, 73
Nyársapát   151, 154
Nyírbátor   436, 442, 446–447
Nyírség (region)   84
Nyitra County   70–71, 73
Nysa   460

Óbuda (part of present-day Budapest)
   140–141, 187–189, 198–199, 252, 310, 333,
   348–349, 391, 434, 449
Ocland (Oklánd, Homoródoklánd)   163
Ocna Dejului (Désakna)   205, 207, 212
Ocna Mureş (Marosújvár)   183
Ocna Sibiului (Vízakna)   183, 205, 213
Őcsény   151, 156
Ónod   242, 248, 265, 269, 413, 468
Opatovská Nová Ves (Apátújfalu)   232
Ópusztaszer (Szer)   161, 199
Oradea (Várad, Nagyvárad, Großwardein)
   199, 309, 312–313, 316, 373, 382–383, 435,
   441, 443, 449, 453
Ordacsehi   161
Ordzovany (Ragyóc)   233
Orgondaszentmiklós (part of present-day
   Karcag)   121, 150, 154
Orosháza   143
Ortut   170
Osijek (Eszék)   333, 420
Ostffyasszonyfa (Asszonyfa)   70
Otok (Gutenwert)   287
Ottoman Empire   3, 90, 117, 131, 217, 225
Oxford   65
Ozora   146, 459

Padua (Padova)   65
Paks   141

INDEX OF GEOGRAPHIC NAMES

Palkonya 140
Pannonhalma 19, 170, 186–189, 191, 195, 198, 249–250, 323–325, 370
Pannonia (province) 67, 284, 286
Pápa 150, 154, 252
Paris 65, 301, 478
Partium (region) 365
Partizanske Ľupča (Németlipcse, Liptsch) 178
Passau 440, 501
Pásztó 14, 164, 326, 328, 375, 420
Patak *see* Sárospatak
Pavia 304
Pécs (Fünfkirchen) 65, 257, 262, 283, 290, 309, 312–313, 321, 324, 338, 419, 435
Pécsvárad 170, 185, 195, 323–325, 422
Pereg (part of present-day Kaszaper) 193
Pereyaslavec 475–476
Perkáta 151, 154
Pest (part of present-day Budapest) 76, 87, 189, 204, 313, 329, 340, 344–346, 355, 387, 408, 421, 434, 437, 443, 448, 450, 453–454, 481, 500–501
Pest County 74, 76, 226, 443, 451
Péterhida (Peterhyda) 73
Peterhyda *see* Péterhida
Petrovaradin (Pétervárad) 197, 328
Pezinok (Bazin) 173
Pilis *see* Pilisszentkereszt
Pilisszentkereszt (Pilis) 13, 140, 163, 189, 191, 198–199, 246, 248, 252, 326, 328, 461
Pisa 301, 497
Plymouth 182
Poland 109, 166, 182, 206–210, 243, 260, 327, 448, 480, 483, 485–486, 492–493
Pomáz 328, 375, 390
Pontigny 326
Pornó *see* Pornóapáti
Pornóapáti (Pornó) 189, 191, 199
Porolissum (part of present-day Moigrad) 187
Poroszló 214
Potaissa (part of present-day Turda) 183
Pozsega County 263
Pozsony County 275–276, 278, 389, 441, 446
Prague (Praha) 148, 382, 476
Prešov (Eperjes, Preschau) 8, 144, 171, 182, 199, 266–267, 341–342, 350, 368, 370, 443, 449

Ptuj (Pettau) 287
Pula 331

Rába (Raab river) 73, 76, 241, 268
Rábahídvég (Hídvég) 73
Rábaköz (region) 239–241, 247
Rácalmás (Szigetfő) 423
Ráckeve 443, 448–449, 454
Radna (Óradna) 167
Rákos (fields; part of present-day Budapest) 501
Rákos *see* Fertőrákos
Rann (mountain) 287
Râșnov (Barcarozsnyó, Rozsnyó) 69
Rechnitz (Rohonc) 250
Rednek *see* Vrdnik
Regéc 265
Regensburg 464, 467, 478, 481, 500, 504
Rendek (part of present-day Mannersdorf an der Rabnitz) 167
Rhine (region) 305
Rhine (river) 147, 481, 486
Rhine-Maas Region 458, 480
Rimavská Baňa (Rimabánya) 173, 178
Rimetea (Torockó) 177
Rodna (Óradna) 169
Rohonca (part of present-day Satu Mare) 199
Röjtökőr (part of present-day Röjtökmuzsaj) 75
Rokoszovo (Rakasz) 75, 435
Roman Empire 67, 183
Romania 21, 24, 27, 31, 63, 117, 183, 205, 282, 305, 339, 364–365
Rome (Roma) 65, 320, 329
Rona de Sus (Felsőróna) 205
Roșia Montană 166
Rovišće 270–274, 276, 452
Rožňava (Rozsnyó, Rosenau) 10, 177
Rudabánya 167, 436, 442
Rudna (Rudna) 167
Rudník (Rudnok) 167
Rudnok *see* Rudník
Rum 70
Russia 148, 475, 178, 481

Ság *see* Šahy
Šahy (Ipolyság, Ság) 446
Sajó (Slaná; river) 140

Sajólád 243
Sălacea (Szalacs) 184–185, 187, 189, 191, 194, 208, 256
Salaföld (part of present-day Diakovce) 324
Sálfölde (part of present-day Palkonya) 68
Sály 150, 154, 375
Salzburg 182, 286, 460, 467
Sâmbăteni (Szabadhely) 184, 187
Samobor (Szamobor) 260
Sankt Pölten 436
Sankt Veit 287
Santiago de Compostela 65
Sărata (Sófalva) 183
Sărăţeni (Sóvárad) 183
Sardinia (island) 182
Sarmizegetusa (Várhely) 183
Sáros County 205, 423, 425, 448
Sárospatak (Patak) 153, 158, 448
Sárszentlőrinc 141
Sarud 150, 154
Sarvaly (part of present-day Sümeg) 107, 151, 154, 378, 461
Sárvár 269, 399, 436
Sárvíz (river) 66, 84
Săsarm (Szészárma) 77
Sátoraljaújhely 333
Satu Barbă (Bártfalva) 435
Satu Mare (Szatmárnémeti, Szatmár) 214, 216, 339–340
Sava (Száva; river) 210, 485
Schlaining (Szalónak; part of present-day Stadtschlaining) 250, 329
Schwäbisch Hall 342
Segesd 117, 124, 133, 148, 151–152, 154, 156, 158, 165, 330, 331
Şeitin (Sajtény) 193
Semmering Pass 67
Senj (Zengg) 494
Serbia 339, 423, 495
Sibiu (Nagyszeben, Szeben, Hermannstadt) 31, 302–304, 306, 341, 382, 448, 486, 496
Sic (Szék) 183, 205
Sicily (island) 182
Siena 301
Sighişoara (Segesvár, Schäßburg, Schäsbrich) 332–333, 382
Silesia 460, 483, 486, 489
Şimleu Silvaniei (Szilágysomlyó) 183

Simontornya 439
Sîniob (Szentjobb) 187
Sióagárd 150, 154
Siófok 42
Slavonia 51, 210, 263–264, 274, 281, 287, 326, 329, 361, 363, 396, 399, 494, 503, 506
Slovak Ore Mountains 169, 175, 177, 380
Slovakia 8, 21, 30, 72, 82–83, 117, 182, 205, 217, 260, 339, 364, 395, 444, 454
Slovenj Gradec (Windischgrätz) 287
Smolenice (Szomolány, Szomola) 70
Smolník (Szomolnok) 283
Soest 182
Sokoró (hills) 427
Solivar (Sóvár, part of present-day Prešov) 171, 182, 205, 208
Solotvino (Aknaszlatina) 183
Sólyomkő (part of present-day Aleşd) 435
Somlóvásárhely 334
Somogy County 66, 68, 73, 211, 216, 223, 270, 278, 321, 380, 427, 452
Somogyfajsz 380
Soponya 70
Sopron (Ödenburg) 8, 62–63, 76, 85, 102, 184, 189, 209, 219, 256, 270, 272, 329–331, 338, 341, 343–345, 352, 354–355, 358, 368, 370, 375–376, 387, 434–436, 450, 461, 463, 491
Sopron County 71, 74–76
Sopronkőhida 71
Sopronkövesd 75
Southern Europe 102
Sóvidék (Salzgebiet, Ţinutul Ocnelor) 183, 205
Spain 182, 472
Špania Dolina (Úrvölgy) 179
Spiš (Szepesség, Zips; region) 60, 63, 95, 108, 263, 382, 389, 484, 486
Spiš-Gemer Ore Mountains (Gömör–Szepesi-érchegység) 175
Spišská Belá (Szepesbéla) 260
Spišská Nová Ves (Igló) 232, 382
Split 310
Sremska Mitrovica (Szávaszentdemeter) 326
Srijem (Szerémség, Srem, Syrmia; region) 68, 85, 109, 240, 283, 290, 310, 312–313, 427, 481

INDEX OF GEOGRAPHIC NAMES 633

Stadtschlaining *see* Schlaining
Stari Jankovci 271–272
Steyr 144, 374, 461
Štítnik (Csetnek) 177, 449
Struga (part of opresent-day Sveti Đurđhoz) 271
Šturovo (Kakat, Párkány) 187
Štvrtok na Ostrove (Csütörtök) 441
Styria 327, 454
Styrian Prealps (mountains) 67
Şugatag (Aknasugatag) 183
Sülysáp 333
Sümeg 151, 154, 461
Susa (part of present-day Ózd) 224
Swabia 458
Switzerland 392, 467
Syrmia *see* Srijem
Szabolcs 124, 151, 156
Szabolcs County 226, 232
Szádvár (Szárd) 265
Szakácsi *see* Nagyszakácsi
Szamos (Someş; river) 192, 197, 208
Szárd *see* Szádvár
Szarvas 150, 154, 161
Szatmár County 172, 444
Szécsény *see* Vasszécsény
Szeged 129, 184–185, 188–189, 195, 197, 199, 208–209, 214, 216, 256
Szekcső *see* Dunaszekcső
Székely Lands (Székelyföld, Ţinutul Secuiesc) 205, 211, 364, 382
Székesfehérvár (Fehérvár) 128, 152, 158, 165, 185, 199, 215, 310, 338, 344, 408, 420, 443, 445, 453, 469
Szekszárd 152, 156, 199
Szemenye *see* Muraszemenye
Szendrő 134, 141, 151, 156
Szentfalva (part of present-day Budapest) 450
Szentgotthárd 189, 191–192, 195, 198–199, 319, 326–327
Szentkirály 102, 128, 153, 158
Szentlászló (part of present-day Budapest) 141
Szentpál (part of present-day Bagod) 436–437, 442, 452
Szentpétermártír (part of present-day Budapest) 355

Szepes County 75, 232–233, 260
Szepnice (part of present-day Zagreb) 77
Szer *see* Ópusztaszer
Szerémség *see* Srijem
Szerencs 444–445
Szigetfő *see* Rácalmás
Szigetmonostor 189, 198
Szolnok 77, 152, 156, 214
Szombathely 355, 423

Tállya 265
Tapolca 252
Târgovişte 448
Târgu Mureş (Marosvásárhely) 163, 331
Tárkány 167
Tata 251, 445
Tăutelec (Hegyköztóttelek, Tóttelek) 442
Temes County 401
Temesköz (region) 401
Thames (river) 45
Thienen 483
Tihany 189, 191, 195, 198, 223, 249, 425, 437
Tilaj 230
Tileagd (Mezőtelegd) 482
Ţinutul Ocnelor *see* Sóvidék
Ţinutul Secuiesc *see* Székely Lands
Tisza (Tisa; river) 74, 84, 139, 142, 208–209, 241–242, 324
Tiszagyenda 150, 154
Tiszalök 120, 150, 154, 161
Tiszalúc 444
Tiszavarsány 443
Titel (Titel) 199, 310
Tófalu (part of present-day Felsőmarác) 77
Tokaj 74, 85, 214, 216, 265
Tolna County 34, 66, 69
Tömörd 167
Topoľníky (Nyárasd) 275
Topolovac *see* Zrinski Topolovac
Topusko (Topuszkó, Topuszka) 326, 328
Tóttelek *see* Tăutelec
Tournai 482
Transdanubia (Dunántúl; region) 12, 63, 67–68, 83, 102, 120, 141, 167, 225–226, 249, 269, 366, 452
Transdanubian Mountains (Dunántúli-középhegység) 83, 88, 108
Transtisza (Tiszántúl; region) 43, 186

Transylvania (Erdély, Siebenbürgen)   12, 30–31, 51, 57, 60, 63, 68, 82–83, 95, 108, 166–167, 169, 171–172, 177, 182–183, 187, 191, 193–197, 205–206, 208–215, 216–217, 225, 262, 283, 302, 305–306, 309, 311–312, 316, 324, 325, 332, 337, 341, 361, 364, 377, 380, 382, 389, 401, 408, 435, 443, 448, 454, 482, 484, 486, 490, 496
Transylvanian Ore Mountains (Erdélyi-érchegység, Munţii Metaliferi)   166, 169, 172, 380, 401
Trenčin (Trencsén)   209, 396, 399, 414–416, 486
Trencsén County   232, 439
Trhová Hradská (Vásárút)   275–276
Trnava (Nagyszombat, Tyrnau)   209, 260–261, 275, 352–353, 471, 486
Trnávka (Csallóköztárnok)   276
Troisfontaines   326
Trstenik (part of present-day Marija Gorica)   66
Tulln   471, 490
Turda (Torda)   171, 183–184, 186, 205, 212–214, 216
Tureň (Zonctorony)   275
Túrkeve   151, 154, 161
Turňa nad Bodvou (Torna)   436
Turóc County   446
Tuzla   182

Ugocsa County   75, 340
Ugod   146, 152, 156
Ukraine   183, 205, 339
Üllő   161
Ung County   75, 227, 258, 283, 435
Úrhida   73
Uzsa   331

Vác   15, 59, 110, 128, 140, 142, 149, 151–153, 156, 158, 165, 262, 309, 312
Váh (Vág; river)   141, 324
Valkó County   58, 263
Váralja   151, 156
Varasd County   413, 452
Varaždin (Varasd)   396, 482
Vas County   34, 70, 73, 75, 77, 170, 226, 230, 306, 436
Vásárhely see Kisvásárhely

Vasas (part of present-day Pécs)   167–168
Vasszécsény   70
Vasvár   167, 170, 184, 209, 256, 324
Veľký Šariš (Nagysáros)   333
Venice (Venezia)   67, 129, 147, 169, 175, 182, 301, 391, 457, 466, 479, 481, 489, 493–497, 506–507
Verecke Pass see Veretskyy pereval
Veretskyy pereval (Verecke Pass)   67
Verona   502
Vértesszentkereszt   332
Veszprém   68–69, 215, 248–249, 275, 309, 312–314, 348, 350, 389, 425, 455
Veszprém County   66, 68–709, 107, 226, 236, 277, 378
Veszprémvölgy (part of present-day Veszprém)   148, 334, 389, 455
Vienna (Wien)   63, 67, 129, 140, 242, 250, 281, 289, 300, 352, 408, 411, 436, 439–440, 443, 448, 460–461, 464, 471, 478, 481, 486, 490, 501, 503–504, 507
Vinohradiv (Nagyszöllős, Szőllős)   75
Virovitica (Verőce)   270–271, 482
Visegrád   13, 117, 122, 126, 133, 135, 144–145, 147, 150–152, 154, 156, 161, 165, 282, 326, 331, 375, 381–382, 390–391, 466, 486
Vistula (Wisla; river)   480
Víziváros (part of present-day Budapest)   376
Vlky (Vők)   275, 278
Volga (river)   45
Vranov nad Topľou (Varannó)   444
Vrdnik (Rednek)   167

Waldenburg   469
Wallachia   31, 131, 306, 486
Western Europe   10, 23, 45–46, 56–57, 67, 88, 102, 147, 220, 223, 239, 244, 247, 252, 293, 310, 318–319, 321, 325, 329–333, 368, 383, 460, 465, 469, 480, 482, 484–485, 489, 492, 495
Wieliczka   182, 208
Wiener Neustadt (Bécsújhely)   63, 436
Wrocław   460
Wulkaprodersdorf (Vulkapordány)   71

Ypres   482
Yugoslavia   21

INDEX OF GEOGRAPHIC NAMES

Zadar (Zára)   310, 329, 494, 497
Zagreb (Zágráb)   189, 198, 209, 260, 273, 283, 309, 312, 329, 422, 494, 506
Zagyva (river)   209
Zala County   68, 71, 73–76, 185, 226, 232, 236, 427, 435–436, 442
Zalaapáti   76
Zalavár (Mosaburg)   41, 66, 71, 74
Zaránd County   401, 405
Ždiar (Zár)   260
Žehra (Zsigra)   75
Zeiselbüchel (part of present-day Budapest)   355
Zela *see* Dolné Zelenice
Zeligrad (Sóvár; part of present-day Blandiana)   184
Zemplén County   70, 74, 444
Žilina (Zsolna)   486
Zirc   141, 190, 326, 328
Žitný ostrov (Csallóköz; island)   275–278, 443
Zlatna (Zalatna)   166, 169
Zólyom County   75
Zombor *see* Mezőzombor
Zrinski Topolovac (Topolovac)   270, 273
Zselic (hills)   277
Zselicerdő   324
Zselicszentjakab (part of present-day Kaposvár)   378, 437
Zsolca *see* Alsózsolca
Zvolen (Zólyom)   75, 340, 444

Index of Personal Names

Acciaiuoli, family 492
Acsády, Ignác 18
Agendorfer, family 343
Ahorn, János, court judge 412
Ajtony, chieftain 93, 185, 194
Albert, king of Hungary 305
Albeus, abbot of Pannonhalma 324, 370
Alfani, family 492
al-Garnati, Abu Hamid, traveler 168, 476–477
Álmos, prince of the Magyars 187
Andrásfalvy, Bertalan 241
Andrew I, king of Hungary 285, 425
Andrew II, king of Hungary 73, 184–185, 188–191, 194, 197, 199, 258, 260–261, 263, 285–286, 289, 311, 326, 339, 464, 481, 494
Andrew III, king of Hungary 78, 206, 257, 282, 313, 495
Anonymus, chronicler 169
Arnold of Lübeck, chronicler 477
Arnolt, Hans, juror of Buda 449
Arnulf, Carolingian emperor 184
Attavante, family 506

Bácskai, Vera 28, 359, 361, 364–366
Bakóc, Tamás, archbishop of Esztergom 314–315, 448
Ban, Herbert 287
Bándi, Zsuzsa 321
Barbara of Cilli, wife of King Sigismund 299
Bardi, family 492
Bartosiewicz, László 35, 118
Bátky, Zsigmond 23
Bátori, family 446
Batu Khan, Mongol ruler 479
Baumgartner, Egon 287
Beatrice of Aragon, queen of Hungary and Bohemia, wife of Matthias Corvinus and Wladislas II 210, 506
Bebek, family 274
Beheim, Bernhard, chamber count 302
Bél, Matthias, Lutheran pastor and scholar 140
Béla, I, king of Hungary 423

Béla, II, king of Hungary 186–187, 195, 262, 285
Béla, III, king of Hungary 188, 191, 194, 196, 255, 262, 282, 285, 311, 326, 328, 477–478
Béla, IV, king of Hungary 62, 73, 78, 101, 172, 178, 189, 195, 197, 206–208, 264, 316, 333, 370–371, 374, 379, 383, 421–422, 429, 500
Béla, prince, son of Béla IV 264
Belényesy, Márta 23, 25–26
ben Meir, ha-Kohen, rabbi and Talmudic scholar 257
Benedict (II), bishop of Oradea 313
Benjamin of Tudela, traveler 478
Benkő, Elek 33
Berend, T. Iván 28
Bernardi, Francesco, chamber count 290, 505
Bertrandon de la Brocquière, traveler and diplomat 212
Besskó, József 114
Blanchard, Ian 32
Bogdán, István 192–193
Bökönyi, Sándor 114, 118
Boleslav the Pious, duke of Greater Poland 382
Boleslav V the Shy (the Chaste), duke of Sandomierz 208
Bonfini, Antonio, chronicler 251
Bornemissza, Péter, judge of Buda 448
Brummel, Gyula 114
Butkai, Péter, chamber count 214
Buza, János 300
Buzás, Gergely 35

C. Tóth, Norbert 453
Carnesecchi, family 501
Casimir III the Great, king of Poland 486
Cavalcanti, family 506
Charles I, king of Hungary 173–175, 180, 208, 260, 262, 279, 283, 290–293, 295–296, 298, 483, 485–486, 488, 495
Coloman (the Learned), king of Hungary 184, 187–188, 258, 261, 264, 282, 286, 310, 425–426, 428, 477

INDEX OF PERSONAL NAMES

Csánki, Dezső 361
Csapi, family 442
Csóka J., Lajos 320
Csőre, Pál 219
Csuti, András, burgher of Körmend 453

Deák, Antal András 241
del Bene, family 492
del Bene, Filippo di Giovanni, businessman 493
Dernschwam, Hans, merchant 212–213, 302
Ders, Márton (of Szerdahely), master of cupbearers 270
di Bernardo da Carmignano, Francesco, businessman 503
di Cambio, Vieri, businessman 493
di Piero Fronte, Fronte, businessman 503
di Pietro Bini, Antonio, businessman 507
di Simone Capponi, Filippo, businessman 503
di Stagio, Felice, businessman 507
di, Bardo, Nofri, businessman 498
Domanovszky, Sándor 21–22
Dózsa, György, peasant leader 364, 368
Draskóczy, István 30, 33, 452
Druget, family 225, 227
Dyer, Christopher 14

Edlasperger (Edlasperg), Peter, burgher of Buda 449
Eizinger, Ulrich, count of Cili 212, 302–303
Elizabeth of Poland, wife of King Charles I 333, 348, 484
Emeric, king of Hungary 188–189, 199, 286
Emeric, saint, son of King Stephen I 382
Engel, Pál 31, 227, 290
Erdélyi, László 18
Ernuszt, János, bishop of Pécs and royal treasurer 273, 299–300
Ernuszt, Zsigmond, royal treasurer 51

F. Romhányi, Beatrix 34–35, 206
Falcucci, Giovanni di Niccolo, businessman 491
Fara, Andrea 31–32
Feld, István 35
Ferber, György, burgher of Košice 449, 451

Ferdinand I, king of Hungary and Bohemia, Holy Roman emperor 212, 300, 408, 415, 446
Ferenczi, László 35
Fleischer, Jakob, burgher of Nuremberg 507
Fontana, Francesco, envoy 303–304
Forster, György, judge of Buda 449, 451
Frederick Habsburg, prince of Austria 486
Frederick I (Barbarossa), Holy Roman emperor 258
Frederick III, Holy Roman emperor 300, 468
Freiherr, Ulrich, captain of Magyaróvár 410
Frescobaldi, family 492
Fronte, family 501
Fügedi, Erik 31, 248, 339, 359, 429, 438, 484
Fugger, family 177, 212, 302, 504

Garai, Miklós, palatine of Hungary 224
Gedai, István 282, 287
George (saint) 382
George, margrave of Brandenburg–Ansbach 276, 396, 399, 401, 403, 405, 408, 410, 413
Gerhard (saint), bishop of Cenad 3, 93, 185, 194, 371
Geszti, János, vice-castellan of Belgrade 371
Géza I, king of Hungary 423
Géza II, king of Hungary 186–188
Giugni, family 506
Gregory III, pope 120
Greniczer, Ágoston, judge of Košice 302
Gritti, Andrea, doge of Venice 496
Gritti, Lodovico, businessman, son of the doge of Venice 496
Gyerőfi, family 435
Gyöngyössy, Márton 35
Györffy, György 28, 31
Györffy, István 23

H. Gyürky, Katalin 464
H. Kolba, Judit 457
Haller, family 448
Haller, Hans, burgher of Buda 449
Haller, Ruprecht, burgher of Nuremberg and Buda 449
Hankó, Béla 114
Hartvik, bishop of Győr, hagiographer 76

Heckenast, Gusztáv 29
Heltai, Gáspár, chronicler 265
Herman, Ottó 22
Hermann, István 290
Hervay, F. Levente 320–321
Holl, Imre 460–461, 466–469
Hóman, Bálint 21, 285, 290, 295–296
Horváth, Mihály 265
Horváti, family 274
Hunyadi, John, regent of Hungary 215, 302, 303, 305, 446
Huszár, Lajos 281, 289–290

Ibn Ya'qūb, Ibrāhīim, traveler 475–476
Inárcsi, Miklós, nobleman 451
Ippolito d'Este, archbishop of Esztergom 314–315
Ivan, comes of Okič 260

Jiškra, Jan, captain-general 301, 303, 305
John of Capistran (saint), Franciscan preacher 371
John of Luxemburg, king of Bohemia 486
John Szapolyai, king of Hungary 279, 406, 408
John the Baptist, saint 292–293
John XXIII, pope 493
Jordan, William Chester 56

K. Németh, András 66
Kakas, János, nobleman 389
Kalász, Elek 319, 326
Kammerer, Ulrich, chamber count 447
Kanczlyr, Angelus, burgher of Buda 448
Kanizsai, family 399
Kanizsai, László, treasurer 452
Károlyi, Zsigmond 241
Kellenbenz, Hermann 437, 439
Kemény, family 435
Kenyeres, István 248
Kinga (Kunigunda), daughter of King Béla IV 208
Kiss, Andrea 56–57
Knapp, Éva 321
Koch, Bernhard 287
Kohn, Sámuel 288
Kolozsvári, György, sculptor 382
Kolozsvári, Márton, sculptor 382

Kovács, Éva 457
Kovács, László 282, 285
Kováts, Ferenc 19, 29, 290, 298
Kristó, Gyula 31
Kubinyi, András 28, 29, 31, 34, 209, 226, 290, 297–298, 361–362, 399, 401, 429
Kunigunda of Brandenburg, spouse of Prince Béla 264

Ladislas I (Saint), king of Hungary 186–188, 282, 285, 292–293, 324, 373, 382–383, 423, 425–428, 477–478
Ladislas IV (the Cuman), king of Hungary 77, 260, 481
Ladislas, V (Posthumous), king of Hungary 302–303, 467–468
Landus, Hieronymus, papal nuncio and Latin archbishop of Crete 303
László, Gyula 23, 284
Lászlóffy, Woldemár 241
Laszlovszky, József 35
Lékai, Lajos 320
Louis I (the Great), king of Hungary and Poland 78, 175, 180, 268, 289–294, 318–319, 329, 377, 421, 439, 484
Louis II, king of Hungary and Bohemia 397
Louis, VII, king of France 476
Lovag, Zsuzsa 460
Lukačka, Ján 453

Makkai, László 28, 247
Maksay, Ferenc 27, 250, 365
Mályusz, Elemér 24, 28–29, 215, 299, 359, 361
Mandelló, Gyula 20
Manini, family 452
Marcus of Nuremberg, chamber count 503–504
Margaret (saint), Dominican nun and daughter of King Béla IV 371
Marsigli, Luigi Ferdinando, diplomat, traveler and cartographer 131, 141–142
Martin V, pope 332
Mary of Habsburg, wife of King Louis II 397, 401, 408, 410–411
Mary the Virgin 285
Mary, queen of Hungary 291–292, 294
Matolcsi, János 118

INDEX OF PERSONAL NAMES

Matthias Corvinus, king of Hungary   60, 62, 176, 210, 214–215, 217, 251–252, 277–278, 294, 299–301, 303, 305, 333, 367, 392, 446, 465, 470, 499, 506–507
Matthias II, king of Hungary and bohemia, Holy Roman emperor   439
Maximilian II, king of Hungary, Holy Roman emperor   446
Melanesi, family   501, 505
Melanesi, Giovanni, businessman   505
Melanesi, Simone, businessman   505
Melanesi, Tommaso di Piero, businessman   503, 505
Méri, István   27
Modrár, Pál, businessman   302
Mollay, Károly   434
Mordovin, Maxim   33
Moritz, Paul, businessman   435, 437, 447, 491
Morosini, family   495
Mozzi, family   492
Münzer, Johann, juror of Buda   448

Nadler, Michael, judge of Buda   503
Nagy, Balázs   35
Nagy, Lóránt   288
Neumann, Tibor   51
Nógrády, Árpád   452

Oberländer-Târnoveanu, Ernest   301
Odo de Deogilo, chaplain to King Louis VII, chronicler   476
Oláh, Miklós (Nicolaus Olahus), archbishop of Esztergom, chronicler   142
Olga (saint), ruler of Kiev   475
Opus, count   186
Oszvald, Ferenc Arisztid   320
Otto of Freising, bishop of Freising, chronicler   3, 258
Otto of Wittelsbach, king of Hungary   279
Óvári, family   419

Pach, Zsigmond Pál   28, 31, 496
Pakucs, Mária   31
Palaiologos, Byzantine ruling dynasty   479
Panciatichi, family   501
Papp, László   23
Pastor, Giovanni, tax officer   506
Pataki, József   411

Paul of Levoča, sculptor and altar maker   389
Paul the Hermit (saint), desert hermit   330
Paulinyi, Oszkár   29, 184, 298–300
Pazdics, family   444
Pecorari, Jacopo, papal nuncio   185
Perényi, family   447–448
Perényi, Gábor (Gabriel), exchequer   202
Perényi, Imre, palatine of Hungary   265
Peter, abbot of Cîteaux   327
Petrovics, István   454
Petrus Andreas, faience master   392
Petrus de Crescentiis (Pietro de' Crescenzi), jurist, agricultural writer   245
Pipo of Ozora *see* Scolari, Filippo
Pitti, family   506
Pitti, Niccolo, chamber count   507
Pitti, Piero, businessman, burgher of Buda   499
Pohl, Artúr   281, 301
Posztós, Mihály, judge of Timişoara   435

Rádóczy, Gyula   288
Rengjeo, Ivan   281
Réthy, László   281, 288
Roger (Rogerius), canon of Oradea, chronicler   481
Rosetti, Gionaventura, manual writer   147
Rucellai, family   506
Rupp, Jakab   280

Saltzer, Ernő   282
Sanuto, Marino, chronicler   507
Sárkány, Ambrus (Ambrosius), count of Pozsony and Zala Counties   202
Schaider, Peter, chamber count   303
Schalk, Carl   294, 300–301
Scheiber, Sándor   288
Schönvisner, István   280
Schulek, Alfréd   289
Scolari, Filippo, royal treasurer   210, 215, 498
Siebenlinder, Johann, judge of Buda   448, 503
Sigismund of Luxemburg, king of Hungary and Bohemia, Holy Roman emperor   9, 78, 127, 140, 202, 209–210, 214, 270, 274, 279, 294, 297, 299–301, 304–305, 331, 346, 387, 391, 443, 446–447, 496, 498, 503, 505–508

Simon, Zsolt   31, 341
Sixtus IV, pope   332
Solymosi, László   323, 372
Štefánik, Martin   30
Stephen I (Saint), king of Hungary   67, 76, 93, 147, 168, 180, 185, 194, 258, 261, 282, 284–285, 309, 371, 382, 423, 476
Stephen III, king of Hungary   187
Stephen V, junior king and later king of Hungary   74, 78, 207, 263, 421, 479, 494
Stibrányi, Máté   66
Stoss, Veit, sculptor   389
Sviatoslav I of Kiev, grand prince of Kiev   475
Szabó, András Péter   341
Szabó, István   27, 269, 359, 401, 413
Szabó, Péter   35
Szakály, Ferenc   364–365
Szapolyai, family   265, 395, 399, 404–415
Székely, György   359, 364, 449
Szenczi Molnár, Albert, linguist, dictionary writer   397
Szende, Katalin   35
Szép, István, burgher of Pest   448
Szerdahelyi Dersfi, family   271–274
Szerecsen, family   290
Szilágyi, Elizabeth, mother of King Matthias Corvinus   305
Szily, Kálmán   231
Szűcs, Jenő   26, 359, 429, 479, 485

Tacitus, Ancient author   166
Tagányi, Károly   18–19
Takács, István   118
Takács, Károly   239
Tallóci, family   210, 215
Tárcai, János, count of the Székelys   306
Teke, Zsuzsa   30
Telegdi, Csanád, archbishop of Esztergom   371
Teleki, Pál   24
Theophilus Presbyter, arts compendium writer   146, 369

Thurzó, family   395, 414, 416
Thurzó, György chamber count   302
Thurzó, János (Jan Thurzo), burgher of Cracow, businessman   177, 302, 504
Tolnai, Máté, abbot of Pannonhalma   325
Tóth, Csaba   35, 295, 300
Trommellenk, Jakab, burgher of Buda   436

Újlaki, family   399

V. Székely, György   287
Vermes, László   288
Vieri dei Medici (Vieri di Cambio de Medici), businessman   493
Visky, Károly   23
Viviani, family   506
von Ebengreuth, Arnold Luschin   287
von Stamp, Jacob, castellan of Magyaróvár   410–411
von Stromer, Wolfgang   30, 489, 496
Vörös, István   118

Weisz, Boglárka   35, 186, 347
Welser, family   504
Wenceslas, king of Hungary   279
Wenzel, Gusztáv   29
Werbőczy, István, chief justice and palatine of Hungary   228–230, 235–236, 244, 360, 433, 507
Werner, György, humanist, royal counselor   300
Weszerle, József   280
Weygel, Johannes, craftsman at Spišska Nova Ves   382
Winter, Heinz   287
Wladislas I, king of Hungary and Poland   294, 300, 305, 446
Wladislas II, king of Hungary and Bohemia   306, 436, 439
Wullam, Syr, merchant   479

Zimányi, Vera   129, 276
Zolnay, László   479, 482